Richard George found the courage to start writing at 66 years of age. For 13 years, he was increasingly forced into 'living in his head' by the progressive disabling of his body by Motor Neurone Disease. The upside of this was the time to indulge his love of British history and historical fiction. His writing is characterised by his anti-establishment stance on most issues and his determination to challenge the accepted view of British history and the culture it has created.

To Jess Phillips M.P.
With the sincerest best
wishes for the future.
Richard G.

Richard George

The Most Undeserving Case

Austin Macauley Publishers™
London • Cambridge • New York • Sharjah

The story, experiences, and words are the author's alone.

A CIP catalogue record for this title is available from the British Library.

ISBN 9781398459113 (Paperback)
ISBN 9781398459120 (Hardback)
ISBN 9781398459137 (ePub e-book)

www.austinmacauley.com

First Published 2023
Austin Macauley Publishers Ltd®
1 Canada Square
Canary Wharf
London
E14 5AA

I owe an enormous debt to Wikipedia, the free internet encyclopaedia, for providing much of the knowledge, without which the intention of this book would fail and its content would be somewhat lacking. Through this encyclopaedia, I have been able to access writers and their articles and books. All those referenced in the book, I thank and acknowledge.

My second debt is to JSTOR, which describes itself as follows: "a digital library for the intellectually curious. We help everyone discover, share and connect valuable ideas."

My third is to the Internet Archive, which describes itself as follows: "a 501(c)(3) non-profit, is building a digital library of Internet sites and other cultural artifacts in digital form. Like a paper library, we provide free access to researchers, historians, scholars, the print disabled and the general public. Our mission is to provide Universal Access to All Knowledge."

My fourth is to Amazon Kindle for books and essays I would never have been able to access through any other medium.

I owe my sincere thanks to Goodreads and BrainyQuote for the quotes at the beginning of each chapter.

Table of Contents

In Memoriam

Christine de Pizan, born Cristina da Pizzano (1364-c. 1430)—French poet and writer.
Denis Diderot (5 October 1713-31 July 1784)—Writer and philosopher.
John Stuart Mill (20 May 1806-7 May 1873)—Writer and politician.
Jeanne d'Arc (c. 1412-30 May 1431)—French soldier and prophetess.
Anne Askew (1521-16 July 1546)—Writer, poet and Protestant martyr.
Lady Anne Clifford (30 January 1590-22 March 1676)—Countess
George Fox (July 1624-13 January 1691)—Founder of Quakers.
Margaret Fell/Fox, born Margaret Askew (1614-23 April 1702)—Co-founder of Quakers.
Olympe de Gouges, born Marie Gouze (7 May 1748-3 November 1793)—French writer.
Nicolas de Condorcet (17 September 1743-29 March 1794)—French writer and philosopher.
Etta Palm d'Aelders (April 1743-28 March 1799)—Dutch spy and feminist.
Mary Wollstonecraft (27 April 1759-10 September 1797)—Writer and philosopher.
Mary Bowes (24 February 1749-28 April 1800)—Countess
Georgiana Cavendish, born Spencer (7 June 1757-30 March 1806)—Duchess and writer.
Henry Hunt (6 November 1773-13 February 1835)—Politician.
William Thompson (1775-28 March 1833)—Writer and philosopher.
Caroline Norton, born Sheridan (22 March 1808-15 June 1877)—Writer.
Barbara Bodichon, born Leigh Smith (8 April 1827-11 June 1891)—Educationalist.
Henry Fawcett (26 August 1833-6 November 1884)—Politician.
Elizabeth Anderson, born Garrett (9 June 1836-17 December 1917)—Physician.
Millicent Fawcett, born Garrett (11 June 1847-5 August 1929)—Dame and politician.
Havelock Ellis (2 February 1859-8 July 1939)—Physician and sexologist.
Magnus Hirschfeld (14 May 1868-14 May 1935)—German physician and sexologist.
Fatema Mernissi (27 September 1940-30 November 2015)—Moroccan writer and sociologist.

Introduction

Even the strongest city will fall if there is no one to defend it, and even the most undeserving case will win if there is no one to testify against it.
Pizan, Christine. The Book of the City of Ladies (Penguin Classics) (Kindle Locations 890–891). Penguin Books Ltd. Kindle Edition.

Being a woman is a terribly difficult trade since it consists principally of dealings with men.
– Joseph Conrad, Chance

To call woman the weaker sex is a libel; it is man's injustice to woman. If by strength is meant brute strength, then, indeed, is woman less brute than man. If by strength is meant moral power, then woman is immeasurably man's superior. Has she not greater intuition, is she not more self-sacrificing, has she not greater powers of endurance, has she not greater courage? Without her, man could not be. If non-violence is the law of our being, the future is with woman. Who can make a more effective appeal to the heart than woman?
[*To the Women of India* (*Young India*, Oct. 4, 1930)]
– Mahatma Gandhi

La Querelle des femmes (the dispute about women), originally a French cultural debate in the 15th century, was translated into English as The Woman Question. My whole adult life I have seen the world (of men?) as fundamentally unjust. The greatest injustice of the development of civilisation has resulted from the biased misconstruction of that question. It should be The Man Question. The story of civilisation, HIStory, is the story of the civilisation of men's behaviour. Men's treatment, understanding and expectations of women should have been the principal concerns of the Man Question because no other injustice has touched the lives of half the human race. Very few victims of injustice seek out, indict, prosecute and eradicate the cause and call to account the perpetrator of the injustices done to them. Women have. They have with their lives fought for more than 600 years **the most undeserving case**.

None of the common justifications for the accusation by most men, of female inferiority, has acquired permanency because, in what should be a universal morality, all human beings are 'deserving' of equal rights and equal value, a sine qua non of humanity, at least since the humanist, human centred, reasoning of the modern era that began in the Renaissance of Classical knowledge in 15th century Europe. The history of the 'undeserving' case, as the German scholar,

Heinrich Cornelius Agrippa, had done as long ago as 1529, raises The Man Question. Did men in society oppress women because of some natural law, or because they wanted to keep social power and status for themselves?

Is this a story of the longest standing oppression in the history of humanity? I leave you to decide for yourself.

If many of the arguments in this book, in fact, its whole tenor, seem familiar, they are; it is. In 1869, an essay was published, written by John Stuart Mill, the English philosopher and politician, made great by his respect for a reasoning that adheres to the two fundamental moral tenets of civilised behaviour: do not do anything to others you would not want them to do to you, the so-called Golden Rule, and look at your own behaviour and faults before blaming or criticising others, the antidote to hypocrisy. *The Subjection of Women* put the incontrovertible case for the equality of women to men.

This book is a compendium of stories to nudge the reader to reconsider the case. Around 1750, Denis Diderot took up the challenge of editing the *Encyclopédie* in the belief that only comprehensive knowledge would have "the power to change men's common way of thinking." The facts that he was imprisoned in 1749 for his radical views and that the *Encyclopédie* was banned by the government of the absolute monarch, Louis XV, and the Papacy under Pope Clement XIII, the two institutions sustaining the conservation of patriarchal control, as well as inspiring the more rational aspects of the French Revolution make him one of my favourite historical figures. In his honour, this book is encyclopaedic in structure.

Each chapter can be read in its own right but the whole gives, I hope, a comprehensive account of the undeserving case. Each chapter has a preamble which explains why it has been written and the testimony it provides to the consideration of the justification, or lack of it, of the case.

Chapter 1
Allogamy: It Takes Two

What would men be without women? Scarce, sir…mighty scarce.
– Mark Twain

11: (Nevertheless, in the Lord woman is not independent of man nor man of woman; 12: for as woman was made from man, so man is now born of woman. And all things are from God.)
– 1 Corinthians 14

Preamble

There was a popular quiz show on television in the 1990s called Catchphrase *in which contestants had to make sense of an animated cartoon, often involving a robotlike figure called Mr. Chips, and liken it to a familiar phrase or saying. The host, a Northern Irish comedian, Roy Walker, was frequently driven to repeat Step 1 of the process of decoding the picture, 'Say what you see'. Applied to Homo Sapiens, regardless of ethnicity, colour, age or location, we see two distinct versions, male and female, not only with different anatomical kit but, on average, the male distinctively larger and more muscular than the female. Observing their public lives and external appearance, the male is superior to the female in physical task completion, taller, more massive, faster and stronger. However, only the female carries the foetus, gives birth to the offspring and nourishes them after birth. When considering the value placed on these two different individuals 'saying what you see' is a good place to start.*

Charles Darwin, in his 1876 book, "The Effects of Cross and Self Fertilisation in the Vegetable Kingdom" (pages 466-467) summed up his findings in the following way.

> "It has been shown in the present volume that the offspring from the union of two distinct individuals, especially if their progenitors have been subjected to very different conditions, have an immense advantage in height, weight, constitutional vigour and fertility over the self-fertilised offspring from one of the same parents. And this fact is amply sufficient to account for the development of the sexual elements, that is, for the genesis of the two sexes."[1]

---

[1] en.wikipedia.org/wiki/Fertilisation#Allogamy_and_autogamy. Accessed 31/10/2016.

Like most plants and animals, human beings are allogamous; we cross fertilise. This seems to be the best method for survival of the species, a particular interest of the Great Charles, producing a variety of Homo Sapiens arguably more interesting and powerful, *certainly a tad more complex*, than an earthworm, flatworm or sea cucumber who do not employ it! That we are two sexes, therefore, seems the best way forward. Making new human beings is why the two sexes have different external features and internal workings, the differences being triggered by hormones released soon after the male's sperm has fertilised the female's egg.

The instruction to do this is contained in chromosomes present in every male sperm. Half have the X chromosome identical to the chromosome in the female's egg and half have the Y chromosome not present in the egg. The code on the Y chromosome is contained in the SRY gene. If the former gets to the egg first XX fuses to produce a female. If the latter gets there first XY fuses to produce a male.

With the female rests the biological power to produce another human being. With the male rests the biological power to produce another male human being. Biologically, therefore, regarding the principal purpose of all living things, to reproduce and survive, neither sex is more powerful or important than the other. However, when it comes to biological, social and familial duty, the female's is far greater than the male's. The fight for survival is the male's principal duty in which dominance is a key requirement.

In our hitherto patriarchal, patrilineal, male-dominating Western culture there is, no matter what the scientific or blatantly observable facts to the contrary, the underlying conviction that 'nature meant it to be this way'. Men-on-top is the natural, God-given way of things, who are we to contradict it? In the most summary and unscientific way, I need to set about examining this claim of 'natural' male superiority and, among many other digressions, its assertion and implementation over 2,000 years, at least, of British history.

Childbearing and child rearing are very time consuming and tiring activities. The female homo sapiens is fertile for about 30 years, say from 15 to 45 years of age. On 20 August 1997, Dawn Brooke gave birth to a healthy son at the age of 59[2]. Weaning an infant from breast feeding is culturally different in terms of when it happens but can occur at around 6 months. The female is certainly ready to conceive again about 10 months after the birth of her last child.

Biologically, therefore, a child per year throughout that 30-year period is a possibility. Multiple births account for large numbers of births to a single mother. 69 is the largest claimed to have taken place—the wife of Feodor Vasilyev, a Russian peasant who lived in the 18th century[3]. A more verifiable case is that of Elizabeth Greenhill of Abbots Langley who had 39 children in 38 births in 17th century England.

---

[2] www.telegraph.co.uk/news/uknews/1560739/UK-woman-59-worlds-oldest-natural-mother.html. Accessed 04/11/2016.

[3] en.wikipedia.org/wiki/List_of_people_with_the_most_children. Accessed 04/11/2016.

> She had 39 children by one husband. They were all born alive, and baptised and all single births save one. The last child, who was born after his father's death, was a surgeon in King-street, Bloomsbury, and wrote the above book, which he was desirous to bring into fashion. She was heard to say by a credible witness, with whom I [the person whose signature attests it] was well acquainted, that she believed, if her husband had lived, she might have had two or three more children. [signed] Rich. Ashby, a clergyman.[4]

On the basis that the exception proves the rule it is probable that in an era of unchecked conception millions of women were bearing large numbers of children. Excessive population increase was prevented by failure to go full term, still births, infant mortality due to failure to wean successfully, pre-natal and post-natal fatalities in childbearing females and fatal disease which also took a high proportion of child-producing adults (the average age of an English peasant woman could well have been as low as 25.)[5]Child rearing like childbearing, was equally hazardous and unpredictable in terms of its principal biological aim of bringing two babies to reproductive maturity, i.e., replacing yourselves. One way to check out this probability is to look at the childbearing and rearing histories of those females who do appear in verifiable historical records; queens. The fertility of queens should not have been any different to any other human female although the physical labour of child rearing was mostly carried out by servants and, therefore, a great deal less draining and injurious to their longevity.

- **Matilda of Flanders** (1031-1083): 11 births, 9 survivors. Last birth 1068
- **Eleanor of Aquitaine** (1122-1204): 10 births, 9 survivors. Last birth 1166
- **Isabella of Angouleme** (1188-1242): 14 births, all survived. Last birth 1229
- **Eleanor of Castille** (1241-1290): 16 births, 9 survived. Last birth 1284
- **Philippa of Hainault** (1314-1369): 13 births, 9 survived. Last birth 1355
- **Elizabeth Woodville** (1437-1492): 12 births, 10 survived. Last birth 1480
- **Catherine of Aragon** (1485-1536): 6 births, 1 survived. Last birth 1518
- **Anne of Denmark** (1574-1619): 9 births, 3 survived. Last birth 1606
- **Henrietta Maria** (1609-1669): 9 births, 6 survived. Last birth 1644
- **Queen Anne** (1665-1714): 17 pregnancies, 0 survived. Last pregnancy 1700

---

[4] en.wikipedia.org/wiki/Thomas_Greenhill_(surgeon). Accessed 04/11/2016.
[5] en.wikipedia.org/wiki/Women in the Middle Ages #Peasant women and health. Accessed 25/06/2017.

- **Charlotte of Mecklenburg-Strelitz** (1744-1818): 16 births, 13 survived. Last birth 1783
- **Queen Victoria** (1819-1901): 9 births, all survived. Last birth 1857
- **Mary of Teck** (1867-1953): 6 births, all survived. Last birth 1905

This modest sample shows a fertility rate (number of children per female) of 11.4 on average whereas the world fertility rate in 2014 was 2.4.[6]

The biological imperative of survival of the species, therefore, it has been argued for hundreds of years, determined the woman's social role and located it in the home just as the man's role was determined by food production which took place outside the home, hunting, herding, gathering or farming. This division of labour applied to ancillary work as well: domestic chores for women—cooking, cleaning, washing, clothing production and maintenance—and territorial defence or expansion of land, the source of food, for men.

As previewed in the preamble, anatomically male apes are bigger and stronger than females and, therefore, could exercise their physical advantage over them and do! -

> Approximately 85,000 women and 12,000 men are raped in England and Wales alone every year: that's roughly 11 rapes (of adults alone) every hour. These figures include assaults by penetration and attempts. Nearly half a million adults are sexually assaulted in England and Wales each year.

- 1 in 5 women aged 16-59 has experienced some form of sexual violence since the age of 16.
- Only around 15% of those who experience sexual violence choose to report to the police.
- Approximately 90% of those who are raped know the perpetrator prior to the offence.

These figures come from *An Overview of Sexual Offending in England and Wales*, the first ever joint official statistics bulletin on sexual violence released by the Ministry of Justice (MoJ), Office for National Statistics (ONS) and Home Office in January 2013.[7]

This physical advantage is considerable; in height alone, the male human, regardless of ethnicity, is 10 to 15 cm. taller than the female. If we look at some world record holders, we can examine the advantage in terms of task completion.

Body Mass Index (BMI) relates weight to height. While it is a measure of obesity, assuming weight is increased by fat, it is also a measure of frame and muscularity if fat is absent as it is in most athletes. The adjective 'massive' is

---

[6] data.worldbank.org/indicator/SP.DYN.TFRT.IN. Accessed 08/11/2016.

[7] rapecrisis.org.uk/statistics.php. Accessed 10/11/2016.

used equally for both types of appearance, abnormal fatness and abnormal height, frame and muscularity.

Sprinting

- **Men's 100m**: **9.58s**—Usain Bolt; H. 1.95m (6ft 5in); W. 94kg (207lb); BMI. 24.7 (Normal)
- **Women's 100m: 10.49s**—Florence Griffith Joiner; H. 1.77m (5ft 7in); W. 57kg (126lb); BMI. 18.2 (<Normal)

Bolt's time is 8.7% faster than Joiner's. His height advantage is +15% giving a stride length advantage of c.11%. He is 35.7% more massive.

Long distance

- **Men's 100km: 6h: 09:14**—Nao Kazami; H. n/a; W. n/a; BMI. n/a
- **Women's 100km: 6h: 33:11**—Tomoe Abe; H. 1.49m (4ft 11in); W. unknown; BMI. Unknown.
- Kazami's time is 6.5% faster than Abe's.
- **Men's 20km Walk: 1h: 16:36**—Yusuke Suzuki; H. 1.69m (5ft 6 ½ in); W. 57kg (126lb); BMI. 20.0 (Normal)
- **Women's 20km Walk - 1h: 23:49 –** Yiang Jiayu; H. 1.63m (5ft 4in); W. 48kg (106lb); BMI. 18 (<normal)**Men's 3000m Steeplechase: 7m 53.63s**—Saif Saeed Shaheen; H. 1.74m (5ft 9in); W. 60kg (132lb); BMI. 19.8 (Normal)
- **Women's 3000m Steeplechase: 8m 44.32s**—Beatrice Chepkoech; H. 1.7m (5ft 6in); W. 54kg (119lb); BMI. 19.1 (Normal)
  Shaheen's time is 10.7% faster than Chepkoech's. His height advantage is +3.6% giving a stride length advantage of 4.1%.

Swimming

- **Men's 50m Freestyle: 20.91s**—Cesar Cielo; H. 1.95m (6ft 5in); W. 88kg (194lb); BMI. 23.1 (Normal)
- **Women's 50m Freestyle: 23.67s**—Sarah Sjostrom; H. 1.82m (6ft 0in); W. 76kg (168lb); BMI. 23.0 (Normal)
  Cielo's time is 13.2% faster than Sarah's. His height advantage is +6.9%. He is equally massive.
- **Men's 1500m Freestyle: 14m:31.02**—Sun Yang; H. 1.98m (6ft 6in); W. 89kg (196lb); BMI. 22.7 (Normal)
- **Women's 1500m Freestyle: 15m:20.48**—Katie Ledecky; H. 1.80m (5ft 11in); W. 70kg (155lb); BMI. 21.6 (Normal)

Yang's time is 5.63% faster than Ledecky's. His height advantage is +10%.

Weightlifting

- **Men's 61kg Clean and Jerk: 174kg**—Eko Yuli Irawan; H. 1.60m (5ft 3in); W. 60.95kg (134lb); BMI. 23.8 (Normal)
- **Women's 64kg Clean and Jerk: 145kg**—Deng Wei; H. 1.59m (5ft 2 ½ in); W. 62.34kg (137.4lb); BMI. 24.7 (Normal)

Eko has lifted a 20 % heavier load than Deng. His height advantage is only +0.6% and they are similar in weight and mass.

- **Men's 81kg Clean and Jerk: 207kg**—Lu Xiaojun; H. 1.72m (5ft 8in); W. 80.75kg (178lb); BMI. 27.28 (>Normal)
- **Women's 76kg Clean and Jerk: 156kg**—Zhang Wangli; H. n/a; W. 73.95kg (163lb); BMI. (>Normal)

Lu has lifted a 32.7% heavier load than Zhang. He is 9.2% heavier.
[Correct at 18.08.2021]

Clearly, their greater muscular strength, body size and mass enable males to outperform females in physical task completion. This mirrors our three ape cousins, the orangutan, the gorilla and the chimpanzee. Male orangutans are significantly taller and heavier than females. Male gorillas are on average twice the weight of females, taller and with a longer arm span. Male chimpanzees also are heavier, taller and have a wider arm span than females although the differences are not so marked. In fact, the differences, known as sexual dimorphism are greater the more distant the hominid cousin—orangs display the greatest dimorphism and humans the least.

All the Great Apes or hominids have a common ancestor from which they have evolved, and all have retained this bodily dimorphism.

> Within the Hominoidea (apes) superfamily, the Hominidae family diverged from the Hylobatidae (gibbon) family some 15-20 million years ago; African great apes (subfamily Homininae) diverged from orangutans (Ponginae) about 14 million years ago; the Hominini tribe (humans, *Australopithecines* and other extinct biped genera, and chimpanzee) parted from the Gorillini tribe (gorillas) between 9 and 8 million years ago; and, in turn, the subtribes Hominina (humans and biped ancestors) and Panina (chimps) separated about 7.5 to 5.6 million years ago.[8]

However, there are no physical challenges in which males engage that cannot be taken on by females. Even the need for impregnation is now up for re-interpretation as science explores the phenomenon of parthenogenesis—virgin

[8] en.wikipedia.org/wiki/Human_evolution. Accessed 27/06/2017.

birth—which has been observed in some plants and animals. The inequality exists only in the superior task completion of males which intelligence, teamwork and technology can and do render and have rendered less significant anyway.

Furthermore, there is one combined physical task unique to females, the carrying of a foetus, the delivery of a baby and the breast feeding of an infant and, as the modern house husband has proved, the male's superior bulk and strength does not preclude him from carrying out any of the tasks ancillary to that process and normally assigned to females (assuming a willingness for 'bottle' to replace 'breast').

Professor of Anthropology, Barry Hewlett, and his wife, Bonnie, have spent a long time living alongside and observing the Aka Pygmy people of the Central African Republic. They found a culture where male and female roles are interchangeable. Men mind children while the women hunt, and women mind them while men cook. While in their phase as primary carers, i.e., breast-feeders, women go back to work either taking the baby with them or leaving it with the father who even allows it to suckle his nipples for comfort.

> "There is a sexual division of labour in the Aka community—women, for example, are the primary caregivers," [he says]. "But, and this is crucial, there's a level of flexibility that's virtually unknown in our society. Aka fathers will slip into roles usually occupied by mothers without a second thought and without, more importantly, any loss of status—there's no stigma involved in the different jobs."[9]

Compare this with William Langland's word picture of life for a peasant woman in England 600 years ago in his poem, *Piers Plowman*.

> "Burdened with children and landlords' rent;
> What they can put aside from what they make spinning they spend on housing,
> Also on milk and meal to make porridge with
> To sate their children who cry out for food
> And they themselves also suffer much hunger,
> And woe in wintertime, and waking up nights
> To rise on the bedside to rock the cradle,
> Also to card and comb wool, to patch and to wash,
> To rub flax and reel yarn and to peel rushes
> That it is pity to describe or show in rhyme
> The woe of these women who live in huts."[10]

---

[9] www.theguardian.com/society/2005/jun/15/childrensservices. familyandrelationships. Accessed 13/11/2016.

[10] en.wikipedia.org/wiki/Women_in_the_Middle_Ages#Peasant_women _and_health. Accessed 28/06/2017.

Chapter 2
Procreation

Even evolutionary explanations of the traditional division of labour by sex do not imply that it is unchangeable, "natural" in the sense of good, or something that should be forced on individual women or men who don't want it.
– Steven Pinker, How the Mind Works

We start out postulating sharp boundaries, such as between humans and apes, or between apes and monkeys, but are in fact dealing with sandcastles that lose much of their structure when the sea of knowledge washes over them. They turn into hills, levelled ever more, until we are back to where evolutionary theory always leads us: a gently sloping beach.
– Frans de Waal, *The Age of Empathy*

Preamble

While the facts support the argument that the superior 'brute strength' of the male human animal makes him more suited to and more efficient in heavy-duty tasks and the unique primary care biology of the female occupies much of her time and much of her physical effort, they are not conclusive in delineating two different animals incapable, due to their anatomical differences, of more than adequately fulfilling the social roles of the other. Is there, then, something else other than muscular mass and baby production driving the sexes to self-select themselves for their social roles? The most believed suspects are hormones; two, in particular, testosterone, the primary male sex hormone, and oestrogen, the primary female one.

Both hormones are present in both sexes and trigger many sexual responses in both. There is a correlation between the former and aggressive and competitive behaviour in males who produce 7-8 times more of it than females. The latter stimulates and regulates the menstrual cycle in females which can, not inevitably does, lead to mood swings and stress. Different aspects of Premenstrual Syndrome (PMS) have been reported by 20-30% of women. In 3-8% of cases the effects are severe.[11]

Whereas muscularity and aggression are useful advantages for dominant behaviour (Please remember that over 1 million women per year suffer domestic

---

[11] en.wikipedia.org/wiki/Menstrual_cycle. Accessed 15/11/2016.

violence in the UK.) there is a great deal more complexity in attaining dominance than these alone (some 700,000 men suffer as well). Dominant animals in mixed sex groups dominate the majority—of both sexes—and in single sex groups there is still a dominant male (gorillas) or female (elephants). Furthermore, there are no corresponding studies showing that oestrogen has a strong tendency to make females submissive.

Genghis Khan, who is said to have sired at least 1000 children throughout one of the greatest Empire's the world has seen, is also said to have been killed by one of his female conquests—*submissive but deadly*. The world's first Black Widow, Mary Ann Cotton from Sunderland, is thought to have murdered 3 out of her 4 husbands, 11 out of her 13 children, her lover and, possibly, at least 21 people in all; not for aggressive lusts or revenge but for money. She was hanged in 1873, 15 years before her male counterpart, Jack the Ripper, terrified the East End with his mere 5 deeply disturbing sexually motivated murders. The spiders named in her honour, renowned for their highly poisonous and distressing bite, show that nature does not universally favour the male of the species.

> According to Canadian Geographic, black widows are primarily solitary, with the exception of late spring when mating occurs. Female spiders can live up to three years. Males typically live for one or two months.

Black widows get their name because "females [carry] out sexual cannibalism after mating." The female often kills and eats the male, which explains the males' short lifespans. Sewlal said that scientists theorise the practice occurs "so that the females would get a ready source of protein, which would be beneficial to the offspring now developing inside her. However, she continued, "this is mostly observed in laboratory conditions so that males cannot escape."[12]

A further biological argument for male domination relates to sexual behaviours. At least four behavioural patterns are commonly cited to support the proposition that the natural necessity of male sexual dominance leads to his 'natural' dominance in family, community and society.

- Greater strength, aggression and competitiveness make males a sexual threat to and protector of females, a situation that, for reasons of survival, requires male-only regulation i.e., patriarchy.
- In this situation, males compete for females—fittest wins.
- Monogamous females ensure survival or the prolongation of the male genome.
- Face-to-face sex is the best and most natural human way of copulating—male on top.

[12] www.livescience.com/39919-black-widow-spiders.html. Accessed 15/11/2016.

In what I'm going to say next I'm almost certainly going to display great ignorance or naivety or both! However, when faced with mind-bogglingly clever scientific knowledge it seems to me important that both its content and its relevance need to be revealed in such a way that non-specialists can grasp its importance to their daily existence.

The first two of these behaviours above suggest that hominids might have evolved from a common ancestor whose sexual behaviour was that of a 'tournament' species. This is what Wikipedia has to say about tournament species.

> Tournament species in zoology are those species in which members of one sex (usually males) compete in order to mate. In tournament species, most members of the competing sex never win the competitions and never mate, but almost all members of the other sex do mate with the small group of winners.
> Tournament species are characterised by fierce same-sex fighting. Significantly larger or better-armed individuals in these species have an advantage, but only to the competing sex. Thus, most tournament species have high sexual dimorphism. Examples of tournament species include grouse, peafowl, lions, mountain gorillas and elephant seals.
> In some species, members of the competing sex come together in special display areas called leks. In other species, competition is more direct, in the form of fighting between males.
> In a small number of species, females compete for males; these include species of jacana, species of phalarope, and the spotted hyena. In all these cases, the female of the species shows traits that help in same-sex battles: larger bodies, aggressiveness, territorialism. Even maintenance of a multiple male "harem" is sometimes seen in these animals.
> Most species fall on a continuum between tournament species and pair-bonding species.[13]

Although helpful in the acquisition or protection of food supplies or warding off predators it does seem that the massiveness has more to do with competition for mates in same-sex battles. The purpose of winning would seem to be, on the male's part, to ensure the transmission of his genes, via his sperm, to future generations and, on the female's part, to make sure she gets the best genes for her eggs that will be her contribution to the next generation. Nature has a number of schemes that try to avoid this mutually satisfactory outcome being the result of intra-species bloodshed.

In the avian world, the male's design for 'getting the girl(s)' is to make himself irresistibly attractive. He can call (the Screaming Piha), dance (the Bird

[13] en.wikipedia.org/wiki/Display_(zoology). Accessed 26/11/2016.

of Paradise), build a home (the Bower Bird) or, in most cases, just show off (*Hm! Definitely a human trait. Having brought up 4 boys and been one myself I recognise this behaviour only too clearly!*). He can show off with colour (Parrots [*my favourite is the Australian King Parrot where his gorgeous red head and body and green feathers are matched by her more muted green head and feathers and less conspicuous red body*]), hunting skills (Shrikes: [Shrikes hang their kills on a thorn, even a barb-wire fence, possibly partly to show off what good hunters they are.]) or secondary sex characteristics such as the peacock's tail.

The avian equivalent of Miss World is a strictly male affair—*Mr World?*—called a lek. The Capercaillie which lives in Scotland adopts the Mick Jagger approach with a solitary male wooing several females with his vocalisations and having sex with them all. The sage grouse of North America have a proper contest in which the males strut around, the winners take centre stage, and the females choose which ones are the most suitable mates.

Lekking behaviour does occur in some mammals and at least one primate, the mountain gorilla, a sub-species of the eastern gorilla. In these lekking species looks matter and, in many, males have exaggerated secondary sex characteristics which can function as armaments, for instance antlers. If appearances, such as exceptional body mass or armaments such as antlers, are not enough to deter fighting then aggressive behaviour is tried. For example, mountain gorillas, observed to be basically shy and gentle creatures, will fight, even to the death, to gain or preserve mating rights. First, however, a male silverback will try intimidation.

> The ritualised charge display is unique to gorillas. The entire sequence has nine steps: (1) progressively quickening hooting, (2) symbolic feeding, (3) rising bipedally, (4) throwing vegetation, (5) chest-beating with cupped hands, (6) one leg kick, (7) sideways running four-legged, (8) slapping and tearing vegetation and (9) thumping the ground with palms.[14]

A lot like the fearsome Maori War Dance, the Haka, performed by the All Blacks before every Rugby Test match!

The preference for display or threatening behaviour over fighting makes 'natural' common sense. Fighting is a real threat to natural fitness, taking abnormal amounts of energy which would be better used for food gathering and reproduction. It can also result in external wounds or internal injuries that leave the male temporarily or permanently incapacitated in which latter state death is the likely outcome.

Although, therefore, lekking is primarily an avian behaviour, using elaborate display features of colour and add-ons, it does occur in mammals with the

[14] wikipedia.org/wiki/Mountain_gorilla. Accessed 14/07/2017.

attendant aggression that is present in competition of any kind. Is it fanciful to see traces of this type of behaviour in the human phenomena of discos and night-clubs, make-up and fashion, six-packs and plastic surgery, groupies and ostentatious wealth, sports cars and mansions, Friday night punch-ups and macho-male posturing?

However, what humans do that is most similar to lekking, I would suggest, is speed dating in which process hitherto estranged males and females have a limited time period to introduce themselves, find an attraction, choose a mate and possibly engage in reproductive behaviour, the female's mate choice depending on physical attraction and that most powerful of male secondary sex characteristics, charm!

In lekking, the females seem to have an important, if not decisive, say in with whom they mate and, therefore, the transmission of the genome most likely to ensure survival of the species. Herd animals like ruminants, deer, antelope, sheep etc., have a mating season when females are on heat (in oestrus) which triggers male-male competition, including fighting. The reward for the winner is to mate with as many females as he can, thus transferring control of the genome to the dominant males.

A third rather more considerate approach is for a male to gain and keep control of a territory in which there are many females who will mate with him when in heat either voluntarily or, in some species, compulsorily. A good example of this among hominids is the orangutan. More solitary than the other great apes, males gain control of a territory in which females range. If they have the characteristic cheek flanges of the fully mature male females, when in heat, will most likely mate with them. The unwilling ones are often coerced into mating. Flanged males dominate the unflanged but those of similar maturity will fight.

In all three of these cultures, lekking, rutting and territory-establishing, the male has little or nothing to do with parenting and deposits his genes as widely as possible. He is polygynous. An additional safety procedure provided in his genome by Mother Nature is the compulsion to hang on to the partners with whom he is gene sharing, known as mate-guarding. For all you hot-blooded males out there who think that a polygynous lifestyle sounds like your idea of heaven Nature paints a different picture. For those mammals that lead the polygynous life, like Red Deer and Elephant seals, mate-guarding is energy sapping and ultimately unsuccessful, involving continuous fighting and mating, both exhausting, continuous watchfulness and chasing-off. There is little chance of complete success due to a high probability of being cuckolded.

The origins of the word cuckold, true to its natural word root, cuckoo, show the natural rather than the social downside to be more important. To the cuckolded ruminant or pinniped, it is not so much about the infidelity of one of his 'wives' but the natural waste of survival energy involved in bringing up another male's offspring. When a male lion is certain that offspring are not his, such as when he has just taken over a group of females, he will very probably kill the cubs who are suckling to stop the mother lactating thus allowing her to go back into oestrus.

Infanticide in the natural world, the mammal world, for compelling reasons of gene transmission is far from rare. It has been observed in common chimpanzee communities and well documented throughout human history, albeit for different reasons such as poverty (e.g., inability to pay the dowry of a female child) or deformity (physical inability of a child to contribute to family subsistence).

Chapter 3
Polygyny: The Harem

Now that Arab women are pouring into the streets by the million, men discover with dismay that they, not women, were the captives of the harem dream.
Fatema Mernissi

Preamble

Fatema Mernissi was a Moroccan writer and an Islamic feminist who herself grew up in a harem and whose PhD dissertation, Beyond the Veil, confirmed my almost total lack of understanding of Islamic culture and ensured, above all, that any socio-religious, cultural or intellectual superiority that I, as a Briton raised in the Judeo-Christian tradition, may have felt about Islamic culture was utterly misplaced, misconceived and uneducated. Understanding of other cultures is not a betrayal of one's own cultural practices but it is a way of modifying that age-old tendency to assume that one's own way is the best, in every way superior to all others; more civilised, more worthy of life, more divinely approved.

Harem culture is an ancient and common feature in human social development. Although it has been strongly associated with Islamic countries in the Middle East the practice pre-dates Islam having been a feature of Byzantine and, earlier still, Greek, Assyrian and Persian noble life. The etymological relationship between Harem and Polygyny is like that between Hoover and vacuum cleaner. Harem carries with it connotations of seclusion particularly of female members of a family group. With nineteenth century Romanticism and Orientalism, stoked by poets like Byron (*Turkish Tales*), travellers like Burton (*The Book of the Thousand Nights and One Night*), painters like Ingres (*Grande Odalisque*) and composers such as Mozart (*Die Entführung aus dem Serail*, "The Abduction from the Seraglio"), it became metonymic of a hidden, sexually charged world of available females at the disposal of a single male that fed the polygynous fantasies of the repressed generations of nineteenth and pre-1960s twentieth century Western men, and women, as they gobbled up the latest newspaper reports of cases brought by guardians of public morals such as the Society for the Suppression of Vice under the esteemed provisions of the Obscene Publications Act 1857 or paid their 27 cents to watch *The Sheikh* in the autumn of 1921.

Together with its co-practice of veiling in public this secretisation (purdah) of females by a society in which males make the rules (patriarchy) mirrors the genetic imperative of many tournament males in many different species of ensuring that it is their genes that are passed on to the offspring in which, to a greater or lesser extent, they invest their energies with the self-determined objective of bringing them to a sexual maturity that in its turn will secure the survival of the species.

It is a male-driven natural behaviour generated from the natural fact that a female always knows her offspring whereas a male does not, *thus giving females the unique strength of knowledge of and certainty over the future of their genes to which males can only aspire by gaining control of the conditions within which fertile females can be impregnated.* In Roman law, this was known as 'Mater semper certa est' (the mother is always certain). This anxiety, this gene jealousy, has driven male conduct towards women to the point almost of hysterical and certainly unjust irrationality.

Harem culture in the world of Homo Sapiens, therefore, did incorporate many features found in tournament species. Most obviously it embraced the dominance of the alpha male whose power was measured in financial or possession-based wealth rather than muscular strength but who nevertheless expended much of that financial power in fighting to assert his superiority and mate-guard the harem that was his most ostentatious reward for accumulating it.

Secondly, the investment of his wealth in all the mate-guarding apparatus of the harem, palaces like the Topkapi in Istanbul, eunuchs, household servants and expenses and, finally, an army and civil service to aid in its retention, exhausts it sooner or later. The huge natural advantage for his genes was that they got the best of both worlds: they were spread widely in search of the perfect female match and the resultant offspring and inheritors of his wealth, his natural human advantage, and were 99% certain to be his.

The sexual frisson of pre-Victorian and Victorian Orientalist pornography was provided in the dual fantasies of all these available and nubile females in bondage to the male will, for example, *The Lustful Turk*, and the possibility, despite all the investment in mate-guarding with eunuchs, less than real men who did not have to demonstrate the iron will of the Victorian gentleman over their sexual urges—of cuckolding with one, or preferably several, of them as was the case in *A Night in a Moorish Harem*.

Last, but not least, harem cultural practices were the exclusive province of the rich and powerful. Ordinary hewers of wood and drawers of water could neither afford multiple mates nor the mate-guarding paraphernalia that went with them. When not actually producing or nurturing offspring the mates had to contribute to the resources that would keep their offspring alive and allow them to grow to sexual maturity. Work, in the fields, marketplaces or workshops, meant that women mixed with men to earn the bread of life. Work was communal and public and provided the resources for child-rearing as a joint enterprise.

In conclusion, therefore, the harem culture of the ruling class in many species, including some mammals, some hominids and some groups of Homo sapiens, was a genetic response to survival which involved polygynous groupings around alpha males and necessitated that those males made the rules by which every member lived—a male world delineated and controlled by males—which, with much exaggeration and personalisation, we call a patriarchy. It is not, however, the only approach to genome transmission, the secret to survival, nor is it probably the most primitive which brings us on to a consideration of its opposites; Monogamy and Matriarchy and the related issues of morality and sexual dominance.

Although it is recorded that Harems were populated by many females other than wives and concubines, the potential breeding partners for other alpha males, such as close female relatives of that male and even princes of the royal blood until they reached puberty they were clearly about gene transmission not a finishing school for potential noble brides or royal princes nor a sort of human adornment of the wealthy. The acquisition of human bling by the alpha males of today attracts the attention of feminists the world over.

Therefore, the harem stands historically as a response, as in non-human animals, to a natural drive connected to the survival process. The overwhelming evidence for this and the most extraordinarily savage aspect of the whole Harem apparatus was the primary mate-guarding component, eunuchs, who provided the muscular-mass potential (or its equivalent in intellectual acumen) to enforce a protective and incarcerative regime designed to ward off sexual predators and competitors without the capacity to be one themselves.

Harem culture in human beings, unlike in non-human animals, institutionalised the emasculation of sexual competitors in addition to their subjugation and in so doing demonstrated an intellect generated by their larger brain capable of unimaginably greater violence in its controlled savagery than that shown by any tournament male in his attempt to impose some kind of savage control.

Chapter 4
Monogamy

Only about 3 percent of animal species are monogamous. A couple of penguins, some otters and a few other oddball critters. To these select few it comes natural to mate for life and never look at another member of the opposite sex. Humans are not part of that little club. Like the other 97% of species, humans are not monogamous by nature. We just pretend that we are.
– Oliver Markus, Why Men And Women Can't Be Friends

Preamble

I need to continue this more general scientific perspective—anthropological would perhaps best describe its gist—to examine the much-debated natural context for the history of gender inequality in British history and, to do that, introduce you to some leading academic lights reading of whose works, which I have not done, would almost certainly offer incredible insight into this mysterious world of sexual behaviour, reproduction, and survival. My brief inexpert acquaintance with them, however, prompts me to issue two massive caveats and a plea for patience.

Firstly, there is no single definitive answer to the mystery of why human beings behave as they do or, more accurately in terms of my quest, have done in the relationship between the sexes.

Secondly, in a previous reference to the anthropology of Bronislaw Malinowski in my other amateur companion to me, 'An Armchair of Dissent', I took on board the caution concerning the subjectivity of observers—seeing what you want to see rather than what you do see—which in the theatre of 'gender warfare' can be further distorted by 'political' motives. This added to the reluctance of some observers and writers about sexual behaviour, particularly those inflicted with a sense of Victorian morality, 'to say it how it is' must prompt us to be very cautious about the predictability and explicability of human gendered behaviour.

Bearing these in mind, I will return to the case of the deliberate and systematic suppression of one sex by the other in British history and tradition, but it will be a long and possibly circuitous journey on which I ask you to accompany me.

The history of modern British society is at most 2,000 years old. The history of settled agricultural, urban society is approximately 10,000 years old. The history of Homo Sapiens is 200,000 to 100,000 years old. At some time in this era monogamous behaviour was tried and, in some cultures, including that of Western Europeans, became established as the morally correct and socially preferred sexual behaviour. On the most likely assumption that at some stage in the past all hominids were promiscuous something must have happened for some to favour monogamy. Sergey Gavrilets, Professor at the University of Tennessee, applies maths to evolutionary conundrums such as this.

In an article in the Health section of *Time* Magazine, 29 May 2012, Maia Szalavitz reviewed Gavrilets' 2012 paper 'Human origins and the transition from promiscuity to pair-bonding' (*Proceedings of the National Academy of Sciences* 109(25):9923-9928). She sees in Gavrilets' study the possibility of a sexual revolution greater than that of the 1960s when promiscuity—without life-changing consequences due to the contraceptive pill—became fashionable and undermined the Victorian morality that had underpinned the quintessentially 'British' sexual culture of monogamy, *in which I was schooled*, for well over a hundred years.

Human males below the alphas and betas still had the instinct to ensure the survival of their genome thus presenting them with several choices. Most of these involved competing or careful mate-guarding for which they were not suited physically, socially, or politically. Szalavitz records Gavrilets' own statement of his proposition:

> "What happens is that for guys at the bottom of the hierarchy who are weak or small and who would never be able to win competitions, mate-provisioning becomes a very valuable option" says Gavrilets. "They start provisioning the females first and then females develop a preference for provisioning, and then [begins] the whole process of the co-evolution of male provisioning and female faithfulness."[15]

Then the evolutionary process takes over:

> Both male and female choice drove evolution. "Female faithfulness increases as a result of males selecting more faithful females and male provisioning grows as females select for better providers and they co-evolve in a mutually beneficial way," Gavrilets says.[16]

What I like about this proposition is its placement of the unempowered, the inferiors if you like, at the heart of an evolutionary process that produced a homo sapiens that we recognise as modern. The question of what drives social change has exercised most philosophers (*feel free to read Hobbes, Rousseau or Marx, Aristotle or Aquinas, Russell or Dawkins*) and if we slightly alter it to 'who' drives social change, the movers and shakers or the anonymous multitude of the ordinary Jacks and Jills, it becomes even more of a fascination. Furthermore, it

---

[15] healthland.time.com/2012/05/29/the-ancient-sexual-revolution-that-may-have-spurred-human-monogamy/. Accessed 05/09/2017.

[16] Ibid.

seems to fit with my reading of human ingenuity summed up most memorably by Richard Buckminster Fuller:

> "You never change things by fighting the existing reality.
> To change something, build a new model that makes the existing model obsolete."

I first came across Buckminster Fuller as a student in 1967/8, a developing dissenter struggling with a worldview of unfairness and personal feelings of inadequacy and mundanity. I was loving my study of Keynesian economics and the growing threat of Friedman and his free market Monetarism, but my head was full of new stuff of which I was thus far totally unaware. One of my subsidiary courses was the Economics of Development and it fed my prejudicial feelings about the astonishing inequality that was omnipresent in the world in which I lived and, to some extent, of which I was an overprivileged product.

My darker thoughts were of kwashiorkor, the burning of grain surpluses, set aside, famine, disease and the shanty towns of South America and South Asia. I was very concerned about feeding the world, for heaven's sake—such a beautiful world as shown by the iconic photos from Apollo 8 -, 16 years before Sir Bob aroused some global concern for doing so among the powers that be. I would like to think that, along with the absurdly long hair and equally absurd high heels (YouTube Brotherhood of Man "Save Your Kisses for Me", 1976. That was me in my 20s!), many of my generation had the compassion necessary to kickstart a different view of the Third World that lasted only too briefly to be replaced by Al Qaeda, the Twin Towers, the Iraq War, Robert Mugabe, General Pinochet, Boko Haram, Isis etc.

Buckminster Fuller published a book in 1968 entitled 'Operating Manual for Spaceship Earth' which added to my concern for feeding the world the equally grave concern for 'powering' it. That metaphor for Planet Earth, Star ship Planet Earth, 'God Bless all those who sail in her', has stayed with me all my life. Feeding the crew and fuelling the engine get the cargo (the human race) safely home. Bucky's new model 'states that we "must operate exclusively on our vast daily energy income from the powers of wind, tide, water, and the direct Sun radiation energy".[17]

I hope, with all the angst of that 19 year-old me, that the rightness of Bucky's new model and Henry George's (George also shared Bucky's metaphor of SS Planet Earth but some 90 years before) assertion that the land and its natural resources are a free gift to all mankind, all of whom are entitled to an equal share of it making profit or gain from it only from the effort or investment they make in their exploitation of it, combine to form the new evolutionary model that will guarantee the survival of the human genome.

The ingenuity or downright sneakiness required in this model was shown by the lower ranking males given that the mate-provisioning at the core of this

---

[17] en.wikipedia.org/wiki/Operating_Manual_for_Spaceship_Earth. Accessed 06/09/2017.

behaviour was just another male ruse to get the female in oestrus to mate only with him thus no different from other more overtly competitive ruses employed by potential alphas and betas. Szalavitz considers the reaction of another noted evolutionary psychologist, Sarah Hrdy who cast doubt on Gavrilets' model by considering the female side of such a revolutionary compact.

Firstly, Hrdy believes that the significant evolutionary factor in cooperative child rearing was the cooperation of groups of females rather than a pair bond between a single male and a single female. Secondly, she casts doubt on the reliability of males being sufficient to engender faithfulness in females:

> "Some men will do anything to remain near their children. Others, even some [who are] certain of their paternity, act like they do not even know they had children," Hrdy says. "I don't think human mothers in the past could count on the long-term survival and fidelity of provisioning mates any more than mothers today can. It looks to me like males are responding to a wider range of factors than can be represented in such a model."[18]

However, if we look at chimpanzees, our closest species-evolutionary relatives, there are signs of a troop culture with fission-fusion—breaking up and reforming larger social groups—grouping behaviour and sufficiently frequent peaceful relations between groups for there to be sexual relations between single females from outside the group and single males within the group. Finally, there is enough evidence of political scheming in chimpanzee communities to believe that their evolution could result in a new hierarchical and social model of bonding and child-rearing behaviour.

Dr Jane Goodall's observations of the Kashakela community in the Gombe National Park in Tanzania in the 60s and 70s showed that power could be gained from alliances; non-alphas, for instance, could oust the alpha with the help of others or put their energy into mating rather than maintaining their dominance.[19]

The assumption that chimpanzee behaviour is somehow representative of less evolved human behaviour must be made with due caution. In acknowledging the fact that we share a common ancestry, first brought to widespread attention by Charles Darwin's book, *The Descent of Man,* in 1871, we tend to be drawn into the misapprehension—given credence almost immediately after the book's publication in the editorial caricature published in the satirical magazine, *The Hornet*, of Darwin's head on the body of an Orangutan (it actually looks more like a chimpanzee)—that the common ancestor looked like and, more importantly, behaved like one of our great ape cousins, the Pongos/Orangutans, the Pans/Chimpanzees, or the Gorillas, thus forgetting that the current versions of these three cousins have been evolving for as many million years as has our

[18] healthland.time.com/2012/05/29/the-ancient-sexual-revolution-that-may-have-spurred-human-monogamy/. Accessed 06/09/2017.
[19] en.wikipedia.org/wiki/Kasakela_Chimpanzee_Community. Accessed 07/09/2017.

version. They are not earlier versions of us. They are current versions of themselves.

What we do have from the mathematical analysis of Gavrilets and the field observations of Goodall are the natural components of potentially monogamous behaviour in hominids and homo sapiens as a species of hominid; most particularly, sharing of food, rearing of offspring and greater certainty of paternity.

Chapter 5
The Monogamous Human

What a piece of work is a man! How noble in reason, how infinite in faculty, in form and moving how express and admirable, in action how like an angel, in apprehension how like a god—the beauty of the world, the paragon of animals!

William Shakespeare, *Hamlet, Prince of Denmark, Act II, Scene 2*

Preamble

Of course, we human beings are the current version of ourselves as well. It is worth a moment's thought on what evolution has fashioned in us that is different from other animals and, more particularly other hominids.

If you're looking for incontrovertible proofs or even probabilities, as they say about football scores on the News, look away now!

There are some quite obscure differences and some well touted ones but none, contrary to common misconceptions, unique. The human chin, for instance, is quite unique. No one has a definitive idea about what it is there for or why it has evolved. Elephants have something similar, possibly to assist in some heavy duty chewing and crunching. Could that have been the case in an eater of raw meat and roots—most other apes, with the exception of Pans, stick to fruitarian or vegetarian food—whose brains made the cultural move to cooking, i.e., using heat energy to soften hard and fibrous matter (*I do not see much evidence of a marine or savannah or rainforest McDonalds catering for non-homo sapiens!*)?

Certainly, homo sapiens is the only hominid with a chin and there seems some archaeological evidence showing that human ancestors did not have a chin, but a bony jaw reinforcer called a simian shelf like all other great apes. It seems that the space taken up by this bony structure could be filled with more muscles that would allow more movement of the tongue and jaw to facilitate human language.

What is the relevance of a chin to monogamy, you may well be asking? Its connection to language is maybe a positive start!

As humans were evolving their language acquisition the ape-like jaw was receding into the face removing the natural pout configured around the simian shelf. Homo sapiens can still pout to communicate attractiveness or dissatisfaction but it is not a necessary behaviour except for babies who need it to latch on to the nipple to suck. Human females, unlike other great ape females have essentially conical shaped breasts that project and isolate the nipple which enables the flat-faced human baby to latch on even with a limited pout.

Without this conicality, the face would be pressed against the chest of the mother who would have to press the suckling baby to her nipple rather than just hold it and allow it to reach for it, rather like a mid-air refuelling operation. Breasts, sexual behaviour and mate-guarding in the form of policing that behaviour do have relevance to monogamy as, in its way, does language.

No, the human brain is not the largest on the planet! Like all other things whose size is being measured we could do it two ways, either measuring its volume or its weight. As brain volume tends to increase with body volume it will not surprise you to know that elephants, sperm whales and killer whales have larger brains. They also have heavier brains as do bottlenose dolphins; the blue whale, however, being the largest living creature on the planet, has a smaller brain than a sperm whale's 18 pounder, thus contradicting the expected result. Neanderthals, once close cousins to humans, had a larger brain than modern man. More relevant than sheer size is the brain mass/body mass ratio. In this respect, elephants are lower than and shrews are equal to humans who have the highest encephalisation quotient on the planet (7.4 as compared to a chimpanzee's 2.2).

Of course, size alone is not the most important factor in animal intelligence; it is what is done with it that counts. Larger animals need more brain capacity to handle more muscle functions in their larger bodies. Brain activity depends on neurons, their size and number, and, among primates, humans have a brain three times larger than Pongos, Gorillas and Pans and, therefore, more and larger neurons. Even in this league we are not top; the long-finned pilot whale having 37.2 billion (US measure) compared to a human 20 billion. Anyway, the logic that we are pursuing here is as follows; most animals are polygamous: most humans are monogamous: humans are smarter (only in terms of cognitive ability, it must be said) than most animals: so, monogamy is a smarter survival strategy than polygamy. *Hm!*

We walk on 2 legs. We are bipedal. Bipedalism is far from unique. Birds hop and flightless birds walk (and run very fast!)—an ostrich at full speed can reach 40mph (*the Great Usain could only reach about 26 and a four-legged cheetah about 60*)—and kangaroos hop at great speed. Birds, however, hold their bodies horizontal or at an angle to their legs as do Roos whereas Homo Sapiens walks upright and, along with its ancestors, has done for millions of years with its skeleton slowly evolving into the perfect upright, bipedal human that is Usain Bolt.

Part of that evolutionary process, of course, will involve the brain. For instance, the brain directs the coordination of two organs whose use is highly elevated by bipedalism, the hand and the eye. Without needing to understand the physiological techno-speak, read how we achieve hand-eye coordination, essential to tool making, tool use and tool carrying.

> The neural control of eye-hand coordination is complex because it involves every part of the central nervous system involved in vision: eye movements, touch, and hand control. This includes the eyes themselves, the cerebral cortex, subcortical structures (such as the cerebellum, basal ganglia, and brain stem), the spinal cord, and the peripheral nervous system. Other areas involved in eye-hand coordination that have been studied most intensely are the frontal and parietal cortex areas for the control of eye saccades and hand-reach. Both of these areas are believed to play a key role in eye-hand coordination and the planning of movements during tasks.[20]

In 1974, Lucy came out of the closet (more accurately, the ground), discovered 'in Africa, near the village Hadar in the Awash Valley of the Afar Triangle in Ethiopia, by paleoanthropologist Donald Johanson of the Cleveland Museum of Natural History.'[21] Lucy was the nickname given to a find of bones, officially known as AL 288-1, believed to be a significant part of the skeleton of a human ancestor. Small in stature with a small brain similar in size to that of a chimpanzee and a large stomach and digestive system equally similar, Lucy definitely walked. She was bipedal. Almost certainly a forager, Lucy would have had an advantage both in being able to use her hands and extend the range and number of habitats in which she could gather food.

Lucy, *Australopithecus afarensis*, lived over 3 million years ago. In the same region of Africa, a skeleton over 4 million years old was also discovered but Ardi, *Ardipithecus ramidus* as she is known, probably walked bipedally yet had an opposable big toe as well as an opposable thumb whereas Lucy had flat feet. Humans are not the only primates or mammals with opposable thumbs and, of course, birds would have a hard time perching without an opposable digit! In Lucy, however, we begin to see the unbeatable physiology of ape brain, forward sight, arms, hands with opposable thumbs and flat feet that in their co-evolution have produced the most successful, in survival terms it should be emphasised, hominid ever.

Evolution has left 7 extant species of hominids:

Genus Pongo:	Sumatran Orangutan.
	Bornean Orangutan.
Genus Gorilla:	Western Gorilla.
	Eastern Gorilla.
Genus Pan:	Common chimpanzee.
	Bonobo.
Genus Homo:	Homo sapiens.

---

20 en.wikipedia.org/wiki/Eye%E2%80%93hand_coordination. Accessed 13/09/2017.

21 en.wikipedia.org/wiki/Lucy_(Australopithecus). Accessed 15/09/2017.

The following table lists the estimated number of great ape individuals living outside zoos:

Species	Estimated number
Sumatran orangutan	6,667
Bornean orangutan	61,234
Western gorilla	200,000
Eastern gorilla	6,000
Common chimpanzee	100,000
Bonobo	10,000
Human	7,364,930,000[22]

Beware of feeling superior! Compared with ants we are insignificant survivors.

> *Ants do pretty well in the numbers game too, with estimates of their global population ranging from 10,000 trillion to a quadrillion (a million trillion). While counting ants is difficult and these estimates could be out by a good few zeros, it's pretty safe to say ants are the most numerous insects in the world.*[23]
> *Like all insects, ants have six legs. Each leg has three joints. The legs of the ant are very strong so they can run very quickly. If a man could run as fast for his size as an ant can, he could run as fast as a racehorse. Ants can lift 20 times their own body weight. An ant brain has about 250 000 brain cells.. A human brain has 10,000 million so a colony of 40,000 ants has collectively the same size brain as a human.*
> *The Army Ant (Ecitron Burchelli) of South America, can have as many as 700,000 members in its colony.*[24].

With those flat feet taking them gradually across the globe and those shorter arms and opposable thumbs making and using a greater variety of tools, the branch Homo evolved larger brains from their need to respond to a bewildering variety of environmental and technological cognitive challenges and opportunities. As well as scavenging meat those legs could be used to hunt it and those arms and hands to make and deploy weapons that improved the efficiency of the hunter-killer, made all the more deadly by hunting in cooperative groups. After some two and a half million years, Lucy's descendants arrived in Europe, having already settled in Asia and the Middle East.

As a hunter, Homo erectus was a formidable unit. There may be thousands of potential conquerors of Usain Bolt in the animal world but there are, despite

[22] en.wikipedia.org/wiki/Hominidae. Accessed 27/06/2017.

[23] www.bbc.com/earth/story/20150211-whats-the-most-dominant-life-form. Accessed 09/06/2018.

[24] www.lingolex.com/ants.htm. Accessed 09/06/2018.

its multitudinous variety, very few terrestrial Mo Farahs or Abebe Bikilas. The human hunter was relentless with a stamina and persistence unrivalled by his prey. Secondly, from stick poking or hitting or stone cutting or hitting to missile propulsion would be a pointless transition if the human arm did not provide the necessary propulsive strength to hurl a spear or throw a weight. Its ability to do so is unique.

World records

- *Shot Put:* *Randy Barnes-23.12m.* *Natalya lisovskaya-22.63m.*
- *Discus:* *Jurgen Schult-74.08m.* *Gabriele Reisch-76.80m.*
- *Hammer:* *Yuri Sedych-86.74m.* *Anita Wlodarczyk-82.96m.*
- *Javelin:* *Jan Zelezny-98.48m.* *Barbara Spotakova-72.28m.*
- *Unproven world record for a cricket ball: Roald Bradstock-132.66m.*
- *The Pakistani fast bowler Shoaib Akhtar delivered the fastest delivery officially recorded at a top speed of 161.3km/h.*

Whether during this period of Homo habilis and Homo erectus, the monogamous behaviour hypothesised by Gavrilets began to emerge in these hunting groups can only be conjectured but it is not unimaginable or infeasible. The next technological phase, however, agriculture, which replaced gathering and hunting with planting and animal domestication, might well have favoured monogamy. Along with clothing and language, agriculture was the invention of recognisably modern humans, homo sapiens, who ousted or outlasted their only competitor, *Homo Neanderthalensis*, some of the later survivors of whom might well have been clothed and spoken a less polished language, some 40,000 years ago.

Three other fairly unique human features made the more uni-locational food provision of agriculture highly suitable for a nuclear family, one male, one female and multiple offspring, in which the food-providing and child-rearing tasks were shared out within the family unit.

Firstly, that increasingly clever primate who could conquer and consume other animals and meet the challenges presented by different climates and habitats, needed more and larger neurons to make the necessary connections of knowledge, movement, memory and communication. The adult brain was growing and needed time and space to grow. It caused human foetuses to be proper bigheads! And that hand-eye coordination and bipedalism which gave them their evolutionary edge over other life forms needed some time to kick in. That big head, as billions of women throughout the ages would have testified and billions more who do and will testify, takes some shifting through a pelvic girdle designed for upright locomotion.

Natural evolution has done a lot to help.

- The pelvic girdle of a female human surrounds a larger more circular space.

- The four bones that make it up have joints which can expand during childbirth.
- The skull of a human baby is softer than an adult's and its six sections have sutures at the joints that allow the head to expand and contract.
- The normal birth position of headfirst, nose facing spine presents the narrowest part of the head to the pelvic space.
- The baby's head makes a subtle adjustment to make sure the broadest part of the head passes through the broadest part of the pelvic space.

Amazing! What a piece of work is a woman!

Much can go wrong with this intricately smooth process. About 4% of babies do not turn producing many problems associated with a breech birth. Access to modern technology in the form of a caesarean section is the human bighead's evolved solution to, well, being an evolved bighead, but nutrition and a secure food supply obviate a lot of the problems, including deaths of both neonates and mothers, caused by obstructed delivery, itself frequently caused by stunted growth or malformation of the pelvic girdle. UNICEF has estimated that: "Globally, more than one quarter (26 per cent) of children under 5 years of age were stunted in 2011—roughly 165 million children worldwide." and "In sub-Saharan Africa, 40 per cent of children under 5 years of age are stunted; in South Asia, 39 per cent are stunted."[25]

Forms of infant mortality include:

- *Deaths of babies due to obstructed delivery or breech presentation are included in a measure of infant mortality.*
- *Perinatal mortality is late foetal death (22 weeks gestation to birth), or death of a new-born up to one week postpartum.*
- *Neonatal mortality is new-born death occurring within 28 days postpartum. Neonatal death is often attributed to inadequate access to basic medical care, during pregnancy and after delivery. This accounts for 40-60% of infant mortality in developing countries.*
- *Post neonatal mortality is the death of children aged 29 days to one year. The major contributors to post neonatal death are malnutrition, infectious disease, troubled pregnancy, Sudden Infant Death Syndrome and problems with the home environment.'*[26]

Measured by number of deaths per 1000 live births: 'The infant mortality rate of the world is 49.4 according to the United Nations and 34.1 according to the CIA World Factbook.'[27] .

---

[25] en.wikipedia.org/wiki/Stunted growth. Accessed 21/09/2017.

[26] en.wikipedia.org/wiki/List of countries by infant mortality rate. Accessed 21/09/2017.

[27] ibid.

A difficult birth can have serious, even fatal, and long term, consequences for the mother. Indeed, the caesarean procedure is likely to have been used to rescue a live baby from a dead mother—joy and sorrow exemplifying the journey of the emotional human being.

> *'The maternal mortality rate (MMR) varies from 9 per 100,000 live births in the US and Europe to 900 per 100,000 live births in Sub-Saharan Africa. Every year more than half a million women die in pregnancy or childbirth.'*
> *'The world maternal mortality rate has declined 44% since 1990, but still every day 830 women die from pregnancy or childbirth related causes. According to the United Nations Population Fund (UNFPA), this is equivalent to "about one woman every two minutes and for every woman who dies, 20 or 30 encounter complications with serious or long-lasting consequences. Most of these deaths and injuries are entirely preventable."'*[28]

One of the most unpleasant long-term conditions caused by a difficult delivery is obstetric fistulas, holes in the soft tissues between the vagina and the bladder or rectum. 'An estimated 2 million women in sub-Saharan Africa, Asia, the Arab region, and Latin America and the Caribbean are living with this injury, and some 50,000 to 100,000 new cases develop each year.'[29]

'Symptoms of obstetric fistula' include:

- *Flatulence, urinary or faecal incontinence, which may be continual or only happen at night*
- *Foul-smelling vaginal discharge*
- *Repeated vaginal or urinary tract infections.*
- *Irritation or pain in the vagina or surrounding areas*
- *Pain during sexual activity*

> *Other effects of obstetric fistulae include stillborn babies due to prolonged labour, which happens 85% to 100% of the time, severe ulcerations of the vaginal tract, "foot drop", which is the paralysis of the lower limbs caused by nerve damage, making it impossible for women to walk, infection of the fistula forming an abscess, and up to two-thirds of the women become amenorrhoeic.*
> *Obstetric fistulae have far-reaching physical, social, economic, and psychological consequences for the women affected.*
> *According to UNFPA, "Due to the prolonged obstructed labour, the baby almost inevitably dies, and the woman is left with chronic*

[28] en.wikipedia.org/wiki/Maternal death. Accessed 21/09/2017.
[29] en.wikipedia.org/wiki/Obstetric_fistula#Risk_factors. Accessed 21/09/2017.

incontinence. Unable to control the flow of urine or faeces, or both, she may be abandoned by her husband and family and ostracised by her community. Without treatment, her prospects for work and family life are virtually non-existent."[30]

Please read this summary of the social consequences of this condition which you may or may not have heard of and I will think this digression worthwhile.

Physical consequences of obstetric fistulae lead to severe sociocultural stigmatisation for various reasons. For example, in Burkina Faso, most citizens do not believe an obstetric fistula to be a medical condition, but as a divine punishment or a curse for disloyal or disrespectful behaviour. Other sub-Saharan cultures view offspring as an indicator of a family's wealth. A woman who is unable to successfully produce children as assets for her family is believed to make her and her family socially and economically inferior. A patient's incontinence and pain also render her unable to perform household chores and childrearing as a wife and as a mother, thus devaluing her. Other misconceptions about obstetric fistulae are that they are caused by venereal diseases or are divine punishment for sexual misconduct.

As a result, many girls are divorced or abandoned by their husbands and partners, disowned by family, ridiculed by friends, and even isolated by health workers. Divorce rates for women who suffer from an obstetric fistula range from 50% to as high as 89%. Now marginalised members of society, girls are forced to live on the edges of their villages and towns, often to live in isolation in a hut where they will likely die from starvation or an infection in the birth canal. The unavoidable odour is viewed as offensive, thus their removal from society is seen as essential. Accounts of women who suffer obstetric fistulae proclaim that their lives have been reduced to the leaking of urine, faeces and blood because they are no longer capable or allowed to participate in traditional activities, including the duties of wife and mother. Because such consequences highly stigmatise and marginalise the woman, the intense loneliness and shame can lead to clinical depression and suicidal thoughts. Some women have formed small groups and resorted to walking to seek medical help, where their characteristic odour makes them a target for sub-Saharan predatory wildlife, further endangering their lives. This trip can take on average 12 hours to complete.

Moreover, women are sometimes forced to turn to commercial sex work as a means of survival because the extreme poverty and social isolation that result from obstetric fistulae eliminate all other income opportunities. With only 7.5% of women with fistulae able to access treatment, the vast majority of women end up with the consequences of

[30] Ibid.

> *obstructed and prolonged labour simply because options and access to help is so limited.*[31]

The second, possibly unique, feature of homo sapiens is that her babies are born totally helpless. Intense post-natal aftercare is not just advisable or necessary, it is essential—as much part of being human as technological aptitude, intelligent problem-solving, environmental adaptation and walking upright. Human babies are unique among mammals in this secondary altriciality; i.e., a second post-natal phase of complete helplessness.

> So, the consequence of secondary altriciality is that the new-born requires a period *after* birth of getting its needs satisfied in the same complete way as it did prior to that in the womb. This is a characteristic of *Homo sapiens.* It is another one of those very few things that definitively distinguishes us from all other species known. That is, the human infant is in a more dependent state, when born, than any other species, when its young is born. The human infant at birth in terms of its degree of development, is at a level corresponding to that at which, in every other mammal, it would still be in the womb. In other words, we are born, comparatively, "premature".[32]

While in the womb the mother provides all the environmental and nutritional care the baby needs automatically thus not interfering with her ability to make a group contribution either socially, culturally, economically, or politically—obviously, her physical contribution would be impaired by her pregnancy. Why not a longer period of gestation then?

> Indeed, by one estimation a human foetus would have to undergo a gestation period of 18 to 21 months instead of the usual nine to be born at a neurological and cognitive development stage comparable to that of a chimpanzee new-born.[33]

Clearly, size of the baby has a lot to do with it—a meadow mouse gestates for 3 weeks; an elephant for 95 weeks (a human for 40 weeks)—but brain size plays a part as well. The human brain is less than 30% of its adult weight at birth (300g. as compared to 1400g.)—a chimpanzee's is about 40%—whereas the largest believed to exist is that of the Weddel seal at 70% of its adult weight.

> Scientists have found over the years that animals born into hostile environments tend to have larger brains at birth to help them survive. Zebras and wildebeest, for example, must be able to run with the herd just hours after being born—their relatively mature brains at birth help

[31] Ibid.

[32] angelsinnature.wordpress.com/tag/secondary-altriciality/. Accessed 22/09/2017.

[33] blogs.scientificamerican.com/observations/why-humans-give-birth-to-helpless-babies/. Accessed 22/09/2017.

> them to not only run, but respond in appropriate ways when predators appear. Likewise, Weddell seal pups must be able to undertake what few other mammals are willing to dare, regardless of age—swim long distances under stretches of sea ice. Doing so is dangerous because there is always the risk that a seal won't be able to find a hole in the ice or an air pocket in time to prevent drowning.[34]

Large brain size at birth, therefore, seems to correlate highly with independent negotiation of environmental challenges exceedingly early on in life's journey. The utter inability of a human infant to do this has been explained by the incompatibility of a 21-month-old human brain and the bipedal restrictions placed on the birth canal and the pelvic girdle. Mother Nature over millions of years has decided that such a cranium could not be delivered. A second idea is put forward by Professor Holly Dunsworth and her researchers, suggesting that the human mother cannot share her energy with the foetus for longer than 40 weeks:

> Dunsworth and her collaborators conclude that "if the human reproductive system poses a dilemma between competing needs, then foetal energy needs and maternal energy supply are the competitors, rather than [brain expansion] and bipedalism."[35]

In his report on Weddel seals, Bob Yirka gives us an insight into the energy-sapping potential of a large-brained neonate.

> The pups, the researchers found, require 30 to 50 grams of glucose per day to survive, all of it coming from their mother's milk—28 grams of it is consumed by the brain.[36]

Exhausted, their mums leave them to fend for themselves at just six weeks old!

By contrast, the human infant's brain is not out of the second gear of its brain growth. By the time it is 3 the infant's brain will be about 90% of its adult size or weight not reaching full capacity until its user is 9-14 years of age. Throughout this very long period of dependence, unlike that very young Weddel seal who needs to be ready to meet environmental challenges, the helpless human is taking a learning, elastic approach to them, not only adapting but memorising how to react to the stimulation the environment provides. Working out 'how' creates a culture.

For her article on why human infants are born helpless, Kate Wong asked for the views of a palaeoanthropologist, Karen Rosenberg. The conclusion seems to

---

[34] phys.org/news/2013-05-weddell-brains-birth-mammal.html. Accessed 22/09/2017.
[35] blogs.scientificamerican.com/observations/why-humans-give-birth-to-helpless-babies/. Accessed 4/09/2017.
[36] phys.org/news/2013-05-weddell-brains-birth-mammal.html. Accessed 24/09/2017.

ask the question "Is or was monogamy an essential cultural addition to the whole care package?"

> Rosenberg additionally noted—and I found this especially fascinating—that the authors mention the possibility that the timing of birth actually optimises cognitive and motor neuronal development. That idea, first proposed by Swiss zoologist Adolf Portman in the 1960s, is worth pursuing, she says. "Maybe human new-borns are adapted to soaking up all this cultural stuff and maybe being born earlier lets you do this," she muses. "Maybe being born earlier is better if you're a cultural animal." Food for thought.[37]

One thing is certain. When that care package goes wrong the consequences for the infant or the future teenager or adult are fatal or counterproductive to an enduring and improving survival of their genes.

> Globally, 9.2 million infants and children die each year before their fifth birthday; more than 60% of these deaths are seen as being avoidable with low-cost measures such as continuous breast-feeding, vaccinations, and improved nutrition.[38]

In a world before advanced medical care and technology, how was nutrition and prenatal, neonatal and post-natal care provision guaranteed in sufficient quantity to ensure survival and growth of population? Impressive though it was until the 1820s, world population is estimated to have been 1 billion by 1820. It now grows at 1 billion every 15 years or so. If agriculture was the mega technological, social and cultural change that provided the nutrition, was a monogamous unit essential to its delivery in sufficient quantities to mother and infant in order to ensure not just survival but population growth, however modest by modern standards?

> Low birth weight makes up 60-80% of the infant mortality rate in developing countries. *The New England Journal of Medicine* stated that "The lowest mortality rates occur among infants weighing 3,000 to 3,500 g (6.6 to 7.7 lb.). For infants born weighing 2,500 g (5.5 lb.) or less, the mortality rate rapidly increases with decreasing weight, and most of the infants weighing 1,000 g (2.2 lb.) or less die. As compared with normal-birth-weight infants, those with low weight at birth are almost 40 times more likely to die in the neonatal period; for infants with very low weight at birth the relative risk of neonatal death is almost 200 times greater."

---

[37] blogs.scientificamerican.com/observations/why-humans-give-birth-to-helpless-babies/. Accessed 4/09/2017.
[38] en.wikipedia.org/wiki/Infant mortality. Accessed 24/09/2017.

> Infant mortality due to low birth weight is usually a direct cause stemming from other medical complications such as preterm birth, poor maternal nutritional status, lack of prenatal care, maternal sickness during pregnancy, and an unhygienic home environment. Along with birth weight, period of gestation makes up the two most important predictors of an infant's chances of survival and their overall health.[39]

The third quite unique human feature concerns the female's baby-production engineering. This wonder of nature, being a mammal, takes place inside the body of the female homo sapiens and consists of two processes; one that produces an egg and one that produces the kit to take that egg (endometrium, the inner lining of the womb), once it is fertilised, forward to being a viable baby. No egg—no baby; no kit—no baby. Each egg has its own kit or its own version of the kit. If the egg is not fertilised the kit is rejigged or got rid of altogether, mostly—and here, I'm no expert—a bit of both.

Being a result of natural evolution, there are many versions of these two processes, most notably, perhaps, marsupials for which the nourishing part of the kit, the placenta, is in a pouch outside their body and the even more remarkable monotremes, the platypus and the echidna, who actually lay eggs (not like birds' eggs but, in the case of the platypus, so well on in their development that the young emerge very soon after the eggs are laid or, in the case of the echidna, the eggs are laid in her pouch).

However, there are two common versions. Most mammal species do these two processes in cycles, the ovulation cycle and the menstruation cycle and for most they are seasonal, happening once, twice or more times per year (rabbits many more than this, hence their phenomenal capacity to breed!). When the cycle starts the females advertise it and, while it lasts, very little is on any individual's mind other than reproduction. Most commonly for the millions of grazers this time is known as a rut. The females, in our everyday experience mostly cats and dogs, for farmers cows, sheep and horses, come into season, on heat, ready for being fertilised (in oestrus); the eggs and the kits are there, brand new and raring to go (interestingly, cats only get theirs ready when intercourse has occurred).

In this oestrus-based version, female readiness is made sensually apparent and stimulates males to respond. If there is no response and the female is not fertilised, the egg and the baby-growing kit are absorbed or rejigged ready for the next ovulation. Given normal health, this cycle continues until death. As pointed out before, mammal species in which this seasonal oestrus occurs are polygynous and males play no part in raising offspring.

In version two, which applies to Great Apes, Old World monkeys, some other primates, some species of bats and the elephant shrew the whole baby-making kit and caboodle is removed in a discharge of blood from the vagina, in the case of humans every 28 days or so (menstruation), and, in some cases, notably chimpanzees and humans, at some stage the whole process stops (the

[39] Ibid.

menopause) leaving older females who are no longer fertile. Much rarer is, most obviously in a human female, the absence of any visible sign that she is in the fertile part of her cycle and, therefore, receptive to mating (concealed ovulation). In this case, the human case, mating behaviour would seem to need to be different with the male concentrating on one female with whom he mates frequently both ensuring her fidelity by providing food and protection and guarding her and her offspring from the attention of other males.

To my inexpert eye there's a big difference between a female communicating to males, "Don't bother, I'll show you when I'm ready" (most mammals) and one saying, "You can try anytime but it will be obvious when you can't" (humans). In the former 'tournament' culture (*sort of?; nature produces such an array of versions—"God moves in mysterious ways; His wonders to perform"!)*, the female intent not to waste her fertility by having no partners or choosing one that is inferior and the male response to it of spreading his genes as widely as possible in competition with other males hell-bent on doing the same embraces polygyny and promiscuity, mate-choice and mate-guarding, infanticide, harems and cuckoldry, with little or no cooperative child rearing between male and female (male chimpanzees are known to stay with their mate for a period of time after the birth—for 30 days or so a baby is totally dependent on the mother).

Above all, assured paternity, in this culture, is either unimportant or achieved by intense, seasonal, energy-sapping, often dangerous stratagems of male ownership and control. In the latter, let us call it, 'concealed fertility' culture, combined with the birth hazards, nutritional needs and child-rearing burden of the bipedal, large-brained human, are the opposites, monogamy and female fidelity, more appropriate to survival?

The answer is important because if the moral code by which we live combined with the socio-political regime of patriarchy could have a definite 'natural' rationale it would justify much of the unequal treatment of women throughout the ages, distinguishing neatly the 'pre-scientific enlightenment' attitude to women from the modern, 21st century, strides towards gender equality, on the grounds of a social solution to a genetically transmitted compulsion to survive that is evolving as human techno-scientific culture 'advances'. *Unfortunately, those seeking a clear 'Yes' or 'No', whatever their motives or subjective perspective, will not find one here!*

Before attempting some sort of response, it is necessary, I feel, to clarify what various people say about monogamy. From Wikipedia:

> Biologists, biological anthropologists, and behavioural ecologists often use the term monogamy in the sense of sexual, if not genetic, monogamy. Modern biological researchers, using the theory of evolution, approach human monogamy as the same in human and non-human animal species. They postulate the following four versions of monogamy:

- Marital monogamy refers to marriages of only two people.
- Social monogamy refers to two partners living together, having sex with each other, and cooperating in acquiring basic resources such as shelter, food and money.
- Sexual monogamy refers to two partners remaining sexually exclusive with each other and having no outside sex partners.
- Genetic monogamy refers to sexually monogamous relationships with genetic evidence of paternity.
- When cultural or social anthropologists and other social scientists use the term monogamy, the meaning is social or marital monogamy. Marital monogamy may be further distinguished between:

1. marriage once in a lifetime.
2. marriage with only one person at a time (**serial monogamy**), in contrast to bigamy or polygamy;[40]

The cultures of the majority of the nearly 8 billion humans on this planet promote a practice of monogamy that embraces all these aspects, except version 1 of marital monogamy, although, Wikipedia goes on to point out, of the cultures thus far discovered the majority are not monogamous.

> According to the Ethnographic Atlas, of 1,231 societies from around the world noted, 186 were monogamous; 453 had occasional polygyny; 588 had more frequent polygyny; and 4 had polyandry. However, this does not take into account the relative population of each of the societies studied, and the actual practice of polygamy in a tolerant society may actually be low, with the majority of aspirant polygamists practicing monogamous marriage.[41]

Human 'nature', however, frequently fails to conform to the cultural expectation of sexual and genetic monogamy (*Enter Jeremy Kyle, the tabloid press and the majority, I'm guessing, of the world's myths, drama and literature!*) whilst human society overwhelmingly coalesces units of various sizes (nuclear and extended families) formed by serial socially monogamous relationships. *Hence the 'bleeding obvious' conflict between brain and body, head and heart, intellect and emotion, control and instinct that is the hitherto inexplicable, insoluble even, human condition.*

That greedy, energy-sapping human brain, therefore, has evolved a survival strategy that ensures the best possible conditions to protect the body in which it lives and on which it depends for energy, nutrition, oxygen and fluids and the transmission of a genome that is most likely to ensure the survival of its descendants for generations of bodies to come. This magic formula consists of cooperative provision of food, water and shelter by monogamous social units,

---

[40] en.wikipedia.org/wiki/Monogamy. Accessed 09/10/2017.
[41] Ibid.

cooperative child-rearing within and between those units and the physical and emotional capacities for frequent sexual activity and empathetic attachment that strengthens these pair bonds, the latter also strengthening the social bonds; all policed by a moral code that works about as well as that poor elephant seal lumbering around the beach trying to ensure sole access to his harem of female beauties!

The real question in all this that requires an answer is: Is there anything, other than superior body mass and some superior physical aptitudes, that naturally determines the male human's position of dominance over the female?

- The male's need to be certain of his paternity of the offspring he is provisioning is as great as the female's need to reproduce and rear her offspring until they, in their turn, can reproduce. Is Monogamy mutually beneficial?
- The energy required for family provisioning is no greater than that required for family production and rearing.
- The roles played in the reproduction and survival scenario are equally important.
- The rationale for cooperation is equally compelling for both sexes.
- The ability to be hierarchical is no less for the female than the male in many species, including primates such as homo sapiens.

The one inequality between the male and female human that is proven and will always be there until there is an acceptance of extra-uterine, asexual conception concerns the certainty over the genetic origins of the female's offspring. She knows, unless she is seriously promiscuous, but he can never be sure. Patriarchy is as much about fear as it is about possession. Possession is as much about certainty as it is about acquisitiveness.

Chapter 6
Matriarchy

I sometimes try to imagine what would have happened if we'd known the bonobo first and the chimpanzee only later—or not at all. The discussion about human evolution might not revolve as much around violence, warfare and male dominance, but rather around sexuality, empathy, caring and cooperation. What a different intellectual landscape we would occupy!
– Frans de Waal, *Our Inner Ape: A Leading Primatologist Explains Why We Are Who We Are*

When we hear the word "matriarchy", we are conditioned to a number of responses: that matriarchy refers to the past and that matriarchies have never existed; that matriarchy is a hopeless fantasy of female domination, of mothers dominating children, of women being cruel to men. Conditioning us negatively to matriarchy is, of course, in the interests of patriarchs. We are made to feel that patriarchy is natural; we are less likely to question it, and less likely to direct our energies to ending it.
– Love, Barbara; Shanklin, Elizabeth (1983). "The answer is matriarchy". In Joyce Trebilcot. *Mothering: Essays in Feminist Theory*. New Jersey: Rowman and Allenheld.

Preamble

Wikipedia defines Matriarchy as follows:

> ***Matriarchy** is a social system in which **females** (most notably in mammals) hold the primary power positions in roles of political leadership, moral authority, social privilege and control of property at the specific exclusion of **men**—at least to a large degree.*[42]

Not only are we given four specific aspects of human culture by which to attempt an assessment of whether, how and why a society is matriarchal or patriarchal:

- *Primary power positions in roles of political leadership*
- *Primary power positions in roles of moral authority*
- *Primary power positions in roles of social privilege*

[42] en.wikipedia.org/wiki/Matriarchy. Accessed 16/10/2017.

- *Primary power positions in roles of control of property*

but a non-subjective, overarching benchmark statement on the existence of either by simply replacing the bold words in the definition with the correctly gendered alternative. What an amazing statement of the obvious that is, you're thinking, but, in defence of it, the topic is so rife with subjective and highly politicised points of view that I feel the need for an anchor to counteract the tendency to drift in no particular direction!

In its overview of matriarchy, Wikipedia points to a disputed 'list of human cultural universals (viz., features shared by nearly all current human societies)' compiled by anthropologist Donald Brown in which he includes men being the "dominant element" in public political affairs. Earlier in the article it states that: 'Most anthropologists hold that there are no known anthropological societies that are unambiguously matriarchal, but some authors believe exceptions may exist or may have.'[43] These two statements seem to be suggesting that a matriarchal society does not exist and has not existed. We could dispute this or draw a conclusion that patriarchy of the unambiguous variety is the current evolutionary survival model and the one that has covered the last, say, 10,000 years of recorded or verifiable history of homo sapiens. If this is the case, we have to pursue an investigation of abuse of power rather than abuse of nature. Either way male homo sapiens is in the dock accused of gross unfairness on both counts. Before we do this let us look at how a matriarchy may look in the animal world and has been thought to have looked or possibly does look in the human world because when John Stuart Mill wrote his essay in the 1860s on the abuse of masculine power, *The Subjection of Women*, he, man of reason that he was, had to admit that there were no definitive examples of matriarchy to provide a reasoned comparison.

> ... the opinion in favour of the present system, which entirely subordinates the weaker sex to the stronger, rests upon theory only; for there never has been trial made of any other:[44]

As pointed out earlier in Chapter 5, gene sequencing has delineated the 3 Hominid genera into 2 species each. However, these 7 species share over 95% of their gene characteristics, the closest being humans and chimpanzees who could well have 99% in common. Although consideration of Pongos and Gorillas would throw and already has thrown up factors that have led to their speciation (development into separate species who do not share genes i.e., do not engage in reproductive behaviour together) and that would inform the student of human behaviour, I suggest that a look at the genus Pan and the differences between the common chimpanzee and the bonobo would be more enlightening.

---

[43] en.wikipedia.org/wiki/Matriarchy. Accessed 16/10/2017.

[44] Mill, John Stuart (2012-05-11T23:58:59). The Subjection of Women. Kindle Edition.

The Congo river dominates southern central Africa. It runs through the second biggest rain forest in the world, the natural habitat of chimpanzees. Formed about 1.5-2 million years ago it is commonly believed to be the natural barrier that led, about 1 million years ago, to the separate speciation of the common chimpanzee, which lives exclusively north of the river, and the bonobo which lives exclusively south of the river. Similar in physical appearance and with similar eating (mainly frugivorous, occasionally carnivorous and classified as omnivorous) and socialising (fission-fusion groupings of males and females) habits, these two closely related cousins have cultures in which aspects of their social behaviour, particularly their sexual behaviour, are remarkably different.

Cutting to the chase, observations of these two speciated societies and cultures see that of the common chimpanzee as a hierarchical patriarchy in which dominant males make decisions and have sexual control over females, resolving conflicts, most particularly territorial, sexual, familial and social, with aggression that can escalate to killing of their own kind. On the contrary, bonobo society is seen as a more egalitarian matriarchy in which male status is derived from the mother's status, significant groups of females can make decisions or overturn those made by males and the majority of conflicts, including those between different communities, are resolved peacefully, often with sexual intercourse (in its broadest sense) that is homosexual, heterosexual and intergenerational.

We owe much of our knowledge of common chimpanzees to the remarkable career of Jane Goodall whose continuous over-50-year observation of Eastern chimpanzees in the Gombe Stream National Park has cemented our respect for all non-human life but particularly for the 'humanity' of our chimpanzee cousins. Her expertise and knowledge are matched, in the case of the bonobo, by that of Frans de Waal, a Dutch primatologist who lives, writes and teaches in the USA and is principally known for his 'make-love-not-war' interpretation of bonobo social behaviour.

Both eminent experts have their detractors and critics, primarily because their work is 'political' if it is used to make inferences about human behaviour, especially in the arenas of 'gender warfare', thus far only words or social and private actions within communities, and 'territorial warfare' in which the intra-species death toll of homo sapiens would be unimaginable in the non-human world, especially that of our closest genetic cousins. Goodall is criticised for her anthropomorphism, evidenced by her naming of the chimps she observed rather than the strict ethological practice of numbering them.

The observations of both are subjected to scepticism because they are of animals in semi-captive situations rather than in their natural wild surroundings—*hardly fair in the case of bonobos when their natural habitat in the Democratic Republic of Congo has been the backdrop for a human civil war, known as 'Africa's World War', for 20 years. Current UK Government advice to would-be visitors:*

> *The security situation in eastern DRC remains unstable. The continued presence of armed groups, military operations against them,*

intercommunal violence and an influx of refugees from neighbouring countries all contribute to a deterioration in the political, security and humanitarian situation. There are continued reports of kidnappings, including of staff from international NGOs ...[45]

Despite these criticisms, I find their academically expert observations sufficiently convincing to demonstrate a clear contrast between the cultures of common chimpanzees and bonobos and that Bonobo culture strongly suggests that patriarchy was not the only possible evolutionary outcome for early homo sapiens. Is it, however, 'unambiguously matriarchal' and, if so, what behaviours are the result of being so?

In the political life of the bonobo troop—conflict resolution, group decision-making and group survival strategies—alliances of females predominate. Female-female bonding is strong and often strengthened by homosexual activity as well as cooperative child-rearing and grooming. Social status is determined matrilineally. Among male bonobos it is mum's status that counts because female promiscuity renders dad's identity uncertain, unimportant and insignificant. Morally, although conflicts occur and decisions are made, bonobos are largely peaceful beings often resolving tensions, disagreements and overexuberance with sexual behaviours—what mums say and do is 'right'.

In terms of property/territory rights tensions do occur within and between troops but disputes are usually resolved peacefully, often with grooming, sex and food provisioning. Female teenagers frequently leave their troop to join another, gaining acceptance by grooming, sexual bonding and alliances. On the four criteria, therefore, Bonobo society is unambiguously matriarchal; its promiscuous, sexual and essentially peaceful nature contrasting with the promiscuous, male-dominated, essentially aggressive tendencies of its cousins north of the river. Both cousins share the empathetic, intuitive and cognitive traits that link them so closely to humans, but the female-ruled bonobos seem to lack the savagery.

If we accept that the so-called 'Western' culture to which British culture largely conforms has evolved along the lines of the common chimpanzee, are there any signs in homo sapiens that the 'bonobo' route was ever chosen? Are there or have there been any unambiguous human matriarchies, human bonobos?

One much studied, much written about and now much visited culture is that of the Mosuo people in Yunnan province in the southwest of China, bordering Tibet. This beautiful mountain region centred on Lake Lugu is known, mostly for tourist purposes, by several names:

---

45 www.gov.uk/foreign-travel-advice/democratic-republic-of-the-congo. Accessed 06/07/2017.

> The lake is also well known in Chinese travel pamphlets as the region of "Amazons," "The Kingdom of Women" and "Home of the Matriarchal Tribe", this last name highlighting the dominant role of the Mosuo women in their society. The marriage rites of the Mosuo people are known as "azhu marriage" ceremony and this unique aspect of their social culture has given the title "exotic land of daughters" to the area. It is also known as "A Quaint Realm of Matriarchy. "The matriarchal and matrilineal society of the Mosuos is also termed the "Women's World."[46]

Media accounts of Mosuo culture tend to highlight exotic sexuality—*zouhun*, which many Chinese interpret as "free love", matriarchy—a land where women rule; and primitivity—a society that has not evolved.[47]

The truth, of course, is about to get in the way of a good story, I'm afraid!

In the Mosuo cultural tradition, property and the control of property are in the hands of women. The family structures and duties are determined by a matriarch whose house it is and whose powers of control are passed on to another woman. Women control and carry out all domestic and business activities except those associated with fishing, livestock management and death. The civic affairs of the community, its politics, are also left largely to men. There is no joint ownership of property and no joint responsibility for child-rearing because there is no western and Chinese-style nuclear family because there is no marriage.

Sons and daughters, grandsons and granddaughters live all their lives in the house of the matriarch. The male role models are maternal uncles. Women, the potential participant and the matriarch, have control over sexual relationships via the cultural tradition of 'walking marriage' in which chosen and approved male partners visit at dead of night for the purpose of reproduction and walk away before daybreak.

> Azu marriage is the way of living of the Mosuo people, and *Azu* in the local Mosuo language (which does not have its own script) means "intimate sweetheart". It is a convenient arrangement in which the partners come and go as they like. Three types of Azu marriages have been mentioned namely, the "travelling marriage," which is marriage without cohabitation; and the second type is the marriage with cohabitation that have developed into deep feelings after living under "travelling marriage" practice; they then live together and raise children as a family. The third type of marriage, which is linked to the history of Mongolian people occupying Lugu Lake who inculcated the practice of monogamous marriage among the Mosuo people, is called as "One on one marriage."

---

[46] https://en.wikipedia.org/wiki/Lugu_Lake. Accessed 27/10/2017.
[47] https://en.wikipedia.org/wiki/Mosuo. Accessed 27/10/2017.

> However, in all the three types of marriages, women have the rightful ownership of land, houses and full rights to the children born to them. The children carry their mother's family name and pay greatest respect to their mothers who in turn enjoy high social status. It is for these reasons that Mosuo people of Lugu Lake are an attraction. The male companions are known as "axias" and they work for the women.[48]

What excites the patriarchal world media is their mythical interpretation of this tradition as a world of promiscuous free love which has led to many a male tourist nursing not only a bruised ego, protests from Mosuo women that they know the paternity of their children and a generally accepted anthropological conclusion that the practice is akin to serial monogamy not promiscuity. Nevertheless, this combination of female prerogative in mate choice, female ownership of property and moral, familial, and social privilege and judgements residing in a female head of the non-nuclear extended family constitutes an unambiguous matriarchy with major survival advantages.

> Other than the child receiving exceptional care and attention from the extended family, there are many inconspicuous advantages for participating in a walking marriage. For example: divorce is never an issue because the man and woman are not legally bound together, thus sharing very few of the same responsibilities. There are also never any disputes over who owns custody of the child since the child belongs to the mother's extended family and takes the mother's last name. In the case of a parent's death, the child still has a prodigious amount of care and affection from the extended family.[49]

The sexual frisson excited by a world full of dominatrixes and the implication that such a society is by definition 'primitive' and 'less evolved'—a euphemism for 'inferior'—is a biased politicisation of the concept of Matriarchy that has existed in the patriarchal world, be it of Britain, of China, of the west or the east, and that has prevented a balanced assessment of these two opposite versions of human culture for thousands of years.

[48] en.wikipedia.org/wiki/Lugu_Lake. Accessed 27/10/2017.
[49] en.wikipedia.org/wiki/Mosuo. Accessed 27/10/2017.

Chapter 7
The Amazon Fetish

Why can't a woman be more like man?
Men are so honest, so thoroughly square
Eternally noble, historically fair
-A Hymn to Him, My Fair Lady, Alan J. Lerner

How can a woman be expected to be happy with a man who insists on treating her as if she were a perfectly normal human being?
-Oscar Wilde

Preamble

The patriarchal worlds of Greece and Rome and the even more ancient cultures of the Middle East did not neglect the visualisation of matriarchies in their myths and legends. Mostly, however, they portrayed matriarchal women as having the same qualities as men in terms of making their way in and preserving their portion of the world, aggression and competition via trade, diplomacy and warfare. This we might call the 'Amazon fetish' which had certain basic tenets.

- *Amazons were physically 'hench'. Their right breast, so one myth goes, was cauterised so that it would not grow to hinder their archery or spear throwing.*
- *Amazons lived beyond the 'civilised' world of the Mediterranean Sea; either north in the lands of the Scythians (modern Ukraine) or the Germaniae (modern Germany) or south in the depths of Africa.*
- *Amazons were an all-female society. Strabo, a geographer and traveller who lived in the early Roman Empire explains that the Amazons lived near the Gargareans, an all-male tribe. They interbred, with the female offspring staying with the Amazon mother and the male offspring going to be adopted by a Gargarean father. Hm!*
- *Amazons were brutal and savage warriors and conquerors.*
- *Only 'real men' such as Heracles, Achilles and Theseus or 'civilised' patriarchies such as Athens could best them.*

Amazonomachy, a sort of ancient Greek war of the sexes, was the inspiration for much Greek art. It was not, however, a recognition of the possibility of matriarchy, more of the love-hate relationship with women of the patriarchal male. Its not so covert motifs, of women being only able to rule women, competition with males by the development of male traits, not the least of which were physicality and the use of lethal weaponry, which compromised their femininity and led to their eventual defeat by and submission to patriarchal civilisation, came from the sexual uncertainty of the self-defining dominant male not the folk memory of a matriarchal prehistory.

Most of the famous women of the ancient world and Dark Age Europe were warrior queens—the legendary Queen of the Amazons, Hippolyta, Tomyris of the Massegetai, Zenobia of Palmyra and Boudicca of the Iceni, to name a few, but although they were Queens regnant (queens who ruled solo not wives of kings) they, with the exception of the mythical Hippolyta, were still heads of patriarchal societies. We have to go to Vietnam to ingest a legend of matriarchal triumph.

> After two centuries of Chinese rule, the Vietnamese rose up against them under the leadership of two sisters, Trung Trac and Trung Nhi, who gathered an army of 80,000. They trained 36 women to be generals and drove the Chinese out of Viet Nam in A.D. 40. Trung Trac was then named ruler and renamed "Trung Vuong" or "She-king Trung." They continued to fight the Chinese for three years, but eventually, unsuccessful, they committed suicide.[50]

No Queen Regnant of the United Kingdom before Elizabeth II, matriarchal though they may have been as individuals, ruled with female ministers or advisers or in the era of female enfranchisement or elected representatives at the national level and even 'Gloriana', arguably the most matriarchal of them all, had to deny her femininity to inspire a warlike determination in her male soldiery. From her famous Tilbury speech to the troops in 1588, these are the words that have historically defined Elizabeth I:

> I know I have the body of a weak, feeble woman; but I have the heart and stomach of a king, and of a king of England too.[51]

Probably the most 'bonobo-like' matriarchal queen in antiquity was Cleopatra VII Philopator, the last ruler of the Ptolemaic kingdom of Egypt—*yes, that Cleopatra, celebrated by Shakespeare, Shaw and Elizabeth Taylor.* Confronted by the frightening might of the Roman military under the command of its most successful general ever, Julius Caesar, she was faced with the greatest challenge of her rule—how to preserve her dynasty and the integrity of her country.

Egypt in the 60s to the 40s BC was not the Egypt of the great ancient Queens such as Hatshepsut and Nefertiti. Cleopatra's ancestors were Greek Macedonians—Ptolemy was one of Alexander the Great's most trusted generals—who went 'native' in their ruling style, for instance, adopting the co-

[50] www.thoughtco.com/ancient-women-warriors-121482. Accessed 31/10/2017.
[51] en.wikipedia.org/wiki/Speech to the Troops at Tilbury. Accessed 31/10/2017.

ruler and incestuous practices of the ancient dynasties. However, there is no doubt that the rule of the Egypt in which the young Cleopatra grew up was patriarchal as was the imperial Roman rule of most of its neighbours in the Near East. She was no angelic lover of peace and no stranger to violent warfare and murderous acts and, although only 21 when the 52-year-old master of the Roman world arrived in Alexandria in 48BC, fiercely ambitious. She could give Caesar, a renowned philanderer, what her brother and long-time enemy, Ptolemy, could not.

The bonobo strategy of making love not war worked. Caesar defeated her brother, decided not to annex Egypt as a Roman province and recognised Cleopatra as sole ruler in return for her being his mistress and giving him a son, nicknamed Caesarion, who was named as heir to the independent kingdom.

She was in Rome when her lover was assassinated in 44BC. In the civil war that followed she could not remain neutral and, having allegedly funded the assassins' faction for a while, chose the most powerful of the contenders, Mark Antony, becoming his lover in 41BC, bearing his twins a year later and after a break of four years or so marrying him and bearing a son. Antony made Alexandria his home until their deaths after the sea battle of Actium and the desertion of Antony's army in 30BC.

Had her strategy worked and had Antony won the battle, it is not fanciful to conjecture an entirely different Roman world—a return to a Republic leaving Egypt as a powerful independent country ruled by a Queen, or more astonishing still, a Roman Empire centred on Alexandria with a woman as its most powerful political figure or, as was to happen some four hundred imperial years later, a divided Empire with the eastern part centred on Alexandria not, as was to come to pass, Byzantium. Such was the power that femininity—the sexual allure of softness, sweetness, beauty, intelligence and charm—ruthlessly exploited, could exert over the masculinity of even the most powerful patriarchs.

> Cleopatra was regarded as a great beauty, even in the ancient world. In his *Life of Antony*, Plutarch remarks that "judging by the proofs which she had had before this of the effect of her beauty upon Caius Caesar and Gnaeus the son of Pompey, she had hopes that she would more easily bring Antony to her feet. For Caesar and Pompey had known her when she was still a girl and inexperienced in affairs, but she was going to visit Antony at the very time when women have the most brilliant beauty." Later in the work, however, Plutarch indicates that "her beauty, as we are told, was in itself neither altogether incomparable, nor such as to strike those who saw her." Rather, what ultimately made Cleopatra attractive were her wit, charm and "sweetness in the tones of her voice." Cassius Dio also spoke of Cleopatra's allure: "For she was a woman of surpassing beauty, and at that time, when she was in the prime of her youth, she was most striking; she also possessed a most charming voice and knowledge of how to make herself agreeable to everyone. Being

brilliant to look upon and to listen to, with the power to subjugate everyone, even a love-sated man already past his prime, she thought that it would be in keeping with her role to meet Caesar, and she reposed in her beauty all her claims to the throne."[52]

Her intent to establish a matrilineal dynasty perished with her and the death of Caesarion a year after. Whether, had she succeeded, a new revision of the role of women in Egypt would have followed we shall never know but there is no doubt that she had the skills and the intellectual clout to embark on such a project. Her place in history, patriarchal history, however, is based on the patriarchal view of her as an exceptional female who, instead of mastering masculine skills and traits a la Amazon, attained and retained power by using her femininity, particularly her sexuality in the political arena, as did, in later years, Gloriana and Catherine the Great, by offering it to the alpha-males of her day, unlike Elizabeth who withheld it and Catherine who promiscuously used it as the first task in a job interview. These were exceptional women who made it in a world dominated by men and who remain tolerated sex symbols in the patriarchal opinions of those who would glorify them and enhance their fame.

Conclusion

A woman being the political top dog in an otherwise patriarchal society is not sufficient to redefine it as a matriarchy or form the basis for matriarchal customs and practices because:

- To be unambiguously matriarchal women have to wield political, social and economic power significantly greater than that of men.
- The key to social status is ownership of property and its transmission upon the death or 'abdication' of the ownership rights and titles. A true matriarchy cannot exist unless ownership of property is by females and transmission is matrilineal.
- Finally, control of reproductive activity, its rules and mores, has to be in the hands of females for a matriarchy to exist.

Two further points of cautious objectivity are needed to prevent us running away with the idea that a matriarchal culture would be or would have been fairer or more peaceful.

Firstly, a matriarchy would still involve dominance of one gender over the other; we have no idea whether it would be more egalitarian; the relatively peaceful nature of bonobo society could well be because food is plentiful with few competitors, like gorillas, which common chimpanzees have to deal with. The lack of jealous rivalry in Mosuo villages could result from the simpler, single purpose, agricultural nature of their culture.

[52] en.wikipedia.org/wiki/Cleopatra. Accessed 02/11/2017.

Secondly, so ingrained is the patriarchal culture of human beings that visualising the reversal of dominance is unavoidably subjective, hence the visible absurdity of the 'Amazon fetish' of the patriarchies of Greece and Rome.

Amazingly, the fetish lasted; to feature in quite recent British history. In the late 70s The Two Ronnies was probably the most watched comedy programme on TV. It featured an 8-part story full of innuendo and puns that were the indisputably sexist, although Ronnie Barker was too brilliant for it not to have been an ironic satire of the age in which he lived, trademark of its humour. The story was called 'The Worm that Turned'. It visualised a matriarchal dictatorship in which the secret police, led by Diana Dors, were as ludicrously dressed in PVC hot pants as overtly provocative as Henry VIII's codpiece.

Janet and Betty, Corbett and Barker, dressed in women's clothing and chained to their domestic duties were trying to escape to an all-male refuge in Wales. Apart from clever puns like the renaming of the Tower of London, Barbara Castle, and Mars Bars, Pa's Bars, it was a reliving of the fetish with all its fear of disempowerment, excitement and sexual frissance of domination by women and, above all, its arrogant certainty of an eternal and triumphant patriarchy.

Author's note: I laughed with millions of others! But, given that this was the heyday of 'Top of the Pops', 'Jim'll fix it', 'It's a Knockout', Jimmy Saville, Stuart Hall and Rolf Harris, is it too politically correct to look back at this time as an episode in which patriarchal certainty led to abuse that is completely unacceptable and contrary to the survival of human society (in Western culture, at least) on its irrevocable evolutionary path to a more egalitarian world. Has its subsequent unveiling heralded the beginning of the end, as evolutionarily revolutionary as bipedal locomotion? I hope so.

Chapter 8
Morality, Mores and Culture

Therefore, all things whatsoever ye would that men should do to you, do ye even so to them; for this is the Law and the Prophets.
– Gospel according to Matthew 7:12

…men endeavour to sink us still lower, merely to render us alluring objects for a moment; and women, intoxicated by the adoration which men, under the influence of their senses, pay them, do not seek to obtain a durable interest in their hearts, or to become the friends of the fellow creatures who find amusement in their society.
– Mary Wollstonecraft, A Vindication of the Rights of Woman

Confusing monogamy with morality has done more to destroy the conscience of the human race than any other error.
– George Bernard Shaw

Preamble

Morality should be but is not universal, it is personal and subjective. It is not about what is thought (the secret world of an individual's innermost thoughts can have zones of brilliant light and darkest black) but about what is said or done. It cannot be taught, I think, without also being learned from examples. Most worryingly it can be indoctrinated. It can be compromised by fear, desperation and other emotions or impulses. It is enforced, often by coercion, and can be rejected irrationally or anti-socially as easily as it can be reasonably or altruistically. Above all, it is always ideological and comparative, changeable, and fragile. It struggles eternally to turn back the irresistible tide of the seven deadly sins.

Possibly, the nearest statement to a universal moral principle is the so-called Golden Rule or ethic of reciprocity. Based on the survival model adopted by Homo sapiens of collective living and cooperation its expression of empathy and altruism appears in most religions and cultures old and new. On the BibleGateway website <https://www.biblegateway.com/verse/en/Matthew%207:12> *there are 58 English translations of the words of Jesus Christ in which he stated it. On the Humanist Website* <Think Humanism>, *Maria MacLachlan (October 2007) gives the following examples:*

- *Do not to your neighbour what you would take ill from him.* ***(Pittacus****, 650 BCE)*
- *Do not unto another that you would not have him do unto you. Thou needest this law alone. It is the foundation of all the rest.* ***(Confucius****, 500 BCE)*
- *Avoid doing what you would blame others for doing.* ***(Thales****, 464 BCE)*
- *What you wish your neighbours to be to you, such be also to them.* ***(Sextus the Pythagorean****, 406 BCE)*
- *We should conduct ourselves toward others as we would have them act toward us.* ***(Aristotle****, 384 BCE)*
- *Cherish reciprocal benevolence, which will make you as anxious for another's welfare as your own.* ***(Aristippus of Cyrene****, 365 BCE)*
- *Act toward others as you desire them to act toward you.* ***(Isocrates****, 338 BCE)*
- *This is the sum of duty: Do naught unto others which would cause you pain if done to you. (From the* ***Mahabharata*** *(5:1517), 300 BCE)*
- *What is hateful to you, do not to your fellow men. That is the entire Law; all the rest is commentary.* ***(Rabbi Hillel*** *50 BCE)*
- *Thou shalt love thy neighbour as thyself. (From the* ***Bible****, Leviticus 19:18 1440 BCE)*
- *Therefore, all things whatsoever ye would that men should do to you, do ye even so to them.* ***(Jesus of Nazareth****, circa 30 CE)*[53]

Morality, therefore, is a key component of culture, not value-absolute but tailored to fit that culture's approach to survival. If key elements in that culture are patriarchy, monogamy, patrilineal inheritance and possession of property and social hierarchy then its morality will be devised and enforced by the most powerful beneficiaries of that cultural model, men. In the arena of gender—disability, race, and class also—the Golden Rule was, and still is, conveniently overruled.

It seemed so often to have little relevance to fair treatment of 50% of any society's (unless Amazonian or monastic) population. It is within the streetlight of this revelation of double standards that we need to address the origins of British patriarchal morality and its cultural enforcement by thought word and deed.

The cultural origins of Britain as a nation are generally agreed to be, in historical order, Brythonic and Celtic, Gaelic and Anglo-Saxon, Norse and Norman-French but, like most of Western Europe, the cultural origins of its morality are Romano-Christian. They were, therefore, constructed far away from these shores and, in many ways, quite alien in respect of the social and environmental factors that shaped them.

---

[53] www.thinkhumanism.com/the-golden-rule.html. Accessed 09/11/2017.

Little is known about the role and treatment of women before the age of literacy and, therefore, subject to the assumption that what they were was how it was generally accepted they should have been. What I am trying to get across is that there is a morality of inequality as there is a morality of equality i.e., if inequality got the job done—the job being getting the next generation to a point at which they were in a fit state to produce their next generation—it will have been justified as 'good' within whatever moral framework existed at the time.

Before I begin to look at the mores that may or may not have shaped British values, I just want to share with you a perspective of historical time. In many of your lifetimes, you will celebrate the 1000th anniversary of the Battle of Hastings, on 14 October 2066—in the absence of some cryogenic miracle in the next few years I regret I will be unable to share in it! *For much of my writing I do not celebrate it in any way, shape or form and the following sections will, contrary, no doubt, to the national sentiment, mark it as a black day in British history. Nevertheless, have a good one because all my research suggests that this was the biggest event in recorded British history in terms of its social and cultural impact!*

The current Queen is related to its victor and separated from him by over 25 generations of his progeny. Given greater longevity among the mega rich and better health, nutrition, and medicine over the last 250 years we could hypothesize 1000 years comprising 40 generations of common folk. 200 years ago, one fifth of the second millennium of verifiable recorded history, there were no planes, trains, or automobiles.

For most of the million years that homo sapiens has inhabited the British Isles, they were not 'isles' at all but a peninsular of northern Europe which, with rising sea levels, was steadily cut off from the mainland. As it diminished, it became a land bridge with present day Belgium and southern Holland which the eminent archaeology professor, Bryony Coles, named 'Doggerland'. In the latter half of the sixth millennium BC, Doggerland was deluged and became the North Sea. The island inhabitants to the west of this newly created sea were hunter-gatherers of north European origin, culturally similar to their cousins across the water on the European mainland.

Many anthropologists, such as the Canadian Richard Borshay Lee, believe hunter-gatherer culture to have been significantly egalitarian but, with food supplies becoming harder to forage, Britannic peoples made the transition to agriculture during the Neolithic period, 4300-2000 BC, slowly evolving from a matrilocal, matrilineal culture with common-living and job-sharing to a more separated, tribally territorial, patrilocal and patrilineal arrangement not dissimilar to anywhere else in inhabited Europe at this time.

In these Neolithic years before recorded history, tribes were the organisational units of significance so that by the time Britain was on the written map of the great Mediterranean city states of Athens, Carthage, and Rome it was tribal having gone through innumerable migrations from the north European mainland of what we have come to call Celtic peoples speaking a similar Germanic language and living in not dissimilar ways to their cousins to the east.

Whatever population pressure there was by or on Celtic tribes in the 500 years before the Romans arrived, therefore, would have been created by immigrants from the North European mainland pushing the indigenous populations westwards to what are now the Celtic fringes of Cornwall, Wales, Ireland and the Western islands of Scotland just as did the Belgae, mentioned by Julius Caesar in his account of his Gallic Wars in the first century BC, in pre-Roman Britain, and the Anglo-Saxons in post-Roman times. If, therefore, we were looking for traces of the pre-Celtic culture in the recorded or reliable history of the British Isles they would logically be in the Gaelic culture of western Ireland or the Western Isles of Scotland.

However, as yet, none has been found that shows evidence of their survival of these territorial shifts that resulted in the largely patrilineal, Romano-Christian culture of the Gaels which itself was not challenged until the coming of Norse conquerors in the 8th century CE. The most up-to-date reconstruction of that transitional society, neither wholly hunter-gatherer nor wholly agricultural, has not revealed the status or treatment of women in it.

However, whatever evidence there is of the native Celtic culture that the Romans encountered, briefly in 55 BC and then for the 300 years following the invasion of 43 CE, shows that it was patriarchal although Roman writers, such as Tacitus and Cassius Dio, were captivated enough by powerful Celtic women, such as the renowned warrior queen of the Iceni, Boudicca, whose power passed to her when her husband died and the less renowned Roman ally, Cartimandua, queen of the Brigantes, who seems to have inherited her power in her own right (in legal Latin, *suo jure*), to write about them at some length. Is this enough evidence of a Celtic culture in which women played a natural role in public affairs, a cultural feature reined in by the Romano-Christian patriarchy?

If Cartimandua was Queen suo jure who inherited her right to rule in an otherwise patrilineal culture she would have been a rare phenomenon in the 2000 years anno domini, in Europe at least. Most European Queens in the Common Era were Queen Consorts, wives of Kings—notably powerful examples were Eleanor of Aquitaine, wife and consort of Louis VII of France (1137-1152) and Henry II of England (1154-1189), Isabella of France, wife and consort of Edward II of England (1307-1327) and Queen Regent of Edward III of England (1326-1330) and, in the so-called Wars of the Roses in 15th century England, Margaret of Anjou, wife and consort of the Lancastrian Henry VI of England (1445-1461) and the Yorkist Elizabeth Woodville, wife and consort of Edward IV of England (1464-1483); most Queens Regnant were widows of Kings—among the most famous were Boudicca, widowed Queen of the Brythonic tribe of the Iceni (60-61AD), and Catherine the Great, Empress of Russia (1762-1796).

Some were Queens Regent until their child reached an age of majority, such as the aforementioned Isabella, mother of Edward III (Regent 1326-1330) and, most completely, Catherine de Medici, mother of Charles IX of France (Regent 1560-1563). All these remarkable women were, of course, atypically powerful for their times, and indeed any times, due to the social advantage conferred upon them by their birth into a patriarchal elite. Their power was, therefore, dependent on men as opposed to society in general.

Three remarkable cases of women who were granted absolute power, suo jure, Empress Matilda (1102-1167), daughter of Henry I of England, Mary I of England (1516-1558), daughter of Henry VIII of England, and Maria Theresa (1717-80), sovereign of Austria, Hungary, Croatia, Bohemia, Transylvania, Mantua, Milan, Lodomeria and Galicia, the Austrian Netherlands and Parma, daughter of Holy Roman Emperor, Charles VI, will amaze you later, in Chapter 24, by showing how three of the biggest hitting alpha males in European history were arrogant enough to defy the prevailing patriarchal mores.

The Roman fascination with these powerful 'barbarian' women was, no doubt, partly driven by 'the Amazon fetish' but another possibility could be that it was a foreign custom because women in the Roman elite, over 700 years, were never allowed to participate in public life. In the days of the Republic, they could not vote or hold public office. The mother of the reforming champions of the poor, Tiberius and Gaius Gracchus, Cornelia Africana, daughter of the victor of Zama, Scipio Africanus, was extremely influential in guiding her sons' political opinions. She became an iconic example of Roman womanhood, *which emphasised influence in public affairs exerted behind the scenes.*

In the imperial years there were no Empresses *suo jure* or regnant and those that did wield some power, such as Livia, wife of Augustus Caesar and mother of his successor, Tiberius, and Helena, widowed mother of Constantine the Great, did so through their relationship with their husband or son.

There is one possibility that would contradict this statement. In the late third century AD, after a turbulent few years, a military warlord, Aurelian, became Emperor. His wife, Ulpia Severina, outlived him and there is a substantial amount of evidence, mostly coins minted with her image on them, to suggest that she ruled the Empire before a successor was elected. She is the exception that proves the rule although it is questionable whether her name would be a worthy answer to the trivia quiz question: Did a woman ever rule the Roman Empire? For sure, however, there were no female Roman war leaders like Boudicca.

Interestingly, in the Byzantine Empire, Rome's eastern descendant, some women did wield power as Queens regnant, albeit by their connection to a male spouse or relative.

- Irene Sarantapechaina (797-802 AD)
- Zoe Porphyrogenita (Co-Empress with her sister April-June 1042)
- Theodora Porphyrogenita (Co-Empress with her sister April-June 1042)

Irene of Athens, as she is better known, demonstrated a stereotypically male ruthlessness and tenacity when it came to getting power and holding on to it, having been Queen Consort to Leo IV and Queen Regent to her son, Constantine VI, and only Queen Regnant after she had defeated him, hunted him down and gouged out his eyes, an injury from which he died a few days later. 250 years later, the sisters, Zoe and Theodora, daughters born to the Emperor Constantine VIII, were forced to rule together, Zoe, the passionate beauty, outflanking Theodora, calm, rational and born to rule, with several marriages.

The most famous Co-Empress was another Theodora, Queen Consort and Co-Empress as wife of Emperor Justinian I from 527AD to her death from cancer in 548. She was powerful enough to sponsor legislation to improve the lives of women in the Empire. From humble origins she was firstly Justinian's mistress then his wife and, two years later, she became Empress Consort. Although sources are unreliable which, given the barbarity of the times, is understandable there is much evidence to suggest that she became more than his consort, having equal power to make decisions that affected the lives of people within the Empire. Her Wikipedia biography records her considerable efforts to establish women's rights in areas where they had none.

> Theodora participated in Justinian's legal and spiritual reforms, and her involvement in the increase of the rights of women was substantial. She had laws passed that prohibited forced prostitution "and was known for buying girls who had been sold into prostitution, freeing them, and providing for their future." She closed brothels and made pimping a criminal offense. She created a convent on the Asian side of the Dardanelles called the *Metanoia* (Repentance), where the ex-prostitutes could support themselves.
> She also expanded the rights of women in divorce and property ownership, instituted the death penalty for rape, forbade exposure of unwanted infants, gave mothers some guardianship rights over their children, and forbade the killing of a wife who committed adultery. Procopius wrote that she was naturally inclined to assist women in misfortune. After Theodora's death, "little effective legislation was passed by Justinian."[54]

Very few male rulers in European history have married their mistress. Arguably, Elizabeth Woodville was Edward IV's mistress, but did they consummate their love before their secret marriage? Similarly, most experts would hold the opinion that Anne Boleyn was married to Henry VIII before consummation. In British history, that leaves the current Prince of Wales and his great uncle, Edward VIII, who married his mistress but gave up his crown, and the allegedly bad King John. Although John was married to Isabel of Gloucester when he formed his intention to marry Isabella of Angouleme the proposition that she was his mistress can be quickly dismissed by the fact that she was only 12 when they married in 1200 and 11 when John had his first marriage annulled on the grounds of consanguinity (they were second cousins).

---

[54] en.wikipedia.org/wiki/Theodora (6th century). Accessed 16/01/2018.

Add to that two further facts; firstly, she was clearly made for motherhood, bearing 14 healthy children in her lifetime (5 to John and 9 to her second husband, Hugh de Lusignan), yet did not have her first child, the future Henry III, until 1207 when she was 19, thus showing some delicate concern on the part of her husband for her youth; secondly, there were sound strategic reasons for a political marriage given John's ultimately unsuccessful efforts to hold on to his lands in France, a proposition cemented by the fact that her very powerful and illustrious mother-in-law, Eleanor of Aquitaine, approved the match.

Reputation in this world is a delicate balance between the factors comprehended by it; morality, loyalty, humanity, propriety, and success, to name but a few. Being a bad king, which he undoubtedly was, does not make John universally bad just as being a popular TV host and DJ does not, certainly did not, make Jimmy Saville universally good.

How about the reverse; female rulers and their lovers? Catherine the Great had lovers before and after she had her husband Peter III assassinated but, although she supported the election of one of them, Stanislaw August Paniotowski, to be Stanislaw II Augustus, the last King of Poland, she did not marry them. Isabella of France, Queen Consort of Edward II, co-ruled as Queen Regent of her son, the future Edward III, with her lover, Roger Mortimer, Earl of March, from 1327-1330.

Although he allegedly arranged her widowhood by ordering the death of the King while in captivity they could not marry because he was already married to Joan de Geneville. Likewise, Robert Dudley, Earl of Leicester, alleged lover of Elizabeth I, could not marry her because he was already married to Amy Robsart. Even after Amy's suspicious death in 1560 and having Elizabeth's permission to press his suit he and Elizabeth did not marry for complex political reasons, he being proposed as a consort for Mary, Queen of Scots, and she treading a perilously delicate path between royal suitors from France and Spain, Austria, and Sweden.

That leaves her cousin, Mary, Queen of Scots, as the only possible example of a British queen marrying her lover. She had known James Hepburn, Earl of Bothwell, as a young Queen Consort of Francis II of France. When she married the Catholic, Lord Darnley, father of the future James I, Bothwell, whether a lover or not, was the darling of the Protestant disapproval movement. In 1567, two months after Darnley was killed in an explosion, Bothwell abducted Mary whom he married only 12 days after divorcing his wife, Lady Jean Gordon. Bothwell was accused of being Darnley's murderer, raping and abducting Mary and being her long term on-and-off lover. Only the first two give copious causes for belief.

Many of history's mistresses and lovers, as was Theodora, were very influential—notable-notorious examples being Alice Perrers, mistress of Edward III, Diane de Poitiers, mistress of Henri II of France, Barbara Palmer/Villiers, Duchess of Cleveland/Lady Castlemaine, mistress of Charles II, and the delightfully named Madame de Pompadour (1721-1764), mistress, friend and confidante of Louis XV—but their royal lovers still ruled, argued in all-male councils and made laws suggested or approved (or disapproved) by all-male parliaments.

In the gender reverse, the male lovers—notable-notorious examples being Mortimer and Dudley and, more ambiguously, Robert Carr and George Villiers, Duke of Buckingham, alleged lovers of James I—were possibly co-ruling because of their solidarity with their monarch in councils and parliaments. Carr, for instance, was the King's principal ally in the policy of ruling without a Parliament which dangerous (to James' son, Charles I, in particular) precedent finally came to pass in 1614 and was to last for 7 years. About Dudley, Philip II of Spain is said to have been given this advice:

> Lord Robert has come so much into favour that he does whatever he likes with affairs and it is even said that her majesty visits him in his chamber day and night. People talk of this so freely that they go so far as to say that his wife has a malady in one of her breasts and the Queen is only waiting for her to die to marry Lord Robert … Matters have reached such a pass … that … it would … be well to approach Lord Robert on your Majesty's behalf … Your Majesty would do well to attract and confirm him in his friendship.[55]

Very few of these mistresses came from a non-nobility/gentry background as did Theodora. The most famous actress/mistresses were Moll Davis and Nell Gwynne who were rivals for the favours of Charles II but were more taken up with making their way in a recently liberated man's world than changing it and Lillie Langtry, friend and for 3 years mistress of the Prince of Wales, the future Edward VII. Possibly the most colourful mistress of all time was Lola Montez (1821-1861), mistress of Ludwig I of Bavaria, who rose from humble Irish beginnings to become Countess of Landsfeld and play a major role in Ludwig's downfall and eventual abdication after the 1848 revolutions.

She went on to reinvent herself many times, with many marriages, always surrounded by scandal and, in a more sinister light, death, throughout the western world (Ireland, Scotland, England, France, Spain, Bavaria, India, Australia and America!), dying in America, only 39 years old, from syphilis, the price she paid for a career dependent on sexual intercourse.

Millions of women throughout history must have faced the same realities as Lola and made the same choices and, in their thousands, shared the same fate. In a man's world slavery and prostitution made a commodity of the human body, a commodity to satisfy the wants of men. That world of men treated marriage as a business contract designed to enhance their wealth and property. As part of the deal, sexual intercourse was essential to produce offspring who by their

---

[55] en.wikipedia.org/wiki/Robert Dudley, 1st Earl of Leicester. Accessed 17/01/2018.

marriages would, in turn, expand and enhance the family business, essential but not necessarily desired by or pleasurable to either participant.

The male libido, although mandated by most moral codes to be expressed only in a monogamous relationship, was a force of nature, as we shall see in later chapters, that the patriarchy could not and would not deny. Numerous reasons why the morally approved partner was unavailable—pregnancy, menstruation or just the whole 'female mystery' thing—or undesirable (including for reasons of the man's sexuality) meant those to whom abstinence was impossible sought satisfaction elsewhere.

In the novel 'La Dame aux Camelias' by Alexandre Dumas, fils (in English better known as 'Camille') that formed the basis for Verdi's beautiful opera 'La Traviata' the heroine, Marguerite Gautier (Violetta Valery in the opera) wore a red camelia when she was menstruating, thus unavailable for sex, and a white one when available, showing not only that the primary occupation of a courtesan was that of paid sex worker—no matter what the social wrapping paper—but also the commoditisation of female sexuality.

The extra allure of a female (or male) who also had a libido and no moral qualms about expressing it made a temporary contract, bought, and paid for, as irresistible as it was morally understandable and forgivable. In most patriarchal and hierarchical cultures luxuries were the exclusive preserve of the rich and powerful. Such commodities were more than capable of improvement. In the Athenian Republic, for instance, there were two classes of prostitute, pornai who plied their trade to ordinary punters from off the street and hetairai who were more select and educated to provide sophisticated society and sex.

In the absolute monarchies in the Orient and in Europe, this class distinction was perpetuated by a similar type of superior sex worker known as a courtesan who was socially acceptable in noble circles but largely disapproved of by her monogamous, legitimate, child-bearing female social superiors.

One route to courtesanship was the Stage because it enabled the public display of female sexuality rather than keeping it hidden and private, the duty of a virtuous wife: hence the synonymity of the two professions, 'actress' and 'prostitute'. Had not Justinian's uncle, the Emperor Justin I, changed the law to allow a noble to marry a socially inferior actress, Theodora would never have been able to attain her respectably superior position of power. Aspasia, the 5th century BC partner of the great Athenian leader, Pericles, could not, by law, marry him and is alleged to have wielded her political influence by using her legendary courtesan skills to cast her spell not only over Pericles but also over much of the Athenian intelligentsia.

Another hetaira from the 4th century BC was Phryne whose public nakedness legend has inspired many works of art. Both these hetaira were put on trial for 'impiety' which if proved carried the death penalty. Reportedly nothing came of Aspasia's trial and Phryne is alleged, on the advice of her defender, Hypereides, a famous orator, to have bared her breasts to the judges who felt constrained not to condemn to death 'a prophetess and a priestess of Aphrodite'. Impiety meant lack of proper respect for something sacred. Socrates, for instance was sentenced to death for impiety.

What were sacred, of course, were the cultural values and mores of the power elite mystically reinforced by a religious credo, the precise requirements of which, both moral and spiritual, were only known to a select few and in which the uninformed majority were expected to believe without question. Socrates was impious because he threatened the established elite by questioning its democratic system, its strength, and their wisdom. Aspasia and Phryne threatened to expose the sham of its patriarchal principles by which men's strengths had to be lauded, their weaknesses tolerated, and, above all, their power and wealth preserved and unchallenged.

> *According to Plato's Apology, Socrates' life as the "gadfly" of Athens began when his friend Chaerephon asked the oracle at Delphi if anyone were wiser than Socrates; the Oracle responded that no-one was wiser. Socrates believed the Oracle's response was not correct, because he believed he possessed no wisdom whatsoever. He proceeded to test the riddle by approaching men considered wise by the people of Athens—statesmen, poets, and artisans—in order to refute the Oracle's pronouncement. Questioning them, however, Socrates concluded: while each man thought he knew a great deal and was wise, in fact they knew very little and were not wise at all.*
>
> *Socrates realised the Oracle was correct; while so-called wise men thought themselves wise and yet were not, he himself knew he was not wise at all, which, paradoxically, made him the wiser one since he was the only person aware of his own ignorance. Socrates' paradoxical wisdom made the prominent Athenians he publicly questioned look foolish, turning them against him and leading to accusations of wrongdoing.*[56]

All these examples demonstrate that, in a man's world, one way or another, women could be powerful but, with the possible exception of Theodora, not powerful enough to transform the lot of women or the cultural morality that enforced it.

In 4th century BC Athens hetairai were not permitted to marry an Athenian citizen. In a speech prosecuting a freedwoman, Neaera, for doing so, Apollodorus of Acharnae, summed up the view of women in Classical times.

> We have courtesans for pleasure, concubines for the daily tending of the body, and wives in order to beget legitimate children and have a trustworthy guardian of what is at home.[57]

---

[56] en.wikipedia.org/wiki/Socrates#Causes of the trial. Accessed 23/01/2018.
[57] en.wikipedia.org/wiki/Hetaira. Accessed 25/01/2018.

This Athenian view of women, both separating the uses of women to men and assigning titles to the specialists who would carry them out is representative of a Mediterranean-wide view passed on to northern Europe by the Romano-Christian Empire of the Franks and perpetuated in the Middle East by the Islamic-Arab conquest. Both Judaism and Islam, while recognising the spiritual equality of men and women, even their equal value to God's creation (Judaism does not even gender God), assign this separation of roles with women, on the whole, in control of the home and men in control of the world outside it.

On her very readable website, Judaism 101, Tracey Rich tells us that although there have been many learned women in the Jewish tradition and a wider grant of rights of women over property and marriage the expected role was that of wife and mother.

> There is no question that in traditional Judaism, the primary role of a woman is as wife and mother, keeper of the household. However, Judaism has great respect for the importance of that role and the spiritual influence that the woman has over her family. The Talmud says that when a pious man marries a wicked woman, the man becomes wicked, but when a wicked man marries a pious woman, the man becomes pious. The child of a Jewish woman and a gentile man is Jewish because of the mother's spiritual influence; the child of a Jewish man and a gentile woman is not.[58]

A somewhat less rosy picture, however, was painted by Roland Le Vaux, the renowned Catholic priest, archaeologist, and writer on ancient Israel.

> "The social and legal position of an Israelite wife was inferior to the position a wife occupied in the great countries round about… all the texts show that Israelites wanted mainly sons to perpetuate the family line and fortune, and to preserve the ancestral inheritance… A husband could divorce his wife; women on the other hand could not ask for divorce… the wife called her husband Ba'al or master; she also called him adon or lord; she addressed him, in fact, as a slave addressed his master or subject, his king. The Decalogue includes a man's wife among his possessions… all her life she remains a minor.
> The wife does not inherit from her husband, nor daughters from their father, except when there is no male heir. A vow made by a girl or married woman needs, to be valid, the consent of the father or husband and if this consent is withheld, the vow is null and void. A man had a right to sell his daughter. Women were excluded from the succession."[59]

Islam confirms that there are separate, equally valuable roles but introduces the idea of complementarity.

---

[58] www.jewfaq.org/women.htm. Accessed 29/01/2018.
[59] www.nobeliefs.com/DarkBible/darkbible7.html. Accessed 11/02/2018.

> The emphasis which Islam places upon the feminine/masculine polarity (and therefore complementarity) results, quite logically, in a separation of social functions. In general, a woman's sphere of operation is the home in which she is the dominant figure—and a man's corresponding sphere is the outside world. However, this separation is not, in practice, as rigid as it appears. There are many examples—both in the early history of Islam and in the contemporary world—of Muslim women who have played prominent roles in public life, including being sultanas, queens, elected heads of state and wealthy businesswomen Moreover, it is important to recognise that in Islam, home and family are firmly situated at the centre of life in this world and of society: a man's work cannot take precedence over the private realm.[60]

As things stood around 400 CE in southern and western Europe, including the Roman province of Britannia, and throughout the 'civilised' world—the 'Western version of it at least—in the circles or echelons of moneyed society the woman's sphere of operation was private, in the home, and the man's was public, in the 'civitas', the state.

We can only really imagine what life was like for the rest. I will be trying to grasp the realities of slavery in a later chapter. For a female slave in a man's world I guess the reality would have included abuse of the sexual enticement of her body, given that she was a possession as well as a woman, both objects of a man's desire.

> While rape of Roman citizens had repercussions, forced sexual intercourse in other contexts was not even considered rape. Again, protection of a woman and her security in her own body was not the paramount goal, and Roman sexual legislation emphasised this through the application of rape laws only to those of a certain social status. In many circumstances, acts clearly viewed as modern-day rape were permissible. For example, "a husband could force himself on his wife without breaking any law." Additionally, there were groups of women, including slaves, prostitutes, and foreigners, upon whom rape (stuprum) could not be committed due to their social status.
> Specifically, since 74 the law did not recognise slaves as having legal standing, a master or his sons could satisfy their sexual desires by force or persuasion upon a slave. Moreover, because the Roman slave was merely a piece of the owner's property, slave owners could order their slaves to submit to the demands of others and could hire their slaves out for sexual services.[61]

Even in the mosques and synagogues of today's more enlightened world, women are separated from men, at least partly, on the basis that sexual desire

---

[60] en.wikipedia.org/wiki/Women in Islam #Gender roles. Accessed 29/01/2018.
[61] repository.law.umich.edu. Accessed 04/02/2018.

and spiritual fulfilment do not mix and that men presumably cannot be trusted to contain the former in order to obtain the latter.

Roman agriculture was carried out on large estates on which even the supervisory work was done by slaves, some of whom were able to obtain their freedom after many years' service. On this assumption, the jobs done by men and women may have been different, but their status would have been the same. The children of freedmen were born free. Smaller holdings of land existed, often being granted to retired legionaries. In these cases, their wives and female children would have been able to inherit property and manage it but would not have had the right to vote or play a public role.

In mines and quarries, the situation was no different and I suspect that work for women in them was as backbreaking as it was for men. Only in towns would we have found a middle class of free Roman citizens providing goods and services to paying customers. Among them would have been women. Roman 'urban' 'civilised' culture was undisputed in the Roman Province of Britannia for 300 years, but it must have been modified and 'liberalised' over this immensely long time. *Go back to 1717 and examine how customs, mores and morality have changed.* In the Empire itself much changed.

> The Edict of Caracalla (officially the Constitutio Antoniniana (Latin: "Constitution [or Edict] of Antoninus") was an edict issued in AD 212 by the Roman Emperor Caracalla, which declared that all free men in the Roman Empire were to be given full Roman citizenship and all free women in the Empire were given the same rights as Roman women. Before 212, for the most part only inhabitants of Italia held full Roman citizenship. Colonies of Romans established in other provinces, Romans (or their descendants) living in provinces, the inhabitants of various cities throughout the Empire, and a few local nobles (such as kings of client countries) also held full citizenship. Provincials, on the other hand, were usually non-citizens, although some held the Latin Right. However, by the previous century Roman citizenship had already lost much of its exclusiveness and become more available.[62]

It is, therefore, unwise to assume that the Classical customs, roles and status of groups or individuals remained fixed throughout a millennium of turbulent vitality just because the labels, Greek and Roman, are suitably general to fix and typify an era within a much vaster overview of time. Rome as an undisputed code of rules, laws and social behaviours was under pressure from the third century AD. The departure of the legions from Britannia in 410 CE or of Romulus, the last known Emperor of Rome, in 476 did not necessarily mean the end of Romanised society.

To a large extent, Romanisation has come down to us as being urban in character. Indeed, as cities declined over the last 200 years of the Empire, so

---

[62] repository.law.umich.edu. Accessed 04/02/2018.

urban ways would have declined as well. As wealthy Romans built their villas on their estates out of town, the shortage of essential local finance and administrative skill led to a failure to run urban services like public health and law and order. Towns were centres of trade built near arterial roads or navigable waterways or the sea which were also routes for brigands, bandits and barbarians, pirates, plague and pillagers. Cities shrunk to towns and towns to citadels. Safety was no longer in numbers but in isolation and guaranteed not by an army trained and paid by a central imperial administration but by local magnates who, as warlords, could pay for hired soldiers and demand payment from communities to guarantee the safety of their crops, livestock and modest living quarters.

The urban nature of classical civilisations gave rise to the word:

> The English word "civilisation" comes from the 16th-century French *civilisé* ("civilised"), from Latin *civilis* ("civil"), related to *civis* ("citizen") and *civitas* ("city").[63]

Yet, it came to embrace more, to get a 'Roman' feel about it—*hardly surprising as the Renaissance was the rebirth of Classical learning, so sacred that any new ideas, such as the heliocentric nature of the solar system, were regarded as heresy, not just against God's creation but against the Classical ingredients of 'civilisation'*. There were three further components to the concept: progress, social stratification and elite culture. All were 'men' things; progress was the domination of nature, a male achievement of brute force and masculine contemplation; social stratification was the necessary result of the superiority of one group of males over another; and finally, culture, the cultivation of art and music, religion and philosophy, was man's rise above the carnal towards the spiritual. In a civilised world, women, weaker and subjugated by their biology were inferior, vital to survival maybe but less essential to the male project of civilisation, most definitely a man's word.

Civilisation is the process of setting man free from men.
– Ayn Rand, *The Fountainhead*

This was the 'civilisation' that the Roman Empire brought to Western Europe. Did it subdue a more ancient set of mores that accorded a higher social status to women that was less diluted in the British Isles? A place to start is to plot the progress of this alien culture from its Mediterranean origins to the cold and rainy forested regions to the North and West.

[63] en.wikipedia.org/wiki/Civilization. Accessed 06/02/2018.

Chapter 9
North by Northwest

I say quite deliberately that the Christian religion, as organised in its churches, has been and still is the principal enemy of moral progress in the world.
– Bertrand Russel

There was a time when religion ruled the world. It is known as the Dark Ages.
– Ruth Hurmence Green

Preamble

As a people, we would like to think that there is something unique to being British and maybe the melting pot of Anglo-Saxon, Celt, Brython, Scot, Danish and French has produced a unique cultural blend. The Norman Conquest, however, brought Western European culture to endure and dominate the thinking of our elites. That culture did not bring Christianity, but it brought a brand of Christianity which was Western European, Roman in essence and direction. The discourse and practice of gender roles and status came with it.

This Mediterranean culture, via Roman military might, advanced engineering, central Law and State administration of taxes and public expenditure (generally referred to as the Roman Empire) spread north westwards in a number of successful military campaigns over 170 years, from 50 BC to 120 AD. Although the Empire controlled the banks of the Danube and the Rhine, it never established itself far beyond them. Of course, its northernmost frontier was Britannia's very own Hadrian's Wall. The widespread commonality of the culture was most noticeable in urban living.

In such a setting, women, as pointed out before, had a range of freedom greater than many other Mediterranean or Near Eastern cultures of the time or in antiquity. Although nominally under the authority of her father, not her husband, a Roman woman gained more citizen rights when he died. She had equal rights to inherit, could own and dispose of property and wealth without reference to anyone and increase them by entering into business.

Proceeding with caution because the recorded history that has come down to us is Rome-centred (and then Constantinople-centred from the fourth century CE), recorded by Roman historians, a story unfolds of persistent pressure from peoples who were migrating from east to west and south if they could, eventually swamping the Western Roman Empire and ending its imperial line in 476 AD when Odoacer, a leader in the Roman army of Germanic descent, declared himself King of Italy and recognised the Byzantine Emperor, Zeno, as his overlord.

As they pushed southwards, such peoples as the Vandals, Goths and Huns fused with Romanised peoples such as the Gauls, Celts and Brythons but as they pushed westwards, north of that Danube-Rhine frontier, they displaced further westwards peoples such as the Frisians, Jutes, Angles and Saxons who began pressing on Britannia in the third and fourth centuries CE.

From that rather arbitrary date in history, we move into a period called The Dark Ages, now reconfigured as Late Antiquity or Early Middle Ages. Three contextual factors need to be considered as well as the most important one, namely that the lights might have gone out in the history of the British Isles until switched on again to illuminate the career of Alfred the Great (871-899 CE) but they most certainly did not fail to reveal an amazingly complex power struggle that took place in Central-western Europe.

One of the historiographical features that has eased our understandings of the perplexities of these times is a change of language. If we change 'Anglo-Saxon' to 'Germanic', 'barbarian' to 'non-Mediterranean in origin', 'invasion' to 'migration', 'Romans' to 'those within the Roman Empire', subdividing them according to their citizen status, and break down 'provinces' into 'tribal groupings' we get a far more understandable picture of what happened in the Early Middle Ages.

Firstly, we have no reason to believe that Roman 'civilisation' and culture were unwelcomed in Hispania, Gallia, Britannia, Germania (The Rhineland), Rhaetia (Switzerland, Austria, and Germany) and Noricum (parts of Austria, Slovenia, Bavaria); the constant civil wars of the third, fourth and fifth centuries CE were more about central versus regional control and self-seeking and over mighty military leaders than nationalistic rejection of a foreign way of life. The Pax Romana was probably universally welcomed and resented as much as any centralised government would have been and still is.

I cannot resist a quote from Monty Python's Life of Brian:

> ***Reg**: All right, but apart from the sanitation, the medicine, education, wine, public order, irrigation, roads, the fresh-water system, and public health, what have the Romans ever done for us?*
> ***PFJ Member**: Brought peace?*
> ***Reg**: Oh, peace? SHUT UP!*[64]

For instance, a Germanic people/tribe we now know as the Burgundians, whose origins lay in Sweden, migrated steadily over 500 years southwards and westwards, via the Baltic island of Bornholm, the Baltic coast and Poland, to the

---

[64] en.wikiquote.org/wiki/Monty_Python%27s_Life_of_Brian. Accessed 13/02/2018.

Rhine valley in an area surrounding the modern cities of Worms, Speyer, Strasbourg and Mainz. After territorial disputes with Gallic tribes within the Empire they were granted territory within it by the Emperor Honorius, eventually helping the Empire to maintain the frontier in the province of Germania Superior, with some moving westwards into Germania Inferior.

In the late 430s, they endured a severe mauling by a confederation of eastern Germanic tribes and Huns, working for the Roman general, Flavius Aetius, himself of Germanic stock, led by Attila, the archetypal 'barbarian', but they were again given land further to the south around Lyon. Some, however, remained outside the Empire fighting for Attila in the 450s. Attila was described at second hand by the 6th century Roman historian, Jordanes, himself of Gothic origin, suggesting that he was of Eurasian origin and no more 'barbaric' than the 'civilised' Romans with whom he fought:

> He was a man born into the world to shake the nations, the scourge of all lands, who in some way terrified all mankind by the dreadful rumours noised abroad concerning him. He was haughty in his walk, rolling his eyes hither and thither, so that the power of his proud spirit appeared in the movement of his body. He was indeed a lover of war, yet restrained in action, mighty in counsel, gracious to suppliants and lenient to those who were once received into his protection. Short of stature, with a broad chest and a large head; his eyes were small, his beard thin and sprinkled with grey; and he had a flat nose and tanned skin, showing evidence of his origin.[65]

The displacement of the Burgundians and the destruction of Worms is the stuff of legend in poetry, the Nibelungenlied, opera, Wagner's Ring Cycle, and film, Fritz Lang's 'Die Nibelungen: Siegfried', which became the romantic basis for German nationalism in the 20th century.

When, therefore, having fallen out over broken Roman promises, a final showdown between Aetius and Attila occurred in 451 at The Battle of the Catalaunian Plains, there was an imperial Roman general from Bulgaria (Moesia) allied with a Visigothic King, Theodoric, son of Alaric who had sacked Rome in 410, leading mostly Germanic troops, many of whom were Roman citizens (foederati were from tribes whose leaders traded military service to the Empire in return for Roman citizenship), against an imperial federation of Germanic and Eurasian tribes led by an Iranian former employee of the Roman Empire. There were Burgundians on both sides. *It's not easy to draw many cultural affinities from such political and ethnic diversity.*

If we assume a similar sort of experience to these for Frisians, Angles, Saxons and Jutes with respect to Germanic migrations from the east and their subsequent migration to and settlement of lands formerly within the Roman

---

[65] en.wikipedia.org/wiki/Attila. Accessed 19/02/2018.

Empire we justifiably can build a picture of a similar fusion and non-fusion of cultural mores, including the roles and rights of women.

Secondly, there is no reason to believe that a culture that had been embedded over four hundred years would have been erased overnight. The populations of the terminated Western Empire would be more accurately described as Romano-Germanic, Romano-Celtic, Romano-Gallic and Romano-British. For instance, apart from the first six Emperors very few were Roman Italians and throughout the imperial era very few soldiers and generals were Roman Italians. At the level of the ordinary person the 'coloniae', the highest status Roman cities in Britannia, such as Colchester, Silchester, London and York, were settled by retired legionaries, few of whom would have been Roman Italians. Rome was a culture, a way of life as well as a political, economic and legal system.

We have our own British legends attached to this period when the light of history dimmed. That there was a King Arthur in the 5th century running a kingdom along the lines of Roman imperial law and institutions and using Roman military war strategies and tactics to preserve a Roman style of living is perfectly believable given our knowledge of what happened in Italy, France, Spain, the Rhine and Danube valleys and the North European plain with nomadic hunter gatherers settling down to a rural, agricultural existence protected by urban dwelling warrior kings. The sixth century monk, Gildas, mentions two such figures, Ambrosius Aurelianus and Arthur, both victorious over invading Saxons.

When centralised imperial government disappeared it did not mean that government, even centralised to some extent, disappeared with it leaving a sort of Western European, 'uncivilised', 'barbaric' anarchy. There had always been hereditary kings but when it came to matters of imperial importance, they were subject to the rulings of Roman Governors (Rector provinciae). When these officers, loyal to the Emperor and appointed in Rome, were no longer applicable their powers were taken over by kings. Gregory of Tours, a sixth century bishop and historian of the Franks, talks of one of these kingdoms, the Kingdom of the Romans, now known as the Kingdom of Soissons, in what is now northern central France, north of the Loire, being run by a former Roman commander, Aegidius and his son, Syagrius, along Roman lines with former troops of the Empire. It was eventually defeated by the Franks in the 480s and absorbed into their empire.

Thirdly, the 'collapse' of the Empire as a political and economic system was more of a collapse of world-wide trade which required the Pax Romana for its security, accompanied by a fall in population and a reduction in urban living possibly due to a decentralisation of wealth and decline in health (much new research has revealed possible drought, volcanic activity and plague as well as the loss of that Roman ingenuity that could tame Mother Nature).

Kyle Harper of the University of Oklahoma in his book, ***'The Fate of Rome Climate, Disease, and the End of an Empire'*** has written about a highly plausible chain of 6th century natural phenomena that explain the relatively rapid shrinkage of Roman urban centres and the ruralisation of significantly reduced Western European populations.

> *Two things happened in the 530s and 540s to end that upswing. First, a massive volcanic eruption somewhere in the northern hemisphere made 536 AD the coldest year of the last two millennia. Summer never came. To make matters worse, this was a spike in a long, ongoing cooling trend, which the eruption simply made worse. Another followed in 540, exacerbating an already bad situation. That decade between 536 and 545 was the coldest of the last 2,000 years. The consequences of a drastic, rapid downturn in the climate for a society that depends on agriculture would obviously be pretty bad. They were.*
> *Second, a massive wave of disease hit in the early 540s. The Justinianic Plague, the first great burst of bubonic plague, had arrived. In addition to ravaging cities like Constantinople and Rome, it reached as far as Ireland and remote villages in southern Germany. A recent excavation of a burial site sequenced the bacterium responsible for the outbreak, Yersinia pestis, the same one that would cause the much better-known Black Death in the fourteenth century. According to Harper, the Justinianic Plague was every bit as bad as its later sibling in terms of death toll; we simply know far less about it. Like the Black Death, the plague would stick around in recurrent outbreaks for the next two centuries. This helped to keep the population far lower than it had been during the boom years of the Pax Romana, or even those of the embattled late Empire.*[66]

I am arguing, therefore, that there has to have been some cultural continuity rather than the commonly favoured view of 'a descent into barbaric ignorance and 'uncivilised behaviour'. By the fourth century AD three distinctive features of 'Roman' culture were to ensure its influence over these new kingdoms in Western Europe, including Eastern and Central Britain: Christianity, Roman law and the lingua franca of Late Latin. Our question is: Did they engender a more public, more equal role for women than they had before as imperial subjects or Germanic tribeswomen?

Before we look at what these three cultural ingredients meant to European, including British, women between 500 AD and the Norman takeover in 1066 we need to look briefly at the early days of Christianity, how it became the State religion of the Empire and how it eventually became the religion of western Europe including Britain.

---

66 deadspin.com/climate-plague-and-the-fall-of-the-roman-empire-1822315385. Accessed 14/02/2018.

Chapter 10
The Rise of Christianity

I like your Christ, I do not like your Christians. Your Christians are so unlike your Christ.
-Mahatma Gandhi

In truth, there was only one Christian and he died on the cross.
– Friedrich Nietzsche

If you don't behave as you believe, you will end by believing as you behave.
– Fulton J. Sheen
Of holies'

Preamble

In his first Sherlock Holmes mystery, A Study in Scarlet, Sir Arthur Conan Doyle, one of my literary and lifetime heroes, puts these words into Holmes' mouth:

"What you do in this world is a matter of no consequence. The question is what can you make people believe you have done."

Jesus of Nazareth is no less real than the Prophet Mohammed, the Buddha, Confucius, Martin Luther or King Henry VIII. Like all the others, he said and did things as we all, being living creatures, say and do. Making others believe in a human interpretation of what he said and did as the ultimate Divine is the history of Christianity. The beginning of that world-changing story depended I think, not on who he was and what he said he was or what he did and what eyewitnesses said he did but when and where he lived.

Jesus of Nazareth was a Jew. He lived and died in the recently created Roman province of Judaea. The Roman Empire was run from Rome, some 4000 kilometres away. The first ever Emperor, Augustus, last man standing after a brutal power struggle that effectively ended the Roman Republic in 27 BCE, died during Jesus' lifetime and was succeeded by his stepson, Tiberius, in 14CE whose mother, Livia, was the power behind the throne.

Nazareth was about 150 km, a week's walk, away from Jerusalem, capital city of Herod Antipas, a client king of the Romans, and religious centre of Judaism, an ancient religion dating back 1000 years. Its centrepiece was a great temple built on the site of the Temple of Solomon, the holy of holies that contained the two stone tablets given by Yahweh, the Jewish God, to the patriarch, Moses, and placed in the Ark of The Covenant and which was infamously destroyed by the Babylonian king, Nebuchadnezzar.

Judaea was not a happy or a peaceful region when the Romans took over in 6 CE. There was and had been a lot of infighting in the royal family and much religious disapproval of what the King had done by divorcing his wife and marrying, Herodias, the wife of his half-brother who also happened to be his niece. By pointing out that this was contrary to Mosaic Law, John the Baptist started an antipathy that resulted in his execution and, quite possibly, led to Herod's lifelong fear that Jesus was the resurrected John and, therefore, a good candidate for suffering the same fate as his mentor.

Nazareth was in Galilee, a base for many groups of freedom fighters opposed to paying taxes to Rome. Some nationalists, led by Judas the Galilean, actually rebelled against the tax census conducted by the Governor of Syria, Quirinius, that accompanied the Roman move to direct rule and forms the historical backdrop for the Nativity story. In the 40s CE his sons, Jacob and Simon, rebelled again and were executed by the procurator (the imperial financial official of a province), Tiberius Julius Alexander. Judas' movement of 'Zealots', led by Menahim Ben Judah, possibly Judas' grandson, also played a major provocative part in the First Roman-Jewish War in 66 CE.

In addition to anti-Roman discontent over taxation and land ownership, brutally dealt with by the Roman military, and aristocratic fighting over the client kingship involving brutal repression of opponents and supporters of opponents of the Herodian regime, there was bitter religious disagreement. Zealots, who appear to have been outright nationalists for whom the subservience of Mosaic Law to Roman Law was a political cause of simmering dissent, as was paying taxes to Rome and selling land to Roman landlords and becoming tenants, known as sharecropping, were the most belligerent and anti-Roman of four principal religious groups. The other three were Sadducees, Pharisees and Essenes. While all basically adhering to Mosaic Law and the Abrahamic traditions that were their distinct heritage, they had their religio-philosophical differences, only laid to one side when threatened by a new kid on the block.

There is a wealth of scholarship concerning the differences between the three groups which I am hopefully going to simplify.

Sadducees were mostly from the priestly elite. They maintained the temple in Jerusalem and owned much property and land. They were also the military elite. As for their philosophy, they did not believe in heaven or hell or the resurrection of the dead. After death, shades wandered a featureless landscape for eternity in which the good were partitioned from the evil. More importantly, they believed in free will. God could not be evil or mean evil, but Man could choose between good and evil, the consequences of choosing the latter being of Man's creation not God's. Finally, what God intended for Creation, God's Law as it pertained to a social and moral code, was written down in the Torah, the first five books of the Jewish Bible. For those codes of behaviour Man should look no further.

Pharisees, according to the Jewish historian, Josephus, himself probably a Pharisee who lived in the first century CE, were closer to the common people. They differed from the Sadducees in that they saw the Law as being inclusive of centuries of interpretations of the Torah passed down in an oral tradition. They believed in a resurrection of the dead and an afterlife dependent on how a person lived their life on this Earth. Three classes of people would be denied eternal happiness, 'those who deny the resurrection of the dead, those who deny the divinity of the Torah, and Epicureans (who deny divine supervision of human affairs)'.[67] Finally, God had given Man free will but knew what was going to happen, Man's destiny. Sadducees, by contrast, believed that God had no control over fate.

Essenes believed that all human existence was predetermined. They believed in the immortality of the soul. They were ascetics who lived in communes which embraced poverty, piety and purity. They were reported to be vegetarian, refusing to engage in the ritual sacrifice of animals, often celibate and carrying out ritual cleansing practices including immersion in water. Josephus and others identified a fourth sect, Therapeutae, in the cities of Alexandria and Antioch, who led a clearly monastic existence of exclusiveness, communal living, rejection of worldly goods and pleasures and probable celibacy.

Two further religio-cultural ingredients made up the Judaean melting pot of religious and moral debate. From the East came Zoroastrianism, the religion of the then much less powerful Persian Empire and from the northwest the centuries old Hellenistic influence and its philosophies such as Scepticism, Stoicism, Cynicism and Epicureanism.

An ancient religion, possibly 2000 years old by the time the Roman takeover of Judaea occurred, Zoroastrianism had beliefs that were shared by the three Abrahamic religions, Judaism, Christianity and Islam, such as monotheism, the perfect goodness of God, the virgin birth, the afterlife, the day of judgement and heaven and hell, a messianic figure, Saoshyant ("one who brings benefit") and the purifying powers of fire and water. It was associated with mystery, especially by the Greeks, including magic, originally meaning use of supernatural power to solve natural problems (*miracles?*), and astrology.

One reinvention or reconstruction, the cult of Mithras, which involved elaborate rituals to reveal the mystery of God's creation, i.e., the natural world, was a popular form of worship in the Roman Empire, especially in the Roman Army. Evidence of its influence has been found in China and India as well as Judaea and the Romano-Hellenistic world, showing that religious culture was spreading worldwide long before the Roman conquest of Western Europe.

Sadducees embraced Hellenistic culture, but Pharisees were more nationalistic and rejected it. The Essenes, however, followed the more ascetic path already well-trodden by the Sceptics, Cynics and Stoics in their rejection of

---

[67] en.wikipedia.org/wiki/Pharisees. Accessed 26/02/2018.

worldly wealth as a virtuous pursuit and source of human happiness and belief in a power above and beyond the human spirit. Epicureans, according to some later interpreters both in Roman times and in the much later 18th century Age of Enlightenment, did not deny the possibility of God but attributed to the term an ideal of goodness, a high bar of human behavioural and moral excellence to be aspired to by all. Such a God or gods could not be omnipotent, omniscient and omnibenevolent and allow evil in their creation. Lactantius, a prominent Christian adviser to Constantine the Great, summed up their trilemma over God's governance of all human existence.

> God either wants to eliminate bad things and cannot, or can but does not want to, or neither wishes to nor can, or both wants to and can. If he wants to and cannot, then he is weak—and this does not apply to god. If he can but does not want to, then he is spiteful—which is equally foreign to god's nature. If he neither wants to nor can, he is both weak and spiteful, and so not a god. If he wants to and can, which is the only thing fitting for a god, where then do bad things come from? Or why does he not eliminate them?[68]

Overall, this inflammatory mixture of polytheism and monotheism, atheism and agnosticism, sectarianism, insurrection and political manoeuvring simmered away under the Roman State and its state or civic religion. The Roman Empire's many cultures and ethnicities embraced multifarious forms and styles of religious worship and faith communities, not always in one mixing bowl like in Judaea. Socio-culturally none of them challenged or offered an alternative to the Roman patriarchy strong enough to influence its mores with respect to gender roles and rights. In fact, as pointed out before, the Romanised woman enjoyed more individuality and economic, social, even political, influence than women in any culture swallowed up by the Imperial mission.

In short, 'The Gender Issue' did not get under the Roman skin in the same way that 'The Religious Issue' of Christianity did but in the merging of the two issues Christianity won the religious debate to exert the most powerful influence on Western culture of all but Rome won the gender debate with an equally world-changing impact on the lives of women in Western Europe for one and a half millennia. Christianity changed our world but, in the early days in which it was establishing itself, the world changed Christianity; a process which has continued and continues up to and including the present day. The protector, preserver, pioneer and propagandist for western Christianity for 1200 years or so was, after all, the Roman Catholic church whose heartbeat was in Rome.

Roman *religio* was not unlike many in the known world at that time. It was reverential of the past, particularly in the worship of the *lares*, the ancestral spirits of the home and the state, expiational and celebrational about the present, blaming reversal on and attributing victory to the relationship with the gods who

[68] en.wikipedia.org/wiki/Epicureanism. Accessed 27/02/2018.

needed pleasing and thanking with elaborate ritual and sacrifice, and inquisitive about the future by seeking signs, auspices, from the gods as to what actions would bring success to the Roman mission.

Most of us have some idea about the 12 main deities—Jupiter-Juno, Neptune-Minerva, Mars-Venus, Apollo-Diana, Vulcan-Vesta, Mercury-Ceres[69] ; each of which had power over key areas of human existence, like Mars the god of war and Venus the goddess of love, but are not aware that there were lesser deities many of which acquired a cult following.

Being polytheistic, the Roman State would allow ethnic god-based cults, especially if they had some use. However, they would ban those that they regarded as a *superstitio*, i.e., those that showed an unhealthy relationship with Roman gods or whose gods were a threat to the Imperial mission. Therefore, the mystic cult of Mithras which originated in the old Persian Empire and was, as I said earlier, particularly popular in the Roman military, was acceptable (although occasionally and randomly proscribed) but the cult of the Druids which fostered a cohesive nationalism in provinces such as Britannia and allegedly practised human sacrifice was banned and eventually annihilated.

Julius Caesar did a deal with the Jewish leaders that, due to the ancient reverence they had for Yahweh, their only God, those who worshipped Yahweh and followed Mosaic Laws and mores were exempt from sacrificing to Roman gods. Whether Judaism was not as overtly monotheistic as it has now become or the Roman State chose to see its belief in one God as monolatristic, i.e., saying that there might be many gods but for Jews, Yahweh was the only one, the Romans accorded it the status of a *religio licita*, a lawful religion.

Thousands of Jews, therefore, lived in the major cities of the Empire, particularly the three biggest, Alexandria, Antioch and Rome itself, abstaining from public shows of support for Romanism, and continuing to practise circumcision which the Romans and Greeks saw as barbaric, without persecution.

Such religious toleration was not matched by political toleration when in 70 AD, the religious and political (as in anti-taxation grievances) pots boiled over. The Roman general, Titus, the future Emperor, ended 4 years of savage fighting by destroying the sacred temple in Jerusalem and reportedly lining the city walls with executed insurgents.

Asserting their religious beliefs in the Romano-Hellenistic world was a constant source of conflict for the Jews into which John the Baptist, Jesus, the Apostles and early Christians were drawn being defined as a Jewish sect for at least a century after Jesus' death and for many in the Roman world until the 4th century CE when Christianity became the state religion of the Empire.

In a world in which death was omnipresent, poverty and a subsistence existence was the lot of the vast majority of free people, ownership of another person was never questioned nor, indeed, was the ownership of wealth by a tiny elite who bought or paid for a ruthlessly efficient military machine to police,

[69] en.wikipedia.org/wiki/List of Roman deities. Accessed 08/03/2018.

enforce and expand the status quo, issues such as life after death, the power of gods, the end of the world and how to influence the God or gods who decided these things were a very big deal. The Jews fought among themselves over these things, as I have already pointed out, and looking at Judaism from the Greek and Roman points of view, a people believing that they were the chosen people of one God who would be the only ones to go to heaven at the end of the world which was just around the corner must have seemed like a real and ever-present threat to the hierarchical status quo and an irritating non-conformism especially to the Greeks whose conformity to the laws and mores of the Empire gave them protection and prosperity.

Such a challenge to the power elite and their laws was, has been and is sedition and punishable by imprisonment and, when a source of violent challenge, defined as rebellion, death—usually a gruesome death carried out publicly with the express purpose of deterring others. Jesus was crucified for sedition. Christians were potentially seditious. Jews had already been there and got the T-shirt.

Early Christians, probably the vast majority, were most definitely a Jewish sect, differing only in respect of believing that Jesus was the Messiah, in Greek the Christ, the human fulfilment of the Jewish prophecy in the Old Testament, particularly the Book of Isaiah, whose life and teachings would prepare the world for his Second Coming and the Day of Judgement. To add to his credibility as having the inside track to God Christians widely believed him to be the Son of God.

In the Roman world, people were converting to religious cults all the time in the hope, probably, of avoiding an eternal 'Hell' and the pursuit of moral and spiritual fulfilment. *The Greeks, I think, had a pretty good picture of what Hell was like, the prolongation of unrewarded labour towards or an unquenched thirst for understanding the meaning of life. In the underworld Sisyphus rolled a rock to the top of a mountain only for it to teeter for a moment and roll all the way back down to the bottom and Tantalus, plagued with a raging thirst, stood in a pool of water with a bunch of fruit above his head both of which receded out of his reach when he rose up or bent down to quench his thirst. In his philosophical essay 'The Myth of Sisyphus' Camus, stoically, I think, recommends to us to 'imagine Sisyphus happy'. Hm!*

To join such a club, you had to agree to the terms and conditions which, in the case of Judaism, were quite demanding and crystal clear having been written down in the Torah and known as The Law of Moses. At the Council of Jerusalem held around 50 AD, 20 years or so after Jesus' crucifixion, Paul, himself a convert to Christianity, reached a compromise with James the Just, Bishop of Jerusalem and said to be the brother of Jesus, that non-Jewish converts would not have to agree to all the conditions, the least acceptable of which to a non-Jew, a Gentile, was circumcision.

In the 40 years after the death of Jesus, therefore, Christianity was beginning to diverge from Judaism and appearing not only in the synagogues of Jerusalem but to the north of Judaea in what is now Turkey—Galatia, Ephesus and Antioch, the third largest city in the Empire—Macedonia and Northern Greece—Philippi, Thessalonica and Corinth—and to the west in Egypt, Cyprus and Cyrenicia (Crete and Libya), even in Rome itself; all this against a backdrop of anti-Judaism and Jewish insurrection. As well as the revolts in Galilee in 6 AD and 46 AD, Tiberius had expelled Jews from Rome in 19 AD as did Claudius in 49 AD.

In between these years, Caligula had sent a general, Petronius, to Jerusalem in 39 AD to enforce the erection of his statue in the Temple with a view to Jews worshipping him as a living god. Greek inhabitants of Alexandria are said to have broken into synagogues to set up statues of the emperor, angry at the Jews insistence on wanting the same citizen rights as the Greeks without conforming to Imperial law and custom. (*N.B. We have to be careful in writing about this anti-Judaism in the Empire because such history can be part of the anti-Semitic agenda.)*

Given all these rumblings of tension, it is no surprise that Nero blamed Christians for causing the Great Fire of Rome in 64AD recorded by Tacitus in his *Annals*:

> "Therefore, to stop the rumour [that he had set Rome on fire], he [Emperor Nero] falsely charged with guilt, and punished with the most fearful tortures, the persons commonly called Christians, who were [generally] hated for their enormities. Christus, the founder of that name, was put to death as a criminal by Pontius Pilate, procurator of Judea, in the reign of Tiberius, but the pernicious superstition—repressed for a time, broke out yet again, not only through Judea—where the mischief originated, but through the city of Rome also, whither all things horrible and disgraceful flow from all quarters, as to a common receptacle, and where they are encouraged. Accordingly, first those were arrested who confessed they were Christians; next on their information, a vast multitude were convicted, not so much on the charge of burning the city, as of "hating the human race."[70]

Whether true or not, Christians and possibly Jews, if there were any, were again expelled from Rome and 2 years later there was open revolt in Judaea. Many of the leading lights of the generation that had known Jesus, such as Peter, Paul and James, disappear from history as real people to be venerated with the legendary status of martyrs by Christian writers, apologists with something to prove (Such apologist writings as the Gospels and the Acts are dated as being set down at the earliest in the 60s CE and certainly in the latter years of the 1st century CE). The outcome of the First Jewish-Roman War was that most Jews in Jerusalem were killed or expelled to swell the ranks of Jewish communities elsewhere in the Empire. It is not unreasonable to assume that Jewish Christians, the church of Bishop James, were included among the personae non-grata.

---

[70] www.eyewitnesstohistory.com/christians.htm. Accessed 12/03/2018.

With the Temple destroyed and Christianity on the side of the Pharisaic belief in the resurrection of the dead, the Sadducees petered out. Judaism and Jewish Christianity became the religion of the ordinary person. The tithe that every Jew paid for the upkeep of the Temple became a 2 denarii tax to pay for the upkeep of the Temple of Jupiter in Rome and, under Vespasian's younger son, Domitian, was extended to Jewish converts and even people who 'lived like Jews'. As the Torah contains a mass of rules of living, we could justifiably conclude that Christians, the majority of whom still observed the teachings of the Torah (Jewish Christians: Jewish converts to Christianity; Gentiles who observed all the Torah teachings and Gentiles who observed only those negotiated by Paul for Gentiles), were taxed.

After Domitian's assassination in 96 CE, his successor, Nerva, exempted Christians from the Jewish tax. Would that I had been a fly on the wall! How, in 97 AD, did they convince a far from stupid and unwise Emperor that Christianity was separate from Judaism, a *religio licita*, without raising suspicions that theirs was a *religio illicita* or a dangerously subversive *superstitio*? We know that only 20 years later Christians who did not recant were executed. In a letter from Pliny the Younger, governor of Bithynia, on the Black Sea coast of north-western Turkey, to the then Emperor, Trajan, he summarised what he did to Christians.

> Meanwhile, in the case of those who were denounced to me as Christians, I have observed the following procedure: I interrogated these as to whether they were Christians; those who confessed I interrogated a second and a third time, threatening them with punishment; those who persisted I ordered executed. For I had no doubt that, whatever the nature of their creed, stubbornness and inflexible obstinacy surely deserve to be punished. There were others possessed of the same folly; but because they were Roman citizens, I signed an order for them to be transferred to Rome.[71]

One God—Messiah; apocalypse—resurrection; Healer—Miracle worker; Torah laws—meeting places (synagogues = churches)—how did all those beliefs, mores and morals not constitute 'living like Jews'? There was clearly a need (spiritual and financial?) for Christianity to explain itself—write down what Jesus said and did? (The gospels date between roughly 60 and 110 AD and were written in Greek, a lingua franca of the times. It is always worth remembering that written documents were not for ordinary people because at that time and for another 1500 years or so, ordinary people could not read or write!)

After the destruction of the Temple in 70 CE and the execution and dispersal of thousands of Jews, a new type of non-Temple-centred Judaism was being defined by their own teachers, Rabbis. One could speculate that with Jews defining what their religious teaching was it was easier for Christians to define

---

[71] www.earlychristianwritings.com/text/pliny.html. Accessed 16/03/2018.

what Christianity was by rejecting aspects of Jewish teachings, the Talmud, rather than clarifying to a third party what defining aspects of their religion were.

Many questions could be asked about that little-mentioned meeting or, more likely, series of meetings, not the least of which concerns the identity of those representing 'Christians'. It is unlikely to have been so-called Jewish Christians whose only point of difference with Jews was that Jesus was the long-awaited Messiah from the lineage of David prophesied by Isaiah. Many of these will have been former Pharisees, possibly clever men of substance like their Jewish counterparts. We have some proof of this divergence of views from the 'Incident at Antioch' related in Paul's letter to the Galatians in which Paul rebuked Peter for not eating with Gentiles who did not observe Jewish purity laws:

> When Peter came to Antioch, I opposed him to his face, because he was clearly in the wrong. Before certain men came from James, he used to eat with the Gentiles. But when they arrived, he began to draw back and separate himself from the Gentiles because he was afraid of those who belonged to the circumcision group.[72]

Peter's subsequent acceptance of the rebuke did not go down well with his fellow Christians in Jerusalem:

> The apostles and the believers throughout Judea heard that the Gentiles also had received the word of God. So when Peter went up to Jerusalem, the circumcised believers criticised him and said, "You went into the house of the uncircumcised and ate with them."[73]

It is unlikely to have been so-called Gnostics among whose complex beliefs about 'The God' there was no room for a duality. Jesus was a human with a divine spark—not unlike deified Emperors—but not the Son of God, God made flesh, God on Earth.

We are left, therefore, with the only version of Christians that makes sense; Proto-orthodox or Pauline Christians, followers of the teachings of Paul, formerly Saul, a tentmaker from the Port of Tarsus, a Jewish convert, Roman citizen, preacher and Christian missionary. *I am convinced that it was this template upon which the Christian myth/truth/belief was created and will go on soon to look at what it meant for women. Back to the meeting.*

One would assume that the delegation was high-level, bishops, leaders of 'churches' such as the Pope, Clement I, and deacons, their seconds-in-command. One would also assume that the meeting was in Rome so members of 'parishes', newly created by Pope Anacletus, might have been there to explain the nuts-and-bolts side of things. Were any women there? Pliny, in his letter to Trajan a few years later confirmed that women were involved in churches at a high level.

---

[72] en.wikipedia.org/wiki/Incident at Antioch. Accessed 16/03/2018.
[73] Ibid.

> They asserted, however, that the sum and substance of their fault or error had been that they were accustomed to meet on a fixed day before dawn and sing responsively a hymn to Christ as to a god, and to bind themselves by oath, not to some crime, but not to commit fraud, theft, or adultery, not falsify their trust, nor to refuse to return a trust when called upon to do so. When this was over, it was their custom to depart and to assemble again to partake of food—but ordinary and innocent food.
> Even this, they affirmed, they had ceased to do after my edict by which, in accordance with your instructions, I had forbidden political associations. Accordingly, I judged it all the more necessary to find out what the truth was by torturing two female slaves who were called deaconesses. But I discovered nothing else but depraved, excessive superstition.[74]

Unlike many Jews, some of whom were doing very nicely out of the Pax Romana, it is doubtful that many of the delegation were wealthy—females and slaves were hardly a threat to the mighty Empire. (*No, I haven't forgotten Spartacus but that was 160 or so years before this, when Rome was a republic!*) If earlier leaders were killed for some sort of sedition or blasphemy, it was not because they wielded a social or economic power sufficient to challenge the imperial power elite. Peter was a fisherman and Paul a tentmaker.

In his letter to the Magnesians, Ignatius gives us some clue to the case for there being a clearly discernible difference. Jews had elaborate rituals preparing for and observing the Sabbath day, which was the seventh day of the week, our Saturday. To the third person observer these defined Judaism and its exclusive nature. Ignatius writes about the 'Lord's Day', clearly different from the Sabbath and not subject to the ritual.

> Be not seduced by strange doctrines nor by antiquated fables, which are profitless. For if even unto this day we live after the manner of Judaism, we avow that we have not received grace … If then those who had walked in ancient practices attained unto newness of hope, no longer observing Sabbaths but fashioning their lives after the Lord's day, on which our life also arose through Him and through His death which some men deny … how shall we be able to live apart from Him? … It is monstrous to talk of Jesus Christ and to practise Judaism. For Christianity did not believe in Judaism, but Judaism in Christianity—*Ignatius to the Magnesians* 8:1, 9:1-2, 10:3, Lightfoot translation.[75]

The theological or philosophical or even Christological and soteriological case (*I'm just showing off now with these what the Americans call '$100 words'! Christology is about the nature of Christ and soteriology is about salvation.*), as I have already mentioned, would have centred on the Messiah. From the Roman

---

[74] www.earlychristianwritings.com/text/pliny.html. Accessed 17/03/2018.
[75] en.wikipedia.org/wiki/Ignatius of Antioch #Letters. Accessed 18/03/2018.

point of view, if, as Christians said, Jesus was the Messiah, well … he had come and gone with no real threat to the Empire—he certainly did not lead an insurrection—and the Romano-Hellenic tradition had no real problems with sons of gods. In fact, it had no real problem with gods on earth or in human form, although it reserved that status for former Emperors.

Furthermore, this was the New Testament era and if, as I believe, the Gospels are the fruit of Pauline Christianity then it would have been a prevalent view that it was the Jews who found Jesus guilty of sacrilege rather than the Romans who found him guilty of sedition. How could his followers, Christians, also be followers of his executioners, Jews? It is unlikely that the Christological or soteriological nature of Jesus was fully formed for this meeting but the Recensionists, text revisers, of the 4th century AD put these words into one of the letters of Ignatius written on his way to martyrdom just a few years after this hypothetical meeting.

> But our Physician is the only true God, the unbegotten and unapproachable, the Lord of all, the Father and Begetter of the only begotten Son. We have also as a Physician the Lord our God, Jesus the Christ, the only begotten Son and Word, before time began, but who afterwards also became man, of Mary the virgin. For "the Word was made flesh." Being incorporeal, He was in the body, being impassible, He was in a passible body, being immortal, He was in a mortal body, being life, He became subject to corruption, that He might free our souls from death and corruption, and heal them, and might restore them to health, when they were diseased with ungodliness and wicked lusts. *Letter to the Ephesians*, Ch 7, longer version.[76]

Even if this sort of language were being used, I think the Roman authorities would have just written these, now sacred, words off as a bit of extreme nonsense. Tacitus who was in the process of writing his *Histories* at this time called them 'enormities'. Pliny, a bit later, called them 'depraved, excessive superstition'. What would really have mattered to the Roman State would have been the political nature of Christianity, if any, given that the Jewish diaspora, especially in the Hellenic world, was highly political, potentially insurrectional and a source of unrest among Romano-Hellene citizens.

Was Nerva able to extract a promise from Christian leaders of peaceful behaviour sufficiently convincing to obviate the necessity for the overtly religio-political acts, such as sacrificing to the Emperor and cursing Christ, that Pliny was to demand less than 15 years later and that some Christians, in their 'stubbornness and inflexible obstinacy', refused to do?

Under Trajan, Nerva's successor, in whose name Pliny was Governor of Bithynia, it was clear that Christians were not proscribed—indeed Trajan confirmed that in his reply to Pliny—but still subject to prosecution leading

---

[76] en.wikipedia.org/wiki/Ignatius of Antioch #Letters. Accessed 19/03/2018.

potentially to imprisonment, banishment, even death. Under Roman Law which was largely uncodified an accusation had to be made against an individual and the cases of the plaintiff and the defendant presented to the Governor. The best argument, both factually and rhetorically, won the dispute. An accusation of being a 'Christian'—even though we are not sure whether that title was used in Trajan's reign—was unlikely to have been enough to secure a conviction.

We can speculate as to who the potential accusers might have been and of what offences they were accusing Christians. Accusers were likely to have been those who were proponents and beneficiaries of Roman, Greek and possibly Jewish culture, probably Roman citizens and probably men. Whereas Jews were a direct economic threat, Christians were more of a social, religious, cultural and, as we shall see, indirect economic threat. Their offences if provable, were indeed grievous and, to use a modern term, 'gross'; sedition—they met secretly in private houses in organised groups or 'churches' to spread the teachings of a crucified Jewish rebel; sacrilege, blasphemy and disloyalty—they would not sacrifice to the 'state' gods on feast days, professing allegiance to the Jewish God and basing their refusal on unshakeable loyalty to Him thus rejecting the protective power of the Romano/Hellenistic theocracy and bringing ill fortune to and threatening the prosperity of the God-given Imperial mission.

As far back as the 60s AD, Christians were the first port of call when it came to scapegoats and Jonahs to blame for imperial disasters such as plagues, earthquakes, fires, droughts, famines, social unrest and military defeats and personal disasters such as business failure, bankruptcy, marital breakdown and filial disobedience (Thank you, Jane Austen, for that wonderful phrase!); and, in the eyes of 'Appalled of Nicomedia (capital of the Roman province of Bithynia)', darker offences of incest (Christians were 'brothers' and 'sisters') and cannibalism (the Eucharist).

Is it possible, just possible, knowing the Establishment psyche of a power structure such as the Roman Empire, that, in the first half of the second century CE, Christianity, by offering a viably alternative social, religious and cultural perspective on the meaning and purpose of life, threatened the prevailing patriarchy of Roman, Greek and Jewish culture to such an extent that not only did it gain an ineradicable foothold among all classes and ethnicities (and genders?) of the Empire but envisioned a world so outrageously different in its socio-structural possibilities that the earthbound intellect of the powers-that-be, Christian and Pagan, had to enforce compromises (between the various versions, Judaizers, Marcionites, Gnostics, Valentinians, and with the geographical and cultural origins of Jewish and Gentile converts and the Imperial regime itself) by mythologising, adulterating, dogmatising and revising its message of heaven on earth into a viable, acceptable and resistant human, social construct, Christianity, in which the beneficiaries, as ever, were a property-owning male elite and the losers were the unpropertied, slaves, the lower classes and women for whom in that brief period it had promised so much? Christianity got into bed with patriarchal civilisation and became its soulmate.

In the introduction to his work *The Age of Reason*, Thomas Paine encapsulated my own views on this very possibility.

> *I believe in one God, and no more; and I hope for happiness beyond this life.*
> *I believe in the equality of man; and I believe that religious duties consist in doing justice, loving mercy, and endeavouring to make our fellow-creatures happy.*
> *But, lest it should be supposed that I believe many other things in addition to these, I shall, in the progress of this work, declare the things I do not believe, and my reasons for not believing them.*
> *I do not believe in the creed professed by the Jewish Church, by the Roman Church, by the Greek Church, by the Turkish Church, by the Protestant Church, nor by any church that I know of. My own mind is my own church.*
> *All national institutions of churches, whether Jewish, Christian or Turkish, appear to me no other than human inventions, set up to terrify and enslave mankind, and monopolise power and profit.*
> *I do not mean by this declaration to condemn those who believe otherwise; they have the same right to their belief as I have to mine. But it is necessary to the happiness of man that he be mentally faithful to himself. Infidelity does not consist in believing, or in disbelieving; it consists in professing to believe what he does not believe.*[77]

---

[77] en.wikipedia.org/wiki/The Age of Reason. Accessed 05/05/2018.

Chapter 11
Romanisation, Regimentation, Recension

Strauss believed it was for politicians to assert powerful and inspiring myths that everyone could believe in. They might not be true, but they were necessary illusions. One of these was religion; the other was the myth of the nation.
-Alan Curtis

We want one single, grand lie which will be believed by everybody—including the rulers, ideally, but failing that the rest of the city.
-Socrates in Plato's *Republic* Book 3

Preamble

Christianity and its Bible, as Paine pointed out, are human constructs upon which Christians base(d) their belief and morality. The Septuagint, he argued, can be proved not to be the Word of Moses, nor prophecy the word of prophets thus undermining the direct link between the Creator God, the Messiah Jesus and the Divine will or Holy Spirit. Without proof of the carnal/spiritual essence of the Trinity, he argued, there was no reasonable basis for Christian belief, good man though Jesus was and real though the universal presence of the Creator God must be.

We could extend Paine's argument to question whether Christian morality as applied to social status and behaviour is similarly flawed. We have looked at gender inequality from a natural and a cultural point of view but what if the power of belief, Christian belief, drove a similarly powerful social belief in the inferiority of half the human race?

In the first 50 years of the second century AD, the rebellious tension in the Jewish diaspora in the Eastern Mediterranean and nationalists in Judaea propelled the Jews towards two violent revolts against the Roman authorities, firstly, the Kitos Revolt of 115-7 AD and secondly, the Bar-Khokhba Revolt of 132-136 CE. After the latter, Jews were expelled from Jerusalem and Judaea in their hundreds of thousands. As far as we know, neither Gentile nor Jewish Christians took part in either revolt thus furthering the distance between the two communities. Under Hadrian the proscription of Judaism was particularly severe thus, presumably, taking the heat off Christians although the cases of the aforementioned Ignatius, and Polycarp, bishop of Smyrna, and Pliny's letter suggest that there were instances of Christian martyrdom in these 50 years.

Although statistically unverifiable, one could assume that, free from direct persecution and with its principal rival on the ropes, Christianity spread, taking advantage of the continuation of Trajan's policy of 'live-and-let-live' under the benign and peaceful Antoninus Pius (138-161 CE) and the wise and stoical Marcus Aurelius (161–180 CE). It is no great surprise, therefore, that Romano-Christian historians, particularly those from the 18th century European 'Age of Enlightenment', like Edward Gibbon, who, being less than impressed with democracy, had a pronounced soft spot for benevolent absolutism, saw this as a bit of a Golden Era.

> If a man were called to fix the period in the history of the world during which the condition of the human race was most happy and prosperous, he would, without hesitation, name that which elapsed from the death of Domitian to the accession of Commodus. The vast extent of the Roman Empire was governed by absolute power, under the guidance of virtue and wisdom. The armies were restrained by the firm but gentle hand of four successive emperors, whose characters and authority commanded respect. The forms of the civil administration were carefully preserved by Nerva, Trajan, Hadrian and the Antonines, who delighted in the image of liberty, and were pleased with considering themselves as the accountable ministers of the laws. Such princes deserved the honour of restoring the republic, had the Romans of their days been capable of enjoying a rational freedom.[78]

Gibbon, alleged to have been no lover of organised religion, ironically lauded an age in which the Christian religion was doing just that, organising itself.

In his criticism, J. C. Stobart, author of The Grandeur that was Rome *(1911), wrote of Gibbon that "The mere notion of empire continuing to decline and fall for five centuries is ridiculous...this is one of the cases which prove that History is made not so much by heroes or natural forces as by historians."*[79]

Rejecting any notion whatsoever that I am deserving of the nomenclature 'historian', I am going to do exactly what Stobart accused Gibbon of doing, make a coherent story, a plausible one, I hope, out of a number of related but differently sourced facts.

The oft-quoted suggestion, repeated in Wikipedia's biography, that persecution of Christians increased during the Germanic Wars of Marcus Aurelius in the 170s CE is, in addition to being an excellent example of single source misdirection, all too common in history, a product of the recensionist Christian propaganda machine at the centre of my proposition and, therefore, worthy of a small digression.

---

[78] en.wikipedia.org/wiki/Nerva–Antonine dynasty #Five Good Emperors. Accessed 09/05/2018.

[79] en.wikipedia.org/wiki/Edward Gibbon. Accessed 09/05/2018.

Christianity developed in a Hellenistic culture. The Hellenistic world was characterised by philosophies all of which required complex theological reasoning to link God(s) to nature, the divine to the carnal, explain the human phenomena of good and evil, pain and pleasure and, the old chestnut, reveal the secret of life and what happened when it ended. After two supremely successful soldier Emperors, Trajan and Hadrian, during whose time the Empire reached its fullest and most secure extent, came two philosopher Emperors, Antoninus Pius and Marcus Aurelius (to be accurate Marcus did a lot of fighting too) during whose time the Pax Romana sculpted, as Gibbon, with some justification, remarked, an image of civilised liberty on which the advocates of 19th century imperialism gazed admiringly, about which they eagerly learned and to which they self-confidently aspired.

Marcus Aurelius, as already mentioned, like thousands of other intellectuals in the Greco-Roman world, was a Stoic. In fact, to give him his rightful place in history, he was a Stoic champion, a Stoic hero, especially to 19th century revivalists who studied and, to some extent, revered his writings. If we take a quick glance at Stoicism, there are enough similarities to Christianity to suggest that they might have been allies, not rivals; for instance, they shared views on the virtuous life, the equal value of humans (women? More on that subject later.), no matter what their social status, the futility of entrusting happiness to possessions and wealth and the need for natural justice and peaceful social cooperation. Indeed, when Christianity had established itself in the Romano-Hellenic world in the 4th century Stoicism began to decline. Modern writers such as Maxwell Staniforth see this as an ethical and moral development rather than a defeat of Stoicism or a mere coincidence, a bit like the grey and red squirrel scenario.

It is equally unlikely that the major points of difference—Stoic materialism, resignation to a predestined and rational universal fate and the irrationally 'obstinate' (a word used by Marcus Aurelius himself in his *Meditations*) Christian refusal to participate in religious practices based on human myths, legends and deities (*accepting the Jewish ones instead?*) which may or may not change the present consequences of that fate and its insistence that it would be different and blissfully heavenly for every person who believed in and worshipped the one Jewish God and accepted that their Christ was that God made flesh and was sacrificed to make it so—would have driven Stoics to take out lawsuits against Christians with whom they differed on points of theology.

In fact, Staniforth sees a distinctive commonality in the Christian Trinity and the Stoic Logos (the 'divine', incorporeal spirit driving the universe), seemingly affirmed in the opening words of John's Gospel: 'In the beginning was the Word, and the Word was with God, and the Word was God.'

> In the introduction to his 1964 translation of *Meditations*, the Anglican priest Maxwell Staniforth discussed the profound influence of Stoic philosophy on Christianity. In particular:

Again, in the doctrine of the Trinity, the ecclesiastical conception of Father, Word, and Spirit finds its germ in the different Stoic names of the Divine Unity. Thus Seneca, writing of the supreme Power which shapes the universe, states, 'This Power we sometimes call the All-ruling God, sometimes the incorporeal Wisdom, sometimes the holy Spirit, sometimes Destiny.' The Church had only to reject the last of these terms to arrive at its own acceptable definition of the Divine Nature; while the further assertion 'these three are One', which the modern mind finds paradoxical, was no more than commonplace to those familiar with Stoic notions.[80]

Intellectual battles, however, took place between an elite few literate people who were wealthy enough and powerful enough to indulge in them. Indeed, taking a philosophical stance sufficiently complex in its theology and morality to require intensive instruction, became a source of wealth in itself with the setting up of schools such as the one founded by Origen of Alexandria (of whom more later) in Caesarea in the early 3rd century AD, in which Christianity's rhetoric, history and practices could be taught.

The vast majority of hard-working souls required a headier mixture of demonstrable signs of divinity such as mysteries, mythology and miracles all of which Stoics were prepared to accept as 'human' attempts to tap into that piece of the universal divine Logos that resided in an individual human being, a transcending of the boundaries of nature. *Not that Christianity did not have its mysteries—the three-in-one, the incarnation, the resurrection and the ascension—its mysterious practices, such as the Eucharist, its Jewish mythology and its fair share of miracles in the Old and New Testaments.*

The fourth 'M' in this potent brew was Martyrdom, *the real clincher for an ignorant, incredulous multitude.* Nothing is more convincing of a belief, an emotion or an attachment to a cause than being prepared to die for it. It turns a rebel into a freedom fighter, sedition into martyrdom and the death penalty into a moral, even a spiritual, victory. Stoics had their Martyrs; Socrates died out of principle and duty to be a loyal, if morally dangerous, citizen; Cato the Younger and Seneca the Younger died for their opposition to the tyrannical rule of Julius Caesar and Nero respectively and many more 'Stoic Martyrs' died for their opposition to Nero and Domitian. In his *Meditations* Marcus Aurelius emphasised the reverence in which these Stoic moral role models were held:

> […] that through him I came to know Thrasea, Helvidius, Cato, Dio, Brutus, and to conceive the idea of a balanced constitution, and of government founded on equity and freedom of speech, and of a monarchy which values above all things the freedom of the subject.[81]

---

[80] en.wikipedia.org/wiki/Trinity#Impact of Stoic philosophy. Accessed 29/06/2018.
[81] en.wikipedia.org/wiki/Stoic Opposition. Accessed 08/07/2018.

I need to make a few more contextual points before coming to my 'story' of the early days of Christianity and its relevance to the status of women in Western Europe for the next 1800 years and completing this digression and its relevance.

Firstly, I mentioned the importance of 'when' and 'where' in history. It is equally true of historians. Much of our knowledge of the first four centuries of the Roman Empire and the status of Christians within it comes from the works of very few writers.

Publius Cornelius Tacitus who, in the 90s AD, wrote about the early Empire, roughly 14–70 AD and from whom we know about the Roman Conquest of Britain and from whose *Annals Book 15:44* later writers authenticated a secular confirmation of the existence and crucifixion of Christ and the persecution, torture and execution of Christians. *Worth a full citation, I think.*

> Such indeed were the precautions of human wisdom. The next thing was to seek means of propitiating the gods, and recourse was had to the Sibylline books, by the direction of which prayers were offered to Vulcanus, Ceres, and Proserpina. Juno, too, was entreated by the matrons, first, in the Capitol, then on the nearest part of the coast, whence water was procured to sprinkle the fane and image of the goddess. And there were sacred banquets and nightly vigils celebrated by married women. But all human efforts, all the lavish gifts of the emperor, and the propitiations of the gods, did not banish the sinister belief that the conflagration was the result of an order.
>
> Consequently, to get rid of the report, Nero fastened the guilt and inflicted the most exquisite tortures on a class hated for their abominations, called Christians by the populace. Christus, from whom the name had its origin, suffered the extreme penalty during the reign of Tiberius at the hands of one of our procurators, Pontius Pilatus, and a most mischievous superstition, thus checked for the moment, again broke out not only in Judaea, the first source of the evil, but even in Rome, where all things hideous and shameful from every part of the world find their centre and become popular.
>
> Accordingly, an arrest was first made of all who pleaded guilty; then, upon their information, an immense multitude was convicted, not so much of the crime of firing the city, as of hatred against mankind. Mockery of every sort was added to their deaths. Covered with the skins of beasts, they were torn by dogs and perished, or were nailed to crosses, or were doomed to the flames and burnt, to serve as a nightly illumination, when daylight had expired. Nero offered his gardens for the spectacle, and was exhibiting a show in the circus, while he mingled with the people in the dress of a charioteer or stood aloft on a car.
>
> Hence, even for criminals who deserved extreme and exemplary punishment, there arose a feeling of compassion; for it was not, as it

> seemed, for the public good, but to glut one man's cruelty, that they were being destroyed.[82]

Gaius Suetonius Tranquillus whose *Twelve Caesars*, written around 121 AD, thus including the reign of Domitian, to some extent verifies the history of Tacitus including the existence of a 'Chrestus' whose followers were Jews.

Lucius Cassius Dio whose *History of Rome*, written about 230 AD after 22 years of research, adding the years until 229 AD, is the last of the recognised recorders of Roman Imperial history. All three cross-check to some extent but cover imperial power politics rather than socio-legal history in which sphere Christianity would have fallen unless responsible for serious public unrest or rebellion such as the Jewish revolts all three of which were recorded in some detail. Needless to say none of these histories survives in its original form and none of the copies in its entirety.

Cassius Dio's history of the Antonine Emperors, for instance, comes to us as a personal summary of a copy of the original made by an 11th century monk, John Xiphilinus. The only secular histories of the third century are from the untraceable and unverifiable Herodian who covers the years 180–238 AD and the highly spurious Augustan History which is variously accused of being a parody, a fiction or a piece of pagan propaganda (fake news is not just a Trump era phenomenon!).

The fourth group of writers, it should be emphasised, were historians of Christianity not of the Roman Empire. As such their view of events was far from impartial. Roughly speaking there were four types of early Christian writing. The first involved making the Bible accessible to believers and non-believers alike by collecting, translating, sorting, sifting and dating the different oral and written accounts of the Jewish God and the lives, acts and sayings of Jesus and his apostles. The second, known as exegesis, offered explanations of what the events and sayings in the aforementioned texts meant. Whether this constructed by or was made to fit in with Christian theology is a moot point.

The third were apologies, defences of Christianity which usually followed the same rhetorical style used by existing philosophers, such as Stoics and Platonists, to attack the truth of Christianity whilst asserting the reasoning behind their own philosophy. Finally, when able to do so, Christianity went on to the front foot producing a number of polemics or attacks on other philosophies (with a fair bit of polemic in-fighting as well!) that contained the more extreme threats of hellfire and damnation in contrast to apologies which tended to concentrate on love, salvation and eternal life.

For example, Quintus Septimius Florens Tertullianus, better known as Tertullian, a convert to Christianity who probably lived in Carthage around 200 AD, a time of Stoic dominance and random persecution of Christians throughout the Empire, wrote a defence of Christian belief and practice called the *Apologeticum*. Lucius Caecilius Firmianus Lactantius, however, writing after

---

[82] en.wikisource.org/wiki/The Annals (Tacitus)/Book 15 #44. Accessed 09/07/2018.

Constantine's victory over his rival Maxentius at the Battle of the Milvian Bridge in 312 and the subsequent policy of religious toleration decided in Milan in 313 AD, went on the offensive declaring that not only was Constantine's victory the Christian God's vengeance on his persecutors but also, in his paper *De mortibus persecutorum* ("On the Deaths of the Persecutors"), that their deaths were similarly the result of God's wrath.

> They who insulted over the Divinity, lie low; they who cast down the holy temple, are fallen with more tremendous ruin; and the tormentors of just men have poured out their guilty souls amidst plagues inflicted by Heaven, and amidst deserved tortures. For God delayed to punish them, that, by great and marvellous examples, He might teach posterity that He alone is God, and that with fit vengeance He executes judgment on the proud, the impious, and the persecutors.[83]

A fellow Christian member of and polemicist in Constantine's inner circle was Eusebius Pamphili 260-340 AD, Bishop of Caesarea Maritima from 314 AD, whose *Historia Ecclesiastica* is a major, and sometimes the only, source of information about the early Christian church. Eusebius hung his history on two pegs, heresy—what Christianity was not—and martyrdom—the ultimate sacrifice for the achievement of salvation and eternal life.

By the time he wrote his history of the early Christian church, 140 years had passed since the time of Marcus Aurelius. During those years, there had been persecutory imperial decrees from Decius and Valerian in the 250s AD and by Diocletian and Galerius in the early 300s AD. Equally, there had been times of great tolerance under Philip the Arab in the 240s and Gallienus in the 260s AD. In the times of these persecutions we know that imperial decrees were issued, not specifically against Christians but rather to ensure an open act of loyalty to the Imperial mission from all imperial citizens/taxpayers by observing festivals, sacrificing to the ancient gods to ensure the Emperor's health and the well-being of his Empire.

The various punishments, destructions of churches, confiscations of property, banishments from the local area and, of course, fines, were determined locally. Death was only one of them and, given the Roman concern with taxes and troops (*"You have a choice—Join up or die" has a ring of truth about it in an Empire threatened by widespread insurgency or am I being too 'Dirty Dozen'?*), the least likely and probably reserved for community leaders such as bishops and presbyters—cut off the head and kill the snake. There is no evidence of any such decree being issued by any of the 'Five Good Emperors' and clear, non-Christian evidence, in the form of Pliny's exchange of letters with Trajan, that it was not an assumed, unspoken imperial policy of the nudge-nudge-wink-wink variety.

We know, furthermore, that criminals (from the lower social orders) were thrown to the lions or similarly savage wild beasts in Roman arenas—*damnatio*

[83] people.ucalgary.ca/~vandersp/Courses/texts/lactant/lactpers.html. Accessed 21/07/2018.

ad bestias was thought to have originated in North Africa, possibly brought from Carthage, and not ended in Rome until 681 AD—but only have three references to that being the fate of confessed Christians. The only reference mentioning lions is unsurprisingly from Tertullian, in rhetorical context and characteristic of much of his other writing, with a tinge of sarcastic exaggeration in its tone rather than that of a serious eyewitness.

So, highlighting the ridiculousness of the accusation that Christians were to blame for every natural disaster that befell the Empire, in Chapter 40 he gave us this indelible image made photographically visual by paintings such as *The Christian Martyrs' Last Prayer* by Jean-Leon Gerome in 1863.

> 'If the Tiber rises too high for the walls, or the Nile too low for the fields, if the heavens do not open, or the earth does, if there is famine, if there is plague, instantly the howl is, "The Christians to the lion!" What, all of them, to a single lion?'[84]

(*My particular favourite is his defence of Christian brotherhood: "We share everything except our wives—you share nothing except your wives."*)

Add a Christian matron defying her pagan father and a young lactating slave girl, a prophetic vision or two, a dash of public nudity and bestial savagery and you have the anonymously edited (often attributed to Tertullian, *not his style, I think!*) passion of Perpetua and Felicitas in which the ordeal of facing the beasts is also described, except, although one of the martyrs is severely wounded by a leopard, the women face a maddened heifer.

The third reference is contained in the aforementioned Eusebius's Ecclesiastical History in which he quotes from a letter from Gallic Christians to those in Asia and Phrygia detailing the martyrdoms of the bishops and deacons of Lyon and Vienne and other believers such as a young man called Sanctus and a slave woman called Blandina in which they faced beasts in the arena by command of Marcus Aurelius.

It is not entirely impossible that all three of these references came together in the works of Eusebius and were then embedded into the Christian tradition in the late fourth century when under the emperor Theodosius by the Edict of Thessalonica, 380 AD, Nicene Christianity (proclaiming the trinity, the three-in-one, Father, Son and Holy Spirit) became the state religion of the Roman Empire and its fundamental theology and morality were being fixed in the writings of such iconic Christian 'fathers' as St Jerome and St Augustine of Hippo.

Hence my earlier cautionary reference to single source acceptance of 'truths' such as the Marcus Aurelius' change of policy towards Christians. The fact is that the martyrs that fill Eusebius' work were not killed by beasts. Stephen was stoned, Paul was beheaded (as a Roman citizen he could not be condemned to the beasts), Peter was crucified (upside down?), Polycarp was burned, Ignatius',

[84] www.tertullian.org/works/apologeticum.htm. Accessed 23/07/2018.

although he feared the 'beasts', and Iraneus' fates are unknown, the method of execution of the Scillita martyrs is unknown, Justin the Martyr, Cyprian and Pamphilus were beheaded and Origen died of injuries sustained from torture in prison. *Yet, 'Christianos ad leones' is the archetypal image of martyrdom in the Roman era as powerful as that of the Marian torches of the English Reformation.*

There is serious cause for questioning the 'truths' contained in Eusebius' history arising from an examination of his motives, in no way suggesting that they were malicious or 'unchristian' as in a deviation from the basic human intention for good in the 'divine' message of Jesus but rather a questioning of their possible anecdotal confabulation of 'mythical' tales handed down from generation to generation of Christians with just enough historical content to suck in the ignorant, the fervent and the gullible. Indeed, Justin the Martyr who figures prominently in Eusebius' history referred to the 'gospels' synonymously as 'memoirs of the apostles'.

Eusebius had the Christian provenance to convince the later writers of the authenticity of his history. His teacher and mentor, Pamphilus had studied in Alexandria and been custodian of the library of Origen of Alexandria, the most illustrious Christian apologist of the third century AD, in Caesarea which Jerome claimed provided most of the information that became the New Testament. Origen, being in Alexandria, would have had access to the writings of Christian scholars of the Hellenistic world going back via Cyprian, Tertullian, Iraneus, Justin the Martyr, Ignatius and Polycarp to the actual Apostles such as John, the gospel writer. *Do you know what Jesus actually said and did? Well, no but I have read the record of his words and acts in the work of a writer who studied the work of a writer who studied the work of a writer etc. etc. who knew the Apostle John!*

However, the so-called Edict of Milan was a declaration of tolerance for all superstitions in the Empire and while Constantine may have favoured Christianity there is no real evidence that he pushed it more than any other. That job was left to 'salesmen' such as Lactantius and Eusebius and the selling line of Eusebius was martyrdom. Death for faith was not the end but the beginning of an eternal life not subject to the laws and limitations of natural existence. The quality of the product for those who did their 'due diligence' was its piety and, like all sales patter, that of Eusebius stuck to or embellished the piety of the martyrs and their mystic, prophetic, miraculous link to the God made Man whose death meant salvation for all who believed that He was also just the Jewish son of a carpenter who was crucified 300 years earlier.

Christianity had its competitors. We have already looked at Stoicism. Origen knew in detail the work of Celsus, an influential Epicurean or Eclectic philosopher from the time of the Five Good Emperors because some of his best theological writing in defence of the Christian God and His involvement in the lives of all human beings, his finest creation, was in refutation of the ideas of Celsus and his contention that no single God should prevent people from participating fully in the Imperial polity. Porphyry, a great Neoplatonist philosopher whose treatise, *Adversus Christianos*, was deemed too close to the bone and destroyed in the fifth century by order of the Christian Emperor Theodosius II along with the works of Celsus, was said to have attended Origen's lectures in Caesarea. Outselling these formidable opponents, therefore, was not easy for a polemicist like Eusebius. Edward Gibbon suggests that there were one or two techniques employed that amounted to what he called 'pious fraud'.

- Edward Gibbon openly distrusted the writings of Eusebius concerning the number of martyrs, by noting a passage in the shorter text of the *Martyrs of Palestine* attached to the *Ecclesiastical History* (Book 8, Chapter 2) in which Eusebius introduces his description of the martyrs of the Great Persecution under Diocletian with: "*Wherefore we have decided to relate nothing concerning them except the things in which we can vindicate the Divine judgment. [...] We shall introduce into this history in general only those events which may be useful first to ourselves and afterwards to posterity.*"
  In the longer text of the same work, chapter 12, Eusebius states: "*I think it best to pass by all the other events which occurred in the meantime: such as [...] the lust of power on the part of many, the disorderly and unlawful ordinations, and the schisms among the confessors themselves; also the novelties which were zealously devised against the remnants of the Church by the new and factious members, who added innovation after innovation and forced them in unsparingly among the calamities of the persecution, heaping misfortune upon misfortune. I judge it more suitable to shun and avoid the account of these things, as I said at the beginning.*"
- When his own honesty was challenged by his contemporaries, Gibbon appealed to a chapter heading in Eusebius' *Praeparatio evangelica* (Book XII, Chapter 31) in which Eusebius discussed "*That it will be necessary sometimes to use falsehood as a remedy for the benefit of those who require such a mode of treatment.*"
- Although Gibbon refers to Eusebius as the 'gravest' of the ecclesiastical historians, he also suggests that Eusebius was more concerned with the passing political concerns of his time than his duty as a reliable historian.[85]

Not without significance, given that Platonism was a major rival, Socrates in Plato's 'Republic' justifies the use of the 'noble lie'. The end justifies the means. I lean more towards this opinion on the examination of this ethic of Leo Strauss, the 20th century German American philosopher.

> *In The Power of Nightmares, documentary filmmaker Adam Curtis opines that "Strauss believed it was for politicians to assert powerful and inspiring myths that everyone could believe in. They might not be*

[85] en.wikipedia.org/wiki/Eusebius. Accessed 29/07/2018.

true, but they were necessary illusions. One of these was religion; the other was the myth of the nation."[86]

Whether a 'noble lie' or an 'eternal truth', the 'Word of God' or 'myth' and 'hearsay', 'copying errors' or 'falsified propaganda' the fundamentals of the Christian religion came together, and the product was ready to be sold worldwide by the Council of Nicaea in 325 AD. As one of its chief salesmen it is right that the 'pious fraud' of Eusebius should be put under the microscope.

An article by Richard Carrier, a prolific American author and speaker on philosophy and belief, written in 2017, *The Rain Miracle of Marcus Aurelius: A Case Study in Christian Lies*, gives a good idea of how a myth gains credence in the salesman's patter and the customers' inclination to buy sufficient of it to make a firm sale take place.

In the Piazza Colonna in Rome is a victory column to celebrate the victory of Marcus Aurelius over the Germanic tribes on the Danube frontier at some time in the 170s AD. One carved scene shows a lightning bolt destroying an enemy war machine and another a deluge of rain falling on a battle. Cassius Dio, the Roman senator, provincial governor and historian, writing 50 years or so after the battle almost certainly erroneously conflates both events giving one simultaneous picture of a miraculous rainstorm quenching the thirst of the Roman troops while lightning bolts strike down their enemy. This miracle, not quite borne out by the facts, Dio attributes to divine intervention, standard practice for an age, 1500 years before scientific understanding of the weather, in which the outcome of battles was decided by the gods and victory given to those whom they favoured.

Enough of Dio's writing is extant, some in entirety and some in fragments, to confirm the reality of his existence although scribal and translation errors, oral embellishment and lapses or inventions of memory could have affected the accuracy of facts and details about the events about which he wrote. Unfortunately, no original fragments of the chapters covering these wars exist only an abridgement or epitome of them written in the 11th century by the aforementioned John Xiphilinus, a Christian monk, by order from the Byzantine Emperor Michael Dukas VII who reigned from 1071–8 CE.

Upon some authority, Xiphilinus perpetrates a blatant piece of recension, not only revising Dio's text but haranguing him for getting the wrong end of the stick!

> The Romans, accordingly, were in a terrible plight from fatigue, wounds, the heat of the sun, and thirst, and so could neither fight nor retreat, but were standing and the line and at their several posts, scorched by the heat, when suddenly many clouds gathered and a mighty rain, not without divine interposition, burst upon them. Indeed, there is a story to the effect that Harnuphis, an Egyptian magician, who was a companion

[86] en.wikipedia.org/wiki/Noble_liehttps://en.wikipedia.org/wiki/Noble_lie. Accessed 29/07/2018.

of Marcus, had invoked by means of enchantments various deities and in particular Mercury, the god of the air, and by this means attracted the rain.

[71.9] This is what Dio says about the matter, but he is apparently in error, whether intentionally or otherwise; and yet I am inclined to believe his error was chiefly intentional. It surely must be so, for he was not ignorant of the division of soldiers that bore the special name of the "Thundering" legion—indeed he mentions it in the list along with the others- a title which was given it for no other reason (for no other is reported) than because of the incident that occurred in this very war. It was precisely this incident that saved the Romans on this occasion and brought destruction upon the barbarians, and not Harnuphis, the magician; for Marcus is not reported to have taken pleasure in the company of magicians or in witchcraft.

Now the incident I have reference to is this: Marcus had a division of soldiers (the Romans call a division a legion) from Melitene; and these people are all worshippers of Christ. Now it is stated that in this battle, when Marcus found himself at a loss what to do in the circumstances and feared for his whole army, the prefect approached him and told him that those who are called Christians can accomplish anything whatever by their prayers and that in the army there chanced to be a whole division of this sect. Marcus on hearing this appealed to them to pray to their God; and when they had prayed, their God immediately gave ear and smote the enemy with a thunderbolt and comforted the Romans with a shower of rain. Marcus was greatly astonished at this and not only honoured the Christians by an official decree but also named the legion the 'thundering' legion.

It is also reported that there is a letter of Marcus extant on the subject. But the Greeks, though they know that the division was called the "thundering" legion and themselves bear witness to the fact, nevertheless make no statement whatever about the reason for its name.[87]

Why was Xiphilinus so certain that Dio was wrong? Were there other records that contradicted Dio's version of events? There were at least two from around the time that this event occurred. The first is from Apollinaris, Bishop of Hierapolis. The second is from the aforementioned Tertullian. There are serious problems with both. We only know about Apollinaris second-hand in Eusebius' history in a passage in which Eusebius tries to verify the Christian miracle of the Rainstorm by citing non-Christian and heralded Christian writers as sources.

This story is related by non-Christian writers who have been pleased to treat the times referred to, and it has also been recorded by our own

[87] www.livius.org/sources/content/cassius-dio/dio-on-the-rain-miracle/. Accessed 30/07/2018.

people. By those historians who were strangers to the faith, the marvel is mentioned, but it is not acknowledged as an answer to our prayers. But by our own people, as friends of the truth, the occurrence is related in a simple and artless manner. Among these is Apollinaris, who says that from that time the legion through whose prayers the wonder took place received from the emperor a title appropriate to the event, being called in the language of the Romans the Thundering Legion.[88]

Eusebius also mentions Tertullian's telling of the story, but the original is extant. Unfortunately, it is contained in a letter allegedly written by Marcus Aurelius to support protection of Christians from accusations of subverting Roman rule, which is obviously a fake, not the only one it seems by which Tertullian was taken in. It is perfectly possible that this fake began the whole sorry tale. Incidentally, the letter cleverly combines well known facts with the Christian message—there was a 12th Thunderbolt Legion, but it dated back to the time of Julius Caesar and it did serve in the region of the Melitene in Eastern Turkey in which Christianity flourished in the 2nd century AD. *All very believable.*

Conclusion

Confabulation, conflation, storytelling, embellishment, myths, mysteries, miracles, martyrdom, pressure selling, ignorance and gullibility all play their part in the Christian story as does syncretism, the attempts to Christianise Roman history and to Romanise Christian history (By 385 AD, in an extraordinary turn around, punishment for heresy became the Roman state punishment of execution and the first Christian martyr of Christendom, Priscillian, was put to death for being a bit outré and cultish for the proto-orthodox Christian thought police) but once organised and dogmatised into a Bible, a Liturgy, and all the 'ologies' it took an incredibly powerful hold on that spiritual part of the human individual we call the soul for the sake of which obedience to the morality was essential.

In amongst all this was decided the status of half the Christian brotherhood—its sisterhood. My contention is that its definition followed much the same route as martyrdom and miracles. What God said was right and good was right and good but what God said was decided after debate by all too human individuals.

Author's note

It is important to remember that nothing I have said in this chapter is original or 'right'. Debates about theology and philosophy, politics and religion, power and belief are as long-lived as the written word. I am supremely unqualified to delve into their truths but to understand the complexity of the male's treatment of the female I am convinced that you must start there. I am passingly familiar with the work of Adam Curtis but not that of Richard Carrier. It will not surprise

[88] www.richardcarrier.info/archives/12480. Accessed 30/07/2018.

you that throughout this chapter, the voice of Thomas Paine was in my head whose writing and life, I admit, have had a huge influence on my thinking.

I have tried not to be biased but I am what I am. I am not an atheist like Carrier, and I am as equally suspicious of the use of power as Curtis. I have all my adult life shared the views of Paine who has inspired this lengthy prologue to my treatment of the unequal treatment of women in British history.

Chapter 12
The Word of God: Not!

Man makes religion, religion does not make man.
– Karl Marx

"Heresy", by the way, simply means "choice". It came to mean "thoughtcrime", implying it was blasphemy to presume to choose your own belief instead of swallowing what the bishops spoon-fed you.
– Robert M. Price

Preamble

What God said was the Truth in Christianity, the religion based on the teachings of Jesus of Nazareth, the Christ—"I am the Way, the Truth and the Life" (John 14:6)—whose insistent message of carnal shame and spiritual hope insinuated itself into and captivated the collective mind of believers. The reality, however, was that the Word of God was decided by the many apologists and polemicists mentioned in the previous chapter and Councils of Christian leaders, bishops, all men, starting with the Council of Nicaea called by the Emperor Constantine in 325 AD. What was not the Word of God acquired a name, Heresy, a school of thought that was not correct or Orthodox.

What was correct in 325 AD was decided by a majority vote from around 250 to 300 of the 1800 bishops of the time, a significant minority elite of the all-male elite, the reinforcement of which, adopting the same minority model, has become the Christianity that has guided Britain's morals for 15 centuries.

Was the 'school of thought' that women should have an equal opportunity to play all roles in Christian society ever God's Word and, if so, when did it become a heresy and whose decision was it to bury the idea for $14^{1/2}$ of those 15 centuries? From 100 AD many heresies were identified, nowadays we would call them freedom of worship or freedom of conscience. Six of those were most vigorously declaimed, even persecuted, by proto-orthodox Christianity; Gnosticism, Valentinianism, Marcionism, Montanism, Arianism and Nestorianism. *Fear not about all the -isms they can be easily boiled down into plain understandable scenarios!* As you would expect the -ologies of these heresies relate to the nature of God and Jesus but there is, *I think*, a strong gender theme running through them.

For three centuries Gnostic beliefs were a serious rival to proto-orthodox Christianity. Unlike Stoicism and other Platonist philosophies, they were not pagan but an alternative view of the Christian God, Jesus Christ, the 12 disciples and the apostle Paul. They were heterodox. They were of sufficient concern to be firstly challenged by such hallowed Christian theologians as Tertullian, Irenaeus of Lyons and the 3rd and late 4th century heresiologists, Hippolytus of Rome and Epiphanius, bishop of Salamis, on the basis of whose refutations they were subsequently suppressed in the usual persecutive ways, recension, polemics, prohibition of teaching and possession of them and text burning.

All that was known, therefore, or allowed to be openly discussed, of Gnosticism was from proto-orthodox condemnations of it, probably miscopied, altered and regularised, which were allowed to circulate in the early, middle and early modern ages, i.e., the second to the mid-eighteenth century, of Western Christendom.

Then, in 1774, James Bruce, a sort of 18th century Scottish Indiana Jones, presented a copy of the Book of Enoch, an apocryphal text lost for hundreds of years but known to exist in Ethiopia, that he had purchased while on his travels, to the Bodleian Library in Oxford. Among other stuff in the codex he had purchased were the Gnostic texts known now as the Books of Jeu which, in 1893, were sorted out and translated into German by the eminent Coptologist, Carl Schmidt. They were translated into English by Violet McDermott in 1978. The Books of Jeu are mentioned in the *Pistis Sophia*, a Coptic translation of the Gnostic text, which was purchased in 1785 by the British Museum from the heirs of Dr Anthony Askew, an avid book collector.

In 1896, another codex, purchased in Cairo the year before and brought back to Berlin, was brought to the attention of Carl Schmidt. Known as the Berlin Codex it contained the *Gospel of Mary,* the *Apocryphon of John*, *The Sophia of Jesus Christ*, and an epitome of the *Act of Peter*. Not much interest was shown in the contents of the codex being Gnostic until the discovery in 1945 near the settlement of Nag Hammadi in Upper Egypt of 13 vellum codices of Gnostic texts among which were the latter three from the Berlin Codex. Gnosticism was very much back on the agenda for scholars of early Christianity.

Valentinus and Marcion were almost certainly Gnostic Christians and sufficiently influential to attract the refutation of their theology and practices by orthodox Church Fathers, Tertullian in his mocking polemics *Adversus Valentinianos* and *Adversus Marcionem*, Irenaeus in his *Adversus Haereses* and Epiphanius in his *Panarion*. Tertullian expounds the Gnostic creation myth in order to demonstrate that it is too ridiculous to be believable and Irenaeus attacks Marcion for his rejection of the Old Testament Hebrew God of wrath and vengeance on the grounds that He was not the God of love and forgiveness about which Jesus taught.

Another movement that caused Irenaeus concern was Montanism or the New Prophecy which, founded on the idea that the presumably Gnostic God had yet more to reveal about the 'unknown' through prophets who were able to leave the carnal and psychic world and commune with the spiritual God of the universe, often produced public displays of trancelike ecstasy and visions. This behaviour gave 'peaceful' Christians a bad name with the Roman authorities and challenged the accepted Christology that Jesus was the Word and the Way, the ultimate and only route to the perfect ethereal God and was the fulfilment of the Hebrew prophecies chronicled in the Old Testament.

Assuming that these heresies were still around in the fourth century the succession of ecumenical councils must have plumped irrevocably for the mystic and mythological gobbledygook of the old Hebrew books that now constitute the Old Testament, rejecting the Gnostic gobbledygook of Valentinus, Marcion and Montanus as 'false prophesy' (a phrase common to Christianity, Judaism and Islam). According to the orthodox lobby, the Jesus of the Gospels had warned them to watch out for and some of the apostles had actually encountered 'false prophets'. There is no doubt, therefore, that orthodox Christianity was committed to the Old Testament as the Word of God.

Back to Sherlock Holmes. Power over life and death is the ultimate power. Politics has given individuals and groups, like Hitler and the Nazis, this ultimate power throughout history but religion has achieved it over the masses of ordinary people whose lives and deaths make and have made the world go around for the whole of human existence. It has done so by harnessing that potential in all of us to believe anything that assuages pain, fear and doubt, explains the inexplicable and gives hope to those who despair. It has no boundaries only, to paraphrase the great detective, 'what it can get people to believe of what it says and what people have done in its name'.

The tool of persuasion is language. Make it as mysterious and mystic, as multi-layered and impenetrable, as vague and visionary as you can and then gather a group of 'scholars' and 'chosen/ordained' ministers to whom the exclusive interpretation of that language is their gift from God, and you have the makings of a religion. Finally, make sure that somewhere in what is said there are warnings that what non-believers or other interpreters say are the words/language of 'false prophets' and the package is complete. God is/was the Logos, the Word. If you suspect you have heard some of this before of course you have. I will give you the full quote from Karl Marx:

> *The foundation of irreligious criticism is, "Man makes religion, religion does not make man" (Marx). Religion is, indeed, the self-consciousness and self-esteem of man who has either not yet won through to himself or has already lost himself again. But man is no abstract being squatting outside the world. Man is the world of man—state, society. This state and this society produce religion, which is an inverted consciousness of the world, because they are an inverted world. Religion is the general theory of this world, its encyclopaedic compendium, its logic in popular form, its spiritual point d'honneur, its enthusiasm, its moral sanction, its solemn complement, and its universal basis of consolation and justification. It is the fantastic realisation of the human essence since the human essence has not acquired any true reality. The struggle against*

religion is, therefore, indirectly the struggle against a world whose spiritual aroma is accessible via religion.

Religious suffering is, at one and the same time, the expression of real suffering and a protest against real suffering. Religion is the sigh of the oppressed creature, the heart of a heartless world, and the soul of soulless conditions. It is the opium of the people.

The abolition of religion as the illusory happiness of the people is the demand for their real happiness. To call on them to give up their illusions about their condition is to call on them to give up a condition that requires illusions. The criticism of religion is, therefore, in embryo, the criticism of that vale of tears of which religion is the halo.[89]

As to the belief that the Bible is the Word of God, even if we write off the Old Testament creation story as myth, its story of the establishment of Judaea as history, its psalms as poetry and its prophets as, *well*, prophets there is still the incredible story of Jesus, his virgin birth, his miracles, his amazing words, his crucifixion and his ascension to heaven, to wonder at and believe in. Its truth is triangulated in the synoptic gospels of Matthew, Mark and Luke. Who are we to disbelieve its essential components, with the obvious caveat that, as they were (*as these are*), they are the 'words of others'? Yet the New Testament does not end there. There is a fourth gospel, attributed to 'John' but whose identity is the subject of 'scholarly debate', written, allegedly, by the same writer as three letters and an extraordinary apocalyptic revelation or vision with which the canonical bible ends.

There are other gospels—The Gospel of Truth (sometimes attributed to Valentinus), The Gospels of Thomas, Philip, Judas and Mary—but, being Gnostic, they did not make the cut. They were rejected and, therefore, not the Word of God. There are letters or epistles, Paul's, of course, the letter to the Hebrews, James, Peter and Jude. The overwhelming content of these relates to resisting persecution and false teachers, maintaining the faith and advice on how to live as a Christian but the three attributed to John, like the gospel attributed to him, are somewhat different.

Gnostics did not believe that the Jewish God who made the world was the supreme divine who was unknown and unknowable without unlocking the secrets of the universe. Jesus could not, therefore, be flesh and blood, the Son of a supreme spirit. He must be that spirit mystically capable of convincing those who knew him that he was a person. An alternative explanation could be that he was a human being, in no way a god, whose divine spark enabled him to reveal the secrets that showed the 'Way' up the levels to the Supreme Spirit God. The Johannine writings, using scenarios and language Valentinians and Montanists would empathise with, seem to hammer away that Jesus was the supreme deity made flesh, the Trinity of God, Son of God and Holy Spirit—the Word and the Way—all the same; what the Greeks called 'homoousios', 'one in being'.

[89] en.wikipedia.org/wiki/Opium of the people. Accessed 01/09/2018.

A large number of followers of Jesus Christ, for a long time, found this idea illogical. If Jesus was the Son, then he had a beginning as opposed to God who was eternal and supreme. Jesus, therefore, was less than God, not equal, a begotten-God. When Arius propounded this logic in the fourth century it did not go down well with orthodox theologians and all his writings were burned. This Arian idea, however, did not go away but became tied up with the nature of Jesus. Nestorius, the Patriarch of Constantinople, took it up a side-track.

> Nestorius emphasised the dual natures of Christ, trying to find a middle ground between those who emphasised the fact that in Christ God had been born as a man, insisted on calling the Virgin Mary *Theotokos* (Greek: Θεοτόκος, "God-bearer"), and those that rejected that title because God as an eternal being could not have been born. Nestorius suggested the title *Christotokos* (*Χριστοτόκος*, "Christ-bearer"), but this proposal did not gain acceptance on either side.[90]

The Nestorian dispute dragged on with the Assyrian Orthodox Church until 1994 when a joint statement produced this agreement on the Word of God.

> The Word of God, second Person of the Holy Trinity, became incarnate by the power of the Holy Spirit in assuming from the holy Virgin Mary a body animated by a rational soul, with which he was indissolubly united from the moment of his conception. Therefore, our Lord Jesus Christ is true God and true man, perfect in his divinity and perfect in his humanity, consubstantial with the Father and consubstantial with us in all things but sin. His divinity and his humanity are united in one person, without confusion or change, without division or separation. In him has been preserved the difference of the natures of divinity and humanity, with all their properties, faculties and operations. But far from constituting "one and another", the divinity and humanity are united in the person of the same and unique Son of God and Lord Jesus Christ, who is the object of a single adoration.
> Christ therefore is not an "ordinary man" whom God adopted in order to reside in him and inspire him, as in the righteous ones and the prophets. But the same God the Word, begotten of his Father before all worlds without beginning according to his divinity, was born of a mother without a father in the last times according to his humanity.[91]

It further resolved the dispute over whose mother Mary actually was.

The humanity to which the Blessed Virgin Mary gave birth always was that of the Son of God himself. That is the reason why the Assyrian Church of the East is praying [to] the Virgin Mary as "the Mother of Christ our God and

---

90 en.wikipedia.org/wiki/Council of Ephesus. Accessed 13/08/2018.

91 en.wikipedia.org/wiki/Common Christological Declaration Between the Catholic Church and the Assyrian Church of the East. Accessed 13/08/2018.

Saviour". In the light of this same faith the Catholic tradition addresses the Virgin Mary as "the Mother of God" and also as "the Mother of Christ".[92]

Having established the components of the Word of God and before going on to examine what it said about women I think it would be instructive to look at what 'that which was not the Word of God' had to say, the stance it took, especially on the status of women, and whether there is a possibility that that had to do with its suppression.

[92] Ibid.

Chapter 13
Gnosticism: A Missed Opportunity

Perfection only happens when one has both faith and gnosis.
– Karim El Koussa

Theology being the work of males, original sin was traced to the female.
– Barbara W. Tuchman

Preamble

The protagonists in the story of Christianity are a male God, male interpreters of His purpose for the world He created, like Moses, Abraham and Isaiah, His Son, Jesus, and his male Apostles and missionaries, especially Paul, Peter and John. The persons who messed the whole thing up are female, Eve, of course, and various bit players like Jezebel. The villain of the piece, according to John's Revelation, the Antichrist, is also female; the Whore of Babylon upon whose forehead is written "MYSTERY, BABYLON THE GREAT, THE MOTHER OF HARLOTS AND ABOMINATIONS OF THE EARTH".

I, therefore, get the distinct impression that the transition of the Hebrew God of wrath and vengeance into the Christian God of love and salvation was achieved despite the continuously frustrating and, at its worst, diversionary existence of the feminine half of the human race.

Gnosticism, on the other hand, in many ways, places the feminine in the limelight. A female, or feminine spirit, Sophia (Wisdom), is still responsible for the world's imperfection but Her redemption is frequently the narrative theme of Gnostic theology. Rightly so, I think, the whole 'begetting' thing is a big deal in the Gnostic story because a male can only beget by inseminating a female. So obvious and widely known and experienced was this fact of carnal life that no religion was likely to have remained unquestioned about it and errors or slippages were made in the continuity of the story.

My favourite is in the Matthew 1:42 begettings which linked Jesus to Abraham in a narrative that established begetting as an exclusively masculine activity. However, the 41st begetting produced Joseph who had no biological link to Jesus the whole point of whom was that he was the Son of God! *Surely, it was Mary's earthly lineage that mattered not Joseph's! Matthew uses Joseph's adoption of Jesus as sufficient reason for the earthly life of the Son of God. Mary's earthly lineage was later deemed to be irrelevant (and her unique bodily ability to take in a male produced sperm, provide an egg with which it can link and nurture the resulting embryo into a fully viable human being) by the doctrine of her own immaculate conception without sin and Jesus' virgin birth.*

In the Gnostic text, *The Sophia of Jesus Christ,* in a passage a bit like Churchill's description of Russian policy—'a riddle, wrapped in a mystery, inside an enigma'—the Supreme God is described as 'Self-Grown'. Its likeness, Immortal Man, is androgynous, both male and female in appearance, with a consort, the Great Sophia. Mortal Man is their creation and, though at first perfect and androgynous, made imperfect by Sophia's desire to know the Supreme God.

> "I want you to know that he who appeared before the universe in infinity, Self-grown, Self-constructed Father, being full of shining light and ineffable, in the beginning, when he decided to have his likeness become a great power, immediately the principle (or beginning) of that Light appeared as Immortal Androgynous Man, that through that Immortal Androgynous Man they might attain their salvation…"[93]
>
> "I want you to know that First Man is called 'Begetter, Self-perfected Mind'. He reflected with Great Sophia, his consort, and revealed his first-begotten, androgynous son. His male name is designated 'First Begetter, Son of God', his female name, 'First Begettress Sophia, Mother of the Universe'. Some call her 'Love'. Now First-begotten is called 'Christ'."[94]

In this version, the feminine plays an equal part in creation and the perfect 'Man' is both male and female. The Supreme God is an ineffable spirit without gender. The route to heaven is a joint venture, a combination of feminine Wisdom, Sophia, and masculine knowledge, Gnosis. *Makes sense; wisdom without knowledge is as imperfect as knowledge without wisdom.*

> In some gnostic myths, a partner, Christos, was created for Sophia and that partnership is an aid to humans. Sophia is thus simultaneously part of patriarchal myths that devalue women (she is the cosmic "fall" just as Eve is the material "fall") and represents liberation from them.[95]

I somewhat dismissively referred earlier to this rather mystical sort of theologising as gobbledygook, but I am no more convinced that utterly rational, provable science has produced (or ever will, dear Stephen) a cosmology that gets any nearer to answering that crunch group of questions that religious belief since the beginning of human thought has tried to answer.

If I have it correctly: Jesus, in Gnostic theology, was the Gnosis, the Word, the Knowledge through which those who were ethereal enough attained

---

[93] gnosis.org/naghamm/sjc.html. Accessed 20/08/2018.
[94] Ibid.
[95] www.kenyon.edu/Depts/Religion/Projects/Reln91/Gender/Gnosticism.htm. Accessed 21/08/2018.

immortality. He was the masculine, never human but an emanation capable of appearing human. If Sophia, the Wisdom, the Truth, was the feminine, apart from Eve and all the bad women from Hebrew history, did she also appear as human? A likely candidate, albeit conflated or misinterpreted or just hijacked, could be Mary Magdalene.

The Church or cult or school of Valentinus, probably, as I said before, an offshoot of Alexandrine Christianity centred on Carthage, rejected the ecclesiastical hierarchy regarded as essential to the orthodox Church in favour of the principle of equality of individual believers. Women, therefore, were more prominent, healing, preaching, conducting the Eucharist and influencing the affairs of the church as presbyters or elders, possibly even priests. Certainly, Irenaeus encountered in Southern Gaul Valentinians like these who followed the lead of Marcus, a pupil of Valentinus, dismissing the whole thing as a sect of 'silly women'.

Marcus encouraged women to 'prophesy' which was also the main feature of Montanism in which Montanus and his two prophetesses Priscilla and Maximilla pioneered the practice of public meetings in which they had visions direct from God that led to a sort of mass hysteria. This may well have been the cause of the Lyons persecutions mentioned by Eusebius. Montanist groups certainly had female presbyters and bishops. However, before getting too carried away with this line of thought, Tertullian, who had a penchant for the Montanist New Prophecy was also able to write in his *De Cultu Feminarum*:

"Do you not know that you are, Eve? The judgment of God upon this sex lives on in this age; therefore, necessarily the guilt should live on also. You are the gateway of the devil; you are the one who unseals the curse of that tree, and you are the first one to turn your back on the divine law; you are the one who persuaded him whom the devil was not capable of corrupting; you easily destroyed the image of God, Adam. Because of what you deserve, that is, death, even the Son of God had to die."[96]

If this was orthodox thinking on the status of women according to the Old Testament it is small wonder that Marcionism which rejected it as unacceptably harsh was also deemed heretical.

Whoever or whatever Mary Magdalene was, wise or wayward, sinner or saviour, prostitute or priestess, companion or consort, soulmate or sister cannot detract from the fact that a widespread corpus of early Christianity gave her great prominence, considerable column inches and a credible influence on the movement as a whole. Its relevance to the gender debate does not relate to its credibility, her actual status or personality, whether the Gnostic Mary predates the biblical Mary and the multiple translations of Greek words into 'consort' or 'wife' or 'sister' but that someone, ostensibly Christian, was raising a female figure above males or at least making her their equal in areas of theological debate, testimony on Jesus and foundation of the movement.

---

[96] en.wikipedia.org/wiki/Tertullian. Accessed 22/08/2018.

Author's note: There is a mass of academic literature, much of it from the USA, on this topic. Wikipedia refers heavily to the very readable and fascinating book by Bart D. Ehrman, *Peter, Paul and Mary Magdalene: The Followers of Jesus in History and Legend.* To him should go the credit for my argument here.

In the canonical Gospels Mary is mentioned some 13 or 14 times (Given that Mary was a very common Jewish name the epithet Magdalene is important when identifying her, I think). She is mentioned nowhere else in the Authorised Bible. In the Gnostic tradition, she is given an equal, even leading, say in the *Gospels of Thomas* and *Philip*. She has a Gospel named in her honour in which she is blessed with a vision as abstruse as John's *Revelation*.

Of the 64 questions asked of Jesus in the *Pistis Sophia* (Faith wisdom or *why the Gnostic Jesus is the Saviour*) Mary asks 39. Other women, Mary, the mother of Jesus, and Salome, also ask faith-related questions. The introduction to the *Sophia of Jesus Christ* makes it explicit that Jesus revealed his secrets to 12 disciples and 7 women but only Mary questioned him. The authors of Gnostic texts seemed to be consciously selecting Mary for a leading role. Indeed, in the *Gospel of Mary* she does lead, steadying the frightened male disciples like a commander rallying her troops.

> "Do not weep or grieve or be in doubt, for his grace will be with you all and will protect you. Rather, let us praise his greatness, for he has prepared us and made us truly human."[97]

In the *Pistis Sophia*, the *Gospel of Philip* and the *Gospel of Mary,* Mary is established as superior to the male disciples, closer to Jesus and with a greater understanding of his teachings.

> "Mary, thou blessed one, whom I will perfect in all mysteries of those of the height, discourse in openness, thou, whose heart is raised to the kingdom of heaven more than all thy brethren".[98] [*Pistis Sophia*]
>
> And the companion of the saviour was Mary Magdalene. Christ loved Mary more than all the disciples and used to kiss her often. The rest of the disciples were offended by it and expressed disapproval. They said to him, "Why do you love her more than all of us?" The Saviour answered and said to them, "Why do I not love you like her?[99] [*The Gospel of Philip*]
>
> Peter said to Mary, "Sister we know that the Saviour loved you more than the rest of woman. Tell us the words of the Saviour which you remember which you know, but we do not, nor have we heard them". Mary answered and said, "What is hidden from you I will proclaim to you". And she began to speak to them these words: "I", she said, "I saw

---

[97] en.wikipedia.org/wiki/Mary Magdalene # Apocryphal early Christian writings. Accessed 26/08/2018.

[98] Ibid.

[99] Ibid.

> the Lord in a vision, and I said to Him, Lord I saw you today in a vision".[100] [*The Gospel of Mary*]

This caused jealousy and disdain in some of the males, led by Simon Peter and his brother, Andrew, and some apprehension in Mary about their sexist attitude. In the *Pistis Sophia* there is this three-way conversation between Jesus, Mary and Peter.

> Simon Peter, annoyed at Mary's dominance of the conversation, tells Jesus, "My master, we cannot endure this woman who gets in our way and does not let any of us speak, though she talks all the time." Mary defends herself, saying, "My master, I understand in my mind that I can come forward at any time to interpret what Pistis Sophia [the divine being who gives wisdom] has said, but I am afraid of Peter, because he threatens me and hates our gender."[101]

In the *Gospel of Mary*, in which Mary is asked to relate her vision, Andrew and Peter again demonstrate their disdain for her.

> Andrew challenges Mary, insisting, "Say what you think about what she said, but I do not believe the saviour said this. These teachings are strange ideas." Peter responds, saying, "Did he really speak with a woman in private, without our knowledge? Should we all listen to her? Did he prefer her to us?"[102]

Levi, the J.S. Mill of the disciples, rebukes them.

> "Peter, you are always angry. Now I see you arguing against this woman like an adversary. If the saviour made her worthy, who are you to reject her? Surely the saviour knows her well. That is why he loved her more than us."[103]

Jesus finds himself in the middle of a gender debate. In the *Gospel of Thomas*, this exchange takes place.

> Simon Peter said to them: Let Mary go forth from among us, for women are not worthy of the life. Jesus said: Behold, I shall lead her, that I may make her male, in order that she also may become a living spirit like you males. For every woman who makes herself male shall enter into the kingdom of heaven.[104]

---

[100] Ibid.
[101] Ibid.
[102] Ibid.
[103] Ibid.
[104] Ibid

This is entirely open to interpretation which, no matter what effort is made by the interpreter, will be influenced by individual subjectivity. Whatever I say, therefore, is most unlikely to influence those who already have strong opinions on feminism or the Bible or Gnosticism or all three. To me the statement is about gender not sex and spirituality not carnality. 'Make her male' embraces the dual concepts of equal divinity, male and female, and equal socio-cultural status, male and female—such a dangerously revolutionary idea for Hebrew and Hellenistic social mores, the maleness of the supreme Hebrew God and the Roman property-based patriarchy.

At no point is the Gnostic Jesus or the biblical Jesus, the Son of God, the Word, the route to salvation and eternal life, sexist, except, challenged by Gnostic writings, in respect of his choice of 12 male apostles. However, the Word of God post-325 AD was more than the sayings and doings of Jesus. Setting aside for a moment the Old Testament, the permanent side-lining of which led to Marcion's excommunication circa 144 CE, the gender debate arises in the New Testament Pauline Epistles and Johannine writings.

In his first letter to the Church at Corinth, a troubled and troublesome lot, Paul tried to cut down the factionalisation which was a feature of early Christian communities. Clearly one of the complaints by the church leaders was like that of the Gnostic Simon Peter, namely that women members were so vocal that services were interrupted, and men could not get a word in edgeways. Paul's now famously controversial advice was as follows:

> "As in all the congregations of the Lord's people. Women should remain silent in the churches, They are not allowed to speak, but must be in submission, as the law says. If they want to inquire about something, they should ask their own husbands at home; for it is disgraceful for a woman to speak in the church." 1 Corinthians 14:33-35(NIV)[105]

Similar advice was given to or by a church leader in Ephesus, Timothy.

> Likewise, I want women to adorn themselves with proper clothing, modestly and discreetly, not with braided hair and gold or pearls or costly garments, but rather by means of good works, as is proper for women making a claim to godliness. A woman must quietly receive instruction with entire submissiveness. But I do not allow a woman to teach or exercise authority over a man, but to remain quiet. For it was Adam who was first created, and then Eve. And it was not Adam who was deceived, but the woman being deceived, fell into transgression. But women will be preserved through the bearing of children if they continue in faith and love and sanctity with self-restraint. 1 Timothy 2: 9-15 (NASB)[106]

---

[105] en.wikipedia.org/wiki/Paul the Apostle and women. Accessed 28/08/2018.
[106] Ibid.

Most opinions and arguments in defence of and attack on these passages relate to whether the author of them was Paul, whether the translation of key Greek words should be this or that and what Paul really meant given the context in which they were written. They are, however, and have been for the best part of two millennia, the Word of God and blatantly discriminatory.

By way of contradiction, the Gnostic Jesus, in answer to her fear that Peter hates her gender, assures Mary with these words. *Do not interpret them, just read what they say in support of a woman disciple in fear of the sexism of male disciples.*

> "**Any** of those filled with the spirit of light will come forward to interpret what I say: no one will be able to oppose them."[107]

The Johannine Jesus is equally and consistently all-embracing:

> "I am the light of the world. **Whoever** follows me will never walk in darkness but will have the light of life." John 8:12

Even Paul who, allegedly, said some very discriminatory things wrote the biblical clarion call for equality:

> There is neither Jew nor Gentile, neither slave nor free, nor is there male and female, for **you are all one** in Christ Jesus. Galatians 3:28 [my highlighting]

All the letters in the New Testament are written to men or by men or to groups, except one. The second letter from John is addressed to a woman although it slides later to 'dear friends'. It is a warning not to listen to 'deceivers' who might 'come to your meeting' and tell you that Christ did not come 'in a real body'.

> **6** Love means doing what God has commanded us, and he has commanded us to love one another, just as you heard from the beginning. **7** I say this because many deceivers have gone out into the world. They deny that Jesus Christ came in a real body. Such a person is a deceiver and an antichrist. 2 John 6-7

If this is a warning against Gnostics, is it also a warning against a feminist outlook? If so, Gnosticism existed a lot earlier than is thought or this letter is not by the apostle John but within the anti-Gnostic Johannine tendency and written a lot later.

---

[107] en.wikipedia.org/wiki/Mary Magdalene #Apocryphal early Christian writings. Accessed 31/08/2018.

One final word on Gnosticism. In defence of the mystic mix of metaphors, parables, poetry or psalmistry and mysterious gobbledygook of religious writings we are often asked to interpret what was said or accept the words of an ordained priest who has sermonised his interpretation. A story, poem, or picture that can be interpreted to reveal a hidden meaning, typically a moral or political one we call an allegory. In a flight of hypothesising fantasy let me suggest an allegorical reading of the *Pistis Sophia* and the *Gospel of Mary*.

What if it is about factional voices—Mary, the voice of the female Christian, Peter the voice of the domineering Roman Christian, Andrew the voice of the more questioning Eastern, Alexandrine and Phrygian Christian and Levi, 'the lawyer', the voice of reason. There is a suggestion here that Christ, the champion of equality, of oneness, was 'Christianised' by the early Christian patriarchy, whether or not under the influence or in fear of the Greco-Roman and Mosaic patriarchies of that era, and the door was slammed on gender equality for over 1500 years with the eternal locksmith, the Church, continuously reinforcing the bolts so that not only the Gnostic secrets would remain hidden but, even more preciously, the true Words of God.

If this is remotely the case then a fifth-century Gandhi, possibly a Gnostic, would have been fully justified in using the Mahatma's words, "I like your Christ, I do not like your Christians. Your Christians are so unlike your Christ."

Chapter 14
Women in the Word of God

Unto the woman he said, I will greatly multiply thy sorrow and thy conception; in sorrow thou shalt bring forth children; and thy desire shall be to thy husband, and he shall rule over thee.
– (Genesis 3:16)

Wives, submit yourselves unto your own husbands, as unto the Lord. For the husband is the head of the wife, even as Christ is the head of the church: and he is the saviour of the body. Therefore, as the church is subject unto Christ, so let the wives be to their own husbands in everything.
– (Ephesians 5:22-24)

Preamble

Of the four components into which I divided the canonical Bible, the Word of God, I have dealt with the Gospels and the Johannine texts and some of Paul's letters. I now want to look at the Old Testament. Experts have argued long and hard about the Bible's treatment of women, but I am only interested in what it says, or in this instance what God (the Hebrew version) says.

The gender positioning and the culturisation of women in the Old Testament is primitive, certainly by modern social standards (by which they should most definitely not be judged) but even by those of the immediate post-Roman era or the Romano-Christian Middle Ages or Early Modern period of Western European civilisation. For instance, no remotely moral, caring father in that 1500 years would have looked at the story of Lot and his daughters with its gang rape and drunken incest as socially approved paternal behaviour no matter how important your visitors in the case of the former or your need to continue your family line in the case of the latter (*although the Habsburgs, for example, with their uncle/niece pairings came fairly close!*).

Nor is the Old Testament lacking in female role models, good like Miriam, Deborah and Esther or evil like Delilah and Jezebel, who played important parts in the history of Israel, God's chosen people. Renaissance art (e.g., *Lot and His Daughters*, Joachim Wtewael, painted in the 1620s) shows the level of awareness of these biblical stories centred on women but these representations while drawing attention to the female, albeit to its tempting sexuality, did nothing to enhance its social standing, merely reinforcing the sexist positioning of the prevailing patriarchy.

However, these stories did not record God's command to commit incest, etc. and, therefore, only have the directive or exemplary authority of episodes in the history of Israel in a cultural era, say 1000-300 BC, in which the status of ordinary women was that of pieces of their fathers' or husbands' property.

In her journal chapter, 'The Social Status of Woman in the Old Testament', Caroline Breyfogle gathers together the biblical references in her summary of the situation:

> Legally, the wife was the property of her husband. He was her Baal, master, or owner (Exod. 21:3, 22; Prov. 31:11); she was his Be'ulah, or chattel (Gen. 20:3 [E]; Deut. 22:22; Isa. 54: I; 62:4). In the law, she is listed with his ox and ass (Exod. 20: 17; cf. Deut. 5: 21), ranked after his children (Deut. 29: ii), and dropped altogether from the family list, where her personality is completely merged into that of her husband (Deut. 12:12; Num. 18:11, 19). As chattel, she may be surrendered for the protection of a guest (Judg., chap. 19), be made to serve the commercial advantage of her owner (Gen. 12:13, 15, 16; 20:2 ff.), be disposed of with the ancestral estates (Ruth 4:3-5), be brutally punished (Gen. 38:24; Lev. 2I :9), or be expelled at will from the home (Deut. 24: i). Injury to her person was rated as damage to property, compensation for which was accepted by the male in authority over her (Exod. 21:22; Deut. 22:19).[108]

In this ancient Semitic culture, therefore, women were inferior. Breyfogle nails down the reason why.

> The subjection of woman to the man during this period is due less to the weakness of the woman than to the mastery of the man over life. The predatory life, so long experienced in Arabia, the warfare characteristic of the settlement in Canaan, created in the man an attitude of mastery toward life and toward that group more closely associated with himself in the family.[109]

The God, therefore, of such a culture would inevitably be male and, in His creation, men would come first. This is confirmed in the creation story or is it? *Is it just my interpretation or are there not only two versions or instances of creation but two different stories?*

- Version/story 1: Genesis 1 26-28.

> Then God said, "Let us make mankind in our image, in our likeness, so that they may rule over the fish in the sea and the birds in the sky, over

---

[108] www.journals.uchicago.edu/doi/pdfplus/10.1086/474296. Accessed 11/09/2018.
[109] Ibid

the livestock and all the wild animals, and over all the creatures that move along the ground."

27 So God created mankind in his own image, in the image of God he created them; male and female he created them.

28 God blessed them and said to them, "Be fruitful and increase in number; fill the earth and subdue it.

- Version/story 2: Genesis 2.

7 Then the LORD God formed a man from the dust of the ground and breathed into his nostrils the breath of life, and the man became a living being.

18 The LORD God said, "It is not good for the man to be alone. I will make a helper suitable
for him."

21 So the LORD God caused the man to fall into a deep sleep; and while he was sleeping, he took one of the man's ribs and then closed up the place with flesh.

22 Then the LORD God made a woman from the rib he had taken out of the man, and he brought her to the man.

23 The man said, "This is now bone of my bones and flesh of my flesh; she shall be called 'woman,' for she was taken out of man."

Genesis 3

16 To the woman he said:
"I will make your pains in childbearing very severe; with painful labour you will give birth to children.
Your desire will be for your husband, and he will rule over you."

These few verses have spawned a wide diversity of Christian viewpoints—Biblical fundamentalism, Evangelicalism, Creationism, Complementarianism, Literalism, Criticism, infallibility and inerrancy, to name but a few—all of which can be used to make an 'intellectual' or 'religious' point, justify a moral, social, even cultural lifestyle or explain a type of spiritual or material belief of direct relevance to the social status of women.

Luther and Darwin are the two Christian gentlemen most responsible for all this diversity and controversy. Luther challenged the material wealth of the Papacy and the infallibility of the Pope's interpretation of the Christian message as revealed by the Bible, God's Word, and Darwin, more seriously, I think, suggested an alternative explanation to life on earth to the Genesis creation myth.

Until the 16th century, official, orthodox Christendom had sailed under one flag in western Europe and another flag in Eastern Europe and the Middle East. The western, Roman Catholic, flag was flown by the Pope in Rome, apostolic successor to Christ's Number Two, Peter, and God's representative on earth. Whenever, whatever his earthly sins, he spoke ex cathedra (from his throne) his pronouncements could not be wrong. They were/are infallible. These papal encyclicals and decrees known as 'bulls' after the lead seal that confirmed their authenticity went to the all-male area leaders, bishops, and on to the all-male local leaders, priests. *Much as I would like to enter the debate on all male, celibate clergy I am not sure that it is pertinent to my discussion here being a symptom rather than a cause of male domination in the Christian world.* For instance, in 591 CE Pope Gregory I, Gregory the Great, fixed the pre-feminism character of Mary Magdalene for 1400 years.

> She whom Luke calls the sinful woman, whom John calls Mary, we believe to be the Mary from whom seven devils were ejected according to Mark. What did these seven devils signify, if not all the vices? It is clear, [brothers] that the woman previously used the unguent to perfume her flesh in forbidden acts. What she therefore displayed more scandalously; she was now offering to God in a more praiseworthy manner. She had coveted with earthly eyes, but now through penitence these are consumed with tears. She displayed her hair to set off her face, but now her hair dries her tears. She had spoken proud things with her mouth, but in kissing the Lord's feet, she now planted her mouth on the Redeemer's feet. For every delight, therefore, she had had in herself, she now immolated herself. She turned the mass of her crimes to virtues, in order to serve God entirely in penance.
> — Pope Gregory the Great (*homily XXXIII*)[110]

The omission of the word 'brothers' ('fratres' on p.295 of the original Sancti Gregorii Magni, Romani Pontificis, XL homiliarum in Evangelia libri duo *published in 1892) in the Wikipedia text of James Carroll's article in the Smithsonian Magazine, June 2006, is interesting—suggesting some skulduggery?—and sufficient for me, contrary to my promise not to enter into this debate, to publish Carroll's opinion on the sexist nature of the whole episode.*

> The address "brothers" is the clue. Through the Middle Ages and the Counter-Reformation, into the modern period and against the Enlightenment, monks and priests would read Gregory's words, and through them they would read the Gospels' texts themselves. Chivalrous knights, nuns establishing houses for unwed mothers, courtly lovers, desperate sinners, frustrated celibates, and an endless succession of preachers would treat Gregory's reading as literally the gospel truth. Holy Writ, having recast what had actually taken place in the lifetime of Jesus, was itself recast.
> The men of the church who benefited from the recasting, forever spared the presence of females in their sanctuaries, would not know that this was what had happened. Having created a myth, they would not

[110] en.wikipedia.org/wiki/Mary Magdalene #Patristic era. Accessed 17/09/2018.

> remember that it was mythical. Their Mary Magdalene—no fiction, no composite, no betrayal of a once venerated woman—became the only Mary Magdalene that had ever existed.
> This obliteration of the textual distinctions served to evoke an ideal of virtue that drew its heat from being a celibate's vision, conjured for celibates. Gregory the Great's overly particular interest in the fallen woman's past—what that oil had been used for, how that hair had been displayed, that mouth—brought into the centre of church piety a vaguely prurient energy that would thrive under the licensing sponsorship of one of the church's most revered reforming popes.
> Eventually, Magdalene, as a denuded object of Renaissance and Baroque painterly preoccupation, became a figure of nothing less than holy pornography, guaranteeing the ever-lustful harlot—if lustful now for the ecstasy of holiness—a permanent place in the Catholic imagination.
> Thus, Mary of Magdala, who began as a powerful woman at Jesus' side, "became," in Haskins' summary, "the redeemed whore and Christianity's model of repentance, a manageable, controllable figure, and effective weapon and instrument of propaganda against her own sex." There were reasons of narrative form for which this happened. There was a harnessing of sexual restlessness to this image. There was the humane appeal of a story that emphasised the possibility of forgiveness and redemption. But what most drove the anti-sexual sexualising of Mary Magdalene was the male need to dominate women. In the Catholic Church, as elsewhere, that need is still being met.[111]

The only bit of nit-picking we might do with Carroll's inference is that a homily was not an edict or bull issued ex cathedra and, therefore, not infallible. Ordinary, largely illiterate, believers would not have known that either and what was good enough for the Pope was good enough for them.

When the challenge came with the development of the evolution hypothesis first from Lamarck then Darwin and Wallace and their students like Huxley the Roman Catholic Church had to raise its theological standard. It was clear that the twin incompatibility of the literal interpretation of the Bible and, therefore, the Old Testament account of the Creation and the intellectual force of geological (Uniformitarianism) and biological (Evolution) science, at the very least in its challenge to the obvious absurdity of the six-day Creation myth, could not continue. The volume and intensity of the protest among the Catholic fraternity suggest the depths to which the roots generated from a literal reading of the Genesis versions of Creation had become established.

However, of equal significance was the silence and relatively non-committal response from the dogma watchdog of the Vatican, the Magisterium, which had the infallible power to pronounce acceptance of evolution as anathema and place Darwin's as yet untested theory of evolution on the *Index Librorum*

---

111 www.smithsonianmag.com/history/who-was-mary-magdalene-119565482/#sODKRT6gRlP5RLlu.99. Accessed 17/09/2018.

Prohibitorum (English: List of Prohibited Books), a list of publications deemed heretical, or contrary to morality. This tacit acceptance of the rational truth of Science has led to a reconciliation with the Biblical truth of God's Word which is labelled 'theistic evolution' or 'evolutionary theology'. The *Catechism of the Catholic Church* now states this about the Old Testament.

> 121 The Old Testament is an indispensable part of Sacred Scripture. Its books are divinely inspired and retain a permanent value, for the Old Covenant has never been revoked.
>
> 122 Indeed, "the economy of the Old Testament was deliberately SO oriented that it should prepare for and declare in prophecy the coming of Christ, redeemer of all men." "Even though they contain matters imperfect and provisional, the books of the Old Testament bear witness to the whole divine pedagogy of God's saving love: these writings "are a storehouse of sublime teaching on God and of sound wisdom on human life, as well as a wonderful treasury of prayers; in them, too, the mystery of our salvation is present in a hidden way."
>
> 123 Christians venerate the Old Testament as true Word of God. The Church has always vigorously opposed the idea of rejecting the Old Testament under the pretext that the New has rendered it void (Marcionism).[112]

Contrast the reasonable tone of this statement with that of the 1616 Decree of the Holy Congregation for the Index against Copernicanism.

> DECREE
>
> of the Holy Congregation of the Most Illustrious Lord Cardinals especially charged by His Holiness Pope Paul V and by the Holy Apostolic See with the Index of books and their licensing, prohibition, correction, and printing in all of Christendom. To be published everywhere.
>
> In regard to several books containing various heresies and errors, to prevent the emergence of more serious harm throughout Christendom, the Holy Congregation of the Most Illustrious Lord Cardinals in charge of the Index has decided that they should be altogether condemned and prohibited, as indeed with the present decree it condemns and prohibits them, wherever and in whatever language they are printed or about to be printed. It orders that henceforth no one, of whatever station or condition, should dare print them, or have them printed, or read them, or have them in one's possession in any way, under penalty specified in the Holy Council of Trent and in the Index of prohibited books; and under the same penalty, whoever is now or will be in the future in possession

---

112 www.vatican.va/archive/ENG0015/__PR.HTM. Accessed 19/09/2018.

of them is required to surrender them to ordinaries or to inquisitors, immediately after learning of the present decree. (…)

This Holy Congregation has also learned about the spreading and acceptance by many of the false Pythagorean doctrine, altogether contrary to the Holy Scripture, that the earth moves, and the sun is motionless, which is also taught by Nicolaus Copernicus' On the Revolution of the Heavenly Spheres and by Diego de Zúñiga's On Job. This may be seen from a certain letter published by a certain Carmelite Father, whose title is Letter of the Reverend Father Paolo Antonio Foscarini, on the Pythagorean and Copernican Opinion of the Earth's Motion and Sun's Rest and on the New Pythagorean World System (Naples: Lazzaro Scoriggio, 1615), in which the said Father tries to show that the above-mentioned doctrine of the sun's rest at the centre of the world and of the earth's motion is consonant with the truth and does not contradict Holy Scripture.

Therefore, in order that this opinion may not advance any further to the prejudice of Catholic truth, the Congregation has decided that the books by Nicolaus Copernicus (On the Revolutions of Spheres) and by Diego de Zúñiga (On Job) be suspended until corrected; but that the book of the Carmelite Father Paolo Antonio Foscarini be completely prohibited and condemned; and that all other books which teach the same be likewise prohibited, according to whether with the present decree it prohibits, condemns, and suspends them respectively.

Paolo Sfrondati, Vescovo di Albano Cardinale S. Cecilia
Luogo † del sigillo. Registr. Fol. 90.
F. Francisco Maddaleni Capodiferro OP, Segretario
ROMA, Dalla Tipografia della Camera Apostolica, MDCXVI.[113]

It is widely thought that the pain from getting its fingers so severely burnt on the scientific flame lit by the Galileo episode took centuries to disappear. Would that a modern 'Galileo' would emerge to bring about the same caution, compromise and change over Birth Control and relieve the emotional and physical pain and suffering of millions of the world's poorest people and most fervent Catholic adherents.

The fundamental difference between a Roman Catholic and a Protestant perspective on the Word of God was the role of the Pope whose interpretation of and ruling on theological and moral issues raised by it carried equal weight to the original. For Protestant fundamentalists, among whom were the new approaches of Evangelicalism, such as Methodism and Baptism, only the original was true. For the Anglican Establishment, the viewpoint was more political. If it accepted that the Old Testament truths were questionable then the divine veracity of the New Testament ones, such as the Immaculate Conception,

[113] inters.org/decree-against-copernicanism-1616. Accessed 19/09/2018.

the Virgin Birth, the Last Supper, the Resurrection, the Ascension and the Coming of the Holy Spirit to the Apostles, arguably more important foundation stones of Christianity but equally subject to scientific disproof, would be called into question.

Thousands of Christians, particularly in USA, still believe in biblical inerrancy—the Bible is not spiritually or morally wrong—which was the majority view until the late eighteenth century before nineteenth century Liberal or Modernist Christian theologists began to take the centre ground dragging the Anglican Establishment, sometimes reluctantly, along with them. Having tried some rather naff pseudoscience of their own (In 1654, Reverend James Ussher, based on historical records, declared that the world was created during the night of 22 October 4004 BC.), the position after Darwin was to let science have its day, requiring it to incontrovertibly disprove Old Testament historicity and factual accuracy, and, when it did, ride the knockout potential of the punch and adjust in the sure belief that religion and science could, would have to, coexist both being equally important to human health just as the heart and mind are.

It is not helpful to compare modern Britain with the far more God-centred and Establishment-deferential Britain of the late eighteenth and nineteenth centuries because Christianity has ceased to cast its spell over the social and moral affairs of the nation. If we postulate that the USA is the only modern Anglo-Saxon state where such dominance still exists these figures give us some idea of how it may have been (A Gallup Poll correctly predicted the outcome of the 1936 Presidential Election).

> A 2011 Gallup survey reports, "Three in 10 Americans interpret the Bible literally, saying it is the actual word of God. That is similar to what Gallup has measured over the last two decades, but down from the 1970s and 1980s. A 49% plurality of Americans say the Bible is the inspired word of God but that it should not be taken literally, consistently the most common view in Gallup's nearly 40-year history of this question. Another 17% consider the Bible an ancient book of stories recorded by man."[114]

It is quite safe to assume, therefore, that prior to the late 18th century CE most western European Christians, whether Roman Catholic or Protestant, accepted the divine truth of the Old Testament and, therefore, the Creation and, therefore, the absolute and relative status of Man and Woman. When 19th century science began to cast reasonable doubt on all this the Divinity of Creation stood up quite well in the absence, it should be pointed out, of The Big Bang Theory. Very few Christians (some Young Earthers still do today) saw the need to defend how God's work in Nature unfolded itself and how long it would take to reach perfection or, as Thomas Paine had explored, the historical accuracy or authorship of the narratives.

---

[114] en.wikipedia.org/wiki/Biblical literalism. Accessed 20/09/2018.

This still left two serious impediments to a lasting accommodation. Firstly, Creation was God's design, it had a purpose, and Darwin's work seemed to suggest a total lack of design, nature, even human beings a la 1850s, being the result of some random accidents, catastrophes, and Nature's selection process not God's. Again, this concern was easily alleviated. John Newman, a towering nineteenth century figure, both Anglican priest and Roman Catholic cardinal, wrote about it to a friend.

> As to the Divine Design, is it not an instance of incomprehensibly and infinitely marvellous Wisdom and Design to have given certain laws to matter millions of ages ago, which have surely and precisely worked out, in the long course of those ages, those effects which He from the first proposed. Mr. Darwin's theory needs not then to be atheistical, be it true or not; it may simply be suggesting a larger idea of Divine Prescience and Skill. Perhaps your friend has got a surer clue to guide him than I have, who have never studied the question, and I do not [see] that 'the accidental evolution of organic beings' is inconsistent with divine design—It is accidental to us, not to God.[115]

Secondly and more problematically, Man was God's ultimate creation, created in His image to rule over, have dominion over, all the creatures on land and sea. He, therefore, could not be some transmuted, more complex version of some of them. The Church Establishment's point of view was that evolution might be applicable to other plant and animal species but not to Man. In 1860 a group of German Catholic bishops made this statement.

> Our first parents were formed immediately by God. Therefore we declare that the opinion of those who do not fear to assert that this human being, man as regards his body, emerged finally from the spontaneous continuous change of imperfect nature to the more perfect, is clearly opposed to Sacred Scripture and to the Faith.[116]

So, for 1800 years or so, this is how millions of Christian believers, as revealed by the inerrant Word of God and explained/interpreted by the Apostles, the Pope, and ordained priests, saw human beings.

- God is supernatural—He created all things natural, but Man was special being the natural form of God Himself; God is male, and He created Man first and Woman from Man—Woman's role is to help Man.
- God Designed Man and Woman for a Purpose which He reveals/will reveal over time (to Men only?).
- Man is Designed to work toward the Purpose.
- Woman is Designed to help although Her Design also gets in the way by diverting Men from doing God's Will and sinning.

---

[115] en.wikipedia.org/wiki/Catholic Church and evolution. Accessed 20/09/2018.
[116] Ibid.

- God sent His Son, His Male child, to show God's Purpose and provide a route to get God's forgiveness.

Apart from the last bit we find that narrative in the Old Testament and can believe the Truth of it factually, allegorically, metaphorically, or spiritually. The last bit is contained in the Gospels with the last all-male addition of 12 Apostles, all men.

One quarter of the New Testament is devoted to the interpretation of all this by a tentmaker, from Tarsus, a major port now in modern Turkey, but brought up in Jerusalem, who was a Romanised Jew but converted to Christianity. Although probably expert on the Jewish Tanakh, the Hebrew Bible, from his education, none of his knowledge of Jesus was first-hand. As an interpreter of the meaning of the Christian story, theological, moral, and practical teacher and enforcer and much travelled messenger and encourager of putative, nascent, and established Christian communities his, other than those of Jesus and the Pope, was the voice of the western Christian Church. It spoke/speaks to Christians with questions.

I looked earlier at what Paul or whoever hijacked his name said about the public status of Christian women. He further defined female roles within the family so clearly that his advice would have been used as authoritative guidance on families handed down from God to His ordained, all male, ministers. In his first letter to the community at Corinth Paul made it clear what the pecking order was in the family of Christ and the Christian family—and why.

> 3: But I want you to understand that the head of every man is Christ, the head of a woman is her husband, and the head of Christ is God. 4 Any man who prays or prophesies with his head covered dishonours his head, 5: but any woman who prays or prophesies with her head unveiled dishonours her head—it is the same as if her head were shaven. 6: For if a woman will not veil herself, then she should cut off her hair; but if it is disgraceful for a woman to be shorn or shaven, let her wear a veil. 7: For a man ought not to cover his head, since he is the image and glory of God; but woman is the glory of man. 8: (For man was not made from woman, but woman from man. 9: Neither was man created for woman, but woman for man.) 1 Corinthians: 14.

Just in case they missed it he repeated the message later in a letter to the community in Ephesus.

> 21: Be subject to one another out of reverence for Christ. 22: Wives, be subject to your husbands, as to the Lord. 23: For the husband is the head of the wife as Christ is the head of the church, his body, and is himself its Saviour. 24: As the church is subject to Christ, so let wives also be subject in everything to their husbands. 25: Husbands, love your wives, as Christ loved the church and gave himself up for her, ... Ephesians: 5.

Furthermore, just in case they missed that confirmation of the patriarchal nature of the relationship he repeated it again in a letter to the community at Colossae.

> 18: Wives, be subject to your husbands, as is fitting in the Lord. 19: Husbands, love your wives, and do not be harsh with them. Colossians: 3

Only now does it matter who said these words, what he meant by them and what they should mean to us. Until well into the twentieth century after the birth of Jesus they were always the Word of God to be followed and to be ignored or challenged on pain of eternal damnation.

If I go back in my imagination to my farm in rural Kent (my ancestors come from the peasant stock of Kent and East Sussex) in 1381, the year of the Peasant's Revolt, I am sure that I would have had a truly clear idea of my place, my purpose, my duty, and my destiny as a man in God's Design. Seething with the unfairness, the inequality even, of my condition compared to that of the plump Prior at the Priory, the haughty squire and Justice of the Peace and the Lord of my property, an absentee landlord to whom I pay enormous rent I can barely afford and, last but not least, the callous jobs worth of a tax collector and his henchmen out of London with their Chancellor's seal, I doubt that I would have been thinking that my wife had anything to do with it, after all her job and Christian duty was to look after the children, feed me and keep house.

Who told me this? Who said this was so? My father who died of the plague when I was two years old? My mother who died giving birth to my fourth sister when I was eight years old? My Uncle who married my mother after my father's death? My Lord whom I met on market day two years ago when I last paid my feudal dues and who said nothing when I touched my forelock and knelt before him? My King, a fourteen-year-old boy who has never done a day's work in his life, two years older than my eldest who had been helping on the farm since he was six.

No, all that I would have known about life and death was from Father Timothy, who had taught me reckoning and my letters, and his Bible given to him by the Bishop who, it was said, had once been to the holy city, thousands of miles away and met our Father, the Pope of Rome. Equality of respect and treatment was an issue between men in a world run by men.

President Jimmy Carter—the finest, most morally decent post-war President of the USA, in my opinion—very wisely, I think, signalled a sea change to western patriarchy.

When our mothers, wives, sisters, and daughters are considered both different and inferior in the eyes of the God we worship, this belief tends to permeate society, and everyone suffers.

-Jimmy Carter, A Call to Action: Women, Religion, Violence and Power

Chapter 15
Dogma

The Christian faith is the most exciting drama that ever staggered the imagination of man—and the dogma is the drama.
– Dorothy L. Sayers

Some men are so indoctrinated that they sincerely believe that other than cooking and cleaning, the only thing that a woman can do better than them is being a woman.
– Mokokoma Mokhonoana

Preamble

In 597 AD, approximately 200 years after the recorded departure of the Roman legions and roughly 200 years before the crowning of Charlemagne as Holy Roman Emperor, a group of Christian missionaries sent by Pope Gregory I (the Great) and led by an abbot from Rome called Augustine landed in Kent at the invitation of the King's wife, a Christian Frank called Bertha, via her priest, Liudhard, a Frankish bishop. Very quickly the pagan King Aethelberht was himself converted as were many others.

It is most unlikely that the Anglo-Saxon kings were unaware of the Christian message. Some of the people on mainland Britain may have retained the family version of Christianity from Roman times and, particularly in the west and north, may already have been converted by missionary monks from Ireland who also provided a bible-based education, possibly with secular subjects as well, from which the children of some Anglo-Saxon nobles benefitted.

When Alfred the Great, therefore, faced the incursions and eventual invasion of the pagan Vikings some 300 years later he was a confident Christian king of an established Christian nation, primarily of Celtic and Germanic ethnic origin, strong enough to resist then convert the pagans rather than revert to paganism itself. After Alfred's victory over the Viking war band at the Battle of Edington in 878 CE, their leader, Guthrum, not only settled many of his followers in the East Midlands but he also converted to Christianity and by ancient custom so did they.

139 years later, Canute was crowned the first Scandinavian King of England and united the Anglo-Saxon kingdom of Wessex in the south with the Danelaw that then covered much of the Midlands and north-west, Mercia controlling the West Midlands and Northumbria the north-east. Canute was already a Christian.

This ethno-cultural mixture of Germanic, Celtic, Scandinavian and Anglo-Saxon Christian converts was what the Normans conquered in 1066 and the Domesday Book recorded 20 years later.
I would simply love to say that these pagan cultures were surprisingly egalitarian and that it was their Christianisation by an alien South Mediterranean and Middle Eastern cultural and spiritual force steeped in the patriarchal tradition that changed the course of their history. I cannot.

The facts all suggest that the Celts, Franks, Angles, Jutes, Saxons, and Scandinavians embraced a patriarchal Christianity because they themselves were deeply patriarchal. The status of women was ascribed, allowed even, by men. Brilliant academics like Professor Christine Fell (*Women in Anglo-Saxon England*, 1984.), although they have very little evidence on which to base their conclusions—gravestones, grave goods, sagas and the odd letter or reference in what was otherwise HIStory—nevertheless, verify this aspect in all these pre-Christian North European cultures.

What evidence there is of higher-class women in both Anglo-Saxon and Scandinavian culture suggests that instances of Queenship, battle leadership and land ownership by inheritance and widowhood, although very rare, were not a particular social or cultural problem. The daughter of Alfred the Great, Aethelflaeda, Lady of the Mercians, is almost universally cited as an Anglo-Saxon example of woman power, another 'Boudicca'. Furthermore, as daughter of an all-powerful king, she is contrasted with the Norman 'Boudicca', Mathilda, daughter of Henry I, who, some 250 years later, never quite made it in the power game of Snakes and Ladders, always throwing a four, three steps forward and one back, when a three was needed to win absolute, undisputed power.

However, Anglo-Saxon daughters were still used to increase influence in the patriarchal power game through advantageous marriage as were widows with land. Anglo-Saxon and Scandinavian sagas speak of *freothuwebbe*, peace-weavers, women who were married off to an enemy to cement a peace agreement. Canute himself married the defeated Aethelred's widow, Emma of Normandy, in 1017 in order to secure peace between his Danelaw and the kingdom of Wessex ruled by Aethelred's son from his first marriage, Edmund Ironside.

Emma, daughter of Richard, Duke of Normandy, through her peace-weaving marriages, was the link between Anglo-Saxon, Scandinavian and Norman England as wife of two kings, mother of two kings and great aunt of the conqueror king who brought the whole thing together. As such, great though her power and influence must have been, it was granted by the patriarchal big hitters of the time from all three cultures.

It is not difficult to accept that it was the Christian wife, Bertha, who persuaded the pagan husband, Aethelberht, to convert. On the other hand, it is anachronistic to believe that it was to promote the Christian principles of equality, love and peace. Saxon leaders lived in a world of conflict in which might was right, and battles were won because the gods were on your side. There were few certainties but the Christian God, represented in the right way, eliminated some of the uncertainties. Throughout the nearly three centuries before Alfred there was a fair bit of backsliding and mixed messaging but Christianity, being highly syncretic—blending in with pagan traditions—won through by making a clear mortal hierarchy; Christian kings ruled by the grace of God, subjects had a moral obligation to obey their rulers, wives their husbands, children their parents, servants their lords and slaves their masters. If everyone knew their place in God's creation and obeyed God's law, they would all go to heaven.

A conflated view of pre-Christian Anglo-Saxon culture, therefore, would suggest that it had similar patriarchal interrelationships but on a might-is-right-might-is-male logic rather than a God's-creation-God-is-right basis despite the added magical and mysterious power of the latter being written down. There is scant evidence of a cosmology of how the world began or what lay beyond the grave nor, some historians suggest, a heartfelt spiritual need to have one.

> Adopting the terminology of the sociologist of religion Max Weber, the historian Marilyn Dunn described Anglo-Saxon paganism as a "world accepting" religion, one which was "concerned with the here and now" and in particular with issues surrounding the safety of the family, prosperity, and the avoidance of drought or famine. Also adopting the categories of Gustav Mensching, she described Anglo-Saxon paganism as a "folk religion", in that its adherents concentrated on survival and prosperity in this world.[117]

There is no really informative evidence of a belief in heaven and hell, although the Sutton Hoo find suggests a clear visualisation of an afterlife not being dissimilar to the mortal one, leaving us to contemplate a visualisation similar to that of the Norse people's Valhalla, the reward for a true warrior's death in battle. Was pagan belief also apocalyptic as in Norse culture in which the chosen warriors feasting in Valhalla will fight for Odin during the Ragnarök, the last great battle in which many of the old gods will be destroyed before the world submerges under the sea to emerge anew and be re-populated by the Norse version of Adam and Eve?

Three cornerstones of the Christian church, the Creation, the Patriarchy and the Day of Judgement, brought a unifying purpose and order to communal identity as the confederations of villages and towns became earldoms and kingdoms and eventually countries and empires. The fourth cornerstone, God's Law, was more difficult to discern and already a mixture of Mosaic, New Testament and Roman components of morality. From Christian writing, mostly from monks such as Gildas, Bede and Orderic Vitalis and the 12th century chronicler, William of Malmesbury, we have a fairly clear idea of the impact of Christian scriptural morality, including the 'proper' status of women, in God's

---

[117] en.wikipedia.org/wiki/Catholic Church and evolution. Accessed 20/09/2018.

kingdom and the divine guidelines for conduct by and towards them. Just to briefly recap:

- Man came first.
- A woman was the cause of sin in the world and the reason why mankind fell from God's grace.
- Sin is lawlessness.
- Sex is impure and sexual immorality and adultery high on the list of sins.
- Sex should only take place in a God-sanctioned marriage.
- Widows can remarry.
- Wives obey their husbands.
- God regards as sin a divorce for any reason other than adultery.

It is possible that sex was looked upon more liberally, or less sinfully, by Germanic peoples with less importance attached to chastity and monogamy. Certainly, when Christianity brought these two requisites to the table they were and always have been a challenge. The Catholic Church seemed comfortable with turning a blind eye to the extra- or pre-marital sexual activity of men, as long as they confessed it or paid enough to the Church in cash or kind, but were particularly unforgiving of women who failed to observe them, even managing, dating from the conduct of the first woman, Eve, to lay most of the blame on them for attracting the attention and arousing the sexual interest of men.

Both attitudes, contrary to a key aspect of Christian morality, led to unfair conduct towards unmarried mothers, adulteresses and sex workers and, in a different sense, to propertied widows, a hypocrisy that was to last well into the 20th century. Indeed, the last substantial pre-Norman Christian king, Canute (Edward the Confessor, having been brought up in Normandy, was heavily influenced by Norman culture), had two wives, Aelfgifu of Northampton and Emma of Normandy, the former being 'set aside', *whatever that means*, to marry the latter but still entrusted with great political power not the least of which was that her children should inherit on grounds of seniority and bloodline rather than legitimacy in the eyes of the Church.

The Roman Catholic Church, because of its role as a major political player, has never quite been in sync with the Bible, particularly the teachings of Jesus. Of relevance to this point is the acceptance in a monogamic theology of concubinage, a concubine being a woman of status who shared the husband's bed and bore him children without the legitimisation, consecration even, of a Christian marriage ceremony, a tacit deference to the polygamous nature of the human male and his attempt to reduce his fear of not passing on his estate to his offspring by hypocritically binding his wife to a divinely sanctified promise of chastity the breaking of which would have dire social and spiritual consequences for her.

We tend to forget that this defiance of Paul's advice on the conduct of a faithful Christian only applied to key members of a temporal power without whom the Church would have been impoverished, powerless and insignificant if it existed at all. The stark fact is that the Church traded commitment to its spiritual and moral purity for temporal power. Human experience has rarely shown that power and morality were ever a marriage made in heaven.

Finally, on this point, like most pre-scientific cultures, in pre-Christian northern European culture women had a separate purpose to men, a separate social role, namely, to bear and run the family and its home as distinct from fighting to protect it. Taking Scandinavian society as an exemplar, this role was respected and valued, and women were not seen as sexual temptresses. Laws preventing unwanted sexual attentions from men carried severe punishments. As noblewomen were still used in political power brokering as marriage goods and public duties such as speaking in Things, Scandinavian councils, dispensing justice or being credible witnesses were denied to them this was definitely not a society of equality of social contribution.

It was, however, one in which women's work was as valued as that of men and in which, if there were no men around as in the case of a widow whose husband and sons had all been killed in war or adventuring, the woman was believed capable of, supported politically in and socially accepted as doing the man's job, including managing and fighting to protect the family property. We could say that they were complementary which would have been one step in the direction of equality of esteem rather than the opposite path to inferiority and disdain.

Internet browsers will list websites that are full of modern apologies for Biblical complementarianism, especially from Americans, using interpretations of the biblical passages from Pauline epistles to argue that the side-lining of women from leadership roles in the Church and home does not signify gender inequality in God's creation just that the God-ordained roles of men and women are different and complement each other. Germanic and Scandinavian warrior culture was far too busy with fighting to protect or expand territory to philosophise about -isms thus allocating socially needed tasks on the simple, pragmatic basis of men fight and women bear, nurture and ensure the survival of the next generation of warriors.

Important though food, shelter and clothing were to a family, in an acquisitive world, protecting the source of all three, in addition to the essentials of agricultural production, land and water, required might and strength, strategy and training, cohesion and leadership, warrior things, man things. Complementarianism was the pragmatic outcome, unquestioned, flexible and adaptable to changes in circumstances. It was not dogmatic.

Interestingly, after centuries of misdirection, misinterpretation and, at times, blatant hijacking, the Roman Catholic church has arrived at a dogmatic position in defence of an all-male clergy and leadership of Catholic communities that is akin to the complementarianism that not only preceded Christianisation but preceded the full Christian egalitarianism that millions of non-Catholic and non-

fundamentalist Christian churches now practice. In his 1994 letter, Ordination Sacerdotalis, John Paul II, the Polish Pope, wrote:

> *"She [the Catholic Church] holds that it is not admissible to ordain women to the priesthood, for very fundamental reasons. These reasons include: the example recorded in the Sacred Scriptures of Christ choosing his Apostles only from among men; the constant practice of the Church, which has imitated Christ in choosing only men; and her living teaching authority which has consistently held that the exclusion of women from the priesthood is in accordance with God's plan for his Church."*
> *The presence and the role of women in the life and mission of the Church, although not linked to the ministerial priesthood, remain absolutely necessary and irreplaceable. As the Declaration Inter Insigniores points out, "the Church desires that Christian women should become fully aware of the greatness of their mission: today their role is of capital importance both for the renewal and humanisation of society and for the rediscovery by believers of the true face of the Church."*

An all-male priesthood is dogma. The accompanying requirements of celibacy and non-marriage are only regulations and could be changed tomorrow.

Dogma is so important to religion-based morality that I want you to share in what it really means. In the definition box there are four concepts none of which I am comfortable with. Please stay with me. I will not philosophise.

- Tenet or doctrine. *Something **held**, giving a physicality to an abstract idea. Something **taught**, suggesting the involvement of an agency other than oneself.*
- Official Authority. *An idea or set of ideas that are accepted as **right** because they are enforced by someone in an indisputable position of power.*
- Prescription. *Something, in this case a **truth,** recommended to you by someone else who has a quality or qualities that give them the authority to be **right**.*
- Unquestionable truth. *A **truth** from someone the status and authority of whose knowledge cannot be challenged or questioned.*

Of Latin and/or French origin: Dogma, tenet, doctrine, official, authority, prescription, question.

Of Anglo-Saxon origin: Hold, teach, right, truth.

1. an official system of principles or tenets concerning faith, morals, behaviour, etc., as of a church.
2. a specific tenet or doctrine authoritatively laid down, as by a church: the dogma of the Assumption; the recently defined dogma of papal infallibility.
3. prescribed doctrine proclaimed as unquestionably true by a particular group: the difficulty of resisting political dogma.[118]

Dogma is defensive. It is used to defend with superior force, power or authority a moral or behavioural requirement or rule that cannot be proved, reasoned or sensationally experienced to be incontrovertibly right or true. The law determines which behaviours are right or wrong. There are three bases for law, the social rules of right and wrong; Nature, based on what is visible, audible, tangible, odorous and gustable; God, based on God's word as revealed in scripture; Man, based on a human interpretation of what is right or wrong. None of these on its own is able to cope with the awesome cognitive power of the human brain and the complexity of behaviours resulting from human social grouping. The law of a Creator God transcends nature-based law and man-made law because the Creator God transcends Nature and Man because both are His/Her/Its creations.

This single all-knowing, all-powerful **male** God that Christianity advocated as an updated version of the Hebrew God was good not bad, always right and just, totally unlike most polytheistic regimes of divines in pre-Christian Europe.

Natural law, was universally applicable to issues such as the right to survive, reproduce, avoid pain and embrace pleasure, but insufficient to deal with spiritual issues such as emotions and beliefs which are God-given yet similarly universal. Man-made law related to particular, local or personal circumstances should have been made with due consideration to natural and divine moral and ethical precepts, but more often reflected the self-interest and subjectivity of the lawmakers. The 17th century jurist, Matthew Hale, hinted at the impossibility of separating the three bases of the law.

> Hale's definition of the natural law reads: "It is the Law of Almighty God given by him to Man with his Nature discovering the morall good and moral evill of Moral Actions, commanding the former, and forbidding the latter by the secret voice or dictate of his implanted nature, his reason, and his conscience." He viewed natural law as antecedent, preparatory, and subsequent to civil government, and stated that human law "cannot forbid what the Law of Nature enjoins, nor Command what the Law of Nature prohibits."[119]

[118] www.dictionary.com/browse/dogma. Accessed 05/11/2018.
[119] en.wikipedia.org/wiki/Natural law. Accessed 07/11/2018.

Those who did not hear God's voice or ignored it temporarily or permanently were sinners, out of God's grace. Natural law, however, was also God's law, both told or dictated to human beings by this one male God—BUT God could not be proven to speak and those who claimed that He did gave mixed messages about what he meant, all of which I have explored in previous chapters. Hebrew writers wrote about what He said to the Israelite patriarchs, Abraham, Isaac and Jacob, and what He said to or through prophets such as Moses, Elijah and Isaiah. He came in human form as His Son, Jesus, and showed and said what was good and bad, right and wrong. His biographers wrote it down. Jesus left it to his closest friends to tell the world, but the most recorded collection of writings, advice and interpretations was from a converted Roman citizen, Paul.

People who knew people who knew people etc. who knew these friends and followers of Jesus, such as Origen, Tertullian and Clement had their words and deeds recorded by historians such as Eusebius. All this stuff was considered and debated by councils of men who decided what was on the song sheet from which all Christians should have been singing. *I know that I have been through most of this before but that was to illustrate the political survival of Christianity and its social and moral message that emerged. This time it is in order to understand its impact on British culture.*

God's Word, God's law, was/is a divine concept generated in and hijacked by the human intellect, prone to human error and abuse of power. In Roman Catholic Europe at the time of the Norman Conquest the Christian church organisation was highly structured and, like anything touched by Roman imperial culture, hierarchical. It had its own quasi-divine emperor, the Pope, whose words *ex cathedra*, from his bishop's throne, were God's word, God's law.

His primacy, as Bishop of Rome, successor to the first bishop, Peter, the first man to really get the whole Christian thing, was as dogmatically sine qua non as the Trinity, the Immaculate Conception, the Crucifixion and the Resurrection, the Ascension and the Day of Judgement. It was the dogmatically promulgated interpretation of God's word in the Gospel of Matthew 16:17-19. (Made more dogmatic by the total lack of factual proof that the said Peter had ever been Bishop of Rome!)

> Blessed art thou, Simon Bar-Jona. For flesh and blood hast not revealed this to thee, but my Father who is in heaven. And I say to thee, thou art Peter, and upon this rock I will build my church, and the powers of death [gates of hell] shall not prevail against it. I will give to thee the keys of the kingdom of heaven, and whatsoever thou shalt bind on earth shall be bound in heaven, and whatsoever thou shalt loose on earth shall be loosed in heaven.

Unable to be ubiquitous, unlike His God, the Pope delegated his authority to his bishops who, in turn, delegated it to their priests. This act of delegation was an ordination, a consecration underwritten by God which gave the Church representatives an unquestionable spiritual and moral authority. Even when, some 500 years later, Luther questioned the Pope's temporal acquisitiveness he was not questioning his spiritual authority. Luther's insistence that the Bible was the only source of information on God's law was a plea to curb excessive abuse of the Church's application and interpretation of it for earthly gain.

The Protestants who eventually replaced the Pope as God's 'voice' on Earth with the Bible were, at first, civic leaders, rulers, who opposed the Holy Roman Emperor who had the Pope's, and therefore God's, full support for his power, law and justice.

The problem with a dogmatic authority like the Pope or the Bible is one of extent. If the fundamentals of what is said are unquestionable then should not everything that is said be equally unquestioned? Add to this a subjective selectivity in choosing what to observe, practise or, more worryingly, preach of a moral ideology or intent and you have all the elements you need to brainwash people into doing, saying and believing things that increase your power and wealth, such as the inferiority, sinfulness and immoral temptation of women and their exclusion from public life, public office, ownership of property and spiritual leadership.

Biologists tell us that there are three sorts of symbiotic relationship; Commensualist in which one partner benefits and the other is neither helped nor harmed; Mutualist in which both partners benefit; Parasitist in which one partner benefits and the other is harmed. The symbiosis of Church and State is far more evident in history than their rivalry. The relationship began with the Edict of Thessalonica in 380 AD issued by the emperor Theodosius I to the people of Constantinople and gave Christianity the unreserved sanction of the Roman state.

> It is our desire that all the various nations which are subject to our Clemency and Moderation, should continue to profess that religion which was delivered to the Romans by the divine Apostle Peter, as it has been preserved by faithful tradition, and which is now professed by the Pontiff Damasus and by Peter, Bishop of Alexandria, a man of apostolic holiness. According to the apostolic teaching and the doctrine of the Gospel, let us believe in the one deity of the Father, the Son and the Holy Spirit, in equal majesty and in a holy Trinity.
>
> We authorise the followers of this law to assume the title of Catholic Christians; but as for the others, since, in our judgment they are foolish madmen, we decree that they shall be branded with the ignominious name of heretics, and shall not presume to give to their conventicles the name of churches. **They will suffer in the first place the chastisement of the divine condemnation and in the second the punishment of our authority which in accordance with the will of Heaven we shall decide to inflict.**[120]

[120] en.wikipedia.org/wiki/Edict of Thessalonica. Accessed 14/11/2018.

The absolute power implicit in the symbiosis at the very heart of a Roman Catholic state is demonstrated in the threatening language I have highlighted. Even though the Roman Empire disintegrated in Western Europe, those that followed it, the Gothic Empire, the Merovingian and Carolingian Empires and the Holy Roman Empire, realising its power, retained the mutuality of benefit that the Church of Rome provided and the Church grew wealthy with the support of rulers, essentially Germanic in origin (the Germanic successors, and for a time competitors, of the greatest empire the world had ever seen wanted its territory not the destruction of its laws, principles and mores).

When it came to the conversion of peoples who had never co-experienced the whole imperial way of life, the Anglo-Saxons and the Scandinavians, the symbiosis was arguably more Commensualist and less Mutualist, more of a newly grafted than an anciently merged coexistence. Furthermore, by the time of the Norman Conquest the symbiotic relationship of the Church to the State was becoming parasitic with the behaviour of priests and monks and nuns many of whom were married or entertained concubines and approved of and participated in the practice of simony, selling church offices, undermining the doctrines of the spiritual exclusivity, poverty, chastity and purity that were the pillars of Christian authority.

In 11th century Milan, a movement grew up called the *Patrini* which opposed simony and clerical marriage. One of its founding members was Anselm di Baggio who, in 1061, was elected Pope Alexander II. In 1066 he received a delegation from William, Duke of Normandy, asking for the Papal blessing for his proposed invasion of England. Not only did he give his blessing to the enterprise, but he issued an edict to the Anglo-Saxon church instructing them to submit to Norman rule.

Anyone who knows me or has read my take on British, particularly English, history will know that I am a 21st century Digger, a True Leveller, a Gerrard Winstanley, locating and linking nearly everything I find distasteful about Britishness/Englishness to that fateful day, October 14, 1066, on which the 'Norman Yoke' was applied, and Britain ploughed a furrow of class exploitation, injustice and unfairness for a millennium. What I have come to realise, particularly in my research for this book on gender, is that the Norman State, in true mutual symbiosis, brought with it the Norman—a continental/ Mediterranean/Rome-centred version of it—Christian Church.

What, therefore, made the symbiotic bond so strong? Both Pope and Duke were minded to move on territorially. Only 12 years before the Conquest, the issue of leadership of the Christian Church had been resolved by Pope Leo IX's insistence that not only the Bible but a decree of Constantine had stated that it belonged to the Bishop of Rome, the successor to both Peter, the first Bishop, and Constantine, the first Holy Roman Emperor. (The former, as argued above, a matter of opinion and the latter proved to be false by the Church's own investigators in the mid-fifteenth century.)

On his part, the patrino Pope wanted to end the worldly entanglement of Christianity by stopping simony and nepotism in the appointment of lay persons, mostly wealthy and noble, to leadership positions in the Church, insisting that the ground roots priesthood should be aloof from sins of the flesh and the Church leadership equally aloof from the accumulation of wealth, for instance, by holding more than one see.

This Gregorian Reform, named after Alexander's successor, Pope Gregory VII, was accompanied by a new age of asceticism in monasteries and nunneries based on the 'prayer and work' Benedictine Rule. Carnal desires and spiritual transcendence, sex and God's grace, did not mix, especially for those few who were ordained to spread God's word and do His work, priests, bishops, monks, friars and nuns. In the opinion of the five Popes who excommunicated the hugely wealthy Stigand, Archbishop of Canterbury, for holding the two wealthiest sees in England, Canterbury and Winchester, simultaneously, the English/Anglo-Saxon Church was, in most respects, desperately in need of the reforms they were trying to make.

Alexander wanted him out and replaced with a former teacher of his and true advocate of the Pauline interpretation of God's intentions for His Church, an Italian monk from Normandy, Lanfranc. In 1070 he got his way. Stigand was deposed and imprisoned. Lanfranc was installed as Archbishop soon after. William and Lanfranc, Alexander II, Gregory VII and Anselm of Canterbury had history.

To understand the significance of this digression (*I have warned you before about my love of digressions!*), we have to go back to a previous, aforementioned Pope, Leo IX, and even further to Roman law on legal marriage. Roman law, on which much of the canonical law of the 'Latin Rite' Catholic church was based, deemed any marriage within four degrees of consanguinity to be illegal. (With a counting method [A] of up to the common ancestor and down to the prospective partner any marriage was legal in which the common ancestor of the couple was more distant than a grandparent, i.e., they were more distantly related than first cousins.)

At some time in the ninth century, possibly due to recognition of Germanic inheritance law, the impediment limit was widened to the seventh degree but, again only possibly, the calculation method was changed to that of a direct line to the common ancestor [B], thus making the common ancestor the 5X Great Grandparent.

We know that the Pope Alexander II who gave William's conquest of England his blessing and appointed Lanfranc the AoC used calculation method B. However, when William married Mathilda, daughter of Count Baldwin V of Flanders, in approx. 1050-51 CE Pope Leo IX, the second German Pope and the first of three German Popes in a row indicating the influence exerted by German Holy Roman Emperors on Papal elections, a practice ended in 1059 by the Papal Bull, *in nomine Domini*, issued by the French Pope, Nicholas II, declared the marriage illegal by canonical laws. History does not know for certain on what grounds he objected but, given that he had agreed with his Byzantine colleagues in Christ to oppose the Norman incursions into Apulia and Calabria in southern Italy, he was probably anti-Norman enough to make life as difficult for them as he could. A Norman abbot of the time, John de Fecamp, wrote:

> Hatred by the Italians for the Normans has now developed so much and become so inflamed throughout the towns of Italy that scarcely anyone of the Norman race may travel safely on his way, even he be on a devout pilgrimage, for he will be attacked, dragged off, stripped, beaten up, clapped into chains, and often indeed will give up the ghost, tormented in a squalid prison.[121]

Matters came to a head in 1053 when a Norman army defeated in the Battle of Civitate a Papal army of mostly Lombard and Swabian—German—mercenaries and Leo was placed under house arrest in Benevento. Another Norman alpha male and robber baron, Robert Guiscard, completed the conquest of southern Italy and got his teeth into Sicily over the next fifteen years, eventually driving the Byzantines out of the former and the Saracens out of the latter.

William 'the Conqueror' as a sobriquet dates from the 13th century it seems. Our William was mostly known in his day as William 'the Bastard'. Given his Norse heritage it is unlikely that this bothered him much but almost certainly made his noble Christian enemies vaunt their legitimacy as a scoring point against a formidable enemy. It may explain his piety and his need to get along with his Maker and his Maker's representatives on Earth (Normans were noted for their piety. Robert Bartlett noted that they only fought Pope Leo reluctantly.

> "As fervent Christians the Normans were reluctant to fight their spiritual leader and tried to sue for peace but the Swabians mocked them—battle was inevitable."[122]

It is most unlikely to have played a part in Leo's thinking. That leaves us with consanguinity as Leo's stick with which to beat the young rising star. With both calculation methods A and B a first cousin as a marriage partner would have been out of the question. There was a suggestion that Mathilda's mother, Adela of France, had been married to William's uncle, Richard III, before marrying Baldwin when he died in suspicious circumstances allowing his younger brother, Robert, William's father, to take over.

Quite how that made William and Mathilda first cousins I am not sure *but there was a medieval belief that the womb was a mould and a sort of template that made all subsequent children like the first. It is as unlikely that Mathilda was Richard's daughter as it is that the Adela whom Richard married was Mathilda's mother.* Using method B, Rollo, Rolf the Viking, could have been the common ancestor. He would have been within five degrees of William as his

---

[121] en.wikipedia.org/wiki/Battle of Civitate. Accessed 24/11/2018.
[122] https://en.wikipedia.org/wiki/Pope_Leo_IX. Accessed 24/11/2018.

3X great grandfather. It is also suggested that Mathilda's grandfather, Baldwin IV, not only married Mathilda's grandmother but also a great aunt of William's, a daughter of his great-grand father, Richard II.

One daughter of Richard II we do know of. Alice married Reginald I, Count of Burgundy, and their daughter, Alberada of Buonalbergo, married the other Norman conqueror, Robert Guiscard. Robert set her aside in 1058-9 after Pope Nicholas II had invoked the consanguinity rule.

William and Mathilda married despite Pope Leo's ruling. Any declaration of nullity was debated and ruled on by an ecclesiastical council, normally held in Rome, at which the case could be made either to uphold or quash it. William and Mathilda needed an advocate, acceptable to and respected by the Vatican, Italian, a scholar and reachable in Normandy, arguably a Norman citizen. Their eye fell on the Prior of Bec, Lanfranc, largely because he had been so vocal in his opposition to the marriage that William had felt the need to exile him. Somehow, on the verge of going into exile this educated monk did a deal with the illiterate bastard Duke and acted as the advocate. Two of his pupils, Anselmo di Baggio and Hildebrand of Sovano, who must have known what was going on, were to become Popes, Alexander II and his successor, Gregory VII, and a third, Anselm of Aosta, Lanfranc's successor as AoC.

In 1559, Lanfranc won the case posthumously when the French Pope, Nicholas II, removed the impediment. As penance for disobeying Leo's ruling on the canonical propriety of their marriage William and Mathilda built an abbey each, of one of which Lanfranc was to become abbot in 1066. Politically, Nicholas eyed up the Norman penchant for piety, their religious loyalty to the Pope of Rome and their dominant military prowess as a replacement for the growing distance between the papacy and the Holy Roman Emperor and the Latin Rite Church and the Eastern Rite Byzantine Empire.

In the same year, he made Guiscard Duke of Calabria and Duke of Apulia—most of southern Italy—having already recognised him as count of both two years earlier. Under Nicholas' successors, Robert, as mentioned above, undertook a 15-year conquest of Sicily which by the late 1070s recognised the Latin not the Byzantine rite. The issue with the Holy Roman Emperors (and probably most other rulers—William had certainly appointed his fair share of bishops and archbishops) was over the investiture of bishops and abbots and the election of popes. Nicholas laid the foundations for the non-interference of laity in both, coincidentally restoring Latin/southern Mediterranean on and in the papacy and the primacy of Pauline doctrine or dogma.

William, therefore, and these three Benedictine adherents committed to a sexual clean-up of the Church of Rome, not least in Anglo-Saxon England, knew each other well and, both politically and spiritually, needed the support of each other on a personal and an official level. William got a spiritual underwriter for his land-grabbing conquest and the Roman Church got the warrior Christians it needed to fight the threat from the East, be it Byzantine or Saracen, or the threat from the north, the Germanic Holy Roman Empire. Most importantly, William left them to get on with the clean-up assisting them by appointing non-English, mostly Norman Bishops and archdeacons etc., clergy in a strictly organised, hierarchical, 'continental', i.e., Pauline, church structure and allowing the establishment and growth of monastic orders such as Cluniacs, Cistercians and Augustinians with strict rules on the celibate lifestyle, no wives, no concubines.

According to J.P. Somerville, between 1070, the year of Lanfranc's appointment as AoC, and 1140 only one native Englishman was appointed to an English See. By 1250 there were about 700 religious communities, 550 male-only, 150 female-only. At least three Councils were called to enforce clerical celibacy, two by Lanfranc in London (1075) and Winchester (1076) and one by Anselm at Westminster in 1102.[123]

Under these four clerics, Alexander II (Pope from 1061-1073), Gregory VII (Pope from 1073-1085), Lanfranc (Archbishop of Canterbury from 1070-1089) and Anselm (Archbishop of Canterbury from 1193-1107) the Anglo-Saxon Church became the Norman Church and, I think, Anglo-Saxon morality became Norman or 'continental', fiercely organised, dogmatic, centralised under papal supremacy and, most significantly for women, Pauline in its doctrine. None of them lived to see their reforming spirit bear fruit when in 1139 Pope Innocent II placed these dogmatic encyclicals on to the Roman Catholic catechism.

> 6. We also decree that those in the orders of subdeacon and above who have taken **wives or concubines** are to be deprived of their position and ecclesiastical benefice. For since they ought to be in fact and in name temples of God, vessels of the Lord and sanctuaries of the holy Spirit, it is unbecoming that they give themselves up to marriage and impurity.
> 7. Adhering to the path trod by our predecessors, the Roman pontiffs Gregory VII, Urban and Paschal, we prescribe that nobody is to hear the masses of those whom he knows to have wives or concubines. Indeed, that the law of continence and the purity pleasing to God might be propagated among ecclesiastical persons and those in holy orders, we decree that where bishops, priests, deacons, subdeacons, canons regular, monks and professed lay brothers have presumed to take wives and so transgress this holy precept, they are to be separated from their partners. For **we do not deem there to be a marriage which, it is agreed, has been contracted against ecclesiastical law**. Furthermore, when they have separated from each other, let them do a penance commensurate with such outrageous behaviour.
> 8. We decree that the self-same thing is to apply also to women religious if, God forbid, they attempt to marry.[124]

---

[123] faculty.history.wisc.edu/sommerville/123/123%2010%20the%20norman%20church.htm. Accessed 26/11/2018.
[124] www.papalencyclicals.net/councils/ecum10.html. Accessed 26/11/2018.

There are some interesting things in that encyclical:

- *That a man cannot be a temple of God, a vessel of the Lord or a sanctuary of the Holy Spirit if he gives himself up to marriage and impurity (sex? Is impure?).*
- *Marriage is so outrageous it requires a penance.*
- *A religious woman's attempt to marry is forbidden by God.*
  Hm!

As I am palpably guilty of repeating, recorded history is rarely about ordinary people, but it is probably safe to say that throughout this conquered land they took their moral lead from this foreign Norman or Normanised Church in which dogma, doctrine, hierarchy, organisation, architectural magnificence, awe and wonder, fear and duty and infallible papal supremacy were symbiotically linked to the overwhelming military might and savagery of the State.

In this world, I have no doubt whatsoever, *not because I have incontrovertible documentary proof but because they were human beings just like you and me*, that women were regarded as inferior to men for three major reasons. Firstly, they did not fight in protection of what they needed to live, land and water. Secondly, they spent most of their time bearing and nurturing children or, sadly, dying or failing in the attempt. Thirdly, the clergy said that the Bible said they were to blame for the sins of men to whom they must submit their freedom of action, thought, word and deed and, most importantly of all, their body. And who were they to argue! The symbiosis of the Anglo-Norman Fighting Man and Man of God was to shape English and then British cultural attitudes for a thousand years. HIStory!

A 'historical' conclusion

Christine G. Clarke generally concludes that although women's rights might well have declined anyway the Norman conquest greased the wheels of the coach that would drive most of them out of town over the next 500 years.

> It may be difficult to-determine why and exactly when the women of England began to lose their rights. However, it is apparent that Anglo-Saxon women had legal rights and opportunities women coming after them did not have.[125]

Pauline Stafford, however, quite rightly cautions us about seeing the pre-Conquest era as a sort of Golden Age for women compared to the 12th century and beyond a period about which far more documentation is still available to historians intact partly due to the spread of literacy and partly due to the

[125] www.constitution.org/lrev/eng/womens_rights_early_england.pdf. Accessed 1/11/2018.

introduction of a centralised bureaucracy by the Norman regime typified by the Domesday survey of 1086.

The Golden Age appeals to both Conservative and Radical alike. For one it can be a nostalgia for a time of clear and unquestioned hierarchies and relationships, for the other a reminder that changes sought now are merely a return to the past, are possible now because they existed then.[126] *Professor Stafford's article 'Women and the Norman Conquest' should be put in 'The Budding Historian's Handbook'! She cautions about:*

- ***Subjectivity***. *In writing my assessment of the unfairness of the treatment of women in British history I have a clear agenda. Let now be my 'mea culpa' moment! Stafford points to the eulogization of Germanic/Anglo-Saxon women by Tacitus:*
  Society for him is healthy when women are chaste, mothers and controlled by their husbands, not when they visit the theatre and the baths, exchange love letters with their lovers and fail to breastfeed.[127]
  and 800 odd years later John Mitchell Kemble, eminent Victorian historian; Kemble's Teutonic women are a mid-nineteenth-century conservative male pipe dream.[128]
  As commentaries on the behaviour of women of their times, the former to support his opinion that Roman women were to blame for the moral laxity that was undermining Rome's ability to defend itself against and civilise the barbarian hordes and the latter to present an ethnic justification for the model Victorian woman.
- ***Simplification***. *Stafford dislikes, again quite rightly, the classification of a Golden Age or 'the good old days'. The Golden Age phenomenon is largely a simplification to justify a view of the present and as such acquires a subjectivity that undermines its truth.*
- ***Generalisation***. *'Women' is a generalisation. Which women?*
  If Anglo-Saxon England was an age of high status for women which women are we discussing? Noble women only? Noble daughters, wives or widows? An individual noble woman in a particular family context? Was there any common legal of daughters, wives or widows that would encourage such generalisation?
- ***Periodisation***. *1066 is a marker. Things, including the status of women, did not change overnight. Anglo-Saxon England was conquered twice in 50 years. Christianisation took over 200 years to bed in. Normanisation took place under Edward the Confessor. Normans married Anglo-*

---

[126] Stafford, Pauline. "Women and the Norman Conquest." *Transactions of the Royal Historical Society*, vol. 4, 1994, pp. 221–249. *JSTOR*, JSTOR, www.jstor.org/stable/3679222. Accessed 27/11/2018.
[127] Women and the Norman Conquest, Pauline Stafford, Transactions of the Royal Historical Society. 4 (1994), pp. 221-249, www.jstor.org/stable. Accessed 21/10/2018.
[128] Ibid

Saxons in an England in which travel took place at 15 miles per day. Local and individual circumstances altered at different speeds and in a local and an individual context. The attractive juxtaposition of The Golden Age generalisation and that of the Norman Yoke is so tempting but not necessarily accurate or supported by what evidence we have.

Chapter 16
Chivalry

Chivalry is the most delicate form of contempt.
– Albert Guerard

Preamble

In the previous chapter, when I was looking at the semantic breakdown of the word 'dogma', I distinguished between the vocabulary that was Anglo-Saxon or Old English and that which was French or Latin. The key concepts of right and truth were English, the language of the conquered, the intellectual explanations were Latin, the language of the literate, or French, the language of power of the conquerors. One of the claims about William's style of conquest is that he did not disturb too many traditional Anglo-Saxon justice practices.

The other claim is that Anglo-Saxon England was well on the way to Norman, as in European, practice in land tenure, as in Feudalism, before the Conquest. That this impression is too simplistic or just plain wrong—and I must leave its disentanglement to scholars who have devoted their lives to the study of this era—I cannot agree with it.

The Normans brought with them four, *at least*, socio-economic and legal phenomena that had a profound effect on English culture and the status of women, especially noblewomen, within it. Whether they were given their names in a later age of scholarship which enshrined the use of Classical language, whether they were 'continental' rather than specifically Norman, whether they were Frankish, Romano-Germanic and thus pre-dated the Norman occupation of north-western France, in English history they are distinctively Norman, and the language associated with them gives the game away.

- **Chivalry** - Middle English: from Old French *chevalerie*, from medieval Latin *caballerius*, for late Latin *caballarius* 'horseman'.
- **Feudalism** - The word *feudal* derives from an ancient Gothic source *faihu* signifying simply "property" which in its most basic sense was "cattle".[129]
- **Primogeniture** - early 17th century: from medieval Latin *primogenitura*, from Latin *primo* 'first' + *genitura* 'geniture'.

[129] en.wikipedia.org/wiki/Feudalism in England. Accessed 04/12/2018.

- **Inheritance** - late Middle English (formerly also as *enheritance*): from Anglo-Norman French *enheritaunce* 'being admitted as heir', from Old French *enheriter.*
- **Property** - Middle English: from an Anglo-Norman French variant of Old French *propriete*, from Latin *proprietas*, from *proprius* 'one's own, particular'.
- **Coverture** - Middle English (originally denoting a coverlet or garment): from Old French, from *covrir* 'to cover'.

At 2.20 am on 15 April 1912, the Royal Mail Ship *Titanic* slid beneath the icy waters of the Atlantic. Of the 2,222 passengers and crew on board, 792 survived (31.6%). Of the 908 crew members on board, only 23 were female (2.5%). Of the 885 male crew members, only 192 survived (22%). 20 of the 23 females survived (87%). The passengers were divided into three classes, first, second and third. Of the 1,337 passengers, 492 survived (37%). Only 20% of male passengers survived, a stark contrast to the 75% survival rate of female passengers. 61% of the First Class survived, 42% of the Standard (Second) Class and 24% of the Third Class. There were 109 children on board. 53 perished; 1 from first class, none from standard and 52 from third. *My thanks to https://titanicfacts.net (Accessed 16/12/2018) for these facts.*

> In Andrew Roberts's fine new biography of Winston Churchill, I found a letter the great man wrote to his wife, Clementine, just after the Titanic sank in 1912.
> Churchill remarked that the behaviour of the male passengers "reflects nothing but honour upon our civilisation."
> He wrote: "I cannot help feeling proud of our race and its traditions as proved by this event. Boatloads of women and children tossing on the sea safe and sound—and the rest—silence. Honour to their memory… How differently imperial Rome or Ancient Greece would have settled the problem. The swells, the potentates would have gone off with their concubines and pet slaves and soldier guards… whoever could bribe the crew would have had the preference and the rest could go to hell. But such ethics could neither build Titanics with science nor lose them with honour."[130]

Just under 100 years later on 13 January 2012 the cruise liner *Costa Concordia* struck an allegedly uncharted rock necessitating an emergency evacuation not unlike that of the fateful night a century before. So botched was it that, in spite of 100 years of technological advance and international regulation of safety procedures in the event of maritime disaster, 32 people died.

Following reports, for example in the *Daily Mail* under the heading "It was every man—and crew member—for himself", that women and children had to

---

[130] www.wsj.com/articles/did-chivalry-go-down-with-the-titanic-11544829740. Accessed 16/12/2018.

jostle with men to board lifeboats Polly Curtis of the *Guardian* looked into whether the moral necessity, highlighted by the Titanic disaster, had been enshrined in any maritime evacuation code, regulation or law that this alleged behaviour would have contravened. She interviewed three experts, Robert Ashdown, technical, environment and operations director for the European Cruise Council, Ed Galea, an evacuation specialist at the University of Greenwich who specialises in modelling evacuation procedures and Richard Pellew, chief surveyor for the south east region at the Maritime and Coastguard Agency.

Ashdown told her that 'the notion of "women and children first" has always been an "unwritten convention" rather than anything written down in law'. Galea said, "*There are no international regulations as to who goes first. The whole "women and children first" thing comes from Hollywood.*" Pellew concluded with authority, "*Women and children first is a Victorian hangover. There is nothing in policy other than in human nature. The Solas [Safety of Life at Sea] guidance is designed so that everybody gets off.*" Curtis concludes:

> There's no such thing as "women and children first" in the international regulations that set out the evacuation procedures at sea. The only priority that is made is that specially adapted lifeboats are provided for people with mobility problems. In reality, studies show that people tend to behave in relatively selfless ways and help the people who require it. Even if they express fear, true panic is relatively uncommon.[131]

The first publicising of the notion of women-and-children-first was the result of another maritime tragedy which occurred off the coast of South Africa, the British bit of which at that time was only Cape Colony. At 0200 on the morning of 26 February 1852 a troopship, *HMS Birkenhead*, bound for Algoa Bay in the Eastern Cape with young recruits to provide reinforcements in the Eighth Xhosa War, hit a submerged rock and sank. Only 193 of the 643 passengers survived, 113 soldiers (all ranks), 6 Royal Marines, 54 seamen (all ranks), 7 women, 13 children and at least one male civilian, some by swimming to shore, some 40 found clinging to rigging and some, including all the women and children in what small boats the steamer carried that could be launched.

The incident caught the public's attention for three remarkable phenomena; the insistence of the military officers and the ship's captain on the women and children being evacuated before any soldiers or crew, the gruesome predation of sharks on those swimming to shore and the astonishingly stoic discipline of the young soldiers who, despite the ship's captain's order to abandon ship and make for the boats followed instead the command of their officers, who feared that a rush of people trying to board them would capsize the small boats, to remain at attention while the ship sank beneath the waves.[132]

---

[131] https://www.theguardian.com/politics/reality-check-with-polly-curtis/2012/jan/16/costa-concordia-women. Accessed 18/12/2018.

[132] https://en.wikipedia.org/wiki/HMS_Birkenhead_(1845). Accessed 18/12/2018.

All three captains, Smith of the *Titanic*, Salmond of the *Birkenhead* and Schettino of the *Costa Concordia* were to blame, guilty, at the very least, of incompetently putting the safety of their passengers and crew at risk—Smith, by going too fast and failing to have a lifeboat drill; Salmond, by sailing too close to the shore to make a quicker passage; and Schettino by authorising a 'sail-by salute'—but the moral reputation of Smith and Salmond, their integrity and honour unharmed, has been preserved by history. Smith and Salmond went down with their ships, the expected behaviour of ships' captains and team leaders who make a botch of things (Romans who failed fell on their swords as did Japanese—Hara-kiri) but Schettino, though no less guilty of incompetence, arguably no more guilty of manslaughter or causing a shipwreck than his two predecessors, went to jail for 16 years, upheld on appeal, on a number of moral rather than nautical judgements one of which was for abandoning his passengers, in complete contrast to his crew. The labels attached to him by the press at the time, 'Captain Coward' and 'Captain Calamity', 'Italy's most hated man', as well as the unsubstantiated character flaws of daredevilry, insubordination and infidelity (his mistress was on the bridge when the accident happened) are unlikely to be erased by time.

The owners of the *Costa Concordia*, Costa Crociere, avoided any legal blame or moral censure. The President of the Board of Directors of IMM, the owners of the *Titanic*, Joseph Bruce Ismay, was on board and seated himself in the Collapsible C life craft alongside another first-class passenger, William Carter. These wealthy male survivors were vilified by the American press for saving themselves when women and children were still on board the stricken ship. Ismay was labelled "J. Brute Ismay". Two years after the disaster, Carter's wife divorced him citing his cruelty, one example of which was his desertion of her during the evacuation.

> "When the Titanic struck," declared Mrs Carter in her testimony, "my husband came to me and said, 'Get up and dress yourself and the child.' I never saw him again until I was put aboard *Carpathia*. He was leaning over the rail as we climbed up from the boats to the deck, and all he had to say to me was, 'I have had a jolly good breakfast, but I never thought I would make it.'[133]

The sole Japanese survivor, Masabumi Hosono, was also vilified by his homeland press, branded as a coward, ostracised and sacked. Although Japanese morals were powerfully influenced by the long-established Bushido code of the Samurai warrior, Maragaret Mehl, writing in *Encyclopaedia Titanica*, suggests that it was Hosono's failure to implement Western moral values, such as women-and-children-first, that brought dishonour upon him.

---

133 https://www.encyclopedia-titanica.org/titanic-survivor/william-carter.html. Accessed 27/12/2018.

> Hosono's failure to act as the Anglo-Saxon nations evidently expected their men to act caused embarrassment in Japan, but more because of the Japanese acceptance of Western values than because of their own traditions.[134]

What we have here is the pronouncement of a moral, ethical even, judgement on these men based upon an expected code of conduct. In these circumstances what should a good man do? Although steered by the women-and-children-first principle this whole thing is about the behaviour of men, not people in general. The clear public expectation of a good man in Victorian/Edwardian England was that of a chivalrous man. Chivalry was an essential component of being a Victorian gentleman, as important as money and property. However, none of these three was as important as ancestry—blood, family and class. Chivalrous behaviour would be described today as 'classy', 'first class' or 'of a different class'.

Chivalry, class and maleness have always gone together. *Chevalerie,* 'horse soldiery or soldiership', was a European ideal, most definitely not Anglo-Saxon or Celtic. The European version of a horse soldier was tank like. Rather than speedy hit-and-run tactics, often using bows and arrows, of which there are many historical and worldwide examples such as Scythian archers and Plains Indians, the Frankish chevalier/knight developed from Roman heavy cavalry whose purpose was to fight from the back of a horse thus disrupting formations of infantry. Larger horses and technological improvements in saddles, like higher pommels, and the use of stirrups made the horse warrior a formidable opponent.

The training regime required knights to be full-time soldiers. The brute strength required to handle a large horse and sword as well as to wear chain mail, and later plate armour, an essential defence against arrow volleys, meant they had to have the athletic strength of a man. Finally, the kit required—warhorse/destrier, saddle, armour, weapons, groom, squire, riding horse, groom's horse, squire's horse etc., required wealth beyond the reach of an ordinary person.

The source of wealth was land. Thus to gain or defend territory in constant warfare a warrior culture developed in which the game changing weapon was a highly trained, full time soldier on a horse who required a constant, reliable source of great revenue with which to maintain his constant readiness to fight.

As a killing machine, he must have felt, and indeed was, superior. As a man he felt superior—only a man could do his job. As a social being, a member of a community, he was superior, a landowner on whom hundreds of inferiors depended for their lives—a class above. Only two things outranked him (until stratification by size of land owned sorted out various ranks of superior people). His King and His God. As to the former, loyalty to King and Country was a sine qua non of being a good Chevalier although examples of the breaking of this chivalric bond are too numerous to mention.

---

[134] https://www.encyclopedia-titanica.org/last-of-the-last.html. Accessed 27/12/2018.

As to the latter, God's representatives on Earth and interpreters of His wishes regarded killing as a great sin for which, in exchange for a substantial donation—a church, an abbey or a cathedral or a nice piece of gold or silver church ware or, even more desirable, after 1099 CE, a few troops, an army would have been more welcome, to fight the heathen menace in the Holy Land, the Church would provide absolution and intercede with God on the donor's behalf. Adding Christian belief and piety to the chivalric code extended the range of its requirements.

However nobly the Norman Conquest is dressed and however completely it is justified legally or morally, the fact is that William brought with him an army of knights, horse warriors, whose intention was to kill and take over land that belonged to another aristocrat of another race for reasons of wealth and power—on a mission to kill or be killed.

Fighting to the death was an all-male activity which meant that the other opportunity to sin, sex, was absent while on campaign—*not!* Rewriting that assertion in palimpsest, as it were, the opportunity for morally approved sex was rarely available because the married knight's legal wife would be at home and single knights were expected to maintain a sexual continence which, in the testosterone-fuelled community of young, trained killers was a big ask. However, in God's earthly kingdom Woman was the cause of sin and it was her sexual motivation that required control. Men? Well, they could not help themselves when under the seductive spell of a woman. Anyway, they were the superior sex, stronger, more able to run affairs of the world and more able to protect the weaker vessels that were women and children.

Once the Church got involved, the chevalier's life of serious killing and recreational sex was loaded down with sin too great to bear. It required a serious makeover, some seriously cleansing spin! The makeover was chivalry and largely fictional. One further aspect of the chivalric dream was/is that its heyday has always been in the past. The inspiration for this literary chivalric fiction came from writers like Geoffrey of Monmouth whose history of Kings of the Britons talked about a King called Arthur and was widely taken to be true by 11th and 12th century Anglo-Normans.

The Arthurian era with its knightly protagonists, Lancelot, Erec, Yvain and Perceval and their brothers-in-arms such as Gawain and Galahad became the canvas for a beautifully romantic picture of tales of love, honour, duty, broken promises and deeds of valour and treachery told by poets such as Chretien de Troyes in the troubadour tradition and popularised by Eleanor of Aquitaine, Queen and mother of two Kings of England, and her daughter Marie, Countess of Champagne.

Whether Chretien was reflecting a hitherto unrecorded chivalric code or seeking to generate one by referring back to a Golden Age is open to debate. There is evidence that trainee knights had to absorb some Romance literature. The Arthurian deeds of derring-do were matched by those of the French legend,

Charlemagne, and his knights in tales such as the *Song of Roland*. I sense there was more than a little compulsion from the Catholic Church to enforce a code of conduct which was superior to that of the Muslim warrior culture that the Church required knights and their wealth to remove from the holy city of Jerusalem—making the 12th century not only the Golden Age of Chivalry but of Crusading as well.

In the field of propaganda, the Church was a leading promoter of the Establishment line which, until the call to Crusade by Pope Urban II, had been presented to the unruly and warring knights of the 10th and 11th centuries as the *Peace and Truce of God* movement.

What was in fact happening on Crusades was anything but chivalrous. The rapine and pillage following the captures of Antioch and Jerusalem in the First Crusade, 1095-1099 CE, and the slaughter of prisoners at the siege and capture of Acre, 1191 CE, in the Third Crusade, were typical examples of War Rape and Pillage still being employed as a weapon of war terror in the 21st century. We, therefore, look to the past for chivalry to escape the ghastly behaviour of the present; to the Georgian Age of Enlightenment, for instance—Mr Darcy in Jane Austen's *Pride and Prejudice* published in 1813.

The Victorians themselves looked back to the jousting Middle Ages—Sir Walter Scott's *Ivanhoe* published in 1819 but set in the 12th century was a best seller. *I fully admit to taking refuge from my own failings in my admiration of the historical figures of age of chivalry itself, the Anglo-Norman William Marshall (1146-1219), knight-errant, war leader and Regent of England or the French Bertrand du Guesclin (1320-80), one of the last knights-errant, war leader and Constable of France, knowing full well they were not the moral paragons of their legends.*

In this fantastical bygone Golden Age, men were men. The heroes were courageous and hardy, toweringly strong in single combat, overcoming tremendous odds and obstacles, prepared to die for a worthy cause such as their King, the Church or the Lady they loved, dedicated warriors using their strength and skill to overcome evil and protect the weak. William Marshall was certainly hardy, marrying the 17-year-old Isabel de Clare at the age of 43, siring 10 children and leading his troops at the Battle of Lincoln in 1217 at the age of 70. They were expected to be loyal in their relationships with others, especially their feudal lords. Marshall stayed loyal to King John when most of the barons deserted him to ally themselves with King Louis VIII of France.

Furthermore, they were expected to be pious. Elaborate rituals and binding oaths were devised to accompany their knighting ceremonies and to ensure that a knight never went into battle unshriven and unconfessed.

> The knighting ceremony usually involved a ritual bath on the eve of the ceremony (the would-be knight usually dressed in white). Then an all-night prayer vigil would begin, sometimes with the squire's arms on the altar. The kneeling squire would swear an oath, which included some of the following points:

- He would always defend a lady.
- He would speak only the truth.
- He would be loyal to his lord.
- He would be devoted to the church.
- He would be charitable and defend the poor and helpless.
- He would be brave.
- When on a quest, he would remove his armour and arms only while sleeping.
- He would never avoid dangerous paths out of fear.
- He would be on time for any engagement of arms, like a battle or tournament.
- Upon returning to his home or lord's court from an adventure, he would always tell of his escapades.
- If taken prisoner, he would give up his arms and horse to his opponent and not fight the opponent again without the opponent's consent.
- He would fight only one-on-one against an opponent.[135]

Chivalric piety was a long time in the making. Robert II, the second Capetian king of France, 996-1031 CE, and grandfather-in-law of William 'the Bastard' was widely known by the sobriquet Robert 'The Pious'. This, along with a few anecdotes, mostly posthumous, of noble deeds, involving forgiving his enemies and giving alms to the poor, consisted of making enemies, being zealously religious, persecuting Jews and burning heretics. On the suggestion of Warin, Bishop of Beauvais, Robert considered making his knights take this oath. This is a summary. The full oath can be found at <https://books.google.co.uk/books?id=YvEIPYhxqi4Candpg=PA301andlpg=PA301anddq=%27Peace+oath+proposed+by+Bishop+Warin+of+Beauvais+to+King+Robert+the+Pious+(1023)%27,+...andsource=blandots=q8HAQ->

> I will not infringe on the Church in any way. I will not hurt a cleric or a monk if unarmed. I will not steal an ox, cow, pig, sheep, goat, ass, or a mare with colt. I will not attack a vilain or vilainesse or servants or merchants for ransom. I will not take a mule or a horse male or female or a colt in pasture from any man from the calends of March to the feast of the All Saints unless to recover a debt. I will not burn houses or destroy them unless there is a knight inside. I will not root up vines. I will not attack noble ladies traveling without husband nor their maids, nor widows or nuns unless it is their fault. From the beginning of Lent to the end of Easter I will not attack an unarmed knight.[136]

Either the Bishop had a very lively imagination or the deeds that he wanted chevaliers not to do had already been a part of chivalric, as in 'of the chevalerie', behaviour—*I get a picture of fighting monks and nuns, belligerent clerics, feisty*

[135] history.howstuffworks.com/historical-figures/knight3.htm. Accessed 04/01/2019.
[136] en.wikipedia.org/wiki/Peace and Truce of God. Accessed 04/01/2019.

widows, horse and cattle rustling, worker abduction and a winter free-for-all!—confirming what I said earlier about the whole chivalry thing requiring a strenuously applied makeover.

Finally, they were expected to be courteous. Courtly behaviour and courtly language (French, of course. It is said that Henry I tried to learn English but gave up and dropped out. Edward III was the first King of England since Edward the Confessor and Harold Godwinson known to have spoken English, some 260 years after Hastings, although as a second language. His grandson, Richard II, was a highly proficient English speaker but it was probably his cousin and usurper, Henry IV, who, along with his courtiers, actually conducted Court business in English.) were joined, towards the end of the 12th century, by courtly love.

The reasoning behind a strict code of behaviour at the court of a monarch lies in all the semantic nuances of the French word *gentil*. The Court was the monarch's turf, the monarch's playground, well away from the dangers of war and the land-generated disputes of his friends and henchmen who, in toto, represented what he ruled, his domain.

I use the possessive adjective 'his' because Monarchy, Majesty and Mightiness were patriarchal in Europe. Until the reign of Bloody Mary I in 1553, Queen and Her Majesty were titles acquired through marriage to a King. The 5 years of practice served courtiers well for the 45-year reign of her more illustrious half-sister, Gloriana, Elizabeth I. Other medieval countries had problems with the titles of Queens Regnant. Jadwiga, youngest daughter of Louis the Great, King of Hungary and Poland, was crowned King of Poland on 16 October 1384, two years after her elder sister was crowned King of Hungary on 17 September 1382.

Margaret I who ruled Denmark and Norway from 1387-1412, sarcastically named 'The Lady King' by her rivals, adopted the omnigendered title of "sovereign lady and lord and guardian of the entire kingdom of Denmark." Wikipedia informs us that: "This special, double-gendered title bestowed upon the holder the power and authority of a man (lord), of a woman (sovereign lady) and of the gender-neutral guardian."[137]

Those at a feudal court owed everything they had or hoped to have to the monarch's pleasure. They could not afford to incur his displeasure and, in the public glare of court life, could not afford to show any grudge or grievance they held against the monarch or any of their peers or forget their place in the hierarchy of wealth and seniority that the stratified society that made up the crème-de-la-crème at the top of all feudal kingdoms. Behaviour and language had to be publicly gentil/genteel/gentle—nice/inoffensive/non-aggressive/unprovocative—no matter what emotional tensions or perceived injustices or offences festered beneath the surface.

[137] en.wikipedia.org/wiki/Margaret I of Denmark. Accessed 09/01/2019.

Courtly love had to be similarly genteel, given by women to men who had earned it by being incredibly chivalrous in all its aspects, preferably not consummated because sex was for procreation and procreation was about family aggrandisement and class preservation, and, finally, absolutely nothing to do with animal instinct or carnal pleasure. Banishment from court usually meant the end of a career. Getting the whole thing right meant a career based on being at court—a Courtier—less physical than a career on the battlefield but equally perilous and potentially short-lived! A court-based sex worker was a courtesan, her profession being courtesanerie. The art of getting a wealthy wife was courtship.

Much of the analysis of courtesy or court goings-on introduces us to vocabulary whose origin appears to be French—*majeste, royaute, nobilite, civilite, courtoisie, manières, politesse, etiquette*. This is unlikely to be evidence of the British upper classes having a deep felt need or desire to hang on to their 'French' origins. By the time of and during the Hundred Years War, which covered much of the 14th and 15th centuries, English Lords, whilst accepting their Anglo-Norman ancestry, were beginning to see themselves as very separate from their continental equivalents.

In October 1396, Round 1 of the 'Court' Wars took place near Ardres, about 10 miles south-east of Calais, when Richard II, the last Plantagenet King of England, took his court to a summit meeting with Charles VI of France (smaller than the France we know now but still large) to broker a peace, the willingness for which was based on countering the warlike nature of the nobility by getting them to spend their wealth on luxuries and patronage of the arts. War might have been forestalled but competition remained, the winner in this arena being the Court with the most magnificence. This less powerful French Court did not enjoy the unconditional support or wealth of territories to the west, such as Gascony, Aquitaine, Normandy, Brittany and Picardy and quasi-independent duchies to the east, most significantly Savoy, Lorraine and Burgundy, although their leaders owed their feudal homage to the King of France.

The Valois Dukes of Burgundy were a cadet branch of the French royal family—not entitled heirs to the throne by the strict rules of primogeniture—descended from the fourth son, Philip, of John II, the Good, the King of France who was defeated at Poitiers and held for ransom in England—also ruled much of the Netherlands and became enormously wealthy by controlling the trade routes from the cloth producers of Bruges and Ghent, now in modern Belgium, and owning some of the richest farmland in western Europe.

If Round 1 was at best a draw, Round 2 went to the magnificence of the Burgundian Court of Philip the Good, Duke of Burgundy from 1419 to 1467. Burgundy was ideally placed to soak up all the wonders of Renaissance culture. The Renaissance blossomed in an Italy full of city states which evolved from republics based on trade to family domains with the 'Courts' of their ruling dynasties like the Medici in Florence, the Sforzas in Milan and the more oligarchic republic of Venice.

Not only was it driven by the rediscovery of Classical learning the historical marker of which is generally accepted to be the literary output of the Italian poet and 14th century Michael Palin (he travelled widely throughout Europe, allegedly for the sheer pleasure of it), Francesco Petrarca—Petrarch—inspired by his rediscovery of some of Cicero's letters in 1345, but also by the discovery of the Orient.

The subsequent trading links with the Levant, the Eastern Mediterranean, China, via the Silk Road that wound its overland way from modern day Xian in Central China to the Black Sea and Mediterranean ports of the Byzantine Empire, and the Indies, especially after Bartolomeu Dias rounded the Cape of Good Hope in 1488, brought enormous wealth as well as learning. Traders were the medieval equivalent to the world-wide web and dinner conversation was the now long forgotten predecessor to television, computer games and mobile phones. Their tales, since the Crusaders had realised there was a whole strange and 'awesome' world out to the East beyond the holy city of Jerusalem, will have undoubtedly included descriptions of the Forbidden City of Beijing, the Golden Palace of Baghdad and the Palace of Blachernae in Constantinople. Rustichello da Pisa's *Travels of Marco Polo* was a 14th century best seller.

The Renaissance also brought about a more agnostic, philosophical contemplation of the meaning of life which we now call, for want of a better term, Humanism. Inspired by the re-examination of God—over one third of the European population died in The Great Plague of 1347-51 although recent estimates think a higher figure more accurate. Wikipedia quotes medieval historian, Philip Daileader:

> The trend of recent research is pointing to a figure more like 45-50% of the European population dying during a four-year period. There is a fair amount of geographic variation. In Mediterranean Europe, areas such as Italy, the south of France and Spain, where plague ran for about four years consecutively, it was probably closer to 75-80% of the population. In Germany and England … it was probably closer to 20%.[138]

…and the rediscovery of the Greek Stoic philosophers (*hardly a coincidence, I think*) such as Protagoras—"Man is the measure of all things"—'Renaissance Men' looked closely into the body, the intellect, the behaviour, moral and corporal, and the motives of human beings. Thus, the life of great Courts, being visible to and, via their patronage of the observers, i.e., the artists and polymaths, like Da Vinci, sustaining intellectual observation, gave birth to history as we know it, mostly recording the lives of the 'great' and mostly from, until recently, an 'Establishment 'perspective.

The wealth of the Burgundian Valois and the magnificence of their Court were very much on the English radar in the 15th century, as we shall see, not only as a dazzling example of luxurious living but also of another way to accumulate

[138] en.wikipedia.org/wiki/Black Death #Death toll. Accessed 17/01/2019.

stunning amounts of wealth other than ownership of land—trade. Indeed, this new awareness of alternative wealth accumulation was a three-way club; England, Burgundy, as in the Low Countries, and Portugal. At the height of the Hundred Years War between England and France and to which I will come shortly the three were not only linked by political treaties but by the other feudal bonding process, marriage. In 1386, England and Portugal signed the Treaty of Windsor thus beginning the world's longest running alliance—633 years and still running.

It was sealed by the marriage of Philippa of Lancaster, older sister of the future king, Henry IV, to King John I of Portugal. Their sons became Portugal's 'Illustrious Generation' of explorers, empire builders and players on a global stage, and their daughter, Isabella, became the third wife of Philip the Good, Duke of Burgundy.

The luxurious showpiece of Burgundy was only rivalled by that of its neighbour, the Holy Roman Empire, Germany, Bohemia, Italy, Hungary and Croatia, to which it was added by Frederick III, the first Habsburg Emperor, Archduke of Austria. The Dukes of Austria held court at the Hofsburg, 'Castle of the Court', in Vienna which became the winter palace for much of their rule over the Austro-Hungarian Empire. In Renaissance Italy, Vienna and Dijon, therefore, could be found the Style Gurus of 15th century Europe who defined the absolute chic of dress—*costumerie*, hairstyle—*coiffure*, bearing—*comportement*, interior design—*furniture, tapisserie*, food—*banquet, cuisine*, behaviour—*manieres*, language—*politesse* and, last but not least, sex—*amour.*

Yes, sex! Andreas Capellanus, a courtier, probably, in the troubadour court of Marie of Champagne wrote a treatise on Love/Amour/Amore in the 1180s in which he makes this assertion: 'Love is an inborn suffering proceeding from the sight and immoderate thought upon the beauty of the other sex, for which cause above all other things one wishes to embrace the other and, by common assent, in this embrace to fulfil the commandments of love.'[139]
Lust, sexual compulsion and sex itself, all put so delicately and euphemistically!

As I conjectured before, this Frenchification of the vocabulary of courtesy in the English Court was nothing to do with its Franco-Norman origins but more to do with the three-century leadership of France as the exemplar and French as the lingua franca of courtesy, of the upper class, the ruling class. So powerful was the link that during the 17th century French, the language of Court and diplomacy, replaced Latin as Europe's lingua franca for most pursuits requiring a higher education or required of the European nobility, including politics. One of history's most debated anecdotes is the alleged quotation of 16th century Holy Roman Emperor, Charles V, "I speak Spanish to God, Italian to women, French to men and German to my horse."

To understand this whole chivalry chapter in the history of the treatment and perception of women in this country we have to go on our travels, not only back

[139] http://sites.fas.harvard.edu/~chaucer/special/authors/andreas/de_amore.html. Accessed 19/01/2019.

to the 15th century, the golden age of chivalry, but also to France where it originated, flourished and, as a reality rather than a fiction, perished. It was an age of death unparalleled in history in which women played a leading role in the survival of humanity, not only as mothers, wives and sisters but as political pawns and players.

Chapter 17
The French Connection

A Frenchman! Where did you pick up that expression? Are these Burgundians and Bretons and Picards and Gascons beginning to call themselves Frenchmen, just as our fellows are beginning to call themselves Englishmen? They actually talk of France and England as their countries. Theirs, if you please! What is to become of me and you if that way of thinking comes into fashion?
– Bernard Shaw, Saint Joan

Wilt thou be daunted at a woman's sight? Aye, beauty's princely majesty is such, Confounds the tongue and makes the senses rough.
– William Shakespeare, Henry VI, Part 1

Preamble (A classic example of a 'potted' history!)

Although England's early 14th century connection with the French Court was strengthened by the marriage of King Edward II of England to Isabella, daughter of King Philip IV of France, in 1308, the two Kings soon fell out over England's French territories—or France's English territories, particularly Aquitaine—Guyenne and Gascony, Edward's grandfather, Henry III, having renounced England's claim on Normandy in 1259. Philip died in 1314, 4 months after Edward's humiliation at Bannockburn. He was succeeded by his eldest son, Louis X, who died two years later without a son, presenting France with a succession problem it had not had to face for some 200 years.

Louis' wife was pregnant but their son, John I, died 5 days after his coronation, leaving his regent, Uncle Philip, second surviving son of Philip IV, very much in control of France and wanting the throne so much that he had himself crowned at Reims. John, however, had a half-sister, Joan, the four-year old daughter of Louis' first wife, Margaret of Burgundy, whose chief advisors, Uncle Philip's uncle and long-time rival, Charles of Valois, and Joan's uncle, Odo IV, Duke of Burgundy, demanded VAR to which Uncle Philip agreed. The game stopped while the VAR specialists of the time, the Estates-General ('An assembly of prelates, lords, the bourgeois of Paris and doctors of the University'.[140]

studied the video evidence, scrolls of law going back 800 years, in the studio, aka at that time the University of Paris.

---

140 en.wikipedia.org/wiki/Salic law# Applications of the succession and inheritance laws. Accessed 21/01/2019.

Joan was only 4 so Uncle Philip would have to rule France as Regent. Joan was as royal as Uncle Philip, or was she? Her mother, Margaret, had died in prison to which she had been sentenced for adultery in the same period when Joan was conceived. However, her father, on his death bed, had sworn that she was his child. A legal ruling was required.

In short, a woman could not, in France, inherit her father's title and lands. These had to go to his nearest living male relative descended from the male bloodline only. If there were no sons the daughter could inherit the title and lands that her father or any of his male ancestors had obtained by marriage. Odo accepted the decision and the hand of Philip's daughter, Joan, and her county of Artois. Over time, the 'Golden Age' syndrome kicked in and this ruling was referred to as the 'Salic' Law after some ancient law that had applied to certain Frankish tribes living near the Rhine in the 6th century. Shakespeare, that unswervingly loyal Lancastrian apologist and propagandist, popularised the term in his fervently patriotic play, Henry V, to have a dig at the absurdity of French chivalry. After six years Philip V, having died with no sons, was succeeded by his younger brother, Charles IV.

When Charles died in 1328, he, too, left a one-year-old daughter, Mary, and a pregnant wife. Again, a Regent was required and this time it was the son of Charles of Valois, Philip of Valois. Things had also changed in England where, having rebelled against and been complicit in the alleged murder of her husband in 1327, Isabella was Regent for her son, Edward III. Philip was Charles' first cousin, both grandsons of Philip III, King of France (1270-85). Edward was Charles' nephew, great grandson of Philip III. The reckoning of consanguinity at that time made Edward (2 steps) not Philip (3 steps) Charles' nearest living male relative. The muddily clear ruling of 1316 reaffirmed in 1322 had made it clear that title and land could not pass through the female line. Although Isabella was the only one of Philip IV's children still standing, she could not inherit her father's title or territory neither could she pass it on to her son because, in accordance with the so-called Salic Law, it had never been hers to give.

Just because the English were prepared to accept the matrilineal principle, especially if it meant more land and wealth, they could not impose their rules on France. Furthermore, the English continually broke the international convention/law of feudal vassalage by not paying homage to the French King for their French possessions. So, when Edward III refused to do homage once again for Gascony in 1337 the Valois Philip, now Philip VI, King of France, confiscated it. Enraged, Edward declared war and, in a wonderful piece of yah-boo-sucks, asserted his claim to the French throne. When he created his chivalric Order of the Garter its motto was, and still is, Honi soit qui mal y pense—Shame on you who think it/I'm wrong.

Ok, that is a very unsophisticated, no doubt unacademic, run through of the causes of the so-called Hundred Years War with France which, of course, like all historical generalisations and simplifications, is a misnomer. It was not continuous for 100 years nor was it with the whole of France nor did it last for 100 years (It began, as outlined, in 1337 and ended with the defeat at Castillon in 1453.The casus belli was not actually removed until the Treaty of Picquigny in 1475 in which Edward IV withdrew his claim to the throne of France.)! It is remembered for great English (There was no Great Britain for another 300 odd years and Scotland and France were locked into the Auld Alliance, signed by King John Balliol and Philip IV, against the growing power of Edward I's England) victories, Crecy (1346), Poitiers (1356) and Agincourt (1415).

It is remembered for great English heroes, Edward III, his eldest son, the Black Prince, and Henry V and one great French heroine, Joan of Arc. It is also remembered for Henry VI being the only King of France and England from 1422 to 1453. What tends not to be remembered are the French victories at Bauge in 1421, in which Henry V's brother, Thomas of Lancaster, was killed; at Patay in 1429 in which the most important English commanders, Talbot, Scales and Rempston, were captured; at Formigny in 1450 in which Normandy was reconquered by the French commander Arthur Richemont and much of the English army was killed or taken prisoner along with its commander, Sir Thomas Kyriell, and at Castillon in 1453 in which 'Old Talbot' and his son were killed and Gascony lost.

What tended to be avoided in the classrooms of my schooldays, and bears repeating to get the record straight, was the stark fact that the English lost—everything bar the Pale of Calais and the Channel Islands. One of the least performed Shakespeare plays, although there is a considerable volume of criticism of it from a literary, linguistic and dramatic perspective, is/was Henry VI: Part 1 because its theme was this loss and the reasons behind it to which I will come soon.

The Angevin Empire brought to the King of England, Henry II, by his marriage to Eleanor of Aquitaine in 1152, originally much larger than the territory ruled by the then Kings of France, was gone. The excuses—the perfidiously unchivalrous French, the mad and weak King of England (his madness inherited from his mentally ill grandfather, Charles VI of France, like some sort of chemical warfare!), the cowardly and treacherous Fastolf (Sir John Fastolf withdrew his troops at Patay when all was lost and was later pronounced innocent of any wrongdoing) or the witchcraft of Joan of Arc—have always hidden the real reasons for the loss; lack of money and loss of allies.

The expense of taking a feudal host to campaign abroad and the tensions that the fighting in France caused between the aristocracy and King Henry VI combined with the total loss of their French fiefs were major causes of the civil war we now call the Wars of the Roses that lasted 30 years and represented the death throes of the Anglo-French Plantagenet dynasty. Edward III funded much of his fighting himself. The Black Prince was a looter and a pillager and Henry V's Agincourt was little more than a raid that got lucky, taking advantage of the civil war situation in France between the royal Armagnac faction and the hugely wealthy and influential Burgundians. Although these two were observing a truce at the time of Agincourt the Burgundians remained neutral, a significant diminution of French fighting power.

After Agincourt, all parties were financially exhausted, but it was not only the English who were on top, the Burgundians were in control of a whole swathe of northern and eastern France as well as Flanders. Being favoured by the wife of Charles the Mad, Isabeau of Bavaria, the Duke of Burgundy, John the Fearless, gained control of Paris and the King. The new Dauphin, Charles, whose elder brothers had both died while favouring the Burgundian faction, fled south of the Loire river to Bourges. Lured to a second meeting to sort out a truce, John was murdered by assassins from the Armagnac party. The King (or was it Isabeau?) disinherited his son, blaming him for the assassination that had broken the truce. The next in line, Charles of Orleans, the no-longer-Dauphin's cousin, was a prisoner in England, having been captured at Agincourt and forbidden by Henry to be ransomed. This left John's son, Philip III Duke of Burgundy, and Isabeau in charge of Paris and favouring an English overlordship if the mad king should die. Charles the Mad, or Isabeau on his behalf, signed his kingdom over to Henry V at the Treaty of Troyes in 1420 who, in return, agreed to marry his daughter Catherine of Valois. Henry went home to England to show off his wife, to see and be seen and to raise some money to subdue the rest of France.

Dauphin Charles was down but not out. The alliance that was forming between the English and the Burgundians needed some countering. Since 1413 Charles had been engaged to marry Marie of Anjou, daughter of Louis II of Anjou and his wife, Yolande of Aragon. Louis had also been King of Naples and did a lot of fighting in Italy. He died in 1417. While away, Yolande, Duchess of Anjou and Countess of Provence, ran Louis' French territories and then acted as regent for their 14-year-old son, also Louis.

Anjou bordered on Normandy and was, therefore, threatened by the English reconquest of Normandy. Henry was back in England leaving his younger brother and heir to the throne, Thomas, leading the army. They went on the rampage, known as a chevauchee—a la Black Prince 60 years before. Charles needed an army and a soldier to lead them. Enter the Scots and their leader John Stewart, Earl of Buchan, son of the Duke of Albany, Regent of Scotland, honouring their side of the bargain struck in 1295 and known as the Auld Alliance. Victory at Bauge and the death of Thomas of Lancaster boosted the Dauphin's cause but stung Henry into action. He returned.

Further developments occurred the following year, 1422. In April, Charles married Marie, securing the support of her family, particularly her mother, Yolande, without which he would probably not have become King and made France… well, France. In August, the warlike Henry V died on campaign, not King of France because the Mad Charles was still alive and leaving an 11-month-old son and heir. On his deathbed, he named his brother, John, Duke of Bedford, as Regent of France on the tiny Henry VI's behalf. In October, Charles the Mad died leaving the maybe-Dauphin-maybe-not Charles and his mum-in-law proclaiming him to be King Charles VII of France.

As for the other two major players, Isabeau, now a possible Queen Dowager, and Philip III, the 'Good' Duke of Burgundy, the former, having failed to get her son back to Burgundian-run Paris, retired from public life without resolving any of the slurs on her character and the latter began to play the leading role in preventing the dauphin inheriting the French throne out of vengeance for his father's betrayal and death. Philip did not want to be part of France, but he was not objecting to having a part of France which would surely be his reward under a dual English French monarchy.

1423 was a good year for the Dauphin and his Scottish army with victories over English raiders at La Brossiniere and Burgundians at La Buissiere but in a drive to capture Reims so that he could be crowned the Franco-Scottish army of the Dauphin, boosted in numbers by some Aragonese and some Milanese heavy cavalry hired by his mother-in-law Yolande, suffered a bloody defeat at Verneuil on 17 August 1424 in which the Scottish commanders, Buchan, now Constable of France, and Angus, were killed and the French leaders, including La Fayette, Marshal of France and fellow victor at Bauge, taken prisoner.

Instead of marching on Bourges, the victorious Bedford concentrated his efforts on subduing Maine and Anjou. The war was now one of attrition as town after town resisted the besieging English and Charles stayed in the field with Yolande's money, avoiding a pitched battle and slowly losing ground. These five years up to 1429 were the height of the Anglo-Burgundian alliance for the brothers-in-law, Bedford having married Philip's sister, Anne, in 1423. However, they were also the height of Yolande's political powers. There is little doubt who was running the Dauphinist show.

By 1428, not much stood between the Anglo-Burgundians, who were in control of Paris, Reims and Rouen, and the heartland of the loyalist cause. They started to besiege Orleans, a considerable stronghold on the banks of the Loire. Having been on the defensive for so long Charles and his military advisers needed a new approach or all would probably be lost. Verneuil, known by some as the second Agincourt, seemed to add strength to a mindset in the French that the smaller English army had the knack of defeating the larger French led forces in an open battle. But at Orleans the English were not in the field, they were besieging a very large town while garrisoning a huge territory in north-western France stretching from Normandy to Anjou. They were stretched, making Orleans as much a make-or-break situation for them as it was for the French.

As well as a new war strategy, the French and the Dauphin needed inspiration, given that Bedford and the English faced all the same problems, lack of money, lack of support, stretched supply lines, disease and a dodgy reason for carrying on the fight, not to mention a rapidly growing internecine rivalry back in England, potentially equal to that of the Armagnac-Burgundy fall-out that had lasted for twenty years or so.

All change was the order of the day. The new war aim of the French was 'Crown the Dauphin in Reims'. King Charles VII had an altogether better ring to it than 'maybe-Dauphin-maybe-not'. The new war strategy was 'attack not defend' and the new inspiration was a teenage virgin who spoke to God. Enter Joan of Arc. In 1429 the French, with Joan to the fore, began the break-out from Orleans by destroying one by one the mini English redoubts designed to prevent supplies from reaching the town. French morale was good. They knew that they would win because God, via Joan, said they would. Joan was their talisman. She did not fight but bravely took her banner into the thick of the fighting.

Teenage virgins were the reward and victims of the macho fighting man, not his leaders. To the French she was their Virgin Mary (her state of *virgo intacta* was very important to her effectiveness as a morale booster—a myth had been circulating that a Messiah-like virginal saviour would arise, France having been 'lost by a woman (Isabeau)' would be 'restored by a virgin'—and would no doubt have been checked, probably by Yolande).

With Joan calling the shots, the French believed that they were able to achieve the impossible, the supernatural, the will of God. To the English she was, must have been, a witch, servant of the Devil, because God was on their side. After the break-out Joan said to go to Reims and crown the Dauphin. After some mopping up and decluttering in the Loire valley the French caught up with the English reinforcement army at Patay, apparently at Joan's urging, and won a comprehensive victory, killing or capturing a large number of longbowmen who took years to replace and three of the four main English commanders, Talbot, Scales and Rempston (the Earl of Salisbury having been killed at Orleans and the Earl of Suffolk captured in the mopping up operation).

Only Fastolf, as already told, escaped with what remained of the reinforcements, mostly raw recruits. The French marched on to Reims where the Dauphin was crowned Charles VII on 17 July 1429. This event was a supreme piece of symbolic one-upmanship completely trumping the coronation of his rival, Henry VI, in Paris a few months later. Wikipedia tells us:

> The Cathedral of Reims (damaged during the First World War but restored since) housed the Holy Ampulla (*Sainte Ampoule*) containing the *Saint Chrême* (chrism), allegedly brought by a white dove (the Holy Spirit) at the baptism of Clovis in 496. It was used for the anointing, the most important part of the coronation of French kings.[141]

A few days after Henry's coronation, Philip the Good, Henry's Burgundian ally, married his cousin and Bedford's niece, Isabella of Portugal, strengthening the family ties between the brothers-in-law. When the Burgundians captured Joan the following year at the siege of Compiegne, they sold her to the English for 10,000 livres tournois. The rest is history, well legend actually. The following year Anne died of the plague. In 1433, Bedford married Jacquetta of Luxembourg whose uncle, John, had captured Joan at Compiegne and was fervently pro-English. He may even have been the one who sold her.

The Anglo-Burgundian alliance cooled for a number of political reasons, not least Philip's dislike of Bedford's brother, Humphrey of Gloucester, and his ambitions in the Low Countries. In 1435, a Congress took place at Arras in the Pas-de-Calais with a view to ending the war. Bedford died before any treaty was signed and, with a lot of activity behind the scenes, probably invigorated by

---

[141] en.wikipedia.org/wiki/Reims. Accessed 03/02/2019.

Yolande, Philip, having obtained justice for his father from Charles VII, and no longer bound by his personal promise to Bedford, broke with the English and the following year was besieging Calais. England had lost its only ally.

From that point, the war was largely attritional, involving besieging towns, always a slow and costly business, consolidating territory and securing lines of supply. Most of the 1440s were a time of truce with both kings having their problems with their own nobles. In 1445 Henry VI married the niece of Charles VII and granddaughter of Yolande, who had died in 1442, Margaret of Anjou, but to do so he had to cede control of Maine and Anjou to the French king. In 1446, when the news came out in England that this cession of key neighbours of Normandy had been the price of a penniless and remote blood relative of the French king, support for the truce evaporated, although the treasury officials of a nearly bankrupt England and the taxpayers of her French territories welcomed the peace.

While England tried to refill its purse, France modernised its army under Arthur Richemont, a Breton soldier who had fought for both sides at one time or another, been taken prisoner and ransomed, even rebelled against Charles and been forgiven, who was appointed Constable of France. Arthur, also a brother-in-law of Philip the Good until his wife, Margaret of Burgundy, died in 1441, professionalised the French army, creating and training the compagnies d'ordonnances. Roaming out-of-contract mercenaries with their hangers-on were a real problem throughout the thirty years following the Treaty of Troyes so Arthur employed them as paid soldiers of the King and Charles approved a special tax to pay for them. They were organised into a *lance* of fighters all centred on a *gen d'arme*, a heavily armoured cavalryman.

When they were ready, the French broke the truce in 1449 and invaded Normandy. At the Battle of Formigny a year later, the English, *building up their portfolio entitled "How to Snatch Defeat from the Jaws of Victory"*, were devastatingly defeated and Normandy fell. Heavily armoured cavalry was the deciding factor and, for the first time French field artillery played a significant part (guns were not that new having been used by the English at Crecy a hundred years earlier) in a field battle having already, under the direction of the Bureau brothers, given the French a decisive edge when it came to siege warfare.

With Normandy lost, all that was left for the English to defend was Gascony, the key to which was the city of Bordeaux. In 1451, with the destructive power of the Bureaus' canons, the French took Bordeaux and Jean Bureau was made mayor. In 1452, the citizens of Bordeaux, whose livelihoods were inextricably linked to trade with England, rebelled and expelled the French.

They invited the English to have one more throw of the dice, the last ever in southwestern France, as it turned out, after 300 years. Henry VI, never a man of war, agreed to scrape together about 3000 troops for the old soldier, Sir John Talbot, Earl of Shrewsbury, and his favourite and equally warlike son, John, Viscount Lisle, to secure the city. By the spring of 1453, the Earl had retaken Bordeaux and most of Gascony, receiving a further boost when his son turned up with his troops and the promise of reinforcements.

The Bureaus returned, however, that spring with 10,000 troops and 300 cannons. They besieged the town of Castillon, two days march east of Bordeaux, and the Talbots went to the rescue. Having swept away a screen of archers at Libourne, a day's march from Castillon, the Talbots marched on the French armed camp. Having been obliterated by the French artillery, one missile capable of killing 6 foot soldiers, they were routed by a charge of heavy cavalry. Both of the Talbots died, probably as honourably as in Shakespeare's portrayal 130 years later. Bordeaux surrendered on 19th October 1453 rather than being reduced to rubble.

England's fighting days on mainland France, apart from the Pale of Calais, were over. Henry went mad and the Wars of the Roses, having been simmering for years, boiled over to seriously burn the English nobility for thirty more years. France did not look back, annexing Burgundy in 1477. Its centrality to European politics and culture grew ever stronger until the reign of Louis XIV (1643-1715) when, in the 1680s, it became the supreme power in western Europe.

Until Philippa Gregory's trilogy was televised in *The White Queen* series in 2013, and then covered the late 15th century, post 1460, I think it would be fair to say that the Tudor era, as in the 16th century, attracted far more popular historical interest than the two centuries that preceded it—*understandably; not easy to compete with the sex-mad Henry VIII or the Virgin Queen Elizabeth I*—but, in terms of the impact on English character and culture, including its treatment of women, the Hundred Years War has great significance.

I have digressed at length and in some detail into the chronology of its events because, apologies to all you proud nationalists, England lost. I need to just reiterate the scale and significance of the loss. Not only did the Anglo-Norman regime of the Plantagenet dynasty (I doubt that ordinary English folk much cared about the gains or the losses unless they were instructed to do so.) lost what Edward III, the Black Prince and Henry V had gained, it lost all that William I had battled so hard to control prior to 1066 and his youngest son, Henry I, had acquired undisputedly at Tinchebray in 1106 and all that Henry II gained by his marriage to the continental heiress, Eleanor of Aquitaine, in 1154—except Calais. The monarchy lost the base and the ability to reassert its claim to the French throne until it gave it up altogether when the French throne had ceased to exist, and the French Revolutionary government demanded it as a condition of the Treaty of Amiens in 1802. Anglo-Norman nobles who owned land in France and lucrative trading arrangements with Anglo-France lost everything and turned their attention to England as a theatre of war, hence the Wars of the Roses.

400 years after its enforced union, England and Anglo-France completed a separation of nationality. The two nations, however, have retained a sentimental remembrance of a common, stormy past to embark on a future marked by less lethal competition than that of the horse and the lance, the knight and the gen d'arme, in which there has been a difference in the view of a civilised world, a mutual admiration of style, of character, of culture and of history so that now each nation sees itself as very different to but the equal of the other and has replaced war with, if not out-and-out friendship, a mutually affectionate but

respectfully distant entente. From now, in this story about the British, France will be an ever present.

Chapter 18
La Morte Du Chevalier

The knight is a man of blood and iron, a man familiar with the sight of smashed faces and the ragged stumps of lopped-off limbs; he is also a demure, almost maiden like, guest in a hall, a gentle, modest, unobtrusive man. He is not compromise or happy mean between ferocity and meekness; he is fierce to the nth and meek to the nth. The man who combines both characters—the knight—is not a work of nature but of art; of that art which has human beings, instead of canvas or marble, for its medium.

– C.S. Lewis

Preamble

I am insufficiently qualified to analyse or categorise Anglo-Saxon culture, but I feel sure that the chivalrous side of the British character so admired by Churchill is a continental import, conceived in the 11th century Conquest but born and bred, for the English at any rate, on the fields of France where it flourished and withered as a reality in the Hundred Years War continuing only, in the next 500 years, as the Impossible Dream of a 'civilised' world.

No-one was keener to perpetuate the dream than the three larger-than-life superheroes of the 16th century, Henry VIII, King of England, Lord of Ireland, Francis I, King of France and Charles V (*I simply cannot resist his full title[s]. Talk about a multinational business!*):

> Charles, by the grace of God, Holy Roman Emperor, forever August, King of Germany, King of Italy, King of all Spains, of Castile, Aragon, León, of Hungary, of Dalmatia, of Croatia, Navarra, Grenada, Toledo, Valencia, Galicia, Majorca, Sevilla, Cordova, Murcia, Jaén, Algarves, Algeciras, Gibraltar, the Canary Islands, King of Two Sicilies, of Sardinia, Corsica, King of Jerusalem, King of the Western and Eastern Indies, of the Islands and Mainland of the Ocean Sea, Archduke of Austria, Duke of Burgundy, Brabant, Lorraine, Styria, Carinthia, Carniola, Limburg, Luxembourg, Gelderland, Neopatria, Württemberg, Landgrave of Alsace, Prince of Swabia, Asturia and Catalonia, Count of Flanders, Habsburg, Tyrol, Gorizia, Barcelona, Artois, Burgundy Palatine, Hainaut, Holland, Seeland, Ferrette, Kyburg, Namur, Roussillon, Cerdagne, Drenthe, Zutphen, Margrave of the Holy Roman

Empire, Burgau, Oristano and Gociano, Lord of Frisia, the Wendish March, Pordenone, Biscay, Molin, Salins, Tripoli and Mechelen.[142]

...and their children, Elizabeth I, Henry II and Philip II, respectively. Indeed, Round 3 of the 'Court Wars' took place from 7 to 24 June 1520 at Balinghem, just inside the English-held Pale of Calais, when the 'battle' took place known to history as the Field of the Cloth of Gold. Instead of killing each other the two young kings, Henry aged 29 and Francis aged 26, fought with money invested in being as ostentatiously magnificent as their already overstretched national budgets would allow.

The testosterone-fuelled physical rivalry of the young male nobles was satisfied with the sport of jousting, a very dangerous but peacefully chivalrous activity designed to show off the military skills of a horse warrior, a chevalier. The master of ceremonies, papal legate and Cardinal, Thomas Wolsey, did not allow the kings to compete although both had the necessary military skill to do so (Henry was to be seriously injured in a joust in 1536 and, in 1559, Henry II of France, Francis' son, was killed by septicaemia which set in after an eye injury incurred while jousting).

Henry, so the story goes, did challenge Francis to a wrestling match, which he lost. As to the diplomatic success of the meeting, that was equally short-lived, Wolsey putting England's main earner, the cloth trade with the Netherlands and Burgundy, before Henry's pipe dream of becoming King of France. The 20-year-old Charles V with whom he allied England ruled both territories as part of his bounteous inheritance from his grandparents. It must, however, have been an enormously important showpiece at which the courtiers of England would have embraced the essence of a Renaissance court, its dos and don'ts, its must haves and must nots and an unquenchable desire to keep up with Joneses or, should I say, the Valois.

Chivalry and courtesy were shifting from fighting to phantasmagoria, from walking the walk to talking the talk, from battlefield to stately home, from morality to manners and, above all, from a code of conduct designed to restrain the rapaciousness of the noble horse warrior to an expectation and etiquette of propriety and civilised behaviour among his non-combatant yet still noble descendants.

Finally, before leaving the 'Court Wars', please allow me a small digression. Round 4 and victory went to the French king Louis XIV. In 1661, he started to enlarge a chateau built by his father on the site of his favourite hunting lodge in the village of Versailles, about 20 km. from Paris. By the time the first phase was complete in 1678, he had moved his court there with lodgings for his six to seven thousand courtiers. It was further enlarged to its current dimensions during the rest of his reign.

A hundred years before the Revolution the monarchy of France was at the absolute height of its majesty, taking on all comers, hated but envied by the

[142] en.wikipedia.org/wiki/Charles V, Holy Roman Emperor #Titles. Accessed 11/02/2019.

whole of Western Europe of which it was the economic, social, political and cultural number one. Louis' man of war, Sebastien Le Prestre de Vauban put it brilliantly:

> France has its declared enemies Germany and all the states that it embraces; Spain with all its dependencies in Europe, Asia, Africa and America; the Duke of Savoy [in Italy], England, Scotland, Ireland, and all their colonies in the East and West Indies; and Holland with all its possessions in the four corners of the world where it has great establishments. France has … undeclared enemies, indirectly hostile, and envious of its greatness, Denmark, Sweden, Poland, Portugal, Venice, Genoa, and part of the Swiss Confederation, all of which states secretly aid France's enemies by the troops that they hire to them, the money they lend them and by protecting and covering their trade.
> For lukewarm, useless, or impotent friends, France has the Pope, who is indifferent; the King of England [James II] expelled from his country; the grand Duke of Tuscany; the Dukes of Mantua, Mokena, and Parma [all in Italy]; and the other faction of the Swiss. Some of these are sunk in the softness that comes of years of peace, the others are cool in their affections.[143]

The magnificence of Louis' world was his by divine right, his power was absolute. The English (not the British until the Act of Union in 1702) by that time had had enough of that sort of thing and, having chucked out the last king, James II, who claimed his God-given right to rule but became Louis' lodger, went down the route of parliamentary supremacy thus, with the Bill of Rights made law in 1689, decentralising government, dispersing the locations of its functionaries and reducing the importance of a royal 'Court' as such. *They may have rejected the divine right to rule but they retained the divine right to chivalry and courtesy, something the French have always disputed, gentlemanlike behaviour being a uniquely British character trait*!

Three things about the connection between France and England are culturally relevant, I think. Firstly, the Hundred Years War was the testing ground of the Frenchness of the Anglo-Norman elite. During the century of territorial ebb and flow and emotional up and down on the mainland of Europe an English nationality emerged combining a nostalgic sense of loss and admiration for the chivalric culture implicit in their ancestry, part illusory myth and lyrical legend, with the realistic acceptance that they could not reclaim it, own it again or change it. They had to let go, move on as Englishmen, forced by circumstance to give it up and generate their own separate identity but not really wanting to do so. The noble, gentlemanlike maleness of that new identity may not have been French but was, without question, manufactured and test-driven in France.

---

[143] en.wikipedia.org/wiki/Louis XIV of France #Centralisation of power. Accessed 13/02/2019.

Secondly, a new world was being carved out, an underlying factor in the Armagnac-Burgundian civil war (the Armagnacs favoured an economy based on land tenure) and the alliance of England, Portugal and Burgundy. Trade had begun to generate wealth equal to that generated by ownership of land and trade led to the growth of towns and town culture giving rise to a citified, worldly version of sophistication, urbane not rustic. England copied the Portuguese exploration of the world which added a huge variety of exotic luxuries to the textile-based luxuries that enriched England and Burgundy. Citizen armies of equals, protecting a collective, interdependent source of wealth and fighting on foot replaced hierarchically organised feudal hosts and, as proved in the Battle of the Golden Spurs outside Kortrijk in modern day Belgium in 1302, the infantryman's pike had become a match for the heavily armed knight. 175 years later in the Battle of Nancy in which Philip the Good's son Charles the Bold was killed, the Swiss pike men were the decisive force.

Thirdly, the days of the heavily armed tank-like knight/chevalier/horse warrior, despite the invention of highly protective suits of plate armour, were numbered (*Will we ever say that about mobile phones?*). Magnificent though the fully plated Milanese cavalry charge at Verneuil in 1424 must have been, it did not win the day, which was decided by a ferocious bout of hand-to-hand fighting by fully plated foot soldiers, or prolong the days of the horse warrior. The Battle of Castillon, 29 years later was decided as much by artillery, probably operated by Italian mercenaries under the direction of the Bureau brothers, as by the charge of the knights. (*Two months prior to Castillon some 3000km. to the east an end-of-an-era event of much greater global significance occurred. The ancient city of Byzantium fell to the Ottoman Turks. It is said that an ironworker in their pay, Orban the Hungarian, built a bombard cannon, "Basilica", that was 27 feet (8.2 m) long, and able to hurl a 600 lb (272 kg) stone ball over a mile (1.6 km).*)

Arthur Richemont won the Battle of Formigny in 1450 with professional soldiers paid by the State. Paid, trained soldiers meant that loyal support of the monarch no longer had to be in kind but in money through taxation. Gunpowder-powered weapons which were operated by trained experts required finance not hands on operation. In the feudal host the levy was there to fight with the lord not in his stead. The real battle was between one lord or group of lords and another, probably over land which, along with those who made it productive, belonged to the aristocracy.

Fighting was up close and personal; they could smell each other's sweat, hear each other's breathing, see each other's blood and sense each other's pain. It was kill or be killed. Even the leadership led by example. The description of Verneuil that follows firmly belongs to the true age of chivalry during which the life and conduct of a noble was primarily that of a warrior.

> The head-on clash between the superbly armoured English and French men-at-arms on the field of Verneuil, both of whom had marched on foot into battle, resulted, in the words of the British medievalist Desmond

> Seward, in "a hand-to-hand combat whose ferocity astounded even contemporaries". One veteran of Verneuil, Wavrin, recalled how "the blood of the dead spread on the field and that of the wounded ran in great streams all over the earth". For about three-quarters of an hour, Frenchmen and Englishmen stabbed, hacked and cut each other down on the field of Verneuil without either side gaining any advantage in what is often considered to be one of the most fiercely fought battles of the entire war.
> Bedford himself fought in the battle, wielding a fearsome two-handed poleaxe, leading one veteran to recall: "He reached no one whom he did not fell". Seward noted that Bedford's battle-axe "smashed open an expensive armour like a modern tin can, the body underneath being crushed and mangled before even the blade sank in".[144]

The decline of the hands-on noble fighter occurred over two centuries at least. Certainly, Richard III of England and James IV of Scotland died fighting at Bosworth Field in 1485 and Flodden Field in 1513, respectively. George II was the last King of Great Britain to lead his troops into battle at Dettingen in 1743. Both French and German heavy cavalry paraded in their cuirass, a breast and back plate dating back to the ancient world, at the time of World War I. In an article written in 2014 Alistair Lexden noted that:

By the end of 1915, the British death toll included nine peers and an astonishing 95 sons of peers.

This anecdote matches that of Bedford 500 years earlier:

> No peer showed greater bravery than Brigadier-General the 5th Earl of Longford, father of Frank, the Labour minister and prisoners' friend, whose wife was the aunt of Harriet Harman. This very different Longford led a cavalry charge across open ground to capture a strategically important hill in Gallipoli on 21 August 1915. "Don't bother ducking", he told his fellow officers. "The men don't like it and it doesn't do any good". His body was never recovered.[145]

Nevertheless, although the language of chivalry and gallantry has retained its martial connotations of civilised restraint, courage and self-sacrifice for a cause it has slowly acquired the class-based showmanship of the courtier in which largely meaningless etiquette of language and social behaviour signified 'nobility' rather than the skill and character required to be a 'civilised' but effective horse warrior. AND this had a profound effect on the status and treatment of women. The rules and code of conduct of military one-upmanship applied to the same noble class but were hijacked by the social conflict, no less

---

[144] en.wikipedia.org/wiki/Battle of Verneuil#Milanese attack. Accessed 19/02/2019.

[145] www.alistairlexden.org.uk/sites/www.alistairlexden.org.uk/files/ house magazine lords and ww1 0.pdf. Accessed 20/02/2019.

brutal and no less exhausting than hand-to- hand combat, in which all those at Court were involved, to get to the top.

Last but not least, although the English Gentleman became the image of archetypal Englishness—to be replaced by 18-30 lager louts, ladettes and easy lays—its origins and esprit de corps are continental. Would he have evolved had the English won the Hundred Years War? I think not!

Chapter 19
Honorificabilitudinitatibus

Courtesy is as much a mark of a gentleman as courage.
– Theodore Roosevelt

The morals of a whore and the manners of a dancing-master.
– Samuel Johnson

Preamble

To reach honorificabilitudinitatibus (the longest word in the English language with alternate consonants and vowels), a state in which one is able to receive 'honour', one must do 'good', 'good' being what is 'morally right'. In an age where 'might was right', fighting for right, for good, brought honour. As might became less desirable than peaceful debate, the chivalric code of fighting men softened to become the chivalric code of gentlemen.

The pomp and ceremony of Louis' Court were designed to impress, possibly to overawe, his nobles and visitors from abroad such as ambassadors. As pointed to in an earlier chapter, in his court he made the rules. To gain and keep his favour a courtier had to know, observe and obey the rules. It is important to remember that these were not laws the breaking of which, in most Renaissance kingdoms, was frequently construed as treason and usually resulted in the offender losing his head! So complex were these rules that a visitor to court required a written reminder of what was required by a person of his or her status, purpose and social closeness to the King, a sort of ticket or etiquette.

We credit the first usage of the term etiquette in English to Philip Stanhope, Earl of Chesterfield, in letters written to his son in the mid-18th century. A key aspect of etiquette, probably from its ceremonial origins was restraint of behaviour, of language and of emotion, particularly those emotions evoked by intercourse, in the social not the carnal sense, with the opposite sex. To be unable to restrain oneself was vulgar, like 'common people', and a serious social handicap. Here is a piece of Stanhope Pere's advice to his son:

> I would heartily wish that you may often be seen to smile, but never heard to laugh while you live. Frequent and loud laughter is the characteristic of folly and ill-manners; it is the manner in which the mob express their silly joy at silly things; and they call it being merry. In my mind there is nothing so illiberal, and so ill-bred, as audible laughter. I

> am neither of a melancholy nor a cynical disposition and am as willing and as apt to be pleased as anybody; but I am sure that since I have had the full use of my reason nobody has ever heard me laugh.[146]

The multifarious flamboyance of chivalry, observable, for example, in a British coronation, and the delicate precision of courtesy have all the hallmarks of a continental, predominantly pre-Revolutionary French, culture but the prescriptive nature of the rules and the disdain with which any infringement is/was received are classic Anglo-Norman. Women played a major part in this concocted mixture of illusory civilisation and prescriptive propriety, but it was a man's world in which, as we shall see, a woman could have immense power and influence but never equality.

Once educated, well… able to read and write, although it should be noted that the 16th century potentates, Henry, Francis and Charles were seriously well educated and talented in their own right, various highly subjective books were available, known now as courtesy books, written as guidebooks to this world of politeness, manners and courtship.

One of the earliest must-read offerings to the educated, noble Englishman in the 13th century was *The Book of the Civilised Man* by Daniel of Eccles which contained these useful tips:

- Do not attack your enemy while he is squatting to defecate.
- Do not mount your horse in the hall.
- Do not urinate in the Dining Hall if you are a guest.
- "If you are overcome with erotic desire when you are young and your penis drives you to go to a prostitute, do not go to a common whore; empty your testicles quickly and depart quickly."[147]

Daniel offers this very derogatory opinion of women.

> Following a tradition inherited from antiquity, Daniel describes women as lustful and untrustworthy. The poem describes a woman lying in bed with her husband, with her thoughts on to her secret lover: "The lascivious woman throws herself around the neck of her lover, her fingers give him those secret touches that she denies to her husband in bed; one wicked act with her lover pleases the lascivious adulteress more than a hundred with her husband; women's minds always burn for the forbidden." He says she is always ready to fornicate "with a cook or a half-wit, a peasant or a ploughman, or a chaplain… what she longs for is a thick, leaping, robust piece of equipment, long, smooth and stiff… such are the things that charm and delight women". Daniel had a nearly pathological view of the promiscuity of women, but despite this he says, "Whatever your wife does, do not damage your marriage" and he goes

[146] en.wikipedia.org/wiki/Etiquette. Accessed 16/02/2019.
[147] en.wikipedia.org/wiki/Book of the Civilized Man. Accessed 17/02/2019.

on to say "if you are jealous, do not whisper a word about it… when you are jealous, learn to look up at the ceiling."[148]

Clearly, Daniel had a rather more rumbustious view of sex than Andreas Capellanus or Chretien de Troyes. He does, however, demonstrate that in that early, Christianised culture men were struggling with their dual perception of the female vagina, as a depository and relief valve for their testosterone fuelled libido and as the birth conduit of their offspring without which their genes would hit the buffers. To this duo can be added a third perception. An untouched, unpenetrated woman remained pure, unsullied by coitus with a man, closer to God, innocent of the greatest sin and ripe for the Devil.

This trinity of whore, mother and virgin were, have been and still are, for many at least, too much for men to handle reasonably and unhypocritically so they have used what weapons to attack and armour to defend have been available to them to project, mask and indulge their own weaknesses on to, from and with women in a society constructed by men from the one area of existence in which men are, have always been, superior because of the Musculo-skeletal advantages given to them by nature, namely that of fighting.

When Philip the Good married his third wife, Isabella of Portugal, in 1430, he will not have missed the point that she was half English, schooled and educated by the sister and daughter of the greatest landowners in 15th-century England, namely her mother, Philippa of Lancaster. Class-based hierarchical protocol will have been her second nature. At the height of the Anglo-Burgundian alliance, ideas and practices must have mingled into a superior, Franco-Latin-Anglicised version of the honourable, the noble, the ideal life.

So impressed were the English with Philip's devotion to the honourable way that in 1422 he was invited to become a member of the Order of the Garter. He turned down the honour, judging it, very honourably, to be treason to his feudal overlord, the King of France. To celebrate his wedding, therefore, he created his own Order of the Golden Fleece, very Catholic, very pious and very Gallic.

One of Isabella's ladies-in-waiting, Isabel de Sousa, passed on her knowledge of court etiquette and protocol to her daughter, Alienor de Poitiers, who also served the Dukes of Burgundy becoming *demoiselle d'honneur* to Isabel of Bourbon, second wife of Charles the Bold, Philip's son and successor who also married a descendant of John of Gaunt, Margaret of York his great-granddaughter, and became a Knight of the Garter on their marriage in 1468. In the 1480s Alienor, fearing that the current generation were ignoring the importance of the rules of 'perfect' courtesy, began to write an instruction booklet which was published as *Les Honours de la Cour*. The principle that underwrote her manual was extremely classist by modern standards but endured in Britain, having avoided the Republican revolutions and evolutions in 18th and 19th century western Europe, until the late 20th century; Know your place and act accordingly.

---

148 Ibid.

The pinnacle of courteous behaviour was arguably to be found in 16th century Renaissance Italy from which emerged two of the most widely read books of the era, *Il Principe* (The Prince: written in 1513 but not printed and published until 1532) by Niccolò Machiavelli and *Il Cortegiano* (The Book of the Courtier: printed and published in Venice in 1528 and translated into English by Sir Thomas Hoby in 1561.) by Baldassare Castiglione. Holy Roman Emperor, Charles V, apparently had only three books by his bedside, these two and The Bible. Possibly even more popular was a book written and published in Valladolid in the year Castiglione died, 1529, by yet another soldier-diplomat, this time from Castille, Antonio de Guevara.

The subject matter of *Reloj de principes*, the Dial of Princes, was centred on the wisdom and character of Marcus Aurelius. Finally, the Christianisation of power and kingship was comprehensively covered by the much revered Desiderius Erasmus, a Dutch polymath, who spent much of his life in England, in his book, *Institutio principis Christiani*, 'Education of a Christian Prince', published in 1516.

However, the courtesy book that had the most lasting influence, arguably to the present day, and that marked a real shift in the application of courtesy away from its warrior, chivalric origins to its advice on the social conduct and manners of the descendants of that chivalric warrior class and based on the principle of politeness, the ability to avoid offence in one's language, appearance, bearing and carnal pursuits such as eating and drinking, was written by Giovanni Della Casa, a Florentine courtier, and translated into English in 1576 *Il Galateo, overo de' costume* (Galateo: The Rules of Polite Behaviour). This remarkable book structured the world of culture depicted by and handed down to us in the plays of William Shakespeare.

With all this advice, essentially to men, on acquiring and keeping power (Machiavelli), the wisdom and character to exercise it (Guevara), the perfect manners, the *sprezzatura* (nonchalance, sangfroid) with which to demonstrate it (Castiglione), the Christian piety and morality to do God's work on earth with it (Erasmus) and the rules for flaunting it inoffensively (Della Casa) we should have a good impression of where English women fitted into the whole scheme of things, confident in the assumption that court culture and practice were, via the usual channels of family ties, church synods, diplomatic missions, letters and gossip, well observed and shared throughout Western Europe (apart from his history plays the vast majority of Shakespeare's comedies and tragedies are set in Ancient or Renaissance Europe) even before the advent of the printed word.

In fact, in spite of the obvious progression to a generally accepted, upper-class insistence on these genteel, mannered ways of socialising, which will have included social intercourse with women, we see very few signs of equal treatment or regard. In the conversations that make up the substance of *Il Cortegiano*, women are included, and their opinions listened to, contrary to this advice from Christian culture.

> "Men should not sit and listen to a woman…even if she says admirable things, or even saintly things, that is of little consequence, since it came from the mouth of a woman."[149]

Il Galateo tends to reinforce the Classical, biblical and, therefore, prevailing positioning of women in the domestic sphere and Alienor de Poitiers leans towards the view that women are the memorisers of the chivalric pomp and ceremony of court life—important but only in helping and supporting their male kin. Erasmus totally focused on the education of gentlemen and Machiavelli, unsurprisingly, reflected the prevailing misogyny of the Age. Here is his oft-quoted take on the life impact of luck.

> "I conclude therefore that, fortune being changeful and mankind steadfast in their ways, so long as the two are in agreement men are successful, but unsuccessful when they fall out. For my part I consider that it is better to be adventurous than cautious, because fortune is a woman, and if you wish to keep her under it is necessary to beat and ill-use her; and it is seen that she allows herself to be mastered by the adventurous rather than by those who go to work more coldly. She is, therefore, always, woman-like, a lover of young men, because they are less cautious, more violent, and with more audacity command her."[150]

De Guevara, however, took his readers in another direction. Whereas Machiavelli's Prince was defined, so defined in fact that modern evaluators wonder if his whole analysis was heavily satirical rather than genuinely instructional, but hypothetical, de Guevara constructed his about a real, historical character, Marcus Aurelius, about whom I have written sufficiently already. He does, though, point us in another, possibly helpful, direction.

As a student at the University of Birmingham in the late sixties, it was almost infra dig to be anything other than revolutionary. To remind myself of this persona, I had the temerity to assume, later to become a small part of the real me—the middle-class, do-gooder type of socialist, mockery of whom has become the stock in trade of TV satirists, Conservatives and left-wingers alike. I had prints of Karl Marx and Che Guevara prominently displayed on the walls of my various digs. As you will now see, the temerity, the bravado, the mockery and the 'Poster Boys' are nothing new!

> *Ecclesiastes 1:9 King James Version (KJV)*
> ***9*** *The thing that hath been, it is that which shall be; and that which is done is that which shall be done: and there is no new thing under the sun.*

[149] Fragments on 1 Corinthians – Origen. Accessed 09/03/2019.
[150] *The Prince* Niccolò Macchiavelli.

The mega-wealthy of the middle ages, like the twentieth century state-funded student, also looked to their walls for inspiration. Philip the Good, mega-wealthy Duke of Burgundy enlivened his walls with the luxury wallpaper/posters of the day, tapestries—wall carpets/pictures and posters all-in-ones. Favourite Poster Boys, of course, were God, Jesus, the Apostles, saints and mythical figures with 'Girls' well represented, the most popular being the Virgin Mary. One of the popular themes was The Nine Worthies, noted for their warrior qualities, generalship, chivalry, courage and skill at arms. This culturally balanced triad of triads (3 each from Christianity and Judaism and 3 pagans), the Christian Arthur (*was he real*?), Charlemagne whose, hugely demanding, reported Code of Chivalry is below:

> To fear God and maintain His Church
> To serve the liege lord in valour and faith
> To protect the weak and defenceless
> To give succour to widows and orphans
> To refrain from the wanton giving of offence
> To live by honour and for glory
> To despise pecuniary reward
> To fight for the welfare of all
> To obey those placed in authority
> To guard the honour of fellow knights
> To eschew unfairness, meanness and deceit
> To keep faith
> At all times to speak the truth
> To persevere to the end in any enterprise begun
> To respect the honour of women
> Never to refuse a challenge from an equal
> Never to turn the back upon a foe.[151]

...and Godfrey of Bouillon, The Crusader King, who was the first ruler of Christian Jerusalem, the Jewish Joshua, David and Judas 'The Hammer' Maccabeus and the pagan, Hector (*was he real*?), Alexander the Great and Julius Caesar, was first mentioned in *Les Neuf Preux* in a chanson de geste (a sort of epic poem favoured by medieval minstrels), Les Voeux du Paon (The Vows of the Peacock) written by Jacques de Longuyon in 1312.

These nine remained the role models for chivalric behaviour for three hundred years and more (the subject of mockery in Shakespeare's play, *Love's Labour's Lost,* and most ebulliently lauded in the lyrics of the early 18th century patriotic song 'The British Grenadiers' in which Hector and Alexander the Great are hailed as heroes worthy of comparison with the BGs!). In the late 14th century they were given a French flavour by the notoriously anti-English Eustache Deschamps with the addition of a tenth, unsurprisingly French, Worthy, Bertrand

---

[151] www.baronage.co.uk/chivalry/chival1a.html. Accessed 10/03/2019.

du Guesclin, Constable and saviour of France after the devastating humiliation of Poitiers in 1356.

In the mid-15th century, much of the chivalric glamour of the Burgundian court of Philip the Good and his son, Charles the Bold, was chronicled by a famed chevalier, courtier, traveller and diplomat, Jean Le Fevre de Saint-Remy, King of Arms for The Order of the Golden Fleece. His biographies of Charles the Mad and the 15th century Mohammed Ali, Jacques de Lalaing, confirm this as the Golden Age of Chivalry. *I must digress for a short time to highlight some of the life of Jacques de Lalaing.*

In my previous book, I spoke of my pre-pubescent cinematic heroes—I am compelled to include them all because I simply cannot choose between them; Errol Flynn as Robin Hood and Captain Blood, Robert Taylor as Wilfred of Ivanhoe and Gregory Peck as Captain Horatio Hornblower. The Hollywood iconisation of these fictional heroes and the megastars who brought them to life on the screen must have had its equivalent in the past with a similar impact on the imaginations of the boys of their times, noble ones at least, and, like me, for the generations that followed even in an age before technological advance had brought them the printed word.

Who were the heroes of Henry, Francis and Charles and to what extent did they influence and inspire them? Surely, surely Jacques de Lalaing, megastar knight-errant, was the firm favourite of hundreds of pre-pubescent trainee squires throughout Western Europe (We know that he visited Scotland and England.)

Via Wikipedia, the modern summary of de Lalaing's biography first penned by le Fevre in his 'Livre des Faits de Jacques Lalaing' can be found written by S. Matthew Galas, although he bases his essay on the biography of another Burgundian chronicler, Georges Chastellain.[152] *The account reads like a Harry Carpenter trailer for an Ali fight. Lalaing began his knight-errant fighting career in 1445 when he was 22 years old. In 1449 he travelled to Scotland where he defeated their best knights, and England where Henry VI would not allow him to fight. Later that year in Bruges he set up a pavilion and declared a pas d'armes—he would fight all comers on the first day of every month, aiming to claim 30 victories before his 30th birthday. He beat them all, mostly squires trying to make names for themselves.*

He died at the siege of Poucques Castle in modern day Belgium in 1453, ironically, hit by a cannonball against which even he could not defend himself. He who lived by the sword died by the gun! He was 30 years old and, as far as we know, undefeated in 8 years at the top of his game.

It is life stories such as that of de Lalaing that light up the chivalric culture of his day, which, I think we can affirm now prominently featured the warlike, macho male with the modest, god-fearing, courteous nature. Furthermore, it was

---

[152] www.thearma.org/essays/Lalaing.htm#.XIfL0NT7Rkj. Accessed 11/03/2019.

a culture that expected its leaders to embody its qualities so that when the ten-year-old Henry VI entered Paris for his coronation in 1431, he was preceded by 18 allegorical figures. Poor Henry, his qualities, such as piety, patronage of education and the arts and love of beautiful buildings in the Gothic style, were not what were required by a medieval Warlord and which were far more present in his future French wife, Margaret of Anjou, who bravely and at times ruthlessly fought the Lancastrian corner until her defeat at Tewkesbury and the death of her son finally broke her spirit in 1471.

Margaret is just one of the warrior-spirited women of the 14th and 15th centuries who fought for their men; Queen Isabella, mother of Edward III known as 'The She-wolf of France', Yolande of Aragon, mother-in-law of Charles VII of France, Margaret I of Denmark and Norway, ' the Semiramis of the North', the just mentioned Margaret of Anjou, Jacquetta of Luxembourg, mother-in-law of Edward IV, and her daughter Elizabeth Woodville, mother of Edward V, The Prince in the Tower, Margaret Beaufort, mother of Henry VII and Isabella of Castille, wife of Ferdinand of Aragon and ruler of Castille in her own right. Last of these remarkably powerful, actively political women, mostly remembered for her failure to produce sons, high on the job description of a medieval queen, was the daughter of Ferdinand and Isabella, Catherine of Aragon.

For all Henry VIII's belligerent posturing, warriorlike activity and chivalric extravagance, the greatest victory of his reign, the Battle of Flodden in 1513, was achieved when he was east of Calais fighting the French and Catherine was running the country and defending it against the French ally, Scotland.

These women were not icons as such, then or since, although much more attention has been paid to their lives in the last 50 years, mostly by female historians and novelists seeking to redress the gender imbalance in the presentation of Britain's history. Iconic status for a female monarch was, however, in the wings when in 1558 the Gloriana myth began. If anything, they were women who bought into the prevailing culture, seeking to gain from it rather than uproot it. In a way, also, their political significance perhaps shows some willingness in that culture to allow them a role more contributary than those of submissive wife and mother.

In Chapter 14, I spoke of the enduring longevity of 'The Amazon Fetish'. Any attempt to iconise nine worthy women to balance the nine worthy men tended to involve non-descript Amazons until the late 14th century. Once again, we turn to France. Within the strongly misogynistic tradition that existed in the Middle Ages, originating in both the Classical pagan and early Christian literature, mostly written in Greek or Latin, there was sufficient motivation to translate or adapt essays and treatises on women into vernacular language.

Whatever his motivation, Jehan Le Fevre de Ressons, an officer in the parliaments of Charles V and VI of France (The Wise and The Mad) and contemporary of Eustache Deschamps, translated/adapted the *Lamentations of Matheolus*, a deeply anti-women and anti-marriage Latin text, about a hundred years old. Supposedly riddled by guilt, as a penance, Le Fevre wrote the *Livre de Leesce,* The Book of Joy, in order to counter the misogyny that he felt he had promoted in his adaptation. At one point in the *Lamentations* Matheolus asks the question, "Are there any good women?" His conclusion was that even the wise Solomon could not find one so what chance had he. He goes on to defend the power of examples in a discourse. Renate Blumenfeld-Kosinski in her 1994 article 'Jean Le Fevre's Livre de Leesce: Praise or Blame of Women?' gives us this translation of Matheolus.

> So that my doctrine that I am offering you may appear more clearly to you, I am fashioning examples for you according to the poets that cannot be refuted. When we write of times past, we live through examples. Examples indicate to us how to speak of future times ... An example is a kind of argument often used as an integument in logic and that justifies a discourse.[153]

Faced with the argument that there have been no good women in history Le Fevre was pressured into finding some by putting faces to at least nine in order to balance the nine male worthies. Whether he came up with the feminisation we do not know but *Les Neuf Preuses* began to take shape. Le Fevre went with the flow by choosing five Amazon queens, Antiope, Hippolyte, Melanippe, Lampeto and Penthesilia, and four queens from the ancient world, Semiramis, Tomyris, Leipephilene (sometimes Deiphile) and Teuta. It is possible that his contemporary, Deschamps, came up with the same nine 'Worthy Ladies' and even that these were the allegorical figures in Henry VI's (Henry I of France) coronation procession.

We have a third confirmation that the nine worthy ladies were a widespread 15th century phenomenon. In the Castello della Manta in Piedmont in northern Italy, home of Thomas III of Saluzzo, author of *Le Chevalier Errant*, there is a fresco of *I Novi Prodi* and their female counterparts dating from 1420. Finally, a century later in 1519, the eighteen worthies re-appear in the woodcuts of the Bavarian, Hans Burgkmair, only this time more precisely balanced. The three Christian worthy ladies are Helena, Bridget of Sweden and Elizabeth of Hungary. The three from Jewish history are Esther, Judith and Yael and the three pagans are Lucretia, Veturia and Virginia.

My understanding of an allegory is that it is an exemplary figure, often an abstract, like an emotion or an intellectual, moral or social concept like Reason, Virtue or Justice, into which we read a whole lot more once we recognise what qualities the figure represents. It is and was unlikely that the majority of people who saw the figures in Henry's procession in 1431 would have seen them as anything other than symbolic of a chivalrous king in which the same chivalric qualities, primarily of nobility and martiality, were implied in all eighteen worthies, male and female—the Amazon Fetish. However, Deschamps was not unknown for his polemical satire and irony, including railing against the English, heavy taxation and corruption in the nobility, for which he was eventually

[153] www.jstor.org/stable/3040848?read-now=1&seq=7#page_scan_tab_contents. Accessed 16/03/2019.

sacked. The one Englishman he seems to have liked, his contemporary, Geoffrey Chaucer, was not beyond a mordant satirising of his times.

What if Deschamps, who was debatably antifeminist and died in 1406, looked down on that procession delighting in it as a serious case of the Emperor's new clothes? We can address that 'What if?' with a quick examination of why these women were chosen.

The Amazon sisters, Antiope (*Two sources, at least, have her down as Sinope, who is the subject of her own virginity myth but was not an Amazon. How far back that confusion goes or whether it is me that is wrong only a Professor of Greek myths could answer.*), Hippolyte, Melanippe, Lampetho and Penthesilia all met their ends at the hands of male heroes, the three main culprits being Heracles, Theseus and Achilles, giving an allegorical picture of the feisty woman of noble birth eventually falling in love with the male warrior and/or being subdued by him.

The four warrior queens, Semiramis, Tomyris, Leipephiline and Teuta, respectively Babylonian/Assyrian, Scythian, Hellenic and Illyrian, were either mythical or accorded mythical status in most great ancient cultures, Persia, Greece and Rome. All fought against great patriarchies but were eventually subdued despite their wisdom, their ability to rule, their beauty or their skill at arms. The Florentine Giovanni Boccaccio who compiled one of the first lists of famous women *De Mulieribus Claris* (On Famous Women) in the mid-14th century (more of him in a later chapter) said this of Penthesilia, "through practice, Penthesilia and women like her became much more manly in arms than those born male"[154], implying that chivalry required constant training and commitment so that even women could, if so trained, become effective killers, *with the caveat, of course, that the best trained male killer, Achilles, had beaten Penthesilia despite her exceptional, but female, skill and courage.*

In the latter half of the 15th century, a tenth female worthy, Joan of Arc, was added.

Joan's notoriety stems from her historical significance as a war hero which she undisputedly was. Her show trial was a disgraceful demonstration of political expediency over Christian, chivalric, moral virtue. Joan was not executed for opposing and being instrumental in defeating the Anglo-Burgundians, the normal reaction to which would have been ransom. She was tried in an ecclesiastical court for heresy. Heresy was only punishable by death if the accused heretic had committed the offence having ignored a warning. In effect the court required a second instance.

In Joan's case, she was accused of dressing like a man by wearing hose and tunic and wearing her hair short. On Greek pottery, Amazons were depicted wearing armour and Penthesilia must have worn armour for Achilles to have fallen in love with her beautiful face after removing her helmet. In the Castello della Manta, the female worthies although linked by their warlike reputations are

---

154 en.wikipedia.org/wiki/Penthesilea. Accessed 17/03/2019.

all dressed in the height of women's fashions. Again, we have this extreme confusion in the world of men about the position and purpose of women.

About 200 years later, in 1615, the definitive example of Amazonomachy (Amazons at war) the *Battaglia delle Amazzone* by Rubens (or maybe Van Dyke) has a confusing mixture of naked, unarmed, trousered and armoured female warriors, a confusion common at the turn of the 17th century on the Stage in which a number of Shakespeare's heroines, such as Viola and Portia, involved boys playing women pretending to be men. *Hm!*

Burgkmair's nine ladies matched the male triad of triads. His three Christians, Helena, Bridget and Elizabeth, were noted for their piety not their martial skills. His three from the Jewish faith, Esther, Judith and Yael, were killers of Israel's enemies but not soldiers, Esther by persuading her Persian husband to allow the Jews to kill their enemies, Judith by decapitating the Assyrian King, Holofernes, and Yael by driving a nail into the skull of the Canaanite general, Sisera. His three pagans were all from the writings of the Roman historian, Livy; Lucretia, whose rape and suicide led to the revolt that instituted the Roman Republic, Veturia, the mother of Coriolanus whose persuasion of her son to make peace with Rome led to him being killed by his own people and Virginia, whose father killed her rather than let her become the mistress of a Roman nobleman thus causing a revolt that saved the Republic. Piety, loyalty and fidelity seem to link these nine rather than warriorship, seemingly defining honour away from the context of fighting.

Reading between the lines, Boccaccio was concerned that some nobles, defined by their warrior status were becoming soft, as indeed they were. Courtesy, the art of being noble, was taking over from chivalry, the purpose of being noble. We can see this in the de-militarisation of the concept of 'gallantry' which, by the end of the 18th century had acquired a secondary gendered meaning 'Polite attention or respect given by men to women' and then by the end of the 19th century was displaced by the ungendered word 'civility' meaning 'politeness and courtesy in behaviour or speech'.

Conclusion

Many things lay behind the transition from medieval chivalry to modern civility. The advent of gunpowder, guns and cannon, made the face-to-face nature of warfare less of a deciding factor. An opponent's death became more of a long-range thing, no longer involving the crunch of bones, the screams of pain, the sight and taste of blood and the smell of fear. Increasing trade meant more wealth and more cities. Armies could be paid for or made up from citizens desperate to save their homes and livelihoods. Keeping up with the noble Joneses was far more important than fighting them.

Once committed to blood first, from a sanctioned Christian marriage, as the dominant principle of inheritance, discontinuity through death or infant mortality gave noblewomen more important roles as regents, as widowed sources of finance or as marital bargaining chips and, eventually by 1553, queens in their own right, in an England, of course, that was never that convinced by the Salic principle.

Last but not least, despite Henry VIII's desperation to be a Renaissance Prince, chivalry had always been a continental culture, borrowed from the Normans and their descendants, the Plantagenets, and fuelled by the Hundred Years War. He did not lose that war but, according to establishment history, in order to divorce a wife unable to bear him sons, he took England away from that cultural sphere, never to return. Its last flowerings were at The Field of Cloth of Gold and in the language of Shakespeare's history plays. England spent most of the 17th century ridding itself of absolute monarchy, the full splendour of which was to be found in 18th century France before it came crashing down around its ears in 1789. Its culture of social behaviour, however, has had a lasting impact to this very day to such an extent that the great empires of Portugal, Spain, France and Britain felt that they brought civilisation to the world when all it was, in reality, was civility. They were still themselves learning the four cornerstones of civilised behaviour, peace, justice, equality and respect, with the most glaringly obvious group to whom they were denied being women.

The triumph of appearance over reality that chivalry/courtesy/civility represented/represents is replicated in most human social behaviour, the ability to deceive being a key survival technique. The eradication of the impossibility of meeting its medium and long term requirements and goals was always going to be a work-in-progress which it still is but I remain convinced that it is a male w-i-p and that one of the most important areas of civilising change has to be a fundamental re-orientation of the male attitude and behaviour towards women. We live today with the stereotypes, icons and allegories that have emerged from the Golden Age of Chivalry—'The Chevalier'; The Courtier; The Knight Errant; King Arthur; the 'English Gentleman'; the 'Southern [as in states of America] Gentleman' and the 'Band on the Titanic'—without really taking on board their mythical status and the masculine self-delusion and hypocrisy that they represent.

Their literary appeal has been intellectualised as the 'rara avis topos' (the rare bird theme). In every civilised and restrained English Gentleman Doctor Jekyll there was a Mr. Hyde and, in London alone, some 80,000 prostitutes to cater for his less gentlemanlike and less restrained inclinations. The Southern Gentlemen presided over and justified a regime of slavery. The chivalrous Duke of Bedford and Philip the Good allowed the travesty of justice that led to the burning of Joan of Arc.

Chapter 20
Misogyny

Men should not sit and listen to a woman…even if she says admirable things, or even saintly things, that is of little consequence, since it came from the mouth of a woman.
Fragments on 1 Corinthians—Origen

I'm just a person trapped inside a woman's body.
– Elayne Boosler

Gallantry is often a cloak for contempt.
– Elizabeth Peters

Preamble

I would be absolutely amazed if I said anything new about the phenomenon known as 'Misogyny'. The discourse on it has involved philosophers, divines, intellectuals, academics, psychologists and psychiatrists, anthropologists and sociologists, potentates and democrats, feminists, anti-feminists, press and pornographers, playwrights and novelists, poets and singers, judges and juries, sexists and egalitarians, good and bad, men and women.

Therefore, I am going to stay true to my quest for evidence and elucidation of sexual inequality in British society by examining grounds to refute the commonly held view about the evolution of cultural practice and thinking that misogynists were men of their times, more culturally primitive than 21st century man, who knew no better and so were not deliberately or knowingly seeking to gain an advantage of power over women; just doing what they were brought up to do and think.

Secondly, as I have been doing for many chapters now, I will, somewhat prejudicially because of my already emotional, intellectual and personal horror at the unequal nature of British society, outline my understanding of the roots of sexism in our society.

Misogyny comes from Ancient Greek, of course, and, as we all know, means hatred of women. The emotional intensity of hate, I believe, depends on the circumstances that influence an individual, whether by nature or nurture, although large groupings of like-minded individuals can promote its social importance beyond the cultural norms for that society, nation, race or gender. I tend towards Aristotle's definition in which he identifies in 'Hate' the strong desire to destroy, annihilate the hated object. I am sure that such misogynistic psychopaths and sociopaths capable of such hate exist/ed in all cultures and their existence, therefore, makes cultural misogyny seem a less intense yet more pervasive social phenomenon.

The nuances in the synonyms for hatred, dislike, loathing, disgust, contempt, disdain, disrespect and prejudice, are more useful in identifying cultural misogyny because they highlight the cultural rather than physical destructiveness of its ascription by men to women of weakness, physical and intellectual inferiority, inadequacy, unsuitability, uncleanliness, ignorance, emotional and carnal lack of restraint and general unworthiness, rather than a desire for their total obliteration. The longevity and ubiquity of cultural misogyny or sexism, if you prefer, has at least five possible explanations:

- Ruthless and tenacious retention of power by males by all possible means.
- The social result of biological differences.
- Part of God's design of human beings.
- A complementarity of gender roles happily and willingly accepted as essential by both genders and only made less necessary by contraception.
- A process of social evolution exactly like that of physical characteristics.

I have explored the middle three at some length in previous chapters leaving the first and last as opposing possibilities. To accept the last possibility over the first requires sympathetic thinking that involves some serious hijacking of evolutionary science as we know it.
Firstly, I refuse to accept that the intellectual capability of humans 3000 years ago, at the start of recorded history, was one jot inferior to that of modern humans. Secondly, their observation and rationalisation of the world around them was no less keen and insightful than they are now. Thirdly, their ability to debate and convince, their political acumen, if you like, was no less rational and articulate than it is now. All of which implies that their lack of science and technology, particularly anatomy and genetics, meant that the powers-that-be, aka. Men, were unaware of women's abilities and capabilities or unaware of women's aspirations to use them more widely and usefully or convinced that the complementarity and inferiority of a woman's social role was how nature, God's creation, meant it to be. There was no malign intention to have a misogynistic or sexist attitude towards women because no one thought it was wrong, including women. I cannot accept that.

There are many supporters of the view that, on the whole, the Ancient Greeks were misogynistic. If that were the case, one could extrapolate and argue that the Romans followed their cultural example in this respect and then attribute much of the blame for misogynistic tendencies in Western European culture on the whole-hearted acquisition of Classical culture, including disdain for women, without any real challenge. Again, we are back to an apology the essence of which was that male attitudes and treatment of women were due to the Classical foundations of Western civilisation which naturally saw women as inferior beings until challenged by 19th century science and education.

We need to take into consideration these four contextual realities. Firstly, Classical Greek literature was, in fact, Classical Athenian literature (the great Spartan lyric poet, Alcman, for instance, wrote in the Doric dialect which was even less studied than the Attic dialect on which the lingua franca of Alexander the Great's 4th century BC empire, Koine Greek, was based and in which the early editions of the Bible were written) and then, for the purposes of medieval education, presented in a canon rather than a broad range of texts. Furthermore, its authors—philosophers, historians, poets and playwrights—were from an educated and privileged male elite, a fact well hidden by Western European historians, politicians and tract writers with their championing of the all-conquering ideal of Athenian democracy and the corresponding autocracy and military obsession of its nemesis, Sparta. Indeed, there is much evidence to support the view that the Athenian city state or polis was more misogynistic than Sparta and other competing Greek cities.

Secondly, until the Renaissance, translators of Greek dialects were very thin on the ground and the teaching of Latin, a medieval lingua franca, was mostly for grammatical rather than literary purposes.

Thirdly, learning was very much in the hands of the Church and, therefore, subject to its selection and censorship of texts. Therefore, until the Renaissance, any misogynistic views may have been expressed in Latin but were likely to have been more local and personal in origin. The Latin language had long since lost its assumed link with Roman culture and become, as pointed out in the previous point, a medieval lingua franca which few scholars and writers outside the ambit of the Christian church used.

Lastly, most of the Ancient Greek texts were Byzantine or lower Egyptian copies, probably commissioned by wealthy patrons, nearly all fragmented by age and rarely representative of an ancient writer's complete output.

Tempted though I am to digress into this brilliantly interesting world of papyrus scrolls, parchments, vellum and codices, I will simply recommend a very interesting website of the British Library, www.bl.uk, and explode two myths. That the Greeks were the first to store written knowledge is simply not true. Sumerian, Assyrian, Babylonian, Egyptian and Persian civilisations all stored knowledge in Libraries. That Ancient Greek knowledge written down on papyrus scrolls and stored in the Great Library in Alexandria was destroyed in a cataclysmic fire started by Julius Caesar or Aurelian is also a myth giving rise to copycat acts of book-burning such as occurred in Nazi Germany in 1933 or the brilliant 1953 novel by Ray Bradbury, 'Fahrenheit 451'.

We are left, therefore, with fragmentary copies of Athenian scripts of some poets, Hesiod and Homer, some playwrights, the golden four, Aeschylus, Sophocles, Euripides and Aristophanes and the three great philosophers, Socrates, Plato and Aristotle. Their cultural impact on Western European society was/is immense and prolonged. It was prolonged precisely because there was a debate, a difference of approach, a clash of views and forces for conserving tradition and the status quo and forces for change both radical and moderate. Within the presentation of the debate in drama, art or philosophy women and sex were very much foregrounded to the extent that no medieval or renaissance scholar, educator or philosopher king could have missed it. Therefore, if medieval, post-Christianised culture was derived from the Ancient Greeks and Romans, or at least a partial, male reading of it, it was by choice not by an unavoidable natural or social evolution.

Chapter 21
Misogyny in the Classics

From her is the race of women and female kind:
of her is the deadly race and tribe of women who
live amongst mortal men to their great trouble,
no helpmates in hateful poverty, but only in wealth.
– Hesiod, *Works and Days*

Of all creatures that can feel and think,
we women are the worst treated things alive.
– Euripides, *Medea*

Preamble

What might students—outside a career in the Church, they would have been from noble families until the 17th century—have been taught from this group of Greeks? The wealth of Classical scholarship amazes and fascinates me but you might not feel the same so I will stick to my theme while possibly enlightening you in the basics!

The earliest of the group, though disputed, is possibly the epic poet, Hesiod. His two less disputed poems are the *Theogony*, a sort of instructional history of the Olympian Gods, and *Works and Days*, a moan about what hard work farming is. Hesiod was no appreciator of women. The reasons, although wrapped up in his polytheistic creation myth, should contribute to an understanding of why men treat women as they do. For my own enlightenment I am principally indebted to Patricia A. Marquardt.[155]

In his own genealogy of the Olympian gods (Marquardt accepts he has collected various myths from different cultures but thinks it is his own construction), Hesiod introduces us to two female figures of the utmost importance, Aphrodite, the immortal goddess of all things to do with Love and Sex, and Pandora, the first woman, God-given but mortal. Neither of these women, the immortal goddess and the human beauty was conceived in the usual, allogamous way.

According to Hesiod, Aphrodite arose out of the sea foam caused by the genitals of Uranus, the sky-god, which his son Cronus, the youngest of the

[155] Marquardt, Patricia A. "Hesiod's Ambiguous View of Woman." *Classical Philology*, vol. 77, no. 4, 1982, pp. 283–291. *JSTOR*, www.jstor.org/stable/269412. Accessed 02/05/2019.

Titans, had cut off and thrown over his shoulder into the sea. Pandora was fashioned from the earth by Hephaistos, god of artisans, at the order of Zeus, son of Cronos and King of the Olympian Gods. Pandora was Zeus's way of evening things up after Prometheus, mankind's advocate among the gods, had stolen fire and given it to humans. She was their punishment for accepting fire, a bad thing that seemed irresistibly beautiful and good to balance the wonderful gift of fire, a good thing that unmanaged could bring unimaginable destruction.

The other advocate for mankind among the Gods was Prometheus's brother, Epimetheus, who was as stupid as his brother was clever. Despite being warned by his brother not to accept any gifts from Zeus Epimetheus accepted Pandora who brought with her a pithos, a large storage jar (No, not a box! The mistranslation is often attributed to Desiderius Erasmus, the 16th century Dutch humanist, in his *Adagia* written in 1508 *which, at least, proves the works of Hesiod were of interest to medieval scholars!*), which contained all the evils that could afflict mankind including death and the causes of death such as sickness and plague.

Nosy Pandora took the lid off—Erasmus says it was her partner, Epimetheus—and they all escaped, making humans mortal and ending The Golden Age of all-male immortality, pleasure and plenty. Subsequent myths complete the story by repeating the Flood myth. Only two humans survived the Deluge, Deucalion, the son of Prometheus, the clever one, and Pyrrha, the daughter of Epimetheus, the accident-prone not so clever one, and Pandora. *Hm!*

Patricia Marquardt sees more in all this, an indicator of which can be found in these lines 590-3 of *Works and Days:*

> From her is the race of women and female kind:
> of her is the deadly race and tribe of women who
> live amongst mortal men to their great trouble,
> no helpmates in hateful poverty, but only in wealth.[156]

There are elements in Hesiod's interpretation of the Pandora myth that suggest she was a sort of Earth Goddess whose opening up of the earth to be exploited for food and shelter brought life to agricultural communities but only with backbreaking hardship and toil. She also brought death through natural disasters, plagues and famines. As the first woman Pandora brought happiness and sorrow. She brought sexual satisfaction and children but became a drain on resources in times of economic hardship. Her beauty and sexual seductiveness were part of a cruel deception that, all too often, ended in tears. The assets of her beauty were enhanced by the God-given gift of speech which added to the deception in her long-term goal of wearing out her man and taking over his property. The enhancement of their allure with beautiful clothes and enticing company was too expensive for a poor man and, therefore, of no practical use.

[156] Ibid.

> The complexity of Hesiod's view of feminine nature serves as a focus for his anxiety about life in general. Aphrodite, as we have seen, is the procreative urge essential to the human race, as well as deception and seduction. Pandora carries with her the inevitability of hardship and misery, but she is also sexual beauty, which is intrinsically good. There is a direct correlation between the chthonic, unpredictable nature of Pandora as earth-goddess and the economically "evil", deceptive nature of Pandora as woman. As earth-goddess, Pandora means life and death to those who depend on her; as woman, she means happiness and sorrow. This shows how for Hesiod the basic fact of uncertainty in life is seen embodied in femininity. The great and necessary gifts granted by women, especially food and sexual pleasure, are negative as often as positive. There is nothing to which man can completely give himself.[157]

In Hesiod, we begin to see the elements of the sexist treatment of women in Western European culture by which British culture, sorry to keep reminding you, has been strongly influenced:

- *The challenge and consequences of choosing an agricultural lifestyle.*
- *Its cultural origins in the Near East.*
- *The general anxiety it brought to men.*
- *The self-denial in men of the sexual power of women.*
- *The vulnerability to that power of the male ego.*
- *The physical competition that sex presented to carving out a living from agriculture.*
- *The need to blame.*
- *The fear of losing control of the life process.*
- *The narcissism of the male ego.*
- *The rational need in men to defend their way of running the group of humans to which they belonged.*

*When all or some of these subconscious thoughts and feelings were recognised in an individual, Sigmund Freud would have suspected the employment of a defence mechanism he called projection—**Psychological projection** is a defence mechanism in which the human ego defends itself against unconscious impulses or qualities (both positive and negative) by denying their existence in themselves while attributing them to others.*[158]

The Hesiodic view and creation narrative contain enough material of a misogynistic nature to, along with its Hebrew contemporary, the Torah, confirm the hypothesis that misogyny goes back a long way. The female was to blame for mankind's mortality, suffering and sinfulness. For as long as Western European culture has been dominated by an all-male elite, and many would argue

[157] Ibid.

[158] en.wikipedia.org/wiki/Psychological_projection. Accessed 07/05/2019.

that it still is, that particular view, ancient though its origins are, that misogynistic view, has carried some weight with a significant number of men.

Hesiod's contemporary, Homer, an epic poet, an essential read in the canon of Western European literature, projected a different picture of women in his epic poems based on the legendary Trojan War and its aftermath. To begin with, *The Iliad*, his poem about the destruction of Troy, has plenty of female personalities; Helen (Was she abducted by the Trojan prince, Paris, or did they elope?), Andromache and Hecabe, the noble wives and mothers, and Briseis, Chryseis and Cassandra, the noble women made captive slaves and concubines.

The general consensus among academic commentators is that Homer foregrounds the depths of their feelings and emotions, recognising them as fully rounded persons, able to be active but forced to be passive, not the objects that the men in their lives make them out to be. Homer gives them a voice which expresses opinions to which their men do not listen just as Cassandra's prophecies come true but are never believed. In his 1979 article, 'The Portrayal of Women in the Iliad', on the South African website of the journal, *Acta Classica*, Farron makes all of these points and provides an example of the complementarity of male and female roles. Andromache, Hector's wife offers him some sound advice on military tactics which will have the added bonus of him reducing his chances of being killed by Achilles to which Hector, loving husband and family man, replies:

> "But go into the house and take care of your own work, the loom and the distaff, and bid your servants to go about their work. But war will be the concern of the men." (490-492).[159]

Dame Mary Beard, Cambridge academic, writer and documentary maker, in her lecture, *The Public Voice of Women*, which combined with a second lecture, *Women in Power*, made up her book, *Women and Power: A Manifesto*, has made famous a similar pronouncement in Homer's other great epic poem, *The Odyssey*, made by Telemachus, adolescent son of Odysseus, to his mother, Penelope. A bard is singing to an audience of her suitors—arrogant, extravagant spongers—about the problems that Greek heroes are having getting home from the Trojan War. Penelope does not like it and tells him to sing about happier things:

[159] casa-kvsa.org.za/1979/AC22-06-Farron.pdf. Accessed 08/05/2019.

> At which point young Telemachus intervenes: 'Mother', he says, 'go back up into your quarters, and take up your own work, the loom and the distaff… speech will be the business of men, all men, and of me most of all; for mine is the power in this household.[160]

In the world of Homer, therefore, it is clear that women managed the household and remained in their domain, the home. Their skills related to making cloth, spinning and weaving. Men instructed them as to what they should do, where they should be and, most significantly, when they should speak. Speaking in public and going to war were the exclusive preserves of men in this archetypal warrior culture.

Gendered roles and warrior culture, complementarity, would persist as long as warfare was the primary survival strategy, yet there is no real sign of misogyny in these two epic poems in which women, immortal and human, more than play their part as rounded, reasoning, feeling people who do push the boundaries—the goddess, Aphrodite, fights; Hera, wife of Zeus, king of the Gods, while not as powerful, still gives him a good run for his money; Andromache, Hector's wife, has an opinion on battlefield tactics; the semi-goddesses, Calypso and Circe rule their own magical domains in which men do what they say and it is a goddess, Athena, who has control over the fate of Odysseus—sufficiently to suggest an awareness in the male poet that they have the capability to participate in a man's world if not the right.

Homer, therefore, seemed to be edging away from the 'blameworthy—sex object—reproductively necessary but economically draining' characterisation of Hesiod's Pandora/farmer's wife 'Woman'. His women have characters as well as vaginas and are people as well as property. Their qualities, epitomised by Penelope, are fidelity, constancy, loyalty and devotion. They simply cannot help the seductiveness of their beauty. It is God-given. Homer's male heroes are morally and ethically flawed humans although excused, to some extent, by their being the playthings of the Gods. Frankly, much of their behaviour is appalling but excused because of their ability to slaughter their enemies, outwit the Gods and win battles. Hector, the moral hero, the 'good' man, is Trojan not Greek and is killed by the petulant, sulky, savage, woman-hating Achilles. Helen, beautiful and remorseful, seeks forgiveness for her behaviour but Paris, beautiful but feckless, playing out his fate and cursed by the Gods, does not.

Some 300 years later in democratic Athens, we get some more modern insights into the perceptions of women's social impact. *Continuing with my assumption that ancient and medieval people's emotional and intellectual make-up were no different from ours it is not fanciful to assume that, in their world without television and mobile phones, they still made choices about how they spent their time and followed 'popular' trends and recommendations much as we do today.*

---

[160] books.google.co.uk/books/about/Women_Power.html?id=6dU2DwAAQBAJ&printsec=frontcover&source =kp read button&redir esc=y#v=onepage&q&f =false. Accessed 14/05/2019.

Although, therefore, there are many other fragmented writings of many other Athenian playwrights we tend, as probably did Roman and medieval consumers of Greek literature, to concentrate on the big four, all spanning about a hundred years and all living in 'The Golden Age' of Athens in the 5th and 4th centuries BC, Aeschylus, Sophocles, Euripides and the comedian, Aristophanes. All were men; all were from the Athenian elite (Only 10-20% of Athenians had political rights which excluded women, slaves, foreigners and children).

Women figured widely in Athenian tragedies, many of which were eponymously named—e.g., *Iphigenia* (Euripides), *Electra* (Sophocles, Euripides), *Antigone* (Sophocles), *Medea* (Euripides) and *Hecuba* (Euripides)—or contain the word 'Women' in the title—e.g., *Women of Trachis* (Sophocles), *The Trojan Women* and *The Phoenician Women* (Euripides). The inspiration for these extant tragedies is frequently the aftermath of the Trojan War, just as war has inspired and is inspiring much of our drama today, yet to me, rightly or wrongly, there is a whole set of questions being asked about family life, a sort of soap opera, which inevitably involves women. Women are largely wronged by men, otherwise heroic men, but do not take it lying down (*No double entendre intended, please*!).

- In the *Oresteia* trilogy, by Aeschylus, the Greek hero from The Trojan War, Agamemnon, kills his daughter, Iphigenia, to get a fair wind to Troy (although Euripides chooses to say she was spirited away in his play, *Iphigenia in Tauris*), and turns up with a younger woman concubine, Cassandra, his war trophy from the victory over Troy. His son, Orestes, egged on by his sister, Electra, murders his mother, Clytemnestra, for murdering his father.
- In *Oedipus Rex* by Sophocles, the hero kills his father in a road rage incident, marries the mother, Jocasta, who gave him away and, by his actions, is the cause of a deadly plague.
- In *Antigone*, also by Sophocles, the king, Creon, refuses funeral rights to both Antigone's brothers, puts her to death thus causing the death of his son and then his wife.
- In *The Women of Trachis*, one of Sophocles' less well-known plays, Herakles tries to sneak his younger woman, Iole, into his home as a slave having lied to his wife, Deianira, about what he was doing while away at war.
- In *Hecuba* by Euripides, the Greeks, enslave Hecuba, Queen of Troy, allow her daughter, Polyxena, to be sacrificed in honour of their hero, Achilles, and refuse to support her in her case against their ally, Polymestor, who killed her son, Polydorus, in order to steal his treasure.
- In *Medea* the action hero, Jason, having retrieved the Golden Fleece, with, according to the myth, Medea's sorcery skills having played a decisive role in him completing all the tasks he had to accomplish, left her, a foreign princess, for the Greek daughter of Creon, Glauce, thus breaking his promise to marry Medea if she helped him. *What a rotter*!

These wronged women like Iphiginea, Clytemnestra, Electra, Jocasta, Antigone, Hecuba and Medea are key elements of 5th century BC Athenian tragedy as direct avengers or vehicles for vengeance for the wrongs otherwise heroic men have committed. Four of them, Clytemnestra, Electra, Hecuba and Medea are murderers or conspirators in a murder. The other three die as victims of patriarchy. The patriarchal men involved in their tragic stories all suffer terrible fates as if Greek tragedy had/has a message for men in power: Disrespect the woman/women in your life at your peril! It cannot have been lost on the all-male audience of this fictional genre written by men for men and performed by an all-male troop of actors. Although there is no promotion of gender equality in Greek tragedy, to its readers and spectators it conveyed the morals and ethics of chivalry rather than misogyny.

Aristophanes, however, wrote comic plays that lampooned any trends towards modernity, ridiculing new-fangled ideas and philosophies as pretentiousness, with such a heavy use of irony and satire that he dares us to take what he says seriously. Two of his plays, *Thesmophoriazusae* and *Lysistrata,* placed women at the centre of the plot.

In the former, the one with the long name (Aristophanes plays with some other long names in *Lysistrata*, mostly caricaturing female artisans like the *seed-market-porridge-vegetable-sellers* and the *garlic-innkeeping-bread-sellers,* perhaps suggesting that noble women may have been occupied running their homes and having children but that those less well-off not only did all that but worked for a living, very much in public view! *Hm!*), he parodies the tragic playwright, Euripides, for depicting women as so scary—'mad, murderous, and sexually depraved'[161] —that the poet himself, who is a character in the play, fears being killed by them. At an all-women fertility festival, the women meet to decide how to respond.

In farcical manner, Euripides sends a spy disguised as a woman to ascertain what the women intend for him. The spy discovers the women meeting in a democratically constituted council, much like a citizen's Ecclesia to be found in everyday Athenian politics, except that they were men-only affairs. In the debate that follows two women air their accusations against Euripides both citing absurd reasons why his portrayal of women has damaged their lives. The spy, *in the reality of the moment, remember, a man playing a man pretending to be a woman in an assembly of women being portrayed by men (Is that funny-ha-ha or funny-peculiar? Hm!)*, then argues that Euripides' characterisation is pretty accurate by telling stories about her morally reprehensible behaviour. Enter a messenger, a homosexual transvestite, who exposes the ruse, and the male spy is arrested and imprisoned for the blasphemy of being at a women-only festival.

After a number of farcical attempts to release the spy, using well known characters from the playwright Euripides' plays, the character Euripides negotiates a peace with the women who agree not to interfere with any escape plans. The plan that works involves the distraction of the prison guard with a

---

[161] en.wikipedia.org/wiki/Thesmophoriazusae. Accessed 08/06/2019.

sexy dancing girl (played by a male) and the misdirection of the pursuing posse by the women.

Whether Aristophanes is mocking men or women, old or new, strong or weak did and does depend on where you were/are coming from and the baggage you, the viewer, were/are bringing to your judgement. The play's motivation was certainly an internecine enmity between a tragic and a comic playwright. The battlefield was drama not gender and his weapons were a lampooning use of parody, sarcasm and caricature not misogyny. Whether it was the double bluff, merely appearing to ridicule challenges to the male dominant status quo while actually ridiculing it, criticising it and showing off its ludicrosities depended/s on the viewer.

There is clear evidence, however, and this is my point, that 2400 years ago, at the very foundations of Western culture there was an alternative and strong view of women and their political capabilities and possibilities that somehow did not get off the ground.

In *Lysistrata*, Aristophanes takes this challenging motif one step further with a 'What if?'. What if women had the upper hand, real power (*Remember The Two Ronnies.*)? The eponymous heroine has the idea that women on both sides of the conflict between Athens and Sparta, known to history as the Peloponnesian War, could make their men stop the fighting by refusing to let them have sex until they made peace. With her Spartan ally, Lampita, Lysistrata calls a sex strike. Meanwhile, old women manage to occupy the city treasury denying the government the money to buy weapons. After various farcical exchanges involving men with large 'bundles' under their tunics and a magistrate of the old school who lays the blame for the strike on men who cannot control their womenfolk the men give in and peace is made between men and men and between men and women.

Much scholarly effort has gone into analysing this play a review of which I am not competent to write even if I had the time or space. Only Aristophanes knew what his real message was. Was it about sex, war, government, patriarchy or all or none of them? Did it honour or show disdain for women? Like all art the interpretation lies with the individual who experiences it. There is something enduring about the motifs of the sex strike, the gender role reversal, gender stereotyping and, even, men in drag that western culture has generally found amusing. Maybe that was all Aristophanes was attempting to be.

What the play does show is that, even in powerful, misogyny-tending cultures, there was a publicly acknowledged appreciation by men of women's power, women's political views and women's sexuality. Whether that induced fear or love, respect or disdain was tested out in *Lysistrata* for centuries to come. Its challenge to sexism, intended or unintended, has been largely unrecorded for two and a half millennia while its fictional whimsy has been much copied without any of these fundamental questions being answered until very recently, yet it is difficult to deny, which, in itself, is of huge significance to the history of women, that from the 5th century BC, the concept and components of 'Girl Power' were out there, in a fictional world if not in reality.

Chapter 22
The Philosophers: Aristotle

...from the hour of their birth, some are marked out for subjection, others for rule.

...the male is by nature superior, and the female inferior...

For although there may be exceptions to the order of nature, the male is by nature fitter for command than the female...

For the slave has no deliberative faculty at all; the woman has, but it is without authority, and the child has, but it is immature...

Silence is a woman's glory.
Extracts from Aristotle's *Politics*, Book 1

Preamble

In this Golden Age of Athens, however, intellectuals were also very good at searching for the fundamental source of knowledge and reality; in fact, they invented the word for the study of them—philosophy. The canon of Ancient Greek philosophy elevates above the many others three 5th and 4th century BC Athenian philosophers, Socrates (d. 399 BCE) whom, wisely favouring the spoken word over the written word as a vehicle of truth and thus writing nothing down, we mostly know through his lampooning critic, Aristophanes, and his two pupils, Plato and Xenophon; Plato (d.347 BCE), Socrates' more adoring student, whose philosophy was often propounded out of the mouth of his hero, and, therefore, his hero as a literary character, in Plato's fictional dialogues; and Aristotle (d.322 BCE), Plato's student and possible educator of Alexander the Great.

The two most studied books were/are Plato's Republic in which the literary character, Socrates, in conversation with his student friends tries to construct the components of a perfectly virtuous State and Aristotle's Politics in which, in instructional format, he tries to do much the same. Aristotle's ideas were influential in the Western Roman Empire and, thus, in medieval Western Europe whereas Plato's went the other way to the Eastern, later to become Byzantine, Empire and only made their way west in full after the fall of Byzantium in 1453 CE.

They were, however, clearly an influence on Roman political thinking. Cicero, in his work on the Roman constitution, De Re Publica, written in 51/50

BCE, imitates Plato and the method of the Socratic dialogue. As Reason and Science began to replace God and Belief the writings of these three ancient world thinkers formed a baseline, a starting point almost, from which the modern track to such revolutionary movements as egalitarianism and feminism began.

As the point of view that I have taken or want to take is that of the historic consumer rather than that of the historic or present-day analyser, my chronological sequencing will come from who came first in terms of influence on Western European readers—Aristotle, Plato—rather than whose life and literary production preceded the other—Plato, Aristotle.

We need a likely candidate for a powerful ruler who could have read Greek philosophers and been influenced by what they said and, having analysed it on his own, with educators or with advisers, used his power to advance the status of women, maintain the status quo or set it back for misogynistic reasons; and we have one who was English, royal, intellectual, learned, literate and a lawmaker.

Alfred the Great was a king for 28 years, 871-899 CE, first of Wessex and then of Anglo-Saxon England. Although we are told that the only scholars at this time who were able to translate Greek resided in Ireland there is no reason to believe that Alfred, a very outward-looking king, was unable to access Aristotle's *Politics*. Alfred went to Rome twice in his lifetime and, on the second occasion, spent time at the court of the King of the Franks, Charles the Bald. He would almost certainly have spoken Latin in which case he would have been able to access via borrowing or receiving as a gift a translation by someone like Boethius whose *Consolation of Philosophy* was a medieval bestseller or one of the Islamic scholars via the Muslim Caliphate of Cordoba that covered modern day Portugal and south and central Spain and definitely engaged in transfers of cultural ideas and practices with the Frankish Empire to the north.

If Alfred had read or obtained a copy of *Politics*, he would surely, in an age without Coronation Street or Twitter, have shared the gist of it, at the very least, with his court. What would he have learnt about women from Aristotle?

In *Politics*, Aristotle philosophises about the perfect State by considering its component parts. He begins by looking at households, as a State is a collection of households. In household management which he is happy to call 'rule' there are three relationships and one necessary task, the accumulation of sufficient wealth to house, clothe and feed all the family. Of the three relationships—master/slave, husband/wife and father/child—he deals with the first before the others *which says something about the level of concern for gender issues amongst the male elite.* His egalitarian credentials appear in this discussion.

Author's note

I am not even going to attempt to analyse the text in order to convince you of the non-egalitarian, anti-feminist or misogynistic nature of its reasoning. The words speak for themselves and will probably confirm your opinions on these issues, make you reconsider them or leave you just as confused as you were before! My understanding of the logical sequence will be in bold print. The *translation that I have found is by Benjamin Jowett (1817-1893), a renowned Oxford scholar, friend, as we shall see, of Florence Nightingale, and Classics professor of the Victorian era, conservative but liberal enough for his translation to be reasonably objective. The number of typos suggests that his translation has been transcribed for the website <classics.mit.edu> The Internet Classics Archive which is the source of my quotations.*

What is a slave?

> 'Hence, we see what the nature and office of a slave is; he who is by nature not his own but another's man, is by nature a slave; and he may be said to be another's man who, being a human being, is also a possession. And a possession may be defined as an instrument of action, separable from the possessor.' (Book 1, Part IV)

Is a slave a natural creation?

> 'But is there any one thus intended by nature to be a slave, and for whom such a condition is expedient and right, or rather is not all slavery a violation of nature?
> There is no difficulty in answering this question, on grounds both of reason and of fact. For that some should rule, and others be ruled is a thing not only necessary, but expedient; **from the hour of their birth, some are marked out for subjection, others for rule**.' (Book 1, Part V)

Who, for example, is marked out for subjection?

> 'At all events we may firstly observe in living creatures both a despotical and a constitutional rule; for the soul rules the body with a despotical rule, whereas the intellect rules the appetites with a constitutional and royal rule. And it is clear that the rule of the soul over the body, and of the mind and the rational element over the passionate, is natural and expedient, whereas the equality of the two or the rule of the inferior is always hurtful. The same holds good of animals in relation to men; for tame animals have a better nature than wild, and all tame animals are better off when they are ruled by man; for then they are preserved. Again, **the male is by nature superior, and the female inferior**; and the one rules, and the other is ruled; this principle, of necessity, extends to all mankind.' (Book 1, Part V)

But most slaves are either born slaves and, therefore, know no other nature or are made slaves and, therefore, were once free.

> 'But that those who take the opposite view have in a certain way right on their side, may be easily seen. For the words slavery and slave are used in two senses. There is a slave or slavery by law as well as by nature. The law of which I speak is a sort of convention- the law by which whatever is taken in war is supposed to belong to the victors. But, this right many jurists impeach, as they would an orator who brought forward an unconstitutional measure: they detest the notion that, because one man has the power of doing violence and is superior in brute strength, another shall be his slave and subject'. (Book 1, Part VI)

Also, not all rulers are superior in their nature neither are all freemen.

> 'But then we must look for the intentions of nature in things which retain their nature, and not in things which are corrupted. And therefore we must study the man who is in the most perfect state both of body and soul, for in him we shall see the true relation of the two; although in bad or corrupted natures the body will often appear to rule over the soul, because they are in an evil and unnatural condition'. (Book 1, Part V)
>
> 'What does this mean but that they distinguish freedom and slavery, noble and humble birth, by the two principles of good and evil? They think that as men and animals beget men and animals, so from good men a good man springs. But this is what nature, though she may intend it, cannot always accomplish'. (Book 1, Part VI)
>
> 'We see then that there is some foundation for this difference of opinion, and that all are not either slaves by nature or freemen by nature, and also that there is in some cases a marked distinction between the two classes, rendering it expedient and right for the one to be slaves and the others to be masters: the one practicing obedience, the others exercising the authority and lordship which nature intended them to have. The abuse of this authority is injurious to both; for the interests of part and whole, of body and soul, are the same, and the slave is a part of the master, a living but separated part of his bodily frame. Hence, where the relation of master and slave between them is natural they are friends and have a common interest, but where it rests merely on law and force the reverse is true'. (Book 1, Part VI)

What about the relationships between husband and wife, father and children?

> 'Of household management we have seen that there are three parts- one is the rule of a master over slaves, which has been discussed already, another of a father, and the third of a husband. A husband and father, we

saw, rules over wife and children, both free, but the rule differs, the rule over his children being a royal, over his wife a constitutional rule. **For although there may be exceptions to the order of nature, the male is by nature fitter for command than the female, just as the elder and full-grown is superior to the younger and more immature.**

But in most constitutional states the citizens rule and are ruled by turns, for the idea of a constitutional state implies that the natures of the citizens are equal, and do not differ at all. Nevertheless, when one rules and the other is ruled, we endeavour to create a difference of outward forms and names and titles of respect, which may be illustrated by the saying of Amasis about his foot-pan*. The relation of the male to the female is of this kind, but there the inequality is permanent. The rule of a father over his children is royal, for he rules by virtue both of love and of the respect due to age, exercising a kind of royal power.

And, therefore, Homer has appropriately called Zeus 'father of Gods and men,' because he is the king of them all. For a king is the natural superior of his subjects, but he should be of the same kin or kind with them, and such is the relation of elder and younger, of father and son.' (Book 1, Part XII)

* *The saying about Amasis comes from Herodotus, where Amasis, after becoming ruler of Egypt, found people grumbling against him because he had once been a commoner like them. He proceeded to refashion a foot-pan in which people had washed their feet as an idol, and, seeing the people marvel at it, he told them that he was like the idol in that he was once common but had been refashioned as their ruler. The Egyptians then accepted him as their ruler. (Histories ii 172.)*[162]

What makes a free man so superior that he is the natural ruler over slaves, women and children?

The whole nub of Aristotle's reasoning comes in Part XIII of Book 1. It is difficult to take extracts without affecting the structured reasoning of the whole argument so I will quote the whole passage and highlight what I think are sections relevant to my point.

'Thus, it is clear that household management attends more to men than to the acquisition of inanimate things, and to human excellence more than to the excellence of property which we call wealth, and to the virtue of freemen more than to the virtue of slaves. A question may indeed be raised, whether there is any excellence at all in a slave beyond and higher than merely instrumental and ministerial qualities—whether he can have

[162] books.google.co.uk/books/about/Women_Power.html?id=6dU2DwAAQBAJ&printsec=frontcover&source=kp_read_button&redir_esc=y#v=onepage&q&f=false. Accessed 14/05/2019.

the virtues of temperance, courage, justice, and the like; or whether slaves possess only bodily and ministerial qualities. And, whichever way we answer the question, a difficulty arises; for, if they have virtue, in what will they differ from freemen?

On the other hand, since they are men and share in rational principle, it seems absurd to say that they have no virtue. **A similar question may be raised about women and children, whether they too have virtues: ought a woman to be temperate and brave and just**, and is a child to be called temperate, and intemperate, ... So, in general we may ask about the natural ruler, and the natural subject, whether they have the same or different virtues. For if a noble nature is equally required in both, why should one of them always rule, and the other always be ruled? Nor can we say that this is a question of degree, for the difference between ruler and subject is a difference of kind, which the difference of more and less never is.

Yet how strange is the supposition that the one ought, and that the other ought not, to have virtue! For if the ruler is intemperate and unjust, how can he rule well? If the subject, how can he obey well? If he be licentious and cowardly, he will certainly not do his duty. It is evident, therefore, that both of them must have a share of virtue but varying as natural subjects also vary among themselves. **Here the very constitution of the soul has shown us the way; in it one part naturally rules, and the other is subject, and the virtue of the ruler we maintain to be different from that of the subject; the one being the virtue of the rational, and the other of the irrational part. Now, it is obvious that the same principle applies generally, and therefore almost all things rule and are ruled according to nature. But the kind of rule differs; the freeman rules over the slave after another manner from that in which the male rules over the female, or the man over the child; although the parts of the soul are present in any of them, they are present in different degrees. For the slave has no deliberative faculty at all; the woman has, but it is without authority, and the child has, but it is immature.**

So, it must necessarily be supposed to be with the moral virtues also; all should partake of them, but only in such manner and degree as is required by each for the fulfilment of his duty. **Hence the ruler ought to have moral virtue in perfection, for his function, taken absolutely, demands a master artificer, and rational principle is such an artificer; the subjects, on the other hand, require only that measure of virtue which is proper to each of them. Clearly, then, moral virtue belongs to all of them; but the temperance of a man and of a woman, or the courage and justice of a man and of a woman, are not, as Socrates maintained, the same; the courage of a man is shown in commanding, of a woman in obeying.**

And this holds of all other virtues, as will be more clearly seen if we look at them in detail, for those who say generally that virtue consists in a good disposition of the soul, or in doing rightly, or the like, only deceive themselves. Far better than such definitions is their mode of speaking, who, like Gorgias*, enumerate the virtues. **All classes must be deemed to have their special attributes; as the poet says of women, "Silence is a woman's glory",** but this is not equally the glory of man. The child is imperfect, and therefore obviously his virtue is not relative to himself alone, but to the perfect man and to his teacher, and in like manner the virtue of the slave is relative to a master. Now we determined that a slave is useful for the wants of life, and therefore he will obviously require only so much virtue as will prevent him from failing in his duty through cowardice or lack of self-control.

Someone will ask whether, if what we are saying is true, virtue will not be required also in the artisans, for they often fail in their work through the lack of self-control? But is there not a great difference in the two cases? For the slave shares in his master's life; the artisan is less closely connected with him, and only attains excellence in proportion as he becomes a slave. The meaner sort of mechanic has a special and separate slavery; and whereas the slave exists by nature, not so the shoemaker or other artisan. It is manifest, then, that the master ought to be the source of such excellence in the slave, and not a mere possessor of the art of mastership which trains the slave in his duties. Wherefore they are mistaken who forbid us to converse with slaves and say that we should employ command only, for slaves stand even more in need of admonition than children.

So much for this subject; the relations of husband and wife, parent and child, their several virtues, what in their intercourse with one another is good, and what is evil, and how we may pursue the good and good escape the evil, will have to be discussed when we speak of the different forms of government. **For, inasmuch as every family is a part of a state, and these relationships are the parts of a family, and the virtue of the part must have regard to the virtue of the whole, women and children must be trained by education with an eye to the constitution, if the virtues of either of them are supposed to make any difference in the virtues of the state. And they must make a difference: for the children grow up to be citizens, and half the free persons in a state are women.** (Book 1, Part XIII)

**A Platonic dialogue on Virtue. Remember, Aristotle was Plato's pupil.*

What do you make of all this? More importantly, what did the pre-Renaissance reader make of it? Given that we are at the mercy, respectively, of at least one scribe, an untold number of recensionists, one translator and one transcriber, all with their own agendas, possibly, you have read the actual words of Aristotle, a major influence on Western European culture and, therefore, presumably, on Western European attitudes to women. You, however, are reading him with a 21st Century eye and I am back a thousand years, at least 300 lifetimes, wondering what a reader like Alfred the Great, Henry I (I mention Henry because he tried so hard to secure his throne for his daughter, Matilda, albeit after he lost his son, William, in the White Ship disaster.) or Pope Gregory the Great made of the great man's words.

I just need to remind you of the extracts from the introduction to this chapter.

- From the hour of their birth, some are marked out for subjection, others for rule.
- The male is by nature superior, and the female inferior.
- For although there may be exceptions to the order of nature, the male is by nature fitter for command than the female.
- For the slave has no deliberative faculty at all; the woman has, but it is without authority, and the child has, but it is immature.
- "Silence is a woman's glory."

To me, Book 1 of *Politics* is an attempt to justify the prevailing patriarchy of a warrior culture with which, in my 21st century version of a Western European cultural product, I feel deeply uncomfortable to the point of abhorrence and total rejection. To Alfred, and here I am conjecturing—*a most unhistorian-like thing to do*, its assertions of male fitness to rule, natural, and intellectual, rational and rhetorical superiority would have merely confirmed his already Christian dogmatic education that this was the intended cultural status quo of God's creation. To Henry, it contained enough recognition of exceptions to press the case for a suitably high-born and educated woman, i.e., his daughter, to rule his Anglo-French dominion. To Gregory, it would have been one of the few non-heretical pagan texts that confirmed his commitment to an all-male priesthood of which he, a man, was the leader, second only to the male Almighty himself.

Would they have seen the acceptance of Aristotle that there were alternate ways of looking at some of his propositions or would the generalisation of men's right to rule slaves, women and children, enforced by his juxtaposition of the three categories of subject have helped these alpha males to ignore them? Someone must have noticed what I am about to debate but we do not hear much about early medieval atheists or feminists in the acceptably mainstream histories of Britain.

Aristotle's assertion of male superiority is not based on any argument. It is a fact—nature has made the male of all living things superior. Yet, in his debate about slavery he recognises that some jurists, students of the law, reject that muscular might is a right basis for superiority of one individual over another. Furthermore, he accepts that things do not always turn out as nature intended; slaves can have attributes that their masters do not, and masters can lack the attributes that they need to be perfectly fit to rule. The juxtaposition strongly implies that the same can be true of men and women. Also, the natural fitness to rule can be corrupted so that men rule badly, without moral rectitude.

Finally, he accepts that slaves and women can be as good as freemen—they are not without 'virtue'—but this virtue should be used differently, primarily to obey, definitely not to rule. As morally good as men they may be but have they the same degree of virtues needed to rule? Here, we hit the same problems of translation and interpretation that have plagued the 'Truth' for millennia. Our translator is a Victorian academic, Jowett, in an era where gender equality was a subject of considerable disputation. He has chosen these translations for what I would call 'reasoned, moderation', 'intellectual ability' and 'resolve or mental toughness', all essential in a good ruler's emotional and intellectual make-up and character. Jowett chooses to translate these essentials as 'temperance', 'deliberative faculty' and 'courage'.

Aristotle, disagreeing with Socrates and Plato, is adamant that a woman's temperance and courage are not equal to those of a man. She has the intellect (deliberative faculty) but no authority to turn it into a direction or a decision. He does not exemplify the former assertion or explore or admit what the outcome would be if a woman were given the authority in the law to rule over men.

He does, however, distinguish between women and slaves and children when it comes to how they should be ruled. The man's rule of the household should be constitutional which I take to mean that there are some things in which the woman of the house has the final say or some matters on which the patriarch should listen to her advice. Nevertheless, when it comes to the affairs of a State women and children are a very important consideration and should be educated, in the broadest sense of the term, to play their part. When it comes to that part his philosophy shouts out two things about the woman's part:

- **In the *Politics* of the household OBEY your husband.**
- **In the *Politics* of the State STAY SILENT.**

Chapter 23
The Philosophers: Plato

If women are expected to do the same work as men, we must teach them the same things.
– Plato, *The Republic*

That the useful is the noble and the hurtful is the base.
– Plato, *The Republic*

DNA is not the heart's destiny; the genetic lottery may determine the cards in your deck, but experience deals the hand you can play.
– Thomas Lewis, *A General Theory of Love*

Preamble

All my non-fiction writing is motivated by a desire to understand human behaviour—come to think of it, most people's writing is! Somewhere along the road we all encounter the nature-nurture dichotomy. Equally, somewhere along that same road we get a twinge of the 'if-only'—if only it could all be different; good, kind, loving, peaceful, painless, forever? Regardless of whatever grandiloquent language in which it is wrapped up this urge to understand the incomprehensible is what motivates philosophy. We are all in our own way philosophers.

Do not be daunted by mention of Aristotle or Plato; the essence of their thinking is no different to yours or mine. My own philosophical awakening was in 1964. I was 14/15, hormones raging, anatomical exploration in its infancy, rebellion against the Christian message at the experimental stage, when I watched a play on television called 'In Camera'. Jean-Paul Sartre wrote his play, No Exit, in 1944. Its French title is 'Huis Clos' which is best translated as In Camera. Its message that 'Hell is other people' had a profound effect on my burgeoning atheism/irreligiosity and switched on my philosophic thought processes.

> *"All those eyes intent on me. Devouring me. What? Only two of you? I thought there were more; many more. So this is hell. I'd never have believed it. You remember all we were told about the torture-chambers, the fire and brimstone, the "burning marl." Old wives' tales! There is no need for red-hot pokers. HELL IS OTHER PEOPLE!"*

On an everyday, every person's level of understanding the main difference between Plato (who, as I pointed out in the previous chapter, came first chronologically but whose ideas, I am supposing, became widely known in Western Europe after Aristotle's) and Aristotle is that Plato postulated that human nature, in all its individual versions, was innate, determined before birth, and unlocked by life experiences whereas Aristotle believed that a new-born child was a blank slate, a tabula rasa, whose nature would be determined by life experiences—nature v. nurture.

Both, being products of a patriarchal elite, saw a constructed regime of control as the solution to a better world but Plato, via his literary Socrates discussing his if-only moment with some friends, modelled his perfect State in which justice—fairness and virtue—and good would be achieved for every individual whereas Aristotle seemed happy to defend and work with the patriarchal status quo.

Plato's *Republic* is a book about Justice, asking the question, 'Can Justice and Happiness exist alongside each other in a City State like Athens'? His mouthpiece, Socrates, hypothesises a State in which every citizen contributes and benefits according to their nature which divides them into three groups, rulers or guardians, warriors, and artisans or workers. As for the latter, working for a living requires gender equality because daily toil does not allow any time for public service, assessing the suitability of one's rulers or educating oneself, all of which are the focus of the *Republic* (In Greek, Plato's work was known as the *Politeia* or 'how a city-state is run'. Cicero gave it the name *res publica,* 'public matters' which bears little resemblance to our definition of a Republic, 'a state where the sovereign power is the people'.).

As for the classes of rulers and warriors, they were the ones who played crucial roles in sustaining the *polis* of Athens and were exclusively male. However, in *the Politeia*, Plato's Socrates makes a logical case for women to be included. More of that in a moment.

The majority of Plato's most powerful writing occurred in a series of *Dialogues* between his hero and teacher, Socrates, and various others, Athenians and outsiders, young and old, friends, acquaintances and students. (Only his *Laws*, written allegedly when he was older, does not involve his Socrates in some way.) Much debate has raged over the centuries about various dichotomies in his writing; feminist/misogynist, traditionalist/modernist and ownership of only Socrates' or all the speakers' views. Being a rather simplistic appreciator of philosophy and Plato in particular I sit most comfortably with the view that the literary Socrates in the Dialogues is the voice of Plato himself, which on many occasions challenges the rationality of traditional viewpoints, presented by Socrates' interlocutors, such as Meno and Timaeus, with a modernist take on death, the afterlife, the immortality of the soul, the cosmos and the rights of women.

In the *Dialogues*, therefore, the reader will see examples of thinking that does relate to a traditional, ingrained culture of misogyny but not from the Platonic

Socrates. Much the same can be said of whiffs of phallocentrism and homoeroticism. What you will see, as well as some, seemingly inescapable, classist stuff about philosopher kings and eugenic breeding programmes is an underlying sexist assumption of natural male supremacy.

As to whether the whole corpus of Plato is representative of his views or those of the historical Socrates, if we are prepared to accept Matthew, Mark, Luke and John as the biographers of Jesus, who, like Socrates, wrote nothing down, why shouldn't we accept Plato as the biographer of Socrates? It is important for me, therefore, in what I am about to say that I make clear who is speaking what opinion within the assumption that Aristotle was a fully indoctrinated member of the hierarchical elite, serving and educating them, and Plato or the Platonic Socrates (the Historical Socrates has gone down in history as having fallen foul of the regime by corrupting its youth and blaspheming its religion) was more prepared to challenge it.

Without going at a tangent to a lengthy digression, I need to reiterate that these historical superstars were people just like you and me. For decades psychologists have been interested in the phenomenon of motivated perception or 'seeing what you want to see'. Part of Aristotle's popularity in the Middle Ages was due to his sophisticated, for the times, observation-based examinations of the natural world, especially anatomy, which were taken up in the 2nd century AD by the Greek medical researcher, Aelius Galenus, Galen, who, re-popularised in the 12th century by the Arab influence in southern parts of Western Europe such as Sicily and Spain and then introduced into the curricula of universities in Salerno, Bologna, Naples and Montpellier for example, dominated medical thought until the proliferation of dissections, begun in the late 13th century by Mondino de Liuzzi in Bologna.

Both Aristotle and Galen dabbled in psychology but, unlike many of their anatomical observations, when it came to women's character and intellect, they saw what they wanted to see, i.e., their inferiority. The inconsistencies and inaccuracies intermingled with the scholarly observations and philosophy were accepted by the awe-inspired scholars in medieval Western Europe as a basis for treatments of physical and mental illness. Here is Aristotle's presentation of the character/nature of women from Book IX of The History of Animals (This translation is by D'Arcy Wentworth Thompson):

> Of the animals that are comparatively obscure and short-lived the characters or dispositions are not so obvious to recognition as are those of animals that are longer-lived. These latter animals appear to have a natural capacity corresponding to each of the passions: to cunning or simplicity, courage or timidity, to good temper or to bad, and to other similar dispositions of mind.
>
> Some also are capable of giving or receiving instruction, of receiving it from one another or from man: those that have the faculty of hearing, for

instance; and, not to limit the matter to audible sound, such as can differentiate the suggested meanings of word and gesture.
In all genera in which the distinction of male and female is found, Nature makes a similar differentiation in the mental characteristics of the two sexes. This differentiation is the most obvious in the case of humankind and in that of the larger animals and the viviparous quadrupeds. In the case of these latter the female, softer in character, is the sooner tamed, admits more readily of caressing, is more apt in the way of learning; as, for instance, in the Laconian breed of dogs the female is cleverer than the male. Of the Molossian breed of dogs, such as are employed in the chase are pretty much the same as those elsewhere; but sheepdogs of this breed are superior to the others in size, and in the courage with which they face the attacks of wild animals.
Dogs that are born of a mixed breed between these two kinds are remarkable for courage and endurance of hard labour.
In all cases, excepting those of the bear and leopard, the female is less spirited than the male; in regard to the two exceptional cases, the superiority in courage rests with the female. With all other animals the female is softer in disposition than the male, is more mischievous, less simple, more impulsive, and more attentive to the nurture of the young: the male, on the other hand, is more spirited than the female, more savage, more simple and less cunning. The traces of these differentiated characteristics are more or less visible everywhere, but they are especially visible where character is the more developed, and most of all in man.
The fact is, the nature of man is the most rounded off and complete, and consequently in man the qualities or capacities above referred to are found in their perfection. Hence woman is more compassionate[1] than man, more easily moved to tears[2], at the same time is more jealous[3], more querulous[4], more apt to scold[5] and to strike[6]. She is, furthermore, more prone to despondency[7] and less hopeful[8] than the man, more void of shame[9] or self-respect[10], more false of speech[11], more deceptive[12], and of more retentive memory[13]. She is also more wakeful[14], more shrinking[16], more difficult to rouse to action[17], and requires a smaller quantity of nutriment[18].
As was previously stated, the male is more courageous[19] than the female, and more sympathetic[20] in the way of standing by to help. Even in the case of molluscs, when the cuttlefish is struck with the trident the male stands by to help the female; but when the male is struck the female runs away.

In this mishmash of observations, we see Aristotle's authority on a woman's character and disposition (I have emboldened them in the text) coming from observations of some gender-based behavioural differences in breeds of dogs, and genera of animals—including cuttlefish?—none of which are scientific nor following a method of enquiry that distinguishes physical attributes from intellectual ones.

I have numbered 20 qualities he attributes to woman, of which 4 may be construed as socially positive, although somehow, I guess that her compassion, her retentive memory and her wakefulness are not seen as such by the dominant male in her life! At least she is cheap to feed! These are not objective observations they are the heavily biased views of a male supremacist and could be rightly construed as misogyny cloaked in a mist of quasi-scientific, quasi-rational facts of life.

It is hardly surprising, therefore, that in the male supremacist culture of Norman Britain such views were highly influential—male supremacist Classical Age learning providing 'proof' for what Men in male supremacist Early Medieval Western European culture were going to do anyway, in the way they perceived and treated women, because, given the emphasis on physical superiority in their warrior culture, they could. Moral theory and philosophy confirmed moral actuality—motivated perception.

> In Plato, however, we see a challenge to male supremacy from his Socrates for which he uses dialectical logic not motivated perception of behaviour but demonstrates that he too, as we are about to see, is unable to escape being a cultural insider—a man—and beneficiary of the Athenian status quo. The problem was that until the 14th century not much Platonic logic was around and about.
>
> In the case of Plato, the Middle Ages for all practical purposes had only the first part of the *Timaeus* (to 53c), hardly a typical Platonic dialogue, in a translation and commentary by a certain Calcidius (or Chalcidius). The *Timaeus* contains Plato's cosmology, his account of the origin of the cosmos.
>
> There were also translations of the *Meno* and the *Phaedo* made in the twelfth century by a certain Henry Aristippus of Catania, but almost no one appears to have read them. They seem to have had only a modest circulation and absolutely no influence at all to speak of.
>
> There had been a few other Latin translations made even much earlier, but these vanished from circulation before the Middle Ages got very far along. Cicero himself had translated the *Protagoras* and a small part of the *Timaeus*, and in the second century Apuleius translated the *Phaedo*, but these translations disappeared after the sixth century and had very little effect on anyone (Klibansky [1982], pp. 21-22). As Saint Jerome remarks in the late-fourth or early-fifth century, in his *Commentary on the Epistle to the Galatians*, "How many people know Plato's books, or his name? Idle old men on the corners hardly recall him" (Migne [1844-64], vol. 26, col. 401B).
>
> This state of affairs lasted until the Renaissance, when Marsilio Ficino (1433-99) translated and commented on the complete works of Plato.

> Thus, except for roughly the first half of the *Timaeus*, the Middle Ages did not know the actual texts of Plato.[163]

Plato's Timaeus, as pointed out earlier, was supportive of Plato's view that soul and body were present in every human, the former, immortal, and the latter created by a craftsman entity whom he called the Demiurge, a word we have come across in our investigation into Gnosticism, and which made all physical things in the Universe. A soul was without gender and lived in many bodies determining a person's reasoning, feelings and drives. A person's virtue, their ability to do and be good, was determined by how much their soul influenced them to be rationally wise, emotionally courageous and physically temperate. The *Timaeus* dialogue came after *The Republic*, a sort of 'going back to the basics' to see if Socrates' proposal of the ideal state matched the Creator's design of the ideal Creation.

Plato's Socrates asks Timaeus to explain the Creation of the Universe, the Earth and the Biology of Humans because he is an Astronomer. Timaeus uses Observation of the Mortal Body, the Eternal Truths of Mathematics, the Four Chemical Elements, Fire, Air, Earth and Water, and the Immortality of the Soul (Scientific ideas that lasted well into the Renaissance era) to explain the Perfectly Good Creation intended by the Creator. The nature of the soul causes the Creator to choose a body for its mortal life on Earth. The extent to which that life is virtuous determines the soul's route through various other lives to the divine. The nature and functions of bodies is left by the Creator father to the Gods making Creation a two-legged affair as we can see in the following passage from *Timaeus*:

> …and as human nature was of two kinds, the superior race would hereafter be called man. Now, when they should be implanted in bodies **by necessity**, and be always gaining or losing some part of their bodily substance, then in the first place it would be necessary that they should all have in them one and the same faculty of sensation, arising out of irresistible impressions; in the second place, they must have love, in which pleasure and pain mingle; also fear and anger, and the feelings which are akin or opposite to them; if they conquered these they would live righteously, and if they were conquered by them, unrighteously.
> **He** who lived well during his appointed time was to return and dwell in his native star, and there he would have a blessed and congenial existence. But if he failed in attaining this, at the second birth he would pass into a woman, and if, when in that state of being, he did not desist from evil, he would continually be changed into some brute who resembled him in the evil nature which he had acquired, and would not cease from his toils and transformations until he followed the revolution of the same and the like within him, and overcame by the help of reason

[163] plato.stanford.edu/entries/medieval-philosophy/#AvailabilityOfGreekTexts. Accessed 18/08/2019.

> the turbulent and irrational mob of later accretions, made up of fire and air and water and earth, and returned to the form of his first and better state.
>
> Having given all these laws to his creatures, that he might be guiltless of future evil in any of them, the creator sowed some of them in the earth, and some in the moon, and some in the other instruments of time; and when he had sown them, he committed to the younger gods the fashioning of their mortal bodies, and desired them to furnish what was still lacking to the human soul, and having made all the suitable additions, to rule over them, and to pilot the mortal animal in the best and wisest manner which they could, and avert from him all but self-inflicted evils.

Not being an expert on Plato, I hope that I have the gist of this right, i.e., the link between the philosophic life, the immortality of the soul, the functional opposition of the body to virtue and the route to divine perfection via the pursuit of a virtuous existence (Only philosophers go to heaven!).

The search for this link is as old as the dawning of the human intellect and very much alive in medieval times suggested by the scholarly interest in the dialogues of Plato; the *Phaedo*, on the soul, the *Meno* on the virtuous life and the *Timaeus* on Creation. Timaeus having given his erudite quasi-confabulation of the Creation finishes, almost as an afterthought, with this explanation of the creation of animals.

I have to give it all to you. Read it carefully and see if you understand it as I do. The highlighting and numbering are mine. In what I say next I do not intend any disparagement of Academia. However, am I wrong to observe that careers, livelihoods and reputations, mostly of men, have been built and millions of spoken and written words used, mostly by men—among whom is our esteemed translator, Benjamin Jowett, in search of the meaning of these passages, far too many, I feel, in support or justification of an already established point of view, far too frequently that of the dominant male.

My inexpert reading of it is of a staggeringly absolute exposition of male supremacy (confirmation that the use of the term 'man' in the passage above does indeed mean man as opposed to woman not man as in Mankind.) in which the proposed inferiority of women is likened to that of animals by reason of their inferior or non-existent powers of rational thought. Its final passage, in Jowett's translation, is as follows.

> Thus, our original design of discoursing about the universe down to the creation of man is nearly completed. A brief mention may be made of the generation of **other animals**[1a], so far as the subject admits of brevity; in this manner our argument will best attain a due proportion. **On the**

subject of animals, then, the following remarks may be offered. **Of the men who came into the world, those who were cowards or led unrighteous lives may with reason be supposed to have changed into the nature of women in the second generation[1b].** And this was the reason why at that time the gods created in **us**[2] the desire of sexual intercourse, contriving in man one animated substance, and in woman another, which they formed respectively in the following manner.
The outlet for drink by which liquids pass through the lung under the kidneys and into the bladder, which receives then by the pressure of the air emits them, was so fashioned by them as to penetrate also into the body of the marrow, which passes from the head along the neck and through the back, and which in the preceding discourse we have named the seed. And the seed having life, and becoming endowed with respiration, produces in that part in which it respires a lively desire of emission, and thus creates in **us** the love of procreation[3].
Wherefore also in men the organ of generation becoming rebellious and masterful, like an animal disobedient to reason, and maddened with the sting of lust, seeks to gain absolute sway ; and the same is the case with the so-called womb or matrix of women ; the animal within them is desirous of procreating children, and when remaining unfruitful long beyond its proper time, gets discontented and angry[4], and wandering in every direction through the body, closes up the passages of the breath, and, by obstructing respiration, drives them to extremity, causing all varieties of disease, until at length the desire and love of the man and the woman, bringing them together and as it were plucking the fruit from the tree, sow in the womb, as in a field, animals unseen by reason of their smallness and without form; these again are separated and matured within; they are then finally brought out into the light, and thus the generation of animals is completed.
Thus were created women and the female sex in general. But the race of birds was created out **of innocent light-minded men**[5], who, although their minds were directed toward heaven, imagined, in their simplicity, that the clearest demonstration of the things above was to be obtained by sight; these were remodelled and transformed into birds, and they grew feathers instead of hair. The race of wild pedestrian animals, again, came from **those who had no philosophy in any of their thoughts**[6], and never considered at all about the nature of the heavens, because they had ceased to use the courses of the head, but followed the guidance of those parts of the soul which are in the breast.
In consequence of these habits of theirs, they had their front-legs and their heads resting upon the earth to which they were drawn by natural affinity; and the crowns of their heads were elongated and of all sorts of shapes, into which the courses of the soul were crushed by reason of disuse. And this was the reason why they were created quadrupeds and

polypods: God gave the more senseless of them the more support that they might be more attracted to the earth. And the most foolish of them, who trail their bodies entirely upon the ground and have no longer any need of feet, he made without feet to crawl upon the earth.

The fourth class were the inhabitants of the water: **these were made out of the most entirely senseless and ignorant of all**[7], whom the transformers did not think any longer worthy of pure respiration, because they possessed a soul which was made impure by all sorts of transgression; and instead of the subtle and pure medium of air, they gave them the deep and muddy sea to be their element of respiration ; and hence arose the race of fishes and oysters, and other aquatic animals, which have received the most remote habitations as a punishment of their outlandish ignorance. These are the laws by which animals pass into one another, now, as ever, changing as they lose or gain wisdom and folly.

In the section I have marked (1a), there is the extraordinary separation of men from all other animals (To be fair, I think the word animal is used here to mean living, moving life form, as opposed to inferior, less intelligent life form but as we are about to see, 'If the cap fits…'), among which are included women who are only on this earth because allogamous procreation is the only way mortal life can perpetuate itself. The Demiurge, the Creator/father, does not create women and other animals. The imperfect souls of his creation, men, reincarnate into them. Cowardly and Unrighteous men's soul/bodies become women (1b). Jowett's choice of 'unrighteous' implies a moral as opposed, say, to a physical defect (uncontrollable instinct) but is consistent with his translation of Timaeus's earlier assertion that the righteous man can control his feelings and his emotions.

Those whose Reason controls their soul/body remain immortal, living in heaven among the stars. Those whose Reason does not control their feelings and emotions assume a body, fashioned by the lesser gods, and will only attain immortality when Reason not carnal Necessity rules their life, i.e., they are free of evil. If their life as a woman embraces evil they will be trapped in a more and more brutish embodiment. Women are not God's creation. They are intellectually inferior. Men would not need sex if women did not exist. Bodies are not God's design. Their construction was subcontracted to inferior creators and the part of their design that procreates is the source of evil.

The 'us' at (2) is clearly referring to men only. Men's sexual desire, created by the lesser gods, exists because women exist (*Well, of course it does! However, if it is the cause of imperfection, a prevention of reaching the divine, of becoming immortal, the root of sin, someone needs to take the blame—women? Hm!*). After some all-male biology linking desire, erection and ejaculation the 'us' is repeated and again refers to men only (3). Timaeus then likens the intensity of female desire to that of men but, whereas its physical response in men, an erection, is obvious, he goes into a strange theory about the bodily response in women (*which, I confess, I still do not understand*), mentioning discontent, anger, disease, and constriction of breathing and a proper time to be fruitful (4). Is this the male interpretation of menstruation, feminine hormones, happiness and even orgasm? If it is, the Timaeus solution has been perpetuated over the millennia in all macho males; to be happy women need regular sex and children (Timaeus does not actually use the word 'child').

I have to interject for a brief thought about the word 'extremity' which I have underlined in the passage. The 'extremity' of female behaviour, hysteria being one example (more of this in a later chapter), was a popular topic of debate in Victorian Britain and a frequent justification of the male view that women were not temperamentally suited to positions of importance. Is that what Timaeus means here? Does he mean physical extremity, i.e., as in danger to health or does the phrase 'all varieties of disease' euphemistically refer to mental issues (on Jowett's part rather than that of Timaeus)?

In her book *Beyond the Veil* Muslim feminist writer, Fatema Mernissi, offers the hint of a third possibility, the extremity of female desire. In the introduction she writes about pre-Islamic Mecca in which it was said that women offered themselves in the street to handsome men and a section of writing by a 9th Century Islamic scholar, Ibn Habib al-Baghdadi, entitled 'The Men who had to Use Turbans as Veils for Fear of Being Attacked by Women because of their Beauty'! She also cites evidence of such behaviour from Babylonian times, the 18th century BC. Her book is a fascinating review of two genders and two cultures, masculine and feminine and Western and Eastern.

In human sexual interaction, who is the active party and who the passive? Who is the strong and temperate and who the weak and intemperate? Who is in control of their desire and who not? Both Western Christian and Eastern Islamic culture come to a similar conclusion, she reasons. Men are weak in the face of female sexual allure. Western culture dealt with this by establishing a patriarchy that made sexual control an implicit part of religio- cultural education/ brainwashing whereas Islamic culture dealt with it explicitly by taking a woman's beauty out of the general public gaze of men, allowing its effect to fall on one male only, the father of her children, and making it part of their religious law. *Either way, it seems to me, it leads to male projection of their own weakness and lack of self-control on to women and then seeking to make the facts fit the fantasy.*

In another dialogue with a wealthy young man called Meno, Socrates defends women against this limiting stereotype by disproving Meno's proposition that for different people goodness or virtue, the route to divine immortality, is limited to the purpose for which they were created.

> Let us take first the virtue of a man—he should know how to administer the state, and in the administration of it to benefit his friends and harm his enemies; and he must also be careful not to suffer harm himself. A woman's virtue, if you wish to know about that, may also be easily described: her duty is to order her house, and keep what is indoors, and obey her husband. Every age, every condition of life, young or old, male

or female, bond or free, has a different virtue: there are virtues numberless, and no lack of definitions of them; for virtue is relative to the actions and ages of each of us in all that we do. And the same may be said of vice, Socrates.

Socrates then convinces Meno that goodness relates not to what you are or what you do but to the way you do it.

Soc. And can either house or state or anything be well ordered without temperance and without justice?
Men. Certainly not.
Soc. Then they who order a state, or a house temperately or justly order them with temperance and justice?
Men. Certainly.
Soc. Then both men and women, if they are to be good men and women, must have the same virtues of temperance and justice?
Men. True.
Soc. And can either a young man or an elder one be good, if they are intemperate and unjust?
Men. They cannot.
Soc. They must be temperate and just?
Men. Yes.
Soc. Then all men are good in the same way, and by participation in the same virtues?
Men. Such is the inference.
Soc. And they surely would not have been good in the same way, unless their virtue had been the same?
Men. They would not.
Soc. Then now that the sameness of all virtue has been proven, try and remember what you and Gorgias say that virtue is.

No wonder the might-is-right brigade of Athenian oligarchs thought he was dangerous!

The designation of women as animals created from imperfect or unrighteous male soul/bodies is confirmed/classified by Timaeus mentioning them in the same breath as other second-generation general life forms; birds generated from 'lightminded, innocents' (5), Pedestrian land animals generated from ' those who had no philosophy in any of their thoughts' (6), the most senseless being snakes, and the fourth class being sea creatures generated from 'the most entirely senseless and ignorant of all' who had 'a soul which was made impure by all sorts of transgression' (7).

Two aspects of this monologue unfortunately allow for interpretation which in a patriarchal culture where men have control of scholarship is unlikely to be pro-female.

Firstly, in Jowett's words, the monologue is show-cased as an 'entertaining discourse'. There are four basic types of discourse: argument, persuasion, narration and exposition. Timaeus is clearly not arguing or persuading because no one in the dialogue is disagreeing or doubting. Before he starts his discourse another party in the gathering, Critias, tells the story of Atlantis but, whether he believes it or not or tries to persuade his listeners of its truth, he makes it clear that it is a story, a myth, a legend. However, Timaeus' Creation discourse is an exposition, a lecture, intended to be credible knowledge. Its concentration on mathematical perfection, anatomical explanation and the migration of souls suggests strongly it follows a Pythagorean school of philosophising which was well established in the Hellenistic world of the 4th century BC.

His views on the place of women in Creation, therefore, can be taken as established theoretical knowledge of many scholars in Greece at the time not entertaining storytelling, prejudicial opinion, irony, sarcasm or mockery.

Secondly, because Plato's Socrates does not comment on or question what Timaeus says, we will never know whether these are Plato's views or establishment views with which he disagreed. To a medieval Christian scholar, steeped in Christian patriarchy and the Renaissance of Classical learning, *and here I am guessing*, it would confirm rather than confound any of the views on women expressed by Timaeus.

What we do know is that in *The Republic* Plato's Socrates reasons away any exclusion of women from a place in the political life of a state. (It is rare indeed, especially when your life perspective is anti-establishment and your political views are held by a minority of people in your native land, to find someone, quite by chance, whose perspectives on a piece of thinking, in this case Plato, his Socrates and the rights of women in Western European culture, match your own to the extent that the author of them could be you! Therefore, I need to bring your attention to the Serbian Professor of Ancient Philosophy at the University of Belgrade, Irena Deretic, whose essay, *Plato on Women*[164], must share a place in what I am about to say.)

To refocus, in his dialogue, *The Republic*, Plato's Socrates is intent on eliciting from his interlocutors, Adeimantus, Glaucon, Plato's brothers, and Thrasymachus, a Sophist teacher, approval for the structure of the perfect State in which Justice, Virtue and Happiness are all achievable. Having sorted out the male ruling structure his companions want him to explain where women and children fit in. Socrates had hoped to avoid this tricky subject, knowing that logical reasoning will take him down avenues and to conclusions that would be controversial, even ridiculous, to the Athenian patriarchy of the 4th Century BC, requiring a culture change in gender equality that was to take another 2300 years to complete. *Indeed, if we take gender equality as a key component of Western civilisation and Hellenistic culture which gave us Plato, Roman culture, the Bible and so much more as one of its key cornerstones then if, as Deretic suggests, this was the first attempt to justify equality for half the human race, the*

---

164 www.academia.edu/36447117/PLATO_ON_WOMEN.pdf. Accessed 24/09/2019.

length of time it has taken to come to fruition suggests to me deliberate repression of the idea rather than ignorance of the issues on the part of the other half.

The **first** question that Socrates asks concerns whether females given the same advantages of birth and education could do the same jobs as males. He uses working dogs for his analogy.

> Are dogs divided into hes and shes, or do they both share equally in hunting and in keeping watch and in the other duties of dogs? or do we entrust to the males the entire and exclusive care of the flocks, while we leave the females at home, under the idea that the bearing and suckling their puppies is labour enough for them?

Thrasymachus replies that males and females do the same jobs. He further agrees that it then follows that if women are to do the same duties as men they must have the same nurture and education. The education for male guardians has already been agreed to be music and gymnastics.

The **second** question is a trickier one and needs some innovatory thinking to answer.

> Then women must be taught music and gymnastic and also the art of war, which they must practise like the men?

The sight of women, particularly older women, wrestling naked, wearing armour and riding horses might be thought socially ridiculous and, therefore, unacceptable but Socrates argues that public nakedness of men was not an Athenian custom but imported from other parts of Greece to improve Athenian fighting skills and became the norm because the reasonable and practical benefits overcame the social discomfort. Anything should be acceptable if the reasoning behind it confirms that it is for the general improvement of the State.

The **third** question relates to whether this inclusion of women in the educational programmes of men contradicts one of the founding principles agreed by Socrates and Glaucon to be essential to the *Kallipolis*, the beautiful city, namely that 'everybody was to do the one work suited to his own nature'.

> Let us come to an understanding about the nature of woman: Is she capable of sharing either wholly or partially in the actions of men, or not at all? And is the art of war one of those arts in which she can or cannot share?

Socrates and Plato's brother, Glaucon, get to work on refuting the contradiction. They, firstly, agree that men and women have very different natures (again, as with the word 'animal' used by Timaeus, or Jowett, in his translation of Timaeus' word, it is possibly unwise to apply the 21st Century connotations to the Ancient Greek or Victorian uses of the word 'nature' which now far more leans towards 'temperament' than natural characteristics, such as appearance, and abilities, such as muscular strength) and, therefore, should have different pursuits but that the word 'different' requires more refinement to its use and meaning.

Michel Breal, a late 19th French Professor of Philology (everything to do with language), is credited with being the founder of Semantics, the importance to logic, vocabulary and semiotics (the meaning of symbols), of establishing the main meaning of a word, sentence or symbol.

Socrates leads.

> I said: Suppose that by way of illustration we were to ask the question whether there is not an opposition in nature between bald men and hairy men; and if this is admitted by us, then, if bald men are cobblers, we should forbid the hairy men to be cobblers, and conversely?
> That would be a jest, he said.
> Yes, I said, a jest; and why? because we never meant when we constructed the State, that the opposition of natures should extend to every difference, but only to those differences which affected the pursuit in which the individual is engaged; we should have argued, for example, that a physician and one who is in mind a physician may be said to have the same nature.
> True.
> Whereas the physician and the carpenter have different natures?
> Certainly.
> And if, I said, the male and female sex appear to differ in their fitness for any art or pursuit, we should say that such pursuit or art ought to be assigned to one or the other of them; but if the difference consists only in women bearing and men begetting children, this does not amount to a proof that a woman differs from a man in respect of the sort of education she should receive; and we shall therefore continue to maintain that our guardians and their wives ought to have the same pursuits.

Having established that women are capable of accessing the same education as men and that nothing in their different nature would make some women—not all, due to the same variability in individual aptitude and suitability that means that not all men would be just because they were men—any less gifted as rulers of the State, they check the equal rights proposal one last time.

> And those women who have such qualities are to be selected as the companions and colleagues of men who have similar qualities and whom they resemble in capacity and in character?
> Very true.
> And ought not the same natures to have the same pursuits?

> They ought.
> Then, as we were saying before, there is nothing unnatural in assigning music and gymnastic to the wives of the guardians—to that point we come round again.
> Certainly not.
> The law which we then enacted was agreeable to **nature**, and therefore not an impossibility or mere aspiration; and the contrary practice, which prevails at present, is in reality a violation of **nature**.

Plato's Socrates, having covered all the angles, defiantly and joyously declared his triumph of Reason over Prejudice.

> Then we have made an enactment not only possible but in the highest degree beneficial to the State?
> True.
> Then let the wives of our guardians strip, for their virtue will be their robe, and let them share in the toils of war and the defence of their country; only in the distribution of labours the lighter are to be assigned to the women, who are the weaker natures, but in other respects their duties are to be the same. And as for the man who laughs at naked women exercising their bodies from the best of motives, in his laughter he is plucking a fruit of unripe wisdom, and he himself is ignorant of what he is laughing at, or what he is about—for that is, and ever will be, the best of sayings, That the useful is the noble and the hurtful is the base.

It is a great pity, I think, that Socrates ended this piece of incontestable logic with this defiant message to those who would have ridiculed it as eccentric, unpragmatic, socially unacceptable pie in the sky. Its juxtaposition with *The Republic's* three other eminently mockable ideas, the abolition of the private family, a eugenic breeding programme for the ruling class and the Philosopher King, and Socrates' admission that his Kallipolis was, at least in part, the product of daydreaming ('let me feast my mind with the dream as day dreamers are in the habit of feasting themselves when they are walking alone') not only spawned a genre of satirical literature that has proposed all sorts of Utopian alternatives to the unpalatable realities of the real world but possibly consigned literature on equal rights for women to the same shelf in the library, a shelf marked 'fiction' rather than fact.

Professor Deretic does point out, however, that in *The Laws* an older, more pragmatic Plato, via the discourse of an unnamed Athenian (himself? Socrates?), attempts to postulate a more workable State, Magnesia—his 'second best city', but still advocates educational, social and political opportunities for women, although they are not allowed to own property.

Consequently, at 805c6-d2, he stresses: "In education and everything else, the female sex should be on the same footing as the male". Without the equal participation of women in all the political activities open to men, the polis would only be half a state with only half of its potentialities and strengths developed. Accordingly, any genuine unity and harmony and *eudaimonia* of the polis depended on making women as equal as possible to men in the performance of social and political functions.[165]

Epilogue

General opinion on Plato, it seems, is that he was/is very influential on Western thinking, religious and secular, social and political, fictional and non-fictional and, of course, philosophical. His writings are full of ideas, which had their renaissance in 15th century Florence under the patronage of the enormously wealthy and influential Medici family, Cosimo, his brother, Lorenzo, and his grandson, Lorenzo the Magnificent, patron of Botticelli and Michelangelo. Cosimo was clearly a Plato fan. In 1462, he re-founded Plato's Academy, placing Marsilio Ficino in charge. Cosimo was also an avid book collector, financing numerous trips to places all over the Middle East in search of manuscripts among which were all the extant Platonic Dialogues. Ficino translated them into Latin, the lingua franca of medieval Western European literati.

We know that Sir Thomas More, the prominent Tudor lawyer and widely travelled Tudor diplomat who was to become Henry VIII's Lord Chancellor—before losing his head for refusing to recognise said king's claim to be England's spiritual leader and sanction his divorce from Catherine of Aragon—must have read Plato's *Republic*. In 1516, his satire, *Utopia*, was published. *Utopia* had too many similarities to not have been Plato-inspired. By the time it was translated into English, the original neologism, *ou-topia*—'no place', had become *eu-topia*—in More's own words (he, too, saw the homophones), 'a place of felicitye' in which pronunciation and meaning it has captured our attention more than Plato's *Republic* or *Politea* or *Kallipolis* or More's original tale.

Over time, inevitably from my experience, Plato's big ideas have been intermixed, misinterpreted, hijacked and stigmatised. (*I will not say misunderstood because, like works of art and religious beliefs, ideas are for personal interpretation not indoctrination, social or commercial, academic or political. Liking or disliking, adopting or rejecting ideas is a very personal human trait, highly susceptible to Plato's three parts of the soul—reason, spirit and appetite.*) The contemplative beauty of the ideas of the Perfect Good, the abstract perfection of every named natural thing and the Immortality of the Soul graces the cognitive process of everyone with time to think rather than grind out or enjoy the fruits of their existence. The idea of the Philosopher King—a benevolent tyrant or tyrannical leadership/ruling class—who produces justice and happiness by considering laws and actions suggested by philosophising as

165 www.academia.edu/36447117/PLATO_ON_WOMEN.pdf. Accessed 26/09/2019.

well as fighting—has rarely, if ever, caught on in the post-*Utopia* world. His Communism (more Hippie than Marx), rejection of private ownership and abolition of the nuclear family have also been consigned to the fringes of human social experimentation (e.g., Winstanley's 17th century Diggers, Robert Owen's 19th century New Harmony, Indiana, and New Lanark, Scotland, America's 20th century Hippie Communes or Israel's Kibbutzim.) or mutated into mega-socio- and politico-economic phenomena such as the USSR or, on a much smaller scale, British Rail, British Steel and British Gas. Some of his ideas, for instance, those on perfect love, particularly in the *Phaedrus* dialogue, being socially unpalatable due to their homoerotic tone, have led to the merit of others being ignored or tarred with the same brush of social unacceptability.

It is hard for me to feel objective about the fact that the one big idea that failed to ignite any flame to shed light on or burn away a glaring injustice blocking the road to Utopia concerned the treatment and status of half the human race. Plato had argued convincingly—rationally and reluctantly—that women, given the same educational and nurturing opportunities, were capable of equal social, economic and political achievement, except any activity that required specifically male muscularity, and suggested the practical and moral benefit of their inclusion in the regulation of a state. His literary Socrates had also challenged the inferiority of the female soul and the limitation of their virtue, their potential to do good or contribute to the communal good, to the domestic arena.

Was More influenced by Plato? In his biography in Wikipedia it tells us that More, contrary to the family convention of his time, invested heavily in the education of his three daughters, Margaret, Elizabeth and Cicely and his two foster-daughters, one of whom, Margaret Clement, like his eldest daughter, Margaret, was a renowned scholar of her day. Many noble families followed his example.

Chapter 24
The Monstrous Regiment

To promote a Woman to bear rule, superiority, dominion or empire above any realm, nation or city is repugnant to nature, contumely to God, a thing most contrarious to his revealed will and approved ordinance, and finally it is the subversion of good order, of all equity and justice.
– John Knox

Preamble

According to Wikipedia, in total contrast to the opinion of Mr. Knox:

> *Queen Elizabeth II became the longest-reigning British monarch on 9 September 2015 when she surpassed the reign of her great-great-grandmother Victoria. On 6 February 2017, she became the first British monarch to celebrate a Sapphire Jubilee, commemorating 65 years on the throne.*[166]

At the business end of government, on 4 May 1979 Margaret Thatcher became the first woman Prime Minister of the United Kingdom, 19 years after the first ever elected woman Prime Minister in world politics, Simiravo Bandaranaike of Ceylon, now Sri Lanka, and 60 years after Nancy Astor, the first woman MP to take her seat in the House of Commons (Of the 650 MPs in the 2019 House of Commons 191, 29%, are women). When appointed, Margaret Thatcher was a 54-year-old wife and mother of two children. She served as the UK's most powerful person for nearly 12 years. On 18 July 2020, Elizabeth II will have been Head of State for 25,000 days. Her grandson said this of his grandmother:

> *"I think I speak for my generation when I say that the example and continuity provided by The Queen is not only very rare among leaders but a great source of pride and reassurance."*

Two and a half millennia after he proposed it, is 2019 Britain Socrates' Kallipolis? Does it conform to his logic that some women of the right class, given the right education and nurture, can do the 'Man's' job of ruling a State in which Justice and Happiness are hand in hand? Far more important as a question to

---

166 en.wikipedia.org/wiki/List_of_monarchs_in_Britain_by_length_of_reign. Accessed 11/10/2019.

be asked is, "Why has it taken 2,500 years, 10,000 lifetimes, to reach a cultural point in time at which we might even have some good news for Socrates—namely that Reason is beginning to prevail?"

On 16 December 1740, most of Western European civilisation, in the full glow of the Age of Enlightenment, the Age of Reason, went to war over a woman's right to rule the realm she had inherited from her father.

The father was the Habsburg Holy Roman Emperor, Charles VI, the woman in question was his daughter, Maria Theresa Walburga Amalia Christina. The inheritance was Austria, Hungary, Croatia, Bohemia, Transylvania, Mantua, Milan, Lodomeria and Galicia, the Austrian Netherlands, and Parma. By her marriage to Francis Stephen, she was Duchess of Lorraine, Grand Duchess of Tuscany and, in 1745, was to become Holy Roman Empress. *Of course, this extraordinary decision was a bit more complicated than the answer to the 'querelle des femmes', the 'Woman Question', yet, on the other hand, more simple too; territorial greed.*

The constitutional and inheritance laws of the Habsburg Empire were based on the law of the Salian Franks that we have met before, codified by King Clovis around 500 AD. By the medieval Salic law, a woman could not inherit, nor own land be it a fief or a kingdom. Charles VI's brother, Holy Roman Emperor, Joseph I, only had two daughters, Maria Josepha and Maria Amalia. Under the watchful eye of his father, Leopold I, Charles made an agreement with Joseph, The Mutual Pact of Succession, that Joseph's daughters would succeed Charles if he died with no male heirs and take precedence over any daughters that Charles may have.

Sure enough, Joseph died in 1711, Charles became Emperor but had only two surviving children, both daughters, Maria Theresa and Maria Anna. In 1713, six years before he had any children, Charles had secretly amended the Pact issuing an edict, known as the Pragmatic Sanction, allowing a female to succeed in the absence of any male Habsburgs.

Both his nieces had married while his own daughters were infants. Maria Josepha, the elder, married Frederick Augustus who was to become Elector of Saxony and King of Poland and her sister, Maria Amalia married Charles Albert who was to become Elector of Bavaria and Holy Roman Emperor. Charles VI spent over 10 years persuading and paying Europe's major players to sanction this exception to Salic law. It is worth considering the phrase 'Pragmatic Sanction'—official approval for a sensible or workable course of action—suggesting that Reason might have prevailed on this occasion (nothing to do with the fact that Austria-Hungary and the Holy Roman Empire was a huge player on the European economic and political playing field, of course?) but the moral—humanitarian cause had not really been advanced.

Great Britain's and the Dutch Republic's approval cost Charles a lucrative share in the tea trade with the East Indies. France agreed in exchange for the Duchy of Lorraine. Frederick Augustus of Saxony agreed in return for Charles' support for his election to King of Poland and Duke of Lithuania. (Habsburg support for Frederick in the War of the Polish Succession, 1733-5, and subsequently for Russia in the Russo-Turkish War, 1735-9, cost the Empire territories in Italy and the northern Balkans as well as bankrupting the Treasury.) Frederick I of Prussia agreed out of loyalty to his Emperor.

However, his niece's husband, Charles Albert of Bavaria, a growing power, agreed to the sanction but, clearly, did not approve, citing, in 1740, Uncle Charles' repudiation of the Mutual Pact of Succession and the Salic Law. Charles may have won over minds but not hearts because within two months of Maria Theresa's accession France, Spain, Prussia, Saxony and Bavaria had withdrawn their approval and declared war hoping to get a slice of the Austro-Hungarian cake.

After 7 years, 10 months and 2 days of the War of the Austrian Succession, the Treaty of Aix-La-Chapelle confirmed Maria Theresa as Archduchess of Austria and Queen of Hungary. Most of the territory she inherited from her father, with the notable exception of the mineral-rich region of Silesia which had been seized by Prussia early in the War, remained under the rule of the new Habsburg-Lorraine dynasty. When her husband died in 1765 her eldest son became Holy Roman Emperor, a position she had ensured for her husband, Francis, in 1745 by recognising the cession of Silesia to Prussia. After her husband's death her full title was:

> Maria Theresa, by the Grace of God, Dowager Empress of the Romans, Queen of Hungary, of Bohemia, of Dalmatia, of Croatia, of Slavonia, of Galicia, of Lodomeria, etc.; Archduchess of Austria; Duchess of Burgundy, of Styria, of Carinthia and of Carniola; Grand Princess of Transylvania; Margravine of Moravia; Duchess of Brabant, of Limburg, of Luxemburg, of Guelders, of Württemberg, of Upper and Lower Silesia, of Milan, of Mantua, of Parma, of Piacenza, of Guastalla, of Auschwitz and of Zator; Princess of Swabia; Princely Countess of Habsburg, of Flanders, of Tyrol, of Hainault, of Kyburg, of Gorizia and of Gradisca; Margravine of Burgau, of Upper and Lower Lusatia; Countess of Namur; Lady of the Wendish Mark and of Mechlin; Dowager Duchess of Lorraine and Bar, Dowager Grand Duchess of Tuscany.[167]

Was she true to her 'natural' woman's role?

> Over the course of twenty years, Maria Theresa gave birth to sixteen children, thirteen of whom survived infancy. The first child, Maria Elisabeth (1737-1740), was born a little less than a year after the wedding. The child's sex caused great disappointment and so would the births of Maria Anna, the eldest surviving child, and Maria Carolina (1740-1741). While fighting to preserve her inheritance, Maria Theresa

---

167 en.wikipedia.org/wiki/Maria_Theresa. Accessed 16/10/2019.

gave birth to a son named after Saint Joseph, to whom she had repeatedly prayed for a male child during the pregnancy. Maria Theresa's favourite child, Maria Christina, was born on her 25th birthday, four days before the defeat of the Austrian army in Chotusitz.

Five more children were born during the war: Maria Elisabeth, Charles, Maria Amalia, Leopold and Maria Carolina (1748-1748). During this period, there was no rest for Maria Theresa during pregnancies or around the births; the war and childbearing were carried on simultaneously. Five children were born during the peace between the War of the Austrian Succession and the Seven Years' War: Maria Johanna, Maria Josepha, Maria Carolina, Ferdinand and Maria Antonia. She delivered her last child, Maximilian Francis, during the Seven Years' War, aged 39. Maria Theresa asserted that, had she not been almost always pregnant, she would have gone into battle herself.[168]

Was she a capable ruler?

> According to Austrian historian Robert A. Kann, Maria Theresa was a monarch of above-average qualifications but intellectually inferior to Joseph and Leopold. Kann asserts that she nevertheless possessed qualities appreciated in a monarch: warm heart, practical mind, firm determination and sound perception. Most importantly, she was ready to recognise the mental superiority of some of her advisers and to give way to a superior mind while enjoying support of her ministers even if their ideas differed from her own. Joseph, however, was never able to establish rapport with the same advisers, even though their philosophy of government was closer to Joseph's than to Maria Theresa's.[169]

For most of her forty-year rule (1740-80), Maria Theresa's constant ally, the Russian Empire, was also ruled by women, both usurpers. Empress Elizabeth had overthrown her first cousin twice removed, the infant Tsar, Ivan VI, in 1741 and ruled until her death on Christmas Day 1761. Her successor, her nephew, Peter III, was overthrown by his German wife, Princess Sophie of Anhalt-Zerbst, after only six months in charge. Princess Sophie had been reinvented by Empress/Aunt Elizabeth as Yekaterina Alekseyevna, known to history as Catherine the Great.

I most definitely disagree with many of their opinions and enactments—e.g., Maria Theresa's anti-Semitism and Catherine's suppression of serfs—but matched up with the rulers of their time and, for that matter, rulers anywhere at any time they were certainly competent, capable and, for the most part, effective in the public domain while enduring the inevitable biological complications of their femaleness.

[168] Ibid.
[169] Ibid.

These three women, Elizabeth and Catherine from Russia and Maria Theresa from Austria could be said to be of a radically different cultural sphere of influence, East rather than West European, Slavic and Germanic rather than Celtic and Frankish, Byzantine rather than Roman and Russian Orthodox and rigidly Roman Catholic rather than Protestant or Secular. None of this really washes, however, because Peter the Great, Elizabeth's father and Catherine's grandfather-in-law, westernised Russia in the late 17th century and the Habsburgs were fully part of and fully involved in the Western European political intriguing against the power of Louis XIV, le Roi Soleil. What this exceptionally rare circumstance really demonstrated was that blood was more important than gender and that if Daddy were powerful enough he could do anything including, against all the pressure of the 'warrior culture' that prevailed in medieval and early modern Europe, make his daughter his successor.

After 1713, Charles VI, Holy Roman Emperor, spent the rest of his life safeguarding his Pragmatic Sanction against the moral and legal pressure exerted by the Salic Law that has repeatedly exemplified the male supremacy that was an implicit trait in the Western European ruling class. Incidentally, you will recall that this same legal restriction on inheritance of a female or a male of the female line had caused the Hundred Years War and was to prevent the greatest empress of all, Queen Victoria, from inheriting Hanover from her uncle, William IV. The measure of the maleness of Charles VI's power was that within months of his death those most likely to break their oaths to him did so. *Their disdain for women in general and a female ruler in particular as well as their desire to dismember the Habsburg Empire must have been a factor in the volte face of these long-established patriarchies. Such disdain seems not to have prevailed in Russian culture as the central component of the all-male warrior culture, the army, was prepared to support two female usurpers in 20 years.*

No such constitutional limitation seems to have resided in the political DNA of the Anglo-Norman ruling class of England, Wales and Ireland. Its monarchy was legitimised by a trial of strength, The Battle of Hastings 1066, and when it was wobbled by civil war—The Anarchy 1135-54, The Usurpation by Henry IV secured in the Battle of Shrewsbury 1403, The Wars of the Roses, 1455-85, ended by the Battle of Bosworth 1485, The English Civil War, 1642-51, ended by The Battle of Worcester 1651, and The Glorious Revolution of 1688 secured by The Battle of the Boyne 1690 and the Battle of Culloden 1746—a stellar cast of alpha males (William I, Henry I and II, Richard I, Edward I, III and IV and, of course, the 'Daddy' of them all, Henry VIII) continuously proved that 'Might Was Right'.

Founded by a bastard, usurped, inherited matrilineally, abolished, occupied and battled over by Roman Catholics and Protestants, even handed over to foreigners, the British throne has survived intact to produce its longest ever occupant, a Queen Regnant, Elizabeth II, the current incarnation of many Queens Consort (e.g., Margaret of Anjou), Queens Regent (e.g., Isabella of France), some of whom I have mentioned, and a few Queens Regnant that have played their part in British history all, in their own way, as capable of ruling as any man.

Mary I, to whom we will come very soon, was the first Queen Regnant of Great Britain and Ireland but she was not the first heir apparent or heir presumptive (an heir presumptive can be displaced by future children of the reigning monarch). That honour fell to the only legitimate daughter of Henry I, the Empress—a title that was disputed because she and her husband were not actually crowned by the Pope in Rome—Matilda, widow of the Holy Roman Emperor, or King of the Romans, Henry V. Henry I of England had two legitimate children by his first wife, Matilda of Scotland, great granddaughter of the Anglo-Saxon King Edmund Ironside. Matilda was the eldest and William Adelin (a Norman French Latinisation of the Anglo-Saxon *Aethling* meaning 'royal prince eligible to be King'), Henry's heir apparent who, born in 1103, was a year younger. His cousin, also William, son of his father's older brother, Robert Curthose, Duke of Normandy, was known as William *Clito*, another variant of *Adelin*. These names suggest that male-preference primogeniture, possibly with the approval of the leading lights, temporal and spiritual, of the ruling class established a king/*cynig* whose primary jobs were to make war by leading the war band in battle and keep the peace by dispensing justice according to the law.

Nevertheless, when William Adelin was drowned in the White Ship disaster in 1120, despite his plethora of nephews, Theobald and Stephen of Blois, sons of his sister, Adela, and the aforementioned William Clito, and bastards like Robert, 1st Earl of Gloucester, Richard de Dunstanville, 1st Earl of Cornwall, Henry Fitzroy, all supporters of their half-sister in The Anarchy, and Richard of Lincoln who also died in the White Ship disaster Henry made Matilda his heir presumptive. Hoping not to need her he married again in 1121. His bride, the 18-year-old Adeliza of Louvain, despite 14 years of marriage to her previously prolifically fertile husband, then 35 years her senior, produced no heirs for him (In her later marriage to William D'Aubigny, 1st Earl of Arundel, she had seven children!)

An established alpha male like Henry could do what he wanted, including defying presumed ancestral customs of inheritance, but he needed the 'Sanction' of his top fighters and potential rivals to his choice of heir, just as Charles VI did 600 years later. When Henry V died the English Henry recalled his widowed daughter to the Norman court declaring her to be his heir presumptive and then at Westminster during the Christmas period in 1126 he made his nobility take an oath to recognise Matilda and her offspring as his dynastic successors.

Among them were Matilda's cousin, Stephen of Blois, who was speedily to break his promise when Henry died in 1135 by seizing the throne and her stepmother, Adeliza, who, in 1139, was to betray her and her brother, Robert, by inviting them to England, in defiance of her then husband, William D'Aubigny, and then handing Matilda over to Stephen when he besieged Arundel castle. It is suggested that Adeliza made some amends by brokering a truce under which

Stephen released Matilda. Like Maria Theresa, Matilda had no choice but to fight for her rightful inheritance.

In June 1141, after the victory of her forces under her half-brother, Robert of Gloucester, at the Battle of Lincoln and the capture of the King, Matilda arrived in London to be crowned, having persuaded the clergy to recognise her as 'Lady of England and Normandy'. However, the AoC was reluctant to crown her Queen there and then. On 24 June, the London militia and guildsmen took to the streets and chucked her out. Her chance to be Queen Regnant, *feme sole* ('a woman alone') as she referred to her claim, was gone.

I can only conjecture on how much of the reluctance of the nobles and the Church, the establishment if you like, and the hostility of the London merchant class was to do with Matilda's gender. Other powerful forces such as snobbery and greed or, more moderately put, class and money determine loyalty although the patriarchal version of these times would prefer to foreground the manly, chivalric virtues of honour, oath-keeping and kinship. Indeed, one such line of explanation follows just this, i.e., Stephen was a 'nice chap', chivalrous, brave and pious whereas Matilda was a bit of a 'snooty madame' with an unbending will and a foul temper to boot. Why did Stephen let her go in 1139? His chivalrous nature is as good an explanation as any—true noble warriors did not make war on women etc. He was, however, quite happy for his wife, another Matilda, to carry on his fight while he was in prison, following in the 'chatelaine' tradition of defending the home, as in the castle(s) that protected his landed wealth, while the husband was away on campaign.

In an article for *History Extra* David Crouch, Professor of Medieval History at the University of Hull, confirms this view of Stephen:

> "London was a huge city in medieval terms, and the opinions of its people carried great weight," says Crouch. "Stephen's appeal to Londoners lay partly in his personality—he was by all accounts a very affable man—but also with the fact that his wife was Countess of Boulogne, a town that was a point of access for trade on the continent. Stephen's coronation, therefore, was seen to be in London's best interests."[170]

…and Matilda:

> "Stephen's treatment in Bristol reveals much about Matilda's character," says Crouch. "He was placed in leg irons, despite being an anointed king; this seemingly vindictive act shocked his subjects and did little to increase the empress's popularity.
> "Matilda's lack of discretion and sensitivity in the way she treated her magnates at court is well documented by medieval chroniclers. After Stephen's capture, her route to the throne looked clearer than it had ever

[170] www.historyextra.com/period/medieval/history-explorer-stephen-and-matildas-fight-for-the-throne/. Accessed 01/11/2019.

> been, yet she is described in contemporary sources as alienating members of her court with her uncontrollable and spiteful behaviour."
>
> With Stephen imprisoned and unable to marshal his support, Matilda seized the initiative and made it as far as Westminster in her bid for the crown. There, she was accepted by the population of London—as Stephen had been some six years earlier—and preparations began to take place for her coronation.
>
> "By 1141, victory looked to be well within Matilda's reach," says Crouch. "Her rival to the throne was in prison and the inhabitants of the most important city in England had accepted her as their reigning queen. But the tables turned dramatically when, just two days before her coronation, she alienated both new and old sources of support.
>
> "As tradition dictated, Matilda was petitioned by Londoners for tax concessions and other favours in the run-up to her coronation. But, instead of wooing her new subjects with generosity and magnanimity, Matilda, as was her way, granted no favours, shrieked at her petitioners and banished them from her presence. In one fell swoop she had lost the city and its support."
>
> Realising they would gain nothing from Matilda's reign, the rejected Londoners returned to the city where they proceeded to ring the bells. Men of London's militia poured into the streets and an angry mob advanced on Westminster, forcing Matilda to flee to Oxford for her own safety.[171]

The political brain behind Stephen was his youngest brother, Henry of Blois, Bishop of Winchester and Papal Legate. If palms needed greasing Henry and Stephen were well placed to do it, being, probably, the two wealthiest English nobles. Money, brains and command of people's souls meant that Henry had a political voice that a noble ignored at his peril. Henry was probably behind Stephen's daring dash to claim the vacant throne in front of Matilda and their older brother, Theobald of Blois. His was certainly the argument that exonerated those nobles who cared about breaking their promises to Henry I. He was certainly pragmatic, brokering truces and prisoner exchanges and the final deal that brought the peace that ushered in the Angevin era.

However, in his arguments and justifications of his brother's rule was he also biblical enough to regurgitate the divine opposition to female rule? To get the hint of an answer, we need to leap forward 400 years to the period before, during and after the reign of the first English Queen Regnant, Mary I, daughter of the biggest daddy of them all, Henry VIII.

Before we take that leap, I just want to look at the words of a medieval feminist spin doctor who tried to counter the misogyny of those times by promoting the goodness and usefulness of historical women whose exemplary

---

[171] Ibid.

qualities countered those who suggested that women were content to play second fiddle and get on with the social role assigned to them by the patriarchy.

Chapter 25
Christine De Pizan

Even the strongest city will fall if there is no one to defend it, and even the most undeserving case will win if there is no one to testify against it.
– Pizan, Christine. *The Book of the City of Ladies* (Penguin Classics) (Kindle Locations 890-891). Penguin Books Ltd. Kindle Edition.

Preamble

Do you believe in Ghosts—dead souls who haunt a place or a person? From the native Australians and Americans to the Spiritualists and Theosophists of 19th and early 20th century USA and Western Europe the dead have had something to say to the living. History performs the same function with, at times, the same spooky intensity—the past seems to be talking to us or we seem to be transported back to it. Such an experience came over me when I read the translation by Rosalind Brown-Grant of The Book of The City of Ladies when I was heavily into the Hundred Years War and the whole chivalry thing having read Bernard Cornwell's '1356'. It was like Christine was there speaking to me and these words in particular inspired me to write this book.

> *The female sex has been left defenceless for a long time now, like an orchard without a wall, and bereft of a champion to take up arms in order to protect it. Indeed, this is because those trusty knights who should by right defend women have been negligent in their duty and lacking in vigilance, leaving womankind open to attack from all sides. It's no wonder that women have been the losers in this war against them since the envious slanderers and vicious traitors who criticise them have been allowed to aim all manner of weapons at their defenceless targets. Even the strongest city will fall if there is no one to defend it, and even the most undeserving case will win if there is no one to testify against it.*[172]

Cristina da Pizzano was born in Venice in 1364. Her family moved to Paris when she was four when her father was appointed as king's astrologer to Charles V, King of France. She married in 1379 and had three children. Her husband died in 1389 and her father the year before. To support her mother and children Christine de Pizan, the French version of her name, became a writer good enough

[172] Pizan, Christine. The Book of the City of Ladies (Penguin Classics) (Kindle Locations 886-891). Penguin Books Ltd. Kindle Edition.

to secure the patronage of some very important French nobles, Louis I, Duke of Orleans, Philip the Bold and John the Fearless, both Dukes of Burgundy. Christine was a professional writer prepared to write about anything with an educated woman's perspective. She was surprisingly popular among a readership who enjoyed literature that perpetrated a misogynistic view of the traditional roles of mother, daughter and, principally, wife.

I have already pointed to that medieval perspective in Chapter 19 in the context of the death of chivalry, picking out for particular notice *Lamentations* by Matheolus. More popular still was *The Story of the Rose, Le Roman de la Rose,* an allegorical story of the impediments encountered in the pursuit of true love containing lots of sexist advice on how they might be overcome by the true and false application of the arts of chivalry and lots of vitriol about their origins in the social institutions of the age, particularly marriage. There are characters in *Roman de la Rose* who can only be described as misogynistic, at least, in the part added by Jean De Meun, putting women in the company of the usual targets for satire, the rich, the poor, the young, the old, the Church, the Castle, the zealous and the idle, the sincere and the hypocrite; all very male!

The first part, written by Guillaume de Lorris in circa 1230, is far sweeter and more 'courtly' than De Meun's, written about 45 years later, suggesting a growing disillusionment with the knightly inspiration of courtly love throughout the 13th century that, followed by 150 years of plague, death, disputed kingship, civil wars and military defeat (see Chapter 17 on The Hundred Years War) that decimated the French nobility, totally undermined faith in the 'male' ruling class and a hatred of all things upper class, including the need for a man to marry for status not love.

However, all this zeitgeist conjecture is only my subjective opinion. History is about what people do and say. Hindsight is good to read or hear but it is opinion not History.

Why would a book that was 125 years old still be popular and the cause of a serious literary and, I would suggest, cultural squabble that lasted 4 years involving some pretty high-status people? The first part is easier to answer. *A Tale of Two Cities* and *Alice in Wonderland*, respectively written 160 and 154 years ago, are still in the top ten list of best sellers of all time and Shakespeare's Sonnet 18 is over 400 years old.

La Querelle de la Rose started in the context of a trio of circumstances, the Hundred Years War, the Papal Schism and the usurpation of the English throne by Henry IV. Christine de Pizan, as well as the Bible, The Church Fathers and Aristotle, had some fairly new ammunition, Bocaccio's *De Mulieribus Claris*—Concerning Famous Women—written in 1362, and sufficient status via Christine's patrons to declare war on Matheolus' lamentation that there were 'no good women' and de Meun's lascivious depiction of women as sex objects and the slanderous, self-pitying suggestion of both that women, particularly whores and wives, were the main cause of male misery.

As explained in Chapter 17, from Edward III's reign English kings had asserted their right to be kings of France, but the claim was based on inheritance via a female. Henry IV, being more warlike, *I think it is fair to say*, than his cousin, Richard II, was a serious threat to Charles VI's throne. He was also politic enough to forget that his claim to the English throne, although he cemented it on the might-is-right criterion, was not the senior one which belonged to the daughters, Marie and Phillipa de Coucy, of his father's, John of Gaunt, older sister, Isabella.

Richard's heir presumptive, Edmund Mortimer, a great grandson of Edward III via his mother, Phillipa, daughter and only child of John of Gaunt's older brother, Lionel of Antwerp, also had a superior claim based on seniority that after a few more family twists and turns was to become the Yorkist claim in the 15th century Wars of the Roses. Arguing, therefore, that his right to the English throne was superior to that of the de Coucys or the Mortimers because his link to Edward III was patrilineal whereas theirs was matrilineal he conveniently forgot that his claim to the French throne was also matrilineal via Edward III's mother Isabella, granddaughter of Philip III (*Sorry about the partial repeat of Chapter 17 but if we are looking at the historical role of noble women we need to remember that it takes two to produce a child.*)

Isabella's father Philip IV was the older brother of Charles of Valois ancestor of Charles VI making Henry IV's claim, eventually ratified for his grandson, Henry VI, senior to that of Charles VI. Hence, there was a fundamental difference between English succession customs and French. In 14/15th century England females could not rule but males descended from a female (e.g., Henry II) could. In France not only were females not allowed to rule but neither could males descended from females. Back to the Salic Law!

When Louis XVI was deposed on 21 September 1789, France had never had a Queen Regnant. When, after a brief swansong from 1814-48, the monarchy was abolished it was still the case. An interesting aside is that, although the Second French Republic granted universal male suffrage in 1848, 70 years before the UK, France did not put universal female suffrage on the statute book until 1944, 16 years after the UK. Does that tell us anything about the two cultures?

On the establishment side defending *La Roman de la Rose* as modern poetry, representative of French, as opposed to Italian, culture, that tackled the whole love/sex thing from a more human less divine perspective following the pagan views of the classical Roman satirical poets, Ovid and Juvenal, and the philosophers, Aristotle and Cicero, were some powerful men in the administration of France, the court and the literary elite in Paris, John de Montreuil and the brothers, Gontier and Pierre Col. On the more 'Roman Catholic' side were Christine de Pizan, defending moral, respectful behaviour towards women and sex and Jean de Gerson, Chancellor of the University of

Paris and tireless worker for the ending of the Papal Schism. Christine and Jean found the *Roman* immoral, misogynistic and obscene so let us have a bit of a taste.

The poem is about a young man's quest for his true love, *more cynically sex with the object of his desire*. The abstracts of his mental and emotional journey, like Shame and Joy, are personalised. He has three main advisers. The old woman has 'been there' and seen the tarnish on the prize of the rose as well as having an insight into the sexuality of a woman. Friend is worldly wise and cynical in his warnings about the realities of consummated love. Genius, as a priest hearing Nature's confession about what a mess she has made of mankind, launches into a tirade about the 'nature' of women.

Here is Friend on Marriage.

> They knew well the saying, neither lying nor foolish, that love and lordship never kept each other company nor dwelt together. The one that dominates separates them.
>
> "Ah! If I had believed Theophrastus, I would never have married a wife. He considers no man wise who takes a wife in marriage, whether she is beautiful or ugly, poor or rich, for he says, and affirms it as true in his noble book, Aureolus (a good one to study in school), that married life is very disagreeable, full of toil and trouble, of quarrels and fights that result from the pride of foolish women, full, too, of their opposition and the reproaches that they make and utter with their mouths, full of the demands and the complaints that they find on many occasions. One has great trouble keeping them in line and restraining their silly desires.
>
> He who wants to take a poor wife must undertake to feed her, clothe her and put shoes on her feet. And if he thinks that he can improve his situation by taking a very rich wife, he will find her so proud and haughty, so overweening and arrogant, that he will again have great torment to endure her. And if, in addition, she is beautiful, everybody will run after her, pursue her and do her honour; they will come to blows, will work, struggle, battle, and exert themselves to serve her; and they all will surround her, Marriage is an evil bond, so help me Saint Julian, who harbours wandering pilgrims, and Saint Leonard, who unshackles prisoners who are truly repentant when he sees them lamenting. **It would have been better for me to go hang, the day I had to take a wife, when I became acquainted with so quaint a woman."**[173]

[173] archive.org/stream/LorrisGuillaumeDeTheRomanceOfTheRose/Lorris%2C+Guillaume+de+-+The+Romance+of+the+Rose_djvu.txt. Accessed 18/11/2019.

Here's Friend insulting a flirty wife.

> Now may the flesh and bones that have brought me such shame be given over to wolves and mad dogs! It is through you, lady slut, and through your wild ways, that I am given over to shame, you riotous, filthy, vile, stinking bitch.[174]

Here's Friend despairing of finding a 'chaste' wife.

> I do not say these things on account of good women, who establish restraints through their virtues; but I have not yet found any, however many I may have tested. Not even Solomon could find them, no matter how well he knew how to test them, for he himself affirms that he never found a stable woman.[175]

Here's Genius on the 'nature' of women.

> But it is also true, without fail, that a woman is easily inflamed with wrath. Virgil himself bears witness—and he knew a great deal about their difficulties—that no woman was ever so stable that she might not be varied and changeable. And thus she remains a very irritable animal. Solomon says that there was never a head more cruel than the head of a serpent and nothing more wrathful than a woman, and that nothing, he says, has so much malice. Briefly, there is so much vice in woman that no one can recount her perverse ways in rhyme or in verse. Titus Livius, who knew well what the habits and ways of women are, says that women are so easily deceived, so silly and of such pliable natures that with their ways entreaties are not worth blandishments. Again, Scripture says elsewhere that the basis of all feminine vice is avarice.[176]

Finally, never trust a woman!

> Whoever tells his secrets to his wife makes of her his mistress.
> No man born of woman, unless he is drunk or demented, should reveal anything to a woman that should be kept hidden if he doesn't want to hear it from someone else. No matter how loyal or good-natured she is, it would be better to flee the country than tell a woman something that should be kept silent. He should never do any secret deed if he sees a woman come, for even if there is bodily danger, you may be sure that she will tell it, no matter how long she may wait. Even if no one asks her anything about it, she will certainly tell it without any unusual coaxing; for nothing would she keep silent. To her thinking she would be dead if

174 Ibid.
175 Ibid.
176 Ibid.

> the secret did not jump out of her mouth, even if she is in danger or reproached. And if the one who told her is such a person that, after she knows, dares strike her or beat her just once, not three or four times, then no sooner than he touches her will she reproach him with his secret, and she will do so right out in the open. He who confides in a woman loses her.[177]

All this is pretty offensive stuff, no matter what the time period; immoral because of the degree of its denigration of God's creation—of which women are a somewhat essential component!—misogynistic because of its fairly direct suggestion that women are good for nothing except sex, whether it be procreational or recreational, and obscene in its language (at one stage mentioning what Pizan called a woman's 'secret parts'). Its bawdiness and cynicism probably explain its popularity but its targets, particularly the clergy and women, were much discussed in France at the turn of the 15th century with its mad king, allegedly flighty queen and its own Pope (at one time there were three claimants to be God's 'sole representative on earth'); unusual times made more unusual by the powerful and respected presence at Court of a woman writer one of whose patrons it seems was France's deadly enemy, Henry IV of England.

For the last time, I promise, I will urge you to think of people in history as talking, acting and thinking in much the same way as we do today. Books about history are frequently academic or literary—which is not really how the world is or was. Is it?

The quarrel lost its intensity with the 1405 publication of Christine's literary response, *The Book of the City of Ladies*.

I'd like to think this was the result of Christine's courteous and rational refutation of the sexist implications in the text of the poem but cynically it probably had more to do with the tightening of his grasp on power of her patron, Jean the Fearless, Duke of Burgundy, whose Burgundian faction was responsible for the deaths of Christine's opponents, and presumed Armagnacs, in the quarrel, John de Montreuil and Gontier Col, in the 1418 sack of Paris.

Christine's City of Ladies—the City being her Book—was built and populated by women who were chosen by her allegorical advisers, Reason, Rectitude and Justice, as examples of everything, such as propriety, constancy, fidelity and rationality, that characters in the *Roman* implied they were not and could not be. She chose her characters carefully to prompt a defence of women that showed male criticism of women to be irrational, their views to be morally and ethically wrong and their judgements and treatment to be unjust.

---

177 Ibid.

The dialectic skill with which she cemented the core of this refutation, which was narrative examples of 'good' women from Classical and Biblical times, is what captures my interest because such a sequence of questions could be used today to challenge the attitudes of 21st century British males.

Here are her questions. Firstly, she questions Lady Reason.

- But please tell me exactly what it is that makes so many different authors **slander women** in their writings because, if I understand you correctly, they are wrong to do so. **Is it Nature** that makes them do this? **Or, if it is out of hatred, how can you explain it?'**
- In reply to Reason's answer that some men who criticised women did so with good intentions Christine asked, "Were they right to do so, since they were acting with good intentions? **Isn't it true that one's actions are judged by one's intentions?'**
- The Roman poets like Ovid were much read and revered in medieval times. Christine's next question was, "My lady, why is it that Ovid … made so many **derogatory remarks** about women in his writings …?"
- Christine cites an Italian Renaissance writer. "However, I've seen another book by an Italian writer called Cecco d'Ascoli … In this work, he says some **extraordinarily unpleasant things** which are worse than anything else I've ever read, and which **shouldn't be repeated by anybody with any sense."**
- Christine cites another Latin work. "My lady, I've also come across another little book in Latin, called On the Secrets of Women, which states that **the female body is inherently flawed and defective in many of its functions.**"
- Christine also remembers, "… after going on at great length about **female children being the result of some weakness or deficiency in the mother's womb**, he claimed that **Nature herself is ashamed when she sees that she has created such an imperfect being**."
- Christine brings up the philosophy of Cicero (*called Tully in Le Roman*). "…wasn't it Cicero who said that **man should not be subject to woman and that he who did so abased himself because it is wrong to be subject to one who is your inferior**?"
- Christine refers to a saying attributed to the Roman orator, Cato, "My lady, it was one of the Catos, the one who was a great orator, who declared that **if woman hadn't been created, man would converse with the gods.**"
- Christine brings up another saying by Cato. "It was also this Cato Uticensis who said that **a woman who is attractive to a man is like a rose which is lovely to look at but hides its sharp thorns underneath.**"

- On how women look, Christine asks, "My lady, is it true what certain authors have said about **women being by nature gluttonous and prone to overindulgence**?"
- Christine continues on women's appearance. "… some writers make out that, in fact, **women go to church all dressed and made up in order to show themselves off to men and find themselves lovers.**"
- Christine asks about women's nature. "Yet, there is another author who has said that **women are by nature weak-minded and childish, which explains why they get on so well with children and why children like being with them.**"
- Christine asks about male mockery of women. "My lady, men have made a great deal of mileage out of mocking women because of a Latin proverb which says that **"God made woman to weep, talk and spin"**."
- Christine remembers "something that makes me smile, something silly which I've heard men and even foolish preachers say **about Christ appearing first to a woman because he knew she couldn't keep her mouth shut and so the news of his resurrection would spread all the faster.**"
- Christine seeks an explanation as to "… **why women are allowed neither to present a case at a trial, nor bear witness, nor pass sentence since some men have claimed that it's all because of some woman or other who behaved badly in a court of law.**"
- Christine asks about the physical nature of women. "Yet, despite what we've said about intelligence, it's undeniable that **women are by nature fearful creatures, having weak, frail bodies and lacking in physical strength**. Men have therefore argued that it is these things that make the female sex inferior and of lesser value. To their minds**, if a person's body is defective in some way, this undermines and diminishes that person's moral qualities and thus it follows that he or she is less worthy of praise.**"
- Christine asks further about women's intelligence and aptitude for learning. "… please tell me if, amongst all the other favours He has shown to women, **God ever chose to honour any of them with great intelligence and knowledge**. Do they indeed have an aptitude for learning? I'd really like to know why it is **that men claim women to be so slow-witted**."
- Christine asks about women's ingenuity. "However, I'd like to ask you if you know of any **woman who was ingenious, or creative, or clever enough to invent any new useful and important branches of knowledge which did not previously exist.**"
- Christine asks about women's judgement. "… I'd be keen to know whether women's minds, which both you and my own experience have proved to me to be **capable of understanding the most complex matters in sciences and other disciplines, are just as proficient at learning the lessons which good judgement teaches us**."

Using dialectic logic and examples from history, Christine shows that it is **irrational** for men:

- To criticise women indiscriminately whatever their reasons or intentions.
- To cite the remarks of Classical or Renaissance authors as true just because of their reputation as poets or philosophers.
- To assert that the female body is a flawed creation and female children the result of a procreational defect.
- To refuse the opinion and direction of a woman because she is an inferior creation to a man.
- To suggest that without women men would get closer to God.
- To suggest that female beauty is a painful trap for men.
- To suggest that women are overindulgent.
- To state that women only dress attractively in church to attract men.
- To suggest that women without exception talk too much.
- To suggest that women due to their lack of physical strength lack courage.
- To deduce that the physical frailty of a woman compared to a man leads to a moral frailty.
- To cite this as a reason for women to be unreliable witnesses in court and unsuitable lawyers or judges.
- To conclude that women are less intelligent than men and more slow-witted.
- To state that women are less ingenious and inventive than men.
- To imply that women display poor judgement and cannot learn from their experiences.

Are we certain that we do not recognise such sexist attitudes even though the Sex Discrimination Act in 1975 was passed 570 years after Christine's Book was written? Is her Book not proof that the roots of sexism were understood long ago and ignorance of them was not the result of cultural immaturity on the part of Western European civilisation?

Secondly, Christine addresses Lady Rectitude.

- "… when wives are pregnant and give birth to a daughter, their husbands are very often unhappy and disgruntled that they didn't bear them a son. But why is it, my lady, that they are so displeased? Is it **because girls are more trouble than boys or less loving and caring towards their parents than male children are**?"
- "… it being **the fault of women and their shrewish, vengeful nagging that the married state is such a constant hell for men**?"

- "… the philosopher Theophrastus, whom I mentioned earlier, said about **women hating their husbands when they're old and despising men who are scholars or clerks**."
- "… that a man should avoid telling a woman anything which he wants kept secret because **women are incapable of keeping their mouths shut**."
- "My lady, though I can see that women have brought countless good things into the world, **these men still claim that they have brought only evil.**"
- "That's why I'm all the more amazed at the opinion of some men who state that they are **completely opposed to their daughters, wives or other female relatives engaging in study, for fear that their morals will be corrupted**."
- "So why is it that these men say that **so few women are chaste**?"
- "My lady, from what you've told me, these ladies were no less chaste for all their attractiveness, whereas lots of men claim that it **is hard to find a lovely woman who is also pure**."
- "It therefore angers and upsets me when men claim that **women want to be raped** and that, even though a woman may verbally rebuff a man, she won't in fact mind it if he does force himself upon her."
- "Yet, of all the vices that men, and especially authors, accuse women of possessing, they are unanimous that **the female sex is unstable and fickle, frivolous, flighty and weak-minded, as impressionable as children and completely lacking in resolution**."
- "Yet men often say that, despite all the protestations of fidelity that a woman in love may make, **she not only flits from one lover to another but is also extraordinarily unfeeling, devious and false. They assert that this fickleness in women comes from their lack of moral character**."
- "Yet, those women who want to look lovely by dressing elegantly come in for a lot of criticism, because it's said **that they only do so in order to attract attention from men**."
- "As far as I can see, it's even untrue what they so often say about **avarice being the most prevalent of all the female vices.**"

Lady Rectitude provides historical examples of women/wives who were chaste, constant, sensible, decisive and intelligent as well as gentle, caring and considerate. Her frequent defence is not that women are perfect, some are seducers, and some are fickle and greedy, but that, in general, women are no less moral than men and in many cases better than men, better as wives, better as daughters—certainly no more expensive to bring up than sons!—and better as people. Lady Reason has a symbolic mirror suggesting heavily that people, in this case, men should avoid hypocrisy and take a good look at themselves in their own mirror.

In the third part of her book, Christine discusses with Lady Justice who should live in the City of Ladies as paragons of the female sex.

> 'We shall thus prove that God loves the female sex by showing that He endowed women, just as He did men, with the strength and fortitude needed to suffer terrible martyrdoms in defence of His holy faith, despite the fact that these women were only tender, young creatures. The whole of womankind can benefit from hearing about the lives of ladies such as these, whose heads are crowned with glory, for the lessons which they impart are more edifying than any others.'[178]

Christine's illustrious women came from stories of Christian martyrdom in which the villain was a pagan tyrant and the heroine a Christian virgin or widow or virtuous wife and the sinful cause of the latter's martyrdom and the former's cruelty was lust. One, St Afra, was the token repentant prostitute.

Christine was seeking equality of value and respect for women in the context of God's creation. In this respect she was successful in her refutation of sexist prejudice and misogynistic male supremacy. She could not conceive of the social possibilities for women opened up by science and medicine, education and industrialisation. Virgin, wife, mother, widow was the life path of a woman in the 15th century. Sex was procreational or occupational not recreational. Morality was determined by God or the spokesmen of God within the guilt trip that was the Christian religion. Life after death in heaven not hell was what kept people going when mortality was ever-present.

Having established that women were equal and of equal value in the sight of God her advice as to how to take that forward was bound to be influenced by this context. Here it is. Wives first.

Those wives whose husbands are loving and kind, good-natured and wise, should praise the Lord.

> Those wives whose husbands are neither good nor bad should none the less thank the Lord that they're not any worse.
>
> Those wives with husbands who are wayward, sinful and cruel should do their best to tolerate them… Even if their husbands are so steeped in sin that all their efforts come to nothing, these women's souls will at least have benefited greatly from having shown such patience.
>
> 'So, my ladies, be humble and long-suffering and the grace of God will be magnified in you. You will be covered in glory and be granted the kingdom of heaven.

---

[178] Ibid.

Now virgins.

> 'As for you girls who are young virginal maidens, be pure and modest, timid and steadfast, for the wicked have set their snares to catch you. Keep your gaze directed downwards, say few words, and be cautious in everything you do.

And widows.

> 'As for you widowed ladies, be respectable in the way you dress, speak and hold yourselves. Be devout in your words and deeds, prudent in the way you run your affairs, and patient, strong and resilient in the face of suffering and aggravation, for you will have sore need of such qualities. Be unassuming in your temperament, speech and bearing, and be charitable in your actions.

What about sex?

> O my ladies, fly, fly from the passionate love with which they try to tempt you! For God's sake, fly from it! No good can come to you of it. Rather, you can be sure that though it may seem to be superficially attractive, it can only be to your harm in the end. This is always the case, so don't think otherwise.

And men?

> My dear ladies, remember how these men accuse you of being weak, flighty and easily led, and yet still use the most convoluted, outlandish and bizarre methods they can think of to trap you, just as one would a wild animal.
> Have nothing to do with such men beneath whose smiling looks a lethal venom is concealed, one which will poison you to death.
> My ladies see how these men assail you on all sides and accuse you of every vice imaginable. Prove them all wrong by showing how principled you are and refute the criticisms they make of you by behaving morally.

Christine saves her greatest honour for a Mother, the Virgin Mary, of course, whom Lady Justice persuades to become Queen of the City.

> Rather, you should follow the example of your queen, the noble Virgin. On hearing that she was to receive the supreme honour of becoming the mother of the Son of God, her humility grew all the greater as she offered herself up to the Lord as His handmaiden. Thus, my ladies, since it is true that the more virtuous someone is, the more this makes them meek

> and mild, this city should make you conduct yourselves in a moral fashion and encourage you to be meritorious and forbearing.

Christine de Pizan made a powerful case for the natural and inherent human rights of women, so powerful, in fact, that it would be hard to argue that such ideas were unknown to the sexists and misogynists in the following 500 years of Western European history. To call her a feminist would be anachronistic because she could not even dream of the electoral, civil or economic rights for which, respectively, women like Emmeline Pankhurst in 1903, Rosa Parks in 1963 or The Dagenham strikers of 1968 fought so effectively. Her largely fictional catalogue of female biographies and sermon-like advice on how a good Christian woman should behave to earn respect are very much of the culture of her time.

To have civil rights, you must be a 'civis', a functioning member of the 'civitas' which is/was a geographical site with buildings on it and land in between them. (In the Hellenistic world, where all this language was developed, a 'City' State was the City and all the farmland which surrounded it.) You have to be a citizen, someone with legal status, i.e., an owner, occupier or user of the land or the buildings.

Culturally, property in the 21st century is inanimate mineral or vegetable material or non-human animals such as domesticated farm stock and beasts of burden but for hundreds of years AD, human beings could also be legal property. The laws of the civitas relate/d to the ownership and use of the buildings and the land and can/could be irrelevant in the might-is-right scenario in which the actors were men. (A Queen could raise and direct an army but the generals, captains and soldiers would be men.)

Christine makes a powerful case for Natural Justice not Legal Justice which largely pertains to property, those buildings and land and who owns and uses them. Ownership or 'Title' to property was, apart from widows, in the name of men, fathers and husbands, a la Roman model. Armed retainers necessary to defend property rights of the nobility were, again except for widows, maintained by Lords. As we shall see later it took another 450 years for entitled women to prevent their property legally passing to their husbands as a matter of course.

Christine avoids acknowledging this reality in Lady Reason's reply to her question about the absence of women in the legal process and the courts which administered it. While fiercely defending her stance that it is not women's 'natural' behaviour, rational incapability, intelligence or inability to deal with a legal education that prevented this—they could do the job if called upon—she engages in a bit of, by modern standards, sexist stereotyping.

> But, dear Christine, to come back to your question, you might as well ask why God didn't command men to perform women's tasks and women those of men. In answer, one could say that just as a wise and prudent lord organises his household into different domains and operates a strict division of labour amongst his workforce, so God created man and woman to serve Him in different ways and to help and comfort one

> another, according to a similar division of labour. To this end, He endowed each sex with the qualities and attributes which they need to perform the tasks for which they are cut out, even though sometimes humankind fails to respect these distinctions.
> God gave men strong, powerful bodies to stride about and to speak boldly, which explains why it is men who learn the law and maintain the rule of justice. In those instances where someone refuses to uphold the law which has been established by right, men must enforce it through the use of arms and physical strength, which women clearly could not do.
> Even though God has often endowed many women with great intelligence, it would not be right for them to abandon their customary modesty and to go about bringing cases before a court, as there are already enough men to do so.[179]

When faced with the chance to become a fully-fledged feminist, Christine becomes disingenuous. What tasks? Why couldn't women of means hire the heavy mob? Is she saying that God created women to be 'modest'—to keep quiet about their capabilities and to know their place?

It is too easy to say that the 15th century world was not ready to understand a more equal, more contributory role for women of the upper classes. The ideas were out there but if Western Europe's first proto feminist was too reluctant to take the next step the male dictatorship was certainly not going to help her. So, by the time Henry VIII began executing his wives for failing to do what God intended them for (Anne Boleyn) or behaving in an inappropriate, unchaste and immodest fashion—or behaving, in fact, just like men—(Catherine Howard), the chance had been missed.

---

[179] Ibid.

Chapter 26
Queen Regnant: Succession

There is nothing more difficult to take in hand, more perilous to conduct, or more uncertain in its success, than to take the lead in the introduction of a new order of things.
– Niccolò Machiavelli

Preamble

Before we go to Mary I, the first constitutionally legal Queen Regnant of England and Wales it is obvious but necessary to note that there were forces at play other than gender compelling the ruling classes represented in the two Houses of Parliament, the Lords, Spiritual and Temporal, and the Commons, the knights of the shires and the burgesses of the towns, to accept such a radical break with cultural and constitutional tradition. Wealth, religion and class are/were the three usual suspects.

The landed wealth of the core families of the Anglo-Norman ascendancy was the source of their power and, for some, not all, throughout history the opportunity to increase their wealth or the necessity to defend it have superseded any moral or ethical consideration or reservation that they may have had. Religion was the guardian of those morals and ethics and, in 16th century Britain, as we shall see in this chapter, was still a major factor in the 'Woman Question'.

I am not going to attempt to compete with writers such as Marx and Engels on the socio-economic and political importance of class (My eyes were opened by reading a learned but revelatory volume by David Cannadine, The Decline and Fall of the British Aristocracy.) but I do think we need to question the innateness of human hierarchy in whatever social model history has investigated. A ruling class, no matter by what criterion it was/is defined, either has no rules or the power to change any moral, ethical or spiritual rules that culture, tradition, God or The Law have seemingly established in a society. A Queen Regnant was a case in point and the fact that the Anglo-Norman ruling class of Britain were the first Western European 'civilised' patriarchy to 'give it a go' says something about British culture. I leave you to decide or deduce what that is!

Mary's story has its beginnings in the 14th century when just the sort of King that England was looking for married just the sort of Queen of whom any medieval patriarchy would have approved; genteel and gentle, kind and caring, chaste and obedient, god-fearing and loyal and, above all, fertile. Philippa of Hainaut, a territory now in Northern France that was key to the wool trade and, like England, pro-Burgundian, more than did her duty in giving birth to 13 children including 5 sons who survived to adulthood.

Unfortunately, royal successions throughout patriarchal culture have always had a 'Son' problem—0: not helpful; 1: better than 0 but all the hard preparation and training for kingship depends on his fragile mortality; 2: younger brother gets ideas above his station; 3 or more: recipe for plotting against the Crown—and that applies only to those born of the legitimate Queen Consort! Kings and Emperors had a strong tendency to 'beget' children out of wedlock.

The solution was to find a system that covered every possibility.

- Rule 1—Royal Blood—To apply for the job of 'King' you had to be related, at least a fingertip full of Royal Blood essential.
- Rule 2—Legitimacy—Once the Church got its teeth into Kingship it became 'Divine' and that meant only sons from a sacred union, marriage, counted.
- Rule 3—Primogeniture—The first-born got the Crown. If he died with sons, they got it not his brothers. If he died without sons, then brother No.2. If he died, No.3 and so on.
- Rule 4—Male Preference—The Salic Law, operational in France since 1328, meant searching high and low for male relatives with that fingertip full of Royal Blood. In other cultures, like England, well… And that brings us to Mary!
- Rule 5—In any legal dispute in England the tradition for making an adjudication, deciding a case, demanded referral to the Common Law which meant a thorough look at all the cases where judgements had been made in the past. As Kingship was divine that search included a thorough trawl through the moral and ethical issues raised by God's Word—What God said and did—and likewise for His son and His apostles and those who were inspired by God, Church Fathers, Prophets, Popes and preachers.

Other ways of settling who would inherit were tried. For instance, Elective monarchies of one kind or another had occurred prior to the 16th century, most notably in Anglo-Saxon England (Remember that it was the witenagemot, an assembly of the ecclesiastical and secular great and good, who elected the warlord, Harold Godwinson, as King in 1064) as well as in the crusader Kingdom of Jerusalem, Poland/Lithuania, Scandinavia, Bohemia, Venice and, later, the Dutch Republic.

The old Gaelic/Celtic method of tanistry left the choice of successor to the reigning King. The Tanist would be a member of the Sept, the Royal family. Strictly no females allowed in ancestry or actuality! The French Dauphin was similarly appointed. It was tried only once in England before the 16th century when Henry II crowned his eldest son, known to history as Henry the Young King, in 1170. It ended in tears! He died of dysentery while campaigning against his father and brother, Richard, because he had been given no realm over which to be King!

These rules for a peaceful succession had evolved over time. Yet other, seemingly fair, methods had been used. Partibility, the practice of sharing the patrimony among sons was common in Brythonic—and, therefore, Welsh—and Viking—thence, Norman—culture (William I left Normandy to his eldest son, Robert, and England to his second son, William II.) but not easy to apply if the patrimony was not sufficient to satisfy a large number of sons.

There were also clear precedents for which rules overruled which, notably The Great Cause of 1290 in Scotland when 13 claimants were whittled down to John Balliol whose claim was confirmed by King Edward I of England after nearly two years and, incidentally, settled absolutely nothing helpful to peace in Scotland.

In more complex medieval cases, the sometimes conflicting principles of proximity of blood and primogeniture competed, and outcomes were at times unpredictable. Proximity meant that an heir closer in degree of kinship to the lord in question was given precedence although that heir was not necessarily the heir by primogeniture.

- The Burgundian succession in 1361 was resolved in favour of John, son of a younger daughter, on basis of blood proximity, being a nearer cousin of the dead duke than Charles, grandson of the elder daughter. Proximity sometimes favoured younger lines (directly contrary to the outcome from applying primogeniture), since it was more probable that from a younger line, a member of an earlier generation was still alive compared with the descendants of the elder line.
- In dispute over the Scottish succession, 1290-91, the Bruce family pleaded tanistry and proximity of blood, whereas Balliol argued his claim based on primogeniture. The arbiter, Edward I of England, decided in favour of primogeniture. But later, the Independence Wars reverted the situation in favour of the Bruce, due to political exigency.
- The Earldom of Gloucester (in the beginning of 14th century) went to full sisters of the dead earl, not to his half-sisters, though they were elder, having been born of the father's first marriage, while the earl himself was from second marriage. Full siblings were considered higher in proximity than half-siblings.

However, primogeniture increasingly won legal cases over proximity in later centuries.[180]

Of course, these were just the peaceful solutions to succession. Very few successions settled in any of these ways led to peace within the newly led kingdom. No matter how the new monarch was selected and crowned the

[180] en.wikipedia.org/wiki/Primogeniture#Preference_for_males. Accessed 10/12/2019.

principle of might-is-right could overrule any settlement (*still can!*). Kings, whose job was essentially to make war or peace with their foreign enemies, had as much to fear, often a lot more, from their own nobles who, all too frequently, could be their own relatives. Conquest, civil war, assassination, abdication, usurpation, regicide or just plain disinheritance were all alternatives to a smooth, peaceful, universally recognised and approved succession.

If Henry VIII or Edward VI had had younger brothers, the transition to their successor would have been straightforward, although there would have been no guarantee of a more peaceful reign than Mary's with less bonfires. For example, if true that Henry VIII was his father, even Edward and Mary's illegitimate half-brother, a larger than life soldier of fortune called Sir Thomas Stukley, the least likely to succeed Henry, had more than a little Catholic sympathy throughout his life, plotting with Spain against his half-sister, Elizabeth, and as a renowned recusant (refuser of Anglican rites) involved in one of the wilder plots to free Mary, Queen of Scots, and place her on the English throne.

The possibility of a reversal of Henry's UDI from the Catholic Church was not really removed until 16th April 1746 when Butcher Cumberland defeated Bonnie Prince Charlie on Culloden Moor, 550 miles away from the epicentre of the events of July 1553. (Nearly 200 years, say 8 lifetimes, is a long time for a political shadow as long and as great as this one to dominate the planning of Great Britain's future, short, medium and long-term.)

Both Edward and his father, however, had two sisters apiece, in Edward's case half-sisters. Dad's sisters, Edward's aunts, Margaret and Mary, both died before he was 5 years old in 1541 and 1533, respectively. Both left first cousins with Tudor blood alive and very much kicking when Edward was born in 1537.

- James V, King of Scotland—25—son of Margaret and James IV, King of Scotland.
- Margaret Douglas—22—daughter of Margaret and her second husband, Archibald Douglas.
- Lady Frances Grey, nee Brandon—20—daughter of Mary and her second husband, Charles Brandon, Duke of Suffolk.
- Lady Eleanor Clifford, nee Brandon—18—daughter of Mary and Charles.

By the time of Edward's fatal illness and the widespread concern for his successor in 1553, James V had died 3 weeks after his defeat by his uncle's army at Solway Moss in November 1542 and Lady Clifford, never very well, had died in 1547, leaving a 7-year-old daughter, Margaret. Lady Douglas, Countess of Lennox, was 38 with an 8-year-old son, Henry, Lord Darnley, who, via his father, Matthew Stewart, Earl of Lennox, was descended from James II of Scotland via his eldest daughter, Mary. Lord Darnley, therefore, was Edward's first cousin once removed.

When he died, James V had a six-day-old daughter, Mary, who was Queen of Scots, although Scotland was ruled by Regents, James Hamilton, Earl of Arran (1542-54), second in line to the throne, also via Mary, daughter of James II, and then the Queen's mother, Mary of Guise. Queen Mary was also Edward's first cousin once removed, as was Margaret Clifford. Edward's other first cousins once removed were the Grey sisters, Lady Jane, 16, Lady Katherine, 13, and Lady Mary, 8.

To summarise, therefore, the potential successors to Edward VI from oldest to youngest:

1. Lady Margaret Douglas, 38. First Cousin.
2. Mary Tudor, 37. Half-sister.
3. Lady Frances Grey, 36. First cousin.
4. Elizabeth Tudor, 20. Half-sister.
5. Lady Jane Grey, 16. First cousin once removed.
6. Lady Katherine Grey, 13. First cousin once removed.
7. Lady Margaret Clifford, 13. First cousin once removed.
8. Mary, Queen of Scots, 11. First cousin once removed.
9. Lady Mary Grey, 8. First cousin once removed.
10. Henry, Lord Darnley, 8. First Cousin once removed.

Edward, of course, had a mother as well as a larger-than-life father and, therefore, maternal uncles and cousins. Through her mother, Margery Wentworth, Jane Seymour could trace her ancestry back to Edmund Langley, fourth surviving son of Edward III. It has been suggested that this was a highly attractive quality in Henry's decision to marry her. With Jane's marriage the Seymour family, 3 brothers and 2 sisters that we know of, did very well. Of the three brothers two were very ambitious. Edward, the elder, arguably the best soldier of his day, became Earl of Hertford and, when his 9-year-old nephew became king, Lord Protector of the Kingdom (leader of a Regency Council of which his brother, Thomas, was also a member), awarding himself the Dukedom of Somerset.

The younger uncle, Thomas, countered that by marrying the king's stepmother, Catherine Parr, Henry's extremely wealthy widow. A younger sister, Elizabeth was married to Gregory Cromwell, son of Thomas, architect of the English Reformation. By the end of January 1552, the young king had had both his controlling maternal uncles beheaded leaving John Dudley, Duke of Northumberland, running the country. Dudley had displaced Seymour in what we might call a coup d'état in 1550 demonstrating that the possibility of a coup d'état, a Seymour coup d'état was a reality during the Regency of Edward VI. Wikipedia tells this story.

> On the night of 16 January 1549, for reasons that are not clear (perhaps to take the young king away in his own custody), Seymour was caught trying to break into the King's apartments at Hampton Court Palace. He

entered the privy garden and awoke one of the King's pet spaniels. In response to the dog's barking, he shot and killed it. The next day, he was arrested and sent to the Tower of London. The incident, being caught outside the king's bedroom, at night, with a loaded pistol, was interpreted in the most menacing light, even casting suspicion on Elizabeth's involvement with Thomas.

On 18 January, the council sent agents to question everyone associated with Thomas, including Elizabeth. On 22 February, the council officially accused him of thirty-three charges of treason. He was convicted of treason, condemned to death and executed on 20 March 1549.[181]

Coups d'état were not unheard of in the Anglo-Norman monarchy and uncles and cousins were a serious threat to a young monarch. In 1135, Stephen of Blois won the race for the crown from his cousin and heir presumptive, Matilda, daughter of Henry I, whose own role in the deaths of his two elder brothers, Richard and William, both while hunting in the New Forest, is a conspiracy theorist's dream, and his elder brother, Theobald of Blois (See Chapter 24), who by the common law precedents of primogeniture and male preference was the heir in waiting. Whether or not, 250 years later, John of Gaunt, who was running England at the time of his father's death in 1377, was well enough placed to usurp his 10-year-old nephew, Richard II's throne is open to question but his son, Henry IV's victory at Shrewsbury, 22 years later, strongly suggests that, as probably the wealthiest man in the kingdom, he was.

More famously and more recently, Richard, Duke of Gloucester's imprisonment (and murder?) of his nephews, 12-year-old Edward and 10-year-old Richard, in 1483, while serving as Lord Protector, named by his brother, was a successful ploy that resulted in his coronation on 6 July 1483 as Richard III.

The 'wicked uncle' figure in inheritance plots, with Shakespeare leading the way with his hunchbacked Richard III and Hamlet's uncle/stepfather, Claudius, owed more than a little to real life. My favourite piece of avuncular abuse comes from Ralph Nickleby, uncle of Dickens' eponymous hero, Nicholas.

Over the Channel, the French were stuck with the Salic Law as were the English in their opposition to it. In the same year, 1547, as Henry VIII, one of France's greater kings, Francis I, also died. His predecessor, Louis XII, had died without a son as had his predecessor, Charles VIII. In search of a patrilineal male successor, the French establishment turned to Louis as a second cousin of Charles—they shared the same great grandfather, Charles V who died in 1380. Francis was Charles VIII's third cousin and first cousin once removed to Louis XII. Those were the lengths to which the French would go in order to observe the Salic Law because, if they did not, the Kings of England would have had a very strong matrilineal claim to the French throne. *Sacre bleu!*

---

[181] en.wikipedia.org/wiki/Thomas_Seymour,_1st_Baron_Seymour_of_Sudeley#CITEREFSkidmore2007. Accessed 25/12/2019.

When the grandson of Francis, Henry III, died with no male heir in 1589, having already succeeded two elder brothers, the patrilineal principle had to be stretched back 10 generations to find an ancestor, Louis IX (1226-70), of Henry's in common with his successor Henry IV! The generation gap of Henry VIII from Henry II was 11.

If the Anglo-Norman monarchy in England had denied its matrilineal descent, it would have also denied its claim to the French crown (The fleur-de-lys was not removed from the royal standard until 1801) besides which without emphasising 'nearness in blood' as opposed to 'male preference' the Tudor dynasty, descended from Margaret Beaufort, mother of Henry VII and great-great-granddaughter of Edward III, would have denied its own legitimacy as the English royal family. In fact, it would have been unable to do a 'Henri Quatre' because although William the Bastard conquered, and like Henry VII, 419 years later, killed his nearest rival for the throne, the existing King, his 'nearness in blood' claim to be Edward the Confessor's successor came via his great aunt Emma, Edward's mother, making William Edward's first cousin once removed, the same relationship to Edward VI as most of his potential successors.

We have already looked at the case of Mathilda, Henry I's daughter, who continued the bloodline in the absence of any sons. Indeed, without these three Anglo-Norman women, Emma, Mathilda and Margaret, ensuring the continuance of the ancient English/Danish bloodline, the monarchy which is so much a part of Britishness could well have looked very different by 1701, the time of the Act of Settlement when, via another woman, Sophia of Hanover, Protestant granddaughter of James I, the modern Germanic but constitutional, Anglican monarchy was shaped and approved.

It would be naïve of us to think that all these factors were not being considered as Edward's illness worsened during the first months of 1553. However, there were two other more dominant issues, *if we exclude male supremacy*, emanating from the cultural politics of those times, religion and legitimacy, the latter arising from the former and riddled with the same sort of establishment delusion and hypocrisy from which women had suffered for millennia. So intertwined are they that it is difficult to know which one to take first.

The whole Anglo-Norman supremacy of which all the players in this drama were a part was founded by a bastard, the illegitimate son of a Duke and a tanner's daughter. The Conqueror, an epithet awarded to him by Establishment history, overcame all the problems that plagued him throughout his life by his military prowess and religious devotion, taking full advantage of the Roman Catholic doctrine that good deeds, mostly those that enriched and added to the majesty of the Roman Church led by the Pope, could atone for any sin and effectively buy a place in heaven. Might was right and moral Right was adjudicated by the Pope in Rome.

The Tudor dynasty was doubly open to taunts concerning its legitimate right to the throne. At Bosworth Field Henry VII had seen off his main Yorkist rival, Richard III, and claimed the Kingship by 'right of conquest' but it took until 1525 before the hybrid Tudors saw the back of claims by descendants of Richard of York with the death of Richard de la Pole, Edward IV's nephew, while fighting for France at the Battle of Pavia but who had twice assembled a mercenary army to invade England and win the throne. An elder brother, William, died in prison in 1539 but there were still descendants of George, Duke of Clarence, Edward IV's brother, with a claim to the throne that did not have to defend itself from accusations of illegitimacy. We will meet Margaret, Countess of Salisbury, and her children with Richard Pole in the next chapter. *I fear it will end in tears!*

John Beaufort, Henry VII's great-grandfather, was born in 1371 to his father, John of Gaunt's mistress, Katherine Swynford, while Gaunt was still married to his second wife, Constance of Castille, although he was declared legitimate on two occasions by the English Parliament, 1390 and 1396. The issue was finally settled when John, his father, had married Katherine, by a dispensation from the Pope, Boniface IX, in 1396. However, his son John and his two Beaufort brothers were officially barred from succeeding Richard as King, a bar confirmed by Richard's usurper, Henry IV.

Elizabeth of York, Edward VI's grandmother, was also declared illegitimate by her uncle, Richard III, when he seized the throne in 1483 as Protector of his 12-year-old nephew, Elizabeth's brother, Edward V, on the grounds of a claim that his father, Edward IV's marriage to their mother, Elizabeth Woodville, was bigamous. It was claimed that Edward, a serial womaniser, had undertaken a secret marriage to or signed a pre-marriage contract with Lady Elizabeth Butler, nee Talbot. In 1484, Richard III persuaded parliament to pass an Act to this effect all copies of which Henry VII then had destroyed while also seeking a papal dispensation to marry his third cousin, Elizabeth. True or false, foreign and native enemies of the Tudors had plenty of fuel to fire their challenge to the upstart dynasty.

On the death of his father in 1509, the multi-talented, highly intelligent 17-year-old Henry, once Duke of York now Duke of Cornwall, Prince of Wales, must have felt that it was all up to him to restore the military glory and royal majesty of the era of his great great-great-great grandfather, Edward III, and the ability of his great-great-great grandfather, John of Gaunt, to produce sons. Almost his first decision was to determine the rest of his life, the history of England and the status of English women. He decided to observe his father's last wish, or so the official spin went, and marry his brother's widow, Catherine of Aragon.

We will come to the consequences of that decision in the next chapter, but I would like to interject a small piece of genealogy because there was a time before the story of Edward VI and his half-sisters when they may have looked at a very different future as would we all.

From 17 May 1536 to 12 October 1537, when his third wife, Jane Seymour, gave birth to the future Edward VI, Henry was, after two annulled marriages and with two daughters, not fit for purpose (Henry Fitzroy, a viable alternative, being male and of royal blood, died on 23rd July—in fact, the session of parliament that ratified the annulment of his father's marriage to the Lady Anne Boleyn and the illegitimacy of his two half-sisters was the last time he was seen in public.), without an heir apparent or presumptive. 17 months was a long time in the 16th century, with the sweating sickness, typhoid, tuberculosis, smallpox and the plague ever present and the state of Henry's health after his fall and his mortal existence about to extend to 45 years on the 28th of June.

Furthermore, although rebellion was not in the southern air it was fomenting in the north and finally erupted in October 1536 in the so-called Pilgrimage of Grace. Although the King was never in danger—his closest advisers the Dukes of Suffolk, Charles Brandon, and Norfolk, Thomas Howard, and George Talbot, Earl of Shrewsbury, dealt with it—it could have been a real threat. Had Henry died who would have replaced him? More to the point, were there any legitimately begotten males of royal blood in the wings ready to take over the starring role? *Yes, you have guessed it! We must go back to Edward III.*

Edward and Philippa had 6 children who grew to child begetting or childbearing age, 1 daughter and 5 sons, Edward the Black Prince, Isabella, Lionel, John, Edmund and Thomas. Between them they produced 16 grandchildren, 9 girls and 7 boys. Isabella and Lionel only had girls, 2 and 1, respectively. The 7 boys should have been enough for a patrilineal succession, but they were not.

John of Gaunt had 4 boys who grew to adulthood but only 2 who begat children; Henry IV who deposed his first cousin, Richard II, son of Edward the Black Prince, and left him to die in prison and whose male line ended with the death of his great-grandson, Edward of Westminster, at the Battle of Tewksbury in 1471 and John Beaufort, great-great-grandfather of Henry VIII but via his granddaughter, Lady Margaret Beaufort, wife of Edmund Tudor. Edmund of Langley, Duke of York, had 2 sons but only Richard, Earl of Cambridge, had children.

John Beaufort had 4 sons but only 2 had children. John, his eldest, only had Margaret, Henry VIII's grandmother, leaving the male line dependant on his youngest son, Edmund, and Richard's son, Richard of York. Only one of Edmund's 3 sons, Henry, had a child, his illegitimate son, Charles Somerset whose son, Henry, Earl of Worcester and Baron Herbert, at 40 years old, was father of 3 sons in 1536, William, 10, Thomas, 7, and Francis, 4/5.

Richard of York and his wife, Cecily Neville, had 12 children, 4 of whom were sons who grew to adulthood, Edmund of Rutland who died with his father during or shortly after the Battle of Wakefield in 1460, the 2 Yorkist kings, Edward IV and Richard III, and George, Duke of Clarence. Clarence's daughter, Margaret, Countess of Salisbury, as previously mentioned, will figure later in the story when her great nephew, Henry VIII, was on the throne. Edward IV's sons were the Princes in the Tower, but he did acknowledge an illegitimate son known as Arthur Plantagenet. Richard's son and heir, Edward of Middleham, died in 1484 aged 10 and his acknowledged illegitimate son, John of Gloucester, if history has read it accurately, died around 1499, possibly executed.

Therefore, in 1536-7, not including Henry VIII whose continuous bloodline was through his grandmother, Margaret Beaufort, there were 5 males alive carrying the patrilineal bloodline of Edward III, Arthur Plantagenet, Henry, William, Thomas and Francis Somerset. Their succession impediment was illegitimacy.

Matrilineal succession was certainly more acceptable in England than in France, which in the end adopted a semi-Salic approach, i.e., women counted when no men were there to count, but once we introduce it we meet many of the top nobility of Britain and much of the royalty of Europe as well as confronting the genealogical perplexities caused by illegitimate offspring. We also get 3 new categories that broaden the field: the daughters of Edward III's grandsons, the sons of his granddaughters and the daughters of his granddaughters.

Edward III died in 1377, 160 years before his recently divorced 4x great grandson had to really think about his heir presumptive. Henry was the grandson of a granddaughter of a grandson of Edward III. The most distant of his relatives who had that thimbleful of Edward III's blood—or DNA, to be more accurate—would have been fifth or fourth cousins or either of those once removed. Recent studies have shown that the consanguinity of these distant relatives would have been minute. In Andrew Millard's fascinating article 'The Probability of Descending from Edward III'—fascinating, of course, if you are into Genealogy, Maths and Royalty!—some remarkable statistics and surmises can be found. From the website of Leo van de Pas, <Genealogics>, Millard records that:

> *In the fifth generation he lists 321 descendants, of whom I count about 245 as 'English' (though distinguishing English from Welsh and Irish nobles in this list is difficult).*[182]

Henry VIII was in the sixth generation. (The degree of possible cousinship is always one less than the number of generations from the common ancestor.)

Millard concludes that:

> *Conclusion: there is an extremely high probability that a modern English person with predominantly English ancestry descends from Edward III, at a very minimum over 99%, and more likely very close to 100%. The number of descendants of Edward III must therefore include nearly all of the population of England, and probably much of the populations of the rest of the UK and Eire, as well as many millions in the USA, former British colonies and Europe, so 100 million seems a*

[182] community.dur.ac.uk/a.r.millard/genealogy/EdwardIIIDescent.php. Accessed 18/02/2020.

conservative estimate. Documenting one's own descent from Edward III is, however, another matter![183]

Amazing! Good to know I am royal with less than a 1% chance of proving my genetic link with my august ancestor and royal hero.

There were, therefore, some 300+ possibilities for Henry to choose from including his Seymour in-laws. Jane and her brothers were 7x great grandchildren of Edward III via his son, Lionel of Antwerp, and his only daughter, Philippa Plantagenet, 5th Countess of Ulster. Jane was Henry's fifth cousin twice removed with the DNA of some of the great families of the Anglo-Norman supremacy; Plantagenet, Mortimer, Percy, Clifford, Wentworth and Seymour. Both were direct descendants of Henry II.

On the overtly Yorkist side of his family, his father's in-laws as it were, women played a key role, not least by drawing in Edmund Langley's other two brothers, Lionel of Antwerp via the marriage of his great granddaughter, Anne Mortimer, to Edmund's son, Richard of Conisburgh, Earl of Cambridge, and Thomas of Woodstock via the three marriages of his daughter, Anne of Gloucester, to the two Earls of Stafford, the brothers, Thomas and Edmund, and William Bourchier, Count of Eu.

Although her marriage to Thomas was childless the daughter of her marriage to Edmund, Anne Stafford, through her children, formed a kinship connection to other great families such as the Nevilles, the Lancastrian Hollands and Greys, Mowbrays and the de la Poles, ancestors of the last Yorkist pretenders, and, of course, the Thomas Stanley, Henry VII's step-father, whose failure to intervene combined with the intervention of his younger brother, William, on the Lancastrian side won Henry the Battle of Bosworth.

The son of her third marriage to William Bourchier, Henry, married Isabel of Cambridge, sister-in-law of Anne Mortimer, making the Bourchier family staunch Yorkists for whose cause two of their grandsons died at the Battle of Barnet. The elder of the two, William, was married to Edward IV's sister-in-law, Anne Woodville, and his son, Henry, Henry VIII's second cousin, was a distinguished courtier and soldier, still alive in 1536 but possibly at 64 years old not a good prospect as heir presumptive. He predeceased his second cousin by 7 years.

The female line was the primary source of Henry VIII's foreign kinship connections. Edward III's granddaughter, Marie de Coucy, daughter of his eldest daughter, Isabella, married Henry Bar, Count of Soissons, and although their son, Robert, died at Agincourt, their granddaughter, Jeanne, married Louis of Luxembourg. Their grandson, Charles, was a contemporary of the young Henry VIII, his fifth cousin, and whose granddaughter, Franziska of Luxembourg, was ancestor to much of Europe's royalty. Wikipedia tells us:

[183] Ibid.

Charles (1488-1530), his successor as Count of Ligny, through whose granddaughter Franziska of Luxemburg, famous descendants were produced which includes: Queen Mary of Great Britain, Alexander I and Nicholas I of Russia, Queen Anna Paulowna of the Netherlands from whom the current Dutch royal family is descended, German Emperor William II, Charles Napoléon, Elizabeth II of the United Kingdom, and Juan Carlos I of Spain.[184]

Philippa de Coucy married Robert de Vere, Earl of Oxford, but their descendants did not extend the blood royal for more than a generation. John de Vere, Earl of Oxford, who won the Battle of Bosworth for Henry VII, was not Philippa's descendant. When her husband died the title passed to his uncle.

We have looked at the Yorkist link from Philippa, Countess of Ulster, Lionel's only daughter (*We will look at her bloodline to Jane Seymour in the next chapter*), and Anne of Gloucester, Thomas's daughter. It was 2 of the 4 daughters of John of Gaunt who spread the kinship group far and wide. Although his daughter, Elizabeth, married an English noble, John Holland, step grandson of the Black Prince, and became ancestor of Lady Jane Grey, the 9-day queen, and another daughter, Joan Beaufort, married Ralph de Neville, Earl of Westmoreland (their daughter, Cecily, married Richard of York, making her mother of two Yorkist kings, Edward IV and Richard III.), Philippa and Catherine, half-sisters 13 years apart in age, married into European royalty.

If you love conspiracy stories and scandal and family sagas—Who remembers 'The Forsyte Saga'? I watched all 26 episodes, captivated by the performances of the brilliant Eric Porter as Soames, the lovely Kenneth More who bore a remarkable resemblance to my father and the stunningly beautiful Susan Hampshire and Nyree Dawn Porter (C'mon, allow an old man his memories!)—this period is amazing. Was Edward IV really Richard's son? Was Edmund Tudor the son of Owen or the result of his mother's affair with Edmund Beaufort, Margaret's father?

Either way, Cecily, along with Margaret, of course, make that Beaufort DNA, the result of an affair between the son of a king and his daughter's governess, a powerful component of the royal bloodline! Wikipedia reminds us of what a key player Cecily Neville was in that line. As well as the mother of 2 kings, the grandmother of another and the great-grandmother of another.

> *She was the aunt of Richard Neville, 16th Earl of Warwick, one of the leading peers and military commanders of his generation, a grand-aunt of queen consort Anne Neville who married her son Richard III, and a great-great-grand-aunt of queen consort Catherine Parr, sixth wife of her great-grandson, King Henry VIII.*[185]

---

[184] en.wikipedia.org/wiki/Anthony_I,_Count_of_Ligny. Accessed 20/02/2020.

[185] en.wikipedia.org/wiki/Cecily_Neville,_Duchess_of_York. Accessed 21/02/2020.

Philippa of Lancaster married John I of Portugal with whom she had 5 sons and a daughter whom the Portuguese call 'The Illustrious Generation'. Her sister, Catherine, whose mother was Constance of Castille, gave up her claim to the throne of Castille because Catherine agreed to marry Henry, the future King Henry III of Castille. In 1445, Catherine's grandson, John II of Castille, married Philippa's granddaughter, Isabella of Portugal. Their daughter, the formidable Isabella of Castille, married Ferdinand of Aragon in 1469. Their daughter, of course, was Catherine of Aragon, first wife of Henry VIII.

These connections with European royalty gave Henry and his successors cousins who were friends and cousins who were enemies. Although these affinities were largely achieved through the women of Edward III's bloodline, Anglo-Norman mothers and daughters, they resulted in, at best, distant cousins. The most significant marriage for the future of Great Britain was that of Joan, the daughter of John Beaufort, granddaughter of John of Gaunt and great-granddaughter of the patriarch, Edward III.

On 12 February 1424, the 20-year-old Joan married the 18-year-old James I of Scotland. In the 13 years they were together, they had 8 children—6 daughters and 2 sons. Five of the daughters married into the nobility of Europe, France, Brittany, Savoy, Holland and Austria and the sixth, Joan, who was deaf and dumb, married the Earl of Morton. The two boys were twins, one of whom, Alexander, died and the other of whom became James II of Scotland.

When, therefore, Lady Margaret Tudor, sister of the future Henry VIII, married her fifth cousin, James IV, Joan's great grandson, on 25 January 1503, the blood and genes of their illustrious ancestors, John Beaufort, John of Gaunt and Edward III, were re-merged. They were proportionately increased when Margaret's grandchildren from this and her second marriage to Archibald Douglas, Earl of Angus, Mary, Queen of Scots, and Henry Stuart, Lord Darnley, produced a male heir, James VI of Scotland and I of England, with a lot of Beaufort blood and genes.

However, on 17 May 1536, Mary, Queen of Scots, had not been born (8 December 1542). Just to recap quickly, Henry had one illegitimate son, Henry Fitzroy (soon to die, remember), one illegitimate uncle, Arthur Plantagenet, and one 'illegitimate' (His father, Charles, claimed to have been legitimised.) first cousin, Henry Somerset, Earl of Worcester. He had one legitimate male first cousin with the Beaufort blood coursing through his veins, James V of Scotland, his enemy, a Catholic and a foreigner.

There was, however, another male first cousin but he was on the Woodville side and, therefore, with no more blood of the Beaufort ancestry than me! *Back we go again to the 15th century.* The final group of Yorkist women I shall be looking at are the 7 daughters of Edward IV and Elizabeth Woodville. The Woodvilles, although comfortably wealthy, were not of the first rank of the English nobility. The Queen's mother, Jacquetta of Luxembourg, was descended from English and French royalty but Sir Richard, her father, was of 'middle rank'. Therefore, the 'crème de la crème' of the English upper class were far from sympathetic to the marriage and the rise of this upstart family.

Nevertheless, the children of the royal couple did have the royal blood of the revered Edward III, if not the large slice of Beaufort.

Of the 7 daughters, the eldest, Elizabeth, became a queen; the youngest, Bridget, became a nun; one, Margaret, died in her first year; and one, Mary, in her mid-teens. The other 3, Cecily, Anne and Catherine, Henry VIII's aunts married but only Catherine gave birth to a cousin for him. She married William Courtenay, Earl of Devon, a supporter of Henry VII. Their son, Henry Courtenay, Marquess of Exeter, was Henry's only other legitimate first cousin.

The fate of Henry Courtenay will be revealed in the next chapter when these other factors, legitimacy and religion, become intertwined with the tried and trusted determinants of royal inheritance and produce the first instance of an English Queen Regnant.

Postscript

How did Henry resolve the absence of an heir presumptive? Who, you ask, did he choose and why? What evidence is there of whom he had in mind? The answer is that Henry became the half mortal half God on whom his religious reformation was founded. He gained control of the After Life—well, his afterlife anyway—by getting Parliament to agree to whomever he named in his will as his successor. The fact that this happened must have deluded him into believing that he was the new Emperor, the new Augustus, whereas, in reality he was to become a new Caligula with a monarchical tendency to take out troublemakers with the 'final solution' that took another 110 years to expurgate when the ghosts of all those decapitated lords spiritual and temporal—oh and common folk too!—got their own back in dramatic fashion on his elder sister's great grandson to end an afterlife over which he had no control and which he never wanted.

Chapter 27
The Great Matter

Render unto Caesar the things that are Caesar's, and unto God the things that are God's.
– Matthew 22:21

I am born in a rank which recognises no superior but God, to whom alone I am responsible for my actions
– Richard I 1193

A prince never lacks legitimate reasons to break his promise.
– Niccolò Machiavelli

Preamble

When Henry's older brother, Arthur, died in 1502, both his father and Catherine's mother, Isabella I of Castille, were keen to maintain the Anglo-Spanish alliance that had been sealed by the marriage. What better way to achieve this than for the younger brother and now heir to the throne to marry the young widow. Was the idea spurred on by Catherine's claim that in the 20 weeks they had been married no act of consummation had taken place, made more believable by the fact that Arthur and Catherine were only 16? Or did the pious and virtuous Catherine only reveal this not so unbelievable fact when forced to defend the legitimacy of her marriage to Henry in 1527 in a surprisingly public hearing to determine whether the Pope, Clement VII, would grant him an annulment?

Of course, most of the witnesses who testified that consummation had taken place were English and most of those who did not, including Catherine's Dresser and constant and intimate companion, were Spanish. We will never know but when Catherine died in 1536, she was buried in Peterborough Abbey in a grave marked as the resting place of Catherine, Dowager Princess of Wales thus denying that her Queen Consortship had ever taken place in which case Mary was not the issue of a sanctified and sanctioned marriage. She was a bastard.

On the JSTOR website, <https://www.jstor.org/stable/30094870? read -now=1andrefreqid=excelsior%3A0d31a3bb948c36757b3bfc9277a06203 andseq=3#page_scan_tab_contents.Accessed 06/01/2019> there is a learned article written by Herbert Thurston in *Studies: An Irish Quarterly Review* Vol. 21, No. 81 (Mar.1932), pp. 55-72 (18 pages) entitled 'The Divorce of Henry

VIII', which, in my opinion, settles the issue of the legality of Henry's actions (*you'll have to wait a while longer for the verdict!*), in which there is a powerful case made that Henry VII knew that, for no other reason than the state of Arthur's health, the marriage had not been consummated but that the Spanish did not. Hence, his surviving son's reluctance to sign a document of consent to the proposal on reaching the age of 14 was most likely a political ploy in case political conditions meant that Henry VII wanted to change his mind about the arrangement.

Henry, however, in 1502 was only 10, old enough to be bound by a marriage contract but too young to cohabitate with a young woman five or so years his senior. By the time he was 14, old enough to make his opinions known, his beloved mother had died as had Catherine's and their fathers had fallen out over her dowry. As suggested above, it was made to seem that Henry was not keen on the match at all. Nevertheless, Catherine stayed in England representing her father as his ambassador. It was a bit of a surprise, then, when a few months after his father's death and his own accession to the throne in 1509 Henry quietly married his intended.

His father, or, more believably, the Spanish had already sought and got a papal dispensation from Pope Julius II in December 1503 for Henry to marry Catherine. The dispensation was to set aside the impediment to their marriage of affinity, i.e., that Catherine was his brother's wife, on the grounds, according to Thurston, that the marriage was a vital component in maintaining peace between Spain and England. *Right, here we go! Ten things you have to know about Henry VIII and his 'Great Matter'*:

1. The Law

In the Middle Ages, they recognised three types of law: Divine Law, Natural Law and Man-Made Law. If you believed, as all Christians did, in a Creator God then natural law was divine anyway. Canon Law consisted of man-made Church rules intended to deal with the way in which the Church could guide the individual to salvation and eternal life by avoiding or atoning for sin, some of which concerned marriage. God's Law, natural law and canon law were all simplified into the Will of God, the chief interpreter of which was the Pope. He could prevent sin and forgive sin or mollify sinning by adding a bit of pragmatism to the Word of God which consisted of the Bible, Old and New Testament, and the answers to prayers or prophecies of holy men.

2. Leviticus

Christians in the time of Henry VIII believed that the words and deeds of Moses, the Old Testament patriarchs and prophets, Jesus and the Apostles revealed the Will of God. The moral, behavioural rules (including sexual behaviour) and punishments revealed to Moses when he spoke with God on

Mount Sinai are in the third book of the Bible, Leviticus. The two that pertained to Henry's marriage to Catherine were:

NIV < Leviticus Ch.18 v.16: "Do not have sexual relations with your brother's wife; that would dishonour your brother."

NIV < Leviticus Ch.20 v.21: "If a man marries his brother's wife, it is an act of impurity; he has dishonoured his brother. They will be childless."

The New International Version of the Bible was published in 1978. If we go back to 1611 the King James or Authorised Version gives a better idea of the sexual and social impropriety implicit in marrying your brother's wife.

KJV < 18:16 "Thou shalt not uncover the nakedness of thy brother' wife: it is thy brother' nakedness."

KJV <20:21 "And if a man shall take his brother' wife, it is an unclean thing: he hath uncovered his brother's nakedness; they shall be childless."

Even more revealing is the William Tyndale version published in Antwerp in 1530. It was against the law to publish the Bible in the vernacular in England but allowed everywhere else in Western Europe. Tyndale was accused by Establishment figures of making multiple errors in his translation using original Hebrew and Greek scripts.

In 1530, he wrote a paper criticising Henry's wish for an annulment, The Practyse of Prelates, which the big man did not appreciate but he had also written a paper in 1528, The Obedience of a Christen Man, advocating that monarchs should be the heads of their own churches which was certainly read by Henry, allegedly on Anne Boleyn's recommendation. He was burnt as a heretic in 1536 on the orders of the Holy Roman Emperor, Charles V (more of his part in all this in a short while).

TYN < 18:16 "Thou shalt not vnheale the secrettes of thy brothers wife, for that is thy brothers preuyte."

TYN < 20:21 "Yf a man take his brother's wife, it is an vnclene thinge, he hath vncouered his brother's secrettes, they shalbe childlesse therfore."

These more contemporary versions with their mention of a woman's 'nakedness' and 'secrettes' and the uncovering of a man's 'preuyte' property (Yes, a wife was a husband's property! More of this in a future chapter.) being an act of defilement and moral filth, an 'vnclene thing', do seem to make the sin more abhorrent.

3. Affinity

Affinity is about honourable sexual and marital conduct within a kinship group. It includes incest due to consanguinity but casts its net wider to cover the honourable, morally 'clean' implications of marriage in terms of bringing the spouse's relatives into one's own kinship group. In the time of Henry VIII moral honour and obligation followed Divine Law meaning that your brother's wife was your sister and your husband's brother was your brother. You were related in the first degree of kinship and, although not subject to the incest taboo, instructed by God not to marry.

4. Annulment

In the famous pupil mnemonic for Henry VIII's marital history, I'm sorry to say that all you millions out there have been deceived! Neither of Henry's divorces was a divorce. They were annulments. It was the Legatine Court and, later, Archbishop Thomas Cranmer who, correctly for the time when divorce was not a legally defined term and meant 'marital separation', first took us into this world of euphemism, which has become Establishment history. Who cares, you might ask? Well, Catherine and Mary did, Lady Jane Grey did, Sir Thomas More and Bishop John Fisher and some 250 martyrs of Bloody Mary's reign did, and the 85 million Anglicans worldwide should. Prepare to be corrected!

Until 1857 when the Matrimonial Causes Act allowed divorce proceedings to be heard in a civil court, the dissolution of a marriage was an ecclesiastical affair because marriage in a Catholic world was/is a sacrament, a ceremony favoured by God and granting salvation, not just a property contract. God's salvation was sealed by sending his Son, Jesus Christ, to die for the sins of the world. The Church who believed this was very much against divorce, the termination of a marriage, because Jesus said in Mark 10:11-12 KJV < **11** "And he saith unto them, Whosoever shall put away his wife, and marry another, committeth adultery against her. **12** And if a woman shall put away her husband, and be married to another, she committeth adultery.">

From 1697, a very wealthy husband could, by obtaining a dispensation from Parliament, in the form of an Act of Parliament, dissolve his marriage by a law sufficiently rigorous and indisputable that he could marry again (in theory, a wife could do this as well but with far greater difficulty) but this was not a legal recourse available to Henry. He, therefore, had to resort to the fairly common practice among the noble classes of western Europe of seeking papal approval of annulment. The crucial difference between a divorce and an annulment is/was that the former was the termination of a legally recognised contract whereas the latter rendered the contract null and void, as if had never happened. Children from the former would have been legitimate, of the latter, illegitimate.

5. The Pope

Approval of an annulment in an era when the Pope was a seriously political player in addition to his widely recognised religious supremacy was a you-scratch-my-back-and-I'll-scratch-yours arrangement. Indeed, Henry and his representatives persistently reminded Pope Clement of the book that he had written in 1521 in support of the papacy, *Assertio Septem Sacramentorum.*

As mentioned before, Henry lived in an age of big hitters—Francis I, King of France, Charles V, Holy Roman Emperor and Suleiman the Magnificent, Sultan of the Ottoman Empire completing the quartet. The threat to and fear in the Christian world that Suleiman generated cannot be underestimated but Christian rulers whose wealth and armies would be needed to repel his significant incursions into central Europe were locked into longstanding hostilities over territory in France, the Netherlands and Italy. Clement knew all three Christian rulers having met them in the largely diplomatic role he played prior to his papacy playing a significant part in the continuous cycle of wars, treaties and shifting alliances with which, as Pope, he had to cope as a temporal ruler against a background of spiritual duty to promote peace, counter the challenge to his spiritual supremacy posed by Lutheranism and prevent the advance of Islam into Christian Europe.

In December 1527, when one of Henry's most long serving and trusted diplomats, William Knight, had arrived to plead Henry's case for annulment, Pope Clement was trapped in the Castel Sant'Angelo by mutinous troops of Charles V who had sacked Rome on the 6th May. After a lot of money changed hands in January 1528 Clement was free and approved a commission to hear Henry's case for an annulment. More significantly Clement adopted a far more conciliatory attitude towards Charles which probably involved some sort of agreement not to agree to the annulment of his Auntie Catherine's marriage, not just for family reasons but because it suited Charles, having just celebrated the birth of a son and heir, the future Philip II of Spain, that his great rival Uncle Henry had very little chance that his now 41 year old wife would produce one for him. *Poor Charles, he would have turned in his grave when his son married Aunt Catherine's daughter, Mary, his first cousin, failed to return England to the Catholic fold via a diplomatic marriage and was then thwarted in his attempt to return it by conquest by the daughter, Elizabeth, of his Aunt's rival, Anne Boleyn.*

Lastly on this point, it was up to Henry to prove that the circumstances of his marriage warranted an annulment. Having failed to get an instant answer from Clement he had to prove his case in an ecclesiastical court/Commission in England where the principal adjudicators/Commissioners were Cardinal Thomas Wolsey, Lord Chancellor of England and papal legate, Lorenzo Campeggio, the last ever Cardinal Protector of England. This Legatine Court was a political nicety because for at least four very good reasons, personal, political, legal and spiritual, he was never going to grant the annulment that Henry was seeking.

Most of what follows is circumstantial supposition based on my oft repeated hobbyhorse that the character flaws, emotional inclinations and personal strengths and weaknesses of the 'great' are no less prone to human frailty than yours or mine!

Giulio di Giuliano de Medici who became Pope Clement VII was himself illegitimate. He never knew his mother or, at least, was never able to acknowledge her publicly. He owed everything to his family, firstly, his uncle, Lorenzo the Magnificent, gran maestro of the Florentine Republic from 1469-92, who adopted Giulio, brought him up and educated him alongside his own sons and, secondly, to his cousin and adoptive brother, Lorenzo, who became Pope Leo X in 1513. Giulio knew all about show trials or papal hearings because Lorenzo held one soon after he became Pope and declared his cousin legitimate on the flimsiest of evidence that Giulio's father and mother were betrothed when he was conceived. Once legitimised Giulio could pursue his career in the Church. It is highly unlikely that he would have done anything without serious consideration that would have led to a princess being declared illegitimate. He knew how that felt.

Furthermore, in 1494, Lorenzo the Magnificent's eldest son, Piero the Unfortunate, lost control of Florence and the Medicis were thrown out. It took 18 years before, with the considerable help of Julius II and the Spanish troops of Ferdinand of Aragon, the family were able to re-establish themselves with Giulio becoming gran maestro in 1519. His debt of honour to Pope Julius and King Ferdinand, I suspect, outweighed any reciprocation of gratitude for the words of support Henry had put in his book.

Politically, Clement was under suffocating pressure to condescend to the wishes of Charles V both to hold on to the Papal States and to repel the Muslim menace. After Charles helped to restore Florence to the Medicis yet again in 1530 he needed him even more to lead the so-called Counter Reformation and was his deferential ally until his death in 1534.

6. The Legatine Court

Legally, Pope Clement, quite correctly, saw no reason for an annulment. The case that Henry put before him started with a confession to his spiritual leader and a plea to relieve him of his guilt over marrying his brother's wife and remove the divine curse of a childless marriage that it brought upon his head. The normal practice to absolve such a sin was to build a church, found an abbey or buy an indulgence not to annul a marriage which was a sacrament intended for life. Canon 1055§1 says:

> ...**matrimony** is the "covenant by which a man and a woman establish between themselves a partnership of the whole of life and which is ordered by its nature to the good of the spouses and the procreation and education of offspring", and which "has been raised by Christ the Lord to the dignity of a sacrament between the baptised."[186]

[186] en.wikipedia.org/wiki/Cecily_Neville,_Duchess_of_York. Accessed 21/02/2020.

Henry's second ploy was to point out that the grounds for the dispensation being to ensure peace in Christian Europe were misperceived. There was no likelihood of war between England and Spain. Henry's claim was somewhat tongue in cheek I suspect, which, given the ambition of the Habsburg family, was at best an opinion, hardly an assertion, and was unlikely to persuade such a politically savvy operator as Clement.

Ploy three was to raise an impediment to the marriage. Henry claimed that he was an unwilling participant in the marriage contract, coerced into it by his father and too young to understand what it really entailed. The subsequent marriage hardly bore that out.

Once Catherine produced the papal bull issued by Julius II, it became clear that the consummation issue was irrelevant because, as Thurston pointed out, it contained the words 'forsan consummavissetis' (perhaps consummated) which meant that—despite Catherine's determination to prove that the marriage to Arthur was not consummated with reference to the qualification of penile-vaginal sexual penetration, which provided some bawdy entertainment, probably, distasteful to the Commission members—the marriage to Henry was sanctioned as legal by the Pope regardless of the circumstances of Catherine's previous marriage.

In desperation, the legatine commission having failed in Wolsey's intention to present an incontrovertible case to the pope for annulment, Henry turned to the parameters of papal power, perhaps the first step towards his need to reject it entirely. By what right had the pope the power to provide a dispensation for a situation that was clearly stated by God in the Bible, God's word, to be sinful? With the practice of indulgences under severe scrutiny, dispensations were also being challenged.

Henry's challenge must have been influenced by Luther's spiritual and theological thinking and has the feeling of a threat rather than an argument. If Clement had granted an annulment on the grounds that his predecessor, Julius, exceeded his spiritual power, he would have accepted a spiritual argument that would have rendered the existence of a Pope as unnecessary to Christianity. The successors of St Peter would no longer hold or ever have held 'the keys to the Kingdom of Heaven' (Matthew 16:18-19). The Papacy would self-destruct.

7. Rule Change

Under the rules that obtained in December 1532, Mary was legitimate because her parents' marriage was legitimate. Only when Henry changed the rules by appointing Thomas Cranmer as Archbishop of Canterbury in October, privately marrying Anne Boleyn in January 1533 and having his marriage to Catherine annulled by Cranmer in May 1533 did she become illegitimate.

Nine times out of 10, changing the rules involves changing the law and I need to repeat my caveat concerning the Law. Always ask whose Law is it? In this case, it was most definitely Henry's. Catherine knew he would get his own way.

In her first appearance at the Legatine court on 21 June 1529, she knelt in front of her king and husband and made a plea for justice. Towards the end, she said this:

> *Therefore, it is a wonder to hear what new inventions are now invented against me, that never intended but honesty. And cause me to stand to the order and judgment of this new court, wherein ye may do me much wrong, if ye intend any cruelty; for ye may condemn me for lack of sufficient answer, having no indifferent counsel, but such as be assigned me, with whose wisdom and learning I am not acquainted. Ye must consider that they cannot be indifferent counsellors for my part which be your subjects, and taken out of your own council before, wherein they be made privy, and dare not, for your displeasure, disobey your will and intent, being once made privy thereto.*[187]

8. Henry's Law

Between 1529 and 1534, Henry morphed from an autocrat to a despot, adding cruelty and oppression to his egotistical exercise of his Royal prerogative; England extracted itself from the Catholic European spiritual, cultural and social fraternity bound together by the Pope and the Anglican Church was born. Before we consider whether this advanced the status of women in England let us look briefly at the legal changes enacted by Henry and his parliament.

For 7 years between 1163 and 1170, the temporal boss of England, Henry II, and the spiritual boss of England, Thomas Becket, had quarrelled about who was the boss of bosses, the one who was the ultimate recourse to justice under the civil/common law, the King, or the one who held a similar status for canon law, the Archbishop of Canterbury, because there were overlaps such as criminal clerics and the appointment of public officials. As far as the nation of England (and the Angevin Empire) was concerned Henry ruled all those who were its citizens and lived under the protection of its laws, including all priests, bishops and archbishops.

But, Thomas Becket, the man, may have been Henry's subject but as Archbishop of Canterbury, he had another foreign boss, the Pope, who was one step closer to God. The quarrel ended in, arguably, British history's most famous episcopicide. 23 years after Becket's death, Henry's son, Richard I, faced a show trial to cover up the fact that, as a crusader, he had been illegally imprisoned and held to ransom. Richard began his defence with these words.

"I am born of a rank which recognises no superior but God".

Henry VIII fancied himself a bit of a warrior king after the fashion of his illustrious ancestor. He wanted his own realm in which everyone accepted that

[187] https://www.theanneboleynfiles.com/21-june-1529-god-commit-cause/ Accessed 22/01/2020.

they were his subjects, totally loyal to him because his law was God's law and only God knew better than an anointed king.

For 350 years or so, the extent of the power and jurisdiction of State and Church had not been agreed by either party. In 1392, for instance, the parliament of Richard II had passed the Statute of Praemunire. Its intention, according to Wikipedia, was to limit the powers of the papacy in England, by making it illegal to appeal an English court case to the pope if the king objected, or for anyone to act in a way that recognised papal authority over the authority of the king.

The supremacy over England's subjects was not, therefore, a new issue but by 1532, it had become, I think, the issue. What had started as a dispute over getting rid of a non-productive wife and marrying one capable of producing a male heir, one who, incidentally the king fancied but who refused to become his mistress, became a 'great matter' involving three loves that ranked higher in Henry's affections than any woman; power, God and his subjects.

Firstly, 7 years after he first conceived his plan to replace Catherine, and growing fed up with the Pope's prevarication and Campeggio's procrastination, Henry made his move to remove the Pope's influence over the justice system of his country and sorting out once and for all who on Earth was the last recourse in dispensing justice in his lands, who had the final say in doing God's will on his patch of His creation.

Wolsey having died in 1530, his successor, Thomas Cromwell, drafted an Act that did just that. By establishing Henry as an Emperor anointed by God and therefore equal in rank to the Pope both in the spiritual and the temporal hierarchy no appeals to the Pope as a higher power were allowed and no papal rulings were legal in England and Wales unless agreed to by the King who, like the Pope, was sanctified by God. The Statute in Restraint of Appeals or the Ecclesiastical Appeals Act, made law in April 1533, 3 months after Henry's bigamous marriage to Anne Boleyn, effectively established the Divine Right of Kings in defence of which principle, 116 years later, Henry's great-great nephew, Charles I, was to lose his head.

Secondly, Henry had to make sure that the English and Welsh clergy submitted to his power in matters spiritual as well as temporal. For this he needed an ally from amongst them. He had been made aware by his future wife, Anne, of a Cambridge don who had acted as the Boleyn family chaplain. Thomas Cranmer joined the working party on the king's annulment and suggested by-passing the papacy by collecting a dossier of theological and historical opinions from learned men throughout Europe. Whether Cranmer intended it or not the dossier, *Collectanea Satis Copiosa,* was used to preface the 1533 Act. In October 1532, while an ambassador to the Holy Roman Emperor, Charles V, he was appointed Archbishop of Canterbury. Although married to a relative of Andreas Osiander, a noted Lutheran theologian and Protestant reformer from Nuremberg, centre of the Reformation, Cranmer was approved by the Pope and made a bishop, Henry having paid for the necessary papal bulls, in March 1533.

The Church had its own talking shop and rule maker, a quasi-parliament, called the Convocation of Canterbury. In May 1532, Edward Foxe, Bishop of Hereford, on behalf of the king, had presented three articles to the Convocation for its approval and ratification.

The three articles which were to become known as the Submission of the Clergy were as follows.

- the Church of England was to renounce its authority to make church law (canons) without royal licence.
- the Convocation was to submit all existing canons to the scrutiny of a committee, which would be appointed by the King. Half of the members would be from Parliament (eight from each house) and half from the clergy. This committee would proclaim void all canons it found offensive.
- the Convocation was to retain the remaining canons with the King's consent.[188]

On 11 May 1532, Henry issued this challenge to the clergy. Where does your loyalty lie? He made this speech to Parliament.

> Well beloved subjects, we thought that the clergy of our realm had been our subjects wholly, but now we have well perceived that they be but half our subjects, yea, and scarce our subjects; for all the prelates at their consecration make an oath to the Pope, clean contrary to the oath that they make to us, so that they seem to be his subjects, and not ours. The copy of both oaths I deliver here to you, requiring you to invent some order, that we be not thus deluded of our spiritual subjects.[189]

When Warham and the lesser clergy showed some hesitation, Henry sent a delegation of great landowners, to whom many of them owed their 'living', to apply some pressure. On 16th May the articles were signed, and Henry had removed all opposition to his view of good and bad, right and wrong. When Warham died on August 22nd any tremor of defiance in parliament or convocation was isolated and silenced in the usual Henrician way (Sir Thomas More and Bishop John Fisher were both executed in the summer of 1535. More on this later.)

Once Cranmer was in place, the issue of the annulment, now called a divorce, was re-presented to the Convocation of Canterbury. On 5 April 1533, the assembled clerics agreed by majority vote on the two issues that were stalling progress.

---

188 en.wikipedia.org/wiki/Submission_of_the_Clergy. Accessed 28/01/2020.
189 Ibid.

> "Notarial attestation of the determination of the Convocation of Canterbury, begun 5 Nov. 1529, on the two points discussed in the King's divorce, determining, 1, that the Pope has no power of dispensing in case of a marriage where the brother's widow has been cognita. The house consisted of 66 theologians. The proxies were 197; the negatives 19. The second question was whether Katharine was cognita. The numbers present, 44; one holding the proxies of three bishops. Decided in the affirmative against five or six negatives. Dated 5 April 1533."[190]

Given the go-ahead, Cranmer now set up the all-English version of the Legatine court to try Henry's case. A fortnight later, on 23 May 1533, Cranmer announced its findings. To marry your brother's widow was against the law of God and the King should be forthwith 'divorced' from Catherine. On 28th May, Cranmer declared Henry's new marriage to Anne was valid. Mary, according to the new rules, Henry's Law, was canonically and civilly a bastard. Anne's daughter, Elizabeth, replaced her as heir presumptive. She was not allowed to visit her mother. The very foundations of her faith were being undermined by a JCB variously called the Reformation, Protestantism, Ecclesia Anglicana, the Church of England. She was 17, single and alone.

9. Reformation and Consolidation

Henry had got his own way, but he needed his subjects' approval. Cromwell and his political cronies needed parliamentary ratification of all that had been rushed through. To summarise, the Pope's interference in England's, for England read Henry, affairs needed removing forever. Two Acts were passed in 1534, The Ecclesiastical Licences Act which removed all direct payments to Rome, including the ancient payment of Peter's Pence, and The Appointment of Bishops Act which removed all interference in clerical appointments by the Pope and all purchases of jobs in the Clergy from the Pope and all yearly payments to hold on to them.

Although 7 September 1533 had resulted in the immediate disappointment of a girl child, Anne had proved her procreative ability and there was every reason to hope boys would follow. It was time then to make official what the last four years wrangling had been about. In the first parliamentary session of 1534, Parliament now in thrall to the MP for Taunton, Thomas Cromwell, passed an Act of Succession. From the wording of this Act we get the official, Establishment version of why Henry had done what he had done over the previous four, maybe, six years.

Its opening statements made it clear that, to avoid the civil strife that had occurred in the past, the rules for the Succession would be made absolutely clear, would be agreed by everyone who had a stake in it and, most definitely (the words used 'abhor and detest' could not have been more definite.), when it came

---

[190] www.theanneboleynfiles.com/5-april-1533-convocation-rules/. Accessed 29/01/2020.

to who would be King, Emperor even, of England and Wales and Lord of Ireland there would be no more interference from 'political' Bishops of Rome who were unduly influenced by foreign leaders. So, who would succeed?

> … that it may be enacted by your highness, with the assent of the lords spiritual and temporal, and the Commons, in this present Parliament assembled, and by the authority of the same, that the marriage heretofore solemnised between your highness and the Lady Katherine, being before lawful wife to Prince Arthur, your elder brother, which by him was **carnally known**, as does duly appear by sufficient proof in a lawful process had and made before Thomas, by the sufferance of God, now archbishop of Canterbury and metropolitan and primate of all this realm, shall be, by authority of this present Parliament, definitively, clearly, and absolutely declared, deemed, and adjudged to be **against the laws of Almighty God**, and also accepted, reputed, and taken of no value nor effect, but utterly **void and annulled**, and the separation thereof, made by the said archbishop, shall be **good and effectual to all intents and purposes**; … every such licence, dispensation, act or acts, thing or things heretofore had, made, done, or to be done to the contrary thereof, shall be void and of none effect; and that the said Lady Katherine shall be from henceforth called and reputed only dowager to Prince Arthur, and not queen of this realm; and that the lawful matrimony had and solemnised between your highness and your most dear and entirely beloved wife Queen Anne, shall be established, and taken for undoubtful, true, sincere, and perfect ever hereafter, according to the just judgment of the said Thomas, archbishop of Canterbury, metropolitan and primate of all this realm, whose grounds of judgment have been confirmed, as well by the whole clergy of this realm in both the Convocations, and by both the universities thereof, as by the universities of Bologna, Padua, Paris, Orleans, Toulouse, Anjou, and divers others, and also by the private writings of many right excellent well-learned men…[191]
> [my highlighting]

The Act also made it clear that the affinity rule by which Henry's marriage to Catherine had been annulled applied to all his subjects. Those within the degrees stated were not allowed to marry and those already married could only be excepted by ordained clergy of the Church of England. Such restrictions were only lifted in the early 20th Century. The Act confirmed male supremacy and the patrilineal rights of sons but went on to recognise daughters of royal blood.

> And for default of such sons of your body begotten, and of the heirs of the several bodies of every such sons lawfully begotten, that then the said imperial crown, and other the premises, shall be to the issue female

[191] www.luminarium.org/encyclopedia/firstactofsuccession.htm. Accessed 01/02/2020.

> between your majesty and your said most dear and entirely beloved wife, Queen Anne, begotten, that is to say: first to the eldest issue female, which is the Lady Elizabeth, now princess, and to the heirs of her body lawfully begotten, and for default of such issue, then to the second issue female, and to the heirs of her body lawfully begotten, and so from issue female to issue female, and to the heirs of their bodies one after another, by course of inheritance, according to their ages, as the crown of England has been accustomed, and ought to go, in cases where there be heirs females to the same; and for default of such issue, then the said imperial crown, and all other the premises, shall be in the right heirs of your highness for ever.[192]

Just in case anyone in his realm disagreed with any of this, the Act made it clear that this was high treason punishable by death and that saying nothing was not sufficient. It required an Oath of Allegiance.

Henry, almost certainly on Cromwell's advice, realised that he needed parliamentary recognition of his God-given status as earthly boss of everything that went on in England and Wales, everything! As such he needed more than the normal feudal oath of allegiance. In the autumn session of 1534 Parliament passed the Act of Supremacy which demanded an oath.

> Be it enacted by authority of this present Parliament that the King, our sovereign lord, his heirs and successors, kings of this realm, shall be taken, accepted and reputed the only supreme head in earth of the Church of England, called Anglicana Ecclesia; ... most to the pleasure of Almighty God, the increase of virtue in Christ's religion, and for the conservation of the peace, unity and tranquillity of this realm, any usage, custom, foreign law, foreign authority, prescription or any other thing or things to the contrary hereof notwithstanding.[193]

Finally, to stick all these changes together within the ruler-ruled compact, Henry and Cromwell needed to update the 1352 Treasons Act to suit the circumstances. These were simple: agree with everything we have done—divorced and married again legally on earth and in heaven, replaced the heir presumptive and affirmed male preference in the Succession, replaced the Pope as Head of the Church of England and diverted any of his income to the Crown—and might yet have to do and swear an oath to signify that you do. If you do not, silence is not enough. Take the oath or be executed for high treason.

Under the Treason Act 1534 Sir Thomas More, former Lord Chancellor and friend and Bishop of Rochester, John Fisher, Cardinal and intractable opponent, were imprisoned, tried and executed in June/July 1535: their offence—malicious silence and malicious conspiracy. The word 'malicious' implies 'harm'. By staying silent both men thought that they were doing no harm whereas, according

---

[192] Ibid.

[193] www.luminarium.org/encyclopedia/actsupremacy.htm. Accessed 01/02/2020.

to their accusers, they were harming a chain of actions that were "to the pleasure of Almighty God, the increase of virtue in Christ's religion, and for the conservation of the peace, unity and tranquillity of this realm". The bonds around the moral wrists of Henry's subjects were tightly secured by the inescapable forces of King and God, the God King of ancient times with power over this life and the next. In more objective terms, Henry's obsession with the succession had turned him into a despot and shaped the insularity of England forevermore.

10. Religion

On 17 May 1536, Thomas Cranmer confirmed the annulment of Henry's second marriage condemning his second daughter to illegitimacy. Elizabeth was 4 months short of her third birthday when she joined her 20-year-old sister in the wilderness. Her mother was executed two days later for all sorts of reasons, incest, adultery and treason being those most mentioned. The somewhat salacious details of her relationships with men have acquired iconic status in Establishment patriarchal history forming a male generated smokescreen whose murky depths have only been investigated by truth-seeking historians. Henry's marriage to Anne was annulled the grounds for which did not include any of the reasons for which she was executed. Cranmer's announcement was as follows:

> "in consequence of certain just and lawful impediments which, it was said, were unknown at the time of the union, but had lately been confessed to the Archbishop by the lady herself."[194]

Cranmer was taking one for the team here, leaving people to infer that Anne had confessed to having a pre-marital contract with the man she wanted to marry, Henry Percy, who was to become 6th Earl of Northumberland. Percy always denied this allegation although his unhappy wife, Mary Talbot, daughter of the Earl of Shrewsbury, always hoped that it might have been true in order that she could obtain an annulment of her marriage.

Cranmer almost certainly said this because the other reason for the marriage to be annulled would have done Henry no credit. Eustace Chapuys, Imperial ambassador, referred back to the fact that Henry had 'known' Anne's sister, Mary, the other Boleyn girl, and thus broken the affinity rule yet again, this time with a bit of incestuous consanguinity involved as well. The adultery of kings was so commonplace that few would have blinked at this revelation—Henry, remember had already recognised one illegitimate child, Henry Fitzroy, son of his mistress, Elizabeth Blount, but the scandalous nature of it and despotic hypocrisy it would have displayed would not have endeared Henry to his people who, generally speaking, were happy to be rid of the influence of Rome but unhappy about the king's new marriage.

---

194 www.theanneboleynfiles.com/17-may-1536-the-annulment-of-henry-viii-and-anne-boleyns-marriage/. Accessed 08/02/2020.

Politician priests were commonplace throughout Europe before the 19th century. In the case of Anne Boleyn Cranmer put his loyalty to his earthly lord above his duty to God. A public platform on which Anne could refute the allegations was avoided by putting her case in front of only a group of Lords. (Only 26 of the 53 who should have sat delivered the verdicts on Anne, her brother and her associates, *leaving us to infer that they were the loyal ones.*)

Cranmer's announcement on 17th May followed an investigation of the marriage circumstances by a group of ecclesiastical lawyers and himself. Finally, he broke the Seal of Confession established by the Lateran Council of 1215—sin and penitent should not be revealed—which under different circumstances could have led to his excommunication. (He was, in fact, already virtually excommunicated under the papal interdict of 31 August 1535 which followed the execution of Bishop John Fisher.) When put later to the Convocation and the Parliament both approved it.

It was just as well because Henry was moving on fast. Three days after the execution, he was betrothed to Jane Seymour and within two weeks, he had married her. Soon after all this, Henry celebrated his 46th birthday, looking forward no doubt to a string of sons with his new wife who at 30 years of age or so had many years of childbearing in her.

Chapter 28
The Yorkist Viper

To gain everything and lose everything in the space of a moment. That is the fate of all princes destined for the throne.
– C.S. Pacat, *Kings Rising*

I've plotted and schemed all my life. There is no other way to be a King, fifty and alive all at once.
– James Goldman, *The Lion in Winter*

Preamble

Henry must, however, have been aware of the high probability, given the average longevity of a man in those times, that even his first son would be a minor and a king. The politics of this would surely have meant planning for a regency, for which the only too powerful and recent examples, Henry VI (the Wars of the Roses) and 'the wicked uncle', Richard III (the Princes in the Tower), did not bode well. The obvious answer was to keep everyone guessing which, by getting agreement to the succession being decided by his will, is exactly what he did.

In early 1537, it became clearer by the day that Jane had conceived and the birth of a male heir apparent would put to bed all worries about the succession. However, for them to sleep peacefully, the 46-year-old Henry would have to live until 1555 no matter how many little princes or princesses Jane bore him. To live to the ripe old age of 65 in Tudor times, you had to be extremely lucky and extremely strong. I doubt, given what he had had to go through to father an heir apparent, that Henry felt lucky. He had said to the Pope that he felt God was punishing him for marrying his brother's wife.

With his recent jousting injury to contend with, I doubt he felt very strong either. What sort of Regency would it be? Catholic leaning or Protestant leaning? I feel sure that work on his will began straight after the birth and Jane's death probably hastened by the papal bull of December 17th finally confirming his excommunication which since 1535 had been suspended hoping for a change of heart.

It is not often highlighted but, although Henry had expelled the Pope and Papism, whatever that was, his decision, with some persuasive pressure from Thomas Cromwell, whose motives are still not clear to this day, was political, probably financial, but, above all, as with everything that concerned Henry, *in my opinion the ultimate egotist*, personal. This highly intelligent and well educated man was rightly full of fear that the thing he had wanted most in the world and for which he had made life changing decisions for himself, his family and his realm, namely a son and heir, was a fragile project over which he would have no control. There was no safe and sure way of allaying that fear except his belief, inevitably forlorn, that his magnificence with all its fear and potency would extend beyond the grave and his will be done. He, the archetypal autocratic despot, put his faith in democracy. *Amazing*!

Henry's religious beliefs and practices had not changed after the break with Rome. They remained faithful to the old ways unlike some reformers in Northern Europe. Henry believed in transubstantiation and clerical celibacy. The Protestant rewrite of the Book of Common Prayer occurred in the reign of Henry's son. The positions taken on religious reform assembled under two banners, not Catholic and Protestant as is generally believed, but conservatives and reformers. Given the choice Henry veered towards the conservative faction. He trusted advisers from both camps.

I think it safe to correct the view that Henry was a Protestant or that the Pilgrimage of Grace, which was triggered more by the Dissolution of the Monasteries and agrarian discontent than a headlong rush into Protestant doctrine and practice, or the Exeter Conspiracy at which we are about to look were dress rehearsals for a rerun of the Gunpowder Plot!

Throughout the year, 1538, following his son's birth, the widower Henry had to deal with the threat of foreign invasion from the newly formed alliance between Charles V and Francis I, some popular discontent with his religious reforms and the Will.

By just about any application of common law, the succession was sorted: Edward and his successors, then Mary and her successors, Elizabeth and her successors, Frances Grey, nee Brandon, elder daughter of Henry's younger sister, Mary, and Eleanor Clifford and her successors. However, as we know, Mary and Elizabeth were both excluded by their declared illegitimacy and Frances had 3 daughters, Ladies Jane, Katherine and Mary and Eleanor had one daughter, Margaret.

In 1538, their father/grandfather, Charles Brandon, Duke of Suffolk, a close friend, trusted adviser of Henry's and top enforcer in any war, was at the peak of his power and as trustworthy as anyone to serve the infant who would be king. His sons-in-law, Thomas Grey and Henry Clifford, possible consorts, stood on opposite sides of the fence, the former a staunch Protestant reformer, eventually beheaded in 1554 by Queen Mary, and the latter a flaky Catholic conservative, accused in Queen Elizabeth's reign of harbouring Popish priests.

Would Henry have seen any of these three as political Svengalis behind a female occupied throne? The other two strongmen and political heavyweights were both potential wicked uncle figures, the conservative Thomas Howard, Duke of Norfolk, who made his move in 1540, by introducing his niece, Catherine, the king's fifth wife, to court as a lady in waiting and Edward Seymour, his brother-in-law. Acutely aware of what had happened to his mother's brothers Henry is unlikely to have contemplated any arrangement involving either of these.

His older sister, Margaret, by sleeping with the enemy, was out of the question. Her son, James, was to die, allegedly of a broken heart, soon after his uncle's soldiers had utterly defeated him in 1542 at Solway Moss and the refusal of the Scots to honour the marriage contract between Henry's infant son and his great niece, Mary Queen of Scots, agreed at the Treaty of Greenwich was another Road Closed. Henry, himself, being the offspring of a similar pacification marriage, was furious and made more so by the decision by the Scottish regency, then under the influence of the very Catholic Cardinal Beaton, to marry off Mary to the heir to the French throne.

The point of all this analysis of the events of 1537-9 and its relevance to the Woman Question is that, effectively, by the time Henry had a male heir apparent the chances of his male heir apparent himself having a male heir apparent had been taken away. If Edward did not make it to a procreative age, which sadly was to be the case, the Tudor dynasty would have no choice but to have a Queen Regnant.

For most of his widowerhood, October 1537 to January 1540, Henry was reminded of the effect of his choices concerning the succession of the previous ten years by the so-called Exeter Conspiracy. Two legitimate Yorkist, Catholic bloodlines had survived the bloody recriminations of the early Tudor era. One came with a definite claim to the throne. The Yorkist kings, Edward IV and Richard III, had a middle brother, George, Duke of Clarence, who married Isabel Neville, daughter of Warwick, the Kingmaker. By the time his brother, Edward, had executed George for treason in 1478, he and Isabel had two surviving children, Edward, whose death, executed by Henry VII for treason in 1499, ended the direct male line from Edward III, and an older daughter, Margaret.

After a bit of a rags to riches story which included two spells as a lady in waiting to Catherine of Aragon and one as governess to Princess Mary 1537, Margaret Pole, Countess of Salisbury, a wealthy woman in her own right, found herself in an unwitting opposition to the king. She had four sons, Henry, Baron Montagu, Arthur, Reginald and Geoffrey, and a daughter, Ursula. Her third son, Reginald, recently made a Cardinal worked under Pope Paul III who excommunicated Henry, Cranmer and Cromwell in 1538 in various enterprises aimed at undermining the English Reformation.

Assailed by a lot of theological questions from Cromwell and others Reginald had snapped and, in a thesis/letter, now known as *De Unitate*, he disagreed with Henry's divorce, questioned his right to Royal Supremacy and called upon the Catholic princes of Europe to depose him. His job for the Pope in 1538-9 was to coordinate an embargo designed to weaken England's economy enough to bring about the fall of the king, possibly by invasion from Europe supported by Francis I and Charles V, or internal rebellion aimed at deposing Henry and replacing him with a Catholic monarch. Who would that be?

Princess Mary was, of course, the front runner, possibly with the extra tweak, as suggested by the Imperial ambassador, Eustace Chapuys, in 1536 of her marrying Reginald, not at that time an ordained priest, but there was the legitimacy problem. Montagu, Henry's second cousin and Reginald's older brother, was also a possibility. He, a great nephew, and Henry, a grandson, of Edward IV both shared the same amount of blood of their illustrious ancestor, Edward III. However, there was an even better candidate. Edward IV and Elizabeth Woodville had 7 daughters. The second youngest, Catherine, Henry's aunt, whom we looked at briefly in the previous chapter, married William Courtenay and it was their son, Henry, the king's first cousin, who was possibly the best alternative to any protestant leaning monarch, male or female.

Henry VIII, although I think he was at heart more of a Lancastrian Tudor was prepared to be generous in his patronage of his mother's Yorkist relatives as long as they were loyal and kept quiet about the cracks in his right to the throne and the basis of their claims to replace him. Margaret, her son, Henry Pole, his brother-in-law, Edward Neville, Henry's child-and teen-hood mucker, Nicholas Carew and, of course, his first cousin, Henry Courtenay (the Courtenays and the Nevilles were also cousins.) were all prominent courtiers and had been given important jobs working in or for the royal household: Margaret, as recently mentioned, was lady in waiting to Catherine of Aragon and governess of Princess Mary; Henry Pole was knighted and given his title, Baron Montagu; Edward had held lots of posts including Gentleman of the Privy Chamber; Nicholas was the king's Master of Horse and a Knight of the Garter and Henry Courtenay had his title of Earl of Devon due to the king's reversal of the attainder imposed by Henry VII and was made Marquess of Exeter in 1525. He was also a Gentleman of the Privy Chamber and sat on the Privy Council.

Reginald Pole who was to become the last Catholic Archbishop of Canterbury in 1556 had irrevocably thrown his lot in with the Papacy and was out of Henry's reach in Rome. The others might not have agreed with what was happening but had had, like many of the nobility, to accept it and join politically the conservative or reformist faction. The rift, if there was any, came with the Divorce. For Reginald it meant a choice. He chose the Pope. For the cousins it was about loyalty to friends, Catherine of Aragon and her daughter, Mary. For Carew it was more personal; a dislike of Cromwell and a personal grievance against Henry and Anne Boleyn had put him firmly in the conservative camp as a vocal champion of Mary.

Friends have things in common, one of which may have been the old faith but more passionate was their abhorrence of the treatment of their friend and mistress, Queen Catherine, and their dislike of the king's fixer, Thomas Cromwell, whose dissolution measures were causing much distress in their heartlands in the southwest of England. They may not have liked what was happening and who was in charge but, like their friend, Princess—or de facto ex-Princess—Mary they had submitted, probably feeling the same shame of betrayal that Mary had felt when she wrote her grovelling letter to her father on Thursday, 15 June 1536.

By 1538, the conservative faction was in the ascendancy. They wanted to go back to how things were, so, naturally, they talked about it. They also must have written to Reginald Pole (When the hue and cry was heard letters and papers were burnt.), he was family after all, and they must have moaned about Cromwell and his reforms, disliked Anne Boleyn and bemoaned the fates of Catherine and Mary and sought answers to my question, What if the king and his infant son died? Cromwell had spies everywhere and monitored their tittle-tattle. When he had heard enough, he picked on the weakest, the least discreet and the neediest.

On 29 August 1538, he arrested Geoffrey Pole, youngest son of the Countess of Salisbury, in considerable debt and of questionable temperament, an ideal candidate for the carrot and the stick. In fear of the rack through which he would betray his family he tried to commit suicide. Failing in that evasion he probably took the carrot, his life for all that he knew about his family and the Courtenays and their dealings with Cardinal Pole. There was not much but we can imagine Cromwell putting two and two together for the ever-unpredictable king who would have deeply resented the failure of his cousins to submit to his power and feared for the future of his newly born son.

All who could be rounded up, were, Henry Pole, his mother, the Countess, wife, Jane and son and heir, Henry, Henry Courtenay, his wife, Gertrude, and his son and heir, Edward, and Henry Pole's brother-in-law, Edward Neville. Their sister, Ursula, married to Henry Stafford, avoided censure (Whether the Staffords were reformist or just neutral is difficult to ascertain but their son, Thomas, rebelled against Queen Mary and was beheaded in 1557 and their daughter was a prominent figure in the court of Queen Elizabeth). In November 1538, the three main names, Montagu, Exeter and Neville were beheaded, in March 1539 and May 1541 respectively. Sir Nicholas Carew and the Countess followed them to the block.

Whatever treasonous serpent, real or imagined, in the King's bosom, the Exeter Conspiracy had spawned, its head, like those involved, had been surgically and savagely removed as had the male rivals to the infant Edward. Henry Pole's son like his wife disappeared in the Tower and Geoffrey, in mental turmoil, went into exile. Reginald remained abroad and Edward Courtenay was not released until his mother's friend, Mary, came to the throne in 1553. Edward, considered at various times as a suitable husband for Mary and Elizabeth, went on to be implicated in Thomas Wyatt's rebellion against Mary's marriage to Philip II of Spain, and die in exile in Venice in 1556 unmarried and childless. With these deaths and the exclusion of his older sister's issue, Henry had only females to consider.

- Princess Mary and her descendants (restored by the 1543/44 Act of Succession)
- Princess Elizabeth and her descendants (restored by the 1543/44 Act of Succession)
- Lady Frances Grey
- Lady Jane Grey

- Lady Katherine Grey
- Lady Mary Grey
- Lady Eleanor Clifford
- Lady Margaret Clifford

Necessity is the mother of invention. Edward III's bloodline superseded gender and, if I dare say it, is the true mark of being 'English' rather than Anglo-Saxon, Anglo-Norman or Anglo-Danish, a re-invention, some might say re-invigoration, which would not have been possible without these largely unheralded 14th, 15th and 16th century noblewomen.

Chapter 29
Tudor Women

Some men are sent to heaven by torturers who thought they were doing god's work by sending them to hell.
– Bangambiki Habyarimana

Saintliness is very odd. When people encounter it, they often take it for something else, something completely unlike it: indifference, mockery, scheming, coldness, insolence, perhaps even contempt. But they're mistaken, and that makes them furious. They commit an awful crime. This is doubtless the reason why most saints end up as martyrs.
– Philippe Claudel

Understand that. The only power they have is in death. The harder they die, the louder their voice, the deeper the echoes.
– Pierce Brown

Preamble

When Henry died in 1547, 142 years had passed since Christine de Pizan had refuted the negative view of women held by men, yet still advocated submission to it. What had changed for the better or worse as far as women were concerned? Just to set the record straight about my focus on upper class women and royalty. I must leave the story of ordinary womenfolk to social historians far more qualified than me to tell it. I can only imagine the daily toil and drudgery of their lives, much like their menfolk, the toll on their vitality of constant pregnancy and birth and the soul-destroying omnipresence of hunger, disease and death.

One or two, like Joan of Arc, raised themselves above the anonymous masses, mostly in the context, like the ordinary men of those times, of challenge, rebellion and desperation at their oppression by the ruling class. We will be meeting one or two.

Henry liked his women to be intelligent but submissive. His mistresses made no demands on him. Catherine had dared to make a stand and Anne Boleyn had spoken her mind and enjoyed society, including the attention of men. Catherine Parr got away with expressing her opinion in 1546 (*see later*) and kept her views to herself thereafter. Catherine Howard was his midlife crisis. (*What was he thinking!*) His favourite queen was Jane Seymour, not just because she did her duty and bore him a son but because she attracted no limelight, no moths to the flame. Anne of Cleves made no fuss about the annulment of their marriage and accepted what was offered, becoming known as the 'King's beloved sister'.

The surest proof of how he regarded them is to be found in how he honoured them in death. When he died, Henry was buried beside Jane in St Georges Chapel, Windsor—together forever. He mourned her for three months. Anne of Cleves was buried by his daughter, Mary, in Westminster Abbey and honoured with the epitaph "Anne of Cleves Queen of England…" Catherine's epitaph in Peterborough we have already discussed. Henry did not attend her funeral and forbade Mary to do so. Anne Boleyn and Catherine Howard were buried in unmarked graves in the parish church of Tower Hill where their heads were removed, St Peter ad Vincula. Wikipedia tells us this:

> A list of "remarkable persons" buried in the chapel between 1534 and 1747 is listed on a table on the west wall. Thomas Babington Macaulay memorialised those buried in the chapel in his 1848 History of England:
>
> > In truth there is no sadder spot on the earth than that little cemetery. Death is there associated, not, as in Westminster Abbey and Saint Paul's, with genius and virtue, with public veneration and with imperishable renown; not, as in our humblest churches and churchyards, with everything that is most endearing in social and domestic charities; but with whatever is darkest in human nature and in human destiny, with the savage triumph of implacable enemies, with the inconstancy, the ingratitude, the cowardice of friends, with all the miseries of fallen greatness and of blighted fame. Thither have been carried, through successive ages, by the rude hands of gaolers, without one mourner following, the bleeding relics of men who had been the captains of armies, the leaders of parties, the oracles of senates, and the ornaments of courts.[195]

Henry was a consummate politician—that the price of political failure was often execution was not exceptionally brutal for his times—but what we have seen, even on this brief visit to his world, is that he was spiteful, no slight went unavenged, and egotistical—as long as you did as you were told he was kind and generous. He was, of course, also a hypocrite, a trait shared over millennia by millions of males, certainly powerful males, blissfully unaware of that weakness in their 'civilised' persona or that it was a weakness at all. His treatment of women reflected the values of his times.

Much as popular history would paint a picture of an all-powerful ruler whose head and heart migrated to his codpiece, his whole life was dominated by the procreative power of women and the political advantage to be gained from his direction of their lives. He displayed a ruthless disregard for those that crossed him ending their treasonous threat with the ultimate silence of death.

---

[195] en.wikipedia.org/wiki/Church_of_St_Peter_ad_Vincula. Accessed 11/03/2020.

Two cases, apart from Anne Boleyn, Catherine Howard and Margaret, Countess of Salisbury, stand out. On 30 April 1534, six people, 5 men and one woman, were hanged for treason at Tyburn. The woman was 28-year-old Elizabeth Barton, known in history as the Holy Maid or Nun of Kent. Barton was an 'ecstatic' prophetess who claimed to see into the future. A domestic servant, Elizabeth, with the help at one time or other of the five men on the gallows alongside her, became a nun and a 'fanatical' Catholic who was regarded as a danger to the state. The reason she was at Tyburn, however, was that she criticised Henry's decision to divorce and remarry, making some frightening prophesies about the fate of Henry, the mortal man subject to God's judgement.

Part of the campaign to discredit her was a denigration of her sex which Henry must have condoned (the Act of Attainder by which she was condemned could not have been law without his signature). Diane Watt convinces me that Elizabeth and her coterie of religious men were far more politically motivated than at first appears. Indeed, ecstatic prophecy or something of the sort was one way in which a woman of no rank could make her views public. The miraculously divine nature of prophesy sat well with the vision of a virgin from whose womb emanated a voice not of this world, convincing enough, apparently, to take in Thomas Cranmer!

Men, generally, did not want to come to other than sexual terms with the mysteries of the female anatomy and physiology. Added to the usual slur of having sex with holy men was the fetish value to some male onlookers of, in the words of Richard Morison, protégé of Thomas Cromwell and apologist for Henry VIII, 'the spectacle of a woman prostrated on the floor, with her body convulsing and her open mouth pouring forth heretical and abhorrent words in a clearly vicious image of female sexuality'.[196]

Henry, who had spoken to Elizabeth at least twice, liked her at first, offering her a position as Abbess, but when she openly criticised, and possibly threatened him with a place in Hell, his vicious streak came to bear on her. Again, the manner of her death was symbolic of the deeper motives behind her execution. She had engaged in treasonable talk and language by challenging the decision to divorce for which she was publicly hanged along with her fellow accused, all people leading a life devoted to God's work but believing that the Pope was their spiritual leader and the King their temporal leader. When it came to his pleasures Henry was courteous and chivalrous to women—if they were submissive—but when it came to his position of power, his majesty, the chivalry of gender was irrelevant. Treason was gender neutral.

Private executions probably took many forms—the famous case of George, Duke of Clarence, Henry's great uncle, and the butt of Malmsey wine comes to mind—but public executions made a statement (they were not abolished until 1868) apart from the obvious one of deterrence by the prospect of savage retribution. There were three methods; beheading, reserved for noble traitors and deemed to be more merciful; hanging, with the added extras of drawing and

---

[196] en.wikipedia.org/wiki/Church_of_St_Peter_ad_Vincula. Accessed 11/03/2020.

quartering, reserved for men only because for a woman it would involve nudity, and burning at the stake, often associated with heresy and, in the following century, witchcraft.

Although the practice of burning heretics at the stake, established in a law, De Haeretico Comburendo, passed in 1401 by Henry IV to suppress Lollardy, was for both genders it had come to be seen as a woman's death for, possibly, sexual reasons. The same sexual imagery a woman's lower limbs writhing and twitching noted by Morison, in theory, was unavoidable in hanging (It was not until 1571 that the infamous 'Tyburn Tree' or 'Three-legged Horse' was built to modernise the process of public hanging. Up to that time, hanging was most often achieved by chucking the condemned off the back of a cart. It was very imprecise and could leave a victim in his or her death throes for up to three quarters of an hour.) and masked by the flames of a good burning, although Wikipedia informs us that the 19th century historian, Jules Michelet, rightly or wrongly pointed out that "the first flame to rise consumed the clothes, revealing poor trembling nakedness"[197]. Elizabeth's head was displayed on a spike on London Bridge confirming her status as a traitor.

The next woman, other than Anne Boleyn, executed for treason was Margaret Stafford/Cheyne/Bulmer. Margaret was burned at the stake on May 25th, 1537, for her part in the northern rebellions, The Pilgrimage of Grace and Bigod's Rebellion. She had committed no act of treason, not even written letters like Elizabeth Barton, except to support the rebellion and encourage her husband to become involved. Both Margaret and her husband, Sir John Bulmer, were tortured behind closed doors in the Tower of London. We do not know to what activities they confessed.

It is commonly believed that Margaret was the illegitimate daughter of Edward Stafford, 3rd Duke of Buckingham, whom Henry had had beheaded for treason on 17 May 1521. This was certainly enough to condemn her, whether justly or unjustly, in Henry's eyes but she was, unlike Elizabeth, of dubious moral character. Her first husband, William Cheyne, had apparently sold her to Sir John who set her up as his mistress and, when the spouses of each of them died, married her. She was also described by one contemporary witness, Charles Wriothesley, as beautiful. We will return to wife sales in a later chapter but there is a strong whiff of Tudor sexism in the difference in their deaths and the perception of non-noble women who engaged in political, public activity.

Elizabeth was a papist nun whose gendered morality clearly survived the PR onslaught from Henry's henchmen. If she was genuine her views were from the patriarchal Christian God. If, as was decided with circumstantial evidence gathered by Henry's pro-divorce legal advisers, she was not genuine her male papist co-accused were influencing her and using her for their own subversive political reasons. A woman used by unscrupulous men was unfortunate but not uncommon in the Middle Ages. Margaret, on the other hand, satisfied her treasonous appetites via men. She persuaded a reluctant husband to not only rebel

---

[197] en.wikipedia.org/wiki/Burning_of_women_in_England. Accessed 15/03/2020.

but to become a leader of rebellion. Such women were dangerous and had to be made an example of. As Ruth and Madeleine Dodds observe:

> "She committed no overt act of treason; her offences were merely words and silence... It [her execution] was intended as an example to others. There can be no doubt that many women were ardent supporters of the Pilgrimage... Lady Bulmer's execution ... was an object-lesson to husbands ... to teach them to distrust their wives."[198]

Do we see here the deeply embedded gender bias of late middle-ages Christian culture playing a major role in what should have been a gender-neutral issue of Establishment politics, namely treason and dissent? A traitress could not have had reasons of her own, she was either the duped plaything of unscrupulous men, deserving of a bog-standard death in front of a mocking rather than adoring, reverential mob or an immoral witch enticing otherwise good, potentially loyal men into countercultural rebellion against the natural and God-created patriarchal status quo with their evil feminine charms, deserving of a death excoriating the female evil inside and out.

The most high-profile person in the realm trying to juggle the procreative, sexual fulfilment and political allure of women was, of course, Henry himself. With the annulment of his fourth political marriage to Anne of Cleves, aimed at strengthening ties with Reformer European states, and the execution of his reform-inclined mastermind, Thomas Cromwell, both in 1540, the Conservatives, led by Thomas Howard, 3rd Duke of Norfolk, regained their influence over the King. On the day Cromwell was executed, 28th July 1540, Henry married Howard's niece, Catherine. The 17-year-old did not last long and was beheaded on 13th February 1542. Interestingly, the men in her life, also received different deaths, Thomas Culpeper being beheaded, and Francis Dereham being drawn, hung and quartered.

It is unlikely that Catherine Howard had much influence on Henry except, perhaps, on his sexual health but his next queen, the wealthy twice-widowed Catherine Parr, whom he married on 12 July 1543, most certainly did. Although brought up a Catholic—her mother was a friend of Catherine of Aragon—and twice married to Catholic husbands she came to be known as a favourer of reform at a time when Howard and his co-conservative religious leader, Bishop Stephen Gardiner, were trying to convince the King to slow down reform in the hope that he would do an about turn and ally England to the Holy Roman Emperor, Charles V.

Circumstantial rumours had led to the downfall of Anne Boleyn and whistle-blowers opened the king's eyes to the indiscretions of Catherine Howard. For treason to be confirmed on the statement of just one person was not uncommon in those times of conspiracy and suspicion. (Thomas More had been convicted

[198] en.wikipedia.org/wiki/Margaret_Cheyne. Accessed 16/03/2020.

on the witness statement of Richard Rich whose willingness to do the monarch's dirty work ensured him, unusually for Tudor politicians, of a long career and a long life.) It seems utterly plausible, therefore, that, after the Catherine Howard failure, the conservative faction should have been gunning for the new Queen Catherine who seemed to have the King's ear and was bringing about the sort of rapprochement in his family that moderates hoped might happen in his realm as a whole.

Before the end of July 1543 Parliament had allowed Mary and her offspring and Elizabeth and her offspring back into the line of succession. The timing of the Act was caused by Henry's intention to prosecute the war with France in France itself but the retraction of the exclusion of his daughters could well have been influenced by his new wife. He signed the Third Act of Succession in February 1544. The Act allowed for him to set conditions on the rights of his daughters to succeed but none was specified. He could, however, specify them later in letters patent or by changing his will. With the family back together and Catherine named as regent in the forthcoming absence of the King the prospects for political opportunists (*male*) were receding fast.

I think we are seeing in the Catherine Parr scenario the dawning awareness in powerful males of the Pandora's box of educated women. Powerful, influential women had always been a force in patriarchal politics, never more so than when the bloodline rights of the alpha male were not accompanied by the robust health and clear-thinking intellect needed to run a country as was the case with Charles VI, the Mad, of France and Henry VI of England whose wives, Isabeau of Bavaria and Margaret of Anjou did a decent manlike job of holding the fort on their husband's behalf, *in the face of all the usual sexist and sexual slurs*. Neither of these women, however, had received the education considered, by the patriarchy that is, essential for a future ruler. Those women who received an education free from the patriarchal brainwashing might well have seen things differently. Certainly, Catherine Parr's ability and desire to bring people together was not the usual intent of power brokers in the last years of a once powerful, now vulnerable, King. Frantic jockeying for positions of power in the new regime was the norm.

Educated women were also to be found among the ranks of religious reformers challenging the archetypal patriarchal institution, the Roman Catholic Church. The doctrine of Henry's new Church of England was Catholic. In 1539 the Act of Six Articles established a law to prevent any diversity of religious opinion in his realm. Its passing was a triumph for the Duke of Norfolk enabling him to get rid of Thomas Cromwell on a charge of heresy as defined under the Act. Reforming bishops Hugh Latimer and Nicholas Shaxton were forced to resign. On the 30th of that same July, Robert Barnes, William Jerome and Thomas Garret, all cronies of Cromwell, were burnt at Smithfield for heresy as in speaking publicly in contravention of the Six Articles.

Even-handedly, on the same day, Henry had three Catholics, Thomas Abell, Edward Powell and Richard Fetherstone, drawn, hung and quartered for refusing to take the oath of Supremacy. Burning was for heretics and drawing, hanging and quartering for traitors. Here are the Six Articles:

- first, that in the most blessed sacrament of the altar, by the strength and efficacy of Christ's mighty word, it being spoken by the priest, is present really, under the form of bread and wine, the natural body and blood of our Saviour Jesus Christ, conceived of the Virgin Mary, and that after the consecration there remaineth no substance of bread and wine, nor any other substance but the substance of Christ, God and man.
- secondly, that communion in both kinds is not necessary ad salutem by the law of God to all persons, and that it is to be believed and not doubted of but that in the flesh under form of bread is the very blood, and with the blood under form of wine is the very flesh, as well apart as though they were both together.
- thirdly, that priests, after the order of priesthood received as afore, may not marry by the law of God.
- fourthly, that vows of chastity or widowhood by man or woman made to God advisedly ought to be observed by the law of God, and that it exempteth them from other liberties of Christian people which without that they might enjoy.
- fifthly, that it is meet and necessary that private masses be continued and admitted in this the king's English Church and Congregation, as whereby good Christian people ordering themselves accordingly do receive both godly and goodly consolations and benefits, and it is agreeable also to God's law.
- sixthly, that auricular confession is expedient and necessary to be retained and continued, used, and frequented, in the Church of God.[199]

Freedom of speech and tolerance of religious diversity were not part of Henry's England. Enforcement of loyalty and suppression of dissent were as essential to the patriarchy in the era of the Divine Right of Kings as they were to the 'divine right' of husbands. To question the Six Articles was to question the religious Establishment which in Henry's England was fused with the political Establishment. Extreme questioning, say of priesthood and sacraments, warfare and worldly wealth, was as unwelcome to Protestant patriarchs as it was to Catholic ones.

Belief is triumphant when it passes the ultimate test of denying, defying even, the actuality of the senses and the reasoning desire of the intellect. The 'Duck Test' encapsulates the abductive reasoning that links an observation to a probable conclusion. If it looks like a duck, swims like a duck, and quacks like a duck, then it probably is a duck.

If it looks like a wafer of bread and a chalice of wine, smells, tastes and feels like them, both before and after they have been blessed, and in the hands of a

[199] everything2.com/title/The+Six+Articles. Accessed 18/03/2020.

priest at the altar and elsewhere both the same, then they probably are a wafer of bread and a chalice of wine. They can symbolise the body and blood of Christ; they can inspire or entrance a person to feel that they are ingesting the incarnate Christ, but they are still only bread and wine.

Why was such a seemingly small challenge to the generally accepted version of the 'truth' so threatening to the Establishment that people had to die? Church and State, God and King, were the hierarchical double act, nailed on in Catholic regimes and often called Magisterial Protestantism in Reformed ones, that maintained and sustained the patriarchy. We need to look at what transubstantiated the bread and wine at the point of ingestion into the body and blood of Christ. It was, of course, the presence and blessing of them while on the altar and the provision of them by an ordained priest whose ordination gave him the mystical power to transubstantiate. By questioning the power of ordination, one questioned the holiness of the priest, the bishop who ordained him, the archbishop who ordained the bishop and the pope who ordained him. In Henry's reforming realm, where no papal decree, action or property was superior to the King's, one was questioning the divine right of the anointed king.

By suggesting that an adult who had awareness of meaning of faith needed re-baptising into God's family denied the priest's power to do that with an infant. Faith dependant on reason was very different to faith based on obedience to the Church and everything it stood for. By opposing private chapels, one denied the power of the prayers of an ordained priest to transport the soul of an acknowledged sinner from purgatory to heaven. By printing and distributing a bible in the vernacular to ordinary people whose salvation rested on the power of their faith alone one did not need a priest to recite, teach or interpret the words of Christ, his apostles and the Old Testament prophets and patriarchs.

Finally, if ordinary people were able to talk to God and hear his word in their own language there was no need for an ordained priest, skilled in Latin, merely a leader of the spiritual community. A Roman trained priest bought and paid for and an ordinary mortal man sanctioned by his blood or military might to rule, under these circumstances, were 'ducks' not some mystical, majestic human being empowered by God to command how people lived their lives and prepared for their deaths. The fear of the loss of the power of male supremacy rather than sexism, many more male heretics were burned than female (obviously because there were many more males in public roles), was behind the need to punish heresy.

Extrapolating, however, on the sexist aspect a bit further, a legal and holy union could not exist unless confirmed and blessed by an ordained priest who also had the power to declare it null and void. Marriage and divorce continued to be regulated by canon law. In 1547, the Roman Catholic Council of Trent decreed that only a marriage conducted by an ordained priest and witnessed by at least two people was valid and legal. Until the 1753 Marriage Act, the Anglican Church had directed that for a marriage to be socially valid banns had to be read and/or a licence obtained, and the ceremony conducted in a church by an ordained priest but for its sacramental/legal validity only the priest was needed. As we shall see later, until the Matrimonial Causes Act of 1857, the Church had sole jurisdiction over divorce. It was not until 1937 that any cause other than adultery, for instance cruelty, could be considered in court. Once married, an independent woman ceased to exist being totally subsumed into the legal entity that was her husband. This was the case until The Married Women's Property Act of 1870.

An independent woman, therefore, with a mind and voice of her own, particularly of a reforming inclination, was a real threat to the patriarchal status quo.

It is both extraordinary and unsurprising that all these issues, both overtly and covertly, should come together in the case of one woman, Anne Askew—extraordinary because history is rarely about women below noble rank and unsurprising because thousands of women had they dared to speak out were undoubtedly experiencing one or more of the same things that made up Anne's all-too-brief life.

Anne Askew was a radical (Protestant) reformer in the most fundamental sense of basing her faith on the Bible. She was also a victim of domestic cruelty, probably violence, from a (Catholic) traditionalist husband from whom she wanted a divorce. There were no laws to help her get away from her situation, indeed, if she enquired about or tried to make a case for divorcing a 'cruel' husband she was, probably the first woman to do so, thus shocking the Established status quo. Whether her husband Thomas Kyme of Lincoln was shocked, ashamed or embarrassed by her behaviour, presumably public on the streets of Lincoln, he disowned her.

By 1545, Anne had rejected her married name and was preaching on the streets of London along with her friend, Joan Bocher. They were probably 'Gospellers', forerunners of 'Hot Gospellers' now very popular on TV and in conventions of believers, mostly in the USA, who centred on the Bible, particularly we now think, the Sermon on the Mount as the Word of God and the last word on how a person should live a pious life and be saved. They would have gathered crowds around them, possibly whipping them up into a religious frenzy.

Such public gatherings would have soon come to the notice of local magistrates whose response would have been to Thomas Kyme to come and get his wife, his property, and keep her under control. This Thomas did in March 1545, but Anne soon escaped to her London friends and resumed her preaching.

In early 1546, she was arrested again and questioned, if we are to believe John Foxe in his *Book of Martyrs*, by higher and higher rank interrogators in grander and grander prisons, until finally coming before members of the Privy Council. By July 1546 she was in the Tower of London being illegally tortured in the presence of the Lord Chancellor, Thomas Wriothesley, and Richard Rich, master of the monarch's dirty business. Both were traditionalists, almost certainly, working for Bishop Stephen Gardiner. The racking of a condemned prisoner was illegal. The racking of a woman was also probably illegal and certainly unprecedented. (Margaret Bulmer had been tortured to give up names of people involved in the Pilgrimage of Grace but not necessarily on the rack.)

According to Foxe, Anne Askew was firstly racked by Sir Anthony Knevet (Knyvett), Lieutenant of the Tower of London, and revealed no names of fellow heretics or traitors. Sir Anthony, the man in charge of torturing in the Tower, bailed out of any further stretching, thinking, given the frailty of the woman, it inhuman to inflict any more pain. Foxe hints that there was also some chivalry involved but his death at the executioner's hand after the Battle of Hartley during Wyatt's rebellion against Queen Mary I's marriage to Philip of Spain in 1554 suggests a politico-religious loyalty as well. With Knevet gone to ask the King's pardon for disobeying orders Wriothesley and Rich decided to continue, turning the handles themselves. Anne was torn apart so badly that she had to be carried to the stake in a chair and chained to it.

What did Anne have to say that required such ruthless cruelty from two members of the king's Privy Council? That she had some secret link to the Queen or her coterie? The Queen and her female friends were reformers and these clever, educated women were married to and thus influential with husbands who were among the most powerful politicians in the realm. Catherine was married to an absolute monarch. Wikipedia mentions four powerful friends:

- Closest to her were her sister and chief Lady-in-Waiting, Anne Parr, who was inspired by Anne Boleyn to adopt the 'New Faith'. Anne married William Herbert, Earl of Pembroke, an irascible soldier who, in matters of religion and ambition, went with the flow, marrying his son to Lady Catherine, Jane Grey's sister, in the Reformist wake of Edward VI and annulling the marriage when Mary came to the throne.

- Anne Seymour, nee Stanhope, descendant, via her mother, of Edward III's youngest son, Thomas of Woodstock, former sister-in-law of the King and Aunt by marriage of the heir apparent. (It is thought that her husband, Edward, the future Lord Protector, had quietly favoured the New Faith for some time.)

- Katherine Brandon, nee Willoughby, fourth wife, and from 1545, widow, of Henry's lifelong friend and former brother-in-law, Charles Brandon, Duke of Suffolk, an open supporter of the New Faith despite her mother, Maria de Salinas, being a close friend and lady-in-waiting to Catherine of Aragon.

- Anne Radcliffe, nee Calthorpe, Countess of Sussex. Anne was the Queen consort's lady-in-waiting, well known for her reformist sympathies and trapped in an unhappy marriage with her Catholic husband.

In Foxe's Book of Martyrs, two other names were given:

- Lady Joan Denny, nee Champernowne, was the wife of Sir Anthony Denny, a Reformist and close confidant of the King, Lady-in-Waiting and close friend of Catherine Parr.

- Askew's/Foxe's 'Lady Fitzwilliam' was probably Lady Elizabeth Fitzgerald, wife of Sir Anthony Browne, the King's Master of Horse. Lady Elizabeth was reported to be a great beauty, known in court circles as 'The Fair Geraldine'. She was close to the Queen Consort and her stepdaughter, Elizabeth, although they fell out when the latter became queen.

These educated young women both flirted with the patriarchy perhaps looking to marry the most alpha male they could attract, or become his mistress, and questioned the source of its power, probably seeing through its justifications and challenging it how and when they could. By educating young women enlightened fathers like Sir Thomas More or mothers like Maud Parr, nee Green, Catherine's mother, alongside or in the same way as young men, the Tudor dynasty was sowing the seed of the gender protest of the next 400 years which would be led by educated upper- and middle-class women, some of whom, like Anne Askew, would die for the cause.

History, or at least John Foxe, records that Anne revealed no names not that there was no conspiracy. If there was a Reformist clique at court it was certainly composed of these women. There is enough circumstantial evidence to suggest that they personally or by proxy knew Anne Askew and her story of domestic abuse, possibly giving an interested, even sympathetic, ear to what she had to say. From her own words Anne was a heretic. Her friend, Joan Bocher, was burned to death for heresy in 1550 after a decade on the radar of the Tudor religious police. Although the decision was that of the Regency Council, it clearly was agreed by Cranmer and possibly the King who had to sign the execution warrant. It is possible that the offending challenge to orthodoxy consisted of questioning the Virgin Birth.

In Sidney Lee's entry in the Dictionary of National Biography, Joan "seems to have first come into notice about 1540 as 'a great dispenser of Tindal's New Testament' to the ladies of HenryVIII's court'" [200].

"According to Latimer, she said that 'our Saviour had a phantasticall body'."[201]Did the ladies close to the Queen Consort dare to say such a thing? Did they dare to say anything like it to their husbands, four of whom were on the Regency Council, Hertford, Browne, Denny and Herbert?

---

200 en.wikisource.org/wiki/Bocher,_Joan_(DNB00). Accessed 23/03/2020.

201 Ibid.

Under the Reformist regime of Edward VI and his two Protectors, his uncle Edward Seymour, self-appointed Duke of Somerset, and John Dudley, Duke of Northumberland, the burnings stopped because the Six Articles were no longer criteria for religious orthodoxy. The only other woman of any note burned at the stake in Edward's reign was Alice Arden for the premeditated murder of her husband. That hardly seems a moral evil equivalent to holding an extreme view on the Virgin Birth but was so because the patriarchal hierarchy was God, King, Lord, Husband. As pointed out earlier the equivalence of retribution and immorality was not questioned for another 200 years.

However, before we get carried away with whither all this is tending, i.e., that progressive religious reform was a woman thing, we need to listen to a certain Scottish cleric, John Knox.

Chapter 30
Tudor Queens and John Knox

And a crown put upon her head, as seemly a sight (if men had eyes) as to put a saddle upon the back of an unruly cow.
– John Knox, *The Historie of the Church of Scotland*

Preamble

Britain's first Queen Regnant, Mary I, daughter of King Henry VIII and his first wife, Catherine of Aragon, has not gone down very well in British history. Clearly, at the time, not least in the eyes of the Calvinist reformer, John Knox, the presence of a female on the throne, a childless Catholic who married a Catholic King, was an enormous threat to the neonatal Protestantism that he espoused. His fury at her policies to reverse the Reformation of the Protestant Church and State of England that had been making so much progress in the reign of her half-brother, Edward VI, unleashed a bible-based tirade against her sex. Was his dormant sexism representative of a more widespread sexism in Tudor England?

When Edward died on 6 July 1553, the succession was all about politics and religion. The politics was to do with the future careers of reformist and conservative council members; both the Duke of Norfolk and Stephen Gardiner were imprisoned in the Tower. Edward's device for the succession, contrary to his father's will, made Jane Grey, from a declared reformist family, his heir. (His exclusion of Mary and Elizabeth was one based on religion not gender although the official reason was that Henry's will had not revoked their illegitimacy. Would a male contender have overridden his religious sensibilities?) Jane was also, pertinently, the President of the Council's daughter-in-law.

The fascinating story of the nine day reign of Lady Jane Grey, Henry VIII's great niece and Edward's first cousin once removed, the volte face of the governing council and Mary's triumphant entry into London is not part of my account and requires an expert historian of Tudor history to bring it to life. Her death, therefore, for me, remains the stuff of legend.

By that Christmastide, Jane was in prison, her father-in-law, John Dudley, was dead, Norfolk and the Bishop were free, and the first Queen Regnant in Europe was resolved to reverse everything her half-brother had done. Reformist clergy, led by Archbishop Cranmer, the editor of a new revised *Book of Common*

Prayer that had made the liturgy a vehicle for Reformist doctrine, Hugh Latimer, Bishop of Worcester and Nicholas Ridley, Bishop of London, were locked up and Catholic priests brought in to replace them. John Knox, the 39-year-old Scot, ordained priest in the Catholic Church, was in England.

He had arrived in 1549 from Scotland with a radically Reformist agenda, after a 19-month spell as a galley slave in a French galleon of Henry II of France's navy which had been brought in to counter the reformist movement by Mary of Guise, widow of James V and Regent of Scotland for their daughter, the 7-year-old Mary, Queen of Scots, who was in France, with the agreed intention of marrying the Dauphin, the 5-year-old Francis, son of Henry II and his wife, Catherine de Medici. Just before his enslavement, Knox was already preaching radically Reformist sermons proclaiming, amongst other things, that the Pope was the Antichrist, the Mass should be abolished along with prayers for the dead and rejecting the idea of Purgatory. He was probably much influenced by the Scottish Protestant martyr, George Wishart.

Given a licence from the Church of England to preach in England, I have no doubt that his sermons contained more of the same. He also got married and refused any ecclesiastical office, a further sign of his radical stance. In January 1554, seeing the way the wind was blowing (On 26th January the Wyatt rebels, led by Reformists, occupied Rochester Castle in Kent intending to prevent Mary's marriage to Philip of Spain. The rebellion failed and the marriage took place in July.) and being urged by his friends to flee, he took ship for Europe and by the summer he was in Geneva where he published a pamphlet attacking Mary, the bishops who had brought her to the throne and her cousin, the Emperor, Charles V. He moved on to Frankfurt where more traditional, Anglican exiles like Richard Cox did not agree with his Calvinist prayer book. He was expelled and via Geneva he was back in Scotland by the autumn of 1555 having totally broken with the Anglicans and on the road to formulating his ideas on a Presbyterian model for the Reformation of Scotland.

By the autumn of 1556, he was back in Geneva with his family where he settled down ministering to the Calvinist community. In the summer of 1558 he published his most renowned paper, *The first blast of the trumpet against the monstruous regiment of women*. His targets were undoubtedly, Mary of Guise, mother and regent for the 16-year-old Mary, Queen of Scots, who was in France awaiting her marriage to the Dauphin and Mary I of England, both Catholic women rulers, one in league with France, the other with Spain. John had already crossed swords with the Franco/Scottish Mary and after 1560 was to repeat the issues with her daughter. Had he not won the battle for Scottish hearts and minds, particularly those of a significant number of nobles, the Scottish Reformation might have taken a turn similar to that of England.

I believe, however, that his pamphlet was specifically aimed at Bloody Mary. By 1558, Mary and her government had:

- Annulled all of Edward's religious reforms and instructions contained in the *Book of Common Prayer*.

- Annulled all of Henry VIII's religious changes since 1529, allowing nobles who had acquired church land to keep it.
- Revived the heresy laws of the late 14th and early 15th centuries.
- Consecrated a Catholic Archbishop of Canterbury, Cardinal Reginald Pole.
- Executed the leaders of Edward's Reformation, John Bradford, John Rogers, John Hooper, Hugh Latimer and Thomas Cranmer, by burning at the stake.
- Burnt some 280 Protestant martyrs at the stake.
- Married a Catholic mega-ruler, Philip II of Spain.

Looking at these 'achievements' which Knox must have thought of as abominations he had plenty with which to attack, verbally assault even, Queen Mary and, by association, Regent Mary. Indeed, in his introduction, he summarised them:

"… how abominable before God is the Empire or Rule of Wicked Woman, yea, of a traitress and bastard."

Wicked?

Well, that's largely how Protestant history has seen Mary, thanks in great measure to John Foxe's 'Book of Martyrs' published in 1563 by the very Protestant religious printer, John Day, in the reign of a Protestant ruler, Elizabeth I. When at our most xenophobic the spectre of burning martyrs in Smithfield seems to strike a very English chord.

For Knox, her wickedness lay in her adherence to the Pope, the Antichrist. Even burning heretics in a brutal age of religious conformity was only wicked if you were on the wrong side of it. As for Mary, following in the footsteps of her sonless father, after the devastating fiasco of her all too public phantom pregnancy and the departure abroad of her husband in 1555, she also put her childlessness down to having offended God not by an incestuous marriage, even though Philip was her first cousin once removed, and, therefore, requiring a papal dispensation to marry Mary, but by allowing religious diversity.

Traitress?

Knox had come to England in 1549 when Edward's regime was most definitely Reformist, building on the break from Rome by working on a reformed liturgy, a reduction in 'idolatry' and a rejection and simplification of sacraments. By reversing all that, Mary could be said to have betrayed her father and half-brother, especially by marrying a Habsburg and raising the prospect of an annexation to their Catholic empire against the interest of Scotland's ally France. Knox, however, was far from being a politician. He was a minister, a 'gospeller', delivering three sermons per week to his flock of exiles and, regardless of his politico-religious significance, no lover of the French.

Bastard?

Henry's Will had not restored his daughters' legitimacy only their place in the line of succession. Edward, in his device for the succession, had officially excluded both of his half-sisters, on grounds of their illegitimacy, even though, unofficially, he feared Mary's Catholic fervour. Had he been put on the spot politically Knox would surely have been a Jane Grey supporter and a Wyatt rebellion sympathiser.

Notwithstanding all this ammunition Knox chose to target Mary's gender. The reason seems obvious. At heart he was a gospeller, God's truth was to be found in scripture, nothing else. The truth of God's creation, the natural world and mankind's place in it was to be found in the Bible, nowhere else. The Old Testament was full of stories of wickedness, treachery and bastardy, all of which served as examples, the lessons of which were no doubt promulgated in his lengthy sermons, but the place in the natural hierarchy of women was established right at the beginning, the Genesis of everything. *If you have come all the way with me on my ramble you will know that I had a good go at all this in Chapter 14.*

In *the First Blast* Knox pulled no punches. Even Calvin had reservations. In a letter to William Cecil in 1559, having learnt that Queen Elizabeth wanted nothing to do with any religious texts emanating from Geneva due to her offence at Knox's book Calvin explained that he had made it clear to Knox that some women were exceptions to the natural order of God's creation 'distinguished from females in private life' both 'by custom, and public consent, and long practice…hereditary right' and that 'it would not be lawful to unsettle governments which are ordained by the peculiar providence of God.' He would have advised against such a book because:

> By reason of the thoughtless arrogance of one individual, the wretched crowd of exiles would have been driven away, not only from this city [of Geneva] but even from almost the whole world.[202]

Calvin's advice was not followed. In the book Knox, although he does not endorse violence or suppression, advocates vigorous preaching against the empire of women. [modernised spelling]

> If any think that the empire of women is not of such importance that for the surpassing of the same any man is bound to hazard his life, I answer that to suppress it is in the hand of god alone but to utter the impiety and abomination of the same, I say it is the duty of every true messenger of God to whom the truth is revealed in that behalf.[203]

---

[202] *The First Blast of the Trumpet against the monstrous regiment of Women*. Ed. Edward Arber, F.S.A. 15 August 1878. Kindle Ed. Accessed 31/03/2020.
[203] Ibid.

By modern day standards here is Knox at his most Aristotelian sexist although I think that it would have been a lot too much even for people of his own time as we shall explore shortly.

> For who can deny that it repugneth to nature that the blind shall be appointed to lead and conduct such as do see? That the weak, the sick and impotent persons shall nourish and keep the whole and strong, and finally, that the foolish, mad and phrenetic shall govern the discreet and give counsel to such as be sober of mind? And such be all women, compared unto men in bearing of authority. For their sight in civil regiment is but blindness: their strength, weakness: their counsel, foolishness: and judgement, phrenesy, if it be rightly considered.[204]

Modern chroniclers of Knox are always quick to point out that his use of 'monstrous' had, in line with the times, the meaning of 'unnatural' but in the same breath he has said that the idea of a woman ruler is 'repugnant' [opposite to nature], 'weak', 'sick', 'impotent', 'blind', 'foolish' and 'ph[f]renetic' [excessively emotional]. Such a ruler to me, male or female, would indeed be a monster!

The book did not get any less sexist, going on to berate husbands who were 'subject' to their wives. His target here was possibly Mary of Guise, Regent of Scotland, or her daughter, Mary, Queen of Scots, who was waiting to marry the French Dauphin. Both Catholics, they could be restrained by a strong husband although the English Mary's husband, Philip, agreed that he would relinquish all say in English affairs should his wife die before him, entirely unlike Mary, Queen of Scots, who signed an agreement to hand Scotland over to the Valois dynasty via her marriage.

The book lost much of its necessity and impact within two years of its publication in the summer of 1558. Bloody Mary died on 17th November and her spiritual rock, Cardinal Reginald Pole, died 12 hours later. On 15th January 1559, the English crowned a new monarch, a woman, for the next 44 years Queen Elizabeth I. In July 1559, Henry II of France, unrepentant persecutor of Protestants, died in July from injuries sustained in a jousting accident. At 15, Mary, great niece of Henry VIII, was Queen of France as well as Scotland with a very good claim to be the second Catholic Queen of England, given that the issue of Elizabeth's illegitimacy had never been sorted out and, until things could change, the Pope, Pious V, was in charge of deciding those issues.

In June 1560, Mary of Guise died and later that year, in December, Francis II died. The new regent of France, with sweeping powers, was Catherine de Medici, the 10-year-old Charles IX's mother and Mary, Queen of Scots' mother-in-law.

---

[204] Ibid.

By December 1561, the parentless 18-year-old widow, Mary, was back in Scotland, no longer Queen of France. John Knox had preceded her. Elizabeth, probably the best educated woman in Europe, possibly the best educated noble in England and certainly the best prepared heir presumptive, by education and experience, realised that the Pope was of no use to her as his position was that she was illegitimate, and no use to an England in which reform either had to be accepted or prevented at a huge cost in human, English lives, as was happening, for instance, in France. (The French Wars of Religion were to last another 30 years and claim some 3 million lives only, after a 20-year lull, to be followed by the Thirty Years War which was Europe-wide and claimed another 8 million lives.)

In May 1558, Elizabeth, a Protestant by inclination, became Supreme Governor, not 'Head', of the Church of England, repealed the heresy laws and restored the 1552 Book of Common Prayer but allowed some Catholic ornamentation, like vestments, to remain in church services. For 12 years her reign was marked by religious toleration. Her policy was guided by her motto, "*video et taceo*" ("I see but say nothing").

From that May of 1558 Marian exiles started to leave Geneva and return. In January 1559 Knox left bound for Scotland. He did not arrive until May because the new Queen would not sanction the issue of a passport to travel in England. Elizabeth, not a submissive woman and no fool, was not going to help any man with those views on women, no matter where they came from and what Christian patriarchs had written in support of it. In July, Knox wrote to William Cecil, leader of Elizabeth's Council of advisers, asking him most respectfully to pass a personal letter to the Queen.

In this letter, we learn a lot about the way in which religion had become a tool of male supremacy to such an extent that preachers like Knox could not help tripping up over their own arrogance. I see this exchange between Knox and the English Queen as somewhat seminal in the gender conflict to come.

The letter dated 12 July 1559 had four main sections or themes. Firstly, Knox, in his letter to Cecil, maintains that the *First Blast* was motivated by religious 'Conscience' not the pursuit of royal favours and monetary gain and had no intent to disturb the peace. *Knox shows in this content that he fully understands the political uses and abuses to which his book and sermonising could be put.*

Secondly, he admits to the Queen that he is the author of the *First Blast* and that he meant nothing purposefully malicious by its main proposition. He could not understand why it had offended her or England and hinted at changing his mind if anything new was proposed that contravened his current view.

Thirdly, it was not specifically aimed at her. It was a product of the time in which it was written, therefore could not have been personal besides which she was the answer to his prayers for a Protestant ruler. As for offending England, who was more of a danger, him, who stuck his head above the parapet to challenge (a favourite theme of his) a Queen for marrying a Catholic and thus endangering England's freedom of religion, or those servants of the country who would agree with and do whatever the monarch (*as opposed to God, or more precisely, the Protestant God*) said? He went on to warn her about toadies and timeservers.

His fourth point was also wrapped up in some sermonising. He recognises Elizabeth's elevation to rule over men as a divine exception to the natural principle that God's creation did not intend it to happen. It was such a miracle that Elizabeth should recognise it to the exclusion of any earthly reason such as bloodline. He finishes with a warning.

> When contrarywise a proud conceit and elevation of yourself shall be the occasion that your reign shall be unstable, troublesome and short.[205]

He concludes by warning that God's law comes before any human laws and that if she bases her justice upon that he will speak and write in justification of her 'aucthoritie and regiment as the HOLIE GHOST hath justified the same In DEBORA, that blessed mother in Israeli.'[206]

Well John, nice try but I do not think that would have appeased someone as clever as Elizabeth! It contains no apology. It is self-deluded in that although he cites Mary's abominable rule there is no doubt his target is all women rulers. I do not think either that his reason for not disclosing that he was the author of such a sexist paper and his "I may be wrong but prove it!" justification for his views would have impressed her nor would his re-assertion that her weakness was only compensated for by divine will. Finally, Elizabeth was fully aware of her place in the divine order of creation and that it was dependant on her divinely ordained status and the approval of all her subjects, not just the ones of whom Knox approved!

> *My lords, the law of nature moves me to sorrow for my sister; the burden that is fallen upon me makes me amazed, and yet, considering I am God's creature, ordained to obey His appointment, I will thereto yield, desiring from the bottom of my heart that I may have assistance of His grace to be the minister of His heavenly will in this office now committed to me. And as I am but one body naturally considered, though by His permission a body politic to govern, so shall I desire you all ... to be assistant to me, that I with my ruling and you with your service may make a good account to Almighty God and leave some comfort to our posterity on earth. I mean to direct all my actions by good advice and counsel.*[207]

---

[205] Ibid.

[206] Ibid.

[207] en.wikipedia.org/wiki/Elizabeth_I_of_England#cite_note-46. Accessed 02/04/2020.

The final hypocritical deceit of the July 1559 letter was that it was clearly political. The Scotland to which John Knox returned was dominated by The Lords of the Congregation, a powerful group of Protestant—more Lutheran than Calvinist—nobles who were winning the battle for hearts and minds against Mary of Guise whose alternative was a puppet regime enforced by French money and soldiers secured by her daughter's marriage to the French Dauphin. Religion was already inextricably bound to politics in Scotland. After some toing and froing centred on Edinburgh and the south-east of Scotland at the end of July Knox set up a secret meeting in Lindisfarne to negotiate some armed help from England. By February 1560, the Treaty of Berwick was signed and by March a significant English army was supporting the Scottish Protestants who the previous October had deposed the Queen Regent. By June 1560 she was dead and every foreigner or soldier in foreign pay was instructed by the Treaty of Edinburgh to go home.

During the time that Mary dallied in France mourning the death of her mother on 10th June and her husband on 5 December 1560 until her disembarkation at Leith on 19 August 1561, these lords, whose newly acquired political fixer, the defector William Maitland, allowed Knox to return to religious matters, began making official the Scottish Reformation and giving birth to the Kirk, the National Church of Scotland.

In August 1560, a large group of lords, burgesses, lairds and bishops convened, calling themselves the Scottish Parliament. By the end of the month they had approved a Calvinist theology and declaration of faith; no masses, two sacraments only, sparsely decorated churches, psalms, not hymns, sermons, not songs, and faith, not gifts for prayers. They also commissioned a group to devise how the Kirk was to be run. The *Book of Discipline* was sort of approved in January 1561. It is beyond any doubt that Knox was the driving force behind the Scottish Reformation for good and for bad. His Old Testament gospelling was too much for Elizabeth and it is at this time, with these exchanges, that the Presbyterian Kirk and the Anglican Communion went their separate ways just as John and Elizabeth failed to agree to disagree. *I believe at the heart of this was Elizabeth's extreme dislike of Knox's sexism.*

From that fateful day in August 1561, Knox and 19-year-old Mary locked horns. One of the many bones of contention was Knox's condemnation of women rulers as expressed in his book. He wrote again to Elizabeth a fortnight before Mary's arrival in Leith. He wanted to inform her of Mary's attempts to get scholars and rulers, far and wide, to reject his ideas as laid out in the book. The English ambassador to Scotland, Thomas Randolph, had already informed Sir William Cecil in March that Knox had somewhat moderated the tone of his views blaming its rigour on the times in which it was written. The purpose of this letter was to ask Elizabeth to beware of Mary's motives. He uses the phrase 'shoot at a farther mark'. *I like to concentrate on the actual words used by historical figures but when they are obscure, we must guess what they meant.*

Wikipedia reports the opinion of Jenny Wormald, a Scottish historian, that Mary's commitment to leave unchanged the religious reforms that had been put in place before her return and her acceptance of a mainly Protestant Privy Council meant that she did not want to disassociate herself from the moderate move to Protestantism taken by Elizabeth in England. She sent Maitland, the fixer, to England to argue her case to be heir presumptive. Elizabeth, however, knew that naming an heir was probably the most dangerous thing she could do, giving a focus to those threatening her, her throne and her religious settlement. Knox's 'farther mark' may well have been the throne of England.[208]

Knox, surrounded by his 'monstrous regiment'—Mary, Elizabeth and Catherine de Medici—had realised that, by association, his sexism had undermined his scripture-based fundamentalism. He tried again to explain that it was shaped by circumstances that threatened the neo-nascent Reformation, an argument he used when first summoned to explain his continued preaching against Mary.

Mary had made it plain, as pointed out above, that she would not attempt to overturn any of the religious reforms devised principally by John Knox but neither had she any inclination to ratify the three Acts of Parliament that would have made them law nor, as moderate Protestants like Maitland and Moray hoped, would she forsake her Catholicism. Like all good Catholics she attended Mass on her first Sunday in Scotland. Knox was not at all pleased and preached against Mary and her attendance at Mass despite his more moderate colleagues advising that it was only one Mass, a small price to pay for non-interference. Knox's reply to this in his sermon the following Sunday was, "One Mass is more fearful to me than if ten thousand armed enemies were landed in any part of the realm of purpose to suppress the whole religion."[209]

Knox was summoned to appear before Queen Mary. She said that she would get scholars to challenge what he wrote to which Knox replied, and we only have his record of the conversation—*somewhat arrogantly?*—that he was more than ready and willing to defend what he had said. Mary then seemed to challenge him with the obvious impression that he was implying that she was not his rightful ruler because she was a woman. Knox's answer was that intellectual disagreement with one's government was not a reason to overturn it. If the people wanted a woman ruler, he was not going to go against them.

> I have communicated my judgement to the world; if the realm finds no inconveniency in the regimen of a woman, that which they approve I will not farther disallow, than within mine own breast, but shall be as well content to live under your grace, as Paul was to live under Nero. And my hope is, that so long as ye defile not your hands with the blood of the saints of God, that neither I nor that book shall neither hurt you or

---

[208] https://en.wikipedia.org/wiki/Mary,_Queen_of_Scots#Return_to_Scotland. Accessed 03/04/2020.

[209] Knox, *The History of the Reformation of Religion in Scotland*, full text in archive.org/details/historyreformat00gavgoog/page/n8/mode/2up. Accessed 04/04/2020.

> your authority: for, in very deed, madam, that book was written most especially against that Jezebel of England.[210]

Come on, John! This answer was completely disingenuous. Philosophy was undertaken in the shadow of religious thought. Morality was likewise argued from a religious perspective. Religion itself was highly political. Therefore, intellectual and religious disagreement may not necessarily in themselves have been seditious or revolutionary but combined with the accelerators of social and economic unrest they were more than capable of lighting and spreading the fire of rebellion.

Mary then said what we all, on following the John Knox story, wanted to point out, "But ye speak of women in general." Knox's opener to his reply was patronising and/or condescending. He suggested that it was imprudent to open a discussion of gender issues when the whole 'woman' thing was not a problem to the current situation. He then made the same point that he had made to Elizabeth, namely that times had changed; *more on this very soon*. Thirdly, and, I think rather obscurely, he argued that had he wanted to use her gender to invalidate her right to rule he would have done so before she arrived back in Scotland to make it a fait accompli.

Using Knox and his bible-based morality as a yardstick for progress in the 'Woman Question' presupposes that his Protestant expectations of behaviour were typical, not just of the times but of the progressive reformers of the times. In his exchange with Mary he said two significant things. When expounding his live-and-let-live approach, he added the clause "than within my own breast" meaning others may moderate the application of God's word as laid out in the Bible but he would not. We must assume that many Presbyterian adherents to the Kirk felt the same, whose views would have been duplicated by the Puritan faction in England.

Secondly, when implying that a change in the times had rendered his views somewhat obsolescent he put it this way, "for of late years many things, which before were holden stable, have been called in doubt; yea, they have been plainly impugned." He cannot have meant that the Bible, the 'Word of God', had been 'impugned', i.e., invalidated, so, for some time now I have presumed, hence the lengthy analysis in Chapter 26, that he was talking about the inevitability of a Queen Regnant due to the absence of legitimate male candidates which was as evident in Scotland as in its neighbour, England.

With the key years of the English and Scottish Reformations overseen by four women rulers, three of them Queens Regnant (Mary of Guise was a Queen Regent), John Knox must have regretted writing the *First Blast*, even himself recognising that "many things, which before were holden stable, have been called in doubt." It is unlikely, however, even though half a century's rule by women must have had an impact on hearts and minds, at least those of the ruling

---

[210] Ibid.

class, that much progress was made on the equalisation of the rights accorded to the genders.

On 8th February 1587, those on the Anglican route were sufficiently confident (whether that included Elizabeth or not is a historical debate into which I will not go) to remove the chief Catholic hope for turning back, Mary Queen of Scots, was removed in the typical Tudor way. The following year they fought off the invasion fleet of the major Catholic power in Europe. However, although they were both significant and seemingly permanent members of the Protestant club, Scotland and England went their different ways, Calvinist and Anglican, respectively.

Postscript

Before I leave the aristocracy of 16th century England, I feel obliged to briefly complete the life stories of the Protestant 'Ladies'. Elizabeth, undoubtedly using all the feminine and intellectual wiles at her disposal, survived to become England's first Protestant monarch and earn her legacy of one of its greatest.

- Katherine Parr sadly died on 5 September 1548 after giving birth to Thomas Seymour's daughter, Mary.
- Anne Parr, her sister, died on 20 February 1552, Countess of Pembroke. Both sisters were worthy products of their highly educated mother, Maud Green, overseer of the Royal Court School set up and supervised by Queen Catherine of Aragon.
- Anne Stanhope became Seymour, Duchess of Somerset, hated sister-in-law of Katherine Parr who apparently called her 'That Hell' and mother of a number of reform minded children, Edward Seymour, husband of Lady Catherine Grey, sister of Queen Lady Jane and 3 daughters, Margaret, Anne and Jane who were the first published English female writers. She died on 16 April 1587 having married her steward, Francis Newdigate and passed out of history.
- Katherine Willoughby became Brandon, Duchess of Suffolk as fourth wife of Charles Brandon. Always an advocate of Reform she married, for love, a member of her household, Richard Bertie. The Berties became Marian exiles finding refuge in Poland. Their children, Susan and Peregrine, named in recognition of his parent's wandering life when he was born, were prominent Reformists in the reign of Elizabeth. Katherine died on 19 September 1580.
- Anne Calthorpe became Radcliffe, Countess of Sussex. Her husband was a second cousin of royalty and had their marriage annulled while Anne was abroad having fled because of her Protestant beliefs. Their son, Egremont, took part in the Rising of the North but escaped execution. He went into exile again after being released from the Tower and was executed in Namur for spying and attempting to assassinate Don John, half-brother of Philip II of Spain. Anne's second husband, Andrew

Wyse, a Royal Officer in Ireland, went home with his wife and family and Anne passed out of history.

- Joan Champernowne became Lady Denny after her marriage to Sir Anthony with whom she had 12 children. She died in 1553, some 4 years after her husband, thus avoiding any conflict with her counter-reforming queen. Lady Joan shared her maiden name with Elizabeth's long-time governess, Kate Astley suggesting that she also was close to the young Protestant princess.
- Elizabeth Fitzgerald became Clinton, Countess of Lincoln, and a larger than life personality at Elizabeth's court. Clearly a Protestant by inclination having supported Lady Jane Grey, she survived Mary's reign and upset the Archbishop of Canterbury, Matthew Parker, no Puritan, *now I am guessing*, for encouraging her friend Elizabeth's more joyful side. She died in March 1590. Henry Howard, the Earl of Surrey and Tudor poet wrote a sonnet about her entitled *The Geraldine*.

From Tuscan' came my lady's worthy race; Fair Florence was some time their ancient seat; The western isle, whose pleasant shore doth face Wild Camber's cliffs, did give her lively heat: Fostered she was with milk of Irish breast; Her sire an earl; her dame of princes' blood: From tender years, in Britain she doth rest With king's child, where she tasteth costly food.

Hunsdon did first present her to my een: Bright is her hue, and Geraldine she hight: Hampton me taught to wish her first for mine: And Windsor, alas, doth chase me from her sight.

Her beauty of kind, her virtues from above; Happy is he that can obtain her love.[211]

---

[211] historywitch.com/2013/01/06/the-fair-geraldine/. Accessed 13/04/2020.

Chapter 31
Nonconformism

There is neither Jew nor Greek, there is neither bond nor free, there is neither male nor female: for ye are all one in Christ Jesus.
– Galatians 3:28

Ordinary people pursue money, simple people pursue power, average people pursue fame, but extraordinary people pursue ideas.
– Matshona Dhliwayo

Sir, a woman's preaching is like a dog's walking on his hind legs. It is not done well; but you are surprised to find it done at all.
– James Boswell. *Life of Samuel Johnson*

Preamble

We need to question the assumption that in Middle Ages Europe hierarchy, philosophically and religiously justified as a natural phenomenon and a part of God's creation, was an accepted part of the life of ordinary people; inevitable maybe, but unquestioningly accepted I very much doubt. The Establishment hierarchy that ordinary people had to accept in 17th century England—God-Pope-King-Lord (Spiritual and temporal)-husband/father—began to open itself to challenge once the Pope had been removed. The Establishment was, arguably had always been, a partnership between Church and State enforced ultimately by fear. To disagree with it was to not conform.

Therefore, to be a nonconformist in religion was, inevitably, to be a nonconformist in politics. In this century dominated by Civil War and Regicide, Republicanism and the Bill of Rights, the proliferation of nonconformist ideas and groups that led to the Age of Enlightenment in the following century was a major feature of the backdrop for all the drama.

As investigated in Chapter 14, the scriptural elucidation of Christianity came from patriarchal cultures, Jewish and Greco-Roman, that placed women below men in the pecking order. The puritanical, Calvinistic interpretation emphasised obedience and submission, procreation and childrearing, help-meeting and home management. However, there were two aspects of Protestant fundamentalism that moved the cause of gender equality forward or, at least, sowed the seeds of its advance into the communal consciousness.

The first emanation of extreme adherence to Scripture that came to be known as Puritanism challenged the notion of the God given hierarchy. Presbyterian government of churches was a clear alternative to the episcopal regime of bishops and archbishops which, in Scotland for instance, led to war in 1639-40, known as the Bishops Wars.

It attacked the trappings of wealth. In the 1559 Act of Uniformity Elizabeth took personal control of things considered to increase the mystery of or 'edify' worship such as clerical vestments. In 1548, John Hooper had objected to clerical garb on the grounds that the vestments were Jewish and Catholic trappings not required by scripture. By the time that Robert Crowley, a Marian exile, wrote a pamphlet opposing them, quoting Psalm 31 on the front page, "I have hated all those that hold of superstitious vanities", it had almost become an act of sedition to express such a view.

In its spin-off, Separatism or Nonconformism, Puritanism was to generate an alternative wealth creator to land ownership, industry and commerce, and a work ethic to ennoble it. As Wikipedia puts it:

> Protestants, beginning with Martin Luther, reconceptualised worldly work as a duty which benefits both the individual and society as a whole. Thus, the Catholic idea of good works was transformed into an obligation to consistently work diligently as a sign of grace. Whereas Catholicism teaches that good works are required of Catholics as a necessary manifestation of the faith they received, and that faith apart from works is dead (James 2:14-26) and barren, the Calvinist theologians taught that only those who were predestined to be saved would be saved.
>
> Since it was impossible to know who was predestined, the notion developed that it might be possible to discern that a person was elect (predestined) by observing their way of life. Hard work and frugality were thought to be two important consequences of being one of the elect. Protestants were thus attracted to these qualities and supposed to strive for reaching them.[212]

In some Presbyterian communities, women, predominantly widows, who ran businesses were elected to the council of elders although the Puritan rules that required submission and silence in church and public affairs and submissive obedience to the husband at home were generally applied. The real gender test of separatist nonconformism would have been a group who challenged, rejected or deemed unimportant the creationist reading of the Old Testament and the Pauline teaching of the New Testament, cleaving to the verse from Paul's letter to the Galatians 3:28: 'There is no longer Jew or Greek, there is no longer slave or free, there is no longer male and female; for all of you are one in Christ Jesus.'

By the 1620s, such a group of 'ordinary folk' was beginning to coalesce but the story starts with another Queen Regnant, Elizabeth I. Unlike her half-sister and like her father, Elizabeth wanted nothing to do with Papal authority nor with

---

[212] en.wikipedia.org/wiki/Protestant_work_ethic. Accessed 09/04/2020.

papist aspects of church liturgy or practice and papist theological dogma. She was, however, not happy with unadulterated Calvinist practice based on God's Word and faith alone being the way to a salvation which was predestined; God's choice, about which nothing could be done (certainly not by handing over money to an already wealthy Church), being the only criterion for entry to heaven. She was a Tudor with God's blessing to rule. She was beneficiary of her father's magnificence, his majesty, his vision of kingship. Her Church would reflect her magnificence but not the Pope's, English not Roman and Episcopal not Presbyterian. Highly educated bishops would be in charge not well-meaning 'elders'. In her Empire everyone's relationship with God would be governed by her Anglican establishment.

In 1559, her parliament passed an Act of Uniformity but repealed the Heresy Laws. Under this Act attendance at her Church was compulsory as was the oath of allegiance/loyalty from clergy required by the Act of Supremacy. The Wikipedia article expresses the intent of her religious policy particularly neatly.

> Anglicanism became defined by the *via media* or middle way between the religious extremes of Catholicism and Protestantism; Arminianism and Calvinism; and high church and low church.[213]

We are told that Elizabeth, though a Protestant icon, was remarkably tolerant of other religious viewpoints. We are also given the impression that the burnings and beheadings stopped. They did not. The reprisals after the rebellion of the Northern Earls in 1569 involved the executions of some 600 people, presumably with Roman Catholic sympathies, very few of whom were of noble birth but we are not often told of the 9, at least, Protestants who were executed for purely 'religious' treason, all of whom, for various reasons, rejected an Established Church: treason was their crime, not heresy, emphasising the reality that Church and State were the indivisible components of English rule.

The social and political divisions that took another 400+ years to be resolved began to be clarified; class, religious belief, wealth and political representation were key issues and still today cast a large shadow over what should be a far less divided society. Gender as a divisive force was less clear but the next century would make it so. The two, to some extent three, Queens Regnant of the 16th century, through their opposing views of faith and religious practice turned Great Britain in the direction of democracy and equality that the next century would, after some extreme experimentation, become enshrined in the hearts and minds of the British people.

Queens Regnant, by definition, were from the ruling class which, thus far, was where the Woman Question joined by the Faith Question resided. Neither Mary nor Elizabeth would have been suitable Monarch material if they had only been taught to sew, cook their husband's tea, bring up his children and, above all in Puritan households, kept their mouths firmly shut! Both were highly educated

---

213 en.wikipedia.org/wiki/Elizabethan_Religious_Settlement. Accessed 11/04/2020.

women, Elizabeth (a fine sewer by all accounts) particularly so, not because they were potential monarchs but because they would be the consorts, mothers and hostesses of kings.

Their Ladies-in-Waiting were the companions and frequently mistresses of monarchs and potential wives and mothers of power brokers at Court. Ambassadors at Tudor courts remarked on how exceptionally educated the 'Ladies' were. However, education of the 'ordinary sort', who included gentry, was generally basic, geared to making a living unless they joined the Church in some capacity or other.

Faith based on the Word of God was no good unless people, including women, could read the Bible. If they could read the Bible, they could read other books, pamphlets and religious tracts. They were educated enough to have their own opinions and be the equal of men of their own social milieu. Protestantism, yes, and Puritanism, much as it practised strict hierarchy, including by gender and generation, inadvertently opened the door to equality.

For this second emanation, education, to have a real social impact, it required, as will be a continuous theme of my last few chapters, some recognition and acceptance by men. Step forward two remarkable men, unremarkably named and not in any way lauded in the Establishment history of Britain because they both had rejection of it in common.

John Knox, as we have seen, was a Roman Catholic priest who rejected the Pope, his boss, much of the dogma, theology, liturgy and practice and created a new denomination within Christianity. The Church of Scotland had bishops but was Presbyterian in nature, very different from the Catholic Church. The Anglican Church, however, embraced people, for the sake of placing them historically they have been called Puritans, who wanted to take their belief and worship a lot further from its Catholic origins. They asked this question, "We can read all we need to know about salvation in the Bible and talk to God ourselves, who needs Bishops, Vicars and fancy, expensive Churches with all their paraphernalia?"

Robert Browne who had an on-off relationship with the Anglican Church which landed him in prison over 30 times in his 83 years was a well-known nonconformist in the reign of Queen Elizabeth. He advocated a separation from the National Church into meeting places where the congregation ran its own affairs. He also had the concept, shared by other separatists, that God's spirit was in all of us waiting to be let out and shared by doing God's will. Both these challenges to an episcopal, priest-led Establishment, opened many minds to women's importance and equality in God's creation. These two traits separated a significant minority from the Established Church and the Puritan wing of that church who wanted a more Calvinist approach both of which, if we look at the words of Knox and the Anglican patriarchy, would not have advanced the cause of gender equality. To these two core tenets was then added the powerful idea that people did not need anyone to reveal God's grace to them because every individual had his or her own relationship with God which was no human being's right to shape or interfere with. On this basis people should be allowed to seek God in their own way.

In a community in Amsterdam at the turn of the century two Englishmen, John Smyth and Thomas Helwys, were putting these ideas into practice, not in churches but in meeting houses where the members worshipped in silence. In these meetings lay the origins of what we now call Baptists. In his remarkable book, *The Mistery of Iniquity*, Helwys made this extraordinary appeal for religious toleration:

> "If the Kings people be obedient and true subjects, obeying all humane lawes made by the King, our Lord the King can require no more: for men's religion to God is betwixt God and themselves; the King shall not answer for it, neither may the King be judge between God and man. Let them be heretics, Turks, Jews or whatsoever, it appertains not to the earthly power to punish them in the least measure." — *A Short Declaration of the Mistery of Iniquity*[214]

Such nonconformist groups were known as Separatists, Brownists and, by the 1620s, Seekers. Having been thwarted by James I's decision to uphold the Established Church of England, rejecting Knox's Calvinist model, even though he was also King of Scotland, Calvinism was not an issue, neither was Catholicism as we have spent some time in understanding. Protestant Nonconformists were illegally not conforming to the Protestant Church of England.

The foundations of Seekers lay in the teachings of three brothers, Thomas, Walter and Bartholomew Legate. Much of what they preached was against the orthodoxy which King James had chosen over the Calvinism of his homeland. They undoubtedly questioned the idea of the three-in-one, possibly the divinity of Jesus and certainly the apostolic succession of bishops. All three of these tenets were essential to the Established Church. Thomas and Bartholomew were imprisoned in Newgate. Thomas died in prison and Bartholomew was eventually burnt at the stake for heresy despite the efforts of the king himself to get him to moderate his views. He and Edward Wightman, an anabaptist, were the last people to be burnt at the stake in England for heresy.

If we take ourselves back in our imaginations to participate in these Seeker discussions, so challenging to the status quo, surely women would have been present and their biblical status of inferiority would have been debated alongside the equal value of the individual, regardless of gender, nationality, creed or class, in the eyes of a loving and fearsome God.

The Seekers were not a sect or a denomination, they were a wide range of individuals, of different classes, professions and incomes seeking different ways

---

214 en.wikipedia.org/wiki/Thomas_Helwys. Accessed 16/04/2020.

to find God and address the carnal evils of a troubling world by debating spiritual solutions. If they had readily agreed we would not have some 40,000 'Protestant' denominations in the world today. The British Museum has a broadsheet circulated in 1647, the time at which a Quaker philosophy was beginning to coalesce, called *A Catalogue of the Severall Sects and Opinions in England and other Nations: With a briefe Rehearsall of their false and dangerous Tenents.*[215], in which several of the offending sects are illustrated.

In 1643, a 19-year-old shoemaker from a small village in Leicestershire, now called Fenny Drayton, became a 'seeker' in the actual sense of the word. By 1647, in a chaotic lapse in a Civil War that was a complex power struggle within the Establishment but also a competition for the hearts and minds of 'ordinary folk', George Fox began to get a reputation as a charismatic itinerant preacher. Given the multiplicity of nonconformist ideas Fox would surely have been the victim of much misquotation and misrepresentation.

The Quakers, a derisive name allegedly given to them by a judge mocking Fox's warning of a wrathful God in this verse from the Book of Isaiah (66:5), "Hear the word of the LORD, ye that tremble at his word; Your brethren that hated you, that cast you out for my name's sake, said, Let the LORD be glorified: but he shall appear to your joy, and they shall be ashamed." Indeed, violence would have followed him and his group of fellow ministers (Were there women among them?) around the country. There was much to hate and blame at this time of public disorder and an itinerant group telling you to lead a less sinful life, which could be read as 'having a lot less fun', may not have gone down well, especially after a few pints at the local inn adjacent to the field or marketplace where they were preaching. In an account of his travels Fox mentions whippings and, of course, imprisonment.

When we admire the Quaker example of non-violent resistance to unjust authority and commitment to Pacifism, we forget their violent origins and I'm personally convinced that the presence of women preachers, one of whom we shall meet soon, and ministers had an influence on this remarkable and unshakeable aspect of their faith. His ability to hold his beliefs under a military dictator, a High Church Anglican and a Roman Catholic, albeit an Indulgent one (James II made his Declaration of Indulgence in 1687), and influence them, he certainly had a close relationship with Oliver Cromwell, was remarkable. He must, therefore, have celebrated the Act of Toleration of 1689—probably questioning its failure to include Catholics, non-trinitarians and non-Christians which would have been in the Seeker tradition. Most nonconformists of the Quaker ilk sought to convert, not to exclude.

By 1652, George Fox was in the north of England. His vision that the divine light of the holy spirit was in every individual meant that he fell afoul of the authorities, the Puritan military dictatorship of Oliver Cromwell. His rejection of

---

[215] https://commons.wikimedia.org/wiki/File:Catalogue_of_Sects.GIF#filehistory. Accessed 18/04/2020.

ritual, the need for priests, churches or sacred objects, including expensive vestments or clothing of any kind, his refusal to fight and take oaths and his encouragement to others not to defer to religious or secular authority in acts such as taking one's hat off in church, bowing and curtsying, combined with his actions of pursuing better treatment of prisoners, more assistance for the poor and those with mental health problems and allowing women to preach in meeting places and out and to speak in meetings when the spirit moved them, which it would, because—he believed this from his earliest days as a seeker—women's souls were the equals of men's souls, pretty much offended any Establishment figure, local or national, that he encountered.

By the definition of those times, as soon as he opened his mouth, he committed blasphemy. (Blasphemy is the act of insulting or showing contempt or lack of reverence to a deity, or sacred objects, or toward something considered sacred or inviolable.) His imprisonments, therefore, were for causing a public disturbance, blasphemy, refusing to take an oath, refusing to fight against the Royal Restoration but never for heresy. Quakers were not anti-trinitarian or anti-Catholic; they always held open meetings. It was difficult to accuse them of sedition because Quakers would not bear arms against anyone for any reason and argued that they showed loyalty by their peaceful, moral and truthful lifestyle even if they did not swear an oath.

In 1652, Fox preached in a church in the Ulverston area of northwest Lancashire, now Cumbria. The power of his witness converted the wife of the local magistrate, Margaret Fell. After some contemplation, her husband accepted her commitment and their home, Swarthmoor Hall, became a centre for the Society of Friends—and still is. Margaret became Fox's right-hand woman, organising the supporters into a unified group and holding them together during a period in the 1660s and 1670s of intense harassment by the Authorities. In 1669, 11 years after her husband's death, the 55-year-old Margaret married her spiritual mentor, the 45-year-old George Fox.

While her first husband, Thomas, was alive, Margaret and her groups of co-believers were protected from prosecutions but, after his death in 1658, she found it increasingly difficult to avoid enquiries into the nature of her meetings and incidents where her refusal to take an oath became an issue. During the Protectorship of Richard Cromwell dissatisfied Presbyterians and Cavalier Anglicans overwhelmed the tolerant moderates and when Charles was restored to the throne the so-called Cavalier Parliament passed five Acts in five years that were to land Margaret, George and other Quakers in very hot water. These were:

> The Corporation Act 1661 required municipal officeholders to swear allegiance the Act of Uniformity 1662 made the use of the Anglican Book of Common Prayer compulsory the Quaker Act 1662 requiring the swearing of the Oath of Allegiance the Conventicle Act 1664 prohibited religious assemblies of more than five people, except under the auspices of the Church of England and the Five Mile Act 1665 prohibited

expelled non-conforming clergymen from coming within five miles (8 km) of a parish from which they had been banished.[216]

Margaret was imprisoned at least three times for her beliefs in her long life. Due to her social status she was a high-profile political player even though she would have denied it. She constantly challenged the Establishment distinction between following one's conscience and committing a crime. Her letters to prominent people and organisations during the Commonwealth appealing for them to show leniency to imprisoned Quakers or those on trial must have kept nonconformism and justice in the public conscience. George Fox spoke at length to Cromwell to try and turn him away from violence and religious intolerance. In the early 1660s she visited London at least twice to petition the King to release imprisoned Quakers; on one occasion her petition was for Fox himself. She says that she spoke to Charles more than once and that he acknowledged receipt of more than one letter outlining the Quaker position.

In 1664, after 6 years of sailing close to the wind, her neighbours, the Kirkby's, had her and Fox arrested for contravening the newly passed Conventicle Act. They were! At her trial, the judge, Sir Thomas Twisden, tried to get her to at least stop holding meetings at her house. In *Women's Speaking Justified and Other Pamphlets*, a paper on her life and beliefs edited by Donarworth J. and Lush R.M, in 2018, this first hearing is described.

> Judge Twisden had threatened that if Fell did not promise to discontinue holding Meetings at her house and attend the Church of England (which was required by law), he would ask her to swear the Oath of Allegiance, an oath that was often used to sift out Catholics but was frequently employed against more radical dissenters as well—although only very rarely against women. Those who refused the Oath were fined and jailed. In response to this threat, Fell explains the Friends' refusal to take any oaths: "Christ Jesus hath commanded in plain words, That I should not Swear at all, Matthew 5, and for obedience to Christ's doctrine and command am I here arraigned this day. So you, being Christians, and professing the same thing in words, judge of these things according to that of God in your consciences."
> Here Fell asks judge and jury to follow their liberty of conscience, the Light of Christ inside them, against the letter of the law. Fell insists that she has been indicted "upon the account of my conscience, and not for any evil or wrong done." The exasperated judge tries again and again to make Fell acknowledge that she has broken a law, and so committed an evil act, but she maintains the clear distinction between evil and crime that liberty of conscience prompts in her. She explains that Friends cannot go to the Church of England "contrary to our consciences." And when the judge offers her "liberty till the next Assizes," she refuses it,

[216] en.wikipedia.org/wiki/Charles_II_of_England#Restoration. Accessed 19/04/2020.

> for she "must keep [her] conscience clear": in precise legal terms, in a witty combination of theological and legal concepts, she chooses liberty of conscience over liberty.[217]

In their next appearance before the assizes, Fox, she says, got off on a technicality but Margaret's case, despite some irregularities, went ahead. The indictment this time was refusing to swear the oath of allegiance. Many of the nonconformist believers based their way of life, their morality, on Christ's Sermon on the Mount, as related in Matthew, Chapter 5. Quakers were no exception.

> **34** But I say unto you, Swear not at all; neither by heaven; for it is God's throne:
> **35** Nor by the earth; for it is his footstool: neither by Jerusalem; for it is the city of the great King.
> **36** Neither shalt thou swear by thy head, because thou canst not make one hair white or black.
> **37** But let your communication be, Yea, yea; Nay, nay: for whatsoever is more than these cometh of evil.

Having assured the judge that she and her fellows meant no harm to the King, nor conspiracy against his rule, nor intent to disobey any of his laws she cleverly put the ball back in his court (no pun intended!) by saying "… I do not deny this oath only because it is the oath of allegiance, but I deny it because it is an oath".

It was not good form to put nonconformist women in prison, so the judge attempted a compromise. At least, would she stop holding the meetings? She would not barter her conscience for her estate or her freedom. She was sentenced to life imprisonment and forfeiture of all her property.

On 6 June 1666, she wrote to the King. Again, she used her reductionist logic to admonish him for punishing Quakers for worshipping God. A code of law (known in history as the Clarendon Code) designed to prevent treason by Catholics, with more effort to dispense justice, need not apply to peaceful, non-violent, law-abiding worshippers. Any man with a shred of understanding of God's justice should be able to see that.

> All this has been without any just cause given at any time by that people, which was the object of this law; so that men, that had but the least measure of righteousness and equity, could never have proceeded on to have inflicted such a height of punishment, without some just ground.[218]

After four years in prison, Margaret was released by order of the King and his Council. Shortly after her release, she married George Fox. When she got

---

217 www.itergateway.org/sites/default/files/OV65extract.pdf. Accessed 19/04/2020.
218 www.hallvworthington.com/Margaret_Fox_Selections/ MargaretMemoir.html. Accessed 20/04/2020.

home she was imprisoned again, and it took her new husband and her daughters a considerable effort to get the King's pardon and order, under the great seal, to reinstate her property. George went to America during which time she was continually harassed, including another few weeks in Lancaster gaol, for fines for holding meetings and not attending church.

When he returned in 1673, he was again imprisoned in Worcester which took a considerable toll on his health. After some months, the indictment was quashed, and the very sick George was nursed back to health at Margaret's home. Margaret delivered a letter to, and possibly met, James II and at 85 wrote to William III to emphasise the peaceful non-threatening devoutness of the Friends. Her husband died in 1690 and she herself died in 1702, having lived under six rulers, one of whom was legally killed by his own people, one of whom was expelled by his own people, two of whom were imported from other countries and two of whom were just 'ordinary folk' like her, and for most of a century when religious tolerance, and, therefore, freedom of conscience were major issues.

Margaret Fell/Fox was a prolific writer. While in Lancaster Gaol in the mid-1660s, she wrote a significant pamphlet entitled *Women's Speaking Justified.* She followed the usual tripartite formula of religious pamphlets at that time, tackling the Old Testament passages, particularly those mentioning prophetesses, instancing Christ's interactions with and sayings about women and re-interpreting Paul's meanings behind his statements on women not speaking in church. Whether, under the semantic or rhetorical microscope, she has made a good case for God's support for women speaking, unlike many critics from the nonconformist community, I am totally unqualified to say. That she was in the minority and brave to try is beyond doubt.

My aim in this book is to write a story of women not the story of women. It is neither a feminist history nor an egalitarian polemic. I do, however, understand that is not possible to introduce Margaret Fell into a story of women without asking two questions. Was she a feminist or precursor of feminism? Was she an egalitarian or precursor of egalitarianism, particularly in a political sense?

In her article on Margaret Fell for the Stanford Encyclopaedia of Philosophy, Jacqueline Broad addresses these two questions. On the first, I agree totally with her conclusion that Margaret was "something of a bridge between the *querelle des femmes* of the late-medieval period and the later feminist arguments of figures". On the second, however, she quotes from Smith, H.L. (1982):

> Most female religious writers simply ignored political or feminist topics. Even Margaret Fell Fox, one of the most forceful supporters of women's being able to speak in Quaker meetings, argued in *Women's Speaking Justified* ... that they should never speak in a way that would usurp authority over men. For the large majority of women writing religious

> tracts during the seventeenth century, the question of women's rights simply never arose.[219]

I think that, if one looks beneath the shroud of biblical language and scriptural imagery, Margaret is challenging the authority of men so strongly as to make them fearful of usurpation of the patriarchy sanctioned by their staunchest ally, God, and His Word or written Covenant, the Bible. I have highlighted her use of the word 'men' to emphasise my understanding of its referring to the gender not the species. Before quoting from her pamphlet we should look at her letter to King Charles II in which she calls him:

> **...to a Consideration**, according to Reason, Righteousness, and Equity, concerning us, as a People, to maintain **our just Liberties and Rights**, as he is engaged by Promise, **to defend us from Wrongs, Injuries, and Violence, done to us by Military and Merciless Men**.[220]

23 years later, 1689, the Protestant Parliament which invited the Protestant husband of Mary Stuart, daughter of the Catholic king, James II, to be King William III of England and Ireland, passed an Act Declaring **the Rights and Liberties of the Subject** and Settling the Succession of the Crown. Of the 13 articles, 2 were foregrounded in Margaret's letter:

- freedom to **petition** the king.
- freedom from **cruel and unusual punishments**, and excessive bail.

The Eighth Amendment of the United States Bill of Rights, ratified in 1791, repeats the words, "Excessive bail shall not be required, nor excessive fines imposed, **nor cruel and unusual punishments** inflicted."

Article 5 of The Universal Declaration of Human Rights repeats the words, "No one shall be subjected to **torture or to cruel, inhuman or degrading treatment or punishment**", a prohibition again repeated in the 1950 European Convention on Human Rights.

Other Puritans, such as John Locke ("All mankind... being all equal and independent, no one ought to harm another in his life, health, liberty or possessions."), far more famous than Margaret and far less compartmentalised as a religious extremist, are credited with the philosophical and humanitarian challenge that brought about this earth-shattering leap into the modern world but her words, that managed to reach the ears of a King, the last but one to invoke his divine right to rule, must have had an impact far more widespread and long-lasting than just on her circle of Friends. Indeed, her husband's friend and fellow believer, William Penn took the Friends to the American colonies in the last

---

[219] Smith, H. L., 1982, *Reason's Disciples: Seventeenth Century English Feminists*, Urbana: University of Illinois Press. In plato.stanford.edu/entries/margaret-fell/#LifeWork. Accessed 22/04/2020.

[220] plato.stanford.edu/entries/margaret-fell/#LifeWork. Accessed 22/04/2020.

twenty years of the century where they thrived. At one time Penn argued, like Margaret, that the Quakers were not a political group and, therefore, not subject to the Clarendon Code. *Hm! As Thomas Mann said over 200 years later, 'Everything is Politics'.*

In the pamphlet, Margaret points out that the failure to acknowledge absolute God given gender equality in the Creation story is a weakness in men. *Had she meant mankind she surely would have said so.*

> And first, when *God created Man in his owne Image: in the Image of God created he them, Male and Female: and God blessed them, and God said unto them, Be fruitful, and multiply: And God said, Behold, I have given you of every Herb,* and c. Gen. 1. Here God joyns them together in his own Image, and **makes no such distinctions and differences as men do**; for though they be weak, he is strong; and as he said to the Apostle, *His Grace is sufficient,* and his *strength is made manifest in weakness,* 2 Cor. 12.9. And such hath the Lord chosen, even *the weak things of the world, to confound the things which are mighty; and things which are despised, hath God chosen, to bring to nought things that are,* 1 Cor. 1. **And God hath put no such difference between the Male and Female as men would make.**[221]

I feel Margaret is throwing out a challenge to men. I think we can get closer to which men or sort of men she is targeting. Kings? She berates Charles II and probably James II not for causing the public intolerance by which her Friends, mostly male, are imprisoned and her female Friends are shunned for 'worshipping God' but for allowing it to happen. In fact, both Charles and James were in favour of toleration.

On 4 April 1660, as part of the deal that would restore his throne to him a month later Charles II had promised in the Declaration of Breda to pass an Act of Parliament that would embrace toleration of nonconformist and Catholic worship. Indeed, in 1661 Charles personally forbade the government of the Massachusetts Bay Colony to execute Quakers. It was the Cavalier Parliament that brushed it aside in favour of the Clarendon Code. Charles tried again in March 1672, issuing his Royal Declaration of Indulgence. Again, he was forced to withdraw by the Cavalier Parliament in favour of the Test Acts which effectively excluded Catholics from any public office.

In April 1687, James II issued his own Declaration of Indulgence which allowed for complete freedom of worship, the removal of oaths and the legal requirement to attend a Church of England every week. It is possible that William Penn helped in the drafting of it. For Quakers and other nonconformists, like Baptists, it was the answer to their prayers. But not for long. Within a year James was in exile after taking on Parliament and losing. The 1688/9 Act of Toleration

---

[221] users.wfu.edu/zulick/340/Felltext.html. Accessed 23/04/2020.

still excluded Quakers because it still required nonconformists to swear the loyalty oaths and forbade them to meet in their own houses.

Although the Established Church had both wings, High and Low, the Catholic and Republican threats meant that these Parliaments were full of High Anglican Royalists, pillars of the patriarchy. It is not hard to understand the misogyny of the scripture-based Puritans if you interpret the Bible in the way that Margaret was challenging. Jacqueline Broad cites a paper from 1655 in which a preacher from Cardiff, Joshuah Miller, clearly in heated dispute with a group of Quakers which included, according to him, some vociferous women echoed the opinions of John Knox expressed a generation before.

> What monstrous Doctrine is this? to suffer Women to be Preachers by way of authority, condemned as against nature *Isaiah* 3.12. I *Cor*. 14. 34, 35. 1 *Tim*. 2. 12. 14. This opinion was first held by the Pepuzians, that women might Preach, because they wickedly affirmed Christ assumed the form of a woman, and not of a man. In *France,* they allow not a woman to be a ruler over the affairs of men's goods: But with us some women will be rulers over, and directers of men's consciences; for so amongst the Quakers, women commonly teach as well as men.[222]
>
> *(We have encountered Pepuzians before but in the 2nd century they were called Montanists and valued ecstatic female prophecy.)*

The natural inferiority argument was still very much alive and kicking. Broad finds a paper by an anonymous writer from 1646.

> In the anonymous *A Spirit moving in the Women Preachers* (1646), the author asserts that women preachers transgress not only the rules of nature but also of modesty, divinity, discretion, and civility. On these grounds, the author concludes that women preachers cannot possibly be moved by the spirit of God but must partake in the spirit of darkness, ignorance, and gross error. To support his point, the author notes that the Serpent approached Eve first, because he knew that women were "the silly and weaker Sex" and "naturally apt unto all mischiefe".[223]

Margaret seems to have been aware of this tendency to assume male superiority. She argues very cleverly—whether accurately or not is very much open to debate—and stridently that without women's voices proclaiming the Spirit of God the Serpent wins.

> Thus much may prove that the Church of Christ is a woman, and those that speak against the woman's speaking, speak against the Church of Christ, and the Seed of the woman, which Seed is Christ ; that is to say,

---

222 plato.stanford.edu/entries/margaret-fell/#LifeWork. Accessed 23/04/2020.
223 Ibid.

Those that speak against the Power of the Lord, and the Spirit of the Lord speaking in a woman, simply, by reason of her Sex, or because she is a Woman, not regarding the Seed, and Spirit, and Power that speaks in her ; such speak against Christ, and his Church, and are of the Seed of the Serpent, wherein lodgeth the enmity. And as God the Father made no such difference in the first Creation, nor never since between the Male and the Female, but alwayes out of his Mercy and loving kindness, had regard unto the weak. Let this Word of the Lord, which was from the beginning, stop the mouths of all that oppose Women's Speaking in the Power of the Lord ; for he hath put enmity between the Woman and the Serpent ; and if the Seed of the Woman speak not, the Seed of the Serpent speaks ; for God hath put enmity between the two Seeds, and it is manifest, that those that speak against the Woman and her Seeds Speaking, speak out of the enmity of the old Serpents Seed ; and God hath fulfilled his Word and his Promise, *When the fulness of time was come, he hath sent forth his Son, made of a woman, made under the Law, that we might receive the adoption of Sons,* Gal. 4.4,5.[224]

So, totally ignoring my own guidelines on the dangers of subjective interpretation of other people's words, what is Margaret saying here? We need, firstly to strip away the scriptural language and imagery and, like modern Terms and Conditions documents, explain who and what is involved.

- ***Church of Christ**: Definitely not a man-made building. The Lord's House, where the spirits of all Christians live? The Body of Christ, all Christians, metaphorically what a Christian should look like?*
- ***Woman**: Feminine?*
- ***Seed**: What starts a living thing? (The anatomical study of the whole egg and sperm thing was in its infancy.)*
- ***The Seed of the Woman**: Human beings.*
- ***Serpent**: Temptation.*
- ***The Seed of the Serpent**: Sin.*

Margaret, therefore, is arguing that the nature of Christianity, what matters in God's house is as much feminine as it is masculine. Jesus would not have been a human that died to atone for the sins of mankind unless born of a woman. No new believers would become Christians, live in the Lord's house, unless born of woman. Due to his temptation of Eve, the seed of woman, human beings, would always be hostile to the seed of the Serpent, sin. The spirit of holiness is as much in women as in men. When it wants to speak, it is as true and powerful from a woman as a man. Lastly, not allowing a woman to speak leaves a space for temptation and sin to speak. Ergo, those who prevent women speaking, are allowing in temptation and sin.

---

[224] users.wfu.edu/zulick/340/Felltext.html. Accessed 23/04/2020.

This is a plea for equality of recognition, equality of access and equality of public importance. The Body of Christ, the Church of Christ would be purer, more righteous and closer to God's grace if women spoke. She finishes with this appeal for change.
And thus the Lord Jesus hath manifested himself and his Power, without respect of Persons, and so let all mouths be stopt that would limit him, whose Power and Spirit is infinite, that is pouring it upon all flesh.[225]

God and Jesus did not make distinctions between men and women—they were/He was (*Careful not to be an anti-trinitarian!*) no 'respecter of Persons'—but the patriarchy did.

Unsurprisingly, although committed to female ministry, not all Quaker men were as enlightened as George Fox. They were far from persuaded that women should have a say in the running of the 'church'. Fox's resolution, supported by his inner circle, was what we identified in Chapter 14 as 'complementarian', defining important roles for men and women in the home and in the church, an approach still adhered to by some groups of conservative protestants. Great importance was placed on motherhood and Women's Meetings alongside men only Business Meetings were set up to vet domestic behaviour and suitability of marriage proposals as well as make observations on religious conduct. George and Margaret spent much time supporting and dealing with criticisms of Women's meetings. However, the very idea was dramatically challenging, a worm in the apple of male supremacy that was not to be substantially built upon, in Britain at least, for another 200 years when Women-only organisations of all political persuasions became a feature of the British gender landscape; The Primrose League (Conservative), The Women's Liberal Federation (Liberal) and the Women's Social and Political Union (Radical).

If Margaret Fell Fox had been the only woman preaching, pamphlet writing, appearing in court, petitioning the King and being imprisoned, I would believe that her beliefs and practices were not widely known but she was not the only one. The stories of these trailblazers make for examples of female courage as thought-provoking as those of suffragettes and civil rights campaigners far more famous. Here is a selection.

- Elizabeth Hooton (1600-1672). Her preaching convinced Fox of the power of women's ministry.
- Mary Fisher (1623-1698). Missionary who visited the Ottoman Empire.
- Dorothy White (1630-1686). Prolific pamphleteer.
- Hester Biddle (1629-1697). Went to persuade Louis XIV to live in peace.
- Sarah Blackborow. Prolific pamphleteer in 1650s and 1660s.
- Rebecca Travers (1609-1688). Prolific pamphleteer, preacher and prison visitor.

[225] Ibid.

- Alice Curwen (1619-1679). Missionary, social activist and abolitionist.
- Dorcas Dole (d. 1719). Prolific west country pamphleteer.

By the end of the century that followed the death of the greatest, certainly the cleverest, queen regnant Europe had thus far experienced, her Protestant choice had become an indispensable part of Britishness. In its way the throwing off of the shackles of Catholic dogma led to a levelling process although her Anglican version, the via media, preserved the social hierarchy and its monarchy in Britain for three more centuries whereas countries such as the American colonies and France, one very Protestant and the other very Catholic, chose the Republican route. The green shoots of gender levelling were appearing on every branch of the hierarchical tree. The root that fed them was education.

The upper classes took advantage of the spread of Renaissance learning via the technological marvel of the printing press by educating future pillars of the local and national establishment. Following the example of major players like Sir Thomas More, alongside the young men were young women, the future wives and mothers of their offspring. Like his great-great uncle, Henry VIII, James I wrote. His two most famous books were on kingship, *Basilikon Doron*, and witchcraft, *Daemonologie*.

His son, Charles I, employed one of the cleverest women of her time, Bathsua Makin, to educate his children. Makin maintained throughout her life that women were the equal of men in terms of intellectual capacity and ability to reason but felt that only women who had the time and money could benefit from a full humanist education. She opened a school for gentlewomen in 1673 in London and wrote an essay entitled "*An Essay to Revive the Ancient Education of Gentlewomen*" which she dedicated to the future Mary II.

Again, Bathsua was not alone. Mary Astell, a well-known writer, was a strong advocate of the education of gentlewomen. She was a member of a circle of literary women, poets and philosophers, such as Lady Mary Chudleigh and Lady Mary Wortley Montagu.

Margaret Fell, if taken at face value, appears to devalue education but, if you look further into her reservations, they are anti-establishment and egalitarian. Her point was that God did not enter the inner light via Oxbridge educated aristocrats. God was spiritual and did not require education or the guidance of educated individuals to be accepted into a person's soul. Her intention was to make ordinary people feel comfortable with their own religious experience and follow the Bible rather than the established church. Quakers were very much in favour of educating girls.

> As early as 1668, George Fox set up Shacklewell School "to instruct young lasses and maidens in whatsoever was civil and useful."[226]

---

[226] www.quakersintheworld.org/quakers-in-action/166. Accessed 26/04/2020.

Women were beginning to refute, albeit only to the ears of men who wanted or had a reason to listen, like George Fox, some of the misogynistic myths that propped up the patriarchy. However, it took 226 years, 8 generations or so, for women to get the vote. Why the delay?

Chapter 32
Coverture

If all Men are born Free, why are all Women born Slaves?
– Mary Astell

I was married to a Fascist and I was married to a Marxist and neither one of them ever took out the garbage.
– Lee Grant

Unto the woman he said, I will greatly multiply thy sorrow and thy conception; in sorrow thou shalt bring forth children; and thy desire shall be to thy husband, and he shall rule over thee.
– Genesis 3:16

Preamble

By the time that two more queens regnant had been crowned, women had made some progress to overcoming the impediments placed on their gender by the Bible-led culture of a now Protestant England. Mary I and Elizabeth I were a real life refutation of John Knox's assertion that a woman could not rule. Women had begun to find their voice, to a limited extent in some communities, and to a far greater extent in writing than in public speaking. More women were being well educated and far more were receiving a basic education enabling them to read at the very least. The first magazine for women, The Ladies' Mercury, was issued in 1693. They were certainly more visible as a social group and some of them proved themselves the equal of some men. However, in one key area of society, they were inferior or, in some respects did not exist at all—The Law!

In 1632, 7 years into the reign of Charles I, the anonymous T.E. (suggested to be Thomas Edgar) wrote a legal guide on the status of women under the law called *The Lawes Resolutions for Women's Rights or The Lawes Provision for Woemen.* 133 years later, in 1765, Sir William Blackstone's *Commentaries on the Laws of England* was published.

A PDF copy of The Lawes can be found in the LSE Digital Library. It is hard to read due to its print format. I have, therefore, used a summary from a website on Caryl Churchill's play on women's rights Vinegar Tom, set in the 17th century.

There is no doubt that the status of women in the 17th century legal system was defined by Chapter 2:22-4 of Genesis backed up by Matthew 19:4-6. It was an outcome of being a Christian woman not a woman. When T.E. outlines his content he defines the three natural states recognised by the law: maid, wife and widow. Her future is likewise determined by the Bible, Genesis 3:16, and numerous letters from the Apostle Paul. T.E. makes it sound somewhat bleak and incapable of change.

> Return a little to Genesis, in the third chapter whereof I declared our first parents' transgression in eating the forbidden fruit, for which Adam, Eve, the serpent first, and lastly, the earth itself is cursed. And besides the participation of Adam's punishment, which was subjection to mortality, exiled from the garden of Eden, enjoined to labour, Eve because she had helped to seduce her husband hath inflicted on her an especial bane. *In sorrow shalt thou bring forth thy children, thy desires shall be subject to thy husband, and he shall rule over thee.* See here the reason of that which I touched before, that women have no voice in parliament. They make no laws, they consent to none, they abrogate none. All of them are understood either married or to be married and their desires are subject to their husband. I know no remedy, though some women can shift it well enough.[227]

133 years later, nothing had changed in that the holiness of a woman's unmarried or married state was entirely a matter for the ecclesiastical courts. Blackstone pointed out that the civil courts were only interested in three aspects of the marriage contract. Were the parties willing to make the contract, able to make the contract and did they sign a paper to that effect? Any impediments to its holiness (*following the will of God*) that might make it invalid in the sight of God had to be considered by the Church.

Nothing had changed since Henry VIII's divorce except the religious beliefs and practices of those that ran the Church. Above all, a woman's status related to her role as a procreator. To be holy, a maid had to be a virgin. To be holy, a wife had to be faithful to her husband, to be one flesh. To be holy, a widow of childbearing age had to remarry and become one flesh with a new husband. Only when she was a widow beyond childbearing age could a woman be holy and have some civil rights as an individual.

As a maid, a young woman had very few rights in 1632.

> The learning is… that a woman hath diverse special ages. At the seventh year of her age, her father shall have aid of her tenants to marry her. At nine years of age, she is able to deserve and have dower. At twelve years to consent to marriage. At fourteen to be *hors du guard.* At sixteen to be past the Lord's tender of a husband. At twenty-one to be able to make a

[227] vinegartom.weebly.com/the-laws-resolutions-of-womens-rights.html. Accessed 29/04/2020.

> feoffement. And *per Ingelton* therein the end of the case. A woman married at twelve cannot disagree afterward. But if she be married younger, she may dissent till she be fourteen.[228]

A feoffement was a transfer of property but, as a wife, she could not carry out any property transaction without her husband's approval and then it was carried out in his name. Once married she was in coverture—feme covert. Her legal person ceased to exist. There was no 'she', no 'they', only 'he'. If the wife held land at the time of her marriage then her husband did not own her land but had the rights to the rents and profits from it. Indeed, by the law of curtesy, if there were children from the marriage he could continue to do so even if his wife died.

Widowhood being a very real possibility, a husband could make a dower gift of some part of his estate upon the income off which his widow could live. Thus, for example, Henry VIII's sixth wife, Katherine Parr, having been married twice was a wealthy widow in 1543 and even more so when she married Thomas Seymour in 1547. Finally, a husband and wife, on marrying, could set aside some property jointly owned that would revert, in the event of one of them dying, to the sole ownership of the party still living (sometimes known as a jointure). T.E. confirms that such an action relied very much on the husband's sense of honour or the tenacity of the bride's parents.

> …All husbands are not so unkind or untrusty as to endamage their wives by alienation of their lands. But contrariwise, the greatest part of honest, wise, and sober men are of themselves careful to purchase something for their wives. If they be not, yet they stand sometimes bound by the woman's parents to make their wives some jointure.[229]

A woman from a propertied family, therefore, who was under 21 when married would never have known one single second of making a legal decision of her own. As to her personal privacy in legal matters she would have known none. The importance of maintaining her virginity would have meant limited social opportunities and little ownership of her own body or emotions and desires. It would be a bargaining chip of the utmost importance when her parents came to choose a husband for her. To disobey her father would have made her a social laughingstock, possibly a pariah, in the marriageable community.

Medieval laws on rape did exist and the punishments in certain circumstances were severe but once a woman agreed to marry she was expected to be good and compliant, 'bonny and buxum', in bed as in every other aspect of her married life. Even when those words were removed from her vows by the Tudor prayer books she was expected to 'obey', love and honour 'for better and for worse'. Marital rape simply did not exist. Once the contract conditions of

---

228 vinegartom.weebly.com/the-laws-resolutions-of-womens-rights.html. Accessed 06/05/2020.

229 Ibid.

'willing and able' had been met and signed up to and consummation had occurred, willingly or otherwise, the state of matrimony existed and the wife, excuse the pun, was feme covert in every respect. T.E. seems to treat sex by force as a last resort rather than a crime.

> When sweet words, fair promises, tempting, flattering, swearing, lying will not serve to beguile the poor soul, then with rough handling, violence, and plain strength of arms, they are or have been heretofore rather made prisoners to lust's thieves than wives and companions to faithful honest lovers. So drunken are men with their own lusts and the poison of Ovid's false precept, "*Vim licet appellant, vis est ea grata puellis*" [Force is ok, girls like to be forced] that if the rampier [rampart] of laws were not betwixt women and their harms, I verily think none of them being above twelve years of age and under an hundred, being either fair or rich, should be able to escape ravishing. This is therefore a matter concerning maids, wives, widows, and women of all degrees and conditions, if either they be or possess anything worth the having.[230]

The two principal modern concerns over rape, violence and a woman's autonomy over her own body, have only been addressed in law quite recently. In 1736, however, the all-embracing law book, *History of the Pleas of the Crown*, written by the prominent 17th-century judge, Sir Matthew Hale, reinforced the power of a baron covert (a husband):

> "The husband cannot be guilty of a rape committed by himself upon his lawful wife, for by their mutual consent and contract the wife hath given up herself in this kind unto her husband, which she cannot retract."[231]

It was not until 1991 that this interpretation was overturned by the House of Lords in the following ruling, "Nowadays it cannot seriously be maintained that by marriage a wife submits herself irrevocably to sexual intercourse in all circumstances."[232]

The 2003 Sexual Offences Act made sex with an otherwise allowed adult without their consent against the law. In 1993, 360 years after the *Lawes* was published, the United Nations Declaration on the Elimination of Violence against Women stated that:

> "violence against women is a manifestation of historically unequal power relations between men and women, which has led to domination over and discrimination against women by men and to the prevention of the full advancement of women, and that violence against women is one

[230] Ibid.

[231] en.wikipedia.org/wiki/Matthew_Hale_%28jurist%29#Writings. Accessed 11/05/2020.

[232] www.theweek.co.uk/98330/when-did-marital-rape-become-a-crime. Accessed 11/05/2020.

of the crucial social mechanisms by which women are forced into a subordinate position compared with men".[233]

Throughout the 17th and 18th centuries, in Britain at least, the Law not only excused marital rape but it allowed what we somewhat euphemistically call Domestic Violence which was, with less political correctness and no real sense of shame, Wife Beating. In 1632 this was T.E.'s fairly flippant perception of the law.

> …If a man beat an outlaw, a traitor, a pagan, his villein, or his wife, it is dispunishable, because by the Law Common these persons can have no action… [But] she may sue out of chancery to compel him to find surety of honest behaviour toward her, and that he shall neither do nor procure to be done to her (mark, I pray you) any bodily damage, otherwise than appertains to the office of a husband for lawful and reasonable correction. How far that extendeth I cannot tell, but herein the sex feminine is at no very great disadvantage, for first for the lawfulness: if it be in none other regard lawful to beat a man's wife than because the poor wench can sue no action for it, I pray why may not the wife beat the husband again? What action can he have if she do?… So the actionless woman beaten by her husband hath retaliation left to beat him again, if she dare.[234]

In other words, a wife was a non-person in terms of accusing her husband of a crime or suing him for damages but in the unlikely event of her hitting him back he had no recourse in law either so if she wanted to punish him hit him back! The only legal redress she could obtain was at the Court of Chancery, a sort of appeals court in which the fairness of the common law was tested, over the harshness of the chastisement. The flippancy of this suggestion arises from the fact that it was common knowledge, at least in legal circles, that only the superrich could afford such a case and the backhanders needed to promote it in the massive queue of cases waiting to be heard (a situation made famous by Dickens in his novel, *Bleak House*).

By 1765, Blackstone was able to record this observation suggesting that there was some recourse if not to the law then to social disapproval.

> The husband also (by **the old law**) might give his wife moderate correction. For, as he is to answer for her misbehaviour, the law thought it reasonable to intrust him with this power of restraining her, by domestic chastisement**, in the same moderation that a man is allowed to correct his servants or children**; for whom the master or parent is also liable in some cases to answer.

---

[233] en.wikipedia.org/wiki/Domestic_violence. Accessed 12/05/2020.

[234] vinegartom.weebly.com/the-laws-resolutions-of-womens-rights.html. Accessed 12/05/2020.

> But this power of correction was confined **within reasonable bounds**; and the husband was prohibited to use any violence to his wife, *aliter quam ad virum, ex causa regiminis et castigationis uxoris suae, licite et rationabiliter pertinet*. The civil law gave the husband the same, or a larger, authority over his wife; allowing him, for some misdemesnors**,** ***flagellis et fustibus*** *acriter verberare uxorem*; for others, only *modicam castigationem adhibere.* But, with us, in the politer reign of Charles the second, this power of correction began to be doubted: and a wife may now have **security of the peace against her husband**; or, in return, a husband against his wife.
> Yet, the lower rank of people, who were always fond of **the old common law**, still claim and exert their ancient privilege: and the courts of law will still permit a husband to restrain a wife of her liberty, in case of any gross misbehaviour.[235] [my highlighting]

Blackstone's use of words makes objective understanding of his meaning far from straightforward but the overall impression from what he is saying is that the socio-cultural attitude towards wife chastisement had become 'politer' after what he calls the Great Rebellion. (Those who called Cromwell's Commonwealth this clearly showed their conservative, pro-monarchist, *and, therefore patriarchal*, credentials.) It seems that he meant by 'the old law' the old common law which often based itself on judgements in past cases. The influence of Roman law would not have helped wives as it gave husbands and fathers absolute power over their wives and daughters. It could have meant Old Testament law, the Law of Moses. Blackstone was a firm believer that law was rooted in Natural Law which, in turn, was God's Law.

> "THIS law of nature, being co-eval with mankind and dictated by God himself, is of course superior in obligation to any other. It is binding over all the globe, in all countries, and at all times: no human laws are of any validity, if contrary to this; and such of them as are valid derive all their force, and all their authority, mediately or immediately, from this original."[236]

There is nothing in the Bible, however, that advocates chastising a wife, only ones servants.

> **26** And if a man smite the eye of his servant, or the eye of his maid, that it perish; he shall let him go free for his eye's sake.
> **27** And if he smite out his manservant's tooth, or his maidservant's tooth; he shall let him go free for his tooth's sake. (Exodus 21: 26-7)

---

[235] www.gutenberg.org/files/30802/30802-h/30802-h.htm#Chapter_the_fifteenth. Accessed 14/05/2020.
[236] Ibid.

While not forbidding physical chastisement, this passage is setting a boundary to how severe a beating could be before warranting losing possession of a person/property. Indirectly, it could have been a moral marker for what was deemed excessive use of force to correct a wife's behaviour. Is this what Blackstone meant by 'within reasonable bounds'? He goes on to point out that civil law, law laid down by the civil authorities such as a parliament, allowed a husband to beat his wife—fustibus means 'with clubs'—in certain cases.

In 1782, James Gillray, on his way to being the most celebrated political and social cartoonist of his time, produced a cartoon called *'Judge Thumb or—Patent Sticks for Family Correction: Warranted Lawful'*. Sir Francis Buller, a senior judge on the King's Bench, was alleged to have passed a remark to the effect that a husband could beat his wife with a stick so long as it was no thicker than his thumb thus contradicting Blackstone's 1765 assertion that, since the 'politer' reign of Charles II (more civilised? Courteous? Refined?), a wife could now have 'security of the peace against her husband'. Gillray's caricature seems, however, to endorse Blackstone's other implication that wife beating was now only favoured by the lower classes. With Judge Thumb dominating the sketch selling his thumb-ended sticks—*Who wants a cure for a rusty wife?*—there is a scene in the background in which a modestly dressed man with a stick is chasing a woman crying "*Murder!*" saying, "*Murder, hay? It's Law you Bitch! It's not bigger than my thumb.*"

In Wikipedia's article on Gillray, as well as remarking on his 'keen sense of the ludicrous', it quotes the Eleventh Edition—1910-11—of the Encyclopaedia Britannica:

> "Gillray is as invaluable to the student of English manners as to the political student, attacking the social follies of the time with scathing satire; and nothing escapes his notice, not even a trifling change of fashion in dress. The great tact Gillray displays in hitting on the ludicrous side of any subject is only equalled by the exquisite finish of his sketches—the finest of which reach an epic grandeur and Miltonic sublimity of conception."[237]

Gillray's targets were, generally, both political and social. In this instance, whether his target was the Law, Sir Francis, the working classes, upper class women or men who beat women, the practice of wife beating must have been of some topical interest and one to which he felt drawn by public scrutiny of and prurience about the sexual behaviour of the upper classes.

Furthermore, the century following Blackstone's *Commentaries,* fuelled by the rise of the novel and the Press (Wikipedia tells us that by the early 19th century there were 52 London newspapers and over 100 other titles), was one of hypocritical outrage, much of it highly sexist, at the 'scandalous' behaviour of women and their male counterparts, husbands and paramours, in and out of the

---

[237] en.m.wikipedia.org/wiki/James_Gillray. Accessed 15/05/2020.

bedroom. The language of scandal—adultery, cuckold, mistress, blackguard, scoundrel, gossip, cad and, of course, rake, harlot and whore—although in existence before the 18th century (much of it had its origin in snobbishness about the lower classes and sexism over what women talked about—*etymonline* suggests the origins of 'gossip' lie in the talk of females attending a birth.), became the lingua franca of marital morality. Gillray followed up *Judge Thumb* on 25th May 1786 with *'Lady Termagant Flaybum going to give her stepson a taste of her desert after dinner'.*

Gillray's caricatures may well be explained by the widespread interest in the marriages of two extraordinary aristocratic women: Lady Mary Eleanor Bowes, Countess of Strathmore and Lady Georgiana Cavendish, Duchess of Devonshire, who, we are told, shunned the services of a wet nurse (the stepson implication will be explained in the next chapter). The lives and marriages of these two women not only discomforted Blackstone's aside that wife chastisement was a lower-class phenomenon but also challenged the established requirement for a wife to be a meek and mild cash cow for her 'lord' and 'master' husband. Furthermore, they were both test cases for what the literate public thought when women had the audacity to behave like men. Apparently they were already dressing as men! *I love the gems that we can find on the internet! I just have to digress!*

In her book, *Maids, Wives, Widows: Exploring Early Modern Women's Lives 1540-1714*, Dr Sara Reid refers to a London based female fashion fad for dressing in men's clothes. She has found a letter from John Chamberlain, a noted 17th century letter writer and observer of King James, to the Bishop of London, relating the King's discomfort over and impatience with it. He had instructed the clergy to preach 'vehemently' against 'their wearing of broad-brimmed hats, pointed doublets, their hair cut short or shorn, and some of them stilettos or poniards'.[238] The word used by James, according to Chamberlain, to describe this behaviour in 'our' women was 'insolency'. *Hm*!

In 1662, Charles II ended the Shakespearean tradition of boys playing female roles, thinking it too was rude and encouraged the 'unnatural vice'. No sooner were women restored to playing women than they began playing women in men's clothes, usually as a disguise as in Aphra Behn's character, Helena, in her hit play, *The Rover.* In the Wikipedia article on the Breeches Role it highlights its prominence in Restoration theatre and opera.

> To see real women speak the risqué dialogue of Restoration comedy and show off their bodies on stage was a great novelty, and soon the even greater sensation was introduced of women wearing male clothes on stage. Out of some 375 plays produced on the London stage between 1660 and 1700, it has been calculated that 89, nearly a quarter, contained one or more roles for actresses in male clothes (see Howe). Practically every Restoration actress appeared in trousers at some time, and

[238] books.google.co.uk., p.59. Accessed 20/05/2020.

breeches roles would even be inserted gratuitously in revivals of older plays.

Some critics, such as Jacqueline Pearson, have argued that these cross-dressing roles subvert conventional gender roles by allowing women to imitate the roistering and sexually aggressive behaviour of male Restoration rakes, but Elizabeth Howe has objected in a detailed study that the male disguise was "little more than yet another means of displaying the actress as a sexual object". The epilogue to Thomas Southerne's *Sir Anthony Love* (1690) suggests that it does not much matter if the play is dull, as long as the audience can glimpse the legs of the famous "breeches" actress, Susanna Mountfort (also known as Susanna Verbruggen):

You'll hear with Patience a dull Scene, to see,
In a contented lazy waggery,
The Female Mountford bare above the knee.

Katharine Eisaman Maus also argues that as well as revealing the female legs and buttocks, the breeches role frequently contained a revelation scene where the character not only unpins her hair but as often reveals a breast as well. This is evidenced in the portraits of many of these actresses of the Restoration.[239]

Sir Peter Lely, the Court portrait painter, painted most of the royal mistresses. Whereas he produced glamourous likenesses of Charles' aristocratic lovers, Barbara Villiers, Duchess of Cleveland, and Louise de Kerouaille, Duchess of Portsmouth, his portrait of Margaret Hughes, actress mistress of Prince Rupert of the Rhine, Charles' cousin, shows her left breast exposed. His 1668 portrait of Nell Gwyn as Venus exposes a great deal more than that.

To complement the sex appeal of the actress, Restoration comedy created the almost stock character of the rake, an immoral man taken up with the vices of sex and gambling but with an irresistible power over women either through trickery or gallantry whose contacts with women either reform him or lead to his downfall. Much of his dialogue was double entendre and either truly or falsely gallant but in both respects matched or countered by the heroine, whether in breeches or farthingale.

The conundrum over which I have always puzzled concerns which came first, or, more precisely, which influenced which most, the chicken of Restoration Society culture or the egg of Restoration comedy and tragedy, the daytime reality of the Court or the night-time fantasy of the Theatre. Many of the actresses became the mistresses of high society men (e.g., Moll Davis and Nell Gwyn/Charles II; Margaret Hughes/Prince Rupert; Nell Gwyn and Elizabeth Barry/Earl of Rochester; Anne Lee/Earl of Dorset.) The King's friends were notorious rakes, the three most powerful of whom, John Wilmot, Earl of

---

[239] en.wikipedia.org/wiki/Breeches_role. Accessed 21/05/2020.

Rochester, George Villiers, Duke of Buckingham and Charles Sackville, Earl of Dorset have gone down in history as just that regardless of what else they did or achieved.

Whether this perception of the era is based on Art imitating Reality or vice versa, at the heart of the Restoration was a sea change in the perception of women. Sex for fun had replaced sex for procreation, men's fascination with a woman's libido—much emphasised by women like Behn—had temporarily superseded their obsession with the productivity of her womb. Womanhood, the sex object, had replaced motherhood, the baby-maker.

Holding on to that thought, before we look at the experiences of these two amazing women and two others whose lives highlighted the private and personal rottenness of the legal status of feme covert, I would like to go back to Blackstone's use of the word 'politer'. Without giving any more examples, many of which are urban legends anyway, history has probably correctly recorded that sea change in social behaviour, whether it was a moral reversal as in the theatre is debatable, as a natural easing during the reign of the Merry Monarch, Charles II, of the puritanical restraint of urges and desires espoused by the Commonwealth.

Not only was the monarchy restored but 'vices' such as the theatre and gambling, both banned in the Interregnum, mushroomed into the favourite indulgences of those with too much time on their hands and too much money to spend. In both of these leisure activities women's social profile proliferated. However, Charles' penchant for mistresses whom he openly paraded in front of his aristocratic circle of friends, courtiers and sycophants, acknowledging his paternity of their children, did not exclude the importance and rank they were required to accord to his wife and Queen Consort, Catherine of Braganza, whom he refused to divorce, despite great pressure on him to produce a legitimate heir, male of course, which Catherine was unable to do. True to the theatre the real-life rakes reformed or turned out to be deserving of more sympathy than they got through their dissolute lives.

> At Charles' final illness in 1685, she showed anxiety for his reconciliation with the Roman Catholic faith, and she exhibited great grief at his death. When he lay dying in 1685, he asked for Catherine, but she sent a message asking that her presence be excused and "to beg his pardon if she had offended him all his life." He answered, "Alas poor woman! she asks for my pardon? I beg hers with all my heart; take her back that answer."[240]

- By the age of 33, Rochester was dying, from what is usually described as the effects of syphilis, gonorrhoea, or other venereal diseases, combined with the effects of alcoholism. Carol Richards has disputed this, arguing that it is more likely that he died of renal failure due to

[240] https://en.wikipedia.org/wiki/Catherine_of_Braganza. Accessed 21/05/2020.

chronic nephritis (Bright's disease) His mother had him attended in his final weeks by her religious associates, particularly Gilbert Burnet, later Bishop of Salisbury.

- After hearing of Burnet's departure from his side, Rochester muttered his last words: "Has my friend left me? then I shall die shortly." In the early morning of 26 July 1680, Rochester died "without a shudder or a sound".[241]
- In hopes of converting him to Roman Catholicism, James sent him a priest, but Buckingham ridiculed his arguments. He died on 16 April 1687, from a chill caught while hunting, in the house of a tenant in Kirkbymoorside in Yorkshire (it is known as Buckingham House and it is located in the town centre), expressing great repentance and feeling himself "despised by my country and I fear forsaken by my God".[242]

… but when his youthful follies were over he appears to have developed sterling qualities, and although the poems he has left are very few, none of them are devoid of merit. Dryden's *Essay on Satire* and the dedication of the *Essay of Dramatick Poesie* are addressed to him. Walpole (*Catalogue of Noble Authors*, iv.) says that he had as much wit as his first master, or his contemporaries Buckingham and Rochester, without the royal want of feeling, the duke's want of principles or the earl's want of thought; and Congreve reported of him when he was dying that he slabbered more wit than other people had in their best health.[243]

There was nothing new or modern about a king having mistresses or acknowledging illegitimate children. Henry I is said to have had 24 illegitimate children, 9 sons and 15 daughters by numerous mistresses. There was nothing new about mistresses like Anne Boleyn, supplanting wives in importance and visibility at court. There was nothing new about mistresses from a lower class, like Alice Perrers, mistress of Edward III. What was new, other than the reversal of Puritan morality, was that mistresses became a part of a wealthy, powerful man's accoutrement and, instead of being hidden away from their female rivals, namely the wives of their paramours, like Henry II's mistress, Rosamund Clifford, they became a consideration, an item of regard, not just socially but financially.

What was new was either the openness of the moral hypocrisy in the patriarchy of that time or the absence of it depending on how you view what was happening. Instead of restraining or denying his lust, a rich, powerful man could indulge it with a mistress and return to his wife and family as a dutiful, responsible husband and father, to his church as a pious follower of God's Word

---

241 en.wikipedia.org/wiki/John_Wilmot,_2nd_Earl_of_Rochester. Accessed 21/05/2020.

242 en.wikipedia.org/wiki/George_Villiers,_2nd_Duke_of_Buckingham. Accessed 21/05/2020.

243 en.wikipedia.org/wiki/Charles_Sackville,_6th_Earl_of_Dorset. Accessed 21/05/2020.

and to his community as a pillar of righteousness, a role model and leader, whether a Prince, a Government Minister, a Peer of the Realm, a Justice of the Peace, an industrial magnate or a well-connected merchant.

And his wife could do nothing about it! Few wives tried, being content to have economic security and a standing in society, albeit vicarious. Her battle was to make sure that her legitimate bond with her husband was stronger than and superior to the illegitimate liaison with his mistress.

With the Restoration, keeping a mistress lost its social stigma. It was officially condemned but unofficially sanctioned. Fornication and adultery were wrong in the eyes of God but unavoidable given the male libido. Political marriage was essential, as was procreation, to the economic reality of owning, expanding, and holding on to property. In Charles' court the mistress and the wife were side by side, the one for impropriety, the other for propriety, although the most serious split occurred in his relationship with Catherine when he suggested making his mistress, Barbara Palmer/Villiers, her lady of the bedchamber.

What was happening in fiction and reality was that women and men's treatment of them was in the public eye. Every aspect of the lives of widely different women and their relationships with the rich and powerful was being considered for its merits and demerits. It was a 'politer' age in that the qualities and faults, strengths and weaknesses were given more consideration, more empathy and more understanding which would probably not have happened had Charles not been the sort of man he was, i.e., a philogynist, a man who liked and admired every aspect of femininity. His best epitaph came from this interchange of wit with his friend, Rochester, over the latter's epigram.

> We have a pretty witty king, Whose word no man relies on.
> He never said a foolish thing, And never did a wise one.
>
> To which Charles supposedly replied, "That's true, for my words are my own, but my actions are those of my ministers".[244]

The Hanoverian Age, though similar in many respects to Restoration, did not follow on immediately after it. The last 30 years of the Stuarts were filled with the reigns of 2 kings and 2 queens and the same old tragic failure of the queens, Mary II and Anne, to procreate, and the dominance of religion in the destinies of the kings, James II, the Catholic standard bearer, and William III, the Protestant.

Both James and William were typical of aristocrats of their time, making highly political marriages, the former losing a crown and the latter gaining one, and having a mistress (William denied that Elizabeth Villiers was his mistress and his wife, Mary II believed him.) or, in James' case, several. They were so

[244] en.wikipedia.org/wiki/John_Wilmot,_2nd_Earl_of_Rochester. Accessed 21/05/2020.

packed with events of national importance that Court life and personalities have not been recorded in such surgical detail as that of Charles II, except, possibly, for Anne's relationship with Sarah Churchill, *The Favourite*.

The devotion of the two sisters, Mary and Anne, to their husbands, William and George was in stark contrast to their uncle Charles but George of Denmark's willingness to defer to his wife was similarly different to his namesake from Hanover whose reign was the first of the Hanoverian era the manners of which were in similarly stark contrast to the Victorian era which followed it.

When George Louis, heir to the Electorate of Hanover and the future George I of Great Britain and Ireland, married Sophia Dorothea of Celle in 1682 it was entirely for political and economic reasons. Whether they were ever comfortable in each other's company they did their procreative duty, producing two children in 4 years, George, the future George II, and Sophia Dorothea who became mother of Frederick the Great of Prussia. George Louis preferred the company of his mistress, Melusine von der Schulenburg, and by 1694 Sophia Dorothea was unhappy enough to want to escape from the marriage. She enlisted the help of a Swedish soldier serving her father-in-law, Ernest Augustus, Philip Christoph von Konigsmarck.

Whether they were lovers trying to elope or he was just trying to be gallant we will never know because he was murdered and she was put in prison for the rest of her life after the dissolution of her marriage on the grounds of abandoning her husband. Clearly, the principle that noble husbands could play away but their wives could not, had not changed since the execution of Catherine Howard in 1542. Melusine accompanied George to his new kingdom in 1714 and was hostess at all his parties, being honoured with titles, Duchess of Kendal and Duchess of Munster, and enriching herself selling offices and patents 'as much the Queen of England as anyone was' according to Robert Walpole, the King's Prime Minister from 1721.

The Hanoverians did not provide any discernible pattern for an Age of Mistresses. George II had many mistresses but was devoted to the German wife he chose, Caroline of Brandenburg-Ansbach. His grandson, George III was completely faithful to his wife, Princess Charlotte of Mecklenburg-Strelitz, with whom he had 15 children between 1762 and 1783. His eldest son, the future Prince Regent, was notorious for his mistresses and failed marriage while his third son, the future William IV, lived equally happily with his actress mistress Dorothea Bland, Mrs Jordan, and, when he had to marry for money, with his wife, Princess Adelaide of Saxe-Meiningen.

It was high society, the 'haut ton', that proved to be the battleground of the sexes that would eventually mean that women gained the toehold in 'Manland' that in the 20th century would move from colonisation to substantial settlement sufficient to replace the patriarchy with a 'politer' culture in which womanhood has established some equal political, economic and social recognition with manhood.

Chapter 33
Feme Covert

This may be my XX chromosomes doing the talking, but it seems to me that divorce is, and always has been, a woman's issue par excellence.
– Amanda Foreman

By the present law, the woman was condemned unheard; and it was quite astonishing that such an anomaly should have so long existed in the laws of a civilised and Christian country.
– Sir George Bowyer

Preamble

I return to my constant theme. In the three centuries delineated as Early Modern Britain, they did not know how to make a rocket powerful enough to take a man to the moon or speak to someone more than 50 yards away, but they were people with feelings and a moral sensibility. They were largely driven by sex and money as we are now. Challenging the rich and powerful Establishment was just as difficult as it has always been, even when by blood, tradition, and/or wealth you were one of them.

We are going to look at the lives of four married women, Lady Anne Clifford from the 17th century, Lady Mary Bowes-Lyon and Lady Georgiana Cavendish, nee Spencer, from the 18th and Caroline Norton, nee Sheridan, from the 19th, not only to demonstrate this challenging behaviour but to show that *ceteris paribus* a woman's fight for equal treatment and regard was never harder than in the 200 years following the Restoration of the monarchy in 1660.

For the details of Anne Clifford's cause I have relied heavily on an article written in 2012 by Professor Carla Spivack of Oklahoma University School of Law, '*Law, Land, Identity: The Case of Lady Anne Clifford.*'

The Cliffords were an established Anglo-Norman family from the North of England. Their ancestor, Robert de Clifford, the 1st Baron, was a renowned soldier, a victor at Falkirk in 1298 who received a writ of summons to parliament in 1299 confirming his baronial status. He died at Bannockburn in 1314. His descendant, Henry Clifford, was made Earl of Westmoreland in 1525. Henry's grandson, the third Earl and 13th Baron de Clifford, was an Elizabethan naval commander and Lady Anne Clifford's father. When Lady Anne was 15 her father died and her legal battle to inherit his estates began.

Just before we turn the spotlight on Lady Anne it is worth a quick reminder about the feudal arrangement of/for land in England. No one owned any part of England except the king. He could not hold on to all of that land without help so he enlisted landholders or tenants to hold on to it for him which usually meant providing soldiers for the king's army, upholding the law and paying taxes, either directly or by collection. His soldiers were his servants, his underlings, his Barons. The bit of land they held was a barony. A Baron had a right to do what he liked to make money from his land and a right to hand over his rights to his heirs if the king approved.

Barons did not govern their holdings—the King shared his governing power with Dukes, Bishops and Earls—but, because every square inch of England that did not belong to the King directly or the Church belonged to a Baron, the King recognised each baron's entitlement to their land by summoning him to his advisory council which came to be his parliament. The writ of summons was a legal recognition of the baron's rights. The rights were legally, by the King's writ, allowed to be passed on to 'heirs of the body' within the principle of primogeniture. Heirs of the body, as a legal term, does not specify gender. Professor Spivack suggests that this was reinforced by a charter of King Edward II using the words 'heirs general', a term which Lady Anne herself used in her writings.

In theory, therefore, the king had an interest in every land issue because it was HIS land. However, he was a busy man so, rather than take every issue into his court, the Curia Regis, Henry II set up another court, The Court of Common Pleas, to settle land disputes.

Finally, the main purpose of jurisdiction in common law courts, especially those dealing with land disputes, was arbitration leading to a settlement rather than investigation of an accusation of a criminal act which took place in a criminal court.

Earl Clifford's will left his estates, which he held as a baron, to his younger brother, Francis, to whom the Earldom passed according to the letters patent of Henry VIII who created it. George Clifford was, by all accounts a real-life Lord Flashheart (*Blackadder fans will know who I mean. The wonderful Rik Mayall RIP*); a renowned jouster, naval commander, buccaneer, and adventurer he was also an equally renowned 'courtier', womaniser, gambler, and debtor. He married Margaret Russell, daughter of the Earl of Bedford. Lady Anne was his youngest child and his only daughter. Both his sons died when infants leaving Anne as his sole heir. When her brother, Robert, died her father began to consider the future of his estates which he had neglected for years while he pursued his stellar career at court or venturing abroad.

In 1591, therefore, aware that he had to pass on his estate to his oldest surviving child, his daughter, Anne, he started a legal process, called '*fine and recovery*' aimed at lifting this common law restriction and enabling him to do what he wanted with his land rights. He wanted them to go to his younger brother, Francis. Why?

We can only conjecture on why he wanted this. When he died, he had huge debts and no sons. Whereas a son could have risen in the service of the monarch or married a fortune or, as he had done, leased or sold parts of the vast estates in Westmoreland and Yorkshire, a daughter would marry and give these latter rights to a husband and their heirs who would bear a different name. A wealthy husband would look to his own land's obligations first.

However, his brother, might be able to amalgamate the Clifford landholdings, pay off the debts and pass on the barony and the earldom to his Clifford heirs in a minimally diminished state. If his reasoning were anything like this it would mean that he fully understood the implications of coverture for the immortality of his family name and achievement. Whether intended or not, in fact his brother and nephew spent the next 50 years or so paying off George's debts.

Being only 15 when her father died, Anne needed a legal guardian and she chose her mother, Margaret Russell, who had been separated from George for some time. In November 1606, on behalf of her daughter, she initiated a claim at the Court of Common Pleas for possession of her father's estates and title of Baroness de Clifford. Her father had left Lady Anne £15,000 on the condition that she did not dispute his settlement with her uncle. *Again, we wonder why and again the answer comes back logically as something to do with the status of women in that society.*

In 1609, Anne married Richard Sackville, 3rd Earl of Dorset, a carbon copy of her father since he had large gambling debts and the seemingly obligatory mistresses. Her legal pursuit of her inheritance caused friction in the marriage because Richard needed ready money to settle his debts. Anne's mother died in 1616, putting Richard in charge of the case because, although it was her inheritance, she was feme covert and leaving Anne feeling that her only genuine supporter had gone. Furthermore, before she died her mother had found documents that proved her daughter's entitlement beyond any doubt by negating her father's fine and recovery device. Without getting too legal, if there was any royal interest in the grant of the barony, which there was, the legal trick of fine and recovery could not be used to change the conditions of the grant.

After her mother's death, Richard changed tack. His aim was to get Anne to agree to convey the ownership of the estate to Francis in return for more money. Even King James became involved pressurising Anne to agree at £20,000. Once agreed, if her husband to whom by coverture the money would pass died before her she, as a feme sole would make no further claim on Francis on pain of forfeiting the original £15,000 and having to pay back the agreed £20,000.

As Blackstone made clear some 160 years later for such a contract to be valid all parties with an interest would have to be willing and able and put their name to the agreed terms in the form of their signature. Anne refused to sign any agreement, defying her husband, the courts, and her King. All she ever agreed to was that her husband could inherit if she died before him without any children.

Dorset died before her in 1624 and Lady Anne was able to pursue her case on her own as feme sole which she did.

Despite marrying again in 1630, to a widower, Philip Herbert, Earl of Pembroke, another quarrelsome and unfaithful husband, she never gave in to the patriarchal pressure to hand over her right to inherit. She also resisted his attempts to choose a husband for his stepdaughter, allowing Isabella to choose her own husband, James Compton, Earl of Northampton. Is it possible that T.E. had this case in mind in 1632 when he admitted the possibility of a woman, the daughter, Lady Anne, in direct line having precedence over a man, the brother, Francis, in a transversal line?

Common law it may have been but Professor Spivack points to research that shows that men had been successfully bypassing it 'legally' for centuries at the expense of female heiresses like Lady Anne who, herself, gained no legal recognition of her rights until all her male rivals were dead; Francis in 1641, his childless son and heir, Henry, in 1643 and her husband in 1650. As a Baroness and feme sole Lady Clifford exercised her baronial rights, investing in her property, collecting her rents and improving her land, in contrast to her playboy father and husbands whose behaviour could be only partially absolved by their royal connection and duties, until her death in 1676.

What was going on here? I agree with Professor Spivack that it is anachronistic to put a feminist twist on Lady Anne's motivation. She clearly accepted the gender norms of the day, referring to Dorset as 'my Lord, my husband', even when disagreeing with him, and accepting the contradiction implicit in being a 'Baron' and 'knight' and a woman in a 'Parliament' from which women were banned, its ancient purpose being to assemble fighting men. She is, however, well enough informed to remind men of Platonic reasoning that some women are better than some men, even in prosecuting war:

> *"...though man in his sex be more excellent than Woman, yet in qualitie we see often Women excel Men therefore no reason to bar them of their rights especially when no detriment thereon ensueth to the Commonwealth as in this case it doth not."*[245]

Furthermore, she clearly recognises an already established reality that a Baroness could delegate the hands-on fighting role to a male relative or retainer. Anyway, within her lifetime, the Tenures Abolition Act 1660 abolished Knight Service in favour of socage, in effect rent.

However, accepting that her case was about her rights as an inheritor of her father's estates, title and name and not a political campaign for women in general nor a political statement but a personal one, she was fighting for her rights as a titled feudal tenant not to be legally dealt with any differently from

---

[245] file:///C:/Users/richa/Downloads/SSRN-id2277099%20(1).pdf. Accessed 28/05/2020.

any others because of her gender. Although the fight for women's universal suffrage was delayed by issues of class and property ownership, in the end it came down to a simple question, "Why do men have the right to vote and women do not?"

Lady Anne was asking a similar question, "Why do men, per se, have the right to inherit property and titles when women, per se, do not?" The retort that only men had the natural equipment to fight was no longer valid.

Lady Anne was from the cream of English aristocracy whose father and husbands were all close to the royal family. She was descended from an ancient Anglo-Norman, an inheritor of the privilege won at the Battle of Hastings, one of the elite. Her claim to be a legal person, a landholder suo jure and an equal subject of her lord, the King, was only made because of her gender. Her allegedly haughty, argumentative, and uncompromising character was a male assessment of her situation not the reason why she never received recognition by the law of her rights.

Whether it was thwarted by her husbands, her uncle, the judges of the Court of Common Pleas, the King himself or the slow turn of the wheels of justice, it is naïve to conclude that her gender had nothing to do with her lifelong struggle. Equally naïve would be a conclusion that it had nothing to do with male supremacy and legally backed repression, oppression or suppression of women by men.

Chapter 34
Marriage A-La-Mode

Moral: don't listen to evil silver-tongued counsellors; don't marry a man for his rank, or a woman for her money; don't frequent foolish auctions and masquerade balls unknown to your husband; don't have wicked companions abroad and neglect your wife, otherwise you will be run through the body, and ruin will ensue, and disgrace, and Tyburn.

– William Makepiece Thackeray

Preface

From Aristophanes to Monty Python, satire has been a diversionary tactic, concealing negative, frequently hostile, feelings by mocking the inhumanity in and abuse of power in a shared atmosphere of fun and laughter. Laughter, however, can be as cruel as it is forgiving and the real injustice and hurt to the women whom Gillray and Hogarth targeted shows in the stories we are about to hear in which truth really is stranger than fiction.

In the early to mid-18th century, the satirical artist and engraver, William Hogarth, turned his perceptive eye on the burning social issues of his day such as wealth, poverty, industry, alcohol consumption and cruelty to animals. His *Beer Street* and *Gin Lane* are probably his most famous works visually, but his work *A Rake's Progress* is probably his most known title. Wikipedia tells us that Sir Alan Palmer, decorated filmographer, saw his series of engravings telling a story as a forerunner to the storyboard. I think they are more than that. They are an early flowering of visual satire in the Monty Python mode or, perhaps, given his talent for caricature, Spitting Image.

A Rake's Progress was the sequel to *A Harlot's Progress* and followed up some 10 years later by *Marriage a-La-Mode.* The 6 plates of *A Harlot's Progress* tell the story of a country girl, Moll Hackabout, who arrives in London seeking work as a seamstress but is procured into a brothel, becomes a mistress to a wealthy Jewish merchant, declines again into prostitution and dies at the early age of 23 of venereal disease. Unlike the fiction of the time—Henry Fielding's *Tom Jones*, Daniel Defoe's *Moll Flanders* or the more intentionally erotic *Fanny Hill* by John Cleland—Hogarth represented real people, such as Elizabeth Needham, a notorious Madame, and Sir Francis Charteris, 'The Rape-Master General', a renowned rapist condemned to death for raping a maid, Anne Bond, but pardoned by George II. In an age of corruption his wealth was used to paper over the cracks of his immorality. Fortunately, given the following character assessment, Jonathan Swift, the satirist, did not write his CV or his epitaph:

"a most infamous, vile scoundrel, grown from a foot-boy, or worse, to a prodigious fortune both in England and Scotland: he had a way of insinuating himself into all Ministers under every change, either as pimp, flatterer, or informer. He was tried at seventy for a rape, and came off by sacrificing a great part of his fortune"[246]

Under a different king, Charles I, 99 years earlier in 1631, he may have not fared so well. Mervyn Touchet, 2nd Earl of Castlehaven, was found guilty of assisting a servant to rape his wife, Anne Stanley, a great-great granddaughter of Henry VIII's younger sister, Mary, and sodomy with another servant. He was executed, all the while protesting his innocence. There were enough shenanigans in his house to at least justify a re-investigation.

This case, however, was noteworthy for 4 reasons. The first, his execution, we have noted for its severe stand on sexual morality. The second was the economic imperative behind marriage to an older widow (Anne was 44 and Mervyn was 31). Thirdly, Amanda Foreman describes Touchet's defence and the judicial rebuttal of it as follows:

> Castlehaven's chief defence was that a wife's body belonged to her husband, to dispose of as he saw fit. According to English law, the prosecutors could not disagree with the first part of his statement, but they rejected the logical conclusion of the latter. The earl was sentenced to death.[247]

Finally, and most significantly, Lady Anne was allowed by the Court to testify against her husband's cruelty and, even more incredibly, given an all-male jury, was believed.

A Rake's Progress charts the life of the son and heir of a wealthy but miserly merchant, Tom Rakewell, who wastes his fortune on wine, women and song, tries to rescue things by marrying a wealthy widow, a la Mervyn Touchet, but ends up in the Fleet debtor's prison and, eventually, in the Bethlem hospital for the insane. In this series of 8 plates it is the places depicted that were all too real—the infamous Rose Tavern brothel in Covent Garden, the Fleet debtor's prison and the Bethlem hospital—and far too frequently visited by those with too much time on their hands and too much money in their pockets.

The 6 plates of Marriage a-la-Mode depict the tragedy of a marriage designed to bail out a bankrupt aristocrat between his son and the daughter of a wealthy merchant. Her lover ends up murdering her husband and once he is hung she poisons herself. Here Hogarth seems to be favouring a marriage for love, a theme that was immortally taken up by novelists like Jane Austen later in the century, although her heroines married upper class, usually wealthy, husbands, helping them to live happily ever after! The reality, however, while coverture formed the legal basis for marriage, sex was the newfound freedom, and gambling the vice

---

[246] en.wikipedia.org/wiki/Francis_Charteris_rake. Accessed 30/05/2020.
[247] www.smithsonianmag.com/history/heartbreaking-history-of-divorce-180949439/. Accessed 01/06/2020.

of choice, demonstrated that some had so much money, or thought they had, that it did not matter if vast sums were lost on the toss of a coin. Industry and commerce were the new sources of wealth, money and not love dominated the marriage motives of the rich and powerful.

Mary Eleanor Bowes, dubbed 'The Unhappy Countess', was the daughter of industrialist and MP, Sir George Bowes, who made a fortune out of a coal cartel in County Durham. When he died in 1760, his 11-year-old daughter, Mary, became, possibly, the wealthiest heiress in Europe. On her 18th birthday, Mary married, with her mother's consent but against her advice, John Lyon, "The Beautiful Lord Strathmore". They had 5 children in the first 6 years of their marriage, the youngest of whom, Thomas Bowes-Lyon, is the Queen's great-great-great grandfather.

We know a lot about Mary through her own "*Confessions*" and a biography written by Jessie Foote, the family doctor for over 30 years. Neither is exceptionally reliable for reasons we shall examine later. Apparently, soon after the birth of their last child in 1773, John began to be ill from tuberculosis and the couple mostly lived apart, he in Bristol and Bath for his health and Mary in London for the craic, he running up debts from his passion, horse racing, and she from her 'licentious' lifestyle. John died on his way to Portugal in 1776, interestingly without his wife.

It is entirely possible that all that John and Mary had in common was physical attraction. Jesse Foote, a far from reliable source and lifelong ally of John's successor, described John as follows:

> "The late Earl of Strathmore was not calculated to make even a good, learned woman a pleasing husband. His Lordship's pursuits were always innocent and without the smallest guile, but they were not those of science or any other splendid quality. A sincere friend, a hearty Scotchman and a good bottle companion were points of his character."[248]

Furthermore, it is likewise entirely possible that their living apart was more than the result of his need to 'take the waters'. Whether they were temperamentally unsuited or could not stand the sight of each other or took steps towards another partner or lover is not the issue. The way history records what happened to them is highly loaded in his favour, partly because his illness and tragically early death is a powerful legacy for those who have not dug deeply into the relationship, *which I do not intend to do either*.

Mary's legacy, on the other hand, arises almost totally out of her behaviour as a teenage girl being wooed by a number of eligible bachelors and what happened to her after the marriage was over. *Similar behaviour to hers—flirting, playing several suitors off against each other, taking a lover, hiding the consequences of sexual activity (in her case by termination, in a man's case by vile creams to cure or alleviate syphilis), neither repressing, suppressing nor*

---

[248] en.wikipedia.org/wiki/John_Bowes,_9th_Earl_of_Strathmore _and_Kinghorne. Accessed 01/06/2020.

oppressing one's libido and going out on the town—in a single man made him a rake, except in the eyes of a realist, and pessimist, like Hogarth, a sort of lovable rogue and in a married man made him a fully paid up member of the patriarchy; wife, mistress, son and heir, landowner, gambler, politician and member of White's, the men only Gentleman's Club still in existence 250 years later.

In the absence of her husband, but before his death, Mary, now in her mid-20s, took a lover, the not entirely reputable George Grey. Such a reputation was a minus in a husband but a plus in a lover. Only Mary's *Confessions* chart the circumstances of the relationship and there is good reason to believe that these were made under some duress. She admits to being flirtatious, unwisely so at times, and being pregnant with Grey's child before her husband's death, as well as inducing miscarriages of three foetuses because of their intimacy. However, she is adamant that she had only had sexual relations with three men, Strathmore, Grey and the husband who forced her to confess, Andrew Robinson Stoney.

Stoney is described in historiography as an 'adventurer' which has the sound of a heroic seeker after unknown knowledge or treasure. To the 18th century ear, however, an adventurer was a gambler, a chancer who got what he wanted by unscrupulous means. Unlike a rake who in most cases squandered his fortune immorally, an adventurer was in search of a fortune to squander immorally. Just like a prostitute who offered her body as a sex object in return for money, usually on a short-term arrangement and from her own lodgings (often in a brothel), an adventurer offered his body as a sex object in return for money but, unlike most of his female counterparts, hoping it would be long-term and provide him with lodgings.

A successful or high-class prostitute/courtesan could transition to a mistress provided with her own lodgings, even co-habit with her lover, but a successful adventurer could transition to a husband and own his own house/manor/mansion, formerly the home of his lover but now, under the law of coverture, his.

There is a wonderful book about Mary Bowes and Stoney Bowes, Wedlock, by Wendy Moore, with which I cannot compete for its comprehensive treatment of the affair. The story is compellingly dramatic and reads like a novel, but Wendy Moore's meticulous research has produced a truth stranger than fiction. I will only concentrate on what is relevant to my focus on the collateral damage of coverture.

As a feme sole, Mary was pursued by many infatuated suitors, young and old, some enamoured and some parasitic. Andrew Robinson Stoney, definitely, and her lover, George Grey, probably, were the latter. Stoney had already married once for fortune, as had Grey. There were rumours about his treatment of his first wife. Stoney was also an accomplished conman and after an elaborate subterfuge got Mary, almost certainly pregnant with Grey's child, to marry him. Once married Stoney exerted his 'property' rights over a feme covert. There seems little doubt that he was an abuser.

> According to a physician who treated him, this man Stoney was 'cowardly, insidious, hypocritical, tyrannic, mean, violent, selfish, jealous, revengeful, inhuman and savage, without a single countervailing quality'. Extraordinarily, this was no exaggeration.[249]

Whether he was as evil or Mary as gullible as they were painted by a voracious and less than truthful press that generated a 24-hour rumour mill which satisfied the feeding frenzy of prurient public opinion is not my concern. That his self-assured male supremacy was the guiding light of his life is almost certainly true. That the behaviours with which he asserted it, such as house confinement, exile, domestic abuse, servant abuse and marital rape, were not unique to him in Georgian culture is equally true. Truest of all was the fact that coverture, added to the moral insistence of the Anglican Church that marriage once entered into could not be undone, allowed this to happen.

The staggering juxtaposition of this case with the American Declaration of Independence—"We hold these truths to be self-evident, that all men are created equal, that they are endowed by their Creator with certain unalienable Rights, that among these are Life, Liberty and the pursuit of Happiness."—makes its denial of the right of personhood to a married woman, especially one in which education, beauty and wealth were such a potent mixture as to attract the attention of all, otherwise 'polite', society makes it all the more extraordinary.

On 28th February 1785, Mary Bowes lodged her suit for divorce on the grounds of her husband's adultery and cruelty with the London Consistory Court, the premier ecclesiastical court in England. The case was to entertain the reading public and implicate hundreds of people, friends, relatives and acquaintances of the warring couple, tenants, estate workers, townspeople, hoodlums and servants, lawyers and judges, every shade of the good and the bad. Despite Stoney Bowes' delaying tactics the case came to court in May 1786. Mary won her divorce—*divortium a mensa et thoro. Job done! Well, er, no!*

In Chapter 27, when we looked at the most famous divorce in history, the word 'divorce' made social sense in that a couple were no longer a couple, they were fully separated, the unity of marriage was split in two. Legally, however, the union had been annulled; it never existed. 'The pursuit of happiness' with another partner was possible although neither Catherine nor Anne of Cleves, unlike the husband they never had, chose it. No real property was brought by the wife to either marriage, no castle or mansion, no agricultural rents, no rights to mine coal. If they had been, they would have had to have been returned, therefore, for a cash strapped noble another heiress would need to be found ASAP.

Husbands whose wealth and title depended on a wife's wealth and title (*jure uxoris*) usually had a replacement lined up before seeking an annulment. When the impeccably noble Viscount Bolingbroke divorced his wife, the former Diana

---

[249] ghostsofglamis.blogspot.com/2016/08/a-tragic-countess-and-sociopath.html. Accessed 05/06/2020.

Spencer, in the 1760s, he was so far in debt he had to resort to the marriage ploy employed by Hogarth's Rake.

> In the meantime, he never stopped searching for an heiress old enough or unattractive enough (and therefore desperate to marry) to wed a man of questionable finances and reputation. This led to laughable "courtships" with well-bred spinsters, including one who herself had lost her fortune to gambling.[250]

Although procreation was the main 'religious' purpose of marriage which intermingled with issues of bloodline in the nobility, it gave the Church a decisive 'political' role. The 'moral' Church, Catholic or Anglican, did not approve of violence, except in defence of its creed and dogma, and wanted people to be happy in their carnal as well as their spiritual existence. While adhering to the biblical teaching of marriage for life an ecclesiastical court was prepared to agree to a separation *a mensa et thoro,* 'bed and board' (live in different places and manage different households), in certain circumstances.

Given the patriarchal culture of the time, it was sufficient for a husband to prove his wife's adultery but a wife had to prove not only her husband's adultery but also his excessive maltreatment, not easy to prove because of the widely accepted view that husbands had a perfect right to correct their wives' behaviour. In exceptional cases the court could grant maintenance payments to the wife but, because by law the income generating estate was his by right of coverture, he was baron covert, that was all she would get to live on, unless he was prepared to grant her a legal settlement. (Henry VIII made extensive settlements on both his ex-wives of residences and estates.) It is hard to see how a woman could argue her case when the legal logic of the condition of feme covert meant that she could not testify against her husband.

A way had been found around this by a private deed between the husband and a trustee appointed on the wife's behalf. Such deeds were mostly legally honoured towards the end of the 18th century under the enlightened Lord Chief Justice, William Murray, Baron Mansfield, about whom we will learn more later. More devastating to the social standing of an heiress like Mary Eleanor Bowes would be the loss of her vast income over which the husband's married status still gave him total control. For the wife, the re-establishment of control over her own body and the right to choose to whom she surrendered it came at a heavy cost, loss of wealth and social standing. The husband lost extraordinarily little. Small wonder that marrying a wealthy widow was an attractive career for an 'adventurer'.

When his wife, the former Lady Anne Pierrepont, daughter of the Marquess of Dorchester, returned home pregnant from an extended stay in London in 1659 her husband, John Manners, Lord Roos, heir to the Earldom of Rutland, was determined to divorce her when she is alleged to have said that no matter who

---

[250] en.wikipedia.org/wiki/Frederick_St_John,_2nd_Viscount_Bolingbroke. Accessed 06/06/2020.

the father was, if the baby were a boy he would inherit the title of Earl of Rutland. To disinherit the boy who subsequently was named Ignoto, John needed a divorce and a court ruling that none of Anne's children born after her return from London would be able to inherit the earldom. Having chucked her out on a bed and board basis in 1663 and obtained his legal ruling by Act of Parliament in 1667, he obtained permission to marry again by Act of Parliament in 1670. Many of the parliamentary sessions were attended by Charles II in person. A way had been found to break a fully legitimate and 'holy' union.

However, in the over 300 divorces obtained this way before 1857, only 4 recorded resulted in a woman's suit being successful. A sanguine look at the three-step process usually followed by an aggrieved husband reveals, more than anything else, the legal status of a woman, the cultural ripples of which still showed in the murky waters of gendered relationships well into my lifetime.

Step 1 was to sue the wife's lover for damages in a civil court. His offence to the husband was having 'criminal conversation' with his wife. If it was proved the level of the damages was decided by the court. In his case, for instance, the hapless and basically idle Viscount Bolingbroke did not receive enough from Topham Beauclerk, the defendant in the case, to pay his debts or keep him in the manner to which he had become accustomed.

In the legal term, criminal conversation, lies the rub for a woman until 1857 and for an unreconstructed man to this very day. 'Conversation' was a legal euphemism for sexual intercourse, but the sexual nature of the intercourse may not have been the clincher for the complaint. Equally strange was the anomalous use of the word 'criminal'.

Just to reiterate, lawyers, like all categories of people in the 18th century were no less knowledgeable or skilful than those we go to for legal help in the 21st century. The logic of what I am about to write was not beyond them nor, in this instance of a life event, subject to any technological or scientific limitation compared with the world in which we live now.

Adultery was not a criminal act in Western Europe. The law it broke was God's law. In some Muslim countries today it is against Sharia law which is essentially God's law but, particularly in Saudi Arabia, a powerful influence on criminal law. The nearest the Christian English ever came to a similar conjunction was in 1650 when the Puritan dominated Rump Parliament of the Commonwealth passed the Commonwealth (Adultery) Act by which the penalty was death. This law, like all Commonwealth laws, was voided in 1660 for lack of Royal Assent.

The 'crime' or sin of adultery was a matter for an ecclesiastical court in which punishment was some form of penance. In theory, crime and punishment for adultery applied to both spouses if found guilty. I will come soon to the gendered injustice of how adultery was conveniently seen as a uniquely female activity when in the eyes of God a large proportion of wealthy men were engaged in and blissfully unaware of the hypocrisy endemic in their take on morality and moral law.

If in pre-Norman times adultery had ever been a crime—and then only for a woman's adultery—it was more a crime against the property of a husband than one against his person. There were/are legally 5 sorts of property; two types of real or fixed property, an abode and land which cannot be moved, and two types of moveable property, attached to the abode, like furniture, or the land, like a herd of cows. Lastly, there was a miscellaneous category of moveable items called paraphernalia, like jewellery. Moveable items, because of an ancient connection to a herding culture, were called chattels. The most common property crime was, of course, theft but interfering with or harming another person's property, including the simple act of being on it or being in contact with anything on it without the owner's permission was a crime of trespass. This was certainly how William Blackstone saw it.

> Adultery or criminal conversation with a man's wife, though it is, as a public crime, left by our laws to the coercion of the spiritual courts, yet, considered as a civil injury (and surely there can be no greater), the law, gives a satisfaction to the husband for it by action of trespass vi et armis against the adulterer. wherein the damages recovered are usually very large and exemplary.[251]

There were three categories of trespass, to the person, to land or to goods and chattels. Was then the criminality implicit in 'criminal conversation' one of trespass in which case there was a strong implication that a wife was a husband's property, his chattel? Arguably, by his actions towards her, this is exactly how Stoney Bowes saw Mary Eleanor.

If a chattel, then a wife was of the same legal status as a slave. Logically, therefore, she could be bought and sold. Even in the mid to late 19th century Thomas Hardy was to open his novel, The Mayor of Casterbridge, with a 'Wife Sale'. Whether it was an indictable offence after the 1857 Act was much disputed but in the 17th and 18th centuries it was a way that a couple, with a meagre income could separate by emphasising the financial burden of having a wife whom a husband did not want. If handled properly it gave the wife freedom from a husband she did not want, in fact, the high Court Judge, Baron Mansfield, considered it a 'conspiracy to commit adultery'.

Judge Mansfield presided over a slavery related case and delivered a landmark ruling of great relevance to women in an unhappy marriage. In 1772, Mansfield heard a case in which a writ of habeas corpus (to release someone from illegal detention or imprisonment) had been applied for to set free a runaway slave, James Somersett, who had been recaptured by his owner, Charles Stewart, an American colonist, and imprisoned in a ship in Bristol harbour,

---

[251] api.parliament.uk/historic-hansard/commons/1854/apr/04/criminal-conversation. Accessed 10/06/2020.

owned by Captain John Knowles, bound for Jamaica where Somersett was to be sold.

As there was no law passed by the English government, unlike the Portuguese, the Dutch and the French, in support of the enslavement of one person by another and no law defining a slave as property, was the imprisonment legal and was the intention of Stewart to sell Somersett in Jamaica an illegal abduction of a British subject? In granting the writ High Court Judge Mansfield made this ruling, one he had tried his best to avoid.

> The state of slavery is of such a nature, that it is incapable of being introduced on any reasons, moral or political; but only **positive law**, which preserves its force long after the reasons, occasion, and time itself from whence it was created, is erased from memory: it's so odious, that nothing can be suffered to support it, but **positive law**. Whatever inconveniences, therefore, may follow from a decision, I cannot say this case is allowed or approved by the law of England; and therefore the black must be discharged.[252] [my highlighting]

What is meant by positive law is a human-made law suited to the circumstances of the time in which it was made. William Murray, Judge Mansfield, was one of history's good men and a great moderniser of the law but even he, although liberal in his judgements to end unhappy marriages, was unable to promote new laws that respected a wife's rights to end a marriage to replace the antiquated common law that totally denied that any such rights existed.

If the analogy with slavery is too extreme and the assumption of trespass too harsh on a typical upper class husband of the time then a look at the second route by which damages could be claimed, known in law as loss of consortium, is equally damning. 'Consortium' refers to the legal constituents of a household belonging to the Head of the Household, the *pater familias* in Roman law. I have dealt with his 5 categories of the property of his household which leaves the people over whom he held sway and for whom he provided economically: his wife, his children, and his servants.

As the primary private economic unit of the state, the law protected the integrity of the family and, to some extent, defined the part each category of member played in that unit. Many of the arguments relating to the consequences of leaving the unit concerned servants and, therefore, services in the aftermath of the Black Death (Statute of Labourers, 1349) when movement to a higher paid employment replaced feudal obligation, often just provision of bed and board in return for work, with wages for services provided.

Wikipedia tells us that the action to set a level of financial restitution to compensate a cuckolded husband was "*per quod servitium et consortium amisit* (in consequence of which he lost [another person's] servitude and marital

---

[252] en.wikipedia.org/wiki/William_Murray,_1st_Earl_of_Mansfield. Accessed 07/06/2020.

services)". These marital services were the household duties of a wife, her care and affection and sex.

In the 1619 case, Guy v. Livesey, it is clear that precedent had been established by that time that a husband's exclusive access to the sexual services of his wife was considered to fall within the concept of 'consortium', and that an adulterer might therefore be prosecuted for depriving a cuckold of exclusive access to the sexual services of his wife. Since adultery could not otherwise be prosecuted in secular courts for most of the period after the twelfth century, loss of consortium became an important basis for prosecution for adultery in English law.[253]

By placing a monetary value on a wife's services, in a 'proprietary undertone', a wife was being likened to a servant. Whether slave or servant, a wife was an exclusive provider of sex, care, and affection to her husband. If the exclusivity was compromised, not necessarily by penile penetration, damages were claimed regardless of the unhappy state of a marriage, especially if an Act of Parliament was asked for to redefine the marital status of the husband. Indeed, when seeking to amend the law regarding criminal conversation in 1851, Sir George Bowyer, MP for Dundalk, pointed out that it was only because Parliament required it to grant a divorce by an Act that such a proceeding needed to take place.

Property, chattel, slave, servant—as if these were not evocative enough an adulterous wife suffered the further indignity of being mute throughout the proceedings. Before the practice of divorce by Act of Parliament was ended in 1857, Sir George, in his introduction to his Bill to end criminal conversation as a civil action condemned it in the strongest terms.

> By the present law, the woman was condemned unheard; and it was quite astonishing that such an anomaly should have so long existed in the laws of a civilised and Christian country.[254]

Only if there was some collusion between the husband and the defendant to obtain a divorce by the only known method of the day was any derogatory mention made of the husband's character. In 1782, Sir Richard Worsley was found to have colluded with his wife's lover by allowing him to see her naked in the bath and awarded 1 shilling in damages having sued for £20,000. (George Bisset proved himself a typical adventurer by leaving Lady Worsley, Seymour Dorothy Fleming, when he found out that Sir Richard only wanted a separation *a mensa et thoro* and he could not marry his fortune. Seymour Fleming was forced to become a high-class prostitute or demimondaine.)

The character of the adulterous defendant would only be used to gauge the level of his intent to trespass on or deprive the plaintiff of his property rights.

---

[253] en.wikipedia.org/wiki/Loss_of_consortium. Accessed 11/06/2020.

[254] api.parliament.uk/historic-hansard/commons/1854/apr/04/criminal-conversation. Accesses 12/06/2020.

Many were proud of and admired for such rakish behaviour. The character and conduct of the wife, however, was central to setting a value on the loss of her contribution to the consortium. Lord Cloncurry was awarded £20,000 when his friend, Sir John Piers, had an affair with his wife and was caught in flagrante delicto in a Lyons House by a fresco painter who was on a ladder in the same room! The public disgrace of being caught cranked up the damages and gave rise to the much-enjoyed cartoon 'Crim. Con'.

To my 21st century sense of fair play, the most extraordinary aspect of criminal conversation cases (apart from the time it took the patriarchal legal system to see the injustice of it) was that the plaintiffs, who frequently went on to apply for an Act of Parliament to complete the divorce process successfully, were, apart from the one case, husbands. Criminal conversation as a tort was not abolished in Ireland until 1981. In 1978, a consultation paper was issued by the Law Commission. Ireland was not an entirely separate state until 1949 but had been free to make its own laws from 1937. Much of its legal case history, therefore, was English. The Working Paper has two passages of relevance to this point.

> The question whether a wife has a right of action for criminal conversation against a woman who commits adultery with her husband has never come up for judicial decision in Ireland. If it did, it would, of course, raise Constitutional issues. The view that no action lies is founded on the argument that historically the action has been based on the "servile" position of the wife relative to her husband. Moreover, the tendency in English decisions relating to negligently caused loss of consortium and to harbouring of a spouse has been to deny a right of action to the wife on the basis that these actions are anomalous and that it is better to confine the anomaly as far as possible rather than extend it further.[255]

Here we have the admission that, in law, a wife's status was 'servile' and that, rather than opening a can of worms by instituting procedures for the rare occasion that a wife might want to sue for her husband's criminal conversation, the law would sit on its hands.

In a citation of a judgement in 1923 by Judge Darling in the case of Gray v. Gee the equal right of a wife to sue in cases relating to marital disharmony was clearly stated.

> "In this country a woman was never the chattel of her husband. He had potestas over her and his children, but potestas and proprietas were very different things. He (his Lordship) had come to the conclusion that there was no distinction to be drawn here to the effect that the husband could

255 www.lawreform.ie/_fileupload/consultation%20papers/wpHarbouringOfaSpouse.htm. Accessed 12/06/2020.

bring the action because his wife was his property and that the wife could not because her husband was not her property. If a man was allowed to bring such an action, why should not a woman? He could see no reason. A woman might not lose quite as much as her husband, but if another woman enticed the husband away she lost far more than necessities, and far more than money could replace.

This form of action had been allowed in the United States and in Canada, and although those decisions were not binding upon a Judge in this country, they laid down what was the old law of England. He thought it was entirely consistent with the principles of our common law, and he thought the reason why such an action had never been brought before was that there had been difficulties of procedure. These had now been swept away by the Married Women's Property Act, 1882. He was of opinion that the rights of the two parties were the same. The difficulty had been, not that there was not the right, but that the remedy had not been devised. The law had devised that remedy by the Act which gave a married woman the right to sue in her own name for her own benefit."[256]

In other words, until the Law was changed, firstly, to disengage the concept of marriage from its sacramental straightjacket and make it subject to civil arbitration and, secondly, to affirm the separateness of a husband and wife as legal persons both of whom could own their own property and earn their own living, i.e., the abolition of coverture, justice in divorce cases, which should have been based on the inalienable right of each party to the 'pursuit of happiness' would neither be done nor seen to be done.

Once this contentious step had been taken Step 2 was to go to the ecclesiastical Court of Arches to obtain *divortium a mensa et thoro.* Once granted the husband had both civil and sacramental proof of being wronged sufficient to petition for a complete break and a legal ruling to allow him to marry again.

By 1801, Mrs Jane Addison, nee Campbell, daughter of Sir James Campbell MP and niece of Sir Archibald Campbell, former MP, General and colonial Governor, moved out of the marital home and returned to Scotland. Her husband, Edward, a wealthy London merchant, had an affair with Jane's elder sister, Jesse. Having gone through Step 1 which was taken by Dr James Campbell, Jesse's husband, who obtained £5,000 compensation for his loss of consortium, Jane was granted a *divortium a mensa et thoro* on grounds of her husband's adultery, as, incidentally, had Jesse's husband on grounds of her adultery. Jane, however, wanted to be free to marry again. She, therefore, petitioned Parliament to grant her a *divortium a vinculo matrimonii* (from the bond of marriage).

Her parliamentary influence and her establishment connections meant that she succeeded. The person with whom Edward had the affair clinched it for Jane. Until 1907, under the rules of affinity, such a great issue in Henry VIII's divorce from Catherine of Aragon, marriage to ones deceased wife's sister was

---

[256] Ibid.

prohibited by the Anglican church which deemed it incestuous. (It had to really since its birth had been the result of the prohibition of such a close affinity—Henry married his deceased brother's wife.)

More than one Act was passed, as well as excepting Jane's divorce from the rule of marriage for life, Jane, very unusually for that time, was granted custody of her children, Mr Addison and Jesse were forbidden to marry ever and Jesse could not marry while her husband, Dr Campbell, was still alive. Jane has gone down in history as the first British woman to get a divorce freeing her from any legal bond implicit in her consent to the contract of marriage. *As far as I know the other 3 cases were about an incestuous or bigamous husband.*

Back to Mary Eleanor Bowes. Mary, from her secret location in London and with no significant funds, devised the most ambitious plan to recover from the folly of marrying Andrew and making a new start after 8 years of extreme domestic abuse. Step 1, her separation from her abusive husband, seemed to be achieved. Step 2, the reinstatement of the prenuptial agreement that Stoney Bowes had forced her to recant was her next aim, Step 3, the custody of her children, Mary, and William, seemed the least likely and most distant of all. That she achieved all three was remarkable for a woman of her time. That she did so in the full glare of publicity that accompanied any 'scandal' and with the full range of sexist stratagems employed to undermine the foundation of all three of her suits was not only immensely brave but history changing.

Having been granted her *divortium a mensa et thoro* in 1786, she had already set about proceedings at the Court of Chancery to overturn the forced negation of her prenuptial arrangement regarding the ownership of her property. To prove that she was forced to sign the retraction by her fear of her husband's brutality much of the evidence used to justify her separation would have to be again presented as it was anyway because Stoney Bowes had appealed against the divorce decision to the Court of Arches.

Stoney Bowes, true to character, played dirty, bribing and threatening potential witnesses, hiring crooked lawyers and employing thugs for the heavy stuff. Most significantly, however, he put a great deal of effort into besmirching Mary Eleanor's character, the licentiousness of which he as a respectable husband was socially expected to curb and questioning her lack of duty and respect due to a husband. Bribery, being a normal part of the political process, as were scurrilous press campaigns, and restraint of termagant wives accepted as the social duty of husbands, he won over a lot of influential people such as Charles Howard, the Duke of Norfolk. (Not sufficiently, it seems! When Stoney Bowes asked his friend to bail him out of jail, the Duke refused.)

Having lost his first attempt to block the divorce, Stoney Bowes resorted to kidnap. When caught he was brought back to London and tried for conspiracy in front of Judge 'Thumb' Buller who was having nothing of his delaying tactics and theatrical antics in court to extract sympathy from the all-male jury. He was jailed for 3 years. None of his legal dealings went well after that despite his investment in the dark arts of publicity and legal filibustering. His appeal to the

Court of Arches failed as did his further appeal to the Court of Delegates, significant for its mixture of ecclesiastical and civil justice.

Mary got back her property in a separate ruling and even, via male trustees, got custody of her younger children, Mary and William. Unable to afford the legal costs of his many appeals and defences or even the £300 p.a. alimony he was supposed to pay to Mary, once his bail was found, he enjoyed a short spell of freedom to harass and threaten his servants and tenants before entering debtor's prison for the rest of his life.

Mary Eleanor Bowes was no pioneer feminist. For all her legal victories she only campaigned to obtain funds to fight her corner. For all her wealth and access to the upper echelons of London society she endured hardship and survived when all of it was taken away. Part of her legal success was due to the appallingly caddish character and behaviour of her opponent, Stoney Bowes, the worst possible—by no means, the only—abuser of the legal power of coverture. No laws were changed for 50 more years and coverture did not die, legally (One could argue that its cultural ripples are still coming to shore), for another 70. Mary and Stoney Bowes remained legally married and unable to remarry. He was not imprisoned for his cruelty but for conspiracy and debt.

What did happen, however, was that the absurdities of coverture were exposed, justice, although decided by all-male judges and juries, was triumphant over male supremacy and class and gender status took second place to human decency. Two wrongs were shown not to make a right. What started out as a sexual scandal turned into a refreshingly condemnatory view on domestic abuse. Whatever their views on women or other issues of the day, the high court judges, Mansfield, Wynne, Thurlow and Buller, did their job. The all-male jurors were not blind to a blatant wrong and those far beneath her socially, the miners, led by her lawyer, James Farrer, and land agent, Thomas Colpitts, who captured the violent kidnapper and the four ladies maids, led by her special friend, Mary Morgan, saved Mary Eleanor's bacon time and again. A true story, brilliantly told by Wendy Moore, more amazing than the fiction based upon it in 1844 by Thackeray, *The Luck of Barry Lyndon.*

PS. There is/was no more 'Establishment' figure than a High Court Judge because The Law can be applied objectively but is not per se objective. It is the law of its time, either made, modified or repealed by an Act of Parliament which requires only a majority of votes from MPs, elected by ordinary adults, in the 18th century only a small percentage of them, by appealing to their moral likes and dislikes, their loyalties and prejudices and, most important of all, their bank balances. In the Georgian patriarchy of 1790, the electors were men, the MPs were men. The 'guardians', as Plato called them, the watchers of the watchers, were the privileged members or beneficiaries of the Anglo-Norman elite, The House of Lords, set the cultural and moral tone of what was and what was not acceptable. If we are looking for someone 'good' to balance the 'bad' of Stoney Bowes it must be a man.

William Murray, 1st Earl of Mansfield and Lord Chief Justice of The King's Bench, and Edward Thurlow, 1st Baron Thurlow and Lord Chancellor, were the power houses of the King's Justice at the time of Mary Eleanor's divorce and influential members of the House of Lords, although Mansfield ceased to attend after 1783. Sir Francis Buller rightly or wrongly mocked as Judge Thumb was Mansfield's No. 2 and his personal choice to succeed him. As in Mary Eleanor's case, Buller stood in for him as his health failed later in his life.

Whereas the status of women was an issue of public interest, there was an issue of greater importance, slavery, and the slave trade, in which the question of people as chattels was being frequently raised. Murray, Buller and Thurlow, as high court judges, were all involved. We have already looked briefly at Mansfield's ruling in the Somersett case in 1772 but, 11 years later, he and Buller were involved in a far more seemingly brutal case known as the Zong Massacre.

The case was between the owners of a slave ship, the Zong, and its insurers. Due to a lack of water, after the ship failed to make landfall in Jamaica, the crew threw more than just sick slaves overboard, allegedly, to save the rest of the 400 or so whom they sold for £36 per slave, on average, when they did finally make landfall. In the case of cargo jettisoned for the safety of the ship, insurers were obliged to pay. In the original trial by jury, presided over by Judge Mansfield, he reluctantly accepted the jury's verdict in favour of the owners which had to be based on the perception of slaves as commercial cargo not human beings. Although to us this was an appalling act of inhumanity, the case was a civil suit based on commercial law in which Judge Mansfield specialised.

Whatever he felt personally he had to abide by the jury's verdict until offered a way out. If the cause of the emergency was the crew's negligence or malpractice the owners had to bear the losses themselves. It seems there was reasonable cause to believe that torrential rain had filled the water barrels when only a portion of the slaves had been jettisoned. The claim was, therefore, inflated, false or fraudulent. The appeal reversed the decision on the grounds of the crew's misjudgement, not murder, not manslaughter or any crime against the person.

Again, both the cases were not about the moral issues surrounding slavery but the practical absurdities and deficiencies of the common law as it related to it. The commercial law which promoted the boom in English trade overseas remained untouched. In his personal life, Murray was remarkably close to the slavery issue. When he returned to England in 1765 Murray's nephew, John Lindsay, a naval officer, brought with him his 4-year-old, illegitimate mixed-race daughter, Dido Elizabeth Belle (Her story is beautifully told in the 2014 film, *Belle*.), for the childless Murrays to bring up. They were already bringing up an orphaned niece, Elizabeth, who was just a year older. Wikipedia records that belief in the objectivity of Establishment figures was not strong. When asked what the outcome of the Somersett case would be a Jamaican planter was reputed to have replied, "No doubt… he will be set free, for Lord Mansfield keeps a Black in his house which governs him and the whole family."[257]

However, after his death in 1793, Mansfield showed his sanguine commitment to the letter of the law by confirming Dido's freedom in his Will, thus seeming to imply that his 1772 judgement was only for that one case rather than a general encouragement to abolish slavery throughout Great Britain. Similarly, his 1783 judgement was a commercial one although, by making the owners responsible for the health of their human cargo, it hastened the end of the slave trade from Britain in 1807 and ended slavery throughout the Empire in 1833. In both of these cases the defence was probably in touch with abolitionist campaigners, most notably Granville Sharp who was to become the grand old man of abolition. (When the Bill abolishing the slave trade was approved, he is said to have fallen to his knees to thank God for the victory.) Sharp supported many issues of the day where clear injustice was involved, American Independence— 'No taxation without representation', Irish legislative independence, Parliamentary reform and the impressment of sailors, to name a few but, although we know about his fights for justice for slaves, colonists, voters and sailors we hear very little about his views on coverture and justice for wives and mothers. *Hm!*

In a cultural context in which society was so blind to everyday injustice that only one of the five signatories to the principle of an inalienable right to 'life, liberty and the pursuit of happiness', John Adams, was not an owner of slaves or involved in the slave trade, as was one of the inspirations for it, John Locke, a stockholder in the Royal Africa Company, the injustice of coverture was a blind spot that is difficult to comprehend. Any change in culture resulting from these highly public cases would not have any effect until the Law of the land reflected it which meant overcoming the status quo that benefitted so many people, most of them men.

257 en.wikipedia.org/wiki/Dido_Elizabeth_Belle. Accessed 17/06/2020.

Chapter 35
Anatomy of an Arranged Marriage

Married! Aye why not? Don't everybody marry? Those who have estates, to get heirs of their own; and those who have nothing, to have something; so, according to my system, everybody marries.
– Georgiana Cavendish, *The Sylph*

Happiness in marriage is entirely a matter of chance. If the dispositions of the parties are ever so well known to each other or ever so similar beforehand, it does not advance their felicity in the least. They always continue to grow sufficiently unlike afterwards to have their share of vexation; and it is better to know as little as possible of the defects of the person with whom you are to pass your life.
– Jane Austen, *Pride and Prejudice*

Only one whom chance had elevated to an eminent position can assume the task of lending weight to the progress of the Rights of Woman and of hastening its success.
– Olympe de Gouges[258]

Preamble

Wealth and bloodline would have bowdlerised most aristocratic eccentricities and silenced most of the persistent critics or judges, amateur or professional, upper, or lower class, of the morals swirling around the behaviour of 18th century upper class women. Nevertheless, many private, or what should have been private, scenarios were avidly followed by the fast expanding number of gutter press literati. As in most scandals extra interest occurs if the cast includes a woman, preferably young, beautiful, rich, and unfaithful, a wealthy but mysterious high-ranking man, and politics, especially women with political views.

Finally, to titillate the moral outrage or jealousy even more, there needed to be an extracurricular activity (not ordinary stuff like frequenting prostitutes, siring umpteen illegitimate children by numerous different mistresses, running up enormous gambling debts or divorcing one's unfaithful wife, all par for the course in the Georgian patriarchy!) extraordinary enough to excite mass curiosity. How about a ménage a trois?

---

[258] en.wikipedia.org/wiki/Olympe_de_Gouges. Accessed 08/08/2020.

For much of the 18th century, Great Britain slid away from absolute monarchy towards a ruling class consisting of wealthy individuals from two pools of stakeholders, landowners, and merchants, each respectively in two levels. Sustained by their inherited estates were the former feudal tenants-in-chief, dukes, marquesses, lords and barons—aristocracy—and their chief retainers, knights and squires, sirs and 'honourables'—gentry. Sustained by trade and industry were the international and intranational merchants and the growing urban middle class of tradespeople.

These two groups began to intermingle, not least by marriage, the landed aristocracy dabbling in trading and industrial enterprises and the merchants buying land. However, the key to the door that led to both national houses of politicians was property as it was for those few with the right to elect the Commons. To involve oneself in local affairs required ownership of property as well. (Interestingly, gender was not among the qualifying criteria. More on this later.)

If the Civil War was the earthquake that altered the political landscape of Great Britain, the events of 1687-8 were the defining aftershock. When James II pushed his absolute right to rule by side-lining Parliament in order to promote his seemingly pro-Catholic agenda, factions within the ruling classes began to form on a Catholic/Protestant basis, the Protestant/Parliament persuasion being anti-Catholic, anti-Absolutism and pro-nonconformist Protestants, the Catholic/monarchy persuasion being pro-monarchy, High Anglican and pre-Civil War traditionalists. These two coalitions—they were never parties as we know them today—were sufficiently different to be labelled.

Although the chosen labels were derogatory to both factional groupings they stuck and began to be worn with pride. Whigs were ultra-Protestant rascals from Scotland and Tories ultra-Catholic rascals from Ireland. Whiggism, loosely speaking, wanted things to change whereas Tories liked things the way they were. Just to recap, the higher echelons of the aristocracy were split half and half; the Whigs took with them the merchant, urban middle class and the Tories were strongly supported by the landed upper middle class, the gentry. Family loyalty required sons and, as we shall see, daughters to inherit the politico-factional loyalties of their fathers. As married women did not own or manage property, the entrance ticket to the political arena, they could do little but support their husbands.

When James threatened to undo 155 years of hard work to Protestantize Great Britain, seven (known as the immortal seven) prominent aristocrats invited William of Orange to replace him. One of the petitioners was William Cavendish, 4th Earl of Devonshire, who, for his loyal service to William III, was made 1st Duke of Devonshire in 1694. The Whig tradition was handed down to the 2nd, 3rd and 4th Dukes, all Members of Parliament with the 4th being Prime Minister for a short time in 1756-7. His 16-year-old son, also William, became 5th Duke in 1764.

In 1643, after his gallant service to Charles I at the Battle of Edgehill, the 22-year-old Henry Spencer, Baron Spencer of Althorp in Northamptonshire, was allowed to purchase the vacant title of Earl of Sunderland for the princely sum of £3000. He held it for just 3 months before being killed by a cannonball at the first Battle of Newbury. His son, Robert, the 2nd Earl, confirmed the family's Whiggery by supporting the Exclusion Bill, opposing the succession of James II and, as a confidant of William III, favouring a choice of close advisers exclusively from the Whig faction. Robert's son, Charles, the 3rd Earl, was a prominent politician under George I and married Anne Churchill, daughter of the Duke of Marlborough, thus cementing the family's position in the uppermost rank of British society.

Their third son, John Spencer, was brought up and educated by his illustrious grandmother, Sarah, Duchess of Marlborough. Like his father, his son, also John, was a Whig politician and major beneficiary of his great-grandmother's inheritance. John, later Earl Spencer, had 3 children. His son, George, grew up to be a prominent Whig politician, serving as Home Secretary in Lord Grenville's Ministry of All Talents in 1805. His 2 daughters, Lady Georgiana and Lady Henrietta, 4 years her junior, particularly Georgiana, now take centre stage.

I cannot begin to replicate the historic impact of Amanda Foreman's biography, 'Georgiana Cavendish, Duchess of Devonshire', or the dramatic impact of Saul Dibb's film, 'The Duchess', but my purpose in telling some of her story might overlap theirs.

At a superficial level, it seems unpromising to argue that the psychologically abused wife of an unfaithful husband in a loveless marriage moved forward the cause of gender equality one millimetre. However, in terms of bringing to the public notice (Here, I am making an arguable generalisation that the prime movers of Victorian morality were the middle classes who were also the prime consumers of the Georgian/Regency press dailies or weeklies and among whom will have been a considerable percentage of women.) the gender relationships of the upper classes, the arrogant hypocrisy of the alpha males and the openly lascivious behaviour of their women, Georgiana's fortitude and resilience showed that among the crème de la crème, the social and political ruling class in complete charge of the direction the nation was taking and would take, the treatment of women by men was less moral than it should or could have been and the nature and character of women could rise above the disadvantage, inferiority and implications of 'immorality' assigned to them by the rampant patriarchy of that era.

Our third post-Restoration marriage from hell began on 7 June 1774 when the 17-year-old Lady Georgiana Spencer married the hugely wealthy 25-year-old William Cavendish, 5th Duke of Devonshire. For both staunchly Whig families, it seemed the ideal match that would increase the battalion strength of the reforming, anti-King, pro-American Independence and, above all, Protestant faction facing a Tory resurgence under the premiership of Frederick 'Lord' North, 2nd Earl of Guildford, a former Whig leading a predominantly Tory government many of whom had also been Whigs. The Cavendish-Spencer alliance was to be further cemented in 1780 when Georgiana's sister, Lady Henrietta, married Frederick Ponsonby, 3rd Earl of Bessborough, grandson of William Cavendish, 3rd Duke of Devonshire.

Incidentally, to continue the Whiggite theme, their brother, George, went on to be Home Secretary in the Ministry of All Talents of 1806-7 and his son, John Charles, 3rd Earl Spencer, known affectionately and somewhat incredulously as 'Honest Jack', served as Chancellor under Grey and Melbourne from 1830-4 in the government that pushed through the Great Reform bill of 1832.

Although her novels were not published until the second decade of the 19th century, the milieu of Jane Austen's novels is middle/gentry class England in the last decades of the 18th. All Austen's heroines—the Dashwood sisters, Elizabeth Bennet, Fanny Price, Anne Eliot, Catherine Morland and Emma Woodhouse—marry the man they love, 5 above their social level and 2 equally. The romantic twists and turns of doing that within the cultural mores and economic realities of the times have struck a chord for two centuries in the hearts of readers of both genders.

If that was the dream future of Lady Georgiana Spencer, it was soon to be shattered. Her marriage was arranged and permitted for political, social, economic, and dynastic reasons. We have often commented on what her side of the bargain entailed, submission, support, house management and, above all, the successful production of sons and heirs and marriageable daughters. Her moral compass was chastity, and her marital compass was fidelity. We often comment on and exemplify the behaviours of the 'great and good' British men who have become household names but never use the same criteria for those few women worthy of inclusion alongside them. *Should I now turn the spotlight on the Duchess or the Duke?*

The political husband

Much of what we know about the Duke, the Duchess and their marriage is second hand, subjective and sensationalised because their contemporaries and readers of books and cinemagoers of today tend to love a good scandal. Boring as it must seem I want to avoid the scandalous titbits of those aspects of their lives to a large extent in search of a meaningful, if not fundamental, change in men and women and their perceptions of each other that opened a door to equality, or a desire for it, a century later.

William Cavendish was rich, rich enough to be thought of as one of the richest bachelors in England. His already wealthy father married Lady Charlotte Boyle who, after the death of her sister, Lady Dorothy, became her father's heir. William's mother died of smallpox, as did her sister, in 1754, at the age of 23, leaving the 16-year-old William to inherit her estates when his father died in 1764 going from the Marquess of Hartington to Duke of Devonshire. According to the Duke's biographer (Michael Durban, 'Cavendish, William, fifth duke of Devonshire (1748-1811)', Oxford Dictionary of National Biography (Oxford: Oxford University Press, 2004).), his estates alone were valued at £36,000, extreme wealth when it took 10 days work for a skilled tradesman to earn £1 and a country gentleman could live comfortably on £500. When our duke's son, William, inherited he got 8 stately homes and 200,000 acres of estates in Derbyshire, Yorkshire, Middlesex, Ireland, and London. Therefore, unlike Stoney Bowes, William did not need to marry for money. His equally wealthy son, the 6th Duke, also William, chose not to marry at all.

William's bloodline was impeccably Anglo-Norman aristocratic, dating back to Norman times and inextricably a part of English history. He will have known this, and it gave him an ascribed social standing second only to the King and the ancient dukedoms, such as Norfolk, Somerset, and Richmond. Preservation of the bloodline by producing a son and heir and enrichment of it by a marriage alliance with another august bloodline was a greater driving force for marriage than love or physical attraction. Among the elite, marriage was dynastic and endogamous, i.e., class based.

The Duke's family were Whigs. Although, as I pointed out earlier, Whiggery was highly factional the Duke's family commitment would have been to the sovereignty of the people whom the King served rather than to the unaccountable sovereignty of the King, a traditional choice of Parliament over Monarch. As the Whigs' political objectives changed from 'Old Corps' to 'Rockinghamite' to 'Foxite' to 'Grenvillite' his family support and considerable financing of the parliamentary grouping did not waver. To ally, by marriage, to a similarly loyal and entrenched Whig family made complete sense.

Whether he shared Fox's admiration for the French Revolution or Wilberforce's repulsion for the Slave Trade or Grey's approval of American Independence or Burke's disapproval of radicalism we can never know but when it came to stomping up the money for Whig candidates or Whig conventions or salons arranged by his wife we assume he did it rather than have to put his views to the approval of Parliament or the electorate as a whole. He had no desire to participate in the political rough and tumble but remained happy to finance and facilitate it, or so it seems.

His reluctance to join the other alpha males, Pitt the Younger, Fox, Sheridan, Portland, his brother-in-law, Burke, Grey et al., might have contributed to historical opinions of him as 'phlegmatic', 'insouciant', 'a boor' but before exploring his nature a brief look at his nurture about which little is known might be revealing.

William Cavendish was born on 14 December 1748. He lost his mother in 1754 to smallpox—she was only 23—and his father in 1764—he was only 44 but had been ill for a long time. Although arranged in their childhood his parents' marriage was happy and loving. When widowed his father did not remarry. His father's main friend and political ally, Thomas Pelham-Holles, Duke of Newcastle (Prime Minister, 1754-6), was also happily married. In his biography in the ODNB, Karl Wolfgang Schweizer alludes to the 4th Duke being an easy-going peacemaker who was solid rather than brilliant, popular, dependable, and dutiful. His wife Charlotte, nee Boyle, probably shared the nature of her sister, Dorothy, who made a very unhappy marriage to George Fitzroy, Earl of Euston, grandson of Charles II, of which, with Fitzroy's death in 1747 and the unfortunate Dorothy's 5 years before, the infant William would have been unaware.

> FitzRoy married Lady Dorothy Boyle, the daughter of Richard Boyle, 3rd Earl of Burlington and 4th Earl of Cork and Dorothy Savile, Countess of Burlington and Countess of Cork, in October 1741. In the biography written in the *History of the Parliament,* Lady Boyle was described as "a girl of the softest temper, vast beauty, birth, and fortune." After she died on 2 May 1742, her mother said that Dorothy was relieved of the "extremest misery", that Lady Boyle's husband exacted on her as what is described as "utmost brutality".[259]

With the death of his maternal grandmother, Dorothy, nee Saville, in 1758, the 10-year-old William was left with only his paternal grandmother, Catherine, nee Hoskins, whose disapproval of arranged marriages, particularly that of her eldest son, caused much tension in the family. Catherine took over the running of Chatsworth until William's marriage in 1774. The 4th Duke had 3 sisters and 3 brothers, William's aunts, and uncles. His aunts had all married politicians. When his father died in 1764, his aunt, Lady Caroline who had married William Ponsonby, 2nd Earl of Bessborough, was dead but her 60-year-old husband was still a prominent figure in British and Irish politics. Their son, Frederick, William's cousin, married Lady Henrietta Spencer in 1780, younger sister of Georgiana, William's wife—he was 22 and she was 19—and became his brother-in-law. Wikipedia says this about Frederick, the man and the husband.

> Bessborough usually made a favourable first impression: quiet, but with "the most mild and amiable manner". On the other hand, he was a notoriously bad husband, alternating between neglecting Henrietta and insulting her in public. While there were arguably faults on both sides—she was also addicted to gambling and had numerous love affairs—society in general judged him to be the greater offender.[260]

William's aunt, Lady Elizabeth, married John Ponsonby, the above-mentioned William's brother, making them brothers-in-law as well as brothers. Lady Rachael married Horatio Walpole, nephew of the great Sir Robert, a prominent Whig MP. Both aunts were in their late 30s when the 4th Duke died.

All three of William's father's brothers were bachelors when their brother died. It appears that they managed the 16-year-old Duke's affairs for him. The oldest, Lord George Augustus, was MP for Derbyshire. His younger brother was Lord Frederick Cavendish who, by 1764, had reached the rank of Major-General. He would go on to become a Field-Marshal. The youngest uncle was Lord John

---

[259] en.wikipedia.org/wiki/George_FitzRoy,_Earl_of_Euston. Accessed 07/07/2020.
[260] en.wikipedia.org/wiki/Frederick_Ponsonby,_3rd_Earl_of_Bessborough. Accessed 07/07/2020.

Cavendish, only 32 when his eldest brother died, he had a highly esteemed career as a Whig MP. He was eulogised by his friend, Edmund Burke, as follows:

> He served the publick often out of Office, sometimes in it, with Fidelity, and diligence, and when the occasion call'd for it, with a manly resolution. At length when he was overborne by the Torrent, he retir'd from a world that certainly was not worthy of him. He was of a character that seems as if it were peculiar to this Country. He was exactly what we conceive an English Nobleman of the old Stamp, and one born in better times.[261]

The 5th Duke had 2 younger brothers and a sister. His sister, Dorothy, hit the jackpot in the marriage stakes. In 1766, the 16-year-old Lady Dorothy married the 28-year-old William Henry Cavendish Bentinck, 3rd Duke of Portland and Lord Chamberlain to King George III, a job he hated, and best friend of the recently resigned Prime Minister. A life-long Whig loyalist, Portland's mentor, had been the Duke of Newcastle and his best political friend was Charles Watson-Wentworth, 2nd Marquess of Rockingham. After his friend's death in July 1782 and the failure of the Earl of Shelburne to form a government, Portland became Prime Minister. In his later career he showed himself to be a 'conservative' Whig in contrast to the 'rakish' reformers personified by Charles James Fox.

The older of the Duke's brothers, Lord Richard Cavendish, was a Whig MP but, plagued by ill health, he died abroad at the age of 29. His youngest brother, Lord George Henry Augustus, was a long serving and loyal Whig MP, ultimately for Derbyshire. In his biography on the history of parliament online website he is described as 'very good humoured, and talkative but not a very vocal MP. If anything he was a Foxite, but was his brother? In these extracts we get a feel for his relationship with his eldest brother and the relationship of the Cavendish family to the Whig cause.

He voted with Fox against the war with France on 17 June.

> In January 1794, Thomas Pelham noted that although Cavendish's brother the 5th Duke of Devonshire was very eager for the war, he was inclined to be against it, 'but I rather think he will not vote against'.[262]

When the Whig opposition had to find a new leader in the House late in 1807, Cavendish assured Lord Grey that he was tired of politics, out of touch and despondent:

---

[261] en.wikipedia.org/wiki/Lord_John_Cavendish. Accessed 07/07/2020.

[262] www.historyofparliamentonline.org/volume/1790-1820/member/cavendish-george-augustus-henry-1754-1834. Accessed 08/07/2020.

> 'I always act in concert with my brother and in deference to his superior judgment'. He concurred in the choice of George Ponsonby.[263]

On George Ponsonby's (Lord George's cousin) death in July 1817, Henry Grey Bennet wrote to Creevey (2 prominent Whig politicians):

> Who is to lead us now? God knows. Some talk of Lord George Cavendish, whom I resist, because I think his politics are abominable and his manners insolent and neglectful: but also because the Cavendish system, with the duke at the head is not the thing for the present day. They are timid, idle and haughty.[264]
> By January 1818, the report was that 'Tierney is to lead and Lord George Cavendish to feed the opposition'.[265]

The Cavendish family were clearly at the centre of Whig politics with the Duke as leader. Younger politicians, even family, were expected to defer to his political choices and decisions. When Lord George bought Burlington House, named after his maternal grandfather, from his nephew, the 6th Duke, in 1815 for £70,000 (£6 million in today's currency) it became the party wining and dining venue as Devonshire House had been in his brother's day. Was his older brother 'timid, idle and haughty'? Was that a family trait? Was that an expected trait of the super-rich?

In some respects, the life of the 5th Duke can be explained with a resounding "Yes!" to all three. In not seeking a parliamentary career or any form of Westminster-based office, he was unusual for his family. In the Liberal Party pantheon, his august descendant, Liberal leader Spencer Cavendish, Marquess of Hartington, also known for his eschewal of high office, was described by Tony Little thus.

> The birth of the modern Liberal Party in 1859 brought together three disparate elements, Whigs, Peelites and Radicals. Hartington, as he was known for most of his political life, epitomised the Whig contribution to government—rich, aristocratic but driven by noblesse oblige to take public office. When he broke with Gladstone in the 1880s it symbolised the end of Whig government and marked the drift of the landed classes into the Tory camp.[266]

The 5th Duke, and this is how Ralph Fiennes plays his character, lacked the noblesse oblige that was embraced by most of his nuclear and extended family most of the time. To explain it we must look elsewhere. "The capacity for

---

263 Ibid.
264 Ibid.
265 Ibid.
266 liberalhistory.org.uk/history/hartington-marquess-of-duke-of-devonshire. Accessed 09/07/2020.

friendship is God's way of apologising for our families."—Jay McInerney, The Last of the Savages

At 16, the wealthy young Duke was too young to become the pater familias and manage his wealth or his income. As mentioned above, those tasks fell to his uncles, Lords George, Frederick, and John. George and John went to school and university and Frederick was educated in the army but, it seems, Devonshire's father had largely been educated at home. Having gone to a school the name of which history is unaware his uncles took the decision not to send William to Cambridge, according to his biographer, Michael Durban, 'for fear people there would 'pay dirty court' to him and that he would contract 'unbecoming friendships' (Lord John Cavendish to Richard Newcome, 11 Oct 1764, Chatsworth MS 428.12).

In 1767, therefore, it was arranged for him to go on an extended visit to Europe. Wikipedia picks up on the fact that his companion was a neighbour, William Fitzherbert, son of William Fitzherbert of Tissington Hall, the hardworking MP for Derby who committed suicide in 1772. Were they friends or just neighbours? Fitzherbert had been to Cambridge unlike Cavendish.

William returned in 1768 after the General Election which ended in May. He was 20 that December, still not old enough to be in legal charge of his estate and, I must guess, living on a generous allowance doled out by his uncles. He was Lord High Treasurer of Ireland and Governor of Cork both inherited sinecures. In these character forming years from 20-24, in many an aristocratic case spent at Oxbridge, what did William do? What was there for him to do? Who were his friends? Where did he live—Chatsworth with a prickly grandmother or Devonshire House in fashionable Piccadilly?

When he became able to manage his own affairs in December 1769, Chatsworth had been finished off by his father's hiring of Capability Brown to do the gardens, Devonshire House had been rebuilt by his grandfather after a fire in 1733 and he did not begin his remodelling of Buxton until 1780. We can only conjecture what life must have been like for England's most eligible bachelor.

Michael Durban uses this quote from Nathaniel Wraxall, after 1780 a Tory MP who supported Pitt the Younger and had a largely unjustified reputation for including unsubstantiated rumours in his history memoirs, to hint at William's character.

> He seemed to be incapable of any strong emotion, and destitute of all energy or activity of mind. As play became indispensable in order to rouse him from this lethargic habit and to awaken his torpid faculties, he passed his evenings usually at Brooks's, engaged at whist or faro. Yet beneath so quiet an exterior he possessed a highly improved understanding, and on all disputes that occasionally arose among the members of the club relative to passages of the Roman poets or historians, I know that appeal was constantly made to the Duke, and his decision or opinion was regarded as final.

Historical and Posthumous Memoirs, 3.344

This must have been observed after 1778 because the name Brooks's was not used until the premises in St James's Street, designed and financed by and named after William Brooks, were finished. Prior to its opening, those who were to form its membership met at 49/50 Pall Mall, a former tavern owned by William Almack. The club known as Almack's had been formed in March 1764 as a place where young Whig nobles could wine, dine and gamble. Among its 27 founding members were the 26-year-old William Cavendish-Bentinck, 3rd Duke of Portland, future Prime Minister, the 24-year-old John Ker, 3rd Duke of Roxburghe—thwarted suitor of the King's sister-in-law, Christiane of Mecklenburg, who remained unmarried all his life, the 22-year-old John Crewe—Foxite MP to be made 1st Baron Crewe, and the 27-year-old John Lyon, 9th Earl of Strathmore, whom we have already met. The next year the 16-year-old Charles James Fox became a member.

In 1770, the 53-year-old Horace Walpole observed that 'the gaming at Almack's which has taken the pas of White's, is worthy the decline of our Empire, or Commonwealth…The young men of the age lose five, ten, fifteen thousand pounds in an evening there.' 6 years later, the 39-year-old Edward Gibbon, another thwarted suiter who never married, praised its intellectually stimulating company.

> The style of living though somewhat expensive is exceedingly pleasant and notwithstanding the rage of play I have found more entertaining and even rational society here than in any other Club to which I belong.'[267]

Wraxall's post-1780 behavioural assessment of the married but childless (not quite childless as we will discover soon) Duke may well have been William's response to his married circumstances and a healthy sprinkling of political prejudice on the part of the Tory observer. It tells us little about his lifestyle between 1768, his return from Europe, and 1774, the year of his marriage. Were his friendships 'unbecoming'? The 1770s were famous for behaviour among young aristocratic males, 'the flower of the English youth' as Gibbon described them, that was 'outré', excessive spending, excessive eating and drinking, excessive carousing, excessive interest in sex, excessive gambling, and excessive fashion.

The icon of the age who allegedly was guilty of all the aforementioned excesses was the now adult, excessively indulged, and intellectually brilliant, Charles James Fox, rising (although not yet fully cooked) star of Whig politics. Whether or not Fox was a 'fully paid up' Macaroni (A group of young aristocrats, with too much time on their hands and copying the Italian and French fashions they had seen on their Grand Tour of Europe, who embraced a narcissistic, debatably effeminate/camp, fashion craze at its height in the 1770s.) he was

[267] en.wikipedia.org/wiki/Almack%27s#
The_First_Almack's_Club,_Brooks's,_and_Boodle's. Accessed 10/07/2020.

certainly a profligate gambler, cards at Almacks and horses at Newmarket, and womaniser—Leslie Mitchell, his biographer, relates that his father arranged for him to surrender his virginity to a Parisian courtesan at the age of 14.

Mitchell also emphasises that throughout the 1770s, he was taking his duties as an MP seriously, resigning from two government appointments, at the Admiralty and the Treasury, in 4 years. Interestingly, when his favourite nephew, Henry, 3rd Baron Holland, married the divorced Elizabeth Webster, nee Vassell, in 1797, Fox objected strongly on the grounds that it would ruin Henry's chances of high office in any future Whig administration.

It is impossible to believe that William Cavendish, only 1 month older, did not encounter the magnetic field that surrounded 'The Eyebrow', Fox's schoolboy nickname, at the very least, at the card table or the races. Did they share an interest in the Classics, both esteemed to be talented scholars of Latin literature, to engage in lengthy conversations over or after a boozy dinner? Were Fox and his cronies the source of the 'unbecoming friendships' William's uncles had sought to prevent? Would any young man who did not fully buy into the Macaroni lifestyle or the Foxite enchantment be thought of as 'torpid'?

Fox had at least four major advantages over the Duke. Firstly, being the second son, he did not have a title and the social and economic duties it brought with it. Secondly, he had a famously indulgent father. In 2 years, between 1772 and 1774, Fox ran up £120,000 of gambling debts (£10.2 million today). His father paid them. Thirdly, he had gone to school and university. He left Eton, being thought a bit too 'wicked', and he dropped out of Oxford, but he had absorbed the wider world culture and relationships they presented to him. Fourthly, and more fundamentally, Fox made and had friends, some for life.

In 1793, Mitchell tells us, they raised £61,000 (£5.2 million today) for him as an annuity. If William's wife, Georgiana, lent him money as his close friend in the 1780s, it would be no surprise, but did the bachelor or the married duke ever do so in the 1770s? Quite simply, was Fox his friend? By the late 18th century when the Whigs as a party were disintegrating, Foxite meant little more than being a friend of Charles James Fox and all the baggage, social, political, and economic that came with him. Lady Georgiana Cavendish, nee Spencer, Duchess of Devonshire was, famously or infamously, a Foxite. Was her husband?

In William's bachelor years, the political spectrum ranged from the very radical, John Wilkes, to the potential absolutist, George III. In the late 70s and early 80s Fox took over Wilkes's title of 'Man of the People', a title to which aristocrats like the 5th Duke would never have aspired. The title passed to the more Tory Sir Francis Burdett for his condemnation of the Peterloo Massacre in 1819, also, incidentally, a member of Brooks's at the turn of the century. Though a political supporter of Reform the Duke would never have been a popular hero. The 'popular press', therefore, would have salaciously condemned his eccentric marriage arrangements rather than celebrated them. His well-loved wife had all the amazement and all the sympathy.

In his 20s, the Duke was on the 'marriage' circuit linked with any of the eligible debutantes to whom he had been introduced and with whom he had danced. He was not looking for sex; he would have had easy access to that in a high-class brothel or, as he seems to have done, buying a hat. I feel that it is somewhat overegging the pudding to describe Charlotte Spencer, a milliner, as his mistress although he did get her pregnant a few months before his marriage, presumably while engaged, certainly while marriage negotiations were taking place—*showing a fairly lukewarm commitment to his forthcoming nuptials?* His wife was introduced to the daughter, Charlotte Williams, when, after the death of her mother, she came to live with her father. Georgiana, seemingly unfazed, liked the little girl and happily brought her up.

It is also important to note that some high-class prostitutes did make the progress from sex object to aristocrat, demonstrating the fluidity of male/female relationships that seemed to be the acceptable norm of the 18th and early 19th centuries. Elizabeth Bridget Armitstead, having been mistress to several of the racing set, the 2nd Viscount Bolingbroke who rescued her from Mrs Elizabeth Mitchell's brothel, the 3rd Duke of Dorset, William's uncle, Lord George Cavendish, the 12th Earl of Derby and even the Prince of Wales, settled down with Charles James Fox whom she married in 1795.

Anne Parsons, Nancy as she was known, became Viscountess Maynard in 1776 having had liaisons with 2 Prime Ministers, the Duke of Grafton and Lord Shelburne, the inevitable 3rd Duke of Dorset, and, while staying abroad in France and Italy in the 1780s, had taken into the other famous ménage a trois of the late 18th century Francis Russell, 5th Duke of Bedford. Nancy's husband, Charles, was 10-15 years younger but the Duke was some 30 years younger than their shared lover who was in her late 40s.

In this marriage market known as 'The Season' William was not, by definition, the only extremely eligible bachelor and Georgiana Spencer not the only glittering prize. There was plenty of choice. Was Georgiana his, or his uncles', second choice? His name was linked with Lady Elizabeth Hamilton, known as Lady Betty, daughter of the 6th Duke of Hamilton and his reputedly beautiful wife, Elizabeth, nee Gunning.

Some 4 years older than Georgiana, Lady Betty, seems to have been rather impulsive, possibly to do with her parents having married the night they met! After what Alan G. Crosby, his biographer in the ODNB, 'a brief and fervent courtship' she married in grand social style, in stark contrast to the private, guest free marriage of William and Georgiana 16 days earlier, Edward Smith-Stanley, Lord Strange and heir to the Earldom of Derby. Like so many in this period, this marriage did not work out well.

In 1779, Lady Betty left her husband for John Frederick Sackville, Earl of Dorset—*not again!*—but with her husband refusing to divorce her and claiming custody of her 3 children she became a Society persona non grata and went into exile abroad. Needless to say, the cad, Dorset, lost interest in her. Her husband, no angel himself with his sporting interests and chums taking up much of his time (He was the founder of The Oaks and The Derby who bred horses to race and cocks to fight and popularised the game of cricket.), soon found a replacement, the actress, Elizabeth Farren, with whom he remained for the rest of her life.

There were three things of note and relevance about their relationship. For 17 years or so he remained faithful despite her refusal to be his mistress by allowing him to consummate the partnership. Secondly, Elizabeth was apparently more than willing to take on the children of the Earl's household in 1797 when they married after Lady Betty's death; the Earl's 2 grown-up children from his first marriage, their own 3 children which she bore well into her late 30s and early 40s, the 4 illegitimate children of Edward's lifelong friend, political patron and uncle by marriage, General John Burgoyne, and his mistress, maybe wife, the opera singer, Susan Caulfield—and her mother, the guardian of her virginity all those years!

Thirdly, her new role as a Society hostess was much admired and mourned when she died. Thomas Creevey said this about it, 'Knowsley without Lady Derby is like a house with all the fires and candles put out.'[268]

The political wife

Whether William courted Georgiana fervently (*unlikely*) or she fell for his charm and good looks (*equally unlikely*) or she was of the same emotional make-up as her younger sister, Henrietta, who famously said "I can never love anyone just *a little*", which is how Keira Knightly plays Georgiana in *The Duchess*, we can only surmise. Most probably, it appeared to the Spencers to be a good social and political match for their daughter to a young man no worse than others on the circuit. To the parentless William, on the advice of his bachelor uncles, it was a step he had to take sooner or later for carrying on the family name and traditions. Not just anyone would do, and sex would be purely procreational. The 'living together' bit would be covered by aristocratic manners, gentlemanly conduct, and marital duty. He was the 'catch' not her. It was her duty, as far as domestic tranquillity was concerned, to make the marriage work!

Unlike her sister, Henrietta, who produced 4 children for her not very affectionate husband, Frederick Ponsonby, William's cousin, in the 7 years from her marriage in 1780 until the birth of her youngest son, William, in 1787, 3 sons and a daughter, Georgiana's pregnancies all ended in miscarriages. In 1779, the Duke preferred to stay in summer camp overseeing the training of his militia rather than go over to Spa with his in-laws. Georgiana had already caught the gambling and partying bugs and was running up considerable debts which she had tried to hide from her husband who the previous year had had a fling with the notoriously adulterous Lady Jersey.

The social conventions of the 1780s on having sex (euphemistically 'an affair', from the French, of course, which made it socially chic, the 'done' thing, almost de rigueur) with people other than your legal spouse seem to have been as follows. For men, during all those prolonged periods when their wives were

---

[268] www.oxforddnb.com/view/10.1093.

sexually inaccessible or 'undesirable'—menstruation, pregnancy, and post-pregnancy—mistresses were and had been for centuries an essential piece of a gentleman's accoutrement. Abstinence was simply not an option. Celibacy was strictly for Catholic priests, being somehow foreign and non-Protestant (even Puritans approved of sex with the proviso that it was within marriage). Masturbation was condemned by the Bible and homosexuality punishable by death.

In 1772, a certain Captain Jones, possibly a Macaroni, was sentenced to death for sodomising a 13-year-old boy. He was pardoned and sent to the Americas. All the usual legal and social drama surrounded the case and the royal pardon but the public outcry against the crime and the licentious behaviour of the upper classes showed that not to marry or have a mistress exposed any young gentleman to the scandalous suggestion and rumour that he was gay. Here is the opening paragraph to the editorial from the London Evening Post about the pardon. *Is it being sarcastic?*

> This day, about two o'clock, a respite of seven days came to Newgate for Capt. Jones, clearly convicted of that most detestable, beyond every other the most abominable crime—that the depravity of the human heart could ever entertain an idea of perpetrating—SODOMY!—O religious Prince! O pious George![269]

For a single woman, there was only one rule, or rather one rule for the rich and another for the poor. A woman—most would now be considered teenage girls—who had sex before marriage was socially damaged goods, even in those enlightened, post-Restoration days, to be hidden away or married to the thief of her virginity tout de suite—unless she was poor and he was rich in which case it was largely seen as the girl's fault for being so desirable. Her future depended on his whim. If he chose to desert or deny her, that future was bleak.

For a married woman of the 'ton', the conventions were more restrictive than those for men but more permissive than for the lower and middle classes where Christian morality was more binding. (As we have seen already, for centuries, money seemed to atone for sin more than apologetic words or deeds.)

Just to reiterate the point, by contrast, for their single, post-puberty daughters on whose suitable virginal marriage the family's fortunes often depended, sexual activity was strictly forbidden and intergender relationships even more strictly regulated and supervised. With the utmost hypocrisy, however, for aristocratic young men such girls, as long as they were from a lower class, were 'fair game'.

Once their procreational duty was complete, having produced at least one son and heir whose blood, i.e., genes, was incontestably her husband's, it seemed to have been socially acceptable, at least in the Foxite universe, for married women to have public admirers, usually young men hoping to make their way on the social and career ladders of the times—aristocratic idleness, army, church

[269] www.rictornorton.co.uk/eighteen/jones4.htm. Accessed 17/07/2020.

and politics—and private lovers, sexual partners who did not compete as potential husbands. Passionately and openly expressed love between women was part of the outré social scene. The possibility that it was sexual in nature was largely unimportant, a world of women that men, the important members of society, did not want to know or attempt to understand.

Sexual love between men was a detestable crime whereas between women a matter of indifference. If the covert sexual liaison became overt, by being caught *in flagrante delicto* or the woman becoming pregnant then grounds for divorce had been laid—criminal conversation. Marriage to a divorced woman was not an enhancer of a political career—even Charles Fox, as mentioned earlier, disapproved when his favourite nephew, Henry Holland, married the divorced Lady Webster in 1797—and for a divorced woman to resurrect her social status was not easy unless her second husband was extremely high up in the patriarchy. Even more damaging than divorce, as in the case of Lady Betty Hamilton, Countess of Derby, was the husband's refusal to divorce which could mean the severest of social ostracism.

Already a fashion icon and social triumph after 1778, the still childless 21-year-old Georgiana threw in her lot with the Foxites attempting to be of use to her husband as well as seeking his approval. The Devonshire House circle of Whigs was the talk of the town. As a hostess she took over from Elizabeth Lamb, nee Milbanke, Viscountess Melbourne, who became her closest adviser. In an 'open' marriage with the Viscount, Peniston Lamb, she had many affairs while he stuck to his mistress, the actress and courtesan, Sophia Baddeley.

Lady Melbourne's longest lasting lover was George Wyndham, Earl of Egremont, almost certainly the father of at least 3 of her children one of whom, William, was to marry Georgiana's niece, Caroline Ponsonby (who, as Lady Caroline Lamb, was to become the persistent lover of Lord Byron), and become Home Secretary from 1830-4 and Prime Minister from 1835-41.

The sexual power these women had over the young, and not so young, politicians in their social circle indirectly gave them immense political power in terms of the popularity of their public images as glamorous, fashionable, sexually adventurous, modern women to some extent freed from the patriarchal moral expectations enough to exercise power over men, not, and this is the point, I think, by acting like men, as a Queen like Gloriana had to, but by emphasising their own attributes of beauty, wit, intelligence and sexual allure to fight their way into a man's world, to be noticed and listened to.

Their sexuality and their desirability, used skilfully, gave some of them, for example, Lady Elizabeth Lamb and Lady Frances Villiers, Countess of Jersey, who, as a 40 year old grandmother was to become the quite domineering mistress of the Prince of Wales running his household for him until replaced by the Marchioness of Hertford, the upper hand.

The genius that was Charles James Fox realised this when he had his 'affair' with the magnetic Duchess, whether or not it was sexual is immaterial, which became a formidable friendship and political partnership. From a personal perspective her political activism compensated for the powerlessness of her family situation and her hedonistic response to her unhappiness that had manifested itself in her gambling addiction and for him Georgiana was a portal to powerful friends and backers, like, most notably, George Augustus Frederick, Prince of Wales, whose company, perhaps, he would not have otherwise chosen and vice versa and a woman who understood his weaknesses and was, nevertheless, 100% supportive of his strengths and beliefs.

In 1778, Amanda Foreman relates, Georgiana made her first 'public' foray into Whig politics. In fear of a French invasion, due to the lack of a standing professional army, the aristocracy gathered together a large militia defence force at Coxheath in Kent. Georgiana, anxious to support the men, organised the women into an auxiliary support battalion suitably kitted out in fashionably androgynous uniforms who paraded *en militaire* with the men for a visit by the King and Queen. This patriotic display captured the public imagination, restoring, to some extent, Whig popularity at a time when their opposition to the American War had reduced their political fortunes to an all-time low. Sadly, in a mini sample of her whole life, while she was taken up with parading the Duke, as I have already related, was committing adultery with Lady Jersey.

Her public reputation as a politically active woman and a staunch Whig supporter was established by her appearance at the Westminster constituency hustings in the General Elections of 1780 and 1784 and the representation of Charles James Fox when he was made Foreign Secretary in 1782. Although her campaigning for Fox in Westminster in 1784 turned a potentially embarrassing loss into a resounding success, the Tory press, particularly *The Morning Post*, mercilessly attacked her private vices and family situation to the extent that she never campaigned again.

After her political help for Fox in March 1782, she met in Bath Elizabeth Foster who was to become her best friend, her husband's mistress and, two years after Georgiana's death in 1806, his second wife and the second Duchess of Devonshire. Against a backdrop of enormous and growing gambling debts Georgiana's life went into a tailspin sufficiently wild to make the Morning Post's word portrait of a sexually depraved woman more than marginally credible.

The menage a trois

By the end of 1782, Bess, a separated, financially strapped, absentee mother of two children whom she was forbidden to see, was living chez Cavendish. The 'World' wondered why.

In this Brave New World, 'You pays your money, and you takes your choice'! I'll plump for sex and money, the standard culprits! What else did Bess have but her looks and her 'winning ways'? Amanda Foreman paints this picture of her.

> She was the same age as Georgiana and already the mother of two sons, yet there was something surprisingly girlish about her. Physically, she was the opposite of Georgiana: slimmer, shorter, more delicate, with thin dark hair framing her tiny face. Her appearance of frailty, coupled with

> a feminine helplessness and coquettish charm, made most men want to protect and possess her. The historian Edward Gibbon, who had known Bess since she was a little girl, described her manners as the most seductive of any woman he knew. 'No man could withstand her,' was his opinion. 'If she chose to beckon the Lord Chancellor from his Woolsack in full sight of the world, he could not resist obedience.'[270]

There seems little doubt that Georgiana was seduced by her. Whether or not it was sexual is immaterial; she was hooked. In a touching passage, Amanda Foreman gives an in-depth assessment of Georgiana's state of mind. She was lonely—her devoted sister was taken up with her husband, her infant son, and their shared gambling habit—unfulfilled—not the least, maternally—riddled with guilt about her 'immoral' lifestyle and desperate to do good. To add to all this personal, private angst her public passion, the Whig Party, could not have been in worse shape.

The downfall of the North administration, engineered in Parliament by Fox, had exposed the factional problems in the Opposition of which her friends, the Foxites, were a major but not decisive grouping. Fox had resigned from his post as Foreign Secretary when Lord Shelburne replaced the Marquess of Rockingham upon the latter's sudden death in July 1782 and Shelburne was struggling to get approval to end the American War. *Shifting into Agony Aunt mode, how often has intellectual, emotional, even vocational disappointment or desolation been purged by a bout of physical passion?*

Georgiana's generous offer, covered up as a job offer to be Charlotte Williams' governess—Charlotte, as mentioned above, was the Duke's child by his pre-marriage mistress, Charlotte Spencer, whom Georgiana had welcomed into the home after her mother died, was no good as a long-term home without the Duke's approval. Bess knew how to get that.

After the 'cure' in Bath, the Duke and Duchess must have renewed their effort to have a baby because, by the New Year, Georgiana was pregnant; she was still only 25. The baby was born in July 1783, Lady Georgiana Dorothy Cavendish, "Little G", much adored but not the son and heir that William required. While Georgiana was controversially breast-feeding Little G the cobbled together ministry of Lord North's Tories, Foxite Whigs and the Rockingham Whigs of the Prime Minister, the Duke of Portland, Georgiana's brother-in-law, was failing to overcome the disadvantage of the King's implacable opposition and total withdrawal of patronage.

The year following the birth of her daughter, 1783–4 was Georgiana's annus horribilis. Overshadowing her ministry- saving mediation between the Prince of Wales and Fox that significantly modified his royal demands over his living allowance and the final ending of the American War in September were the termination of the Coalition in December and the steady rise of Pitt in the early months of 1784. Mitigating the marital pleasure at the birth of their first child

---

[270] Foreman, Amanda. The Duchess (Text Only). HarperCollins Publishers. Kindle Edition.

was the persistent gossip about her relationship with Fox and besmirching the loving heartache of her separation from Bess were the continuous reports of the latter's shenanigans in Naples when she was supposed to be in France.

Destroying the triumph of her Westminster campaign to get her friend elected in the General Election of 1784 were the delay, orchestrated by the King and Pitt *allegedly*, of almost a year in its legal recognition during which, Georgiana, a woman meddling in politics, was subjected to public ridicule and disapproval, and the heavy defeat of the Whigs that extinguished their political hopes for some 20 years.

> Ladies who interest themselves so much in the case of elections, are perhaps too ignorant to know that they meddle with what does not concern them, but they ought at least to know, that it is usual, even in these days of degeneracy, to expect common decency in a married woman.
> Morning Post, 8 April 1784[271]

At the end of October 1783, her father died leaving an estate far reduced from what the family expected. Major suspect was the family's gambling addiction, particularly her mother's. As that uncomfortable chicken came home to roost it was accompanied by Georgiana's own. Same species only far larger. Her secret was out and the toll on her emotional and mental health enough to bring on another miscarriage. Her own gambling debts had spiralled so out of control that she had to tell the Duke who seems to have greeted the news with his usual insouciance. Added to her guilt was the overwhelming feeling that she had led her dearest younger sister, Henrietta, down the same disastrous route. The public persona required for the election rescued her from her private woes, a pattern that was to repeat itself often in her short life.

The defeat of the now Foxite Whigs that summer of 1784 was papered over by their absolute conviction that they had been right all along about the King's despotic tendencies. It had brought about a remarkable change in Charles James Fox who had settled down with his mistress, Elizabeth Armistead, whom he eventually married 11 years later, in their home at St Ann's Hill in Surrey.

The election result might have been a disaster for the Whigs, but it was a public triumph for the Duchess. The manner of her electioneering was subjected to deep disapproval from The Establishment both for its masculinity, its mannishness, contrary to all the femininity expected of a 'lady', and its egalitarianism, her easiness with the lower classes, which offended her aristocratic Whig acquaintances. However, her personal popularity did not at any point suffer the same decline in fortune as her party. The misogyny and supremacy of the patriarchy, as shown in the headlines of The Morning Post, may have been ingrained in British culture but was being challenged by a female political activist, in every respect a politician except for her membership of the

---

[271] Ibid.

two groups whose laws and decisions guided the nation, who was and should have been one of their own. Fox's victory in Westminster could be rightly construed as her victory.

Had she been the candidate there is no doubt, I think, that she would have been elected. Such an event would have to wait another 135 years when another aristocrat, Nancy Astor, would take her seat in the House of Commons on 1st December 1919 and begin her own controversial career as a female politician.

1785 was a year of births. On 29th August, Georgiana gave birth to her second daughter, Lady Harriet Elizabeth Cavendish, "Harryo". Soon after, Bess gave birth to Caroline Rosalie Adelaide, who was to get the surname St Jules. The father of both these girls was the Duke. Bess had returned after the 1784 election and become the Duke's mistress. Foreman feels that she was more surprised by Georgiana's pregnancy than her own.

On 13th November, Henrietta, Georgiana's sister, gave birth to her third child, Lady Caroline. The two sisters enjoyed their infant daughters together while Bess skulked abroad looking for someone to give their name to her lovechild. These 3 autumn babies were to be tied together in the most outré fashion following on predictably from their eccentric mothers.

- Harryo would go on to marry her Aunt Henrietta's long-time lover, Granville Leveson-Gower, in 1809. He was 36, 12 years younger than her aunt, and she was 24. In 1812, her cousins, Harriette, and George, came to live with her, always believing that she was the wife of their guardian not the niece of their mother and, therefore, their stepmother, the wife of their father. The marriage was happy producing 11 children, one of whom, also Granville, became a distinguished Liberal Foreign Secretary and friend of William Gladstone, with another son, Frederick, also a Gladstonian Liberal for over 30 years.
- Caroline St Jules became Lady Caroline's sister-in-law when she married George Lamb, younger brother of Caroline's husband, William Lamb, Lord Melbourne, future Home Secretary and Prime Minister, close to Queen Victoria.
- Lady Caroline, first cousin to both Harryo and Caroline Adelaide Rosalie, in 1805 married William Lamb who was to find enduring fame as Victoria's mentor in the early years of her reign. Both the Lamb men, as mentioned earlier, were sons of Georgiana's close friend and fellow Whig hostess, Elizabeth, Viscountess Melbourne. Caroline continued the family tradition for scandal by becoming the lover of the poet, Lord Byron, as magnetic a scandal maker as Charles James Fox in his heyday.

When the King went temporarily insane in 1788, Fox was on holiday in Italy and the Whig response to the so-called Regency Crisis was handled by Richard Brinsley Sheridan, the playwright and politician, fresh from his triumphant speech demanding the impeachment of Warren Hastings, Governor-General of Bengal. Sheridan was a sort of spin doctor, having rewritten Fox's lie about the Prince's marriage to Maria Fitzherbert in 1785, negotiated the terms of the Prince's Regency and, in 1803, trumpeted the Whig's patriotic resistance to the prospect of a Napoleonic invasion.

He was also obsessed with Georgiana's sister, Lady Henrietta Ponsonby, probably her lover as the events of 1788-9 unfolded, even though replaced by Granville Leveson-Gower as the love of her life, and married to the beautiful opera singer, Elizabeth Ann Linley. Their son Tom was the father of Caroline Norton who features prominently in the next chapter. In 1792, Elizabeth had a daughter with Lord Edward Fitzgerald, the future Irish rebel, for whom Sheridan accepted responsibility after her death but who tragically died the following year. Waiting in the wings was Fox's protégé and Georgiana's future, possibly current (the Duchess, possibly in retaliation or, maybe, imitation of Bess, had turned to the ever available, Earl of Dorset, but he was in France), lover, the 24-year-old Charles Grey, Viscount Howick, 5 years younger than his future opponent, William Pitt the Younger, and 7 years younger than Georgiana.

In this heady mixture of sex and politics were many deep ironies. Firstly, the sisters were deeply involved in it, not just via pillow talk but in terms of real political guidance, even leadership. Stripping away all the politicking Pitt was the 'King's man', and Fox was the 'Prince's man. Fox was still the Whig star but not naturally the guiding star that Pitt had become to the Government, not necessarily Tory, benches. If the Prince became a fully powered up Regent on a long-term basis he could have chosen his own government.

However, The Glorious Revolution of 1688, although it had not produced a written Constitution to establish it in tablets of stone—*not the British way*—had shifted the executive power irrevocably in the direction of Parliament. Kings and, by extrapolation, Prince Regents could not do what they wanted. The parliamentary majority overwhelmingly supported Pitt, not the Whigs and certainly not the Foxite Whigs whose Reformist intentions, pro-French Revolutionary, pro-American Independence, pro-Abolition of the Slave Trade and pro-Parliamentary Reform, not to mention Catholic Emancipation, was a hard concoction for the power brokers, many of whom, like the Duke, were their major financial backers, to swallow all at once.

The astonishing irony, then, was that the absolutist King's man was seeking parliamentary limitation, approval even, of a Prince Regent's possible, given the Prince's reputation, more likely probable, use of absolute Royal prerogative to shoot holes in all that 1688 had achieved.

More ironic still was that the parliamentary star of the day, Charles James Fox, with the very real prospect of a return to power and a re-ignition of a Reformist agenda, was supporting the absolute right of the royal bloodline over the parliamentary power of the House of Commons. The most extreme outcome of the Prince's power to do what he wanted, apart from his already burdening penchant for spending the taxpayers' money, would be the recognition of his 1785 marriage to Maria Fitzherbert, a twice widowed Catholic, at 32, six years older than the Prince. Not only would this have contravened the Royal Marriages Act of 1772, whereby no marriage of a royal could take place without the King's permission, and thus polluted or diluted the bloodline but, far more challengingly, the Act of Settlement of 1701 which forbade a monarch to marry a practising Roman Catholic.

This would have been a step far too far for the Protestant Establishment, including even those Whigs in favour of Catholic Emancipation, a price not worth paying. When he finally became the long-term Prince Regent in 1811, accepting similar restrictions to those that would have been imposed in 1788-9 had not the King recovered, and then King in 1820, his opposition to Catholic emancipation and spurning of Maria Fitzherbert showed just how capricious he could be.

In addition to the unpredictability implicit in their chosen Messiah, the Whigs had an opponent skilled in and dedicated to the political process. Pitt, who did not even describe himself as a Tory but as an Independent Whig, gambled on the King's illness being temporary and the French Revolution ending up in war with France. He was right on both counts meaning that Fox was wrong. Pitt never eschewed reform, putting his own plan forward for the abolition of Rotten Boroughs and befriending Wilberforce in his mission to abolish the Slave Trade, just things that would destabilise the nation when national unity was needed to stave off the French threat. Right again! He even set up a rival social circuit to the Devonshire House Circle.

In Pall Mall, Lady Jane Gordon lavishly entertained the Tories in a manner that rivalled Georgiana's. Pitt and his close friend Henry Dundas, Viscount Melville, were frequent participants. For a time, not in fashion or temperament, Lady Gordon's soirees rivalled the Duchess's. The personal circumstances of these two political hostesses were remarkably similar, both in arranged marriages and both having to tolerate their husband's mistress living in their home.

Both had to endure an illegitimate child born within days of their own. Both had true lovers who were most definitely not their husbands, and both had to separate; Georgiana went back, however. Politics had no bearing on private woes and scandal no matter how much the Morning Post tried to convince its more salacious readers that it did.

The female politician

The second great irony was that Georgiana, and to some extent Henrietta, had a personal life whose need for complex political manoeuvring would have been a daily concern. In May, her friend and the Duke's live-in mistress, Bess Foster, now becoming a more accepted member of the London social scene, not least because of her close friendship with Georgiana's sister, delivered the Duke's third illegitimate child, a son, Augustus Clifford, in France. For the sake of a position for her brother, John, Bess had turned her charm on to Charles Lennox, Duke of Richmond, who had been one of the Rockingham Whigs who deserted to Pitt. His penchant for mistresses to compensate for his childless marriage almost certainly means that the price of the favour was sex with Bess with whom he remained hopelessly in love for many years. *Was Bess Sleeping with the Enemy? Did the Duke have doubts about the child's paternity?*

During her absence, Amanda Foreman tells us, the Duke and Duchess were happy although her involvement with the Earl of Dorset, still charming his way into the beds of the female half of London Society, was certainly more than flirtation. Dorset had involved Georgiana in French politics in which her friend, Queen Marie Antoinette, was playing a leading role. Her death by guillotine in 1793, one of many in the post-revolutionary cull of aristocrats held to have been to blame for the disastrous state of pre-revolutionary finance and society, exemplified a rather nasty side to the Revolution, resulting in the formation of the Committee of Public Safety, which, although supported by many aristocratic Whigs, must have caused an itch in the neck of many others.

In the summer of 1788, Admiral Hood was promoted by Pitt to the Admiralty Board to baby-mind Pitt's brother, John, whom he had made First Lord of the Admiralty. The rules concerning Government office meant a by-election in Westminster had to be held. Fox stood, of course, but one of his racier friends, Lord John Townshend, recently married to Georgiana's divorced cousin, also Georgiana, nicknamed 'Jockey'—*Hm!* after a steamy and scandalous affair, was also chosen. Pitt, anticipating a repeat of 1784, wheeled out his brother's wife, Lady Chatham, a lady of impeccable virtue, to counter the common touch of the Spencer sisters.

However, although Henrietta took to the streets, Georgiana, fearing a repeat of the public defamation of 1784, guided the campaign from headquarters, proving herself a very savvy political strategist, ensuring that Lord John was elected despite the Government Press billing it as "the cause of Decency against Indecency"[*World*,25July1788][272]. *What was not indecent anymore, it seems, was the political activism of women which can be justifiably lauded as Georgiana's historical legacy.*

Her other legacy has captured the historical headlines more, namely the politicisation of sex, or the sexualisation of politics, but in the history of men's treatment of women and their progress towards that being the treatment of equals, it is, I think, equally important. For the alpha male, the maleness of politics, the adrenalin rush of battle, the sweetness of its victories, the bitterness of defeat and the restorative hopes of political resurrection, were not enough for his fragile self-esteem. His sexual drive also demanded conquests which dynastic, arranged marriage, with its compulsory wifely submission rarely provided even if the submissive partner was an equally alpha-rated female. His dynastic duty and his sexual proclivities were rarely satisfied by one woman.

Post-coital conversations between alpha male and wife/business partner/household manager/social hostess/mother of sons and heirs and dynastically marriageable daughters and between alpha male and mistress/bed sharer/sex provider must have been very different, the difference being accentuated if the male was married or single, an established politician or an

---

[272] thehistoryofparliament.wordpress.com/2018/09/06/the-cause-of-decency-against-indecency-lady-chatham-and-the-1788-westminster-election. Accessed 29/07/2020.

aspiring one, promiscuous or faithful, in love or just a sexual user or if the female was a woman of established social standing or merely a sex toy. In these pre-contraceptive days children, legitimate or illegitimate, will have figured prominently and frequently. With Georgiana, all these variations would have been likely. Amanda Foreman never said a truer word than these:

> This sort of intimate friendship combined with behind-the-scenes politics was irresistible to Georgiana.[273]

In the Regency Crisis of November 1788 to March 1789, she was a central character both in her role as a highly skilled political operator and an intimate of all the major opposition players.

- Duke of Devonshire: Major Whig financier and insider. Husband.
- Duke of Portland: Nominal Whig leader and leader in the Lords. Brother-in-law.
- Prince of Wales: Close friend. Former obsessive admirer, possible lover. Intimate friend.
- Charles James Fox: Former lover, allegedly. Intimate friend.
- Charles Grey, Viscount Howick. Future, maybe current, lover and future Prime Minister. Political protégé.
- Richard Brinsley Sheridan. Obsessive lover of her sister. Intimate friend.
- Granville Leveson-Gower. Future, maybe current, lover of her sister. Future son-in-law.
- Elizabeth Lamb, Viscountess Melbourne, mother of William Lamb, future Prime Minister, and fellow Whig hostess. Closest friend.

It is impossible to believe that Georgiana's ability to bring Sheridan, Fox and Grey together and modify the Prince's demands was not in evidence, with a voice much respected and listened to, throughout the crisis, such was her personal and political centrality to the Whig cause.

The national crisis might have been over but the Foxite Whigs could not have been in worse shape, comprehensively defeated, daily diminished, utterly demoralised, and acrimoniously divided. To continue this absurd outburst of alliteration, the Duchess was in deep trouble; the expense of her efforts in Westminster and her lavish attempts to combat the challenge of Lady Jane and hold the Whig support together had more than doubled her debts. Her personal life was about to enter its most precarious and painful few years.

In the summer of 1789, the Duke took the family to Spa via Paris narrowly missing the storming of the Bastille. Much as she was concerned about the safety of her friends, particularly Marie Antoinette, Georgiana was relieved to escape her creditors, having engaged in a pathetic campaign of scrounging from the

---

[273] Foreman, Amanda. The Duchess (Text Only). HarperCollins Publishers. Kindle Edition.

Prince, Thomas Coutts, banker and family friend, and her brother, George—anyone but the Cavendishes—to avoid having to inform her husband about the disastrous state of her finances. One downside for the baron covert, as we shall see in two chapters' time, was his responsibility for his wife's debts about which, when he was as wealthy as the Duke, he did not enquire too often, money, even when you had none, like Stoney Bowes, being the last topic of aristocratic dinner or daily conversation, far behind war, politics, gossip, gardening and gambling.

Spa did the trick. On 21 May, in Paris, Georgiana fulfilled her procreative duty and her dynastic mission with the birth of a son, William Cavendish, Marquess of Hartington, known as Hart. It heralded a period of personal peril, unprecedented but not unsuspected and largely self-inflicted. When the family returned from holiday and Hart was weaned, Georgiana's sister became extremely ill. The Duke rented a house in Bath so that she could recover in the bosom of her family. Having put her relationship with Dorset on a friendship basis and finished breastfeeding Hart Georgiana rekindled her affair with Charles Grey behaving towards him in public rather too solicitously and entertaining him in private when her husband was elsewhere.

By October 1791, she, at 6 months, could no longer conceal the reality that she was pregnant and that it could not be her husband's child. After a tip-off, the Duke arrived unannounced to see things for himself. He was furious and made it clear that the only option was to go abroad with Henrietta and have her baby there. If she stayed with or without Grey, she would never see her children again. Grey, therefore, was also furious that Georgiana chose her children over him. (Her enormous debts, which, after his father's death in 1811, took her son years to settle, must have been a factor.) That autumn, on the pretence of Henrietta's health issues, Georgiana, Bess, Henrietta, Frederick, Caroline Ponsonby and Caroline St Jules set off for Europe to welcome into the world, Eliza Courtney, and await the judgement of the Duke as to whether to turn the separation into a legal divorce. The Duke did not allow them back until the late summer of 1793.

Georgiana, personally chastised by the closeness of the abyss of social ostracism that a divorce, or a separation, as it did for Lady Betty Hamilton, would have brought, and politically and socially challenged by the situation in France (The Reign of Terror), enough, Amanda Foreman tells us, to cement her resolve to disagree with Fox over the Revolution and the need to go to war with the regime, was a changed person, more private than public, more sceptical than zealous, less fashionable and on a gambling detox.

While her sister had found the love of her life in Naples, Granville Leveson-Gower (with whom she was to have two children and who was to become Harryo's husband), Georgiana continued to spurn hers, a heart-breaking sacrifice made all the worse by his marriage to her brother-in-law's cousin, Mary Ponsonby, in November 1794 thus completing another year of disappointment for Georgiana.

The aim of Georgiana's lavish entertaining at Devonshire House had been twofold. She threw herself into the Cavendish family legacy of Whiggery, to which her own family was committed, making many friends, lovers and political allies along the way but with the primary aim of bringing together a coalition of Whig factions, united behind her two dear friends, the Prince of Wales and Charles James Fox. With her absence, however, and, in the light of what I will say in my conclusion, her leadership and the growing pro-War, anti—Republican feeling, even among Whigs, the Party, if it ever was that, fell apart.

Georgiana's sister-in-law, Lady Dorothy Bentinck, Duchess of Portland, died in June, just two days after Admiral Howe's naval victory—the French also claimed it as a victory—off Ushant, known as the Glorious First of June, which seemed to release the Duke of Portland from his tie to the Foxite Cavendish family. He joined the Pittite Cabinet as Home Secretary just a month later. He took with him one of Fox's oldest friends, William Wentworth-Fitzwilliam, and the wealthy George Howard, Earl of Carlisle, all dedicated Whigs but in the conservative anti-French Revolution camp.

In the General Election of 1796, the official opposition, Foxite Whigs, ended up with just 95 seats compared with the Pittite return of 424. Fox and many others, apart from a small group led by George Tierney, broke with Parliament altogether. *One cannot help thinking that Fox and his remaining loyal friends significantly missed the Duchess*. In 1801, having achieved the Act of Union of Great Britain and Ireland, Pitt could not get the King to agree to Catholic emancipation and resigned. Fox came out of retirement to press the new Tory government under Henry Addington, 'The Doctor' (He was the son of Pitt's physician and, therefore, his childhood friend.), bringing Georgiana back into the political scene.

She had already made her triumphal return to the social scene with the coming out of Little G and her sumptuous wedding to Lord Morpeth, heir to the Earl of Carlisle. Her family life, however, was still plagued by secrets such as the true extent of her gambling debts from which she had been temporarily relieved with a large loan from the Duke of Bedford, dedicated Foxite and fellow experiencer of the ménage a trois with Nancy Parsons, mentioned earlier, and hiding her sister's pregnancy from her husband and the rest of the family.

Addington now experienced the factional in-fighting that had extinguished the Whigs as a political force in 1796. In 1802, he got some relief by arranging for peace with Napoleon by the Treaty of Amiens. Less than a year later he was forced to declare war again from a position of weakness, to say the least. The war was now against a renowned and, soon to be, seemingly invincible military dictator, Napoleon Bonaparte, who had seized power in November 1799. The war emotionally tugged on the aristocracy's patriotic heartstrings while practically tugging open their purse strings.

Napoleon came to threaten the island of Great Britain until thwarted at Trafalgar in 1805 but Addington's re-declaration of war was more to do with British colonies and naval control of the Mediterranean than threat of invasion or fighting on the European mainland. Peace was financially pragmatic, naively Francophile favouring Fox's position or dangerously Republican favouring Sheridan's and, therefore, unacceptable to a proud King. Georgiana's principal concern, however, was Reform.

Addington, made Viscount Sidmouth by Pitt in 1806, was a reactionary, a tendency that was to come to the fore in his spell as Home Secretary in Lord Liverpool's Tory Government once Wellington had defeated Napoleon in 1815 heralding an uneasy peace. His watch including the suspension of habeas corpus in 1817, the Peterloo Massacre in 1819 and the passing of the Six Acts has to be one of the most overtly oppressive in post-Glorious Revolution British politics.

On the three great Reform issues—parliamentary reform, Catholic emancipation and abolition of the slave trade—Addington, presumably like the King, was anti. Georgiana, if no one else, saw that with mediated negotiation, a coalition of those who were hotly or tepidly in favour of some or all of these, regardless of party and patronage, could form a centrist opposition to the King's supporters without letting in the more revolutionary tendencies of the Sheridanites. Pittites, Grenvillites, Addingtonites and Foxites could do a deal. Whoever came up with the strategy and the idea of a government of 'talent' rather than 'faction' it was Georgiana who took up the challenge and ran with it for the rest of her natural and political life, justifiably, in historical terms, albeit with hindsight, assuming leadership of the political movement that would result in the momentous Ministry of All The Talents under Prime Minister, William Grenville, 1st Baron Grenville, which began its Ministry on 11th February 1806 after the death of Pitt on 23rd January. HIStory will allude to the coalition of talents as Grenville's idea or the initiative of the Prince of Wales but only Georgiana had the skill and connections to pursue it to a successful conclusion.

Georgiana died on 30th March, tragically young like her political nemesis, Pitt, who was only 46, at 48 years old, 'the doyenne of the Whigs' as Foreman calls her, and much politicking skill sadly unfulfilled. When Addington resigned on May 10th, 1804, it was Pitt's assault on his conduct of the war that undermined his parliamentary majority. Pitt hoped for two coalitions to prosecute the war, one at home and one abroad. The King's refusal to sanction any Government that included Fox scuppered the former, made worse by the Grenvillites and the Addingtonites joining the Foxites in Opposition.

As for the second, he succeeded in combining The Holy Roman, Austrian, Russian and British Empires against the French. 1805 is portrayed as a year of glorious victory for the British largely due to Nelson's decisive defeat of the French fleet at Trafalgar on 5th October which assured Britain's naval supremacy for over a decade and removed the threat of invasion. *What we rarely learn in our Anglocentric version of history is that it was a year of unparalleled triumph for Napoleon the repercussions of which killed William Pitt the Younger and ended his 22-year domination of British politics.*

By the end of 1805, Napoleon, with his comprehensive victories at Ulm and Austerlitz, had squashed all opposition on the European mainland. The Russians went home, and the Austrians and Holy Roman Empire signed the Treaty of Pressburg.

Pitt's natural successor was William Grenville, Pitt's first cousin, who got the King to accept his government with Fox playing a prominent role.

Georgiana's hard work had paid off. Here is the Cabinet of her Ministry of All the Talents.

o First Lord of the Treasury Leader of the House of Lords	The Lord Grenville
o Chancellor of Exchequer	The Lord Henry Petty
o Lord Chancellor	The Lord Erskine
o Lord President of the Council	The Earl Fitzwilliam The Viscount Sidmouth (8 Oct 1806)
o Lord Privy Seal	The Viscount Sidmouth The Lord Holland (8 Oct 1806)
o Secretary of State for the Home Department	The Earl Spencer
o Secretary of State for Foreign Affairs o Leader of the House of Commons	Charles James Fox Viscount Howick (24 Sept 1806)
• Secretary of State for War and the Colonies	William Windham
o First Lord of the Admiralty	Charles Grey Thomas Grenville (29 Sept 1806)
o President of the Board of Control	Thomas Grenville George Tierney (1 Oct 1806)
o Master-General of the Ordnance	The Earl of Moira
• Minister without Portfolio	The Earl Fitzwilliam (Oct 1806)
o Lord Chief Justice of the King's Bench	The Lord Ellenborough[274]

There were non-Cabinet posts for Sheridan, her friends, Lord John Townshend, whose daughter, Lady Elizabeth, went on to marry Augustus Clifford, the Duke's illegitimate son with Bess, the Earl of Derby, husband of the disgraced Lady Betty, the Duke of Richmond, nephew of the one who spurned Bess, the Duke of Bedford, father of Lord John Russell, the future Prime Minister, and son of her former friend and creditor (see above), George Walpole, grandson of the Great Robert, and her cousin, Lord Charles Spencer, great grandson of the Duke of Marlborough.

274 Extract from en.wikipedia.org/wiki/Ministry_of_All_the_Talents. Accessed 04/08/2020.

The Ministry was the culmination of a century of Whig politics, a cause dear to Georgiana's heart and a tribute to her persona; charismatic, well-intentioned, sociable, empathetic, bizarre, secretive, flawed, rakish, sexy, beautiful, and fashionable. Above all, it was a woman who kept Reform alive; her femininity encapsulated the weaknesses of powerful men yet empowered them to achieve, weaknesses that she shared without the socio-legal power to brush them to one side.

As for the Duke, if he is to be condemned or disparaged by history it should be for being a typical 'man of his time' whose irrevocably male persona, a mixture of haughty hypocrisy and selfish narcissism, the end result of centuries of patriarchal male supremacy underpinned by the dynastic principle and legal coverture, was exposed by his wife's extraordinary combination of male and female qualities and weaknesses. Lady Georgiana Cavendish, nee Spencer, Duchess of Devonshire, has a hugely significant place in history, not as the first It Girl or as an aristocratic strumpet or over-spoilt waster but as Amanda Foreman has it in her brilliant biography: The Doyenne of the Whig Party.

Epilogue

It was an act of self-delusion, very much like Georgiana's many such fancies, to believe that this Ministry could achieve a satisfactory solution to all four of the major political issues of its day, peace with France, parliamentary reform, Catholic emancipation, and the abolition of slavery. In March 1807, just before the collapse of the Ministry, an Act to abolish the Slave Trade received royal assent but the King's refusal to allow any sort of Catholic emancipation brought down the government. The one notable absentee from the coalition, Georgiana's brother-in-law, the Duke of Portland, took up the reins to be joined by her never-to-be son-in-law, Granville Leveson-Gower.

Pitt, Georgiana and Fox, who died on 13 September 1806, were all gone from the political scene. After 23 years of Tory governments, during which Napoleon was defeated and exiled bringing a peace with France that has lasted to the present day, Charles Grey, now Earl Grey, in his sixties and father-in-law to Little G's daughter, Lady Elizabeth Howard, fulfilled his former lover's wish by piloting through the Great Reform Act of 1832 and The Abolition of Slavery throughout the British Empire Act of 1833. His Home Secretary, William Lamb, Viscount Melbourne, husband of Georgiana's niece, Caroline, was the son of Georgiana's dear friend, Elizabeth, Lady Melbourne.

Lady Melbourne's daughter, Elizabeth, married Henry Temple, Viscount Palmerston, during whose premiership the Matrimonial Causes Act 1857, the beginning of the end for coverture, was passed. In his cabinet was Fox's nephew, Lord Holland, Little G's husband, Earl of Carlisle, Eliza Courtney's brother-in-law, Edward Ellice and Georgiana's nephew, Honest Jack Spencer, Viscount Althorp. These august descendants, reformers all, are Georgiana's dynastic legacy.

Chapter 36
Liberte, Egalite, Fraternite

For example, have they not all violated the principle of equality of rights by quietly depriving half of mankind of the right to participate in the formation of the laws, by excluding women from the rights of citizenship?
– Nicolas de Caritat, Marquis de Condorcet

...woman has the right to mount the scaffold, so she should have the right equally to mount the rostrum, provided that these manifestations do not trouble public order as established by law.
– Marie Gouze aka. Olympe de Gouges

The government in a revolution is the despotism of liberty against tyranny.
– Maximilien Robespierre

If ever there was a book calculated to make a man in love with its author, this appears to me to be the book.
– William Godwin

Preamble

Until the invention of reliable recording technology in the early 20th century, historical records were written. Private correspondence such as the letters researched by Amanda Foreman between Georgiana and her mother and Georgiana and Bess and their friends and acquaintances give us some idea of the private person behind the public mask. Chroniclers and diary writers like Nicholas Thraxall, Horace Walpole and Fanny Burney give us an insight into gossip and private opinion. Hansard transcripts give us the debated issues of the day rather than the private conversation and behind-closed-doors wheeling and dealing of the principal actors involved.

How I long to have been a fly on the wall at the soirees, the balls and the dinners at Devonshire House or the all-nighters at Brooks's. Who said what to whom and why? What were their concepts in the early 1790s of Liberty, Equality and Fraternity? Were they as empty, prejudiced, hypocritical and self-seeking as those across the English Channel, or indeed the Atlantic Ocean, who claimed to espouse the phrase as their social and political credo? Of course, what I am driving at is, was there any discussion among the Foxites, admirers, at least at first, of the Revolution in France, about women's rights, women's equality under the law, women having the vote, women having a seat in the Commons or Lords?

Two things are worth remembering about this fantasy fly-on-the-wall documentary. Firstly, the educated elite such as Georgiana and Fox were fluently bilingual in French and English and secondly, Georgiana et al. were on the continent during their exile from 1791-3 and, therefore, experiencing events in France without the distortions of British Government spin and censorship and the bias of the Government controlled press or the tracts of pro-Revolution radicals. Clearly, once revolutionary change was underway the revolutionaries themselves expected the full attention of other nations.

> *The irons of Frenchmen have fallen with a clatter. The crash of their fall has paled despots and shaken their thrones. Astounded Europe has fixed an attentive eye on the star that illuminates France, on the August Senate that represents a people who join their love of justice to their will to be free.*[275]

Before we look at the fourth failed British marriage, therefore, we once again need to look to French history. Again, Establishment HIStory distorts reality for its own glorification. The tosh that was the standard version of the French Revolution in my schooldays was as follows:

- *14 July 1789, Bastille Prison in Paris 'stormed'. Goodies, i.e., downtrodden French poor, beat Baddies, i.e., overfed, luxury loving, King, Queen and Aristos, and chopped off their heads. Nasty man, Citizen Chauvelin—thanks to Baroness Orczy more memorable than the real-life master politicians, Maximilien Robespierre and Jean-Paul Marat, of whom he is a fictionally conflated imitation (My favourite is Raymond Massey in the 1934 version of The Scarlet Pimpernel, opposite the peerless Leslie Howard.)—decapitates hundreds of aristos in a Reign of Terror, has his own head removed by those who know better how to run a proper country, i.e., like Britain, who themselves are removed by a jumped up chubby little Corsican dictator who is eventually brought down by two dashing Brits, Nelson and Wellington (9th and 15th in a 2002 list of greatest Britons!), but France leaves the world with the exemplary template for how to rise up and establish human, civil rights in a utopian vision of Freedom, Equality and Brotherly Love—Liberte, Egalite, Fraternite.*

  Be prepared to be disavowed!

It is hard to get to the bottom of what those who espoused the Enlightenment understood by the concept of Liberty, but it clearly resonated with women in pre-Revolution and Revolutionary France (*If it did so in pre-1780 Britain I have*

[275] Racz, Elizabeth. "The Women's Rights Movement in the French Revolution." Science & Society, vol. 16, no. 2, 1952, pp. 151–174. JSTOR, www.jstor.org/stable/40400125. Accessed 14 Aug. 2020.

found it hard to dig up which does not mean it isn't there!). Ordinary folk were ambivalent about kingship in both countries, seeing the evils of tyranny in an absolute ruler but also seeing the benefits of an institution answerable only to God that protected them from factional or class-based tyranny.

When the Scottish poet, James Thompson, put together his lyrics in the 1720s, subsequently used for *Rule Britannia,* his idea of Liberty was of a nation freed from absolute monarchy and freed from the foreign influence of European tyrants who just happened to be treading on the toes of liberating merchants from Britain whose slaves were better off in their unfree condition than they were running round free in Africa, thus helping to make their owners, who, together with their aristocratic brothers, would fight enslavement with their last breath, in the 'mother country' extremely wealthy.

> Thee haughty tyrants ne'er shall tame:
> All their attempts to bend thee down,
> Will but arouse thy generous flame;
> But work their woe, and thy renown.
> "Rule, Britannia! rule the waves:
> "Britons never will be slaves."

Within this perception of Liberty lies the Revolutionary concept of Fraternity, meaning that all Frenchmen needed to put aside their differences and participate in the common cause of keeping France French, a band of brothers. The concept of Liberty without an absolute monarch, free from arbitrary oppression, unjust application of the Law and nepotistic use of the Royal Prerogative, the uncomfortable outcome of *The Age of Reason,* the title of Thomas Paine's polemic against institutionalised religion, asked awkward questions and sought answers that were reasonable. If an absolute monarch was unreasonable, and therefore unjust, what about the other members in the feudal hierarchy of male supremacy, the Lord, the Squire, the father and the husband? What about the male God and the all-male celibate priesthood?

Arguably, by asking his parliament, The Estates-General (The First Estate; the Clergy, the Second Estate; the Nobility and the Third Estate; the Common People.), to gather together the nation's grievances in early 1789 Louis XVI started the Revolution.

As we have just reasoned, there was a degree of consensus about what people wanted freedom from, but, having obtained it, it was accompanied by a puzzling melting pot of things that people wanted to do with it. 'Freedom to' takes and took thinkers and lawmakers into the minefields of human rights, right and wrong and 'Egalite'. In Britain, it was not until the Party that was named after the concept, the Liberals, came to power in the 1850s that the definition combined rights and responsibilities with ethics and morality. John Emerich Edward Dalberg-Acton, 1st Baron Acton, 13th Marquess of Groppoli, KCVO, DL, more modestly known as John Acton MP, close friend and adviser of William Gladstone and author of my own political mantra—

> Power tends to corrupt, and absolute power corrupts absolutely. Great men are almost always bad men, even when they exercise influence and not authority.

—got it right, I think, in saying, "**Liberty is not the power of doing what we like, but the right of being able to do what we ought**." Liberty meant freedom of action within the law, but it also meant freedom to think and debate about what morality that law should support and allow. *As I have pointed out before, the most important question about human law is whose law is/was it?* Furthermore, if everyone was created equal and equally valuable in the sight of God then should they not have the same Liberty, the same rights, leaving only individual differences of character, personality, drive and talent to differentiate human beings in terms of wealth, property or status? A revolution throws off the shackles that prevent debate. On all the issues arising from the concept of Liberty this was precisely what it did.

The French Revolution could not make up its mind about who was to debate and make the law. The Assembly of those deputised to debate, changed five times in six years. On 9 July 1789, the Estates-General was replaced by the National Constituent Assembly. On 1 October 1791, this was replaced by the Legislative Assembly. On the 20 September 1792, this was replaced by the National Convention. On the 2 November 1795 this was replaced by the Directory which lasted until 10 November 1799 when a coup d'état turned the Republic into a Consulship with Napoleon as First Consul, a virtual dictator. On 2 December 1804, Napoleon was crowned Emperor.

In its determination since 1789 to find the right way to achieve Liberte, Egalite and Fraternite, France has had 11 regimes: 2 monarchies, 2 Empires, 1 usurpation, 1 German puppet and 5 Republics. It was one of the last Western European countries to implement universal suffrage by allowing all female citizens to have the vote in 1944, in itself a sure sign of wrestling with the meanings of Liberty and Equality. Not quite, I think, what this much applauded woman market trader hoped for in October 1791 when she made this statement to the Assembly.

> The wise and thoughtful choice which Frenchmen have made gives us reason to hope that the Constitution of this kingdom will be the most beautiful of human monuments.[276]

If we take the pre-Revolutionary years, 1756-1788 when William Murray, Lord Mansfield, Lord Chief Justice of Great Britain and Ireland, was as busy reforming the 700-year-old Common Law as he was applying it without fear or favour the bottle that was France was being shaken vigorously by the Four Horsemen of the Apocalypse—War, Oppression, Famine and Death. When the cork popped, women's issues, along with all the others such as taxes, bread

---

[276] Ibid.

shortages, unemployment, lack of human cannon fodder, political representation and colonial unrest, poured out, full of fizz. When the cork that was Napoleon Bonaparte was found in 1804 strong enough to bottle up France's woes and re-label the bottle as the Napoleonic Empire, they had lost their effervescence.

For most of the 18th century, Prussia, sworn enemy of France, wrestled with codifying its laws and the relationship of its people to them. Whatever resulted from these deliberations is now known as the Frederician code, started by King Frederick I and completed in the reign of his grandson, Frederick II. By 1752, a French version, Code Frederic, was available. On its cover the work proudly announced that it was *Fonde sur la Raison et sur les Constitutions du Pays*.

The rationale of this code supported a justification of patriarchy and paternalism that gave women the role of family member for the purpose of procreation, the master's assistant and household manager. Her biology meant that she could do no more. There was no misogynistic disdain just a statement, instruction almost, of her duties. There was little room for complaint since she had knowingly signed up for it. Here are some extracts:

> The husband is by nature the head of his family. To be convinced of this, it is sufficient to consider, that the wife leaves her family to join herself to that of her husband; that she enters into his household, and into the habitation of which he is the master, and grants him rights over her body, with the intention to have children by him to perpetuate the family.
> As it is in the quality of an assistant that the wife enters into the family with her husband, she ought to enjoy all the rights of the family.
> The right of a father over his children is founded on reason: for the children are procreated in the house of which the father is master; they are born in a family of which he is head; they are born of his seed and a portion of his body; they are not themselves in a condition to provide for their own preservation; and their father is obliged to take care of their education until they arrive at the age of maturity.
> Whence it follows, that the children are properly under the power of their father, and not under that of their mother; and that she has as little power over them, as one who lends his ground to another, to make his seed bring forth fruit in it, has over the fruits which it produces.[277]

This emphasis on the mastery of the male owner of property as husband and father was not a peculiarity of Prussian culture. It was widespread. It did not denigrate the female per se, it gave her a complementary role that was inferior to that of the male whose property or 'estate' provided for the family group. In 1762 the Jacobin's favourite philosopher, owing to his advocacy of popular sovereignty and opposition to absolute monarchy, the Genevan, Jean Jacques Rousseau, wrote a treatise on education called *Emile*.

---

[277] books.google.co.uk/books?id=Wh02AAAAIAAJ&pg=PR45&source=gbs selected_pages&cad=2#v= onepage&q&f=false. Accessed 16/08/2020.

In this very subjective work, while accepting the numerous similarities that confirmed that they were of the same species, Rousseau extrapolated from the fundamental biological differences in man and woman, not least in their primary biological function or purpose, that there was a clear difference in their moral perspective and social behaviour which required a different educational experience. I am very grateful to the following site for access to the primary written sources that follow. This site is a collaboration of the Roy Rosenzweig Centre for History and New Media (George Mason University) and American Social History Project (City University of New York), supported by grants from the Florence Gould Foundation and the National Endowment for the Humanities.

> Once it is demonstrated that man and woman are not, and should not be constituted the same, either in character or in temperament, it follows that they should not have the same education. In following the directions of nature they must act together but they should not do the same things; their duties have a common end, but the duties themselves are different and consequently also the tastes that direct them. After having tried to form the natural man, let us also see, in order not to leave our work incomplete, how the woman is to be formed who suits this man.[278]

He went on to make two further statements of particular interest to this point.

The relative duties of the two sexes are not and cannot be equally rigid. **When woman complains about the unjust inequalities placed on her by man she is wrong**; this inequality is by no means a human institution or at least it is not the work of prejudice but of reason.

These similarities and differences must have an influence on morals; this effect is apparent and conforms with experience and **shows the futility of the disputes over the superiority or the equality of the sexes**—as if each sex, arriving at nature's ends by its own particular route, were not on that account more perfect than if it bore greater resemblance to the other.[279] [my highlighting]

Presuming that Rousseau would not have made these statements if he had not experienced complaints from women about inequality and male prejudice and arguments over the assertions of male superiority, we can conclude that in the 1760s, in France at least, the buds of a women's rights movement were waiting to flower. The Frederician view was not without its detractors. At the time that Rousseau's advocacy of the education of daughters being different from that of sons the newspaper, *Journal des Dames*, edited by a woman, Madame de Beaumer, for women, printed this condemnation of men for suppressing the education of women.

---

[278] "Jean–Jacques Rousseau, Emile (1762)," *LIBERTY, EQUALITY, FRATERNITY: EXPLORING THE FRENCH REVOLUTION*, accessed August 19, 2020, revolution.chnm.org/items/show/393.

[279] Ibid.

> If we have not been raised up in the sciences as you have, it is you who are the guilty ones; for have you not always abused, if I may say so, the bodily strength that nature has given you? Have you not used it to annihilate our capacities, and to enshroud the special prerogatives that this same nature has bounteously granted to women, to compensate them for the material strength that you have—advantages that we surely would not dispute you—to truly appreciate vivacity of imagination, delicate feelings, and that amiable politeness, well worth the strength that you parade about so.[280]

When the King asked the Estates to gather together grievances, there was a petition from working women directly to the King asking him to provide an education and to create and protect employment for poor women to prevent them turning to prostitution.

> We ask to be enlightened, to have work, not in order to usurp men's authority, but in order to be better esteemed by them, so that we might have the means of living safe from misfortune and so that poverty does not force the weakest among us, who are blinded by luxury and swept along by example, to join the crowd of unfortunate women who overpopulate the streets and whose debauched audacity disgraces our sex and the men who keep them company.[281]

How many of the petitions, the grievances known as *cahiers*, were as passionately feminist as this?

> But what means can one employ to establish an equilibrium between two sexes formed of the same clay, experiencing the same sensations, that the hand of the creator has made for one another, who worship the same god, and who obey the same sovereign? And why is it that the law is not the same for both? Why does one sex have everything and the other one nothing?[282]

What is striking about this anonymous French feminist is that she actually made a plea for political rights, for representation.

---

[280] "Madame de Beaumer, Editorial, Journal des Dames (March 1762)," *LIBERTY, EQUALITY, FRATERNITY: EXPLORING THE FRENCH REVOLUTION*, accessed August 19, 2020, https://revolution.chnm.org/items/show/392.

[281] "Petition of Women of the Third Estate to the King (1 January 1789)," *LIBERTY, EQUALITY, FRATERNITY: EXPLORING THE FRENCH REVOUTION*, accessed August 19, 2020, https://revolution.chnm.org/items/show/571.

[282] "A Woman's Cahier," *LIBERTY, EQUALITY, FRATERNITY: EXPLORING THE FRENCH REVOLUTION*, accessed August 19, 2020, https://revolution.chnm.org/items/show/272.

> We do not aspire to the honours of government, or to the advantages of being initiated to the secrets of ministries. But we believe that it is entirely equitable to allow women, widows or girls who possess land or other properties, to bring their grievances to the foot of the throne, and that it is also just to collect their votes, because they are obligated, just as are men, to pay the royal taxes and to fulfil the engagements of commerce.
> It may be alleged that all that would be possible to accord them, is to permit them to be represented by proxy, at the Estates-Generals.
> We reply that inasmuch as it has been demonstrated that a noble cannot be represented by a commoner [*roturier*], nor a commoner by a noble, by the same token a man cannot represent a woman. The representatives should have absolutely the same interests as those represented: therefore women should be represented only by women.[283]

As the legislative power changed in France between 1789 and 1804, so did the executive. At the outset, France intended to be a constitutional monarchy. In August 1789, therefore, a Declaration of the Rights of Man and the Citizen was drafted in which the very first word was 'Men' as in 'Men are born and remain free and equal in rights. Social distinctions can be founded only on the common good.'

This not very promising start prompted some sarcastic but heartfelt words in reply as we shall soon see. The men in charge of the Revolution were full of fine words which did little to alleviate the main concern of Parisian women which was how to buy bread to feed their families. Hearing rumours that the King and Queen and the deputies who made up the National Constituent Assembly were banqueting at the palace complex of Versailles, some 12 miles southwest of the centre of Paris where children were starving, the women resolved to march there and see for themselves.

On 6th October, with hardly any food, particularly bread, in the markets, they did what they had been talking about for months. When the now swollen mob arrived, they met sympathetic deputies, among whom was Maximilien Robespierre, and their representatives met the King who was similarly sympathetic and returned with the marchers to Paris. By his actions that day the King relinquished his prerogative of absolute power to veto any decrees proposed and agreed upon by the Assembly. He became answerable to God and his people not to God alone. The power of the patriarchy was exposed by the will of the people. What we forget about the March on Versailles was that its driving force was women and their desperation over not being able to carry out their assigned social role of producing and bringing up the next generation, a desperation almost entirely due to the failure of men to provide the means with which to do it, their assigned social role.

[283] Ibid.

Following the march the situation failed to improve despite the promises that had been made. The men continued to debate a constitution. From that period we have a copy of what women were thinking. Whether the same hint of sarcasm would have been possible had they been members of the Assembly is an unanswerable question. Although it is very feminist in tone and construction I sense that a man (*Condorcet?*) is behind its authorship. If so, he will deserve his place in the next chapter on the exceptional men who had the courage to advocate women's rights in the 18th and 19th centuries.

In its preamble, the proposal/petition exposes the elephant in the room that hosted the debate on equal rights in the 18th and early 19th century.

> What! you have generously decreed equality of rights for all individuals; you have made the humble inhabitant of the hovel march alongside the princes and lords of the earth. Thanks to your paternal solicitude the poor villager is no longer obliged to grovel before the proud seigneur of his parish; the unfortunate vassal can halt in his tracks the impetuous boar that piteously ravaged his crops; the timid soldier dares to complain when he is run down by the splendid coach of the superb publican; the modest priest can sit down in ease at the table of his most illustrious and most reverend superior;...the black African will no longer find himself compared to a stupid animal which, goaded by the prod of a fierce driver, irrigates our furrows with his sweat and blood. Talent, disengaged from the sorrowful confines of ignoble birth, can be developed with confidence, and he who possesses it will no longer be forced to bow and scrape to get the support of an imbecile protector, to burn incense to an ignorant Croesus and to "Monseigneur" a goat.
>
> At last, thanks to your good influence, a serene day will break above our heads, a new people, a people of citizens, wise and happy, will raise itself on the ruins of a barbarous people, and the stupefied earth will witness the birth upon its very bosom of this golden age, this time of good fortune that until now only existed in the fabulous descriptions of the poets.
>
> Ah! our masters! will we then be the only ones for whom the iron age will forever exist...? Will we be the only ones who will not participate in this astonishing regeneration that will renew the face of France and revive its youthfulness like that of the eagle?
>
> You have broken the sceptre of despotism; you have pronounced the beautiful axiom [that]...the French are a free people. Yet still you allow thirteen million slaves shamefully to wear the irons of thirteen million despots! You have defined the true equality of rights—and you still unjustly withhold them from the sweetest and most interesting half among you![284]...

[284] "Women's Petition to the National Assembly," *LIBERTY, EQUALITY, FRATERNITY: EXPLORING THE FRENCH REVOLUTION*, accessed August 20, 2020, https://revolution.chnm.org/items/show/273.

The letter then proposed these 10 articles:

> 1) All the privileges of the male sex are entirely and irrevocably abolished throughout France.
> 2) The feminine sex will always enjoy the same liberty, advantages, rights, and honours as does the masculine sex.
> 3) The masculine gender (*genre*) will no longer be regarded, even grammatically, as the more noble *genre,* given that all genders, all sexes, and all beings should be and are equally noble.
> 4) That no one will henceforth insert in acts, contracts, obligations, etc., this clause, so common but so insulting for women: *That the wife is authorised by her husband before those present,* because in the household both parties should enjoy the same power and authority.
> 5) That wearing breeches will no longer be the exclusive prerogative of the male sex, but each sex will have the right to wear them in turn.
> 6) When a soldier has, out of cowardice, compromised French honour, he will no longer be degraded as is the present custom, by making him wear women's clothing; but as the two sexes are and must be equally honourable in the eyes of humanity, he will henceforth be punished by declaring his gender to be neuter.
> 7) All persons of the feminine sex must be admitted without exception to the district and departmental assemblies, elevated to municipal responsibilities and even as deputies to the National Assembly, when they fulfil the requirements set forth in the electoral laws. They will have both consultative and deliberative voices…
> 8) They can also be appointed as Magistrates. There is no better way to reconcile the public with the courts of justice than to seat beauty and to see the graces presiding there.
> 9) The same applies to all positions, compensations, and military dignities. In this way the French will be truly invincible, when their courage is inspired by the joint themes of glory and love; we do not even make exception for the staff of a marshal of France; so that justice can be rendered equally, we order this instrument to be passed alternatively between men and women.
> 10) Nor do we hesitate to open the sanctuary to the feminine sex, which has so long rightly been referred to as the devoted sex. But since the piety of the faithful has noticeably diminished, said sex promises and obligates itself, when it mounts the chair of truth, to moderate its zeal and not make excessive demands on the attention of the audience.[285]

Freed from their historic, biblical even, obligation to be silent on political issues the quest for the holy grail of equality for women began to find its female voice. Unlike the petition writer above women writers of all sorts did not seek

---

[285] Ibid.

anonymity. With the help of the Roy Rosenzweig Centre we can look at the words of three of them although there were many more.

Etta Palm d'Aelders was a Dutch woman deserted by her husband who was a courtesan in Paris when the Bastille was invaded. She ran a salon, a high-class *Cercle* of politically minded people and dating agency, frequented by prominent revolutionaries such as Marat. On December 30, 1790, she addressed the National Convention in a *Discourse on the Injustice of the Laws in favour of Men, at the Expense of Women*. As well as salons the revolution saw the creation of political clubs for both sexes and even for women only. (This was not exclusively a revolutionary development. From 1771 William Almack, whom we met earlier, managed a club for both sexes in London where men and women were allowed to vote on admissions of both sexes.)

In Paris, the most famous club that admitted men and women was probably The Fraternal Society of Patriots of Both Sexes, Defenders of the Constitution (French: *La Société Fraternelle des Patriotes de l'un et l'autre sexe, Défenseurs de la Constitution*), founded in October 1790. The most famous of the women only clubs, The Society of Revolutionary and Republican Women (*Société des Citoyennes Républicaines Révolutionnaires, Société des républicaines révolutionnaires*), was founded in May 1793 by Pauline Leon and Claire Lacombe. It lasted about a year before it was banned by the Jacobins; *more of them later*.

The first club for both sexes, however, was the Confederation of the Friends of Truth and it was to one of its meetings Etta Palm d'Aelders made this extraordinary address encapsulating the feelings of women in a man's world that must have remained unsaid for hundreds of years.

> The prejudices with which our sex has been surrounded—supported by unjust laws which only accord us a secondary existence in society and which often force us into the humiliating necessity of winning over the cantankerous and ferocious character of a man, who, by the greed of those close to us has become our master—those prejudices have changed what was for us the sweetest and the most saintly of duties, those of wife and mother, into a painful and terrible slavery…
>
> Well! What could be more unjust! Our life, our liberty, our fortune are no longer ours; leaving childhood, turned over to a despot whom often the heart finds repulsive, the most beautiful days of our life slip away in moans and tears, while our fortune becomes prey to fraud and debauchery…
>
> Oh! Gentlemen, if you wish us to be enthusiastic about the happy constitution that gives back men their rights, then begin by being just toward us. From now on we should be your voluntary companions and not your slaves. Let us merit your attachment! Do you believe that the desire for success is less becoming to us, that a good name is less dear to us than to you? And if devotion to study, if patriotic zeal, if virtue itself, which rests so often on love of glory, is as natural to us as to you,

why do we not receive the same education and the same means to acquire them?

I will not speak, Gentlemen, of those iniquitous men who pretend that nothing can exempt us from an eternal subordination. Is this not an absurdity just like those told to the French on 15 July 1789: "Leave there your just demands; you are born for slavery; nothing can exempt you from eternally obeying an arbitrary will."[286]

Another feminine leading light, possibly founding member, of the Friends of Truth was Olympe de Gouges, the nom de plume of Marie Gouze, a petit bourgeois widow from southwestern France. Olympe was a human rights playwright and pamphleteer, a forerunner of internet bloggers or podcasters, rather than a public speaker like Etta. As such she made serious enemies within the patriarchy. Her abolitionist play, *l'Esclavage des Noirs,* was sabotaged by the slave-owning fraternity and when she turned her attention to equal rights for women she offended the Jacobin hegemony to such an extent that they executed her on 3 November 1793.

Other feminist figures such as Etta Palm D'Aelders, Pauline Leon, Claire Lacombe and Sophie de Condorcet at whose house the Friends of Truth met and whose husband, the Marquis de Condorcet, was guillotined just four months after Olympe, survived the Reign of Terror. It does not take much research to put ones finger on the reason for the harsh finality of Olympe's treatment.

The problem with the Declaration of the Rights of Man and the Citizen as far as Olympe de Gouges was concerned was that first word, 'Men'—*les hommes*, and that other word, 'Citizen'—*citoyen*. Any hope that these two words were being used as common gender nouns was dashed when citizens were split into two groups, active and passive. Active citizens paid taxes above a certain level and owned property above a certain value. Passive citizens—poor men, women, regardless of wealth, children, slaves and foreigners—had no political rights. Only about 1 in a 100 active citizens, the Electors, who were substantial property owners elected the National Convention of 1791.

Olympe penned an alternative Declaration of the Rights of Woman and the Female Citizen. It matched all 17 articles of the official version. As well as starting with the words '*La femme*', its Articles 6, 10 and 15 had powerful things to say about Equality in the process of making the law, Liberty in terms of Freedom of Speech and Fraternity of men and women taxpayers holding government to account.

1. Woman is born free and remains equal to man in rights. Social distinctions may be based only on common utility.

---

[286] "Etta Palm D'Aelders, "Discourse on the Injustice of the Laws in Favour of Men, at the Expense of Women" (30 December 1790)," *LIBERTY, EQUALITY, FRATERNITY: EXPLORING THE FRENCH REVOLUTION*, accessed August 21, 2020, https://revolution.chnm.org/items/show/387.

6. The law should be the expression of the general will. All citizenesses and citizens should take part, in person or by their representatives, in its formation. It must be the same for everyone. All citizenesses and citizens, being equal in its eyes, should be equally admissible to all public dignities, offices and employments, according to their ability, and with no other distinction than that of their virtues and talents.
10. No one should be disturbed for his fundamental opinions; woman has the right to mount the scaffold, so she should have the right equally to mount the rostrum, provided that these manifestations do not trouble public order as established by law.
15. The mass of women, joining with men in paying taxes, have the right to hold accountable every public agent of the administration.[287]

A year after Olympe de Gouges wrote her declaration of rights for women, an English female writer and educationist, Mary Wollstonecraft, wrote *A Vindication of the Rights of Woman.* Mary was a well-educated middle-class woman who had been making her own way in life since 1778 in the jobs available to a respectable, reasonably educated woman without a fortune at that time, lady's companion, governess, schoolteacher and author. After an unhappy relationship with the married artist, Henry Fuseli, she made her way to Paris to join in the Revolution and fight for equal rights for ordinary people, a political position which she had just defended in a powerful answer to Edmund Burke's surprising condemnation of the Revolution in his pamphlet, *Reflections on the Revolution in France*, in the form of a letter to him entitled *A Vindication of the Rights of Men.*

Charles-Maurice de Talleyrand-Perigord, Bishop of Autun, 1st Prince of Benevento, was the archetypal politician, the supreme swimmer with the tide who served royalty, republicans and dictators alike. To keep one's head, excuse the pun, in the turbulent times from 1789 to 1815 it helped to be a flexible thinker to say the least. When the National Convention asked him to compile a report on education in which he argued that women only required a domestic education as men were clearly created to deal with the stresses of public life, Mary, who had always advocated an education for girls that matched that of boys, felt obliged to reply or vindicate the principle of an equal right to an education. The ever-emollient Talleyrand had written:

> Let us bring up women, not to aspire to advantages which the Constitution denies them, but to know and appreciate those which it guarantees them…Men are destined to live on the stage of the world. A public education suits them: it early places before their eyes all the scenes of life: only the proportions are different. The paternal home is better for the education of women; they have less need to learn to deal

[287] "Olympe de Gouges, The Declaration of the Rights of Woman (September 1791)," *LIBERTY, EQUALITY, FRATERNITY: EXPLORING THE FRENCH REVOLUTION*, accessed August 24, 2020, revolution.chnm.org/items/show/557.

with the interests of others, than to accustom themselves to a calm and secluded life.[288]

In her introduction, however, Mary pointed out that he had expressed bewilderment at the exclusion of women from public life.

> "that to see one half of the human race excluded by the other from all participation of government, was a political phenomenon that, according to abstract principles, it was impossible to explain."[289]

There is a difference between a declaration and a vindication. The former is demanding, and the latter is reasoning. The Declaration of Rights that provided the power for the Revolution signified that the talk was over, and action was required. Olympe's quasi-parody is also a demand signifying the end of reasonable debate. Mary's vindications signify that she still felt the argument could be won if she could change the minds of men in power. The problem with that was that she was a woman and, therefore, not fit to even argue the point. Why did the bewildered Talleyrand not, at least, put the question?

The finest, most clear and most elegant statement of the case for women's rights did come from a man who, being a mathematician, had spent his life following premises through to their logical conclusion. Unfortunately, he was also a politician at a time when who you knew was more important than what you knew. Marie Jean Antoine Nicolas de Caritat, Marquis of Condorcet, was an egalitarian philosopher and distinguished mathematician. He was also a newspaperman. In 1790, he wrote an article entitled *De l'admission des femmes au droit de cité* ("For the Admission to the Rights of Citizenship For Women"). Blaming habit for men's denial of equal rights for women Condorcet puts forward an irrefutable logic for them that still reverberates today. Thanks to the Roy Rosenzweig Centre I can share the whole of this remarkable piece of writing with you.

> Habit can familiarise men with the violation of their natural rights to the point that among those who have lost them no one dreams of reclaiming them or believes that he has suffered an injustice.
> Some of these violations even escaped the philosophers and legislators when with the greatest zeal they turned their attention to establishing the common rights of the individuals of the human race and to making those rights the sole foundation of political institutions.
> For example, have they not all violated the principle of equality of rights by quietly depriving half of mankind of the right to participate in the formation of the laws, by excluding women from the rights of citizenship? Is there a stronger proof of the power of habit even among

288 en.wikipedia.org/wiki/A_Vindication_of_the_Rights_of_Woman. Accessed 27/08/2020.
289 Wollstonecraft, Mary. A Vindication of the Rights of Women. Kindle Edition.

enlightened men than seeing the principle of equality of rights invoked in favour of three or four hundred men deprived of their rights by an absurd prejudice [perhaps he is thinking of actors here] and at the same time forgetting those rights when it comes to twelve million women?
For this exclusion not to be an act of tyranny one would have to prove that the natural rights of women are not absolutely the same as those of men or show that they are not capable of exercising them. Now the rights of men follow only from the fact that they are feeling beings, capable of acquiring moral ideas and of reasoning about these ideas. Since women have the same qualities, they necessarily have equal rights. Either no individual in mankind has true rights, or all have the same ones; and whoever votes against the right of another, whatever be his religion, his colour, or his sex, has from that moment abjured his own rights.
It would be difficult to prove that women are incapable of exercising the rights of citizenship. Why should beings exposed to pregnancies and to passing indispositions not be able to exercise rights that no one ever imagined taking away from people who have gout every winter or who easily catch colds? Even granting a superiority of mind in men that is not the necessary consequence of the difference in education (which is far from being proved and which ought to be if women are to be deprived of a natural right without injustice), this superiority can consist in only two points.
It is said that no woman has made an important discovery in the sciences or given proof of genius in the arts, letters, etc. But certainly no one would presume to limit the rights of citizenship exclusively to men of genius. Some add that no woman has the same extent of knowledge or the same power of reasoning as certain men do; but what does this prove except that the class of very enlightened men is small? There is complete equality between women and the rest of men; if this little class of men were set aside, inferiority and superiority would be equally shared between the two sexes. Now since it would be completely absurd to limit the rights of citizenship and the eligibility for public offices to this superior class, why should women be excluded rather than those men who are inferior to a great number of women?
...It is said that women have never been guided by what is called reason despite much intelligence, wisdom, and a faculty for reasoning developed to the same degree as in subtle dialecticians. This observation is false: they have not conducted themselves, it is true, according to the reason of men but rather according to their own. Their interests not being the same due to the defects of the laws, the same things not having for them at all the same importance as for us, they can, without being unreasonable, determine their course of action according to other principles and work toward a different goal. It is as reasonable for a woman to occupy herself with the embellishment of her person as it was for Demosthenes [a Greek orator] to cultivate his voice and gestures.

> It is said that women, though better than men in that they are gentler, more sensitive, and less subject to the vices that follow from egotism and hard hearts, do not really possess a sense of justice; that they obey their feelings rather than their consciences. This observation is truer, but it proves nothing. It is not nature but rather education and social conditions that cause this difference. Neither the one nor the other has accustomed women to the idea of what is just, only to the idea of what is becoming or proper.
> Removed from public affairs, from everything that is decided according to the most rigorous idea of justice, or according to positive laws, they concern themselves with and act upon precisely those things which are regulated by natural propriety and by feeling. It is therefore unjust to advance as grounds for continuing to refuse women the enjoyment of their natural rights those reasons that only have some kind of reality because women do not enjoy these rights in the first place.
> If one admits such arguments against women, it would also be necessary to take away the rights of citizenship from that portion of the people who, having to work without respite, can neither acquire enlightenment nor exercise its reason, and soon little by little the only men who would be permitted to be citizens would be those who had followed a course in public law.
> ...It is natural for a woman to nurse her children, to care for them in their infancy; attached to her home by these cares, weaker than a man, it is also natural that she lead a more retiring, more domestic life. Women would therefore be in the same class with men who are obliged by their station or profession to work several hours a day. This may be a reason for not preferring them in elections, but it cannot be the grounds for their legal exclusion.
> ...I demand now that these arguments be refuted by other means than pleasantries or ranting; above all that someone show me a natural difference between men and women that can legitimately found [women's] exclusion from a right.[290]

Condorcet became fully engaged in writing a constitution for France's First Republic. This constitution was never voted in because of the events of late 1793 and the shift of power to Robespierre and the Jacobin faction who planned to adopt their own Constitution but this too was never implemented as Robespierre and the Committee of Public Safety instigated the so-called Reign of Terror. Neither of these constitutions gave any attention to women's right to vote or to hold public office.

The most extreme shift in perspective seems to have happened in Maximilien Robespierre, in power from the summer of 1793 effectively as a Deputy who had

[290] "Condorcet, "On the Admission of Women to the Rights of Citizenship," July 1790," *LIBERTY, EQUALITY, FRATERNITY: EXPLORING THE FRENCH REVOLUTION*, accessed August 27, 2020, revolution.chnm.org/items/show/558.

built up his revolutionary credentials on his opposition to royalty and class abuse, his opposition to the Catholic Church and the War with Austria, his championing of human rights, his opposition to the death penalty and his welcoming of the Women's March on Versailles. Women were an important component of his personal power base. In 1783, he had championed the inclusion of women in Academies and when President of the Academie of Arras he welcomed the membership of the woman writer, Louise-Félicité de Kéralio. When addressing the Convention in 1792, as his power was growing, Wikipedia tells us:

> As his opponents knew well, Robespierre had a strong base of support among the women of Paris. John Moore (Scottish physician) was sitting in the galleries and noted that the audience was 'almost entirely filled with women'. He is a priest who has his devotees but it is evident that all of his power lies in the distaff. Robespierre tried to appeal to women because in the early days of the Revolution when he had tried to appeal to men, he had failed.[291]

Robespierre and his friend and frequent mouthpiece, Louis Antoine de St Just, chose, at some stage in 1792, to eliminate 'enemies of the Revolution', moderate Girondins on one side and ultra-Radical Cordeliers on the other. Both of these men were blindly committed to the ideology of a perfect republican society which was all-inclusive, based on merit not bloodline, and in which sovereignty would rest with the General Will. However, before this could be achieved the revolutionary government would have to eliminate any possibility of a monarchy or a military dictatorship prompted by widespread unrest amongst the poor spilling over into anarchy and violence.

> What we need is a single will (*il faut une volonté une*). It must be either republican or royalist. If it is to be republican, we must have republican ministers, republican newspapers, republican deputies, a republican government. The internal dangers come from the middle classes; to defeat the middle classes we must rally the people. … The people must ally itself with the Convention, and the Convention must make use of the people.[292]

One radical solution that might have worked would have been the enfranchisement of women but, although he introduced universal male suffrage, this was never considered and the typical male response of terrorising the population into becoming Republicans was preferred. One of St Just's most memorable sayings was "a nation generates itself only upon heaps of corpses". Robespierre's justification of his volte face on capital punishment was as follows:

---

[291] en.wikipedia.org/wiki/Maximilien_Robespierre. Accessed 28/08/2020.
[292] Ibid.

> If the basis of popular government in peacetime is virtue, the basis of popular government during a revolution is both virtue and terror; virtue, without which terror is baneful; terror, without which virtue is powerless. Terror is nothing more than speedy, severe and inflexible justice; it is thus an emanation of virtue; it is less a principle in itself, than a consequence of the general principle of democracy, applied to the most pressing needs of the *patrie* [homeland, fatherland].[293]

During the Reign of Terror, some 17000 people died, many executed on trumped up charges of treason. It was a capital offence to suggest in any way a return to the monarchy. At the beginning of his U-turn in 1792 Robespierre famously made it known. "With regret, I pronounce this fatal truth: Louis must die so that the nation may live." Condorcet fully agreed that the King had betrayed his people but opposed the death penalty. In October along with 21 other Girondin leaders he was proscribed. He escaped the guillotine and went into hiding. He was caught and imprisoned in late March 1793. He was found dead in his cell two days later. Olympe de Gouges disillusioned with the direction that the Revolution was taking also opposed the King's execution, maintaining, unlike the 'new' Robespierre, her moral objection to capital punishment and arguing that he was guilty of being a bad king but not a bad man. In November 1793, she was executed for suggesting that the French people should choose whether they wanted a Republic, a Federation or a Constitutional Monarchy.

When it came to being a political male faced with the 'Woman Question', Revolutionary Man, courting the working classes with promises of universal suffrage, seemed as reticent over women's political rights as aristocratic or middle-class man. Whatever the rationale, the part-time participation in public life of a child-bearing woman or the rarity of female property ownership were two more considered reasons why men opposed, ignored or prevaricated over the idea.

If we set aside the 'reasons' put forward, we are left with the spiritual arguments arising from Catholic dogma or Protestant acceptance of biblical truth both of which we have already explored at great length—bearing in mind that atheism was a strong thread in the patchwork of revolutionary thinking. If we further set aside Reason and God, the intellect and the soul, we are left with emotion, the heart. Was it hatred, fear, distrust or disdain, greed, lust, arrogance, self-delusion or instinct?

One of Robespierre's most memorable statements was this oxymoron:

> The government in a revolution is the despotism of liberty against tyranny.

---

293 Ibid.

His spirit was shown in this abolitionist declaration:

> Ask a merchant of human flesh what is property; he will answer by showing you that long coffin he calls a ship… Ask a gentleman [the same] who has lands and vassals… and he will give you almost the identical ideas.[294]

His tyrannical/libertarian regime did sweep away feudalism, did abolish slavery, did promote religious toleration, including recognition of the importance of Jews to the revolutionary society he was creating, but did not liberate half of the population of France who, by at least one account, adored him. Shortly after Olympe had been executed:

> Pierre Gaspard Chaumette cautioned a group of women wearing Phrygian bonnets, reminding them of "the impudent Olympe de Gouges, who was the first woman to start up women's political clubs, who abandoned the cares of her home, to meddle in the affairs of the Republic, and whose head fell under avenging blade of the law".[295]

Chaumette, an ultra-radical who was executed on 13 April 1794 as a counter-revolutionary and who had many enemies due to his anti-Christian views, could not, surely, have been basing his assessment of women as 'impudent' and 'meddlers' on any scripture advocating that women should know their place. Nevertheless, women's political clubs were banned and although Olympe had not played any part in the Society of Republican Women those who had, Leon and Lacombe, were silenced.

Five days after Olympe's execution another prominent Girondin woman, Mme Roland, a middle-class Parisian version of Georgiana Cavendish, was guillotined.

> *Le Moniteur Universel* wrote disapprovingly that Madame Roland had gone to her death with 'ironic gaiety' and stated that like Marie Antoinette and the feminist Olympe de Gouges, she had been put to death because she had crossed the "boundaries of female virtue."[296]

The day after Olympe's execution, Wikipedia tells us that an anonymous Parisian wrote this:

---

[294] en.wikipedia.org/wiki/Maximilien_Robespierre. Accessed 30/08/2020.
[295] en.wikipedia.org/wiki/Olympe_de_Gouges. Accessed 30/08/2020.
[296] en.wikipedia.org/wiki/Madame_Roland. Accessed 30/08/2020.

"Yesterday, at seven o'clock in the evening, a most extraordinary person called Olympe de Gouges who held the imposing title of woman of letters, was taken to the scaffold, while all of Paris, while admiring her beauty, knew that she didn't even know her alphabet...[297]

Mary Wollstonecraft, herself the victim of male indifference from her American lover, Gilbert Imlay, and struggling to bring up their child, Fanny, in the coldest winter in Paris on record, concern about the death toll from which not only replaced the memory of the Terreur but also the Girondin backlash after the execution of Robespierre on 28 July 1794, started to reflect on the Revolution that she had hoped would change the fortunes of women forever. The final words of Volume 1 of *An Historical and Moral View of the Origin and Progress of the French Revolution and the Effect it Has Produced in Europe* show the disillusion that all idealistic sentimentalists feel when the reality of power changes a moral, ethical, humane even, group of political hopefuls into a ruthless pack of expediency driven individuals for whom human rights must be sacrificed on the altar of the need to 'govern'.

> Let us cast our eyes over the history of man, and we shall scarcely find a page that is not tarnished by some foul deed, or bloody transaction. Let us examine the catalogue of the vices of men in a savage state and contrast them with those of men civilised; we shall find that a barbarian, considered as a moral being, is an angel, compared with the refined villain of artificial life. Let us investigate the causes which have produced this degeneracy, and we shall discover, that they are those unjust plans of government, which have been formed by peculiar circumstances in every part of the globe.
>
> Then let us coolly and impartially contemplate the improvements, which are gaining ground in the formation of principles of policy; and I flatter myself it will be allowed by every humane and considerate being, that a political system more simple than has hitherto existed would effectually check those aspiring follies, which, by imitation, leading to vice, have banished from governments the very shadow of justice and magnanimity.
>
> **Thus had France grown up and sickened on the corruption of a state diseased.[298]** [my emphasis]

She returned to England in April 1795 ostensibly to find Imlay. In May she took an overdose. Rejected by Imlay and her failure to win him back with a highly risky visit to Scandinavia to help him to recoup some of his business losses she attempted suicide again by throwing herself into the Thames. Again

---

297 en.wikipedia.org/wiki/Olympe_de_Gouges. Accessed 30/08/2020.

298 Mary Wollstonecraft, An Historical and Moral View of the Origin and Progress of the French Revolution and the Effect it Has Produced in Europe (London: J. Johnson, 1795). 31/08/2020. <https://oll.libertyfund.org/titles/226>

she was rescued. Just as she found happiness with her long-time friend, William Godwin, she suffered the fate of so many women; 11 days after giving birth to her second daughter, the future Mary Shelley, she died of septicaemia on 10 September 1797. Even she, proto feminist that she was, was capable of a U-turn. Having written two novels in which marriage was seen as an unwelcome trap for a woman, she married a man, whose anarchist philosophy also eschewed marriage, to ensure the legitimacy of their daughter in the patriarchal world neither she nor the Revolution upon which she had pinned her hopes could seem to change.

Was there ever a better time and place to grant political rights to women than Paris the 1790s? Yet, it did not happen. The voice was there, the carrot was there (whether you see it as the sexual allure of a Georgiana, Etta, Olympe or Mary, or the voting potential of women to achieve other politically levelling policies) and the stick was there as demonstrated by the Women's March on Versailles that ended the divine untouchability of a God appointed monarch. Interestingly, just days after Mary left for London in April 1795 two further such starvation-inspired marches took place led by desperate women, but both were met by the unanimity of resolute deputies and the women returned home to suffer their fate in political silence.

Why did it not happen in Britain? The simple answer is Repression. In 1794-5, three Acts were passed suspending Habeas Corpus with *An act to empower his Majesty to secure and detain such persons as his Majesty shall suspect are conspiring against his person and government* and prosecuting seditious speech, writing and meetings under the Treason and the Seditious Practices Acts of 1795. Any talk of reform or rights was officially opposed, disapproved of or banned and, when necessary, punished.

By the end of the 18th century, Condorcet, Robespierre, De Gouges and Wollstonecraft had gone, Leon and Lacombe had passed into obscurity and reform and rights were off the menu. For millions of poor and/or female people the political hope, on both sides of La Manche, of attaining Life, Liberty and the Pursuit of Happiness or its peculiarly Jacobin alternative, Liberty, Equality, Fraternity, was cryogenically entombed. There was, however, another route to find the holy grail of equal rights the story of which we will explore in the next chapter. It had to do with love, the realisation that justice required both sense and sensibility, reason and empathy, intellect and emotion, the head and the heart.

Chapter 37
Motherhood

No woman can call herself free who does not own and control her body. No woman can call herself free until she can choose consciously whether she will or will not be a mother.
– Margaret Sanger

Then she had been a fiancée, a young wife, and a mother, and she had discovered that these words were far too small ever to contain the experience.
– Kim Edwards, *The Memory Keeper's Daughter*

She had married a man she did not love; whom she did not profess to love; for certain advantages—to avoid certain pressing miseries.
– Caroline Norton, *Stuart of Dunleath*

Preamble

Etta Palm D'Aelders, Olympe de Gouges and Mary Wollstonecraft, other than their gender, had two things in common with each other and one in common with Georgiana Cavendish and Mary Bowes. All five, like many thousands of women then and now, had unhappy relationships with men which allows any critic of their feminism to question their subjectivity. What the three writers shared was their middle classness. They were educated but had to work for a living. Mostly barred from the professions—schooling of young children did provide a living for some women, as it did for Mary before she went to France, but medicine, the law, the clergy and the armed and civil services were strictly men only—the arts and writing afforded a paid job to those who were good enough, independent of men and free from dependence on sexual interactions with men, consummated or otherwise.

On the one hand, in aristocratic circles at least, the 18th century saw the growing power over men of women's sexuality. On the other hand, in middle class circles, the growing power of women's voice in their literature where their fictional writing in novels such as Evelina *by* Fanny Burney *and* The Mysteries of Udolpho *by Ann Radcliffe or the poetry of Mary Wollstonecraft showed the importance of 'sensibility' or feeling in relationships. This spilled over into their non-fictional writing on current affairs or philosophical propositions and, according to many male critics, made them irrational and unfit commentators on public life which many more conservative public figures thought required a male willingness to put ends before means and the objective ruthlessness to formulate and carry out policies for the public good. However, the working-class women who marched to Versailles in October 1789 wielded the most powerful weapon of the female human being, motherhood.*

The whole purpose of the patriarchy was to have children, sons to hold and expand the patrimony and daughters to strengthen and, hopefully, expand it via advantageous marriages. Men could not be fathers without women to be mothers. The liberation of the mother through education required men to change, to adapt. The behaviour of women in the late 18th century brought men to a crossroads. In one direction lay the continuation of the tried and tested response of repression, in the other, the recognition of a woman as a fellow being with the same inherent natural rights as a man who should, out of a previously denied male sensibility, have the same civil rights as himself.

For women, two campaign routes also were open to them, the gentler favoured by Mary Wollstonecraft of persuasion and placing the burden on men to change and grant the absent rights to women or the more strident favoured by Olympe de Gouges of wrenching their rights from reluctant men by whatever means. The story of both approaches will appear in this chapter, but, with regard to the latter, I will not be going deeply into the Suffragette movement, simply because there are hundreds of historians and social commentators far more knowledgeable and qualified than me to tell its story.

159 years and 3 months after the adoption of the Declaration of the Rights of Man and the Citizen on 26 August 1789, coincidentally also in Paris, the United Nations General Assembly adopted the Universal Declaration of Human Rights on 10 December 1948. Of the 26 Articles of rights, these three were most definitely shirked as the initial revolutionary idealism of 1789 was repressed.

> **Article 16**
> (1) Men and women of full age, without any limitation due to race, nationality or religion, have the right to marry and to found a family. They are entitled to equal rights as to marriage, during marriage and at its dissolution.
> (2) Marriage shall be entered into only with the free and full consent of the intending spouses.
> (3) The family is the natural and fundamental group unit of society and is entitled to protection by society and the State.
>
> **Article 21**
> (1) Everyone has the right to take part in the government of his country, directly or through freely chosen representatives.
> (2) Everyone has the right of equal access to public service in his country.
> (3) The will of the people shall be the basis of the authority of government; this will shall be expressed in periodic and genuine

elections which shall be by universal and equal suffrage and shall be held by secret vote or by equivalent free voting procedures.

Article 23

(1) Everyone has the right to work, to free choice of employment, to just and favourable conditions of work and to protection against unemployment.

(2) Everyone, without any discrimination, has the right to equal pay for equal work.

(3) Everyone who works has the right to just and favourable remuneration ensuring for himself and his family an existence worthy of human dignity, and supplemented, if necessary, by other means of social protection.

(4) Everyone has the right to form and to join trade unions for the protection of his interests.[299]

We might call these groups, marital rights, political rights and workers' rights. For the latter two groups dealt with by Articles 21 and 23, the initial fight was for inclusiveness—hence the regular use of 'everybody'—which only over time involved gender equality; the husbands of the women marchers of 1789 were no more likely to be enfranchised or adequately remunerated than their wives. Class, property, poverty, nationality, religion and colour as triggers for discrimination came before gender. It is important to remember that two underlying principles, the right of life and equity before the Law, were, despite the efforts of lawyers like Lord Mansfield and a handful of social reformers like Jeremy Bentham (decriminalisation of homosexuality; abolition of capital and physical punishment and slavery; animal rights), Samuel Romilly (abolition of capital punishment and slavery) and William Wilberforce (abolition of slavery), far from being understood as essential human rights.

In 1800, over 220 crimes were punishable by death, including sodomy, slavery was still instrumental in wealth creation in Britain and cockfighting, dogfighting, bull and bear baiting still occurred and were not illegal—And women could not vote, hold public office, divorce, have their own property if married or have contact with their children if separated.

Ironically, the rights of animals received parliamentary and legal attention in 1822 with The Cruel Treatment of Cattle Act and the 1835 Cruelty to Animals Act which banned cockfighting and dogfighting long before The Custody of Infants Act, 1839, The Matrimonial Causes Act, 1857, or the Married Women's Property Act, 1870. The Slave Trade Act, 1807, and The Abolition of Slavery Act, 1833, ended slavery in the British Empire. The 1823 Judgement of Death Act and its successor in 1832 drastically reduced the number of executions and offences that demanded execution were reduced to five by 1861.

The movement for Parliamentary Reform meanwhile came to a climax with The Great Reform Act of 1832 which, by stipulating that the reformed suffrage

[299] www.un.org/en/universal-declaration-human-rights/index.html. Accessed 04/09/2020.

was for 'male persons' (When John Stuart Mill proposed the replacement of the words 'man' and 'men' by 'person' and 'persons' it caused great amusement in parliament.), enshrined in law the exclusion of women from voting just because they were women. In 1848, the French Republic declared universal male suffrage, 70 years before Britain, but gave women the vote in 1944, 16 years after Great Britain.

Incidentally, the first true recognition of the equality of women in their full participation in the political process did not occur until the Grand Duchy of Finland, an autonomous state within the Russian Empire, after the assassination of the universally unpopular Governor General, Nikolay Bobrikov in 1904, took advantage of the distraction provided by the Russo-Japanese War in 1905, to arrange an election in which women could not only vote but also stand as candidates; 19 were elected—by contrast, Liechtenstein did not give women the vote until 1984. It should be remembered that women were allowed to vote in New Zealand in 1893 but not become MPs. In Southern Australia only non-aboriginal women were allowed to vote from 1894.

One could examine at length the reasons or hypotheses as to why the cause of women's rights took so long to gain some truly significant momentum. I will look at two in this chapter.

Firstly, if we look at the abolitionist cause, we see a significant set of circumstances coming together. There was widespread support among all classes, among both genders and in all regions of the nation; Josiah Wedgewood and Henry Thornton (entrepreneurs), James Ramsay from Scotland, William Wilberforce from Hull and Samuel Bowly from Gloucester, Anglicans like The Clapham Set and Hannah Moore, John Wesley, Benjamin Lay, the Quaker Dwarf, aristocrats like Charles Grey, Lord Howick and Selina Hastings, Countess of Huntingdon, women writers like Mary Wollstonecraft and Harriet Martineau and, last but not least, the black writers and speakers, former slaves, Ignatius Sancho, Uttobah Cugoano and Olaudah Equiano, are just a few examples.

There was a national organisation of campaigns, conferences and discussions, pamphleteering, petitioning and public meetings, even a new country, Sierra Leone, by people such as Thomas Clarkson (The Society for Effecting the Abolition of the Slave Trade and The Society for the Mitigation and Gradual Abolition of Slavery) and Granville Sharp and local organisations such as the Chelmsford Ladies Anti-Slavery Association.[300] There was access to the legislature via Wilberforce, leader of the 'Saints', 35-40 abolitionist MPs, and Grey, Foreign Secretary in the Ministry of All the Talents which outlawed the Slave Trade and Prime Minister when slavery was ended throughout the British Empire. Finally, there was a pressing moral, Christian imperative to this cause which drove other causes such as the employment and education of women

---

[300] en.wikipedia.org/wiki/Abolitionism in the United Kingdom. Accessed 08/09/2020.

and children and which had prevented the common law of the Anglo-Norman era from ever enshrining the ownership of one individual by another.

In 300 words or so, I can encapsulate the impact of the abolitionist movement in Britain, an historical episode of which I was totally ignorant throughout my character forming years, whereas doing the same summary of the cause of women's rights would necessarily take us to the suffragette era some 50 years later with the formation of the National Society for Women's Suffrage in 1872. Why? In answering this question one can only offer an opinion and that can be moderately or passionately expressed. It is still only an opinion. The rationale for the opinion needs, for credibility and persuasiveness, to be based on facts which will be subjectively chosen by the author.

To assert its moral 'rightness' requires a sensibility, a spiritual and emotional certainty, which may only apply to a limited range of perceived injustices. To see the rightness of one cause and be blind to the wrongness of another, although, with hindsight, they appear to have stemmed from the same spiritual and moral fundamental, is a behaviour difficult to understand and easy to condemn.

In 1800, as we have seen, the Declaration of Independence of the newly created USA, written by the slave-owning Thomas Jefferson, introduced the idea that the right to life should be the right to 'happy' life, the liberty to pursue happiness, and that the people had a right to overturn a government that did not provide a safe legal environment to promote that liberty. Happiness is hard to define because it is highly variable and highly individual. Equality is more straight forward since it is measurable and definable. Equal is 'the same'. There are no comparatives. One cannot be more equal or less equal, but one can be more happy or less happy.

As no human being is the same as any other human being, all a government can do is provide laws which give one person an equal opportunity to pursue their happiness in the same way and to the same extent as any other and for that to happen the Law must be the same for everyone. Once one accepts equal opportunity and equal treatment under the law of the land then anything other than that is 'unjust', and injustice is a major obstacle to the pursuit of happiness. In a race one cannot guarantee a dead heat finish for all those who run it only an equal start. The Declaration of Independence made it clear when the race started—'All men are created equal'.

The force of the abolition campaign came from the acceptance that slaves were human beings and should be treated as such. Their treatment as human beings was inhuman. Even after the 1833 Act they were not equal to most white labourers throughout the Empire. Many of them were "freed" to be indentured labourers, a work contract now banned due to its resemblance to slavery, only gaining their freedom after a contracted period of employment, frequently unpaid. Slaves were not freed in the land where men were all created equal until 18th December 1865 and given full civil rights a century later.

Furthermore, the millions spent to lessen the pain and soften the economic and social blow to two centuries of habitual abuse went to compensate wealthy slave owners for their loss of profit (Sir John Gladstone, father of the future Liberal prime minister, according to Wikipedia, received £106769 for his 2508 slaves, worth £10.2 million in 2020 based on inflation, and £544.5 million in 2020 based on share of GDP) not to the former slaves for the criminal wrongs they had suffered of kidnap, false imprisonment, rape, torture and physical assault none of which would be allowed to go unpunished in white, Western European, Christian culture at the time.

For instance, on 5 May 1760, Laurence Shirley, 4th Earl of Ferrers, was hung at Tyburn for shooting his steward in a drunken rage but 17 years later the owners of the *Zong* a slave ship whose master threw overboard more than 130 African slaves were only tried for insurance fraud. The former was hailed as a triumph of the equality of the law.

Therefore, the moral imperative to recognise the humanity of black slaves was not generally matched by the morality of the cultural aftermath. As the first huge step towards the recognition of equal rights, however, it was a process flawed by human weaknesses but upheld by the law of the land. It was arguably the first successful campaign for human rights reform enforceable by law and certainly encouraged similar campaigns for political and workers' rights which, sadly, had similarly flawed progress outcomes.

Many reformers at the turn of the 19th century embraced the full repertoire of demands for rights, therefore, I must assume that the debates on the human rights of black African slaves must have triggered the Woman Question and a more than passing consideration of the equity under British common law, reinforced by judgements of the courts, with regard to human beings whose only differences were the exotic origins of their place of birth and the colour of their skin. If a woman were different to a man and her anatomical ability to grow a foetus, give birth to a baby and nourish an infant, not forgetting her physical disadvantage when it came to heavy labour, made her look, behave and function differently, how could that make her, as a wife, a mother and a daughter, even a sex worker, any less a human being?

If laws could be passed to make it compulsory for any legal proceedings to treat all humans fairly, including those of a different colour, by recognising their right to 'life, liberty and the pursuit of happiness' why were women not recognised as legal individuals and *citoyennes*? Even the 1801 constitution of the newly created Haitian Republic, although it recognised the equal rights of all races, did not give women any role in the law-making process.

Lady Anne Clifford did not seek political rights. She was seeking the rights of a property owner and inheritor who fulfilled every qualifying circumstance to be so except for her gender. Lady Mary Bowes was not seeking a change in the marital status of husband and wife but that the law would recognise her right to separate from her husband to pursue her happiness by escaping his abuse and returning her property rights which were her only source of income. Lady Georgiana Cavendish asked a far more fundamental moral/legal question of her marriage, i.e., why should a wife's behaviour in her pursuit of happiness by escaping the restraints of an arranged marriage with her outré sexual behaviour be different from that of her husband and negate her rights as a mother to have access to her children who in law 'belonged' to the father?

In her political activism, she was not seeking a parliamentary role, or even some sort of franchise, but asserting her intellectual, interpersonal and organisational suitability to take an 'active' interest in the world of party politics. Apart from her gender she was no different from her male friends and lovers, politicians all. Lady Georgiana and her sister campaigned for the Whigs, for Charles James Fox, a person not a principle. The women of the Revolution were campaigning for political rights and equity before the law on the simple principle that as human beings living under the government of France, no less productive and no less patriotic than most French men, they were entitled to play a part in the process that defined their happiness or far more basically was supposed to put bread into their children's empty stomachs.

Their campaign foundered on the rocks of male supremacy, even in a regime whose mantra was Liberty, Equality, Fraternity and political expediency. When Henry Hunt MP presented a petition on behalf of Mary Smith, a wealthy Yorkshire spinster who paid taxes, to the 1832 Reform parliament, it caused some 'risibility' and sexist innuendo from Tory MP, Sir Frederick Trench, about mixed juries staying up together in a candlelit room. The example of campaigning for a principle, however, was now set. 'Orator' Hunt was a campaigner for universal suffrage and workers' rights who clearly, as did George Fox, the Quaker, wanted to include women in his movement but did not specifically campaign for women's rights.

Our fourth failed marriage kickstarted or put it into second gear both a campaigning spirit and a shift in the sensibility of male thinking that brought about a change in the law, not by the risible suggestion of women having any role in politics but by the recognition by men of their natural rights as mothers and wives. Until 1919, remember, these key laws were made by men.

On 30 May 1827, the 19-year-old Caroline Elizabeth Sarah Sheridan married the 27-year-old George Chapple Norton, recently elected Tory MP for Guildford. She was the granddaughter of the playwright and Whig politician Richard Brinsley Sheridan and the beautiful opera singer Elizabeth Ann Linley. He was the grandson of Sir 'Bullface Doublefee', Sir Fletcher Norton, Baron Grantley, a Tory Attorney-General, Solicitor General and Speaker of the Commons in the time of Lord North and much mocked, one could say despised, especially by the Whigs, for his legal success and his ability to acquire jobs from the government. Whether he used this or not for his son, also named Fletcher, he was lampooned as a pampered sinecurist when he became baron of the exchequer in Scotland.

If we seek the answers to why such an unsuitable match between a Whig scion and a dyed in the wool Tory, between a lively and talented literary figure with writing in her blood and a lazy, failed lawyer and politician, between a penniless woman with earning potential and a penniless gentleman with no earning skills whatsoever, between the 'Byron of Poetesses' (A tribute from

Henry Nelson Coleridge, son of Samuel Taylor Coleridge) and 'Late George Norton' (From an anecdote in Jane Grey Perkins' 1909 biography of Caroline Norton) we find the sad story of many a married woman's unhappiness not only at being unable to pursue her own happiness but also at having any hope of it blighted by the cruel, neglectful or indifferent treatment of her by her husband.

Caroline had definitely drawn the short straw, so much so it is difficult to say why but it smacks of a touch of desperation on her mother's part. Thomas Sheridan had married Caroline Henrietta Callander. She was from a respectable Scottish family of landed gentry with connections to Irish nobility. Tom, as he was known in theatrical circles, began to suffer, like his mother before him and his eldest son after him, from tuberculosis. He moved to the Cape of Good Hope but died there in September 1817 leaving only a small pension for his widow and seven children.

After their return to England in 1818, due to her father-in-law's royal connections she and her family were able to live rent-free in a grace and favour apartment in Hampton Court Palace. The only sketch of Caroline Callander's character is from a letter written by Matthew Lewis, author of the 18th century blockbuster, *The Monk*:

> "Mrs T. Sheridan is very pretty, very sensible, amiable, and gentle; indeed so gentle that Tom insists upon it, that her extreme quietness and tranquillity is a defect in her character. Above all, he accuses her of such an extreme apprehension of giving trouble (he says) it amounts to absolute affectation".[301]

Caroline Henrietta died in June 1851. Of her 4 sons, Thomas, Francis, Richard and Charles, only Richard went on to achieve any public distinction. According to <thepeerage.com>, Thomas died on active service in the navy the year before his sister's marriage, Francis died in 1843 possibly in Mauritius and Charles died in 1847 in Paris of the family curse of tuberculosis. Richard was a long serving Dorsetshire MP and Deputy Lieutenant of that county. Like Mrs. Bennet in *Pride and Prejudice* Mrs T. Sheridan's main worry would have been her three daughters, Helen Selina, Caroline Elizabeth Sarah and Jane Georgiana. As soon as they were of marriageable age she allowed them 'out' into Society. Here is an example of the impression they made, albeit after they were all married. Fanny Kemble, a noted actor and writer who was herself to suffer from a marriage that turned sour for all the usual reasons made this observation.

> … the mother of the Graces was there, more beautiful than anybody but her daughters; Lady Grahame, their beautiful aunt; Mrs. Norton, Mrs. Blackwood (Lady Dufferin), Georgiana Sheridan—(Duchess of Somerset and queen of beauty by universal consent), and Charles Sheridan, their younger brother, a sort of younger brother of the Apollo

[301] en.wikipedia.org/wiki/Caroline_Henrietta_Sheridan. Accessed 18/09/2020.

> Belvidere. Certainly, I never saw such a bunch of beautiful creatures all growing on one stem. I remarked it to Mrs. Norton, who looked complacently round her tiny drawing-room and said, "Yes, we are rather good-looking people."[302]

In 1824, the 17-year-old Helen, became engaged to naval Captain Price Blackwood, son of the Irish Baron Dufferin and Claneboye. Despite the opposition of his family who hoped for a more financially advantageous marriage they married the following year. They went to Florence to avoid the Blackwood family's disapproval. In 1839 she became the Baroness. In 1830, the youngest and universally acclaimed as the prettiest of the sisters, Georgiana, married the devoted Edward Adolphus Seymour, heir to the Dukedom of Somerset, with the blessing of his father but not, it seems his brother. They fell out when his brother allegedly insulted Georgiana calling her "low-bred greedy beggar woman, whose sole object was to get her hands on the property and leave it away from the direct heirs."[303]

She became the Duchess of Somerset in 1855.

Whether she was a social climber or not, Mrs T. Sheridan was able to use her daughters' good looks and education and the social and political connections of their grandfather to obtain for them a husband above their station. Why then did she push her middle daughter into marrying:

> …a briefless barrister of about 25, well made, though not tall, good looking, and with a fine ruddy complexion; but rather slow and lazy, and late for everything, till he at last gained the cognomen … of the "late George Norton"?[304]

There are hints here and there that George deceived her about his financial prospects. There are further allusions to the bullying nature of his family, certainly those of his grandfather, Sir Bullface Doublefee, and we have at least one reference to her desire to please and not cause an upset. Beautiful and clever her middle daughter may have been, with many admirers, but as far as we know there were no offers of marriage on the table other than that made by a younger son smitten by her beauty as a schoolgirl of 15. Taking a more romantic, Austen-like perspective it is possible that Caroline saw no hope of meeting her Mr Knightley who famously said to Emma, "Men of sense, whatever you may choose to say, do not want silly wives", and took the pragmatic approach in choosing one that would not be an intellectual threat. Looking at all the possibilities, the most likely reason is filial duty, i.e., to help out her mother. In Howard Spencer's biography of George, he writes:

---

302 www.victorianweb.org/authors/norton/biography.htm. Accessed 19/09/2020.

303 en.wikipedia.org/wiki/Edward_St_Maur,_11th_Duke_of_Somerset. Accessed 19/09/2020.

304 www.historyofparliamentonline.org/volume/1820-1832/member/norton-hon-george-1800-1875. Accessed 19/09/2020.

> In 1830, Georgiana Ellis wrote that if Caroline 'were not conceited and affected, she would be a very delightful as well as a very singular person', and noted how in her conversational sallies, 'her poor husband is constantly brought in, in a very ridiculous manner'.[305]

Lady Holland, the formidable wife of Charles James Fox's favourite nephew, Henry, later commented on 'the somewhat indelicate and unguarded language and manners of Mrs. Norton'[306] .

For whatever reason, this July wedding did not bode well for Caroline's future pursuit of happiness. Jane Grey Perkins summed it up with the succinctness and clarity of hindsight.

> She, gifted, impetuous, stormy-tempered, with a reckless, specious tongue, with an instinct for taking the lead and getting possession of everything around her: magnanimous and generous, incapable of hoarding injuries and paying back old scores when once the first ungovernable outburst of resentment against them had subsided; and he that dangerous mixture which is often found in dull natures, weak but excessively obstinate and suspicious when he thought he was being led, narrow-spirited, intolerant, slow-witted, yet not silent; rather with a certain power of nagging comment for everything about him that he was least able to understand; not without surface kindness and humanity, fond of children and animals, but coarse natured and self-indulgent, with a capacity for cruelty and brutality and slow revenge, when once convinced he had been aggrieved, so unlike any quality possessed by his wife that it seemed to confuse and stun her like a blow when she found herself opposed to it.[307]
>
> *Perhaps a word of caution is needed on this assessment of the mismatch. Jane Grey Perkins was the pen name of the noted American suffragist Alice Jane Gray Perkins. Her book, The Life of the Honourable Mrs Norton, can be found on the invaluable website <archive.org>.*
>
> The fact that she bore him 3 sons, Fletcher in 1829, Thomas in 1831 and William in 1833 brought no softening in the hard bitterness between them. In fact, Caroline revealed after their separation that she was subjected to violent mistreatment 'from the earliest period of our marriage … such as is brought before the police courts'[308].

George's mother-in-law used her connections to get him a job as a bankruptcy commissioner which enabled the couple to get a house in Birdcage

305 www.historyofparliamentonline.org/volume/1820-1832/member/norton-hon-george-1800-1875. Accessed 20/09/2020.

306 Ibid.

307 Perkins, Jane Grey. *The Life of Mrs. Norton*. London: John Murray, 1909.

308 www.historyofparliamentonline.org/volume/1820-1832/member/norton-hon-george-1800–1875. Accessed 20/09/2020.

Walk to which many of the great and good from the world of literature and politics, mostly Whigs, frequently repaired despite its rather small reception room. By using his wife's connections George hoped to find advancement. He was already claiming the earnings Caroline had from her writing. However, he was no more successful in politics than he was in the legal profession. In the 1830 General Election he failed to hold on to Guildford, losing out to 2 other Tory candidates. Caroline was not amused. She wrote:

> With that mixture of sanguine hope, credulity and vanity which distinguishes him, he assures me that, although thrown out, he was the most popular candidate; that the opponents are hated, and that all those who voted against him did it with tears. I swear to you this is not exaggerated, but what he says and believes ... I am sorry, not because I ever hoped to see him an orator, but because, after all, it is something lost, one of the opportunities of life slipped through one's fingers.[309]

Behaving like Stoney Bowes Mark II, George was utterly dependent on his wife's connections. Having failed in two professions open to younger sons of the aristocracy, the law and politics, and showing no inclination for the military, like his younger brother, Charles Francis, or the Church and having only a small 'private' income from his seventh share of the family fortune he needed a position within the patriarchy based on his being 'favoured' by the rich and powerful. His wife's Mr. Knightley (*except for the marrying bit*), William Lamb, recently entitled Lord Melbourne after the death of his father in 1828 and appointed Home Secretary in Earl Grey's newly assembled Cabinet, came to the rescue by getting him a job as a stipendiary magistrate and underwriting his newly acquired gentleman's mode of address 'The Honourable'.

To supplement the meagre family income, The Honourable Caroline Norton began to write for a living. She had already had poems published, *The Sorrows of Rosalie: A Tale with Other Poems*, that addressed the romantic tragedy of a woman's love for the wrong man, and turned to article writing and a novel, *The Wife and Woman's Reward*. The novel mirrored too closely Caroline's own experiences and featured men too like her husband and his mysterious distant relative, Margaret Vaughan, who had insinuated herself into their family because George had hopes of an inheritance (which did eventually materialise in 1836 in the form of Kettlethorpe Hall, Wakefield, and some sort of income from Mistress Vaughan).

In 1835, the strain on their relationship made Caroline so ill that she miscarried. Although she returned briefly in response to George's pleading and protestations of remorse, the circumstances became intolerable again and she took flight to her sister's. While she was away, George asserted his control over the children.

---

309 Ibid.

Whatever had motivated The Honourable George Norton before with regards to Caroline—among other more pragmatic considerations, it might well have been physical attraction and passion—probably urged on by his greedy relations, as he later claimed, from 1836 onwards it was money. The Prime Minister, well known for his extra-marital dalliances and not unused to scandal, was an intimate acquaintance of his wife, trusted enough for him to leave Caroline alone at Melbourne's residence, but too intimate for George to rein in his jealousy making him prone to manipulation by his family, most definitely in hope of pecuniary but more pressingly for political gain. In late June 1836, after failing to obtain £1400 from Melbourne to settle the affair, he sued him for criminal conversation with his wife, the Honourable Mrs Norton.

When Charles Grey, now the Earl Grey, whom we have met before as the Duchess of Devonshire's young lover, formed his government in November 1830 it was the first wholly Whig government since 1783. Lord Melbourne was the Home Secretary. The new king, William IV, did not like the reforming direction the government had taken and when Grey resigned in July 1834, he liked his replacement, reforming but not radical, even less. In November, he dismissed the Whigs and asked Sir Robert Peel, leader of the Tory party in the Commons, to form the government, not a good or workable idea when the opposition could outvote them.

After a series of defeats, Melbourne and the Whigs came back in March 1835. Melbourne's second ministry was run by a constellation of Whig stars: Melbourne himself (son of Lady Melbourne, Georgiana Cavendish's friend), Lansdowne (son of Prime Minister Shelburne), Duncannon (Melbourne's brother-in-law, Georgiana's nephew), Russell (son of Duke of Bedford and future PM), Palmerston (Melbourne's brother-in-law and future PM), Holland (nephew of Charles James Fox), Howick (son of Earl Grey), Minto (Russell's father-in-law) et al. Any opportunity to breach this phalanx of Whig reformers was a godsend to the Tories.

Melbourne's marriage was a difficult one. His wife, Caroline, Georgiana Cavendish's niece, suffered from nerves, was physically frail and for whom childbirth was both life-threatening and traumatic. Their son had severe mental health issues and their premature daughter died a few days after her birth. The strain caused them to drift apart. In 1812 she had an obsessive affair with the poet, Lord George Byron. The obsession was on public display and unreciprocated leading to some embarrassing social faux pas.

Melbourne, although allegedly a 'player', remained devoted to her throughout despite his family, most forcefully his mother, urging him to dispose of an embarrassment that could hamper his career. They were separated during the last three years of their marriage which were marked by her addictions and mental instability. At her death in 1828 he made a perilous crossing from Ireland where he was serving as Chief Secretary in the Tory, George Canning's coalition.

Much was, at the time, and has been since, said about the relationship between Melbourne and Caroline Norton. The story is brilliantly told by Dr

Diane Atkinson in her book, *The Criminal Conversation of Mrs. Norton*, as, incidentally, is the story of the suffragettes in her book, *Rise Up Women!: The Remarkable Lives of the Suffragettes*, which is why I shall refrain from attempting them here. In 1836, Mrs. Norton was an unhappy but beautiful wife of 28 and he was a remarkably young looking and self-assured widower of 57.

She was neither the first nor the last young woman to be captivated by his stimulating and experienced company. While in Ireland, in his Dublin offices, in 1828 he was sued unsuccessfully for criminal conversation by the husband of Lady Elizabeth Brandon, nee la Touché. The Reverend Lord Brandon was convinced that the relationship was sexual, but the judge and jury did not find the correspondence and witness evidence convincing enough. Furthermore, much was read into his close relationship with the 18-year-old Queen Victoria which history has decided was that of an 'uncle', even 'father' figure.

There were also rumours about his favourite sexual pastime, a long running ingredient of satire and mockery of the aristocratic and powerful members of the patriarchy. The English Vice, as it was known throughout western Europe, was spanking. In London there were a number of birching parlours in which men could relive the schoolboy pleasure and pain of caning and being caned. (We encountered this before in Gillray's cartoon, "Lady Termagant Flaybum" among whose fellow practitioners was "Lady Harriet Tickletail".)

David Fisher, his biographer on <www.historyofparliamentonline.org>, seems to see the implication that this is what they were up to, as apparently does Philip Ziegler in his 1976 biography. Fisher is fairly sure that Melbourne bought off Lord Brandon (which might have encouraged George Norton to try his arm). When he died in 1848 he left money to Lady Brandon and Caroline, both victims of notoriously unhappy marriages, but Caroline's was accompanied by a letter stating that they had never had a sexual relationship thus implying that that was not the case in his affair with Lady Brandon. If Melbourne got his sexual pleasure from spanking then, as in another famous case in more recent history, he could claim, "I did not have sexual relations with that woman…I never told anybody to lie, not a single time, never."

The Honourable Mrs Norton, as we have already noted, had many male admirers and was systematically accused of having an affair with most of them by those who were jealous of her, those whom her quite acid tongue had offended or those, like George's brother, Lord Grantley, who saw some social and/or political advantage in fanning the flames. Melbourne wrote to her frequently urging her to find a way to remain in the marriage, but he knew that she was too open and proud to swallow her dislike and intolerance of George's shortcomings.

Eventually, he accepted that there was no more that could be done. He wrote to his friend, Lord Holland, "The fact is [George] is a stupid brute, and she had not temper nor dissimulation enough to enable her to manage him."[310] He wrote to Caroline:

---

310 en.wikipedia.org/wiki/Caroline_Norton. Accessed 27/09/2020.

> This conduct upon his part seems perfectly unaccountable...You know that I have always counselled you to bear everything and remain to the last. I thought it for the best. I am afraid it is no longer possible. Open breaches of this kind are always to be lamented, but you have the consolation that you have done your utmost to stave this extremity off as long as possible.[311]

The trial was a bit of a legal damp squib because the evidence presented by the prosecution, once again correspondence and blatantly rehearsed witness statements from servants, was totally unconvincing. Melbourne's legal team, Attorney-General, Sir John Campbell, and his barristers, Sir Frederick Thesiger and Thomas Noon Talfourd, of whom we shall hear more later, tore it to pieces. Thus, George's second ploy to make money out of his marriage which, if successful, would have brought him at least £10,000 and Caroline her freedom failed miserably. As an act of revenge, however, it gave Melbourne some sleepless nights and ruined Caroline's social standing as well as depriving her of the regular income from her magazine editorships, any favours from her royal connections and, most importantly of all, her 'good name'.

The Tory press, ably led by the scandalmongering publisher, Barnard Gregory, in his 19th century version of The News of The World, *The Satirist,* unable to get to grips with the PM and his formidable legal team, savaged Caroline instead. As other papers took up the challenge untruths were printed about Caroline and her sisters. One can only assume that the Nortons were behind this broadening of their targets for revenge. It seems likely because Jane Perkins feels, correctly I think, knowing the characters involved, that the final straw was the refusal of the Sheridan family to have George anywhere near their homes or families although the three boys were always welcomed.

From a legal point of view, both George and Caroline had a poor case for divorce. Neither could prove adultery. He had appeared to condone her private meetings with Melbourne by admitting that he himself had walked her to Melbourne's residence and left her there knowing Melbourne was on his own (none of Melbourne's servants had to be called as witnesses at the trial). As she realised at a later date, she had condoned his violent behaviour, or at least appeared to have forgiven it, by returning to the house after the patched-up reconciliation of 1835.

However, they would never live together again. He had failed to get any significant money from the separation, but Miss Vaughan's will had eased his worries on that score. The issue of what she would live on was his to decide. She had wealthy relatives and could earn a substantial sum from her writing on which he would have a claim.

She began at some point to realise that she was legally powerless. She could not contest his suit, sue the papers for the smears that were ruining her reputation, earn her own living if George chose to exercise his right to her royalties or draw

---

311 Ibid.

up a deed of separation with an allowance to put a roof over her head. After the trial he was constrained to offer her £300 per year providing she did not pursue access to her children; she refused it. Far worse, far more hurtful, than all these was his legal right to prevent her seeing the boys.

The right to the children was to become George's bargaining chip, his reassertion of his male supremacy and the weapon with which he could exact his revenge. She realised in her desperate search for economic survival, social recovery and custody of her sons that the insuperable obstacle was the law of coverture. Legally, a wife to all intents and purposes did not exist. If she could not get moral justice from George she would have to get it from a change in the law which, as the laws were made, changed and repealed in parliament and approved by the monarch, meant that she would have to enter into the world of politics as a petitioner, a campaigner.

She would have to convince men to admit women into their world by relinquishing their absolute rights in certain areas, particularly those relating to relationship breakdown. She knew how to do it as she advised her friend, Mary Shelley, with some use of dissimulation of which Melbourne thought she was incapable.

> As to petitioning, no one dislikes begging more than I do, especially when one begs for what seems mere justice; but I have long observed that though people will resist claims (however just), they like to do favours. Therefore, when I beg I am a crawling lizard, a humble toad, a brown snake in cold weather. My meaning is, that if one asks at all, one should rather think of the person written to than one's own feelings.[312]

I agree with modern feminists that Caroline was not a feminist or even a proto feminist. She wrote to Queen Victoria in 1855, "The natural position of woman is inferiority to man. Amen! … I never pretended to the wild and ridiculous doctrine of equality."[313]

Hers was a personal quest for justice based on the argument that the natural right of the mother to bring up her children and the civil right of a married woman to be a legal person in her own right were both prevented from happening by the law of the land. The latter, by giving the legal rights of a married couple to the husband alone, was acting as a legal barrier to the former which, in turn, gave rise to a personal hurt that she found an unbearable impediment to her inalienable right to pursue her own happiness. About the trial and the breakdown of the subsequent farcical negotiations for settling alimony and access to the children she wrote in her 1854 pamphlet, *English Laws for Women in the Nineteenth Century*:

---

[312] spartacus-educational.com/Wnorton.htm. Accessed 28/09/86.

[313] theconversation.com/meet-caroline-norton-fighting-for-womens-rights-before-it-was-even-cool-53668. Accessed 28/09/2020.

> "After the adultery trial was over, I learnt the law as to my children—that the right was with the father; that neither my innocence nor his guilt could alter it; that not even his giving them into the hands of a mistress, would give me any claim to their custody. The eldest was but six years old, the second four, the youngest two and a half, when we were parted. I wrote, therefore, and petitioned the father and husband in whose power I was, for leave to see them—for leave to keep them, till they were a little older. Mr. Norton's answer was that I should not have them; that if I wanted to see them, I might have an interview with them at the chambers of his attorney. What I suffered on my children's account, none will ever know or measure. Mr. Norton held my children as hostages, he felt that while he had them, he still had power over me that nothing could control."[314]

Caroline Norton has been attributed the role in the feminist movement of a catalyst for the establishment of equal rights for women. I prefer to see these four case studies—Lady Anne, Lady Mary, Lady Georgiana and the Honourable Caroline—as components that drew other key components into the fray. I am writing this in the midst of a pandemic, COVID-19, which will surely have its place in history in years to come. I have lived through two pandemics, however. The tragic impact of the AIDS pandemic of the late 20th century was not reduced by a magic bullet cure but by a cocktail of medical and social measures. I suspect that this will be the same approach that will alleviate the impact of COVID-19.

The sickness of sexism, male supremacy and misogyny is still very much in private and public culture but, thanks to numerous components such as the desperation of a mother deprived of her children who had the education, literate ability, openness and courage to reveal her private travails as polemic exemplars for her argument to change the law, its social incidence and cultural influence are much reduced.

---

[314] spartacus-educational.com/Wnorton.htm. Accessed 28/09/2020.

Chapter 38
A Change in the Law

Unjust laws exist; shall we be content to obey them, or shall we endeavour to amend them, and obey them until we have succeeded, or shall we transgress them at once? Men generally, under such a government as this, think that they ought to wait until they have persuaded the majority to alter them. They think that, if they should resist, the remedy would be worse than the evil. But it is the fault of the government itself that the remedy is worse than the evil. It makes it worse. Why is it not more apt to anticipate and provide for reform? Why does it not cherish its wise minority? Why does it cry and resist before it is hurt? Why does it not encourage its citizens to be on the alert to point out its faults, and do better than it would have them?

– Henry David Thoreau, *Civil Disobedience and Other Essays*

Preamble

Caroline was a kick-starter for campaigns for women's rights. She ran her lap in her way. Indeed as she rose to meet her own challenge the next generation who were to pick up the baton and run with it in their own way, Barbara Bodichon, Emily Davies, Dorothea Beale and Elizabeth Garret Anderson, were in their infancy. Much as it would be historically convenient for reformers to conform to a stereotype, they did not. They came from all classes, all faiths, all political parties, all ages and both genders.

Furthermore, they had their owns reasons for their own causes so we should not be surprised or read anything into the fact that, for instance, Wilberforce did not support women's rights nor did Gladstone, Melbourne was not an abolitionist, the most quoted spokesman for Liberty, John Acton, Liberal MP, supported the slave-owning southern states in the American Civil War and the person whose historical legacy I would most like to be my own, Anthony Ashley-Cooper, 7th Earl of Shaftesbury, the 'Poor Man's Earl', of whom his biographer, Georgina Battiscombe, wrote "No man has in fact ever done more to lessen the extent of human misery or to add to the sum total of human happiness", was a Wellingtonian Tory!

Once resolved to campaign for a change in the law on the custody of children, Caroline assembled her army. Her weapon she already had, her pen. Her ammunition she already had, her personal experience. Her general was her now distant friend, Prime Minister Melbourne. Her recruitment sergeant was the barrister and MP who had defended Melbourne in the Crim. Con. Trial, Thomas Noon Talfourd. The recruits were to be a majority of MPs to vote for the Bill in the Commons and Lords Spiritual and Temporal in the Lords logistically supported by the 650,000 recently enfranchised voters—all men.

In 1837, having been refused by John Murray on the grounds of there being too many actionable passages in it, Ridgeways privately published Caroline's first political pamphlet, *The Natural Claim of a Mother to the Custody of her Children as affected by the Common Law Rights of the Father*. Three strong angles are used; natural justice, chivalry and examples of cases where the bona fide intentions of the father are questionable, but he still has custody.

> A man should hardly be allowed to be accuser and judge in his own case, and yet such is the anomalous position created by the law.[315]

The latter point of injustice is the reason Talfourd gives for moving the Bill in the Commons. The sexist scandalmongers in the press immediately accused him of having an affair with Caroline who, in a letter to Mary Shelley, mentioned that she did not know him personally. (Jane Perkins suggests that her go-between was Abraham Hayward, a noted intellectual in London society and member of the Athenaeum Club of brilliant scientific and literary men to which women were frequently welcomed for discussion and debate.) Here are extracts arguing the first two.

> On what principle of *natural* justice the law is founded, which in cases of separation between husband and wife, throws the whole power of limiting the access of a woman to her children into the hands of her husband, it is difficult to say.[316]
> There are few men who would stand tamely by and see a woman *struck*, even by her husband; there are few men who, even in a common street row, would not interfere to protect the wretched drunken creature whose coarse abuse has provoked the blows of her brutal partner; yet what degree of bodily agony, or bodily fear, can compare with the inch-by-inch torture of this unnatural separation?[317]

The Bill was due to be debated in the Commons on 24 May 1837 but the second reading was postponed for a month. On 20 June, the King died. A month later a General Election returned the Whigs under Melbourne with a much-reduced majority. The second reading, therefore, did not take place until May 1838. Although passed by a substantial majority in the Commons it was defeated in the Lords (or rather the Law Lords who defeated it by 11 votes to 9). There was a strong feeling that, having had her children with her in June and July of 1837 due to a clumsy attempt by George, probably deliberate, to reconcile, parliament did not make laws to settle the disputes of one or two people (even

315 archive.org/details/separationofmoth00nort/page/8/mode/2up. Accessed 29/09/2020.
316 Ibid.
317 Ibid.

though an Act of Parliament could grant a husband a divorce from his adulterous wife!). Talfourd was furious. He published this response:

> "Because nature and reason point out the mother as the proper guardian of her infant child, and to enable a profligate, tyrannical, or irritated husband to deny her, at his sole and uncontrolled caprice, all access to her children, seems to me contrary to justice, revolting to humanity, and destructive of those maternal and filial affections which are among the best and surest cements of society."[318]

Caroline picked up her pen and wrote *A Plain Letter to the Lord Chancellor on the Infant Custody Bill.* She also used all her Whig credentials and connections to exert their influence to make the Bill a law of the land. John Copley, Lord Lyndhurst, was to speak for it in the Lords ably supported by Lord Denman and Charles Pepys, the Lord Chancellor. The principal voice against was that of William Best, Lord Wynford. A copy of Caroline's letter was sent to every MP. In August 1839, the Bill became Law. Lyndhurst's speech to the Lords contained Caroline's arguments. It was as though she was speaking through him.

The rights enshrined in the law by The Custody of Infants Act, 1839 were limited. In short, in cases of separation *a mensa et thoro* or *a vinculo*, where the wife was of impeccable reputation, i.e., not adulterous, yet refused access to her children under 7-years-old she could present a petition to the Court of Chancery for having access to or full custody of them and maintenance money from her husband. In 1873 the age was raised to 16. This act also removed the necessity for the mother to be of impeccable reputation, giving a measure of fairness to any proceedings over custody.

The attempts to deny custody on a character assassination similar to that which Caroline had been subjected would have been rendered far less effective. The 65-year-old Caroline would have been pleased; I think. It emphasised that in future custody would be decided by the needs of the child not the rights of the parents. As I am writing, the guiding principle now relates to the fitness of each parent to meet those needs.

Limited as this change in the law seemed, it contained two very significant factors, both to do with the Chancery Court. Firstly, it became a civil proceeding thus making a small step towards taking the law of marriage, in all its breadth, away from the sacramental perspective of the ecclesiastical court of which the inferiority and procreative duty of the woman was a contentious but well established, almost canonical ingredient.

Secondly, the Court of Chancery was the one legally public arena in which the principles of the common law were subsidiary to the principles of equity. The rights of women, in this instance as mothers, had to be examined in a process in which equality was a major criterion. In light of her own opinion of such things

---

[318] spartacus-educational.com/Wcustody39.htm. Accessed 30/09/2020.

and her open opposition to the feminist side declared in her letter to the Chancellor Caroline had scored an own goal.

> The wild and stupid theories advanced by a few women of 'equal rights' and 'equal intelligence' are not the opinions of their sex. I, for one (I, with millions more), believe in the natural superiority of man, as I do in the existence of a God.
> The natural position of woman is of inferiority to man. Amen! That is a thing of God's appointing not of man's devising. I believe it sincerely, as a part of my religion. I never pretended to the wild and ridiculous doctrine of equality.[319]

Caroline began preparing her petition to the Lord Chancellor for access to her children. Her friend, Abraham Hayward, offered to assemble affidavits, including one from Lord Melbourne, to attest that her behaviour while living in the family home had never involved any suggestion of infidelity. However, she was also required to show that since the separation in 1836 her behaviour had been equally beyond reproach. In 1840, her husband and his brother tried and failed to catch her out by tricking her into going to a brothel with a letter asking her to go to the address on business and employing a snooper to watch her movements and con her into further traps. He was arrested after trespassing by entering her uncle's house, where she lived for many years, without permission.

By 1841, the case had still not come to court and never did because, having failed by fair means and foul to combat it, George granted the minimum access required by the law. Probably because the older boys, Fletcher now 12 and Brinsley 10, had expressed their unhappiness at Eton she wanted more access and a say in their education. In September 1842 her youngest son, William, died from tetanus having been injured falling from his horse. Although George asked her to come to Kettlethorpe and attend to the boy, she was too late. The incident produced a thaw in their relationship and a legal ceasefire. George signed a legal agreement granting Caroline access to their two surviving boys equal to his for half the year and an equal say in their education.

Throughout the 1840s, Caroline lost many of the men closest to her; Melbourne and the Whigs fell from power and her brother-in-law, Lord Dufferin, died in 1841, her son died in 1842, her Uncle Charles with whom she lived died in 1843 (by 1845 she was living alone in Chesterfield Street) as did her brother, Frank, her youngest brother, also Charles, died in 1847 and Melbourne died in 1848. All this sadness must have made her think about the pursuit of her own happiness thwarted by her inability to divorce. She described this time in her life.

> Alone. Married to a man's name but, never to know the protection of this nominal husband, nor the joys of family, nor the every-day companionship of a real home. Never to feel or show preference for any

---

[319] archive.org/details/lifeofhonourable00perkrich/page/150/mode/2up. Accessed 30/09/2020.

> friend not of her own sex, though tempted, perhaps, by a feeling nobler than passion—gratitude for generous pity, that has lightened the weary days. To be slandered, tormented, insulted; to find the world and the world's law utterly indifferent to her wrongs or her husband's sin; and through all this to lead a chaste, unspotted, patient, cheerful life; without anger, without bitterness, and with meek respect for those edicts which, with a perverse parody on Scripture, pronounce that it 'is not good for a man to be alone' but extremely good for a woman.[320]

In 1848, Caroline picked up her pen again to write a political polemic, *Letters to the Mob*, calling for one nation approaches to reform rather than the class warfare that was breaking out all over Europe. (*For someone who had such a radical effect on the road to equal rights for women, you will see, if you read this pamphlet, that she was no radical!*) She was back in the game. She was not just angry with the world; she was having trouble with George and money again. He wanted to raise a mortgage on her marriage settlement to help with Brinsley's university fees and, in exchange, agree to a separation deed.

Deeming it too unfavourable to her, the trust lawyer advised against it. He did, however, draw up a deed, a sort of peace treaty by which George could get a mortgage using her trust as security and in return pay her £500 in living expenses if she undertook to stop running up debts for which he was responsible. The tacit understanding if she signed was that he would leave her alone thereafter.

She signed. Later that year, on 24 November, Melbourne died and left Caroline an annuity of £500. When she was told about it in 1849, she accepted because she had incurred heavy debts looking after her eldest son, Fletcher, travelling to and from Lisbon where he worked; even, on one occasion, almost certainly saving his life. George paid nothing. In June 1851, her mother died leaving her an annuity of £480. Blatantly reneging on his promise of 1848, he stopped Caroline's allowance, her cheques to her—or were they his?—creditors bounced and lawsuits were taken out against him. She was advised to let one of them come to court as a sort of test of the law.

On 18 August 1853, the case of Thrupps v. Norton to recover the cost of carriage repairs began at Westminster County Court. Norton's argument was simple. His wife whose carriage it was, purchased from income from her writing, had ample funds to pay the bill because when he had demanded to see her bank book to his amazement he saw that she had been receiving the annuity from Lord Melbourne. Furthermore, he had only signed the deed once she had promised that she had received no money from Melbourne as hush money over the 1836 scandal.

Having been subpoenaed as a witness, Caroline was faced with all this on the spur of the moment in cross examination. In the cold light of day all that George had said could be easily refuted. He had stopped the maintenance

[320] Ibid. p191.

payments months before he saw Caroline's bank books. Secondly, the deed was signed before Melbourne's death, thus supporting Caroline's assertion that she had never received any money from Melbourne. Thirdly, Leman, the lawyer who had drawn up the deed, confirmed that there was no condition, verbal or written, that mentioned Melbourne or money. To add insult to injury, not only did Norton win the case on the technicality that the bill for the repairs was sent when he was paying regular maintenance, but he argued successfully that his signed agreement to pay was an obligation of honour not law because a husband could not contract with his wife because, in law, they were the same person!

The damage, however, was done. Caroline's alleged dirty washing was hung out in public view once again. The press had a field day playing on the prurient susceptibilities of the readers of all classes and Caroline, being feme coverture, was unable to sue for slander and clear her name—that was her husband's job, and certainly could not sue him because it would be legally suing herself! Against her family's and friends' advice she did not help the situation by having a public slanging match with George via a vitriolic exchange of letters in *The Times*.

Six months previously, in February 1853, a Royal Commission report on The Law of Divorce was published. It was commissioned to look at the legal structure of divorce procedure with its 3-court progress to a divorce *a vinculo*; sue for damages in a civil court, obtain a divorce *a mensa et thoro* in an ecclesiastical court and get a dispensation by Act of Parliament for the divorce *a vinculo* enabling the former legally bound couple to marry again, legally. Its three principal concerns were to reduce the demands on courts, to remove the power to grant a dispensation from parliament, also saving time, and to reduce the expense, making divorce an option for the upper middle classes.

The following year, in June 1854, the Lord Chancellor, Robert Rolfe, Baron Cranworth, introduced the Divorce and Matrimonial Causes Bill whose main proposal was the establishment of a secular High Court to decide all divorce cases and issues. There was no mention of wives having any new right to divorce their husbands or retain their property or earnings once no longer living in his household.

Caroline again took up her pen to ask three very pertinent questions. Why, in an age of humanitarian reform, was the case of the married woman largely ignored? Why did not cases of women like her get the attention or sympathy of otherwise decent men? Lastly, why, in an age of law amendment to protect members of society who were unable to help themselves, was there no consideration of that humanitarian spirit applying to separated women? In her pamphlet, *English Laws for Women*, it was clear that she already knew the answers.

> And now let me ask, is there any reason why attention should not be called to the defective state of Laws for Women in England, as attention has been called to other subjects: -namely, by individual effort? Is there any reason why (attention being so called to the subject) Women alone,

> of the more helpless classes, -the classes set apart as not having free control of their own destinies, -should be denied the protection which in other cases supplies and balances such absence of free control? Are we to believe that the gentlemen of Great Britain are so jealous of their privilege of irresponsible power in this one respect, that they would rather know redress *impossible* in cases which they themselves admit to be instances of the grossest cruelty and baseness, than frame laws of control for themselves such as they are willing to frame for others?
> Will they eagerly restrict the labourer or mechanic from violence and brutality in his wretched home, and yet insist on their own right of ill-usage as a luxury fairly belonging (like the possibility of divorce) to the superior and wealthy classes? Is there,-in the disposition of those who are to legislate,-an insurmountable barrier to fair legislation on this subject? and if not, is there any reason why (to plead the cause of the inferior sex as humbly as possible) the laws and enactments for their protection should not undergo as much revision, with as fair a chance of beneficial alteration, as the regulations affecting the management of pauper children,-insane patients,-and the tried and untried prisoners who occupy our gaols?[321]

Caroline was not alone. 1854 saw another pamphlet on married women and the law. *Brief Summary in Plain Language of the Most Important Laws Concerning Women* was written by Barbara Leigh Smith, also a granddaughter of a Whig radical, William Smith, the noted abolitionist. Here Caroline's very personal crusade based on her own experiences of the injustice, from a 'natural' perspective, of the common law of England gelled with the very young, and radical, feminist campaign for women's rights—to work, to be educated and trained, to own property, to divorce and, most outrageous of all, to vote—that had sprung from the thwarted feminism of the French Revolution, the ideas of philosophers like Jeremy Bentham and William Thompson and the equal valuing of women in dissenting churches such as the Quakers and the Unitarians.

At 30 years of age, Barbara married a Dr Eugene Bodichon in 1857, having resisted marriage for many years knowing that she would lose her legal identity (Her father and mother never married either), and it is by that name that she became a leading figure in one cell of the equal rights movement, known as the Langham Place Circle, founding the *English Women's Journal* in 1858 and Girton College, Cambridge, then known as the College for Women at Benslow House and situated in Hitchin, in 1869 with her friend and fellow feminist, Emily Davies. Her work on parliamentary reform in collaboration with Jessie Boucherette and Helen Taylor, stepdaughter of John Stuart Mill, politicised the fight for women's rights that still continues today.

When Victoria came to the throne in 1837, Radicalism and the newly coined Socialism were firmly established all over Western Europe. They often involved

321 digital.library.upenn.edu/women/norton/elfw/elfw.html. Accessed 02/10/2020.

violence and mass protest. They were laced through with an anti-monarchist sentiment that distracted legislators from considering a topic extracted from the large menu of proposed changes, such as the fairer treatment of women, on its own merit. Her early mentor and the person credited with her political education, Lord Melbourne, had himself had a difficult four years as a Home Secretary with a particular brief to bring an end to street violence and the revolutionary idealism that often fuelled it.

By 1855, 6 of the 8 men who tried to assassinate/harm the queen in her 63 years as a monarch had been dealt with quite leniently in line with the more lenient approach of the day. Although none of them appeared to have made their attempt for any political reason, certainly not backed by any radical or revolutionary organisation, one can understand how she may have felt, as a mother of 7 children and, by Christmas, pregnant with the eighth, about forces for change within her realm, the extreme wings of which were prepared to use violence. (For instance, the Chartist movement which advocated universal male suffrage had a largely peaceful following but could be violent, as evidenced by the Newport rising of 1839.)

A letter, therefore, from a patriotic, loyal mother, seeking justice in law for married women, may well have had more of an impact on her thinking than a tract from a known Radical. On June 2, 1855, Caroline sent just such a letter to the most powerful woman in the world. It made these points:

- A married woman in England has no legal existence.
- No matter how long or absolute their separation husband and wife are still one legal person.
- She has no possessions. All that she has in or brings to the marriage can be disposed of by her husband as he wishes.
- An English wife cannot make her own will.
- An English wife cannot claim her own earnings.
- An English wife may not leave her husband's house. The law allows him to reclaim her, by force if necessary, to restore his conjugal rights.
- Any attempt at reconciliation with a cruel husband nullifies her petition for a separation on grounds of cruelty.
- A husband can divorce an unfaithful wife without her having any legal right to defend herself against false allegations or countersue. She cannot give evidence if he sues her alleged lover for damages.
- A man can divorce a vinculo by Act of Parliament, but a woman cannot, except in the most exceptional circumstances such as his incest, bigamy or sodomy.

Caroline knew that no bill could become law without the monarch's approval, and we will never know Victoria's input because her conversations with Prime Minister Palmerston were never recorded. For sure, the end product by no means addressed all the points she made to her queen. Barbara Bodichon and her circle will also have noted that there was no progress at all towards equality for women in the divorce process.

Now I am going to stick my neck out with an extreme opinion! The debate of 1857 was of huge significance to the evolution of 'civilisation'. The concept of Civilisation is not an absolute nor an abstract idea. It is a man, I emphasise 'man', made highly subjective construct. Most thinkers will see its historical progress as one of evolution. Attempts to demolish the construct and rebuild it with something new, 'revolution', have largely been frustrated by the re-emergence of or the failure to eradicate key elements of the old construct (French Class System, Russian Imperialism, Chinese Absolutism). In the parliament of 1850s Great Britain and Ireland the three strands of Western European civilisation were all there in the debate over Matrimonial Causes: political expediency, moral rectitude and justice.

The victory for political expediency in the partial resolution of this issue, steered through Parliament by the master of political expediency, Henry Temple, Viscount Palmerston, was revolutionary, literally turning the world on its head! In this respect it was most unlike the most celebrated historical revolutions in which expediency, which we might define as 'the necessity of doing something regardless of its moral consequences', destroyed or hijacked moral idealism and common justice, its two crucial companions in the construct of Western European civilisation.

Palmerston, at 72 years of age, was at the height of his personal popularity when he and his Whigs were elected in April 1857 with a substantial majority over Lord Derby's Conservatives. He was a career politician—he needed public office to stave off the family indebtedness. He understood indebtedness. Public indebtedness was a serious concern raised by the Commission whose main brief seems to have been to reform the legal process by which divorce cases were decided by making it simpler, shorter and cheaper. As an experienced Chancellor of the Exchequer Gladstone had always been against any increase in Government borrowing but on this issue, as in many others in his lengthy public service, he took to the moral high ground.

Wilberforce had not supported any suggestion of reform that involved women's rights because the Bible, upon which his morals were firmly based, directed the position that God expected of women in the social and domestic spheres. Gladstone opposed the measure because the priests of the established Anglican Church, at their ordination, gave an unbreakable commitment to God to administer the sacraments, one of which was matrimony. (Matrimony was more than marriage; it was the sacrament of marriage, a channel for God's grace—what he intended for his creation, mankind—which could only be opened up by an ordained priest.) A petition from 9,000 Anglican priests was presented to Parliament.

All the moral requirements directed by scripture were there in the three-fold process; marry once only; the two-into-one status of a legal marriage; the indissolubility of the marriage tie; the sin of remarriage once the oath had been taken and the person to whom it was made was still alive; the primacy of the husband and the submissive absolute fidelity of the wife… And the law of the land as it pertained to matrimony followed them.

However, marriage, as opposed to matrimony, had more of a contractual feel to it, when it was used for the aggrandisement of property ownership and social standing. In this circumstance, as we have seen, the woman was like a good or a chattel acquired by the man to have his children, run his household and satisfy his sexual needs, as well as to extend his wealth-earning potential by bringing him more land or more profitable social connections. Neither matrimony or marriage, sacrament or contract, could regulate emotion, sexual attraction or physical desire once the threat of eternal damnation was neutralised. The wreckage of relationship breakdown, its injuries and disputes, its rights and wrongs, had to be salvaged or cleared away justly and fairly by the law.

To summarise the situation, therefore, adjudication on the aftermath of a breakup in one process that considered issues both of matrimony, the sacrament, and marriage, the contract, involved these three stages: 1. Proof of injury to the husband by an award of damages in a civil court. 2. Approval of the moral benefit of separation of husband and wife in an ecclesiastical court and 3. Approval to dispense with the law forbidding remarriage from the House of Lords. It had become protracted, time-consuming and so expensive that it excluded many of the new political power brokers, the property owning upper middle class. God's Law, however, as presented in scripture was a cornerstone of the Protestant, British/Anglican cultural view of morality and ethics.

British justice was supposed to be a leading light to the world or at least to its growing colonies which were all over the world and its legislature the model of democracy. Given all these different angles the resulting Act was bound to be a compromise that would fail to satisfy all people for all time.

From 1 January 1858, The Divorce and Matrimonial Causes Act became law. It established a civil Court of Divorce and Matrimonial Causes which would take over all proceedings to do with matrimony, current and future, from ecclesiastical courts, allow any High Court lawyer to take on such cases, replace a decree *a mensa et thoro* by a decree of Judicial Separation and hear divorce and separation cases from men and women petitioners. This was undoubtedly revolutionary. Grossly overstating its importance no doubt, this removal of the moral restraint imposed by God's Law as revealed in Scripture, this establishment of a law the rightness of which was against the scriptural grain, this process for resolving a human problem without resorting to divine guidance, was as revolutionarily liberating as the invention of the wheel.

In cases where a judicial separation had been granted, the husband had no claim on income earned or property acquired by the wife after the date of legal separation. This would also be the case if the separation were due to desertion for two years or more. The husband could still sue the wife's lover, who, in a divorce case, had to be named, for loss of conjugal services but the damages went to the court who saw to the needs of wife and children first. A wife could now sue for divorce but had to prove an extenuating circumstance to his adultery whereas were he to seek a divorce from her only had to prove adultery.

Finally, in law, a judicially separated wife was seen as a feme sole who could sue and be sued, sign contracts, own property and make a will. The right to revert to the legal status of a single woman, to change her mind, to rectify her mistake, to reject the hegemony of an unjust man over a woman was now established in line with a subject's moral right to overthrow a sovereign in the best interests of his or her people.

Long before Lord Cranworth presented his bill, the Honourable George Norton had sensed the way the wind was going to blow and restarted making proper maintenance payments to Caroline although he still quibbled about the amount. Caroline was spared the need to petition the new secular Court for a Judicial Separation or an Order for maintenance or protection of earnings but as she hung up her political boots she must have been well satisfied that separated women could.

George died in 1875, leaving Caroline to marry a man who loved her and whom she loved, Sir William Stirling-Maxwell, a widower and long-time friend. All her sons were dead, Fletcher having died in his thirtieth year and the always sickly Thomas Brinsley in July 1877, aged 45 and three months before his mother but just in time to inherit the title of Baron Grantley from his Uncle Fletcher who, we suspect, was behind much of his mother's unhappiness. Her grandson, John Richard Brinsley Norton, was to test the measures his grandmother had helped to put in place when he ran off with his cousin's wife. Her marriage was annulled in time for the couple to marry just five days before the birth of their son.

To be oxymoronic, revolutionary though the 1857 Act was, it was also quite conservative in that it did nothing to improve the legal position of married women who were well treated but far from legally independent and even less for those who were ill-treated. The final loosening of the male grip on the Divorce Laws in the UK did not happen until 1973.

Chapter 39
Double Standards

And I don't quite know how they managed to make this law in their favour, or who exactly it was who gave them a greater licence to sin than is allowed to us; and if the fault is common to both sexes (as they can hardly deny), why should the blame not be as well? What makes them think they can boast of the same thing that in women brings only shame?
– Moderata Fonte, *The Worth of Women: Wherein is Clearly Revealed Their Nobility and Their Superiority to Men*

I believe that what this country needs is not less conservatism. It is more Conservatism of the traditional kind that made us join this party.
– John Major

Preamble

In Chapter 8, we looked at moral issues; The Golden Rule, "And as ye would that men should do to you, do ye also to them likewise." (Luke 6:31. KJV) and Jesus' condemnation of hypocrisy, "Thou hypocrite, first cast out the beam out of thine own eye; and then shalt thou see clearly to cast out the mote out of thy brother's eye." (Matthew 7:5. KJV) In a predominantly Christian culture with morals based on scriptural truth where were these two explicit guidelines in the pecking order?

Equally, the two mantras of political expediency were also dominant in the mid-19th century; the Utilitarian "the greatest happiness of the greatest number" and the Machiavellian "the end justifies the means". In a country throbbing with industrial and imperial energy, how much were they undermining or protecting the traditional way of life and the status quo of its patriarchal pecking order?

Wikipedia extracts this view of mid-19th century Britain from Paul Langford, "The English as Reformers: Foreign Visitors' Impressions, 1750-1850", Proceedings of the British Academy (1999), Vol. 85, pp. 101-19.

> *Meanwhile, a steady stream of observers from the Continent commented on the English political culture. Liberal and radical observers noted the servility of the English lower classes, the obsession everyone had with rank and title, the extravagance of the aristocracy, a supposed anti-intellectualism,* ***and a pervasive hypocrisy that extended into such areas as social reform****. There were not so many conservative visitors. They praised the stability of English society, its ancient constitution, and*

reverence for the past; they ignored the negative effects of industrialisation.[322]

I have highlighted the phrase that we could well apply to the issue of women's rights in the 19th century, however, the dual forces of 'anti-intellectualism' and 'reverence for the past' can be observed at work in the male conservatism for an analysis of which I have relied heavily on a 1995 article by Ann Sumner Holmes (Holmes, Ann Sumner. "The Double Standard in the English Divorce Laws, 1857-1923." Law and Social Inquiry, vol. 20, no. 2, 1995, pp. 601-620. JSTOR, www.jstor.org/stable/828954. Accessed 13 Oct. 2020.)

Surprisingly, with conservative icons such as the Duke of Wellington, Lord Salisbury and Margaret Thatcher to choose from, I have chosen John Major's 1993 Conference speech as the most well-defined statement of modern era conservatism I have ever read or heard.

> … many people, particularly older people, were bewildered and profoundly disturbed by 'a world that sometimes seems to be changing too fast for comfort, old certainties crumbling, traditional values falling away. Week after week, month after month, they see attacks on the very pillars of our society—the Church, the law and even the monarchy, … And they ask where is it going, why has it happened and above all, how can we stop it?

Six years earlier, Mr—now as I write this—Sir John KG. CH., Major had ended a four-year affair with Mrs Edwina Currie, a fellow MP. He went on to serve as Prime Minister for seven years and make that speech on family values three years into his first ministry. His secret was not outed until 2002 during a spell of Labour dominance of the House of Commons and, therefore, not politically damaging, if it ever would have been. Was his behaviour right or wrong, of private or public import, hypocritical or deceitful? A simpler way of describing it would be that it was a blatant case of double standards. It was far from unique, certainly not seminal and even more certainly not a sign of the times!

The Catholic saint and church father, Augustine of Hippo, writing around the turn of the 5th century, spoke out about the sexual double standard in Roman civilisation.

> "God bids you not to commit lechery, that is, not to have sex with any woman except your wife. You ask of *her* that she should not have sex with anyone except you—yet you are not willing to observe the same restraint in return. Where you ought to be ahead of your wife in virtue, you collapse under the onset of lechery…Complaints are always being

322 en.wikipedia.org/wiki/Hypocrisy#Great_Britain. Accessed 13/10/2020.

made about men's lechery, yet wives do not dare to find fault with their husbands for it. Male lechery is so brazen and so habitual that it is now sanctioned [= permitted], to the extent that men tell their wives that lechery and adultery are legitimate for men but not for women." (Sermons 1-19)

Around 1600 AD, some 8 years after her death, the mentor of Modesta di Pozzo di Zorzi, her uncle, Giovanni Nicolo Doglioni, had published under her pen name, Modesta Fonte, a clearly feminist work—all the language is from women and their observations are of men and its Italian title, Giustizia delle Donne (Justice for Women), is gender political—that questioned the double standards of men (See the quote at the start of this chapter). Incidentally, it seems that Modesta was very happily married, so happy was her husband that he returned her dowry signifying that he required no financial inducement to marry her—*well that is my romantic interpretation!*

Finding such views present in the ancient and early modern world gives us a 400-year period in the modern world in which male, conservative resistance to female equality via the application and justification of the double standard was an enforced and accepted theme of the patriarchy while change and reform in most other cultural, social, economic and political areas of life were progressively taking us to the British society we experience in our 21st century.

I purposefully use the small 'c' for conservative because neither political party (the Duke of Grafton was a Whig), nor nationality (Lloyd George was Welsh), nor class (Lloyd George was also middle-class) had to do with the acquisition of the male double standard. The [c]onservatism over women's rights was a male thing. To paraphrase J.S. Mill, it would be fair to say that all male chauvinists are conservative, but not all conservatives are male chauvinists.

There have been a number of criticisms of the 1857 Act. While praising it as 'socially and morally … The most important and useful Act on the Statute Book' the barrister, John Fraser MacQueen, secretary of the Divorce Commission, goes on to observe that the 'labours of the pitchfork are visible in every page'[323].

Some of these criticisms related to the fact that divorce was still expensive if you had to travel to London and stay for the duration of your case and the allied fact that much of the legwork of petitions and court orders relating to alimony or protection of earnings planned to be heard and granted locally lacked clarity and could be legally invalid. MacQueen was further concerned about the language the imprecision of which he found puzzling and prone to legal loopholes.

There were, however, two serious inequalities in this law which tell us a lot about the highly subjective thinking of men, Englishmen, about the

---

[323] A Practical Treatise on Divorce and Matrimonial Jurisdiction under The Act of 1857. Accessed on 16/10/2020 from archive.org/details/apracticaltreat02macqgoog A Practical Treatise on Divorce and Matrimonial Jurisdiction under The Act of 1857.

indissolubility of marriage, its sacramental mystery as an element of their social control, the general status of women in and out of marriage and in their relationships with men in general.

Firstly, the major cause of marital break-up throughout the ages, adultery, had always been sufficient on its own for a husband to divorce his wife. The 1857 Act confirmed that this would still be the case. However, in ecclesiastical court, a wife could only obtain a divorce *a mensa et thoro*, in effect, as we saw with Mary Bowes, a separation, if there were some other extenuating circumstance in her husband's behaviour such as, bigamy, incest (defined by prohibitions for consanguinity or affinity), sodomy, bestiality, rape, desertion or cruelty so extreme that it could bring about judicial separation without proof of the husband being unfaithful. Although the 1857 Act enabled the court to grant a full divorce to a wife it retained the exact same condition. *Why?*

Secondly, the Act required that the man with whom the wife had been unfaithful should be named as a co-respondent to the husband's petition for divorce. Although the Act legislated against a suit for criminal conversation it still allowed the husband to claim damages from his wife's lover. A wife was unable to do the same and the female lover of her husband remained anonymous. Why?

Before we seek the answers, it would be helpful to complete the legal history of divorce that without the historic passing of the 1857 Act might well have been very different or of far longer duration. It was not until 1923 that equality in petitions for divorce was recognised in law. A private members bill, coming 13 years after a Royal Commission report on Divorce Reform, introduced by Lord Stanley Buckmaster, a former Lord Chancellor, was passed with large majorities in the Commons and the Lords, making adultery a single cause for divorce for both wife and husband.

In his introduction to the second reading in the Lords which was echoed in the introduction by Major Cyril Entwistle to its second reading in the Commons, he made it clear that his principal concern was equality of opportunity under the law. 'It is not designed in any way to alter the existing grounds upon which divorce can be obtained… It has this purpose and this purpose alone: to secure that whatever may be the grounds of divorce they shall be the same for both women and men.'[324]

In 1937, the Matrimonial Causes Act extended the grounds for divorce to include adultery, desertion, cruelty, incurable insanity, incest or sodomy, each in their own right. The 1925 Summary Jurisdiction (Separation and Maintenance) Act had already done this for judicial separations. 80 years after the 1857 Act unhappy wives were finally on an even playing field with unhappy husbands. It was not until 1973, however, that unhappiness in a marriage, no matter what the cause, was recognised in law by establishing one cause of divorce, 'irretrievable breakdown' one of the conditions of which could now be 'that the respondent

---

[324] hansard.millbanksystems.com/lords/1923/jun/26/matrimonial-causes-bill. Accessed 16/10/2020.

has behaved in such a way that the petitioner cannot reasonably be expected to live with the respondent'.

Two years later, in 1975, all the hard work of Barbara Bodichon and her fellow campaigners for equal opportunities at work and in education and training finally came to fruition with the passing of the Sex Discrimination Act. In 2021, a Bill will be made law to establish the legality of a 'no fault' divorce. The rectifying of the one inequality in the divorce process will affirm that unhappiness can be a medium- or long-term development in any romantic attachment without blame attaching to either partner.

This recognition of the variability in the solidity and durability of the pair bonding of Homo Sapiens is, beyond doubt, up there with the recognition of other human rights emanating from the concept of Liberty. In cases of adultery a co-respondent, since 1937 of the husband as well as of the wife, is still required by law but the rules established by the 1973 Act, known as the Section 25 Criteria, discourage naming so that most petitions for adultery use the phrase 'with an unnamed person'. The final undoing of the inequalities in the pioneering 1857 Act has been the reorganisation of High Court jurisdiction so that Family Proceedings Courts, sub-divisions of Magistrates and County Courts acting on High Court rulings, now deal with divorces and separations, maintenance, and child custody issues. Damages for anything other than costs of divorce proceedings would have to be sought in civil court.

Since 1937, therefore, the desire within the patriarchy to treat women fairly in all walks of life has ensured steady progress towards equality between the sexes. *I very much doubt, however, that all men have been convinced by the arguments for its inclusion as one of the key requirements of a civilised culture.* The fire that has been destroying male supremacy in the 163 years that have followed the 1857 Act is still burning but less fiercely and the smoke of sex discrimination which the wind of change has failed to disperse totally is still very much in the air.

Who, then, had the final say in the philosophical, social, economic, moral and ethical content of the 1857 Act? Four months previous to the Act being given royal assent 654 MPs had been elected by 6% of the male population of Great Britain and Ireland all of whom were by qualification men of property, 377 sailing under the colours of the Whigs, 264 under those of the Conservatives with 13 Others, all members of the Independent Irish Party. The vote for retaining the distinction between men and women was, as Ann Holmes tells us, 71 to 20 in the Lords and 126 to 65 in the Commons. Palmerston's Whig majority contained about 100–120 Radical MPs, for example, the MP for Sheffield, John Arthur Roebuck, a profoundly upper middle-class barrister, whose friend, the philosopher and women's rights proponent, John Stuart Mill, was not elected to Parliament until 1865, who embodied the complicated personal inconsistencies of mid-Victorian MPs who did not have to declare their party affiliations before voting began.

Where do you place on the political spectrum a man who, according to Wikipedia, in a speech at Salisbury in 1862, alleged that working men were spendthrifts and wife-beaters, but, even though a Palmerston supporter, said of the Whigs in 1852:

> "The whigs, have ever been an exclusive and aristocratic faction, though at times employing democratic principles and phrases as weapons of offence against their opponents. … When out of office they are demagogues; in power they become exclusive oligarchs".[325]

Two years later, the Whigs, Radicals, Peelite Conservatives and the IIP would join in the foundation of the Liberal Party. This Parliament, elected by no working-class voters to some of whom the suffrage was opened up 10 years later, contained no working-class MPs the first of whom, Thomas Burt, was elected as MP for Morpeth 17 years later in 1874—and no women. The High Court judges who were to dispense justice within the law from 1 January 1858 were all male as they were for over 100 years until Elizabeth Lane was appointed in 1965. The barristers representing petitioner and respondent were all male.

The first woman barrister in England was Ivy Williams who was called to the Bar in 1922 just three years after the Sex Disqualification (Removal) Act of 1919 had made law that: "A person shall not be disqualified by sex or marriage from the exercise of any public function … and a person shall not be exempted by sex or marriage from the liability to serve as a juror." The Juries Act 1825 had prohibited women from serving on juries and required a property qualification for those men who did. The property qualification which prevented many women from being jurors was not removed until 1971. In the case of a damages suit, the juries were men only.

The world of Divorce Law, therefore, was firmly, and without exception, dominated by upper- and upper-middle-class men of property—most of whom, regardless of their party-political label, were conservative with a small 'c', i.e., having a large stake in the status quo. Unsurprisingly, therefore, property interest lay at the heart of the double standard.

Having replaced criminal conversation with judicial separation, civil and moral tort decided in both a civil and an ecclesiastical court with contractual tort decided only in a civil court, in order to decide the level of damages a value still had to be placed on the wife and her services to the husband who was losing her. She, therefore, was his asset, his property. Although a wife could now leave an adulterous and immoral husband no value, in law, was assigned to his loss to her, only an amount decided for her proper maintenance as a feme sole.

---

[325] en.wikipedia.org/wiki/John_Arthur_Roebuck. Accessed 20/10/2020.

Chapter 40
The Female Citizen

A married woman shall, in accordance with the provisions of this Act, be capable of acquiring, holding, and disposing by will or otherwise, of any real or personal property as her separate property, in the same manner as if she were a feme sole, without the intervention of any trustee.
– Married Women's Property Act, 1882

I tell you there is no hope for woman, till she has a hand in making the law—no chance for her till her vote is worth as much as a man's vote. When it is—woman will not be fobbed off with a six-pence a day for the very work a man would get a dollar for … All you and others are doing to elevate woman, is only fitted to make her feel more sensibly the long abuse of her own understanding, when she comes to her senses. You might as well educate slaves—and still keep them in bondage.
– John Neal

Preamble

Coverture, the legal hangover of the conquering soldier/aristocrat, now the new British post-1688 aristocratic male, opposed to tyranny but not revolutionary, now the new religiously reformed husband as conscious of his duty to cherish as he was of his wife's duty to obey, had to be addressed and removed from the law. Once removed, the legal status of all women was no different from that of men. That being the case fuelled the campaign for their political status to be the same as well.

The philosophical parameters of Liberty had to be changed from Locke's of 1689 to Mill's of 1859, a shift from Liberty being freedom from harm to it being freedom from any other purpose for the exercise of power than the prevention of harm. A subtle shift from 'freedom from' to 'freedom to'.

> The state of nature has a law of nature to govern it, which obliges every one: and reason, which is that law, teaches all mankind, who will but consult it, that being all equal and independent, no one ought to harm another in his life, health, liberty, or possessions…[326]

[326] oll.libertyfund.org/titles/locke-the-two-treatises-of-civil-government-hollis-ed#lf0057_label_207. Accessed 21/10/2020.

> The sole end for which mankind are warranted, individually or collectively, in interfering with the liberty of action of any of their number, is self-protection. That the only purpose for which power can be rightfully exercised over any member of a civilised community, against his will, is to prevent harm to others. His own good, either physical or moral, is not sufficient warrant. He cannot rightfully be compelled to do or forbear because it will be better for him to do so, because it will make him happier, because, in the opinion of others, to do so would be wise, or even right… The only part of the conduct of anyone, for which he is amenable to society, is that which concerns others.[327] (Mill, John Stuart. [1859] 1869.

The natural, inalienable right of Liberty depends not only on a law that protects the possessions of an individual property owner but also on one that allows anyone to own property in the first place. For instance, the widowed *feme sole* who was a few months ago a *feme covert* was the same person by every possible definition except that, as the former she could legally own and deal in property, her own possessions, based on her own decisions, whereas, as the latter she could not. The Law of coverture demanded that she give up her natural right to Liberty to a husband who had no <u>natural</u> right to take it. The 1857 Act did not address this issue but, by awarding a separated woman the legal status of a *feme sole* it focused attention on a *feme covert* and her natural right to own and make decisions about her own property.

With the attention on the ownership of property, the issue began to fall in with the issues of universal suffrage and women's suffrage and women's access to the professions, particularly law and medicine, via higher education, the former subject to property qualifications and the latter meaning that women were capable of earnings sufficient to own or rent property well above the qualifying minimum for having a vote.

The powerhouse of the 1860s women's rights movement was The Kensington Society which followed on from the Langham Place group mentioned earlier. Founded by mostly unmarried women it was a discussion forum that formulated strategies for the peaceful pursuit of gender equality. In addition to Millicent Fawcett, nee Garrett, a formidable suffragist and sister of Elizabeth, who became the first woman to qualify as a doctor in England, and Agnes, the first woman, with her cousin Rhoda, to be trained as an architect in England, and fellow campaigner and biographer of Josephine Butler, nee Grey (Her father was a cousin of Earl Grey, the Prime Minister and former lover of Georgiana Cavendish), the most formidable suffragist of all, in my opinion:

> The society included: Barbara Bodichon, Emily Davies, Frances Buss, Dorothea Beale, Jessie Boucherett, Elizabeth Garrett Anderson, Helen

---

[327] Mill, John Stuart. [1859] 1869. *On Liberty* (4th ed.). London: Longmans, Green, Reader, and Dyer. p. 21–22. Accessed in https://en.wikipedia.org/wiki/John_Stuart_Mill#Liberty.

> Taylor, Charlotte Manning, Anna Swanwick, Anne Clough, and the tireless worker for disadvantaged girls, Rosamond Davenport Hill. Another early member, Emilia Russell Gurney was the wife of Russell Gurney who introduced legislation in parliament on women's rights to property and to practise medicine. Membership expanded to 33 members by the official founding, a total of 58 members in the following year and 67 by its end in 1868.[328]

With apologies to those knowledgeable in this field, I just need to draw attention to one of my previous assurances. I said that I would not tackle the history of the 'suffragette' movement because I am overwhelmingly underqualified to do so. Butler, Fawcett, Gurney and Manning, to name but a few, were notable 'suffragists', committed to peaceful, constitutional campaigning as opposed to the more physical, law infringing activism of Annie Kenney, the Pankhursts and Emily Davison, the iconic 'suffragettes'. Many suffragist sympathisers turned away from the movement after incidents of suffragette violence.

Wikipedia records this story from 1911 about when Lilias Hallett, a prominent backer of Kenney's Women's Social and Political Union (WSPU), visited the home of Mary Blathwayt who ran a refuge near Bath called Eagle House for suffragettes who had been to prison and whose family had withdrawn from the cause after Prime Minister Asquith's car had been attacked in November 1913.

> *She was invited by Mary Blathwayt and her parents to visit Eagle House in 1911. She had been there in 1908 to chair a meeting but this time she was invited to plant a tree. Like the Blathwayts she had mixed feelings about militancy within the suffrage movement. She was said to have been "made ill" by the militants but she confided that it was the militants that were creating the progress that she spent many years failing to achieve.*[329]

These highly educated middle-class women had fathers, like John Grey and Newson Garrett, who were not only comfortably off but liberal minded enough to invest as much in their daughters' education as their sons' or anyone else's sons for that matter. Small wonder, therefore, that these women were committed to girls and young women having the same primary, secondary and tertiary educational opportunities as boys and young men. They, with hindsight, obviously, went on to question why, with that huge inequality rectified, they should not access the hitherto male-only professions of education, medicine and law and, more shockingly to the patriarchy, participate in public life.

---

[328] en.wikipedia.org/wiki/Kensington_Society_%28women%27s _discussion_group%29. Accessed 21/10/2020.

[329] en.wikipedia.org/wiki/Lilias_Ashworth_Hallett. Accessed 22/10/2020.

The 1860s was a decade of huge challenges to the [c]onservative Establishment. Not only were women petitioning for divorce on the grounds of adultery and mistreatment by their husbands, but those husbands were, according to Mr Charles Darwin, whose book *On the Origin of Species* had been published in 1859, the descendants of monkeys! When Viscount Palmerston, an avid opponent of parliamentary reform, died in 1865 his successor, Lord John Russell, an avid proponent of expanding the franchise, had difficulty holding the Liberal Party together due to a large anti-reform faction known as the Adullamites, led by Robert Lowe, opposing the Radical faction who wanted nothing less than universal male suffrage and some of whom, for example John Stuart Mill, step-father of Helen Taylor, Henry Fawcett who married Millicent Garrett and the Bright brothers John and Jacob, wanted female suffrage as well. The 1867 Reform Act was, therefore, a Conservative measure which Disraeli is said to have felt was a vote winner.

One of the few ways that the unenfranchised, and that included all women, could directly access the political process was to present a petition to Parliament via an MP friendly to the cause. On 7 June 1866 John Stuart Mill presented a petition, gathered and written by his stepdaughter, Helen Taylor and Barbara Bodichon, with 1,499 signatures very politely requesting that female householders should have the vote on the same basis and recognising the same disqualifications as applied to male householders.

Almost a year later, on 20 May 1867, Disraeli's Reform Bill was in its committee stage. Just a fortnight earlier, masterminded by Charles Bradlaugh, founder of the London Secular Society in 1866, and activists from the Reform League of which he was a member and the more middle-class Reform Union, a huge rally attended by 200,000 people had been held in Hyde Park in support of the extension of the male suffrage.

The Commons were to consider amendments to Clauses 3 and 4. The detail and motives for the Bill were questioned and the political spectres of corruption and socialism raised but Clause 3, as amended, was passed. Then Mill spoke to his amendment for Clause 4 in which he proposed replacing the word 'man' with the word 'person' so as to include women of property in the franchise.

In his pitch for the inclusion of women in the franchise, Mill addressed the conservative objections of the patriarchy:

> The difficulty which most people feel on this subject is not a practical objection; there is nothing practical about it, it is a mere feeling—a feeling of strangeness; ... the despotism of custom is on the wane; we are not now satisfied with knowing what a thing is, we ask whether it ought to be; and in this House at least, I am bound to believe that an appeal lies from custom to a higher tribunal, in which reason is judge. Now, the reasons which custom is in the habit of giving for itself on this subject are usually very brief. That, indeed, is one of my difficulties; it is not easy to refute an interjection; interjections, however, are the only

> arguments among those we usually hear on this subject, which it seems to me at all difficult to refute.
>
> The others mostly present themselves in such aphorisms as these: Politics are not women's business and would distract them from their proper duties; women do not desire the suffrage but would rather be without it; women are sufficiently represented by the representation of their male relatives and connections; women have power enough already.[330]

Mill went on to refute all these opinions with reason skilfully applied. It is not these comments, however, that have implications for the legal position of married women. For those, we need to examine the opposition to his proposal that came from Edward Kent Karslake, recently elected and soon to be unelected Conservative MP for Colchester.

Karslake, claiming familiarity with and admiration of Mill's writing on political economy and conceding, probably sarcastically, that the issue was on every Englishman's lips, suspected, probably correctly, that Mill's proposition was a back-door attempt to give the franchise to married women. Given that spinsterhood and widowhood were transitional in many women's lives, and that it was a very precious privilege to have the franchise, he argued, then, faced with the choice of giving up that privilege for marriage, women would agitate to have both. He continued to press his point that the cart was before the horse. MPs, he urged, should decide on the rights and privileges of married women first.

When George Monckton-Arundel, Viscount Galway, the long-serving Conservative MP for East Retford, asked Mill to withdraw his motion so that the Committee could move on to 'more important' business Mill replied that he had no intention of doing so and was very pleased that the speeches against his motion had not challenged the actual intention of it only the potential ramifications, fears even, of greater equality of access to public life—female MPs, female professionals and females in the military, for example, even universal suffrage for both sexes—which he would welcome when the time came as it surely would. *I suspect Mill the campaigner was secretly pleased that he had also drawn out the ingrained sexism of the [c]onservative position on equal rights for women—which brings us back to Edward Kent Karslake.*

Karslake argued that there were two unavoidable things preventing married women having the vote, the law of the land and the expediency or practicality of the consequences for the relationship of the sexes not least those within a marriage. Still doing well in the debate he quite rightly stated the existing situation as to the law of the land.

> It was true that, by means of trustees, you could, through the intervention of the Court of Chancery, give some protection to the property of a married woman. With that exception, the law of the land at the present

[330] api.parliament.uk/historic-hansard/commons/1867/may/20/clauses-3-4-progress-may-17. Accessed 24/10/2020.

day had deliberately settled that the wife should be absolutely and entirely under the control of the husband, not only in respect of her property, but of her personal movements. For example, a married woman might not "gad about," and if she did her husband was entitled to lock her up; some held that he might beat her. He had his doubts about that, and if his advice were asked, as a lawyer, he would say do not do it: but undoubtedly the husband had entire dominion over the person and property of his wife. He thought, then, it was clear that votes could not be given to married women consistently with the rules of law as regarded property and the husband's dominion over the wife's movements.[331]

He expressed no opinion as to whether he agreed with this law or not but when he moved on to the practical implications his guard, in terms of his objectivity, began to slip.

He had an 'inner instinct' that husbands, including those MPs present in the House, would not want to debate for whom they would vote with their wives usurping their right to command as head of the household rather than informing them of other views held by someone close to them who happened to be a woman, conversations that Mill hoped would civilise men away from 'brutal' insistence towards a more respectful acceptance of the views of women. Karslake felt this position of Mill's was too philosophical and social scientific (Karslake called this 'political economy') and lacked 'common sense'.

It was well known that elections were corrupt with a lot of money being outlaid by candidates as bribes and employers pressurising employees and landlords their tenants, both of which many [c]onservatives had no problem with, in fact, earlier in the debate before Mill spoke, the Conservative, John Henley, had called the 1865 Election 'the most expensive and corrupt election that has ever been known'. Was Karslake implying that wives should vote the way their husbands told them to without having a party-political view of their own? A further complication was raised by Sir George Bowyer, Liberal MP for Dundalk, who felt that the appearance of women at the hustings and the polls would be 'indecorous'.

He presumed, however, that the hon. Member for Westminster would propose that they should use voting papers, for it would be manifestly indecorous for them to attend the hustings or the polling-booth; but voting papers, duly guarded, would enable the sex to vote in a manner free from objection.[332]

The Ballot Act of 1872 established the principle of the secret ballot and the tradition of the ballot box but those married women who wanted to were not able to hide a vote contrary to that of their husband until 1918. It was not until the

---

331 api.parliament.uk/historic-hansard/commons/1867/may/20/clauses-3-4-progress-may-17#S3V0187P0_18670520_HOC_77. Accessed 26/10/2020.
332 Ibid

Corrupt and Illegal Practices Act of 1883 that control of electoral expenses established the procedures we have now and that would have allowed women to vote.

Karslake finished his speech with an opinion and an assertion. The opinion encapsulated the [c]onservative, Establishment view of women current in the 1860s which we have circled round for some time now.

> He thought that the Committee would come to the opinion that the hon. Gentleman was wrong in his first principles. In one of his very able works the hon. Member had laid it down that there was no greater difference between a woman and a man than there was between two human beings, one with red hair and one with black, or one with a fair skin and the other with a dark one. He (Mr. Karslake) humbly begged to differ from him, for while he believed that a man qualified to possess the franchise would be ennobled by its possession, woman, in his humble opinion, would be almost debased or degraded by it.
> She would be in danger of losing those admirable attributes of her sex—namely, her gentleness, her affection, and her domesticity. The hon. Member for Westminster, as a scholar, would recollect the words of a great man [*Pericles?*] who, flourished about 500 years before Christ, who, like the noble Earl at the head of the Cabinet, was the great leader, the first orator and statesman of the day. That distinguished individual said, in speaking of women— Let them not struggle to rise above their natural condition which has been assigned to them by Providence; let them desire to fly from the breath of praise almost as much as from the breath of censure.[333]

Finally, possibly with the petition that Mill had presented to Parliament a year earlier, Karslake asserted that:

> As not a lady in Essex had asked him to support the proposition in favour of a female franchise and believing that the women in other parts of England were equally indifferent on the subject, he came to the conclusion that the women of this country would prefer to remain as they were, being content with the happy homes and advantages they now possessed, even with the disabilities referred to by Chief Justice Blackstone.[334]

Almost immediately Barbara Bodichon and Helen Taylor, the instigators of the first petition, and their friends, Lydia Becker and Frances Power Cobbe started collecting signatures from women in Colchester. On 25th July Karslake

[333] Ibid.
[334] Ibid.

presented a list of 129 signatures to Parliament. Mill's amendment had already been rejected by 196 votes to 73.

This was not the end of anything. It was the start of everything.

George Denman, MP for Tiverton and a High Court Judge, who, in the debate on Mill's amendment, had said that he had heard no argument that would convince him to vote against it, questioned whether it needed to be made at all. After the Interpretation Act of 1850, known as Lord Brougham's Act and intended to make parliamentary language less verbose, the use of the words 'he' and 'man' in parliamentary documents meant females as well as males because in law 'it was declared that all words importing the masculine gender should be deemed to include females, unless it was specifically stated to the contrary.' The 1832 Reform Act had specified 'male persons'. Denman pointed to a similar confusion in Australia.

> In one of the colonies of Australia, by the use of the word "person" accidentally inserted in an Act of the Legislature, the female suffrage was given. Subsequently, it was said to have been found that such an advantage had arisen from its operation that they declined to alter it, not wishing to get rid of it.[335]

In the November, 3 months after the Reform Bill had received royal assent, a by-election was held in Manchester. A shop owner, Lily Maxwell, who met all the property requirements of the Act, had somehow found her way on to the list of voters. Egged on by Lydia Becker, she turned up to her local polling booth in Chorlton-on-Medlock, future home of the Pankhurst family of suffragettes, on election day. The returning officer who saw his job as seeing that everyone on the list announced their vote and was recorded properly as having done so allowed Lily into the booth where she announced loud and clear her vote for Jacob Bright, a peace campaigner and supporter of women's suffrage (*thus confounding Karslake's opinion that ordinary women had no interest in being part of the political process!*).

> In January 1868, the *Englishwoman's Review* wrote of Lily: 'It is sometimes said that women, especially those of the working class, have no political opinion at all. Yet this woman, who by chance was furnished with a vote, professed strong opinions and was delighted to have a chance of expressing them.'[336]

Thanks to an article by Serina Sandhu for inews.co.uk, following the work of Krista Cowman, a professor of history at the University of Lincoln, whose book "Women in British Politics, c. 1689-1979" is a far from dry but academic treatment of the ups and downs of the fight for equal political rights for women,

---

335 Ibid.

336 www.thehistorypress.co.uk/articles/lily-maxwell-the-first-woman-to-vote. Accessed 27/10/2020.

and an article by Helena Wojtczak (referenced later) I know more about the aftermath of the Maxwell debacle.

1868, General Election year, presented numerous opportunities for women to try and replicate Lily's moment of fame, some dishonestly by deliberate misspelling their names and some honestly when their name having escaped the check by a revising barrister responsible for checking the list was accepted by the returning officer. It was decided by Lydia Becker and others on the Committee of the Manchester Society for Women's Suffrage to get a legal ruling given that 5750 women were on the list of 'persons entitled to vote. On November 7th, 1868, appeals against being removed from the Manchester list on behalf of Mary Abbott and Phillipine Kyllman were brought to the Court of Common Pleas by the society's lawyer, Thomas Chorlton, against the revising barristers Lings and Kessler, respectively.

The ruling in the case of *Chorlton v. Lings* went against the suffrage campaign when, despite being represented by Sir John Coleridge, who was to become Lord Chief Justice of England, and Dr Richard Pankhurst, future husband of Emmeline, the judge ruled that it was contrary to the common law of England for a woman to vote in a general election.

Researcher and author, Helena Wojtczak, has found that in the General Election that followed in December 1868 "... women are known to have voted: 33 in Ashford (Kent); 13 in Salford; 12 in Gorton; 10 in Levenshulme; 9 in Manchester; two in Dublin and an unknown number in Finsbury, East Kent and elsewhere."[337]

The vote on Mill's amendment was 196 to 73. In the 1865 election 658 MPs were elected, 369 Liberals (the first time that name had been used) and 289 Conservatives. Among those who voted for the amendment were some Conservatives, notably the hugely respected Russell Gurney, MP for Southampton. Among those who voted against was the future Liberal Prime Minister, William Gladstone. Of the 369 Liberal members, 56% did not vote. When Lily Maxwell announced her vote it is said that a loud cheer rang out in the room. The first secret ballot was for a by-election in Pontefract on 15th August 1872. Wikipedia tells us that 16% of those men/male persons who voted were illiterate, requiring special arrangements to be made to record their previously oral vote. *Hm!*

That December Gladstone's Liberals won the Election with an increased majority. The setbacks of 1867 were to some extent offset by some real progress in the participation of women in public affairs albeit at a local level. In 1869 The Municipal Franchise Act allowed female ratepayers to vote for local councillors and serve as Poor Law Guardians. The 1888 Local Government Act extended their franchise to the newly created County and County Borough Council elections.

---

[337] British Women's Emancipation since the Renaissance (https://historyofwomen.org). Accessed 01/03/2021.

In 1870, the Elementary Education Act allowed women to be members of a School Board which established and administered elementary schools. Lydia Becker was on the Manchester Board. The 1907 Qualification of Women (County and Borough Councils) Act allowed unmarried or widowed women ratepayers to serve as Councillors and the recently widowed Elizabeth Garrett Anderson became the first woman mayor in 1908.

Set against this progress, Helena Wojtczak tells us that in the 34 years between 1870 and 1904, the subject was debated 18 times and blocked or postponed on many other occasions. As I return to the issue of married women's rights, it is worth contemplating that William Thompson's book, *Appeal of one half the human race, women, against the pretensions of the other half, men, to retain them in political, and thence in civil and domestic slavery*, was published in 1825. It was 42 years before Mill could raise the issue in Parliament and another 61 years before women had the same right as men to elect those who made laws that indirectly or directly affected 100% of British citizens, nearly 10 years after the first woman MP had joined the ranks of the hitherto male only club. *Why?*

Helena Wojtczak's research found these words from the Revising Barrister for West Kent, Mr W.M. Best, in justification for his striking out of the women put forward by the local women's suffrage society:

> *It was not the fault of women that they were a subordinate sex. They were subordinate by the law of nature, the law of God, by the Constitution, and by universal practice throughout the whole world for 6,000 years.*[338]

In line with the reforming burst of the Liberal government, in 1870, the Married Women's Property Act was passed, the main provisions of which were:

- Wages and investments made by a wife could be held by a wife for her own separate use, independent from her husband.
- A wife could inherit up to £200 in her own right and keep the money.
- A wife was allowed to keep any property inherited from her next of kin as long as it was not bound in trust.
- A wife could hold and inherit rented property.
- The act also held that both parents could be made liable to support children.[339]

However, it was not until 1882 that Gladstone's government, elected in 1880, passed a further Married Women's Property Act that ended coverture and

---

[338] Ibid.

[339] www.intriguing-history.com/married-womens-property-act. Accessed 31/10/2020.
www.intriguing-history.com/married-womens-property-act. Accessed 31/10/2020.

allowed a married woman, a feme covert, to be a legal person with all the rights and responsibilities of a feme sole. Interestingly, the only section still extant is Section 17 which regulates disputes between husband and wife over whose property is whose or what share each is entitled to, further proof that in common law, no matter what their married status, they are TWO separate people! *Coverture, RIP. Citizenship, here we come!*

Chapter 41
Social Purity

Between a man and his wife, a husband's infidelity is nothing… The man imposes no bastards on his wife. A man, to be sure, is criminal in the sight of God but he does not do his wife any very material injury if he does not insult her.

– Samuel Johnson, *Boswell's Life of Johnson*

…there is no comparison to be made between prostitutes and the men who consort with them. With the one sex the offence is committed as a matter of gain; with the other it is an irregular indulgence of a natural impulse.

-*Report of Royal Commission upon the Administration and Operation of the Contagious Diseases Acts*, 1871

Preamble

The double standard in all its different guises was confirmed by new medical knowledge, without contravention by religion, superstition, astrology or any of the other discredited dark or magical arts, to be injurious to health, men's, women's and children's. To return to Locke and Mill, it did 'harm' and, therefore, was immoral as well as unhealthy. In 1879, Josephine Butler wrote a book on 'Social Purity' linking the morality of the sexual habits of men under the double standard to the threat to public health, an idea far more fatal to the patriarchy than a hundred suffragette arrests. There is nothing more humiliating to the male hunter than shooting himself in the foot!

It is hard to argue with Samuel Johnson's pragmatic observation about the differing consequences of a wife's adultery and that of a husband, except it would not have been made were it not for the sacramental significance attached to the wife's role in producing sons to inherit and hold on to the patrimony. In his request to the House of Lords for a second reading for his Matrimonial Causes Bill in 1923 Lord Buckmaster signified his understanding of the husband's fear of bringing up a child who has none of his blood (In the Jeremy Kyle show it is frequently shown that paternity is still a burning issue today but now confirmed 100% by DNA testing).

> I should think there can be no greater tragedy in domestic life than the tragedy of the man of unfailing fidelity to his wife, and of deep devotion—the man, to use the words of Othello: Who dotes, yet doubts;

> suspects, yet strongly loves!—who looks into the face of a child born in his own household and is tortured by doubt as to whether it has the right to call him father.[340]

However, the result of a husband's infidelity could be the birth of an illegitimate child. Ann Sumner Holmes cites the reply of a solicitor, E. Heron Allen, to the 1910 Royal Commission.

> He [the husband] does not introduce [a child] into his own house but he introduces it into the house of someone else—either the house of an unmarried girl or of another married woman, and I think his sin is infinitely greater than the woman who brings a little child into the world who will, at all events, be protected.[341]

Powerful, therefore, though Johnson's aphorism was in the 18th century before and during which the rich and powerful royals, Henry VIII or Charles II, or the great dukes, like William Cavendish, could do what they liked, granting their illegitimate children titles and wealth, as in the case of the former, or bringing them into their household, as did the latter, the economic consequences of the husband's infidelity in the less than mega-rich were not so easily brushed under the carpet.

There were also serious social consequences of male infidelity which brought the married women's property, and the suffrage causes into an alliance with the campaign for equal treatment for women in the law relating to contagious diseases. In no other respects was the cultural double standard more blatant than on the issue of prostitution in the second half of the 19th century.

The two testosterone-fuelled activities of males, sex and violence, were the touch papers for the existence of the prostitute. Warfare was a men-only affair, but the heterosexual sex drive required women. War at sea or in a land campaign required men to be away from the company of women for long periods and in their company for periods too short to form lasting pair bonds, which, even if made, were almost certainly going to be interrupted by long absences in which for soldiers and sailors 'theirs was but to do and die'.

In ports or garrison towns, furloughs were spent indulging in 'wine, women and song'. With the ever-widening empire, such towns and cities and the activities of furloughed military personnel were the perfect recipe for the spread of nefarious businesses and contagious diseases. The ever-increasing world trade network meant that similarly cloistered men in civil employment, such as the merchant navy, were drawn into the lifestyle. Faced with the probability of an early death from disease, starvation or military activity it is understandable that

---

[340] api.parliament.uk/historic-hansard/lords/1923/jun/26/matrimonial-causes-bill. Accessed 02/11/2020.

[341] Holmes, Ann Sumner. "The Double Standard in the English Divorce Laws, 1857-1923." Law & Social Inquiry, vol. 20, no. 2, 1995, pp. 601–620. JSTOR, www.jstor.org/stable/828954. Accessed 03/11/2020.

chastity was a demand too much for the average, illiterate and poor soldier or sailor and often disabled ex-soldier or ex-sailor, however Christian they were.

The sex transaction, therefore, between serviceman and sex worker worked for both parties but was created by the all-male activities of wealth gathering and violence. For a poor, unskilled woman on the breadline and frequently with a family to feed and no father's wage, for whatever reason, all she had to sell was her body with the distinct risks of conception and disease and the fairly short-term attraction of the product she was selling.

In Chapter 3, I introduced you to Fatema Mernissi who, looking from the outside, noted the Eurocentric view of female value being based on youth and beauty. This perception led to the sex trafficking of very young girls, not least by older women, mothers (with the age of consent set at 13 until the Criminal Law Amendment Act of 1885 raised it to 16 it was not unknown for 10-12-year-olds to be ensnared as their contribution to the household finances) and madams.

This trafficking had a lucrative exporting side to it by which young girls from London were sold to European pleasure palaces. For four years from 1881 social reformers had been trying to criminalise this trade and raise the age of consent but it took a newspaper expose by W.T. Stead (The Eliza Armstrong case), the editor of *The Pall Mall Gazette*, to push the House of Commons in particular to make the Bill law in August 1885. It would be fair to say that the involvement of children in the immoral subculture of the capital city induced a moral panic in which the double standard should have been exposed but, with hindsight, seems to have persisted in the all-male establishment especially when it came to apportioning blame for the dreadful state of affairs.

Firstly, when in doubt blame foreigners. Venereal disease, either syphilis or gonorrhoea, acquired many xenophobic monikers. In its first recorded outbreak in Naples in 1495 syphilis was known as "The French Disease" because the French army was invading at the time. It was almost certainly coined by an eminent Italian, what we would now call, epidemiologist, Girolamo Fracastoro, who wrote a poem in 1530 called *Syphilis sive morbus gallicus* (Syphilis or the French Disease) fictionally suggesting that it was a divine punishment for challenging the gods, in this case Apollo.

Malta, Poland and Germany followed suit but the French retaliated by calling it "The Italian Disease". The Russians called it "The Polish Disease", the Dutch called it "The Spanish Disease" and the Turks called it "The Christian Disease". In England 'it was variously known as 'the French disease', 'the Spanish itch' and 'the evil of Naples'[342]. More poignantly, gonorrhoea was known as "The Clap", almost certainly after French brothels, *Les Clapiers*, to the descendants of which young English girls were being sent as late as the 1880s.

Secondly, blame a whole New World. Experts still argue about the origins of venereal disease. As this first recorded mass outbreak was in Naples just three years after Columbus had discovered the New World to the west the suspicion, known as The Columbian Transfer, not yet confirmed by anthropologists or

[342] notchesblog.com/2015/10/20/cfp-the-history-of-venereal-disease. Accessed 08/11/2020.

archaeologists but conveniently nothing to do with imperial Britain, that this curse upon European males from doing (*we will see the argument later*) what came naturally, became widespread. The advantage of this theory was that the women at whom it pointed the finger for being the source of the 'curse' were uncivilised savages unlike the men who either forced, paid or otherwise inveigled them into sex!

Indeed, the monikers mentioned above do not seem to deny that those who spread these fatal diseases were soldiers and sailors. The investigations into the Columbian Transfer have turned up former companions of Columbus who went on to serve in the army of Charles VIII on campaign in the Kingdom of Naples. *In 2020, as I write this, we have first-hand knowledge of how quickly a contagion can pass from the few to the many!*

Thirdly, and most comfortably for the patriarchy, it was easiest to blame the 'source' of the disease, women prostitutes. (Although, we know now, and it was known then, that male brothels also existed but, of all the unmentionable sexual taboos, homosexuality was the most sinful. The Cleveland Street Scandal of 1889 was a shocking eye-opener for the average English, middle-class, Christian, literate couple.) One might think that, given the social standing of the male clientele who spread the disease, prostitution was a lower-class activity but, there were at least three levels of prostitute operating in mid-Victorian England.

In addition to the streetwalkers, there were sex workers, often with their own premises, who catered for clients from the professions (Judges, for instance, were frequently lampooned.) as well as those, at whom we have already looked, courtesans etc., who provided the service for the upper classes. If contagious diseases were principally a lower-class problem they would not have bothered the ruling class that much, I suspect, but in two respects they did.

Firstly, they greatly diminished trained cannon fodder—in the case of good seamen, highly trained—at a time when ever greater numbers were required to expand the empire and enforce the law in the growing number of colonies. Secondly, the diseases and their effects were well known to the ruling class having been passed to a significant number of them via a number of routes; for instance, the Grand Tour for young aristocrats took in the fleshpots of Europe for those too weak to resist and was just one example of the over-indulged youth of such family scions; homosexuality I have already mentioned; and the taboo subject of paraphilias, two of which I have already referred to, flagellation and paedophilia. 'Decent', married men, pillars of the community, with any of these urges turned to prostitutes knowing that, in all likelihood, their secret would never be known, and no questions would be asked.

Any discussion such as that of child sex trafficking or contagious disease that might lead to the secret coming out needed to be nipped in the bud unless its threat to the moral probity and physical well-being of the Empire-building elite tipped the balance in favour of legislation to combat a 'social evil'. The 1864 Act I am about to describe was introduced very suddenly to parliament and with very little debate.

The 1864 Contagious Diseases Act allowed the police in a number of ports and garrison towns (the geographical extent of its use was increased by further Acts in 1866 and 1869) to pick up any woman suspected of being a prostitute, force her, on the authorisation of a magistrate, to be examined and, if found to be infected, transfer her to a lock ward usually in the local military infirmary for a minimum of three months. Lack of space meant the local workhouse infirmary frequently had to be used. If a woman refused to cooperate she could be imprisoned, often subjected to hard labour and, worse still, if picked up and found not to be engaged in prostitution the mere fact of the experience so stigmatised her that she could not find work thus being forced into prostitution!

Josephine Butler, a signatory of the 1866 petition, suffragist and activist for education of lower-class women, coined the term 'steel rape' for the examination the emotional experience and mental trauma of which, even for women used to male dominance over their bodies, we can only imagine. Incidentally, the steel instrument was a speculum, versions of which are still essential for vaginal examination, but the Victorian model does look quite menacing. Josephine Butler, a biography of whom by Helen Mathers, *Patron Saint of Prostitutes: Josephine Butler and a Victorian Scandal*, asks why she is not better known, unlike most of the male legislators, got to know and understand the impoverished women driven to prostitution in Liverpool and gave them an opportunity to speak out. Wikipedia gives us one such voice.

> It is men, only men, from the first to the last that we have to do with! To please a man I did wrong at first, then I was flung about from man to man. Men police lay hands on us. By men we are examined, handled, doctored. In the hospital it is a man again who makes prayer and reads the Bible for us. We are had up before magistrates who are men, and we never get out of the hands of men till we die![343]

Josephine, however, knew that to get these women and children the protection of the law she had to convince those 658 male MPs, mostly upper middle and upper class, elected by one third of British men, all men of property, and 130 or so upper-class Lords, all male, of the immoral and hypocritical nature of the double standard they applied to women and, for that matter, poverty. Child prostitution brought together two legal issues, prostitution and child abuse, both of which were of real concern to Josephine and her National Association for the Repeal of the Contagious Diseases Acts.

In his blog in 2010, Dr Bruce Rosen, now sadly deceased, an Australian expert on Victorian history, pointed out the binary nature of the problem as far as the law was concerned. *As I pointed out earlier, if we add the campaign to end coverture then there were three legal concerns all stemming from one overarching question—The Woman Question, Christine Pizan's Querelle des Femmes!*

---

343 https://en.wikipedia.org/wiki/Contagious_Diseases_Acts. Accessed 11/11/2020.

Dr Rosen quite rightly makes this really important point about child sexual abuse:

> The legal definition must, inevitably, revolve around questions of age and coercion. As well, in a much murkier realm, it must be defined by attitudes towards both the "abused" and the "abuser."[344]

Whereas much had been done to recognise the physical abuse of children, and women for that matter, by overwork and subjection to life-threatening conditions in mills, factories and mines (or the more famous case of chimneysweeps) as well as neglect of their intellectual potential through the lack of free public education, the perception of any female who had reached puberty as a sex object rather than a person or a child, even, was pervasive in the morally repressive Victorian social code. For hundreds of years among the aristocracy the sexual partnership of an older, socially and economically established man and a young fertile woman with years of childbearing in front of her was the propertied classes' dream ticket to ensuring the longevity of the patrimony.

Childhood is a very culturally influenced concept in terms of its physical presentation and duration. I rarely have much time for the excuse that moral standards were influenced by the era in which they were established and enforced but I do understand that times were very different before the Welfare State, universal education and contraception, not to mention female emancipation.

What I do not accept is that any form of 'civilisation' accepted as morally appropriate sexual relations with and impregnation of a girl of 12-years-old and under. The Church, Roman Catholic or Anglican, may have approved the marriage of children to adults for political or dynastic reasons but did not sanction sexual relations as part of the deal.

In working families, children had to pay their way and the crowded nature of living conditions provided cover for perversions such as incest and paedophilia. It does not mean that such sexual activity was approved of. The 1828 Offences against the Person Act confirmed the severe disapproval of child abuse by making having 'carnal knowledge' of a child under 10 a felony punishable by death.

Carnal knowledge of a child aged between 10 and 12 was a misdemeanour punishable by imprisonment with the possibility of hard labour. This remained the case as the rationalisation of criminal law continued throughout the 1830s. By the 1841 Substitution of Punishments of Death Act, sex with a child under 10 remained a felony but the death penalty was replaced by penal servitude, imprisonment with hard labour.

---

[344] vichist.blogspot.com/2010/10/sexual-abuse-and-sexual-exploitation-in.html. Accessed 11/11/2020.

Dr Bruce Rosen recounts an incident from 1849 in which an old man is observed by a policeman importuning a very young girl to go home with him. The policeman is fully aware of the impropriety of the man's behaviour but can do nothing, by law, to prevent it. The man who wrote of the incident to *The Times* was reluctant to identify the man for fear of the shock to his family, if he had one, of the revelation. In the 1860s, a chronicler known only as 'Walter' expressed the viewpoint that a 12-year-old girl was fully competent to judge when she was ready for a sexual relationship and many in London were sexually active. Dr Rosen goes on to examine the precision with which the 1861 Offences against the Person Act defined the propriety of sex with a young girl. In summary:

- Sex with a girl under 10 was a felony punishable in a severe case by at least 3 years of imprisonment with hard labour.
- Sex with a girl between 10 and 12 was a misdemeanour punishable in a severe case by 3 years imprisonment with hard labour.
- Deceitful procurement of a young woman under 21 for sex with any man was a misdemeanour punishable by no more than 2 years imprisonment which was the punishment for the other 2 scenarios if considered to be less severe.

The Offences against the Person Act 1875 raised the age of the first category to 12 and the limits of the second were raised to 12-13 but it was not until the 1885 Criminal Law Amendment Act that the age at which a young woman was competent to consent to sexual intercourse was raised to 16, the level at which it stands today, 135 years later. Interestingly, the discretion over the age at which an adolescent could engage in a legal sexual relationship, i.e., one ratified by marriage, was for hundreds of years left with the parents or legal guardians.

It was not until 1929 that the Age of Marriage Act raised the minimum age at which parental consent could be given from 12 for a girl and 14 for a boy to 16 for both. The fact that the average parent knew for hundreds of years prior to the mid-Victorians the impropriety of post-pubescence sex is confirmed by this Wikipedia entry.

> In most of North-western Europe, marriages at very early ages were rare. One thousand marriage certificates from 1619 to 1660 in the Archdiocese of Canterbury show that only one bride was 13 years old, four were 15, twelve were 16, and seventeen were 17 years old; while the other 966 brides were at least 19 years old.[345]

The issue of child prostitution gave rise to multiple examples of double standards, involving as it did contemplation of the nature of childhood, the consequences of poverty, the nature of prostitution and the culture of class.

---

[345] en.m.wikipedia.org/wiki/Marriageable_age. Accessed 14/11/2020.

Our 21st-century cultural assessment of the rights and, therefore, definition of childhood, comprehends such things as education, pleasure, health and innocence. To a mid-Victorian working-class family on the breadline, these were beyond their wildest dreams whereas to a middle or upper-class family they were provided for due to their wealth, socially reinforced conventions and moral expectations. I very much doubt that these wealthier classes provided child prostitutes, although it was far from unprecedented to quasi-enforce sexual intercourse between a young adolescent, sexually naive woman and a much older sexually experienced man. I very much doubt that post-pubescent working-class girls wanted to be one either.

Their trafficking abroad which caused such moral outrage in the 1880s was due to financial need. The signing on fee, basically the selling price of a child prostitute, would have temporarily alleviated family hardship and the future drain on the family finances from another mouth to feed.

When the choice had to be made of a roof over their head and bread on the table or the chastity expected of them by the Church to which they went on Sunday, their only day off, chastity came a poor second. Without an effective contraception device or regime, the only 100% certain method to avoid a large family was sufficient self-control to abstain from sex. Chastity and self-restraint, which were not part of the upper-class Georgian or Victorian male's skill set, were expected of working-class males in order to prevent the Malthusian outcome of overpopulation whereby population would outstrip resources leading to a lowering of the standard of living sufficient to restore the balance.

For financial and accommodation reasons, the working-class wife and mother would, *surely*, have wanted a small family and her daughters to marry and leave the family home, to the finances of which their wage would be a significant contribution and to the childcare and chores her extra pair of hands would be a blessing, later rather than sooner. Marriage for the poor was dominated by subsistence finance whereas for the upper class it was dominated by procreation and dynastic solidarity. The ideal scenario, therefore, for the former would be a family with as few non-wage earners as possible—unlikely unless her husband exercised self-restraint—with later marriage for the wage-earning daughters and sons, and for the latter a large family and earlier marriage, for the females at least.

Rather than the inhumane outcomes of overpopulation, such as famine, drought and disease, that resolved the imbalance between population and resources through a catastrophic increase in deaths or resorting to equally painful post-conception measures such as abortion and infanticide, it seemed more humane to reduce the birth rate by preventing conception. Yet, when Annie Besant and Charles Bradlaugh published in July 1877 Charles Knowlton's *Fruits of Philosophy* which explained various methods of birth control, they were prosecuted for publishing and distributing obscene material. Sex and the human body were to be kept to private conversations as was the indulgence of the middle-class male's libido.

We tend to think that this tract was responding to a fairly recent phenomenon. We would be wrong. Barrier devices, IUDs and condoms, spermicides and douches had been around for at least 4 millennia and herbal medicines to induce sterility, forerunners of the contraceptive pill, had always been tried. They, of course, indicate that there was a social awareness of the need to limit family size for economic reasons. (Indeed, the notoriety of the 1877 trial meant that sales of Knowlton's work increased from 700 per year to 125,000 per year!)

Charles Knowlton's book was written and published in 1832 in Taunton, Massachusetts leading to his imprisonment and a blasphemy trial for the publisher, Abner Kneeland. It was not the first book published on birth control in Britain. The radical printer, Richard Carlile, had published a book, entitled Every Woman's Book, on birth control and women's emancipation in 1826. Fellow Radical, William Cobbett denounced it as "so filthy, so disgusting, so beastly, as to shock even the lewdest men and women."[346]

The condemnation of such methods, firstly by the Roman Catholic Church and then by the Anglican Church (Fruits of Love was said by a local preacher, Mason Grosvenor, to have been behind a campaign of "infidelity and licentiousness"[347]) , does not seem to accord with their work with and for the poor for whom having too many children was an obvious contributor to overcrowding, poor health, loss or insufficiency of income and sexual impropriety, which was precisely Besant and Bradlaugh's defence to being accused of distributing obscene material.

At that time, before the suggestion that women enjoyed sex and might actually initiate it, the admission by the all-male moral arbiters that contraception was actually socially, morally even, beneficial would dent their centuries old struggle to enforce self-restraint and banish the sin of adultery through denial of the flesh by engaging in the spiritual. Furthermore, it was commonly argued that by removing the consequences of sex, i.e., legitimate or illegitimate children, it would lead to widespread male promiscuity, a dangerously decadent proliferation of the deadly sin of lust.

The middle class also dealt in ideals. A popular fantasy was that of the perfect woman, 'The Angel in the House', taken from a poem by Coventry Patmore which eulogised the chaste, submissive, fully supportive wife and mother. The opposite of the domestic angel was the 'fallen woman' defined by any sexual activity outside marriage, pre-marital sex, adultery, prostitution, even rape. Their Bible-based attitudes, almost certainly a reaction to the loose morals of the 18th century landed aristocracy, were against any regulation that would interfere with God's instruction to go forth and multiply (even so-called Puritans, as pointed out earlier, approved of sex within marriage), relying on chastity of the wife, the self-restraint of the husband and the social pressure of conforming to well entrenched expectations to regulate family size and age of marriage.

---

[346] en.wikipedia.org/wiki/Richarhttpsd_Carlile. Accessed 07/02/2021.
[347] en.wikipedia.org/wiki/Charles_Knowlton. Accessed 07/02/2021.

Finally, the attitudes of legislators, a growing number of whom were middle-class, to poverty were guided by the social, economic and philosophical tenets of the time centred around the two principles of self-reliance and idleness. In addition to the warnings of the Reverend Thomas Malthus, the Poor Laws, following Benthamite principles, were based on the strange logic that not working was more pleasurable than working and, therefore, living on the dole, known as outdoor relief, was better than working long hours for low wages.

To get a handout of food and shelter the poor would have to enter workhouses many of which, as proved by the Andover Workhouse Scandal of 1845, treated those who were desperate enough to go there in an uncivilised and inhumane way. *I would imagine* that anything would be seen as preferrable to that. Indeed prostitutes stood out in workhouses as better fed and better dressed than the desperately ragged and undernourished women who were the standard occupants.

It could be said, therefore, that those who should have provided employment or, when necessary, humane welfare to those who needed a living wage to feed, shelter and clothe their dependants, were supporting a government policy more likely to increase than decrease the moral evil of prostitution with its concomitant threat to health from the spread of contagious diseases. The Contagious Diseases Acts of the 1860s, by blaming the sexual immorality of female sex workers and the lack of sexual restraint in impressed fighting men for the social malaise that such a policy and its consequences they themselves created, were just two examples of the hypocrisy of Victorian moral values which took a century and two World Wars to remove.

As for the involvement of children, the clients who would pay for sex with a child would almost certainly include paedophiles who, in the pleasure palaces of London, Brussels or Paris, for reasons of cost alone, were unlikely to have come from the working class. There is no chicken and egg in this morality. A seller will make no money from a product for which there is no demand; the need for a necessity or the desire for a luxury comes first. There would be no fruit machine if there was no desire to gamble. Male desire for sexual satisfaction gives/gave rise to prostitution just as it does/did to adultery and, therefore, subjected them both to the same moral double standard. In fact, there are at least three instances of the double standard observable in 19th century attitudes to prostitution, each relating to institutional failure within the patriarchal culture.

Firstly, while affirming that the institution of marriage was the solution to male desire, which it clearly was not, being valued as a dynastic and procreational solution rather than a romantic and pleasurable experience, the territorial and capitalist elite created situations, through their wars and trading ambitions, for thousands of men in the armed services and trading enterprise which denied them the opportunity to marry and channel their desire for sex into a socially and morally acceptable, and more healthy, direction whilst the daily press related ever more extreme stories about the aristocratic failures to practise what they preached.

Secondly, Christian preaching that sexual intercourse only belonged within marriage, supported by legal institutions such as coverture, clearly did not work, even with the threat of eternal damnation. Given the high sin tariff of extra-marital sex, particularly among the mid-Victorian middle classes, probably due to their non-conformist Puritan origins, it needed to be kept a social secret and, because God is omniscient, a rationale had to be found for the sin to be shifted away from the actual sinner.

Scripture only needed to be tweaked a little to place the blame on the daughters of Eve among whom was a 'class of sinners', temptresses who, betraying their God given nature to be virtuous by denying their sexuality, led men astray by presenting a temptation too hard to resist. Prostitutes were the sinners, 'fallen women' of 'easy virtue'. Blame for an action implies an intention to do it or a negligence in taking steps to prevent it happening. So, this is how the double standard worked. Men could not help being unable to restrain their sexual desire. It was their nature. Women, therefore, were to blame for extra-marital sex by failing to exercise self-restraint on their willingness to allow men to indulge it because such an intention was a betrayal of their 'nature'.

Thirdly, when W. T. Stead wrote his pieces in 1885, it was not prostitution that caused the moral outrage. It was sex with pubescent girls. A culture that for hundreds of years valued females for their procreative potential, in a time when any number of things could have snuffed it out, was turning away from condoning childbearing in adolescence, with a view to criminalising it as a sexual perversion akin to incest, bigamy, bestiality, sodomy or any one of the more deviant paraphilias. The term paedophilia was being coined by an Austrian psychiatrist, Richard von Krafft-Ebing, at the same time as Stead's articles were being published.

Although Ebing was careful to apply the term to sexual arousal by a pre-pubescent child what had been a discretionary power of the pater familias, i.e., the moral and social acceptability of the age at which a young woman/child could have sex, was being re-examined scientifically in the context of psychiatric disorders.

The exposure to such perverted (Ebing defined 'perversion' very much within the sexual morality of the day, "With opportunity for the natural satisfaction of the sexual instinct, every expression of it that does not correspond with the purpose of nature—i.e., propagation, —must be regarded as perverse."[348]) activity was blamed on mothers, particularly single mothers whose duty it was to urgently seek their own, for widows a new, pater familias.

Unmarried mothers were the lowest of the low with no real examination of their circumstances, again far too often attributed to a sinful lack of chastity. The fact that there was a father somewhere did not seem to concern anyone very much. For the wealthy, money could paper over any problem areas. For the middle class, faith and shame were enough to deter most young women from engaging in pre-marital sex.

---

348 https://en.wikipedia.org/wiki/Richard_von_Krafft-Ebing. Accessed 19/11/2020.

For the majority of fallen women, the discrimination against them and their illegitimate child was intense and widespread, increasing the chance of abandonment (The first Foundling Hospital was opened in 1740 after a long campaign by the philanthropist, Thomas Coram.) and, if female and not abandoned, child prostitution. In 2014, Ruth Richardson, in an article prompted by Dickens' novel, *Oliver Twist*, wrote this about the prospects for unmarried mother and child.

> Few employers would take on a woman with an illegitimate child as a regular worker, partly because childcare distracts a mother, and partly because of the shame of illegitimacy. London was full of poor people seeking work, and without some useful skill, it was hard to find. With a child to care for, it was extremely difficult to make enough money to survive. Images of ballad singers begging on the streets—known as the lowest kind of 'work'—often show a woman with baby to care for. Many unwed mothers, or widows with small children, ended up like Oliver's mother: without a home, in poor health, hungry and exhausted, before they would apply to enter the last place of refuge for the desperate: the workhouse.
>
> There, such women would be expected to undertake some of the drudgery of the institution. These women were singled out in some places by having to wear a special uniform which drew attention to their status as unmarried mothers. Some women became institutionalised and ended up as pauper nurses, others might leave their child in the institution, to try to make a new life outside. Like many women, Oliver's poor mother was too weak when she gave birth, and died, leaving him alone in the world.[349]

Attitudes to prostitution itself, among the religious icons of the middle classes can be illustrated by an extract from a letter to Florence Nightingale from her friend, the Oxford don, Benjamin Jowett, containing some advice for Josephine Butler.

> Prostitutes she was told were 'a class of sinners whom she had better have left to themselves' since they were authors of their own destruction.[350]

Neither Jowett nor Nightingale was ever married, and both were famously chaste. Neither of them was ever financially needy and both were highly educated. Neither of them was unkind or unsympathetic to those less fortunate yet they were unable to see the effects of male domination, from which they both

---

[349] www.bl.uk/romantics-and-victorians/articles/foundlings-orphans-and-unmarried-mothers. Accessed 17/11/2020.

[350] Mathers, Helen. Patron Saint of Prostitutes (p. 12). The History Press. Kindle Edition.

benefitted and which they both supported, on the life choices of these women. In his book, A Promised Land, Barack Obama used this wonderful phrase with which he described David Cameron as 'someone who'd never been pressed too hard by life' which classic example of 'damning with faint praise' implies that such a comfortable life can diminish one's ability to understand those who have, something which Josephine Butler tried so hard to overcome.

For many well-intentioned, law-abiding and moral middle-class Victorian families who probably voted for a Liberal Prime Minister who constantly fended off inuendo about his attempts to help fallen women Obama's description would have been most apt, as it is for Jowett, Nightingale and, for that matter, myself.

Chapter 42
Adultery

Marriage is the triumph of imagination over intelligence. Second marriage is the triumph of hope over experience.
– Oscar Wilde

The Constitution only gives people the right to pursue happiness. You have to catch it yourself.
– Benjamin Franklin

Preamble

Western culture seems to be drifting away from making the link between love and marriage. They no longer go together like a horse and carriage. The image and hope, so cynically referred to by Wilde, relates to the romance of a lifelong partnership that will bring happiness. For those who find it, It is the 'catch' of a lifetime but 'to err is human'. To live with the consequences of a deliberate, reasoned action is equally to be human, a socially responsible human. To avoid living with a mistake, however reasonable the decision seemed at the time, for the rest of your life without any chance to correct it is what divorce is all about.

A law that denies the opportunity to correct it by denying the right to pursue happiness to imperfect, but not evil or otherwise harmful, people living in an imperfect world is contrary to the ephemeral but ever-present concept of freedom.

No other issue, however, demonstrated the double standard more blatantly than that of adultery. The 1857 Act may have taken the divorce issue out of the church courts and away from the noble promise of 'for better or worse' but the morality of marriage was still that of Christianity. The 7th Commandment, 'Thou shalt not commit adultery', and the 10th Commandment, 'Thou shalt not covet thy neighbour's wife', set the moral framework for marriage, even though the Old Testament God seems to have discounted a wife coveting a neighbour's husband. Adultery, therefore, was a sin, it transgressed divine law. Any other sin, such as murder, theft or bearing false witness or failing to honour your parents or observe the Sabbath would carry the same penalty or require the same atonement for both genders.

Just to reiterate some things we have already established, for centuries, the rich and powerful had atoned for sinning with money and gifts and people of all classes and conditions understood penance and confession sufficient to clear all those guilty consciences. This atonement, however, was for God's benefit and not intended for the victim of the sin. As we saw in Chapters 12-15 the principle of Lordship ran through the Christian culture as a matter of fact. It, by definition, implied ownership of property and people to work on it and with it for the benefit of the Lord; slaves or servants, tenants and villeins, vassals and craftsmen. These human beings belonged to the Lord as much as the things that contributed to his wealth.

Among them, at least according to the common law, was his wife. All these people were subject to the Lord's power. Effectively, he could do what he liked to them and with them, including sinning against them. They were his inferiors. The only protection they had was the King and Christian morality whose justice was open to human interpretation, corruption and frequent disputation.

By 1882, after 300 years of significant challenge, the moral high ground of an Established Church, the infallibility of the Pope, the Divine Right to rule of the monarch and the omnipotence of Lordship—in whatever position it displayed itself; landowner, pater familias, husband, master—had all begun to show significant cracks. They were no longer facts of life. In the parliamentary debate on the 1923 Matrimonial Causes Act, when the Conservative MP, Dennis Herbert, was asked why any father would view his son's adultery a lot less seriously than his daughter's, he feebly replied, according to Ann Sumner Holmes, "I am not concerned with the question why; it is a fact." With a vote of 257 to 26 in favour of an equal treatment in the Commons and 95 to 8 in the Lords male legislators, for whatever reasons, did not agree.

When the Married Women's Property Act effectively ended coverture, the common law status of a wife as her husband's property, the double standard over adultery was exposed and one of the two bastions of male supremacy (the other being the exclusive right to make the rules) came under serious siege. The fact that it took another 55 years to fall was more due to the stubborn opposition of its defenders, men, than the strength of its walls. With issues of property, child custody and money sorted, adultery and any resulting judicial separation and/or divorce became a purely moral issue.

One of the definitive indicators of middle-classness was a greater adherence to Christian morality, a higher standard fuelled by a belief in a more demanding and less forgiving God than the God of the Catholic tradition and a Church and Churchmen less easily persuaded by money to intercede on behalf of sinners combined with strict communal enforcement of the moral tenets of the Bible.

Reputation in middle-class culture depended on lifestyle and, unlike the upper classes, could not be bought. From the pulpit every Sunday they were reminded of the 'wages of sin' such as prostitution, unmarried mothers, illegitimate children and venereal disease and several stereotypes, such as promiscuous men, drunken men, homosexual men and adulterous men became targets for 'Social Purists' most of whom were women. These Purist Societies placed the emphasis on male self-control of their sex drive the lack of which the 1857 Act and the double standard seemed to condone.

Instead of women such as prostitutes and unmarried mothers being condemned to a damaged social standing and labelled as 'fallen' by sexual activity with a male client or seducer they wanted a higher moral standard matched by a higher moral standard for men, at least as high as the patriarchal culture expected of wives, daughters and feme soles. In short, if you call yourself a Christian then read Matthew 7:5 and practice what you preach.

Adultery had always, except for that brief period during the Commonwealth, been a civil matter. Some sins, however, such as murder and theft were criminal. The criteria for a criminal conviction involved an assumption of innocence unless guilt could be proved to 12 impartial strangers 'beyond a reasonable doubt'. With regard to adultery men, decent Christian men, not overtly misogynistic, stripped of their droits de seigneur and their privileged place in the queue for God's forgiveness of sin, stood accused of a double moral standard in the Court of Public Opinion.

Their accusers, like Josephine Butler looking at the problem of prostitution in a speech in 1879, pointed to 'the unequal standard of morality; the false idea that there is one code of morality for men and another for women.'[351] The double standard did not go unnoticed in the debate on the 1857 Bill. An out of office William Gladstone made this observation in the Commons: "I believe that the evil of introducing this principle of inequality between men and women is far greater than the evil which would arise from additional cases of divorce."

In the Lords, the Bishop of Salisbury agreed. "an indulgence should not be allowed to the man which was denied to the woman."[352] When the Royal Commission on Divorce and Matrimonial Causes interviewed witnesses in 1910 the minutes recorded this statement from Hensley Henson, future Dean of Durham, "In no respect is the teaching of the New Testament more original than in the emphasis it places on the equality of the sexes."[353]

As a character witness, then, Christianity, in a two-pronged attack, social purism and egalitarianism, overruled the principle of marriage for life at all costs in favour of the removal of moral hypocrisy, higher standards of decency among married men and the alleviation of social evils caused by male promiscuity. *Stoney Bowes must have turned in his grave!*

Having forfeited the guarantee of God's forgiveness, the next defence was that wives did not or should not really mind a husband's infidelity because he could not help himself, it did not mean that he loved his wife and children any less. It was held widely to be against women's God-given nature not to be submissive, understanding, supportive and forgiving. To a husband adultery was a result of sexual desire, 'a surprise of the senses' as one MP put it in 1857, and, in the case of a single act of adultery, a 'lapse' which 'on the part of a man is not

---

[351] Holmes, Ann Sumner. "The Double Standard in the English Divorce Laws, 1857-1923." *Law & Social Inquiry*, vol. 20, no. 2, 1995, pp. 601–620. *JSTOR*, www.jstor.org/stable/828954. Accessed 25 Nov. 2020. Holmes, Ann Sumner. "The Double Standard in the English Divorce Laws, 1857-1923." *Law & Social Inquiry*, vol. 20, no. 2, 1995, pp. 601–620. *JSTOR*, www.jstor.org/stable/828954. Accessed 25 Nov. 2020.

[352] Ibid.

[353] Ibid.

inconsistent with a continued esteem and love for his wife.' The ability to self-sacrifice and the forgiving nature of a cuckquean was described in 1910 as 'most touching and beautiful'.[354]

Adultery by a wife was a 'fall', 'an error of the heart', a 'defiance' of her 'natural modesty' and 'social conventions' that made her action 'a greater degradation and perversion of affection on the part of a married woman than does similar conduct on the part of a man.' Furthermore, in 1857, the Lord Advocate, Scotland's highest legal officer, distinguished between the social perception of forgiveness from a cuckold and a cuckquean.

> Condonation on the part of one sex might be amicable, while on the part of the other it would be degrading.[355]

53 years later, the wind was blowing in the opposite direction. Millicent Fawcett's testimony to the Royal Commission said this:

> If divorce is considered a sin and the patient endurance of degradation and compulsory suffering a virtue, a most serious moral confusion is created. It means that women's self-respect and happiness are sacrificed, and adultery on the part of men condoned.[356]

If this defence that women were acting 'unnaturally', contrary to God's intention, was intended as a political attempt to reduce divorce in order for men to save face or forestall what was seen as a step towards their emasculation it backfired. As Lord Lyndhurst pointed out in the 1857 debate, if that were the true nature of women then only the most extreme suffering would induce a wife to seek divorce.

> Nothing but a long, deliberate, hopeless suffering—nothing but intolerable agony, would overcome her patient endurance.[357]

In such cases, therefore, for a wife to be able to divorce her husband was a moral imperative, not an indulgence.

With this defence masculinity and femininity were being weighed in the balance. In order to preserve the key, one might say selfish, facets of their own nature men were resorting to a tried and tested version of a woman's nature. A [c]onservative stubbornness to recognise that times had changed, blown away by the cataclysmic effects of four years of warfare, means that The Woman Question dominates the social history of the fin de siècle and the first 30 years of the 20th century.

---

[354] Ibid.
[355] Ibid.
[356] Ibid.
[357] Ibid.

Conclusion

During the 107 years, from the Great Reform Act of 1832 to the start of The Second World War, British women cajoled, persuaded, fought, seduced, toiled and suffered to challenge the patriarchy to change and grant them equal and full recognition as legal entities in their own right, citizens fully represented in the running of the nation and, above all, human beings of equal intelligence, ability and value as men while still retaining their miraculous biological function to conceive, develop and produce other human beings. There were still more liberating times to come when choice over their procreative ability and future relationships would change male attitudes and social participation even more. But the job was done, the foundations and cornerstones were laid.

The conservatism of the social purists won the battle of the double standards forcing men to observe a single higher moral standard of sexual behaviour whereas the reformers won the battles for a legal identity and representation in the government of the nation.

However, the issue that had always been there, that runs through this long and winding discourse and was at the heart of the defence of the double standard—always had been—was that, just as in the physical difference in massiveness men were 'superior' and the reproductive function and equipment of men and women were different, it suited the patriarchy to persist with the beliefs that women were 'inferior' and of a fundamentally different nature to men in all human functions of the body, physical, intellectual and emotional, and, even at times, of the soul.

Chapter 43
Sex and Sexuality: Sin

Nature has given women so much power that the law has very wisely given them little.
– Samuel Johnson

When I hear his steps outside my door I lie down on my bed, open my legs and think of England.
– Attributed to Lady Hillingdon (1912)

But no reason, however grave, may be put forward by which anything intrinsically against nature may become conformable to nature and morally good.
– Pope Pius XI, *Casti Connubii*, #54

Preamble

History is largely a record of the public, that which has been seen, heard, written down or witnessed. Once a private act is witnessed and recorded it is no longer private. Once a private thought, emotion or motive is declared in writing or speech it is no longer private. The human intellect's ability to deceive means that the declaration, the outing of the private, cannot be fully believed unless verified by witnessing. Secrecy takes privacy one step further by implying deliberate concealment of thoughts or deeds.

Sexual activity has been private, and a myriad of times, secret, throughout the recorded history of 'civilised' human behaviour whereas sexuality, thoughts and feelings about the physical urge, as basic as hunger or thirst, and the satisfaction of it, has become, with the flowering of psychology and psychoanalysis, less private as to its constituent parts, yet it remains broadly secret at an individual level. The empirical methodology of Enlightenment science, with its emphasis on observation, was copied by social scientists like Charcot, Freud, Krafft-Ebing and Ellis thus giving an unprecedented insight into woman's nature.

The history of civilisation(s) has been a story of the private becoming public which has brought with it the intellectual and moral challenge of what to do with it when it is public. The intellectual challenge, the why-do-people-do-what-they-do bit, will be an integral part of the human journey until that journey comes to its end. The moral challenge, however, has always been taken up by 'religion' which starts/started as an attempt to answer important questions about life—

what are we here for, who or what made us, what happens when we die, is there a God or gods etc.—but is/was taken over by the human need to regulate, to bring order out of chaos, by designing and enforcing a system of doctrine and practice.

In the case of Western European culture, the religion, the moral instruction manual, has been Christianity, a religion of men, run, until recently, by men, interpreted by men and, regulated and enforced by men (I have mused on this at length in Chapters 10-12).

We have met the men who formed Christian doctrine and practice a few times on our journey and discovered and discussed at length their contributions to the Romano-Christian culture that came to Britain with the Norman Conquest. These Church Fathers, such as St Augustine and St Thomas Aquinas, did talk about sex and sexuality. Their doctrine and practice lasted some 1500 years and was a moral lighthouse to the mid-Victorian middle-class reaction to the loose moral activity of the Georgian aristocracy.

I just need to do a simple recap. God created nature. He created man first then woman. When Adam and Eve ate the fruit of the tree of knowledge, any behaviour that was not according to God's purpose was a sin. Sex, particularly sex that was not for God's purpose, procreation, was a sin. To get back into God's grace the sin had to be forgiven or excused. Sin was not just regrettably bad, it was evil. The sacrament of marriage excused the sin of sex. Even sex within marriage that was not for procreation, i.e., touching and kissing, oral and anal sex and positions other than the missionary position, considered for hundreds of years most likely to lead to conception with the help of gravity, was a sin. Sex outside of the marriage bed, masturbation, bigamy, bestiality and, of course, sodomy and homosexuality were abominable sins, too disgusting to contemplate.

The doctrine was clear and the sinful practices to be outlawed capable of definition, description and damnation. As for paraphilia, such as fetishes, BDSM, transvestitism etc., we, as a culture, are still struggling with our response, social, intellectual and emotional, as well as spiritual, to them being publicly acknowledged.

It was not until 31 December 1930 that Pope Pius XI, probably in response to the growing discourse on sexual reform that overtook western European culture in the 1920s, made clear the Roman Catholic Church's doctrine on sex in language we could all understand. The papal encyclical, *Casti Connubii* (of chaste love), clears up three questions of Catholic doctrine:

- Marriage is a sacrament and a means to get into God's good books—to sanctify his grace. The Church is opposed to adultery and divorce.
- The Church opposes abortion and contraception because "… any use whatsoever of matrimony exercised in such a way that the act is deliberately frustrated in its natural power to generate life is an offence

against the law of God and of nature, and those who indulge in such are branded with the guilt of a grave sin."[358]

- There are other acceptable reasons for sexual relations. "For in matrimony as well as in the use of the matrimonial right there are also secondary ends, such as mutual aid, the cultivating of mutual love, and the quieting of concupiscence which husband and wife are not forbidden to consider so long as they are subordinated to the primary end [that is, procreation of children and so long as the intrinsic nature of the act is preserved [that is, all sexual acts must be able to procreate in themselves, which means that no unnatural and non-procreative form of a sexual act can ever be performed without sin]."[359]

Sex, therefore, was a sin dating back to Adam and Eve. Sex for procreation was excused if sanctified by marriage. Sex for pleasure was an inexcusable sin for a man as well as a woman. Men, however, were in control of procreative sex which inconveniently was preceded by the urge to procreate made obvious by the physical manifestation of it, the erection, triggered by sexual attraction to all or some features of the person who was the subject of and object in the 'male gaze'. Lust, an inappropriately strong desire for sex, was one of the Seven Deadly Sins. Temperance in all wants, including sex, was a virtue.

There was no doubt what a man's sexual behaviour should have been—*it is not much different today, 170 years later, although possibly for different reasons*—but, although the criteria were set by men, there had always been a considerable doubt over whether the average man with time on his hands could be temperate enough to control the urge rather than satisfy it by promiscuity, infidelity, self-gratification or some paraphiliac indulgence.

A man had a God-given nature that had within it a propensity to sin that he could not control. If there were no women or if women had no sexual allure, there would be no problem (assuming no homosexual inclination, of course), but neither, as Mark Twain tells us, would there be any more men. Everything had been tried, covering up the parts of women that prompted the urge, silencing their voice, suppressing their intellect, keeping them in the home, brainwashing them to behave asexually and giving them no say in deciding how to resolve the dilemma.

Compromise solutions of acceptance of the inability to be 'chaste', such as prostitution, mistresses and masturbation had to be kept secret from the guardians of morality, the Churches and the social purists. Following their nature with its built-in fault line of 'unchastity', male adulterers and fornicators did not commit a great sin. It was hard, almost against their nature, to be a 'chaste' man.

On the other hand, the God-given nature of women was chaste. God created a woman to be a wife and mother. Procreative sex was a duty, a responsibility, not just to her husband but to God. Adulterous and fornicating women, therefore, particularly prostitutes, were 'unnatural', 'monstrous', God-forsaken, fallen

---

[358] en.wikipedia.org/wiki/Casti_connubii. Accessed 02/12/2020.

[359] www.trusaint.com/sexual-pleasure-and-lust/. Accessed 02/12/2020.

from His Grace. A woman did not have—a virtuous woman should not have—any physical sign of sexual desire and did not need to have an orgasm for the procreative act to be successful, although there was, apparently, a dissenting minority of Victorians that, added to the acceptance that women were capable of orgasm, believed that women would only conceive when their orgasm coincided with that of the man.

That European culture was unaware of the female orgasm is disproved by the practice of clitoridectomy in cases of insanity or paraphiliac masturbation. That it was regarded as against natural 'normality' is demonstrated by the existence of such a medical practice.

The cultural practice of not just clitoridectomy but many more extensive acts of female genital mutilation (FGM) in some regions of Africa now horrifies western European cultural sensibility, and rightly so, but was once a practice approved of by the European Establishment, in the name of Science but under the influence of religion.

Therefore, it was assumed that it was not her 'nature', especially if she was virtuous, to seek sex, prefer one man to another or have any other feelings about it that resulted from her physical biology. *There is still much being found out about female sexuality, but enough has been discovered to suggest that just penetrative sex, with no foreplay or sensual behaviour, with a man for whom she felt no physical attraction, was unlikely to elicit a physical response, even without the social and moral brainwashing that she had been subjected to adjuring her to take no pleasure at all from the activity.*

Furthermore, a woman who was not temperate, submissive and tolerant of a man's propensity to have sex with other women was not acting naturally. The last refuge of or the last stand by men in the battle of the double standard, therefore, was in an arena in which they played out the blame game. In cases of adultery and fornication the male seducer was making a bad choice of which God would take a dim view but would acknowledge that it was partly His fault for creating a sexual being. As for prostitution at all levels a moral blind eye was turned to it because of the fear of what social carnage intemperate men might cause if their sexual urge was denied an outlet, until, that was, the spread of venereal disease became a serious social problem.

On the other hand, the woman who was seduced had betrayed God's purpose for womankind by consenting to sex outside of marriage. His behaviour was an understandable misdemeanour, a lapse (See the discussion in Chapter 36 prompted by the article of Anne Sumner Holmes.), hers was a crime against nature, God's creation. The prostitutes were fully blown sinners, the lowest of the low, not because they offered an outlet for male concupiscence but because they offered non-procreative sex for pleasure, consenting to do so for money. By applying the double standard to the Matrimonial Causes Act in 1857 and compounding it with the Contagious Diseases Acts of the 1860s the Law was condoning a lower moral standard for men and condemning women for being its victims.

The blame on women for male immorality continues to this very day. For instance, whose responsibility is it when sex for pleasure unintentionally produces a child who will completely change the futures of both parents? Whose responsibility is it for the sexual act occurring in the first place, the attractively dressed woman, the dominantly insistent man or that large amount of alcohol they have both consumed? The much-respected feminist author from America, Catharine Mackinnon, still asks this question which should have been asked of the Victorian patriarchy.

> *"The assumption is that women can be unequal to men economically, socially, culturally, politically, and in religion, but the moment they have sexual interactions, they are free and equal. That's the assumption—and I think it ought to be thought about, and in particular what consent then means."*[360]

Conservatism, of which a high moral tone is/was a key component, does/did not support a lowering of moral standards it expects/ed them to be raised—the final straw of confused morality that broke the sexist camel's back! For social purists there was no compromise between God's word and male weakness, there was no moral wiggle-room, and this combination of feminist reformers and Christian conservatives brought about the beginning of the end of millennia of double standards, hypocrisy and blame projection in British and Western European, Romano-Christian culture. The Golden Rule has become the moral benchmark and fostered the prurience that now sells millions of tabloids and fly-on-the-wall documentaries the world over.

We should not mistake the redefinition of sexual sins, to exclude, for instance, homosexuality etc. from the moral status of a sin, to accommodate changes in and modernise attitudes for a lowering of the standard. When it comes to morals the bar of public opinion is as high as ever—as, of course, is the propensity for double standards, hypocrisy and blame projection!

Before I go on to look at the blame game, let me share this with you. In the 15th century, an anonymous commentary on the Ten Commandments was in circulation. In the form of a dialogue between a rich man and a man who had chosen to be poor to be closer to God, it was called *Dives et Pauper.* The denial of the truth contained in the following extract over five centuries is hard to accept.

---

[360] en.wikipedia.org/wiki/Human_female_sexuality#:~:text =Human%20female%20sexuality. Accessed 30/01/2021.

> "Wine and women make wise men dote and forsake God's law and do wrong."
> However, the fault is not in the wine, and often not in the woman. The fault is in the one who misuses the wine or the woman or other of God's creations. Even if you get drunk on the wine and through this greed you lapse into lechery, the wine is not to blame but you are, in being unable or unwilling to discipline yourself. And even if you look at a woman and become caught up in her beauty and assent to sin [= adultery; extramarital sex], the woman is not to blame nor is the beauty given her by God to be disparaged: rather, you are to blame for not keeping your heart more clear of wicked thoughts. … If you feel yourself tempted by the sight of a woman, control your gaze better … You are free to leave her. Nothing constrains you to commit lechery but your own lecherous heart."[361]

This 15th century Franciscan monk knew, surely like many others, where the blame lay for sexual sin, and knew, just as Jesus had, about the self-delusion of hypocrisy, yet as recently as 1857 the double standard persisted with its underlying, ancient and persistent assertion that it was Woman's fault!

The personification of God/gods is as ancient as religion. In polytheistic religions Gods were good and bad. However, in the monotheistic Abrahamic tradition God is the personification of Good. The pressure from ancient beliefs to acknowledge good and evil spirits led Christianity to personify evil, probably after the identification of Woman, as in Eve, as opening human eyes to all things evil. Satan was the personification of Evil.

For at least a millennium, Christianity rejected the idea of evil spirits, demons, possessing human beings and making them do evil in the real world. It recognised but side-lined Satan to concentrate on a wrathful God who would judge all souls, only allowing the good ones into His heaven. It was probably more convincing politically to offer a God to non-Christians who guaranteed an afterlife, offered a way out of evil deeds, and won battles etc., rather than rubbish the polytheistic, nature-oriented beliefs from which missionaries were trying to convert them.

Women have never been damned with an evil nature per se but, in addition to causing Man to suffer evil (Story of Eve), their nature also comprised the potential to be seduced by Satan (Witches), not only to worship him but to allow him into their body to cause evil either directly, by casting spells (Magic), cursing, speaking to or conjuring up the dead (Necromancy) and mixing mysterious concoctions, or indirectly, by tempting men into evil, with their words, their actions or their appearance. Men could do these things as well if they let Satan into their heart but over 80% of those accused of witchcraft were women.

---

[361] Anonymous, *Dives and Pauper*.

Finally, until the mid to late 19th century, much was unknown about the natural world, particularly the workings of the human body, even less about female anatomy than male and most particularly about the workings of the human mind, male or female. Yet, it would be irresponsible and irrational to assume that historical human beings, who, we know, had bacterial or viral illnesses for which there were no scientific explanations, many of which had dire physical consequences, did not have psychological and psychiatric problems that seriously affected their behaviour while falling short of actual and perceivable 'lunacy'.

When the harm that evil spirits caused was unexpectedly cleared up, it was a miracle from a triumphant God. When the harm that they caused came unexpectedly and inexplicably or had dire consequences for an individual, their family or their community there were two major explanations. The first was God's wrath and punishment of sin which required a lot of confession, expiation and atonement, all handled by the Church. The second was the presence of Satan or evil spirits, like the sex demons, the male incubi or their female equivalents, succubae, either in an individual person, family or community.

The former tended to explain widespread catastrophes such as natural disasters, famines and droughts, epidemics and pandemics or more politically, loss of wars and deaths of rulers. The latter tended to explain smaller scale, local and, as I have said, individual mysteries, many of which were, in some respect, related to the procreative functions of women, thus more often than not fixing the spotlight on the relationship between Satan and femininity.

When it comes/came to evil, there are/were no limits to the human imagination, particularly when applied to perversity and depravity. In most people, most of the time, their imaginary scenarios remain/ed just that, in the private/secret world of their dreams and thoughts. For example, incubi and succubae appeared in erotic dreams. When they were immoral, sinful, hateful, even homicidal, the anthropomorphic jump to demons was not so unfathomable. Most cultures have/had a demonology. For that millennium or so after the theological musings of St Augustine and other Church Fathers demons or evil spirits were theologically explained as the personal temptation that resides only in that dream and thought world, probably because pagan religions had given them various realities in the real world.

However, during the 200 years following the theological writings of the Dominican friar, Thomas Aquinas, the Christian Church hierarchy, under pressure to recognise the reality of Satan and witchcraft, found it more and more difficult to stick to the canon law established in the 10th and 11th centuries, *canon episcopi,* which, as we have explained, treated them as phantasms in the dreams and thoughts of women from a pre-Christian set of beliefs or folk lore. *Women's nature, remember, made them more prone to such voices and images emanating from a darker, more evil world!*

Of the four major orders of friars, sort of wandering monks, approved by the popes of the 13th century, Dominicans (black friars), Franciscans (grey friars), Carmelites (white friars) and Augustinians (Austin friars), the former were the most intellectual and dogmatic. The ignorance, fear of death, illiteracy and almost constant grief and loss of the poor people to whom they preached generated a potent susceptibility to a person and a message offering hope and redemption. Being dogmatic, the Dominican order became inquisitors in heresy cases. Heresy belongs to the set of human fears that includes xenophobia which gives us a clue to the possible timing of Wiccaphobia.

For centuries, the blame culture had clear targets, the Jews, Muslims, especially in the Mediterranean area, and whichever European country with which you were at war. After many ups and downs, persecutions and expulsions, Western European Christendom was completing a lengthy cull of Jews with their expulsion from Spain, Austria, Hungary and Germany in 1492 and Sicily a year later. By this time, inquisition was at its most insistent after the publication of the papal bull, *Summis desiderantes affectibus*, by Pope Innocent VIII, and the publication of a witch-hunting manual, *Malleus Maleficarum* (Hammer of the Evildoers), written by Dominican friar, Heinrich Kramer in 1487.

Thus, a ready-made replacement for the Jews, now mostly emigrated to Poland-Lithuania and Russia or into Muslim lands, as scapegoat, was found. Kramer's more illustrious Dominican brother, Tomas de Torquemada, Grand Inquisitor in Spain, had the full backing of the king and queen, Ferdinand and Isabella, to seek out false believers, crypto-Jews, thus linking false belief with heresy, the punishment for which was often death and often by burning. Difference was too frequently associated with evil and misfortune required a scapegoat, someone to blame.

In a Christian world, non-Christians were threateningly different. In a Catholic world religious minorities, particularly of a Protestant persuasion, were disturbingly different. In a French, Spanish or German world, non-French, non-Spanish and non-Germans were strangely different. In a man's world women were sinfully different. In an ignorant world knowledge was fearfully different. In a celibate world sexuality was anathema, officially banned. In a procreative world those unsuitable or unsuited, the old, the barren, the ugly, the deformed, the prostitute and the homosexual, or those too suitable or suited, the young, the beautiful, the fashionable, the talkative and the seductive were unsettlingly different.

What all these different people had in common was their vulnerability to being removed from society by shunning, banning, institutionalising, exiling, excommunicating, imprisoning or killing. Without the sanction of the Law, common, civil or canon, such action against the 'different' would be immoral and/or criminal. Therefore, the papal bull, *Summis desiderantes affectibus*, the royal sanction of some Western European rulers, the huntsmen such as Kramer, Torquemada and our own English Witchfinder General, Matthew Hopkins, and the publicity provided by the printing press for manuals such as the *Malleus Maleficarum* (by no means the first witch-hunting literature but the most widely dispersed, it followed the Dominican writings of Thomas Aquinas, as mentioned earlier and the *Formicarius* of Johannes Nider, written in the mid-1430s) fuelled the natural fears, superstitions and mob hysteria of ordinary folk.

Kramer had been appointed inquisitor in 1474 in the southern areas of the Holy Roman Emperor, but he was banned from doing his work in southern Germany. The year after the bull was issued in 1484 he went to Innsbruck. He became involved in a case involving 7 women including the wife, Helena Scheuberin, of a prominent burgher. The city's bishop became alarmed at Kramer's escalating obsession with Scheuberin's sexuality, before, during and after the trial which found her innocent of murdering a regular visitor to her house by using witchcraft.

Family and neighbourhood feuds often led to accusations of witchcraft and were a common feature in cases against men, often as one half of an accused married couple. Helena is also alleged to have cursed Kramer publicly and accused him of being in league with the devil. Such public insults had long been a local infringement of the law. The perpetrators, men and women, were accused, in England, of being scolds and, if found guilty, were subjected to various forms of public humiliation such as the ducking stool.

Imagining what was said behind the scenes it must surely have included discussion of female sexuality among presumably celibate men in the context of the Devil and witches. Its outcome was for Kramer to withdraw or be withdrawn from active prosecution, a fate that did not befall his brother Dominican, Torquemada, who continued in his role until his death in 1498.

Whatever was said, Kramer set about writing a justification of his actions in the guise of an instruction manual on how to uncover witches and then prosecute them successfully. He authenticated his views and methods by adding a fraudulent approval of his theology from the University of Cologne and a copy of the Papal bull. The end result was *Malleus Maleficarum.*

Many histories of the witch-hunting era that was ignited by this manual go to considerable lengths to point out that many condemned witches were men but miss the point, namely that the zeitgeist of the 300 years or so from 1450 to 1750, with its ingredients of brutality, sexuality and religious zeal and its imagery of seductive beauty, physical ugliness and death agony in the flames, centred on women. If we look at the language of 'witchdom', there are clues.

Although the Anglo-Saxon language has both the male *wicca* and the female *wicce,* one of the Laws of Alfred from the 890s AD banishing various forms of *wiccecraeft* strongly suggests that witches were women. Over time the male equivalent has fallen out of use. By 1601 the phrase 'he-witch' was being used. The change from old hag to sexual temptress was made in 'the sex-mad' 18th century.

> Extended sense of "old, ugly, and crabbed or malignant woman" is from early 15c; that of "young woman or girl of bewitching aspect or manners" is first recorded 1740.[362]

---

362 www.etymonline.com/word/witch. Accessed 01/01/2021.

In the title of Kramer's manual, *Malleus Maleficarum*, not only is the undercurrent of violence emphasised by the choice of *Malleus*, The Hammer, the gender of the Evildoers for whom it is intended is made clear by its Latin which, declines and distinguishes gender.—*arum* is feminine—*orum* would be the masculine.

Finally, the papal bull, *Summis desiderantes affectibus*, contained some telling vocabulary, remarkably similar to that used in the *Malleus Maleficarum* (suggesting some collaboration?) that underlay the link of women, sexuality, evil and heresy. While making it clear that both men and women were suspected of being under the influence of demons, the list of evils to which they had abandoned themselves and the nature of the demons affecting them had a heavy preponderance of things sexual and procreative.

> … have abandoned themselves to devils, incubi and succubi, and by their incantations, spells, conjurations, and other accursed charms and crafts, enormities and horrid offences, have slain infants yet in the mother's womb, as also the offspring of cattle, have blasted the produce of the earth, the grapes of the vine, the fruits of the trees, nay, men and women, beasts of burthen, herd-beasts, as well as animals of other kinds, vineyards, orchards, meadows, pasture-land, corn, wheat, and all other cereals; these wretches furthermore afflict and torment men and women, beasts of burthen, herd-beasts, as well as animals of other kinds, with terrible and piteous pains and sore diseases, both internal and external; they hinder men from performing the sexual act and women from conceiving …[363]

Incubi and succubi—*cum daemonibus, incubis et succubis abuti*—were not just ordinary demons, they were specifically associated with copulation and conception. Although the incubus referred to a male demon who 'lay on' and impregnated a human female and a succubus to a female demon who 'lay under' a human male, the focus was on sex, conception and birth, and, therefore, on women. Impregnation could be direct or achieved by a male demon impregnating a female demon who then turned into a male who impregnated a female human. To make sure all the bases were covered King James I, in his *Daemonologie*, suggested two ways of impregnating females with evil seed from the dead. Either the male demon could steal the semen of a dead man and impregnate or cause the corpse to rise and do the job himself.

Therefore, in a world ignorant of science, the evidence was manipulated to fit the theory generated by the ideology of demonology which diverted attention from real life human sinners (male?) to demons, thus putting the Church back in charge of the cleansing of the social debris caused by the failure to get the message over about the perfection of God's creation and the consequences of extra-marital sex. Hence, the dysfunction of the former, resulting in poor crop

[363] en.wikipedia.org/wiki/Summis_desiderantes_affectibus#cite_note-7. Accessed 02/01/2021.

yields, disease and infertility in domesticated livestock, almost certainly exacerbated, we now know, by the Little Ice Age which came between the warm Middle Ages and the Global Warming of the Industrial Revolution, and the continual presence of epidemic and pandemic disease in animals and humans was the work of the Devil or his human accomplices.

The malfunction of the female reproductive system and, more unacceptably to the patriarchy, the existence of erectile dysfunction and other erection disorders, such as priapism, semi-permanent erection, added to the human attempts to prevent conception, deal with the results of unwanted pregnancy, the effects of the menstrual cycle and the delivery of mentally or physically disabled children were also the Devil's work done through his physical possession of women. Pope Innocent, by making witches official, had his excuse for his God's creation, his apology for his God's failure to alleviate the lot of mankind and his mission to make things right all rolled into one.

Perhaps the most disturbing aspect of the *Malleus* is/was not Kramer's somewhat wilder/weirder (*even for those times?*) claims about the powers of witches, such as penis stealing or turning men into beasts, but his calm and pseudo-rational exposition of the nature of women with heavy, but not misogynistic, so he claims, emphasis on its propensity for wickedness.

In Part I, Question VI, he asks why more women than men are witches. He begins by making the generalisation that some learned men point to three things in nature that have no moderation of goodness or vice: the Tongue, the Ecclesiastics and Woman. Acknowledging the social importance of the words and deeds of good women he cherry-picks examples from the Bible, the writings of Church Fathers and Roman writers to show their capacity for wickedness.

> Now the wickedness of women is spoken of in *Ecclesiasticus* xxv: There is no head above the head of a serpent: and there is no wrath above the wrath of a woman. I had rather dwell with a lion and a dragon than to keep house with a wicked woman. And among much which in that place precedes and follows about a wicked woman, he concludes: All wickedness is but little to the wickedness of a woman. Wherefore S. John Chrysostom says on the text, It is not good to marry (*S. Matthew* xix): What else is woman but a foe to friendship, an unescapable punishment, a necessary evil, a natural temptation, a desirable calamity, a domestic danger, a delectable detriment, an evil of nature, painted with fair colours!
>
> Therefore, if it be a sin to divorce her when she ought to be kept, it is indeed a necessary torture; for either we commit adultery by divorcing her, or we must endure daily strife. Cicero in his second book of *The Rhetorics* says: The many lusts of men lead them into one sin, but the lust of women leads them into all sins; for the root of all woman's vices is avarice. And Seneca says in his *Tragedies:* A woman either loves or hates; there is no third grade. And the tears of woman are a deception,

for they may spring from true grief, or they may be a snare. When a woman thinks alone, she thinks evil.[364]

He then offers these reasons:

- And the first is, that they are more credulous; and since the chief aim of the devil is to corrupt faith, therefore he rather attacks them.
- The second reason is, that women are naturally more impressionable, and more ready to receive the influence of a disembodied spirit; and that when they use this quality well they are very good, but when they use it ill they are very evil.
- The third reason is that they have slippery tongues and are unable to conceal from the fellow-women those things which by evil arts they know; and, since they are weak, they find an easy and secret manner of vindicating themselves by witchcraft.
- That since they are feebler both in mind and body, it is not surprising that they should come more under the spell of witchcraft.

For as regards intellect, or the understanding of spiritual things, they seem to be of a different nature from men; a fact which is vouched for by the logic of the authorities, backed by various examples from the Scriptures. Terence says: Women are intellectually like children. And Lactantius (*Institutiones*, III): No woman understood philosophy except Temeste. And *Proverbs* xi, as it were describing a woman, says: As a jewel of gold in a swine's snout, so is a fair woman which is without discretion.

- But the natural reason is that she is more carnal than a man, as is clear from her many carnal abominations. And it should be noted that there was a defect in the formation of the first woman, since she was formed from a bent rib, that is, a rib of the breast, which is bent as it were in a contrary direction to a man. And since through this defect she is an imperfect animal, she always deceives.
- Therefore, a wicked woman is by her nature quicker to waver in her faith, and consequently quicker to abjure the faith, which is the root of witchcraft.
- And as to her other mental quality, that is, her natural will; when she hates someone whom she formerly loved, then she seethes with anger and impatience in her whole soul, as the tides of the sea are always heaving and boiling. Many authorities allude to this cause.
- And truly the most powerful cause which contributes to the increase of witches is the woeful rivalry between married folk and unmarried women and men.[365] [my bullet pointing]

---

[364] sacred-texts.com/pag/mm/mm01_06a.htm. Accessed 07/01/2021.
[365] Ibid.

The misogyny, implicit but denied by Kramer (and many others!), in this rationale was frequently a part of the process of prosecuting witchcraft. Victims tended to be women on the fringes of village life and those, under the umbrella terms of wise women and midwives, who had an intimate knowledge of women's affairs and biology. The executions per capita in England over the 300 years following the *Malleus* were fewer than those on the Continent but a higher proportion of them were women, 90% compared to 80%. Between 1644 and 1646 in East Anglia it is estimated that some 300 were executed having been proved to be witches by a pair of confidence tricksters, John Stearne and Matthew Hopkins, the self-styled Witchfinder-General. This was more than had been put to death in the previous 160 years.

By the time executions stopped in the mid-18th century, some 100,000 trials of witches had been held in western Europe, about half of which had resulted in execution. Between 500-1000 were executed in England during the same period.

There had always been considerable scepticism about the whole issue of witchcraft which, having been added to the scientific refutation of many religious assertions in the so-called Age of Enlightenment, should have led to a radical re-assessment of the nature of women. However, in the 200 years that followed the end of the witch-hunting era, science and religion were vying for the minds and souls of the human race, not least in Victorian Britain. It was not until the 1870s that a witness who would not swear on the Bible could give evidence in a British court. Charles Bradlaugh, an open atheist, was elected three times before he was allowed to sit as an MP for Northampton in 1886. The last imprisonment for blasphemy occurred in 1842. George Holyoake, the convicted man, became a colleague of Bradlaugh in his advancement of the Secularist movement from the 1880s onwards.

We have looked briefly at the conflict of religion and science in the cases of Galileo and Darwin. It was a conflict to establish ownership of the truth. Science was the new kid on the block challenging 1600 years of undisputed Christian control of thinking about the origin and purpose of the human race.

Chapter 44
Sex and Sexuality: Normality

What a folly it is the way people are kept in ignorance on sexual matters, even when they think they know every-thing. I think almost all civilised people are in some way what would be thought abnormal, and they suffer because they don't know that really ever so many people are just like them.
– Bertrand Russell

What is natural cannot be immoral.
– Magnus Hirschfeld

Preamble

The Enlightenment, by going back to learning before the advent of the Christ, spawned philosopher/scientists who wanted to replace the blind faith of John 20:29—"Jesus saith unto him, Thomas, because thou hast seen me, thou hast believed: blessed are they that have not seen, and yet have believed."—with empiricism—"Seeing is believing"—knowledge comes from sensory experience. However, just like Christianity before the Council of Nicaea in 325 CE, Empirical Science took some time to find its feet. Likewise, truth, being subjective, could have been withheld or tailored under pressure from the prevailing belief of the time enforced and reinforced by powerful institutions like, in 325 CE, the Roman state and, 1500 years later, the Christian Church.

In 1663, 13 years after his death, Pope Alexander VII placed two of Rene Descartes' works on the Vatican List of Prohibited Books. Descartes felt that the soul should be scientifically/empirically investigated like all other aspects of nature. It could be said that the Church's insistence that the soul, the source of thoughts, emotions, ideas and beliefs located in the mind, was the business of the Church set back neuroscience two hundred years.

Finally, in this introduction to scientific belief in the Victorian era, three points have to be considered. Firstly, we see what we want to see—Charcot. Secondly, we accept the interpretation of someone else of what we see for various reasons of character and personality—Nietzsche. The truth is subjective. Thirdly, normal is culture referenced. Those in control of the process by which norms are set, set the norms—Hirschfeld.

In the century and a half from 1850-2000 AD, science and technology altered the perception of the normal but much of the groundwork was done in the 60 years from 1880-1940 AD when the answers to the Woman Question related to

Her nature started to be found but only when Man confronted fundamental questions about His own nature.

Ironically, the two western European countries, Scotland and Germany (not as yet unified), where witch mania was worse than most others were turning into acclaimed centres of medicine. In June 1815, Dr John Gordon, an Edinburgh anatomist, published a paper on "*The Doctrines of Gall and Spurzheim*" in which he criticised the scientific theories and practices of two renowned German doctors, Franz Joseph Gall and Johann Spurzheim. In 1816, Spurzheim came to Edinburgh to defend the science he had called 'phrenology'. Dr Gordon favoured the approach to the powers of the brain of another German doctor, Johann Reil.

The difference in the two approaches was that Reil concentrated on mental disorders of the mind which he called 'psychiatry' whereas others, like Spurzheim felt that mental and corporal dysfunction were linked. If Gordon hoped to debunk phrenology in order to expunge it from the teaching of medicine it was a forlorn hope. For the next 30 years it became extremely popular before going into decline as medical knowledge grew.

Phrenology was simply a theory that the generation of emotions, personality traits and moral character, took place in different areas of the brain. The areas of an individual's more dominant traits would be larger or misshapen, thus causing irregularities in the cranium that explained differences between the temper, personality and character of individuals. It was vague and mysterious enough to prove anything—a gift to those who took great comfort from being superior to someone else: the upper and middle class had skulls that indicated qualities of leadership and industriousness, criminals had bumps that indicated an evil and anti-social disposition, native Australians did not have skulls that indicated a capacity to develop civilised attributes such as art and literature, European colonisers in general had crania that showed overall superiority to the peoples, black African, Indian and Asian, that they conquered and, of course, women's skull shape and configuration showed a marked favouring of brain locations to do with child rearing and nurturing and an inferiority in those to do with the qualities needed for social and political participation.

By focusing on the brain, Gall and Spurzheim had taken a giant step towards understanding of behaviour but their failure to interpret what they saw objectively, in the case of the brain, something scientists are still struggling with, in comparison to advances in surgery, genetics and fighting disease, was in danger of confirming the prejudicial discrimination in existence in the patriarchy of the time and discrediting science before its ethics and morality had been embedded into European culture.

The language of extremist views about witchcraft suggested a tendency to overegg the pudding when it came to the unknown and the inexplicable. The possession of devils caused an almost hysterical fear among ordinary people, especially notable in the women accused of it, those women who were often the accusers and those women who witnessed the behaviour that resulted from it and the all-male justice system that dealt with it. (We tend to forget the fact that of the 19 people executed after the Salem Witch Trials of 1692 five were men, the youth of the accusers and their fear at the inevitable outcome.) Lack of emotional control, emotional weakness, was thought to be linked to physical weakness which was the one undeniable feature of women's nature whereas phlegm, the stiff upper lip, was the expected response of the male.

Egyptian writings from 1900 BC wrote about the causes of emotional excess in women, attributing it to a physical rather than a mental source, the 'wandering womb'. Very personal treatments were used to attract the womb back to its normal place in the body. The Ancient Greeks accepted this explanation, and the disorders of hysteria were named after the Greek word for uterus. When the theories of the Four Elements—earth, air, fire and water—and the Four Humours—blood, yellow bile, black bile and phlegm—became the foundations of medical science until the 16th century the heat of blood (one of Kramer's women's 'carnal abominations'?) was cooled by the phlegm expected of the stereotypical British gentleman.

Once doctors like Andreas Vesalius (1514-64) had cast doubt on anatomical guesses like men having one rib less than women and that the womb wandered, their assertion that the brain governed the emotions as well as muscle movement and sensation became accepted. By 1697, respected doctors like Thomas Sydenham, 'The English Hippocrates', were influential in leading scientists and doctors away from the idea that hysteria had anything to do with the soul or the womb.

This acceptance, however, did not stop ideas that evil spirits could influence the brain or that the reproductive functions of certain women could cause an abnormal mental response that in turn caused physical and verbal behaviour that was against the norm for a human female. The symptoms of hysterical behaviour were noted in men but called something different, lunacy was a favourite, but hysteria was overwhelmingly seen as a female complaint and commonly linked to her procreative cycle and its accompanying biology. Possibly the most renowned neurologist of the mid-to-late 19th century was the Frenchman, Jean-Martin Charcot.

Following in the footsteps of his teacher and mentor, Guillaume-Benjamin-Amand Duchenne (de Boulogne), probably the most famous pioneer of modern neurology, Charcot became director of the insane asylum at the Salpêtrière in south eastern Paris in 1862. He worked and taught there for 33 years. While always insistent that hysterical behaviour was found in men he turned one of his most famous sayings into a self-fulfilling prophecy.

> "In the last analysis, we see only what we are ready to see, what we have been taught to see. We eliminate and ignore everything that is not a part of our prejudices."[366]

Two of his case studies captured the public imagination, whether he intended them to or not. They were both of women and led to the sexualisation of female

---

[366] Jean-Martin Charcot - Wikipedia. Accessed 17/01/2021.

hysteria. In 1875–6, Charcot publicised the case of Louise Augustine Gleizes to draw attention to his technique of hypnosis which unlocked the secret inner tribulations of the mind of a woman with hysteria. He linked hypnotic revelation and female hysteria and, in the firm belief of the empirical scientist that the 'truth' could be found by careful observation, he gave public lectures/ demonstrations and had photographs taken of Louise in various hysterical poses.

Some of the supposedly 'uncontrolled' sounds, expressions, touching and movements were sexually suggestive linking hysteria and female sexuality. Such behaviour, it was thought, so 'infamously' against the nature of a temperate, modest and virtuous woman, must be caused by a mental disorder as yet physically undetected. The ethics of this approach have been further questioned as a result of the allegation that when Louise refused to have more photos taken she was returned to solitary confinement and eventually escaped never to be seen again.

Charcot's second case was even more renowned. Marie Wittman was institutionalised in the Salpêtrière in 1877 and used in Charcot's lectures to demonstrate the hysterical symptoms that he wanted his students to observe at first hand. As with Louise, critics disliked the freak show feel of the experience and doubted their veracity. Actors came to learn from the various emotional movements and sounds that Marie claimed later were genuinely caused by her hysterical state of mind. Among these were some of a sexual nature.

The wide range of observers were captured by the artist, Andre Brouillet, in his painting of one of Charcot's lessons, *Une leçon clinique à la Salpêtrière*. This was the era of reproduction prints which made artistic representation financially accessible to the general public. It is said that one of Charcot's most famous attendees, Sigmund Freud, had just such a print on his office wall, both in his native Vienna and in London when he fled the Nazi occupation.

The photos used by Charcot as evidence for hysteria were taken at Salpêtrière by a medical photographer called Albert Londe. Those who were not familiar with advances in photographic techniques would have believed the photos to have been staged, having been used to the daguerreotype and its successor the collodion processes which, due to the exposure time, required lengthy still posing. Londe, however, was an expert chronophotographer with a camera that could take 12 photos in $1/10^{th}$ of a second. His photos, therefore, of convulsions like the famous *arc de cercle* were probably genuine. If, however, we compare his portrait photos of Louise and Marie and Brouillet's painting of some 30 men watching the hysteric contortions of a partially undressed Marie, they could be said to have been sexualising the whole hysteria issue.

Freud, to whom I shall come very soon, came close to an understanding of what was probably going on here. He called it 'The Madonna-Whore Complex'. Some men experiencing erectile dysfunction in a loving relationship failed to be aroused by a woman whom they respected, adored or even worshipped, their 'Madonna', and turned to prostitutes, 'Whores', debased or degraded women, for sex. "Where such men love they have no desire and where they desire they cannot love."[367]

Freud's separation of desire from love, the first physical and the second emotional, was at the centre of the double standard. The ideally virtuous wife who showed temperance, moderation and self-control, in her emotional behaviour, particularly her sexual behaviour, keeping her sexuality private, if not secret, was not enough to stimulate or satisfy the male sex drive. However, a woman in a situation in which she did not have that control, whatever the reason, money (prostitution and pornography) or illness (hysteria), if Freud was right, stimulated a psychologically uncontrollable physical arousal in men, for some of whom it was the only satisfying way to express their sex drive.

Ecstatic prophetesses, like Elizabeth Barton, The 'Nun of Kent', whom we met in Chapter 28, had arguably, for centuries, with their physical, vocal and emotional intemperateness, induced the same conflicting mixture of physical, emotional and moral responses in men. Another major physical drive, however, intensified the response to Charcot's sessions; hypnosis gave the male hypnotiser control over the female patient. Charcot believed that susceptibility to hypnosis was part of the illness of hysteria, following on from the work of Franz Mesmer and his animal magnetism at the turn of the century. The confluence of scientific concepts such as psychology, Mesmerism and hypnosis arose out of research and practice related to hysteria and replaced the more witchlike vocabulary such as fascination, enchantment and bewilderment but retained the notion of male control of the sexual process.

Control is/was a powerful need in men when it comes/came to sex, and hypnosis was a new and powerful scientific gift for achieving it. The 'evil' of lustful thought, sex for pleasure and the imperative of the male orgasm, all used as excuses for the patriarchal double standard, had a scientific explanation. Science, even the more mystical science of the mind, was confirming by empirical observation that the intemperate male was only following his nature whereas the intemperate female was suffering from a peculiarly feminine range of mental illness that overrode her true nature. Fact?

During the Age of Enlightenment, as science started to reveal truths about the physical world, replacing belief with proof and faith with fact (the great French philosopher, Denis Diderot, explained the change, "Grace determines the Christian's action; reason the *philosophe*'s"), the scientific method of empirical study was applied to society and human relationships. The social science of Sociology 'socialised' the positivism of the empirical scientists who denied any 'truth' not based on observable, factual proof.

To the best of my knowledge the science of mapping the neurological activity of the human brain still could not help us observe, for example, the emotions of hate or love taking place, even though we know the brain is the seat of emotion. To understand the behaviour we have to be sure that it is what we are looking for by collecting enough observations that confirm our hypothesis of the constituents

---

367 en.wikipedia.org/wiki/Madonna–whore_complex. Accessed 17/01/2021.

of hate and love which itself depends on enough observations to be sure that there is a confirmation of those ingredients to eliminate the possibility of a coincidence.

The empirical method used by early social scientists relied heavily on case studies the write-ups of which formed the textbooks for their students. The authenticity of the ideas in these books depended on the reader/student's belief in the expertise of the writer/teacher which, in turn depended on his (In the latter years of the 19th and early years of the 20th centuries they were men) reputation which depended on his acceptability to the medical establishment who, by this time, were becoming an important elite within the patriarchy. The prophets of science had taken over from those in the Bible and their truths were challenging Biblical truth.

Like the great preachers who interpreted biblical truths, these 'biblical' case studies required interpreters of their truths. What if observers saw truths that were unacceptable to the theorist—heresies? What if the truths revealed by the theorist, like Darwin's theory of evolution, challenged the very foundations of social stability? Who were the theorists and what motivated them to become what they claimed to be? At about the time that Freud was developing his sex-based hypotheses to explain human behaviour the German philosopher, Friedrich Nietzsche, was asserting that, "There are no facts, only interpretations." The three well-known writers, Charcot, Krafft-Ebing and Freud, researchers and interpreters in this field, given the name Sexology in the early 1900s, were all men and all have and had critics of their patriarchal methods and conclusions. Freud's 'phallocentrism' and conservatism have received particular attention from feminist critics.

The empirical methodology of Sociology and Psychology in the 20th century has thrived on a philosophical acceptance that truth is subjective, and reality is different for every individual human being. Even the empirical miracle of the computer age, Statistics, are subject to Nietzsche's caution on interpretations of facts—"Lies, damned lies and statistics!". Out of this postmodern perspective has emerged the sociological concept of social constructionism.

> A social construct or construction is the meaning, notion, or connotation placed on an object or event by a society and adopted by the inhabitants of that society with respect to how they view or deal with the object or event. In that respect, a social construct as an idea would be widely accepted as natural by the society.
>
> A major focus of social constructionism is to uncover the ways in which individuals and groups participate in the construction of their perceived social reality. It involves looking at the ways social phenomena are developed, institutionalised, known, and made into tradition by humans.[368]

[368] en.wikipedia.org/wiki/Social_constructionismhttps://en.wikipedia.org/wiki/Social_constructionism. Accessed 19/01/2021.

In the 150 years that have followed the Matrimonial Causes Act of 1857, this two-pronged attack by physical science and social science on 3000 years of traditional knowledge and its institutionalisation has struggled to resist becoming absorbed into that tradition. As the physical knowledge of maleness and femaleness began to rewrite and disprove the traditional beliefs such as the wandering womb, social science slowly managed to start revealing new insights into the social constructs of male and female behaviour, masculinity and femininity.

From the obvious physical and biological phenomena of being, in general, less massive, less strong and inferior to males in physical task completion and their major, time-consuming and frequently precarious role in producing and nurturing children, a social tradition of femininity had become so embedded in Western European culture that it was deemed to come from the natural origin of and purpose for all women. It became a 'taken-for-granted' reality. While science, using mind-blowing technological advances, was revealing the reality of the female anatomy, social science was challenging the realities of the nature of femininity. *From that time civilised humanity, or at least some of it, has learned to take nothing for granted.*

The American Sociologist, Charles Horton Cooley, in his exposition of his idea of the Looking Glass Self, pointed the way to what had to change in order to deconstruct and rebuild the social construction of femininity.

> "I am not who you think I am; I am not who I think I am; I am who I think you think I am."[369]

Having been told what to think and feel for thousands of years by men, education had given women the ability to think for themselves. Their femininity, being constructed for them by men, required them to keep their feelings private. It further required a virtuous woman to keep her sexual feelings, her sexuality, more than private; secret, in fact. The actuality of being the educational, creative and skilful equals of men in all walks of life, probably astonished women more than it did their male counterparts. That women could acquire, display and utilise emotional traits hitherto attributed to masculinity, many conservative Victorian men found, rather than astonishing, somewhat disturbing, challenging and possibly even frightening or to use the more popular version of the times, 'frightful'.

Many extraordinary women of all classes and backgrounds, however, have/had stepped out of the emotional identity assigned to them to succeed in walks of life hitherto thought to have required masculinity.

> Traits such as nurturance, sensitivity, sweetness, supportiveness, gentleness, warmth, passivity, cooperativeness, expressiveness, modesty, humility, empathy, affection, tenderness, and being emotional,

---

[369] Ibid

> kind, helpful, devoted, and understanding have been cited as stereotypically feminine.[370]

I doubt that it had ever been beyond the male psyche to accept the possibility of an extraordinary woman, probably preferring the adjective 'exceptional'. Plato did. Even Knox did.

As we have explored from a plethora of different angles, the nature of woman did not make her a different animal. What the patriarchy knew about the dimorphic physiology of women, as noted above, was being constantly updated by science in the second half of the 19th century, some of the social implications of which, such as birth control and abortion, were profoundly disturbing to the status quo but there was more to come from the social sciences. The 'feminine' human being that the patriarchy had created was imagined not real, at least in the sense that she was not what God/Nature had created.

Just as their own chastity was a hypocrisy in order to live with which had required some serious blame projection, self-delusion and truth denial on their part, Woman's capacity for chastity as the defining point of her nature and the benchmark of all those virtuous feminine traits just mentioned was a social construct to bolster up their denial of their own masculine sexual insecurity.

It would take 4 years of unimaginable destruction of life and property from 1914 to 1918 and the even more destructive replay from 1939 to 1945 before a proper re-assessment of masculinity and virtue took place, replacing the macho posturing of a dog-eat-dog, white, Romano-Christian culture with some of those supposedly feminine traits.

If the whole sexuality-based premise for the double standard which justified the argument to exclude women from key areas of social decision-making was wrong then the whole patriarchal social construct of femininity was in urgent need of re-examination. Although there were Madonnas and Whores, Deborahs and Jezebels, just as there were Saints and Adventurers, Mills and Stoneys, social science was proving that the behaviour of the average Woman was as influenced by her sexuality as was that of the average Man; only the social expectation of what to do with it was different. Female sexuality was not an evil, an illness or a behavioural deviance it was a part of her nature.

Ironically, in view of the public health concerns about sexually transmitted diseases which, in part, led to the downfall of the double standard, one of the first surveys of sexual behaviour was carried out by a French hygienist, Alexandre Jean-Baptiste Parent du Châtelet (Parent Duchatelet), who, after 8 years of research, wrote a book based on 3558 case studies of prostitutes in Paris, *De la prostitution dans la ville de Paris* (*Prostitution in the City of Paris*). Over 100 years later, the Kinsey Reports on male and female sexuality were based on

[370] en.wikipedia.org/wiki/Femininity. Accessed 22/01/2021.

approximately 5,300 males and 6,000 females, respectively. Two features of Parent Duchatelet's study that showed its reflection of the patriarchy were that it rarely mentioned the male clientele and their reasons for being with a prostitute and that his 'hygienic' solution to allowing their continued existence was to form the basis of the Contagious Diseases Acts of 1860s Britain.

Social anxiety about the moral and health implications of prostitution was greater, it has been suggested, in Protestant northern Europe. Coincidentally, Britain and Germany/Austria were the most active centres of sexological study. Gaining a better understanding of hysteria was an accelerant for making a link between neurology, sex and mental illness. Two private worlds, the workings of the human brain, the seat of the soul, and the sexual thoughts and motives of women, the cause of sin, were now being openly investigated some 250 years after Rene Descartes' suggestion that they should be.

However, the greatest of the private worlds was an outcome of male sexuality. Homosexuality, and, to a lesser extent, masturbation, were abominable sins, unmentionable and unadmittable, a closely preserved secret that if outed would undermine the patriarchal construct of masculinity unless Science, as it surely would, proved that it was a neurosis, a mental illness.

Chapter 45
Human Rights and Gender Relations

I am proud, that I found the courage to deal the initial blow to the hydra of public contempt.
– Karl Heinrich Ulrichs

Equality means more than passing laws. The struggle is really won in the hearts and minds of the community, where it really counts.
– Barbara Gittings

Preamble

Investigation into the secret world of female sexuality before World War I uncovered uncomfortable secrets about male sexuality. On the premise of one out, all out, human rights which had centred on the political rights of women, concerned itself with other forms of discrimination—working women, disability, ethnic minority and homosexuality. The variant forms of sexuality and gender identity demanding inclusion in the 'normal' of human sexual behaviour has outgrown the 1990s initialism of LGBT (Lesbian, Gay, Bisexual, Transgender) and will pose further challenges to the definition of normality.

One of the decelerants of the whole issue of sex and sexuality had been a lack of language and an extreme reluctance, refusal even, to call a spade a spade. Wikipedia has this quote from social historian, Henry Perkin.

> Between 1780 and 1850, the English ceased to be one of the most aggressive, brutal, rowdy, outspoken, riotous, cruel and bloodthirsty nations in the world and became one of the most inhibited, polite, orderly, tender-minded, prudish and hypocritical.[371]

On the occasion of the arrest of George Bedborough in 1898, a story we shall look at soon, GBS was moved to venture this view in defence of Havelock Ellis's book on homosexuality.

> In Germany and France, the free circulation of such works as the one of Mr Havelock Ellis's now in question has done a good deal to make the public in those countries understand that decency and sympathy are as

[371] en.wikipedia.org/wiki/Victorian_era#Moral_standards. Accessed 26/01/2021.

> necessary in dealing with sexual as with any other subjects. In England, we still repudiate decency and sympathy and make virtues of blackguards and ferocity."[372]

Even the remarkable ability of Ancient Greek to combine prepositions, adjectives and nouns into long words (remember Aristophanes in Chapter 21!) was insufficient. Speaking of long words, enter Richard Fridolin Joseph Freiherr Krafft von Festenberg auf Frohnberg, genannt von Ebing, a German doctor of Psychiatry, graduate of Heidelberg University and practitioner in psychiatric asylums. Krafft-Ebing specialised in paraphilias (He did not use the word which did not enter the English language until 1913. He used the word 'psychopathy'.), conditions in which sexual arousal is caused by 'atypical objects, situations, fantasies, behaviours, or individuals.' Wikipedia tells us that there are currently 549 on the books.[373]

In 1886, his book of 238 case studies, *Psychopathia Sexualis: eine Klinisch-Forensische Studie* (Sexual Psychopathy: A Clinical-Forensic Study), was published. A significant part of the content investigated homosexuality, a term, along with bisexuality and heterosexuality, he used but did not originate (The terms were first used by Karl-Maria Kertbeny, a Hungarian writer on the anthropological origins of homosexuality.), but he did invent the terms 'sadism' and 'masochism', from the fictional tales of the Marquis de Sade and Leopold Ritter von Sacher-Masoch, for the sexual arousal of giving and receiving pain. The practice of naming disorders after fictional characters is most common when naming 'Complexes' which we will look at soon.

His book, and therefore his findings, were of great interest to lay people (The translator into English of his 7th Edition, Charles Gilbert Chaddock, felt that much of this interest was pornographic.) as well as doctors and scientists, surely creating a general debate, with the usual Chinese whispers, about the previously unmentionable (in polite society) subject of human sex and sexuality. There was plenty to debate, with the trials of Oscar Wilde in 1895, a prominent member of the aesthetic movement with its emphasis on 'decadence' and rejection of Victorian materialism and morality. Wilde was convicted of "gross indecency" under Section 11 of the Criminal Law Amendment Act of 1885 which raised the age of consent from 13 to 16 to protect young pre-pubescent girls from being used in the world of prostitution.

The addition of the so-called Labouchere Amendment by Henry Labouchere, Liberal MP for Northampton and editor of an expose magazine called *The Truth,* to protect male child prostitutes from the attentions of older pederasts. In his article, Famous Trials, Professor Douglas O. Linder gives this assessment of the sexual mores of 1890s Britain.

> One final observation about the Wilde trials, often overlooked, deserves mention. Prior to Wilde's trials, prosecutions for consensual

---

[372] spartacus-educational.com/TUhavelock.htm. Accessed 03/02/2021.

[373] en.wikipedia.org/wiki/Paraphilia. Accessed 26/01/2021.

> homosexuality in England were about as rare as they were in the United States at the end of the nineteenth century. What offended Victorian society about Wilde's conduct was not so much that it involved sex with other males. What people found offensive was that Wilde had sex with a large number of young male prostitutes. Wilde was not prosecuted because he was the lover of a social equal who happened to be male. Wilde was prosecuted because of his participation in a not very discreet prostitution ring. Had Wilde merely pursued relationships with men of his own age--especially men of his own social class--he never would have found himself in the dock at Old Bailey.[374]

Krafft-Ebing, however, fully accepted the construction that sex for pleasure was against nature which gave sexuality to humans for the sole purpose of procreation. Homosexuality and masturbation were, therefore, 'perversions', not only abnormal but unacceptable. It belonged with other paraphilias, mental illnesses for which a cure could be found.

In his introduction to his book, Krafft-Ebing shows that he had bought totally into the social construct of gender stereotyping with no neurological, indeed no scientific, support for his assertions, expert though they sounded. From pages 13-16 he lays out the accepted thinking on masculinity and femininity of the 1880s which reinforced the double standard. Men have a more intense sexual desire, a more powerful natural instinct, which once satisfied leaves them free to run the world.

> With a woman, it is quite otherwise. If she is normally developed mentally, and well bred, her sexual desire is small… It is certain that the man who avoids women and the women that seek men are abnormal.
> Woman is wooed for her favour. She remains passive. This lies in her sexual organisation and is not founded merely on the dictates of good breeding.[375]

He, prior to this insight into a woman's sexual nature, had repeated the long-used get-out clauses for the double standard.

> Natural instinct and social position favour unfaithfulness on the part of the husband, while the wife is afforded much protection.
> The aim and ideal of woman, even when she is sunken in the mire of vice, is, and remains, marriage.
> A man of right feeling, no matter how sensual he may be, demands a wife that has been, and is, chaste.[376]

---

[374] famous-trials.com/wilde/327-home. Accessed 07/02/2021.
[375] archive.org/details/PsychopathiaSexualis1000006945/page/ n33/mode/2up. Accessed 27/01/2021.
[376] Ibid.

This influential work had made some significant progress in understanding sex and sexuality, for instance, in recognising that a woman had to be wooed by a man, Krafft-Ebing was affirming that, as opposed to having the right to refuse a mate chosen by someone else, women chose what happened to their bodies and with whom they shared them, an issue still in need of social and legal resolution 20 years into our 21st century.

However, Krafft-Ebings' juxtaposition of sexuality with mental illness still allowed for the view that immodest and over displayed sexual behaviour in women was contrary to their nature. They, just like homosexuals, described as individuals who were male at birth but had a female psyche, Uranists or Urnings, challenged the gender construct. Homosexual women were similarly described as female at birth with a male psyche. It was not hard, therefore, to assume that women striving to make their way in a man's world were going against their true nature.

Sex and sexuality became of more widespread interest before and after the First World War for a number of reasons. The public image of a woman's ability to fight for the suffragette cause and the male establishment's very physical, brutal even, response and the range of physical, dangerous and exhausting war work undertaken by women went a long way to countering the Victorian view of their physical inferiority and their natural inclination to take a passive role. However, the acceptance of a different less male-defined version of femininity, running parallel in many ways with the fight to accept a less heterosexual view of masculinity was to take three quarters of the 20th century to achieve.

Sigmund Freud, an Austrian Jew, born in Freiberg, now Pribor in the Czech Republic, recently appointed to a professorship at Vienna University, wrote his *Three Essays on the Theory of Sexuality* which was published in 1905. Three ideas from his previous ten years of theorising came together, sexual experiences in childhood, repression and psychoanalysis. Underlying all his thinking was his idea of three elements to the psyche: the *id*, the basic instinct for pleasure, the *super ego*, the centre for high moral thinking, and the *ego* where conflicts between the actions determined by the *id* and the *super ego* are resolved. Freud also added to the private and the secret worlds the existence of a subconscious world of which even the person who inhabits it is unaware.

Introducing into educated debate an open, albeit scientific, discussion of sexuality, even in children whom Krafft-Ebing had labelled *generis neutrius*, sexual abuse, repression of sexual feelings, subconscious feelings, opening up about past events, explanations of 'the love that dare not speak its name' (a phrase attributed to Oscar Wilde's lover, Lord Alfred Douglas) and the suggestion that not only did it reside in all of us but was not a vice or an illness, must have led to numerous reassessments of human nature, masculinity and femininity.

Freud's views did not go without challenge nor did they avoid revision, sometimes by Freud himself. A wonderful piece of self-evaluation on his psychoanalytic method resulted in this 1935 reply to a mother anxious about her son's homosexual tendencies.

> I gather from your letter that your son is a homosexual. I am most impressed by the fact that you do not mention this term yourself in your information about him. May I question you why you avoid it? Homosexuality is assuredly no advantage, but it is nothing to be ashamed of, no vice, no degradation; it cannot be classified as an illness; we consider it to be a variation of the sexual function, produced by a certain arrest of sexual development. Many highly respectable individuals of ancient and modern times have been homosexuals, several of the greatest men among them. (Plato, Michelangelo, Leonardo da Vinci, etc). It is a great injustice to persecute homosexuality as a crime -and a cruelty, too. If you do not believe me, read the books of Havelock Ellis.[377]

Freud's student and collaborator, Carl Jung, felt that Freud's Oedipus Complex (a son's sexual jealousy at his mother's love for his father) was inapplicable to male and female infants introducing the 'Electra Complex', a daughter's sexual jealousy at her mother's love for her father. Staying with child nurturing Freud's long-time friend, Alfred Adler, proposed a different non-sexual explanation of behaviour relevant to the male social construct of femininity, the 'Inferiority Complex'.

It was Jung, while working with Freud, who irrevocably injected the idea of a 'complex', a connected group of repressed ideas, into the body of psychology, although he did not coin it. Over 80 years, the simple version of human nature and gender nature had been replaced by a more complex one involving an understanding of the conscious and unconscious workings of the brain as well as of the dimorphic biology of the two genders. This academic advance in psychiatric science and the revelation of the ways in which personality disorders could be understood drew the more complex issues of social concern into the same political arena. Science and medicine did find workable cures for many diseases and illnesses that alleviated the condition of mankind but, as far as gender issues, such as homosexuality, bisexuality, masturbation, sex for pleasure, prostitution, procreation, masculinity and femininity, were concerned only a start was made by the Freudian School of psychology. The rights of women relating to their sexuality and sexual activity now came under a general umbrella heading of tolerance of varied forms of sexual expression for men and women. Since the 1990s we could use the acronym LGBT although that is now felt not to cover the full range of sexual identities.

In his 1935 letter, Freud had referred the mother to the books of Havelock Ellis. After four years in Australia 20-year-old Ellis returned to England in 1879 and studied to be a doctor as the first step on his ambition to be a sexologist. In 1883 he joined the newly formed *Fellowship of the New Life.* Its founder, the Scottish American philosopher, Thomas Davidson, believed that every human being had it within them to lead a perfect life because there was divinity in every

[377] en.wikipedia.org/wiki/Sigmund_Freud%27s_views_on_homosexuality. Accessed 31/01/2021.

individual. This liberality of acceptance as a human being of every sort of personality and, in particular, sexuality, marked out the somewhat eccentric Henry Havelock Ellis as one of the little known but significant figures of 20th century European cultural change.

Through these connections, he was immersed in contra-conservative ideas such as socialism, pacifism and vegetarianism, meeting socialists like the playwright, George Bernard Shaw, animal rights activists, like Henry S. Salt, and, of course, homosexuals, men such as Edward Carpenter and women such as the women's rights activists, Olive Schreiner, arguably his first love, and Edith Lees who was to become his wife in 1891. As an increasingly listened-to sexology lecturer and writer, he also met the Freudian school of psychoanalysts and in 1914, Margaret Sanger, an American feminist and 'birth control' activist with whom he is said to have had an affair.

Margaret was avoiding America where she faced prosecution for putting her ideas on contraception into print. Her English counterpart, Marie Stopes, was also an acquaintance of Ellis, possibly via Margaret Sanger, but not a fan. She described reading his ground-breaking work on homosexuality, *Studies in the Psychology of Sex*: *Sexual Inversion*, as "like breathing a bag of soot; it made me feel choked and dirty for three months."[378]

This brought Ellis into contact with the Malthusian League, founded by the women's and worker's rights activist, Annie Besant, after her trial in 1877 (See Chapter 37) which, in turn, brought him into contact with Charles Robert Drysdale, a co-founder and first President.

Since 1891, Ellis and Edith had been in 'an open marriage', married but having sexual relationships with others, in Edith's case, women, outside the marriage. One of the consequences of an open marriage and free love was that the children of the network of relationships it created would run the risk of being illegitimate. Ellis and Carpenter supported the Legitimation League which campaigned for the legitimation of illegitimate children. In 1897, the League moved its headquarters to London where its President was Lillian Harman, one of the more anarchist women's rights activists.

Its secretary, George Bedborough, also in an open marriage with his wife, Louie, its treasurer, was arrested on an obscenity charge for selling Volume 2 of Ellis's books on the psychology of sex. The intertwining of sexual reformers, suffragettes and anarchists meant particular attention from the Metropolitan Police and much befuddlement in the minds of the press and the general public who tended to 'tar them all with the same brush.

Charles Drysdale and his partner, Alice Vickery, like Stopes, birth control campaigners, were in a 'free union', a lifetime bond without marriage. They believed in 'free love', the idea that sexual relationships between adults in private should be free from all interference by the state. Furthermore, the state should allow talk and writing about sex and sexuality without resorting to a legal

---

[378] spartacus-educational.com/TUhavelock.htm. Accessed 03/02/2021.

definition of obscenity and accept that sex without conception freed women to live the lives they wanted to live.

The wheel of sexual reform was well on the way to turning full circle when, in November 1921, the son of Charles and Alice, Charles Vickery Drysdale, opened the first birth control clinic in Britain, the Walworth Women's Welfare Centre in East London. The previous March, Marie Stopes and her second husband, Humphrey Roe, had opened the first British family planning clinic, the Mother's Clinic, in Marlborough Road, Upper Holloway in north London.

Marie Carmichael Stopes, like Ellis, was a complex character whose views are possibly too controversial for those seeking an interwar liberal reformer. Her motives for her life's work, educating about and facilitating birth control in working class marriages, sit uncomfortably with the liberality of other sexual reformers but, of particular relevance to this book, her desire to dispel unhappiness of many marriages must have been influential on the thinking of those who liberated women from the inequalities of the divorce laws. In the preface to her book, *Married Love*, she wrote this:

> … I speak to those—and in spite of all our neurotic literature and plays they are in the great majority—who are nearly normal, and who are married or about to be married, and who hope, but do not know how to, to make their marriages beautiful and happy.[379]

The first honorary chief medical officer of the Walworth clinic was Norman Haire, an Australian acolyte of Havelock Ellis but probably more famous due to his lectures to Oxbridge students and tours round Britain. Haire fretted a great deal about his own sexuality but was a dedicated sexologist and sexual reformer. In 1923, with a letter of introduction from Havelock Ellis, Haire went to Berlin to see Magnus Hirschfeld, the renowned German sexologist, and visit his *Institut für Sexualwissenschaft* which was particularly dedicated to research into homosexuality and transgender and other sexual minorities.

Hirschfeld, a homosexual himself, as was Haire, had taken the baton from Karl Heinrich Ulrichs, an openly gay sexologist who fought a futile battle in the 1860s to get anti-gay laws repealed. He was also one of the first activists to take the view that homosexuality was natural and biological, coining the mantra, picked up by Krafft-Ebing, of 'a woman in a man's body'.

Hirschfeld, who travelled extensively throughout his life, saw, as I commented on earlier, a close similarity between gay rights and women's rights. In 1905, he joined the *Bund für Mutterschutz* (League for the Protection of Mothers), set up by the feminist campaigner Helen Stocker to fight for what we now call reproductive rights. The foci of their campaigning were two paragraphs of the German legal code, 175 and 218, the first banning homosexuality and the second banning abortion. Her campaign to legalise abortion and sex education

---

379 archive.org/details/married_love/page/n9/mode/2up. Accessed 04/03/2021.

and equalise the legal treatment of illegitimate children ultimately failed in 1932 but Hirschfeld's advocacy did prevent paragraph 175 applying to women.

Hirschfeld, having always been a target for the Nazis as a Jew and a homosexual, settled in France after another overseas tour. In 1933, the Nazis ransacked the Institute and burnt a valuable collection of books and records on sexuality.

Hirschfeld, being a Jewish, homosexual sexologist specialising in sexual 'perversion/deviance/inversion', whichever characterisation it suited detractors to give it, must have been a serious threat to patriarchal social constructs as well as being aware, every hour of his intellectual life, of the perilous state in which his views placed his very existence. Somewhere in the story of the patriarchal treatment of women is the psychology of 'race' and racism. One of Hirschfeld's last books published posthumously in 1938 and written while on his world tour, *Rassismus* (*Racism*), examines what the socially constructed theory behind the prejudice and/or the policy is all about.

Based on the compelling research of Professor Heike Bauer, Professor of Modern Literature and Cultural History, Department of English, Theatre and Creative Writing at Birkbeck College, London, in her 2017 book, *"The Hirschfeld Archives: Violence, Death, and Modern Queer Culture"*, Wikipedia points to Hirschfeld's affirmation of the deep seated desire of philosophy and then science to validate a prejudice as a social rather than an individual phenomenon.

> Unlike many who saw the *völkisch* ideology of the Nazi regime as an aberration and a retrogression from modernity, Hirschfeld insisted that it had deep roots, going back to the German Enlightenment in the 18th century, and it was very much a part of modernity rather than an aberration from it. He added that, in the 19th century, an ideology which divided all of humanity into biologically different races—white, black, yellow, brown and red—as devised by Johann Friedrich Blumenbach served as a way of turning prejudices into a "universal truth", apparently validated by science. In turn, Hirschfeld held the view that this pseudo-scientific way of dividing humanity was the basis of Western thinking about modernity, with whites being praised as the "civilised" race in contrast to the other races, which were dismissed for their "barbarism"; such thinking was used to justify white supremacy.
>
> In this way, he argued that the *völkisch* racism of the National Socialist regime was only an extreme variant of prejudices that were held throughout the Western world, and the differences between Nazi ideology and the racism that was practiced in other nations were differences in degree rather than differences in kind. Hirschfeld argued against this way of seeing the world, writing "if it were practical, we should certainly do well to eradicate the use of the word 'race' as far as

> subdivisions of the human species are concerned; or if we do use it in this way, to put it into quote marks to show it is questionable".[380]

What Hirschfeld was very carefully repudiating here was twofold. Firstly, he was rightly pointing to the danger that false science was attempting to hi-jack properly conducted science, natural and social, in order to justify the social and institutional prejudices essential to the retention of power and justification of actions by the Establishment. Secondly, he was cautioning against the hypocrisy implicit in the moral horror at and condemnation and demonisation of Germany, Nazism and Hitler that diverted attention away from the reality which was that the social tendencies and prejudices encapsulated by the Nazi regime from 1933 were all present to a less impactful extent—'differences in degree rather than differences in kind'—in every corner of Western civilisation. At the Nuremberg war crimes trials many of the accused pointed to this hypocrisy claiming that the regime had merely practised what others had preached.

Therefore, it is very comforting for amateur historians among the general public, like me, to regard Hitler and the Nazi regime as an aberration in the otherwise steady progress of Western European cultural values from barbarity to civilisation, the triumph of good over evil. Hirschfeld spoke of the 'deep roots' of racism but he knew from personal experience that the roots of other prejudices were equally deep.

In 1907, with similar ingredients to the Wilde affair 12 years earlier—an investigative journalist, a celebrated public figure and a revelatory trial - a long-term suspicion of homosexuality in the Imperial German Army's officer corps came to a head when the German journalist, Maximilian Harden, acting on a tip-off, uncovered a homosexual affair between the Kaiser's close friend and adviser, Prince Phillip Eulenburg-Hertefeld, and a General Kuno Graf von Moltke. Numerous trials for libel, civil and criminal, took place in which other homosexual acts in high places were made public, at least one involving cross dressing.

In 1898, Lily von Elbe, von Moltke's wife, sought a divorce on the grounds of her husband's sexual neglect of her because of his sexual relationship with Eulenburg. For political reasons—Harden was a hard-line imperialist—in 1906 Harden outed the affair. Eulenburg cleverly and quickly cleared his name but von Moltke had to resort to a civil libel case. In order to avoid damages Harden's legal team needed to prove the truth of the story that von Moltke was a homosexual for which they called in an expert witness, Hirschfeld, in line with the theory of the times that homosexuality, which Ulrichs had named Uranism, was a mental illness or psychological disorder. A second witness for the prosecution was von Moltke's wife of 9 years, Lily von Elbe, whose role was to confirm that her husband showed little interest in normal heterosexual relations. The third witness, a soldier named Bollhardt, had witnessed parties involving the

[380] en.wikipedia.org/wiki/Magnus_Hirschfeld. Accessed 05/02/2021.

so-called 'Liebenberg Circle' of known homosexuals at which von Moltke was present.

Prussia, holding on to social codes such as the Frederician Code mentioned in Chapter 34, leading light of the unification of Germany in 1871 under its Iron Chancellor, Otto von Bismarck, was arguably the most conservative country in Western Europe (*as in sexism, racism, homophobia, nationalism and imperialism*) but the unfolding scandal, followed voraciously by the western world's press, was to throw up the private world of racist attitudes, sexual deviance and homophobic paranoia behind the façade of social propriety and moral superiority present in the ruling class throughout *fin-de-siecle* western culture. Relying heavily on Norman Domeier's definitive book on the scandal, *The Eulenburg Affair: A Cultural History of Politics in the German Empire*, Wikipedia tells this amazing story.

Firstly, two of the leading players, Harden and Hirschfeld were Jewish. Eulenburg was an outspoken anti-Semite who called Harden "a rascally Jew". Hirschfeld was an openly gay campaigner for gay rights and the removal of Paragraph 175.

Secondly, Lily von Elbe was a divorced woman who spoke openly about sex as the cause of the marital breakdown in a country in which sex and sexuality were very private, even secret, issues.

Thirdly, Eulenburg was a 'respectably' married man with 8 children descended from ancient Prussian nobility among whom homosexuality was the ultimate taboo in its rigidly masculine culture.

Lastly, while the legal processes were taking things further than the Establishment wanted, a gay rights campaigner, Adolf Brand, producer of the homosexual periodical, *Der Eigene* (The Unique), accused the Imperial Chancellor, Prince Bernhard von Bulow, of having a longstanding homosexual relationship with a Privy Councillor, Max Scheefer, taking the suspicions uncomfortably near to the Imperial throne. Von Bulow sued for slander.

Harden's articles may have been in the context of imperial policy but the gist of them gave a flavour of the views of the times. For 3000 years, at least, men who were unmasculine in their behaviour, preferring intellectual and emotional pursuits to those that were physical and athletic and displaying artistic rather than physical prowess had been subjected to jibes hinting at homosexuality. Harden questioned the martial qualities of toughness and ruthlessness in Eulenburg whose effeminacy and womanly nature rendered him too conciliatory to prosecute the necessarily aggressive expansion of the Second Reich.

It is not much remembered that there was significant opposition, including influential women, to the suffrage movement in Britain at this time leading to the establishment in 1908 of the Women's National Anti-suffrage League which joined with the men's version in 1910. One of their most powerful arguments was that the physical inferiority and moral softness of women meant that they were not suited to making political decisions which were primarily about the use of force or fight for their beliefs as men were called upon to do. A kindly Liberal MP and lawyer, Samuel Evans, put it this way.

> *If women were to be entitled to the privileges of citizenship, they ought to share its responsibilities, and to perform its duties. Would it be desirable that women should have to go out to battle?...*[381]

Harden's implication in his characterisation of the 'Harpist' (Eulenburg) and 'Sweetie' (von Moltke) was that homosexuals should not be in charge of the path towards German greatness not because they were gay but because of the feminine qualities of their gayness. This attitude was made more potent when Brand, citing witnesses to his kissing Scheefer at parties, accused von Bulow of hypocrisy by allowing Paragraph 175 to remain on the statute books while engaging in homosexual behaviour himself. Unsurprisingly, von Bulow was proved innocent and Brand was imprisoned. Wikipedia records the view of American historian Elena Mancini that:

> ...the relentless way that Harden pursued Eulenburg despite constant harassment from the Prussian authorities was due to more than his ultra-nationalism, and that the root reason was Harden's "...thoroughly masculine idea of politics, which was distilled in images of decisiveness and a readiness for war.[382]

When Hirschfeld gave his evidence in the Moltke-Harden trial, it prompted more unsavoury homophobic reaction. While offering his expert opinion that von Moltke was gay, he went further by adding that "homosexuality was part of the plan of nature and creation just like normal love." The statement caused an outrage all over Germany, Wikipedia tells us.

> The *Vossische Zeitung* newspaper condemned Hirschfeld in an editorial as "a freak who acted for freaks in the name of pseudoscience". The *Mūnchener Neuesten Nachrichten* newspaper declared in an editorial: "Dr Hirschfeld makes public propaganda under the cover of science, which does nothing but poison our people. Real science should fight against this!"[383]

Equally disturbing was the sexual frankness of the testimony of Lily von Elbe:

> ... who testified that her husband had only made love to her twice in their entire marriage. Elbe spoke with remarkable openness for the period of her sexual desires and her frustration with a husband who was

381 www.johndclare.net/Women1_EvansArguments.htm. Accessed 09/02/2021.
382 en.wikipedia.org/wiki/Philipp,_Prince_of_Eulenburg. Accessed 08/02/2021.
383 en.wikipedia.org/wiki/Magnus_Hirschfeld. Accessed 08/02/2021.

> only interested in having sex with Eulenburg. Elbe's testimony was marked by moments of low comedy when it emerged that she had taken to attacking Moltke with a frying pan in vain attempts to make him have sex with her. The fact that General von Moltke was unable to defend himself from his wife's attacks was taken as proof that he was deficient in his masculinity, which many saw as confirming his homosexuality. At the time, the subject of female sexuality was taboo, and Elbe's testimony was very controversial, with many saying that Elbe must, in some way, be mentally ill because of her willingness to acknowledge her sexuality. At the time, it was generally believed that women should be "chaste" and "pure", and not have any sort of sexuality at all. Letters to the newspapers at the time, from both men and women, overwhelmingly condemned Elbe for her "disgusting" testimony concerning her sexuality. As an expert witness, Hirschfeld also testified that female sexuality was natural, and Elbe was just a normal woman who was, in no way, mentally ill.[384]

When the jury found in favour of Harden, the judge overturned the verdict assuming that the jury had agreed with Hirschfeld's views which would have set an unacceptable legal and moral precedent, asserting that homosexuals had 'the morals of dogs'.

In the second trial, this time for criminal libel, Hirschfeld had been got at by the Prussian authorities. He downgraded his assessment to that of a homoerotic relationship in which no sodomy was likely to have taken place. More shamefully, he gave in to the acceptable views of the time that Lily was suffering from hysteria due to a lack of sex thus making her perception of her husband's relationship with Eulenburg a figment of her fevered imagination.

When Eulenburg was accused of perjuring himself in the Bulow-Brand trial by denying his homosexuality, his career was over as Kaiser Wilhelm coldly distanced himself from any whiff of homosexuality. In ill health and suicidal, he was never able to be tried for his perjury before his death in 1921. Before we leave him, however, as an example of what was an acceptably 'normal' view Wikipedia, based on Domeier, says this about his racism when ambassador in Vienna.

> A vivid display of Eulenburg's anti-Semitism occurred in October 1895 when he reluctantly attended a Jewish charity concert in Vienna. In a dispatch back to the Kaiser, Eulenburg complained that he was the "sole Aryan" in the entire concert hall and stated his ears were pained to hear of "the indescribable mishmash of German spoken with Austrian, Bohemian and Hungarian accents with international cliquishness"." Eulenburg went on to write of his disgust of the "drooping and enormously crooked noses", "bandy knees", "noses like tapirs", "fat

[384] Ibid.

lips", "prominent cheekbones", "eye teeth like a walrus's", "slanted eyes like slits", "gaping jaws with hollow teeth", and the "exposed and sweaty shoulders" of the Jewish women in their evening night-gowns.

Eulenburg wrote that since the Jews all paid their respects to a "Jewish greybeard" that this proved the old Jew "must have slaughtered and eaten many Christian children, since two dozen long yellow teeth protruded from his ghastly maw" (it is not clear in repeating the blood libel if Eulenburg was making an anti-Semitic joke or if he really believed in the blood libel). Finally, Eulenburg concluded his report to the Kaiser that the "badly behaved" Jewish children at the concert were all repulsively ugly and that the only attractive Jew he saw at the concert was the lead singer, a young woman whom Eulenburg stated was more animal than human, albeit one who could sing very well for a Jew.

Despite his anti-Semitism, during his time as Ambassador to Austria, Eulenburg engaged in a homosexual relationship with the Austrian banker Nathaniel Meyer von Rothschild who liked Eulenburg so much that when he died in 1905 he left Eulenburg one million *krones* in his will.[385]

The shocking nature of the language used in this racist context remained abroad in pre-Nazi western Europe, including Britain, and on other issues. The extreme language of Eulenburg's anti-Semitism in pre-Nazi Germany was not confined to that subject nor that country. When, in 1928, a novel about lesbian love, *The Well of Loneliness*, by the openly lesbian author, Radclyffe Hall, who lived with her partner, Una Troubridge, dressed in men's clothes and was frequently called 'John', the editor of the *Sunday Express*, James Douglas, an advocate of censorship, wrote, "I would rather give a healthy boy or a healthy girl a phial of prussic acid than this novel."[386]

A further disturbing example of the 'normality' of what was to later become 'extreme', even 'evil', was the attachment of sexual reformers such as Ellis, Sanger, Stopes and the Drysdales to the pseudoscience of eugenics. Firstly, Eugenics started in Britain with the work of Francis Galton, half-cousin to Charles Darwin, which interpreted Darwin's theory of evolution to allow the possibility of breeding superior human beings and preventing the 'unfit' from proliferating.

Long before Hitler, in countries like the USA, Canada and Sweden, elimination of the unfit by sterilisation was a reality. More cautious governments such as the British (although they were very close to it in the years running up the Mental Deficiency Act, 1913) were reluctant to legislate, fearing a process to define those unfit to reproduce and shying away from an infringement of an individual's right to do so.

---

385 en.wikipedia.org/wiki/Philipp,_Prince_of_Eulenburg. Accessed 08/02/2021.

386 en.wikipedia.org/wiki/The_Well_of_Loneliness. Accessed 09/02/2021.

Given the threat to the sexually deviant/abnormal/inverted, it is difficult to see what Ellis saw in the movement with which he eventually fell out over its support for sterilisation unless it was his belief that such personality or psychological traits could be passed on in one's genes. As to birth control, there is enough evidence to suggest that Stopes and Sanger did fear the swamping of the superior classes who voluntarily limited their family size by the poor and ignorant who did not.

To be fair, however, there were other factors related to poverty, education, women's health and children's health and happiness that were also of concern to the birth control campaigners. None of them could have foreseen that some eugenic knowledge in the hands of a bigoted tyrant could lead to genocide.

Hitler, most demonised, quite rightly, for his gross anti-Semitism, was also deeply homophobic and fiercely opposed to women being in public positions of responsibility advocating that they concentrated on their roles as wife and mother, incubators of the future ethnically and morally pure race of the Third Reich which would last forever.

- Over 1,000,000 homosexuals were targeted in Nazi Germany. Over 100,000 trials were held with over 50,000 convictions. Over 1000 died in concentration camps where homosexuals were regularly beaten and tortured, subjected to medical experimentation, even used for target practice. Many, like Friedrich-Paul von Groszheim, were forcibly castrated.
- From 1940-3, some 90,000 mentally ill and physically disabled people, including children, were euthanised in the notorious Aktion T4 programme, among them Jewish lesbians, like Henny Schermann, who was murdered in Hospital/T4 Centre in 1942.

Although women supported and became Nazis, Hitler's views were, to say the least, conservative if not regressive. His racism was as gross as that of Eulenburg. His homophobia dated from days of the Eulenburg scandal. One of the links was a certain Houston Stewart Chamberlain, British born anti-Semite writer and racial theorist who was a close friend of Eulenburg and mentor of Hitler, again showing that Hitler was not an aberration but the acme of a 50-year-old ascent into fascism and ultra-conservatism. His sexism had its roots in the deeply conservative reactions to the testimony of Lily von Elbe. He was far from alone.

> In an account of the activities of the Seventh Nazi Party Congress held in Nuremberg in September 1935, "Germany: Little Man Big Doings", *Time* magazine (September 23, 1935) reported: "Fifty thousand German women and girls marshalled by hard-bosomed Gertrude Scholtzklink [sic], No. 1 female Nazi, hailed Herr Hitler with bursts of wild, ecstatic cheering which kept up for the whole 45 minutes that he addressed them in his happiest mood. 'There are some things only a man can do!' cried

> this Apotheosis of the Little Man. 'I exalt women as the stablest element in our Reich because woman judges with her heart, not with her head! ... I would not be here now had not women supported me from the very beginning...We deny the Liberal-Jew-Bolshevik theory of 'women's equality' because it dishonours them! ... A woman, if she understands her mission rightly, will say to a man. You preserve our people from danger, and I shall give you children.' (Cries of 'Ja! Ja! Heil Hitler!')
> Many of the 50,000 women wept as they cheered, and Herr Hitler himself seemed on the point of tears as he concluded: 'When my day comes, I will die happy that I can say my life has not been in vain. It was beautiful because it was based on struggle.'[387]

Gertrude Scholtzklink was Hitler's chosen leader of the Nazi Women's League which, by 1938, had 2 million members. Later in 1935, Hitler said this:

...in reality, the granting of so-called equal rights to women, as demanded by Marxism, does not confer equal rights at all, but constitutes the deprivation of rights, since they draw women into a zone where they can only be inferior. It places women in situations where they cannot strengthen their position with regard to men and with society—but it only weakens them.[388]In 1937, Heinrich Himmler, Hitler's No. 2 and architect of The Holocaust, expressed the Nazi view on gender:

> On the whole, in my view, we have too much masculinised our life, to the point that we are militarising impossible things [...] For me, it is a catastrophe that women's organisations, women's communities and women's societies intervene in a domain that destroys all feminine charm, all the feminine majesty and grace. For me, it is a catastrophe that we other poor male fools—I speak generally, because this does not mean you directly, we want to make women an instrument of logical thought, to educate them in everything possible, that we want to masculinise with time the difference between the sexes, the polarity will disappear. The path to homosexuality is not far. [...] We must be very clear.
> The movement, the ideology cannot be sustained if it is worn by women, because man conceives of everything through the mind, whereas women grasp everything through sentiment. [...] The priests burned 5,000 to 6,000 women [for witchcraft], because they preserve emotionally the ancient wisdom and ancient teachings, and because, emotionally, they do not let go, whereas men, they are logically and rationally disposed.[389]

---

[387] en.wikipedia.org/wiki/Gertrud_Scholtz-Klink. Accessed 09/02/2021.
[388] en.wikipedia.org/wiki/Women_in_Nazi_Germany. Accessed 09/02/2021.
[389] Ibid.

The Second World War was indeed a battle against the evil of Nazism but, in some cathartic way, an internal struggle between the good and the evil, the moderate and the extreme, the right and the wrong in Western European culture. By the time the war started in September 1939, the recognition of women as equal members of the human race entitled to equal treatment under the law regardless of marital status had begun to become an established component of Western European culture made worldwide by the imperial presence of British, French, German, Italian, Dutch, Belgian, Portuguese and Spanish colonies or former colonies and the vast American and Russian spheres of influence.

It still vies with other cultures, such as Islamic, Hindu, Buddhist or Middle Eastern, Far Eastern or African, for the hearts and minds of billions of people, particularly with respect to the treatment of women. Here are some examples.

In Wikipedia's article on the UN Declaration of Human Rights, it records the criticism of Riffat Hassan, a Pakistani-American Muslim theologian and feminist author.

> What needs to be pointed out to those who uphold the Universal Declaration of Human Rights to be the highest, or sole, model, of a charter of equality and liberty for all human beings, is that given the Western origin and orientation of this Declaration, the "universality" of the assumptions on which it is based is—at the very least—problematic and subject to questioning. Furthermore, the alleged incompatibility between the concept of human rights and religion in general, or particular religions such as Islam, needs to be examined in an unbiased way.[390]

Progress, as judged by Western European culture, in a Muslim country subject to Shariah Law is being praised. The America based Borgen Project is a campaigning advocate for addressing world poverty.

> … Sharia law and government played a key role in the development of women's rights in Saudi Arabia. These structures forced women into marriage, domestic abuse was a wide-spread issue and basic human rights eroded, year after year. Women started to see a change in the 2000s and 2010s with the enrolment of females elected to the government. Furthermore, women could vote in 2015 and the driving ban ceased in 2018.
>
> Women in Saudi Arabia do not have certain freedoms that may seem trivial to most women around the world. In 2019, it became legal to allow women to obtain passports or to travel without the permission of a male guardian. Though these reforms do not completely solve the oppression women face, they are a step in the right direction. These reforms allow a sense of freedom to women.

---

[390] en.wikipedia.org/wiki/ Universal_Declaration_of_Human_Rights #Human_rights. Accessed 10/02/2021.

> Saudi Arabia is gradually moving closer to removing its "guardianship system" that subjects women's rights to their male relatives. A new regulation includes the right for a women's hiring without the need for a male guardian's permission. Notably, the law is intended to target and ban employment discrimination laws.
> One of the biggest changes for women in Saudi Arabia is allowing women to be able to register their children's births. Previously, a male guardian or the father of the child did this act. Human rights changes such as these in Sharia law allow for women to be looked at as equal and as "heads of the household".[391]

Lipi Mehta, a socio-political blogger about India, says this:

> One of the starkest observations of growing up in India is seeing how differently young girls and young boys are treated. Not just in our behaviours, but in our language and even in the way we think. Girls are told to be more 'careful' while doing everyday things like going to the marketplace or deciding what to wear. They are perceived as liabilities, as burdens and often, are brought up to be "married off".
> Moreover, in thousands of households across India, girls are unwanted. The phenomenon of son preference in India sees an ugly manifestation in this as well. To fight the decades of patriarchy that is at the root of this thinking, we need to make girls count as much as anyone else.[392]

The post-war inclusion of women's rights in the movement for universal human rights ends my story. The cause for sexual understanding moved to the USA. In 1948 Alfred Kinsey and a team of researchers had their report on *Sexual Behaviour in the Human Male* published in book form. It was followed up in 1953 by *Sexual Behaviour in the Human Female*. Both books, although intended for a scientific readership, became non-fiction best sellers. They confirmed Hirschfeld's and Ellis's views on sexuality; that it was a major part of male and female nature and that the objects of sexual attraction in normal humans were on a spectrum ranging from homosexual to bisexual to heterosexual.

Two further books from scientific research into human sexuality, *Human Sexual Response* and *Human Sexual Inadequacy*, published in 1966 and 1970 respectively, cleared away many of the social myths and denials regarding sexual arousal and orgasm, clearly demonstrating that it was a biological response in women as well as men. The lead researchers, Americans, William Masters and Virginia Johnson, laid the foundations for an era of sexual frankness in language and action, other than pornography and prostitution, even describing their own sexual experiences as part of their research.

---

391 en.wikipedia.org/wiki/Universal_Declaration_of_Human_Rights #Human_rights. Accessed 10/02/2021.

392 www.youthkiawaaz.com/2015/12/difference-in-how-women-and-men-are-treated-in-india/. Accessed 10/02/2021.

Combined with revolutionary changes like the oral contraceptive pill and the opening of Brook Advisory Centres in 1964 to offer it to unmarried women, these enlightened publications of social and physical scientific research were hailed as the 'sexual revolution'. The not guilty verdict in the trial of Penguin Books for their publication of D.H. Lawrence's novel, *Lady Chatterley's Lover*, on 2 November 1960 showed that British society was ready for the change. I will leave the last words to "Paragraph 7.34 of the ICPD Programme of Action". *Sexuality and Gender Relations*. (Archived from the original on 17 August 2007).

> "Human sexuality and gender relations are closely interrelated and together affect the ability of men and women to achieve and maintain sexual health and manage their reproductive lives. Equal relationships between men and women in matters of sexual relations and reproduction, including full respect for the physical integrity of the human body, require mutual respect and willingness to accept responsibility for the consequences of sexual behaviour. Responsible sexual behaviour, sensitivity and equity in gender relations, particularly when instilled during the formative years, enhance and promote respectful and harmonious partnerships between men and women."[393]

[393] en.wikipedia.org/wiki/Human_sexual_activity. Accessed 10/02/2021.

Chapter 46
The Verdict

Even the strongest city will fall if there is no one to defend it, and even the most undeserving case will win if there is no one to testify against it.

Christine de Pizan's observation, one of the inspirations for this book, contains within its 31 words many of the issues raised by the Woman question. In my introduction I suggested that it might be the wrong question. If, indeed, it should be the Man Question then it should be La Querelle des Hommes, the dispute of men. It is a question about Men that Men should be debating, disputing and answering.

When I referred to Churchill's wonderful quote in Chapter 13 about understanding the rationale of an alien culture, he could well have been describing the Woman Question as 'a riddle, wrapped in a mystery, inside an enigma'. That is my excuse for presenting no answers to La Querelle des Femmes. My book contains evidence, mostly second-hand, and opinion, mostly, if it is mine, inexpert. You are the jury. Yours is the Verdict. I have assembled the evidence because to rebut even the most undeserving case requires testimony from witnesses, albeit not, in my case, an eyewitness.

I have sought affidavits from as wide a range of disciplines as I could, not just the usual social, economic, political and historical but the moral, spiritual, ethical, philosophical and cultural and the more scientific perspectives of biology, anthropology and psychology, even sexology.

The moral imperative for writing is emphasised in the preamble to Chapter 39, the double failure of the male supremacist conservative to observe the Golden Rule, *"And as ye would that men should do to you, do ye also to them likewise." (Luke 6:31. KJV)* and to recognise the selfishness behind his blatantly hypocritical view of femininity roundly condemned by his moral guiding star, the human Son of his God, *"Thou hypocrite, first cast out the beam out of thine own eye; and then shalt thou see clearly to cast out the mote out of thy brother's eye." (Matthew 7:5. KJV).*

A large part of my intention was to go on a spiritual journey, looking into the soul of humanity rather than the intellect, following the suggestion of Rene Descartes made 500 years ago, looking for these moral truths. Three wonderful lights were my guide. Each brought in an era of fresh reflection on the nature of humanity and civilisation.

Pauline Christianity, a key component of Western European culture, gives us one of great egalitarian statements.

c.60 AD: 'There is no longer Jew or Greek, there is no longer slave or free, there is no longer male and female; for all of you are one in Christ Jesus.' Galatians 3:28

The other two are from the so-called Age of Enlightenment. Two declarations made 13 years and nearly 4,000 miles apart radically shifted the ideal to which civilisation should aspire.

The American Declaration of Independence gives us one of the great statements on Equality, Liberty and Happiness.

4 July 1776 AD: "We hold these truths to be self-evident, that all men are created equal, that they are endowed by their Creator with certain unalienable Rights, that among these are Life, Liberty and the pursuit of Happiness."

13 years later the slogan of the French Revolution added the concept of Fraternity, though much debated as to its intended meaning, a brotherhood all committed to the same spirit of Liberty and Equality. **Liberty, Equality, Fraternity** was not a part of the famous Declaration of the Rights of Man and of the Citizen ratified by the National Constituent Assembly of the First Republic of France between the 20th and the 26th of August 1789. It became the spirit of the Revolution and all that have followed.

26 August 1789 AD: Liberty consists of being able to do anything that does not harm others: thus, the exercise of the natural rights of every man or woman has no bounds other than those that guarantee other members of society the enjoyment of these same rights. (Article IV)
The law is the expression of the general will. All citizens have the right to contribute personally, or through their representatives, to its formation. It must be the same for all, whether it protects or punishes. All citizens, being equal in its eyes, shall be equally eligible to all high offices, public positions and employments, according to their ability, and without other distinction than that of their virtues and talents. (Article VI)

The same problems accompanying the many intellectual attempts to probe the secrets of the human soul have accompanied the attempts to define the powerful concepts of Liberty, Equality and Happiness, in order to turn their mystifying abstractness into a universally recognised reality. The modern world, or most of it, certainly the Western European sphere of influence of which the UK, through its Imperial mission, has created a major part, has pledged itself to follow the fourth encapsulation of what are the civilised essentials of the soul and spirit of humankind.

The Universal Declaration of Human Rights was signed by 48 out of the 58 members of the United Nations (membership is now 193), then and now the largest and only non-religious global intergovernmental organisation dedicated to safeguarding the soul of humankind from the only too human tendency to be guided by the savagery and selfishness of its bodily fears, desires, prejudices and weaknesses.

> **10 December 1948, Palais de Chaillot, Paris, France: All human beings are born free and equal in dignity and rights. They are endowed with reason and conscience and should act towards one another in a spirit of brotherhood. (Article I)**

In my retrial of the case in which women are accused by men of being inferior human beings, Western European 'Men' are in the dock. By the aforementioned humane standards of freedom, equality, brotherhood and happiness, were women well-treated by men? Was their dignity and humanity decently, i.e. in a civilised way, recognised by men? Did they get justice from the patriarchy? Do they now get these things? What changed? What still has to change? Did and/or do men in general want them to change? Will women and men feel differently after reading this book or particular chapters of it? Do we tell Christine her case is over? Has her testimony and those of many others convinced the jury of humanity?

The tools to change the world, to right wrongs, to allow every human on Earth to pursue happiness with the same freedoms and rights as any other are locked up in the toolboxes of political, economic and social institutions, all subject to the direction of government and its instruction manual, the Law. Much of the book looks at these at length. The Devil is in the detail.

The best system for achieving the greatest happiness of the greatest number in reality – there have never been nor will ever be Utopias—is democracy by which the restraints on total freedom which many Enlightenment philosophers called 'the state of nature', the costs and benefits of living as a group and the extent of protection offered to the individual are decided by all those whom they affect, for better or worse. The misrepresentations, the proliferations of definition and philosophical obfuscations of the meaning and system of democracy all arise from those who have a vested interest in preventing it from happening.

Many credit Jean-Jacques Rousseau with the concept of the General Will, *la volonté generale*, but it is put in its moral and human context by the less well-known, Dennis Diderot, whose *Encyclopédie* inspired the format for this book:

> **EVERYTHING you conceive, everything you contemplate, will be good, great, elevated, sublime, if it accords with *the general and common interest.* There is no quality essential to your species apart from that which you demand from all your fellow men to ensure your happiness and theirs…[D]o not ever lose sight of it, or else you will find that your comprehension of the notions of goodness, justice, humanity and virtue grow dim.**

How a governmental system makes sure that everything does accord with the general and common interest and then makes sure that every person is equally protected and free to act as an individual within that accord doing, in observance of John Acton's definition of Liberty, as they should, not always as they want or can (Chapter 36), plays a major part in the Woman Question.

The entry qualification for any consideration of such a political system has to be universal suffrage of all adults who live within the area to be governed. If all these participants agree with the delegation of the power to debate and pass law on the issues of the day, all the adults within the population (with some exceptions related to mental fitness and criminal status) regardless of gender, age, occupation, class, income group, belief, ethnicity, disability and sexual preference should be allowed to put themselves forward for delegation. Each delegate should represent a section of the population, roughly equal in number to every other delegate's. All those delegated to govern should be chosen by the people in a free and fair election process the outcomes of which should, in terms of delegation, be proportional to the components of the general and common interest (a principle first suggested by J.S. Mill in 1861).

In at least three of these respects, the UK still fails this test of democracy although on *The Economist* Democracy Index it is still classed as a 'full democracy', something which France and the USA, cradles of 18th century democracy, are not, both being classed as 'flawed'. The UK has a hereditary monarchy, a family, descended from a King who claimed his sovereignty by right of conquest not the common interest of the people, who provide the head of state; a first-past-the-post electoral system which denies a representation in debating and passing laws that equates to the proportion of votes cast; and a second chamber or senate of unelected individuals to act as a forum for 'further deliberation'. The two top countries in the Democracy Index, Norway and Sweden, are also hereditary monarchies, but have written constitutions and far fewer symbols of traditional power by conquest.

Such an arrangement surely favours conservatism (See Chapter 39). J.S. Mill challenged its presumption that hundreds of years of tradition and practice made something such as total dependence of women on men right for the common interest.

> No presumption in its favour, therefore, can be drawn from the fact of its existence. The only such presumption which it could be supposed to have, must be grounded on its having lasted till now, when so many other things which came down from the same odious source [*might is right*] have been done away with.[394]

Do we see a barrier to the case for women's participation in the law making process in the conservative bias in the British political system? Is it or was it any more conservative than any other Western European democracy? The cultural

---

394 Mill, John Stuart (2012-05-11T23:58:59). The Subjection of Women. Kindle Edition.

history, of equal importance to the political history, of the UK cannot be written in isolation from Western Europe, particularly France.

The Norman Conquest of the 11th century, the Peasants Revolt of the 14th century, the Mercantilism of the 16th and 17th centuries and the Industrial Revolution of the 18th and 19th centuries all have played their part in defining the three class system in the UK, upper, middle and lower, perhaps more rigidly and respectfully observed than in countries where class difference and exploitation led to revolution ('knowing one's place' still pervades the British consciousness like 'fair play'). Which class led the drive towards gender equality? Gender is and was free of class mores, by which I mean that a biological woman is the same as all others, regardless of wealth or social status, and sex was an ever-present, dominant part of human behaviour as it is now and has always been.

However, class played a huge part in the social management of sexual behaviour. In the chapter on the French Revolution (Chapter 36) we learn more about the attitudes and political wishes of working class French women and have to assume that they were similar among their English counterparts. The great stories I have relayed tend to be of upper- and middle-class women because the crucial importance of education meant that the great female reformers were from an income group that could afford to pay for it. The suffragist and suffragette campaign, however, found a common cause that united the classes of English women although, somewhat ironically, less than their support for the masculine posturing that caused the mayhem of World War I.

In the struggle for equality, two of the greatest human institutions, Religion (Chapters 10-15) and The Law (Chapters 37-39), had to be made to examine themselves and change centuries of traditions that had become an almost unquestioned fact of life. The new institution of Science, physical, medical and social, played a huge part in the gender discourse and strengthened the case for gender equality. Institutional discrimination is different from individual discrimination not just because of its far more weighty and widespread impact on individuals but because institutions are not one individual but many among whom responsibility is dispersed. Their power is faceless and hard to pinpoint.

The institution is a human construct to provide control and control is power. Therefore, those in control of institutions have enormous power, privilege and frequently wealth. Where there is enormous power there is scope for abuse but, more problematically, huge incentive to resist any attempt to say and do things differently. To what extent was the Christian Church an opposing influence to an egalitarian movement for gender equality? Who was behind the resistance to law reform on divorce, marital equality and attempts to understand and recognise in law different perspectives on individual sexuality? Both have been cross-examined at length.

My mind keeps coming back to the process we sometimes glibly describe as civilisation. My own reflection on its meaning and progress will end this book in which, whether you have only dipped into it or read the whole story, I hope that you, male and female readers have found ways to understand better, in my opinion, one of the greatest stories of injustice in human social experience.

The civilisation of that forward facing, flat footed, missile throwing, bipedal, big-brained ape, homo sapiens, is what? A triumph? A disaster? A fiction? A truth?

What is the narrative of its story? What is the plot of its drama? Who are its heroes and villains, protagonists and antagonists? Is there a prequel waiting to be found in a jar in the deserts of Upper Egypt, the dust of the Rift valley, the caves of Transjordan, the high plains of the Andes or the frozen wastes of Siberia? Is it over? Is there a sequel? Who are the authors?

The story is one of sex and violence. It is, therefore, a story of men written by men for men. The protagonist is masculine who often, when suitable, casts femininity in the antagonist role. Most of the heroes are warriors, men steeped in violence, or saints, cultural victims of the fight for their version of right and wrong to get control of the human soul. In the violence scenario, villains are male competitors who threaten territory and trade, the key to physical survival, and occasionally those who threaten the cultural soul and the institutions, like the Church, that maintain it. In the sex scenario they are those who threaten the male's certainty about his ability and opportunity to reproduce and transfer his genome and the institutions, from the tribe to the nation state, that he has constructed to sustain that certainty.

In respect of these reproductive drives to survive, however, his most powerful antagonists are women. His principal weapon for eliminating or neutralising the threat to his survival and the survival of his genes in both scenarios is his superior physical bulk and strength. Her principal weapon, however, is her receptivity to any male impregnation that she allows or is deceived into allowing or is forced to allow. This leads to her having exclusive knowledge of the father of her child or, if promiscuous, her having a complete lack of that knowledge both of which leave the male ignorant of whether the child has his genes or not, making the expenditure of energy, like those pinnipeds on the beach (Chapter 2), and the risk of his life in raising that child, a biological waste of time and energy.

The surest answer to his dilemma, given that impregnating all the females in his world is impossible, is to control the process by extreme mate-guarding behaviour. This has involved complete control over the female, his female, in a pair-bonding relationship by enslaving her, owning her and restricting her freedom by force, extreme oppression, repression and suppression. Many versions, from domestic abuse to harems, from Christian matrimony to coverture, from the punishment of sin to the ostracism and shunning of women for whom this sexual repression has not prevented behaviour contrary to the requirements of the male mate-guarder.

Civilisation is more than a process of moving from brute force savagery as the primary route to survival (War!) to rational thinking, discussion, compromise and acceptance of difference (Peace!). It is the process of men relinquishing sole control of the survival process and sharing it with, in some respects, totally handing it over to, the other half of the species, women. As Mill accepted, Reason had no real material for examining the social effect of handing over complete control to women because no examples of matriarchy had been found or explored theoretically. Mill further accepted that there had been a considerable softening of the oppressive actions of men against women but could not understand the reasons for the continued suppression and repression of them, what he called subjection.

As you watch that elephant seal lolloping, frantically, over the breeding beach to fight off any male attempt to impregnate one of his harem you see a metaphor. He is motivated by fear, fear of his own weakness, his own inadequacy, his own inability to maintain control of the transfer of his genes. He is scared of his own species, his own family most probably, a fear totally different from that caused by the threat to his survival posed by the orca out in the bay. He cannot control his urge to mate or his fear of others getting to one of his females before him.

Civilisation is the overcoming of the reproduction related fear of the human male and the eradication of his total-control solutions to the sexualities and sexual processes which threaten him, expose his fear and underline his weakness. Civilisation is a process that totally relates to behaviour of the human male, his fear of sharing control of the primary purpose of his species, survival, and reluctance to find a route to self-control of his sexual instincts, preferring to devise and sustain institutions to allow them and blame and condemn those that arouse them (the homosexual is still blamed—by some—for the existence of homosexuality and the woman in the short skirt is still blamed—by some—for her rape).

The drama, therefore, is not over and will not be until Western European culture unreservedly hands women complete Liberty by enshrining in law their total right to say what happens to their own body with its unique reproductive kit. No matter how much pressure women put on them the solution to the problems of the source of masculine power residing in their physical massiveness and the domination of their soul by the power of their sexual drives is men's alone.

This book, however, is most about the application of the other pervasive but morally unacceptable survival technique, deception, and the abuse of power exercised to maintain it. The case against women, their inferiority and responsibility for evil, needs to be thrown out of court once and for all. It is a lie that has been deployed to cover up the natural truth of masculine weakness. The truth of the weakness and the knowledge of the lie have taken hundreds, probably thousands of years, to be revealed because the means to construct and cover up the lie and create the replacement truth have been in the hands of the liars.

What makes us human is the extraordinary power of the human intellect not the dimorphic nature of our biology. This has been a story of equality of all human beings delayed in its achievement by two other equalities. The extraordinary intellectual ability of homo sapiens to visualise and discover the truth is unfortunately matched by the ability to obscure and pervert it. The equally extraordinary emotional ability to be selfless and empathise is matched by the incurable tendency to be selfish and unsympathetic.

Men, or many men, have known that intellectually they had no case. For utterly selfish reasons they have turned to the divinity of natural creation and, when science and education challenged that assertion and exposed the mind control, brainwashing would not be too strong a description, implicit in its institutionalisation, turned to a theory of natural instinct. That is what masculinity is, what men are. They cannot help themselves. Until that mindset ceases to hold sway the most undeserving case in the history of Homo Sapiens, like Jarndyce v. Jarndyce, will never be settled. I leave the last words to John Stuart Mill and Denis Diderot:

> **If the authority of men over women, when first established, had been the result of a conscientious comparison between different modes of constituting the government of society; if, after trying various other modes of social organisation—the government of women over men, equality between the two, and such mixed and divided modes of government as might be invented—it had been decided, on the testimony of experience, that the mode in which women are wholly under the rule of men, having no share at all in public concerns, and each in private being under the legal obligation of obedience to the man with whom she has associated her destiny, was the arrangement most conducive to the happiness and well-being of both; its general adoption might then be fairly thought to be some evidence that, at the time when it was adopted, it was the best: though even then the considerations which recommended it may, like so many other primeval social facts of the greatest importance, have subsequently, in the course of ages, ceased to exist. But the state of the case is in every respect the reverse of this.**
>
> **In the first place, the opinion in favour of the present system, which entirely subordinates the weaker sex to the stronger, rests upon theory only; for there never has been trial made of any other: so that experience, in the sense in which it is vulgarly opposed to theory, cannot be pretended to have pronounced any verdict. And in the second place, the adoption of this system of inequality never was the result of deliberation, or forethought, or any social ideas, or any notion whatever of what conduced to the benefit of humanity or the good order of society. It arose simply from the fact that from the very earliest twilight of human society, every woman (owing to the value attached to her by men, combined with her inferiority in muscular strength) was found in a state of bondage to some man.**
>
> **Laws and systems of polity always begin by recognising the relations they find already existing between individuals. They convert what was a mere physical fact into a legal right, give it the sanction of society, and principally aim at the substitution of public and organised means of asserting and protecting these rights, instead of the irregular and lawless conflict of physical strength. Those who**

had already been compelled to obedience became in this manner legally bound to it.[395]

The goal of an encyclopaedia is to assemble all the knowledge scattered on the surface of the earth, to demonstrate the general system to the people with whom we live, & to transmit it to the people who will come after us, so that the works of centuries past is not useless to the centuries which follow, that our descendants, by becoming more learned, may become more virtuous & happier, & that we do not die without having merited being part of the human race.[396]

---

[395] Ibid.

[396] https://en.wikipedia.org/wiki/Encyclop%C3%A9die. Accessed 31/08/2021.

Ingram Content Group UK Ltd.
Milton Keynes UK
UKHW020633050423
419681UK00008B/167